Psychological and Neurological Consequences of AI:

Dependency, Laziness, and Reduced Critical Thinking

Pandimurugan Vellaisamy
Acharya University, Uzbekistan

IGI Global
Scientific Publishing
Publishing Tomorrow's Research Today

Vice President of Editorial Melissa Wagner
Director of Acquisitions Mikaela Felty
Director of Book Development Jocelynn Hessler
Production Manager Mike Brehm
Cover Design Jose Rosado

Published in the United States of America by
IGI Global Scientific Publishing
701 East Chocolate Avenue
Hershey, PA, 17033, USA
Tel: 717-533-8845 | Fax: 717-533-7115
Website: https://www.igi-global.com E-mail: cust@igi-global.com

Library of Congress Cataloging-in-Publication Data

LCCN: 2026017837 (CIP Data Pending)
ISBN13: 9798337394848
Isbn13Softcover: 9798337394855
EISBN13: 9798337394862
British Cataloguing in Publication Data
A Cataloguing in Publication record for this book is available from the British Library.

Table of Contents

Detailed Table of Contents

cognitive psychology, human factors engineering, occupational health psychology, and nursing science. It explores AI systems influence attention, clinical decision-making, memory processes, and cognitive workload in acute care settings. While AI automates many monitoring tasks, it introduces new demands such as interpreting alerts, evaluating algorithmic outputs, and integrating machine-generated insights with clinical judgment. Issues like alert fatigue, automation bias, and increased data complexity may affect decision accuracy and patient safety. The chapter also discusses technostress, autonomy concerns, trust in AI systems, emphasizing the importance of human-centered design, training, and organizational support for effective human–AI collaboration in nursing practice

The widespread reliance on artificial intelligence for cognitive support is increasingly shaping the functional organization of the human brain. Prolonged AI dependency may alter neural activity patterns underlying attention, memory, executive function, and decision-making, raising concerns about long-term effects on brain plasticity and cognitive control. This chapter focuses on the neurological consequences of sustained AI use, examining how reduced cognitive effort and habitual cognitive offloading may influence prefrontal-parietal networks, frontostriatal circuits, and hippocampal-dependent memory systems. It will also provide a neurobiological framework for understanding how AI dependency reshapes brain networks involved in higher-order cognition, highlight emerging neural risks of reduced cognitive engagement, and outline directions for future longitudinal and mechanistic research aimed at preserving neural integrity in the era of intelligent technologies.

Artificial Intelligence (AI) is increasingly integrated into daily life, influencing cognition, emotion, and social behavior. While AI enhances efficiency and decision-making, overreliance can produce neuropsychological consequences, including memory decline, reduced attention and executive function, emotional dysregulation, social skill impairment, and habitual reward-driven behavior. Cognitive offloading, automation bias, and technostress further mediate these effects. Neuroplastic adaptations reflect both functional gains and trade-offs, emphasizing AI-mediated circuits while downregulating underused networks. Strategies such as cognitive training, mindful AI use, digital literacy, and human-centered AI design can mitigate risks. Understanding the long-term impacts of AI reliance is critical for balancing augmentation with cognitive, emotional, and social well-being.

Generative Artificial Intelligence (GenAI) is reshaping higher education by enhancing learning while raising concerns about dependency, cognitive offloading, and critical thinking. This chapter examines the relationships among AI Dependency, Ethical Awareness, Algorithmic Bias Awareness, and Critical Thinking Skills in AI-supported learning. A mixed-paradigm approach combining Systematic Theoretical Synthesizing and Partial Least Squares Structural Equation Modeling (PLS-SEM) was used to analyze data from 110 university students. Results show that all three constructs significantly influence critical thinking, with Algorithmic Bias Awareness as the strongest predictor. Students who recognize AI limitations and biases demonstrate stronger analytical reasoning and metacognitive skills. The study proposes a Mixed-Paradigm Cognitive-Behavioral Triangulation Matrix integrating behavioral dependency, ethical cognition, and algorithmic skepticism. Findings highlight the importance of AI literacy and critical engagement for maintaining cognitive independence in AI-mediated education.

Over-automation in education arises when AI systems move from supportive tools to default authorities in teaching learning system. This is done without proportional safeguards. While AI can enhance personalisation and efficiency, chronic reliance can reshape cognition and behavior by encouraging cognitive offloading, weakening critical thinking, and normalising "output-following" overdependent reasoning. This chapter argues that the most consequential harms emerge from the institutionalisation of AI reliance that diffuses responsibility, reduces learner agency, and embeds

Preface

Artificial Intelligence (AI) has rapidly evolved from a specialized computational technology into an indispensable component of everyday life. AI-powered systems now influence education, healthcare, finance, transportation, governance, scientific research, and countless aspects of human decision-making. Intelligent assistants, recommendation systems, generative AI platforms, autonomous technologies, and predictive analytics have significantly improved productivity, efficiency, and accessibility to information. However, alongside these remarkable technological advances, increasing concerns have emerged regarding AI's long-term psychological, neurological, educational, and societal consequences. As individuals increasingly rely on intelligent systems to perform cognitive tasks that once demanded human memory, reasoning, creativity, and critical thinking, important questions arise about how continuous AI dependence may reshape the human mind.

This book, Psychological and Neurological Consequences of AI: Dependency, Laziness, and Reduced Critical Thinking, addresses one of the most pressing yet underexplored challenges of the AI era. Rather than focusing solely on the technological capabilities of artificial intelligence, this volume examines AI's influence on human cognition, behavior, learning, motivation, and neurological functioning. The contributors explore how prolonged dependence on AI technologies may affect attention, executive functioning, decision-making, cognitive engagement, creativity, autonomy, metacognition, and brain plasticity. At the same time, the book presents balanced perspectives by highlighting responsible AI design, ethical governance, and human-centered approaches that ensure AI augments rather than replaces human intelligence.

The subject of this volume is particularly timely. AI is transforming classrooms, workplaces, hospitals, industries, and public institutions at an unprecedented pace. Students increasingly rely on AI-generated content instead of developing analytical reasoning. Professionals depend on automated recommendations for complex decision-making. Healthcare practitioners incorporate AI-assisted diagnostics into clinical workflows. While these developments create substantial opportunities, they also raise concerns regarding automation bias, cognitive offloading, erosion of independent thinking, reduced intellectual effort, and overreliance on machine-generated knowledge. Understanding these implications is essential for developing AI systems that preserve human agency while maximizing technological benefits.

The interdisciplinary nature of this book makes it relevant to multiple academic and professional communities. It will serve as an important resource for graduate students, doctoral researchers, psychologists, neuroscientists, educators, instructional designers, teacher educators, healthcare professionals, AI researchers, computer scientists, human-computer interaction specialists, cognitive scientists, policymakers, ethics researchers, technology developers, and organizational leaders seeking a deeper understanding of the relationship between artificial intelligence and human cognition.

The chapters included in this volume collectively provide diverse theoretical, conceptual, and applied perspectives on AI dependency and cognitive transformation.

The opening chapter, AI Dependency and Cognitive Offloading: Rethinking Human-Centered Design in the Age of Intelligent Systems, examines how increasing cognitive delegation to AI influences human thinking and decision-making while proposing human-centered design principles that encourage collaborative intelligence instead of cognitive replacement.

The second chapter, AI-Induced Cognitive Atrophy: Experimental, Neuroplastic, and Evolutionary Perspectives on Human Cognition, integrates neuroscience, psychology, and machine learning concepts to explain how prolonged underuse of cognitive abilities may contribute to declining memory, reasoning, and higher-order thinking.

The third chapter, Attention, Memory, and Self-Regulation Under AI Dependence: Executive Functions at Risk, examines how growing dependence on artificial intelligence may reshape core executive functions, particularly attention, memory, and self-regulation. While AI tools can support learning, productivity, and decision-making, their constant availability also invites subtle forms of cognitive surrender.

The fourth chapter, Automating the Thinking Process: Neural and Psychological Implications of Constant AI Support and Assistance, investigates how persistent AI assistance influences executive control, attentional processes, metacognitive monitoring, and intrinsic motivation, while proposing balanced human–AI cognitive cooperation.

The fifth chapter, Automation Bias in Medical Imaging and Large Language Models: Cognitive Erosion from Overtrusting Imperfect AI, focuses on automation bias in clinical and knowledge-intensive environments, presenting intervention frameworks that encourage verification, transparency, and cognitive resilience.

The sixth chapter, Beyond Dependency: Artificial Intelligence as Cognitive Redistribution in Education, reconceptualizes AI not as a replacement for learning but as a cognitive scaffold that redistributes intellectual effort, emphasizing the importance of instructional design and self-regulated learning.

The seventh chapter, Cognitive Dependency and Pedagogical Resilience in AI-Saturated Classrooms: Critical Thinking in the Age of AI, explores educational challenges associated with AI-supported learning and proposes pedagogical strategies that strengthen learner autonomy, cognitive integrity, and critical thinking.

The eighth chapter, Cognitive Offloading to Cognitive Atrophy: A Neuropsychological Framework of AI Dependency, Automation Bias, and the Erosion of Critical Thinking, presents a comprehensive theoretical framework connecting cognitive offloading with neurological and educational consequences while advocating balanced human–AI collaboration.

The ninth chapter, Digital Tools as Educational Resources: Transforming Classroom Practices in the Era of Modern Learning, discusses the educational opportunities and challenges associated with digital technologies and AI integration, emphasizing equitable implementation, teacher preparedness, and ethical considerations.

The tenth chapter, Neurocognitive and Psychological Implications of AI-Based Patient Monitoring Technologies in Modern Nursing, examines how AI-assisted healthcare technologies influence nurses' attention, cognitive workload, decision-making, and professional autonomy while addressing technostress and human factors in clinical environments.

The eleventh chapter, Neuroplastic Consequences of Artificial Intelligence Dependency: Effects on Executive Networks and Cognitive Control, explores the neurological mechanisms through which sustained AI dependence may reshape brain networks responsible for attention, executive functioning, memory, and cognitive control.

The twelfth chapter, Neuropsychological Effects of Overreliance on Artificial Intelligence, examines the neuropsychological consequences of increasing AI reliance, highlighting its effects on memory, attention, executive functioning, emotional regulation, social skills, and cognitive behavior through mechanisms such as cognitive offloading, automation bias, and technostress.

The thirteenth chapter, Examining the Influence of AI Dependency, Ethical Awareness, and Algorithmic Bias Awareness on Critical Thinking: Nudging the Algorithmic Mind, examines the relationships among AI Dependency, Ethical Awareness, Algorithmic Bias Awareness, and Critical Thinking Skills in AI-supported learning.

The fourteenth chapter, Over-Automation in Higher Education: Ethical Risks and Human-Centered AI, investigates institutional overdependence on AI within higher education and proposes ethical frameworks that preserve learner agency, accountability, trust, and responsible educational innovation.

The fifteenth chapter, Students in the AI Age: Learning, Dependency, and Cognitive Growth among Economics Students in Higher Education, examines AI-supported learning through established cognitive theories and introduces a conceptual framework explaining pathways toward either cognitive dependency or cognitive growth.

The final chapter, Toward Human-Centered AI in Economics Education: Designing Artificial Intelligence for Thinking, Not Cognitive Replacement, concludes the volume by presenting human-centered design principles that encourage metacognition, intellectual autonomy, analytical reasoning, and responsible AI integration in higher education.

Collectively, these chapters demonstrate that the future of artificial intelligence should not be viewed merely as a technological challenge but as a human challenge requiring interdisciplinary collaboration among educators, psychologists, neuroscientists, engineers, policymakers, and designers. While AI possesses extraordinary potential to enhance productivity and expand human capabilities, its long-term success depends on preserving the cognitive capacities that define human intelligence—critical thinking, creativity, ethical judgment, reflective reasoning, and independent decision-making.

This volume contributes to the emerging body of scholarship examining AI's psychological and neurological implications by synthesizing insights from cognitive science, neuroscience, psychology, education, healthcare, ethics, and artificial intelligence. It encourages researchers and practitioners to move beyond technology-centric perspectives toward human-centered AI ecosystems that support learning, preserve cognitive resilience, and promote sustainable human development.

We sincerely thank all contributing authors, reviewers, editorial staff, and researchers whose expertise has made this volume possible. We hope this book stimulates meaningful scholarly discussions, inspires future interdisciplinary research, informs responsible AI policies, and contributes to the development of intelligent technologies that enhance—not diminish—the richness of human cognition.

Section 1

Foundations of AI Dependency, Cognitive Offloading, and Human-Centered Intelligence

Chapter 1
AI Dependency and Cognitive Offloading:
Rethinking Human-Centered Design in the Age of Intelligent Systems

Doni Sugianto Sihotang
http://orcid.org/0009-0008-5222-4475
Universitas Negeri Jakarta, Indonesia

Usep Suhud
http://orcid.org/0000-0002-1728-0737
Universitas Negeri Jakarta, Indonesia

Agung Wahyu Handaru
http://orcid.org/0000-0003-0198-8041
Universitas Negeri Jakarta, Indonesia

ABSTRACT

This chapter analyzes the psychological and cognitive consequences of heightened dependence on intelligent technologies, emphasizing dependency and cognitive job delegation in human-technology interactions. This chapter aims to examine how intelligent systems transform cognitive processes, affect critical thinking, and contest conventional human-centered design principles. The discourse emphasizes cognitive advantages, including enhanced efficiency and improved decision-making, while acknowledging concerns such as skill degradation, reduced autonomy, and diminished cognitive involvement. The chapter additionally advocates for design-centric solutions that prioritize collaborative intelligence, ethical governance, and inclusive development frameworks. This chapter advances the development

DOI: 10.4018/979-8-3373-9484-8.ch001

of intelligent systems by re-evaluating user-centered techniques, thereby fostering cognitive resilience, safeguarding human agency, and encouraging sustainable collaboration between humans and technology across educational, professional, and social contexts.

INTRODUCTION

1. The Rise of AI-Driven Cognitive Assistance

Artificial intelligence (AI) has rapidly evolved from a specialized technological tool into a fundamental component of human cognition and decision-making. AI-driven systems, including large language models, recommendation algorithms, and intelligent assistants, are increasingly embedded in daily activities such as writing, planning, learning, and problem-solving. These technologies function as cognitive collaborators that support information processing and influence how individuals evaluate alternatives and make judgments. The growing reliance on AI reflects a transition toward hybrid human–machine cognition, in which intelligent systems assist or partially guide cognitive activities that were traditionally performed exclusively by humans (Muthusamy et al., 2025).

The expanding role of AI in cognition can be understood through several established theoretical perspectives. Distributed Cognition Theory suggests that cognition is distributed across individuals, artifacts, and technological environments rather than residing solely within the human mind. From this perspective, AI systems become integral components of broader cognitive systems that support information processing and decision-making. Similarly, Extended Mind Theory argues that external tools can function as extensions of human cognition when they are consistently used to support memory, reasoning, and problem-solving. As AI systems increasingly perform sophisticated cognitive tasks, they may operate not merely as tools but as cognitive partners that augment human intellectual capabilities.

The incorporation of AI into everyday decision-making contexts has substantial implications for human cognition. AI systems not only automate routine tasks but also shape how users interpret information, prioritize options, and formulate preferences. Recent studies indicate that algorithmic systems can subtly influence human reasoning and decision-making processes, generating new cognitive effects and reshaping notions of autonomy (Rodriguez-Fernandez, 2025). Furthermore, AI technologies simulate various aspects of cognition, including learning, prediction, and problem-solving, although they lack human qualities such as emotional intelligence, contextual awareness, and ethical judgment. This distinction creates a complex interaction in which humans rely on AI-generated outputs while remaining responsible for interpretation and final decisions (Checkonthayil, 2024).

A fundamental concept explaining this transformation is cognitive offloading, which refers to delegating mental tasks to external tools or technologies. Traditionally, cognitive offloading involved instruments such as notes and calculators; however, AI significantly extends this capability by performing advanced cognitive operations, including summarization, idea generation, and analytical reasoning (García-Barrios, 2025). Cognitive Load Theory helps explain why such delegation becomes attractive, as AI reduces mental effort associated with complex information processing. Nevertheless, excessive offloading may decrease opportunities for active learning and cognitive engagement. Moreover, Human–AI Interaction models emphasize that trust, usability, and transparency influence the extent to which individuals rely on intelligent systems. Excessive trust may result in automation bias, whereby users accept AI recommendations without sufficient critical evaluation, potentially weakening critical thinking and cognitive resilience (Peng & Yeh, 2025). Consequently, understanding AI-driven cognitive assistance requires balancing its potential for cognitive augmentation with the need to preserve human autonomy and intellectual engagement.

2. Relevance of AI Dependency and Cognitive Offloading

The rapid proliferation of artificial intelligence (AI) in educational settings, professional contexts, and everyday decision-making has heightened concerns about AI dependency and cognitive offloading. While AI technologies improve efficiency, accessibility, and task performance, their increasing integration into cognitive activities raises important questions regarding human autonomy, cognitive engagement, and ethical accountability. Understanding these dynamics is particularly important within the context of human-centered design (HCD), which seeks to develop technologies that enhance human capabilities while preserving critical thinking and independent decision-making.

A useful distinction must be made between AI augmentation and AI dependency. AI augmentation refers to the productive use of AI systems to enhance human capabilities while maintaining active cognitive engagement and human oversight. In this context, AI serves as a supportive tool that assists users in generating ideas, analyzing information, or improving decision quality without replacing human judgment. For example, students may use generative AI to brainstorm research topics, while professionals may employ AI systems to identify patterns in large datasets before making final decisions. In contrast, AI dependency occurs when individuals increasingly rely on AI-generated outputs as substitutes for their own reasoning, reducing active participation in cognitive processes and limiting opportunities for independent learning and problem-solving.

The relevance of this distinction is increasingly evident in educational and professional environments. Although AI-supported activities can enhance productivity and learning outcomes, excessive reliance may diminish cognitive engagement and analytical reasoning. Research suggests that students who depend heavily on AI-generated responses may experience cognitive fatigue and reduced critical thinking, particularly when they passively accept automated outputs rather than actively evaluating information (Tian & Zhang, 2025). Similarly, prolonged dependence on AI-assisted tools may weaken independent reasoning and problem-solving capabilities, especially when convenience takes precedence over cognitive involvement (Elzerman, 2025).

Beyond cognitive implications, AI dependency also introduces broader ethical and societal concerns. Human-centered AI research emphasizes the importance of designing systems that empower users, promote transparency, and ensure accountability. Failure to address these issues may undermine user autonomy and create asymmetrical relationships between humans and intelligent systems (Usmani et al., 2023). Furthermore, the opaque nature of many AI systems raises concerns regarding fairness, trust, and explainability, making it difficult for users to understand how recommendations are generated (Hofmann, 2025). Human-centered AI approaches therefore advocate collaborative relationships between humans and AI, ensuring that intelligent systems augment rather than replace human cognition while supporting confidence, inclusivity, and psychological well-being (Chandra et al., 2026). Consequently, distinguishing augmentation from dependency is essential for developing responsible AI systems that strengthen cognitive resilience rather than foster technological reliance.

3. Objectives and Contribution of the Chapter

As AI systems increasingly serve as cognitive collaborators, comprehending the relationship between AI reliance, cognitive offloading, and human-centered design (HCD) is crucial. This chapter seeks to examine the impact of AI-driven cognitive support on human cognition and to provide practical frameworks that reconcile technology efficiency with human autonomy. Resolving these concerns is essential to ensuring that AI augments human capabilities rather than undermining cognitive autonomy.

This chapter aims to analyze the increasing dependence on AI systems and their consequences on cognitive offloading. Cognitive offloading occurs when individuals delegate mental tasks to external systems, such as AI-driven technologies capable of advanced reasoning and decision-making. Although AI-assisted settings can improve task performance and efficiency, overreliance may lead to skill degradation and diminished cognitive engagement. Research indicates that AI-assisted learning environments might yield rapid results but may also cultivate dependency if users rely excessively on automated answers rather than actively participating in problem-solving (Karny et al., 2024). This paradox underscores the necessity of meticulously assessing the impact of AI integration on human cognition.

This chapter also aims to examine the role of human-centered design principles in mitigating the hazards associated with AI dependency. Human-centered AI focuses on creating systems that value user empowerment, autonomy, and well-being. By integrating transparency, explainability, and user autonomy, AI systems can serve as auxiliary instruments that augment cognitive involvement rather than supplanting human decision-making. Human-centered AI frameworks prioritize inclusive and ethical design methodologies that ensure AI technologies align with human values and foster human trust–AI collaboration (Chandra et al., 2026).

This chapter synthesizes theoretical and practical findings to create actionable design frameworks for responsible AI systems. These frameworks seek to maintain cognitive autonomy while utilizing AI's capabilities in data processing and predictive analytics. Friction-based design methodologies push users to evaluate AI-generated outputs rather than passively accept them critically. These methods can enhance cognitive involvement and mitigate automation bias in decision-making contexts (Natali et al., 2024).

This chapter also emphasizes the significance of collaborative intelligence, in which humans and AI systems cooperate to enhance decision-making outcomes. Models of human-AI collaboration prioritize preserving user agency during decision-making. Research indicates that collaborative decision-making frameworks can improve performance when AI technologies assist rather than supplant human judgment (Xiaowei et al., 2025).

This chapter enhances the conversation on responsible AI by incorporating human-centered design methodologies into AI development processes. Responsible AI innovation prioritizes iterative design, user engagement, and ethical governance to ensure that AI systems augment human capabilities while mitigating risks (Snehi et al., 2025). This chapter establishes a conceptual and practical basis for reevaluating human-centered design in the era of intelligent systems.

BACKGROUND

1. Historical Evolution of AI and Cognitive Offloading

The evolution of artificial intelligence (AI) signifies a comprehensive change in the interaction between technology and human cognition and decision-making. Initial AI development stemmed from fundamental computational theories in the mid-twentieth century, as academics sought to emulate human reasoning through rule-based systems and symbolic logic. Early systems, such as expert systems and symbolic reasoning models, were developed to automate organized decision-making processes. Despite their limited adaptability, these systems enabled cognitive automation, allowing robots to assist humans with analytical and repetitive tasks (Lynch & Laister Smith, 2025).

The advancement of machine learning in the late twentieth century signified a significant transformation in AI capabilities. Rather than relying on established rules, machine learning models began deriving insights from data patterns, enabling more flexible and scalable decision-making systems. The transition intensified with the advent of deep learning and neural networks, which augmented AI capabilities in natural language processing, computer vision, and predictive analytics. Contemporary large language models and intelligent assistants emulate intricate cognitive functions, including reasoning, summarization, and creative production, thereby considerably broadening the domain of cognitive automation (Mundlamuri et al., 2025).

With the advancement of AI technology, cognitive offloading has become increasingly crucial to human-machine interaction. Cognitive offloading refers to the delegation of mental tasks to external systems, enabling humans to alleviate cognitive burden and enhance efficiency. Historically, humans have employed tools such as writing systems, calculators, and digital devices for cognitive assistance. Contemporary AI systems, however, expand this paradigm by executing higher-order cognitive processes such as ideation, analysis, and decision-making. This transition signifies a profound change in cognitive work, with AI systems increasingly serving as epistemic partners rather than just tools (Espeso-García, 2025).

The advent of generative AI has significantly expedited cognitive offloading and introduced novel consequences for human cognition. Generative AI systems can produce text, graphics, and analytical outputs, enabling humans to assign intricate cognitive tasks to intelligent systems. Although these technologies improve productivity and accessibility, apprehensions have arisen concerning skill degradation and reliance. Studies suggest that overdependence on generative AI may diminish critical thinking, creativity, and autonomous problem-solving abilities, especially in educational and professional environments (Giray, 2024).

Furthermore, generative AI has facilitated novel patterns of skill transformation, encompassing deskilling, reskilling, and upskilling. Although certain conventional cognitive abilities may diminish due to automation, individuals may concurrently cultivate new talents relevant to AI engagement and supervision. This transition is contingent upon user interaction with AI technologies. Excessive reliance may diminish cognitive independence, while balanced involvement may augment human skills (Yang et al., 2026).

The historical development of AI illustrates a progressive transition from the automation of physical and procedural tasks to the enhancement of advanced cognitive capacities. As generative AI advances, comprehending its function in cognitive offloading becomes crucial. This transition underscores the necessity of developing AI systems that enhance human cognition while mitigating the hazards of dependency and skill degradation.

2. Human-Centered Design Principles

Human-Centered Design (HCD) has become a fundamental framework for creating artificial intelligence (AI) systems that emphasize human values, cognitive requirements, and ethical principles. As AI technologies increasingly influence decision-making and cognitive processes, HCD plays a critical role in ensuring that intelligent systems enhance human autonomy rather than encourage dependency. The core principles of inclusiveness, transparency, and ethical responsibility provide a foundation for developing AI systems that augment human cognition while minimizing unintended consequences.

Inclusivity remains a central principle of human-centered AI. Inclusive design ensures that AI systems accommodate users with different cognitive abilities, cultural backgrounds, and levels of technological literacy. Research demonstrates that inclusive AI can improve accessibility and equity across domains such as healthcare, education, and industry. By considering the needs of diverse stakeholders, developers can reduce bias and promote fair outcomes while ensuring that AI technologies remain accessible to a broad range of users (Pyae, 2025). Inclusive design therefore supports equitable participation and prevents the exclusion of vulnerable populations.

Transparency is another essential component of HCD, particularly because many AI systems operate as complex "black boxes." Explainable AI is a practical implementation of this principle, providing users with understandable explanations of how recommendations, predictions, or decisions are generated. Features such as confidence indicators, explanation panels, and decision rationales allow users to critically evaluate AI outputs rather than relying on them unthinkingly. These mechanisms strengthen trust, improve accountability, and reduce the risks associated with automation bias and excessive cognitive offloading (Buschek et al., 2024).

Ethical considerations further reinforce human-centered AI development. Ethical AI seeks to address concerns related to privacy, fairness, bias, and user autonomy. In practice, these goals can be supported through human-in-the-loop mechanisms that require human oversight during critical decision-making processes. Rather than allowing AI systems to make autonomous decisions, human reviewers retain authority to validate, modify, or reject AI-generated recommendations. Such approaches help ensure that AI systems complement rather than replace human judgment (Nizamani et al., 2025).

Implementing HCD also requires adaptive interfaces and continuous user engagement. Adaptive interfaces can adjust the level of AI assistance based on user expertise, task complexity, and contextual needs, thereby maintaining appropriate cognitive involvement. Likewise, user feedback systems allow individuals to report errors, evaluate recommendations, and contribute to system improvement over time. These mechanisms create iterative learning cycles that enhance usability and responsiveness. Nevertheless, implementing such practices remains challenging because human-centered AI development requires interdisciplinary collaboration among engineers, designers, psychologists, and ethicists, as well as adaptation to domain-specific requirements across sectors such as manufacturing, healthcare, and education (Kutz et al., 2023; Snehi et al., 2025).

3. Cognitive Offloading Mechanisms

Cognitive offloading refers to the transfer of mental tasks to external tools or technologies, enabling individuals to reduce cognitive burden and improve performance. The emergence of artificial intelligence (AI) has transformed cognitive offloading from simple tools such as written notes and calculators into sophisticated systems capable of reasoning, prediction, and decision support. AI systems increasingly serve as cognitive extensions, redistributing mental effort between humans and machines and fundamentally changing how people process information and solve problems (Grinschgl & Neubauer, 2022). Research on extended cognition further suggests that AI can serve as an active cognitive partner, enhancing human performance beyond natural cognitive limitations (Chiriatti et al., 2025).

A critical distinction must be made between beneficial cognitive augmentation and harmful dependency. Beneficial cognitive augmentation occurs when AI supports human cognition while preserving active engagement and independent judgment. For example, physicians may use AI-assisted diagnostic systems to identify patterns in medical images, yet final diagnoses remain dependent on professional expertise and contextual evaluation. Similarly, students may use generative AI to brainstorm research ideas, organize arguments, or summarize information before independently analyzing and refining the results. In these situations, AI functions as a cognitive scaffold that expands human capabilities without replacing human reasoning. Such applications can improve productivity, decision quality, and creativity while allowing individuals to remain cognitively engaged (Najem et al., 2024).

However, cognitive offloading also presents significant risks when augmentation evolves into dependency. Trust and perceived reliability often encourage individuals to delegate increasingly complex tasks to AI systems. Research indicates that cognitive offloading is strongly influenced by users' desire to conserve mental resources, particularly when cognitive demands are high (Peng & Yeh, 2025). Problems arise when users begin to accept AI outputs without critical evaluation. For instance, students may directly copy AI-generated responses into assignments without verifying accuracy or developing their own understanding of the material. Likewise, professionals may rely on algorithmic recommendations without independently assessing assumptions, risks, or contextual factors. Such behaviors reduce opportunities for learning, reflection, and skill development.

The long-term consequences of excessive cognitive offloading are particularly concerning. While AI can improve efficiency and reduce workload, prolonged dependence may contribute to deterioration in memory retention, analytical reasoning, and autonomous problem-solving. Automation bias may further reinforce this tendency by encouraging users to place excessive trust in AI-generated recommendations and reducing their willingness to challenge or verify outputs (Skulmowski, 2024). Consequently, cognitive offloading should not be viewed as inherently beneficial or harmful. Rather, its impact depends on whether AI is used to augment human cognition or to replace it. Maintaining a balanced human–AI relationship is therefore essential to preserving cognitive autonomy while still benefiting from the efficiencies and capabilities offered by intelligent technologies.

MAIN FOCUS OF THE CHAPTER

Issues, Controversies, Problems

1. AI Dependency and Reduced Critical Thinking

The rapid integration of artificial intelligence (AI) into educational, professional, and everyday contexts has transformed how individuals acquire knowledge, solve problems, and make decisions. While AI technologies improve efficiency and accessibility, growing dependence on these systems raises concerns regarding critical thinking and cognitive engagement. AI dependency often emerges when individuals rely excessively on automated outputs, resulting in cognitive offloading that reduces the need for independent reasoning and reflective analysis. As AI systems increasingly perform complex cognitive tasks, concerns about declining analytical thinking have become more prominent.

A critical distinction should be made between cognitive augmentation and cognitive dependency. Cognitive augmentation occurs when AI enhances human cognitive performance while preserving active reasoning, evaluation, and decision-making. In this context, AI serves as a supportive partner, assisting users in processing information and generating insights without replacing human judgment. In contrast, cognitive dependency develops when users increasingly substitute AI-generated outputs for their own reasoning, reducing cognitive effort and limiting opportunities for critical reflection. The challenge is therefore not the use of AI itself, but the extent to which human cognitive engagement is maintained throughout the interaction process.

Empirical evidence suggests that AI-supported environments can produce both outcomes. In educational settings, students frequently use generative AI for brainstorming, idea generation, and information organization. When used as a learning aid, AI can enhance productivity and support deeper exploration of complex topics. However, studies indicate that excessive reliance on AI-generated responses may reduce cognitive engagement and encourage passive learning behaviors (Gerlich, 2025). Research further suggests that students who regularly depend on AI outputs may become less likely to evaluate evidence, synthesize information independently, or engage in reflective thinking, thereby weakening critical reasoning skills over time (Yavich, 2025).

Similar patterns are evident in professional environments. AI systems increasingly support activities such as report writing, market analysis, financial forecasting, and strategic decision-making. Cognitive augmentation occurs when professionals use AI recommendations as one input among several sources of information before applying contextual judgment. However, cognitive dependency emerges when individuals accept AI-generated recommendations without verification or critical assessment. Such practices may create what researchers describe as the "automation trap," in which excessive trust in AI reduces users' willingness to challenge outputs, evaluate alternatives, or identify potential errors (Karamuk, 2025).

The implications extend beyond decision quality to creativity and intellectual autonomy. Studies have shown that extensive reliance on AI-generated content may reduce originality and critical engagement, as users increasingly rely on automated suggestions rather than developing their own ideas (Octaberlina et al., 2024). Nevertheless, these risks are not inevitable. Evidence indicates that individuals with higher levels of AI literacy are more likely to critically evaluate AI outputs and maintain cognitive engagement during AI-assisted tasks (Kulal, 2025). Consequently, fostering AI literacy and encouraging reflective use of AI are essential strategies to ensure that AI serves as a tool for cognitive augmentation rather than a source of cognitive dependency.

2. Cognitive Offloading and Skill Erosion

Cognitive offloading has become increasingly prevalent in the age of artificial intelligence (AI), as individuals delegate cognitive tasks to intelligent systems to reduce mental effort and improve efficiency. AI-powered assistants, automated decision-support systems, and generative AI applications now perform activities that previously required active human reasoning and analysis. While this shift can enhance productivity, it also raises concerns regarding skill erosion and reduced cognitive engagement. As cognitive responsibilities are transferred to external systems, opportunities to practice and maintain essential cognitive skills may gradually decline.

Cognitive offloading behaviors are strongly influenced by trust and perceived cognitive limitations. Individuals are more likely to delegate tasks when they perceive external systems as reliable or when they doubt their own cognitive abilities. Research indicates that trust in external tools significantly increases the likelihood of cognitive offloading, particularly in memory-intensive and decision-making tasks (Peng & Yeh, 2025). Moreover, metacognitive judgments often influence offloading decisions, as individuals may choose AI assistance even when they possess sufficient knowledge or capability to complete tasks independently. Such patterns can gradually reduce opportunities for active learning and skill development (Boldt & Gilbert, 2019).

The consequences of cognitive offloading can be observed across multiple domains. In education, AI writing tools enable students to generate essays, summaries, and assignments with minimal effort. While these technologies can support learning by assisting with brainstorming and content organization, excessive reliance on them may reduce opportunities to practice writing, critical analysis, and independent reasoning. Students who routinely depend on AI-generated content may engage less deeply with learning materials and gradually weaken their analytical and communication skills. This illustrates how educational benefits can coexist with risks of long-term skill erosion.

Similar concerns emerge in healthcare. Clinical decision-support systems assist physicians by identifying patterns, suggesting diagnoses, and recommending treatments. These systems can improve diagnostic accuracy and reduce cognitive workload, particularly in complex medical environments. However, prolonged dependence on automated recommendations may diminish clinicians' diagnostic reasoning skills if professionals increasingly defer to AI-generated conclusions rather than conducting independent assessments. Maintaining human expertise, therefore, remains essential even when AI provides valuable analytical support.

Professional decision-making contexts also reveal comparable dynamics. In financial analysis, AI systems can rapidly process market data and generate investment recommendations, while legal professionals increasingly use AI tools for document review and case analysis. These applications improve efficiency and reduce workload, yet excessive reliance may limit opportunities to develop expertise, contextual judgment, and critical evaluation skills. Research on cognitive automation describes this process as a "vicious cycle" in which continuous delegation gradually reduces competence, increasing future dependence on automated systems (Rinta-Kahila et al., 2023). Although cognitive offloading can enhance performance and free cognitive resources for higher-order tasks (Morrison & Richmond, 2020), its long-term effects vary according to task complexity, individual characteristics, and contextual factors (Dong et al., 2025). Consequently, balancing AI assistance with active cognitive engagement is essential to prevent skill erosion while preserving the benefits of intelligent technologies.

3. Human-Centered Design Challenges in AI Systems

Human-centered design (HCD) has become an essential foundation for developing artificial intelligence (AI) systems that prioritize human needs, autonomy, and cognitive well-being. However, implementing human-centered AI remains challenging due to the complexity of intelligent systems, ethical concerns, and interdisciplinary requirements. As AI technologies increasingly influence decision-making and cognitive processes, addressing these challenges is crucial to preventing overreliance and cognitive dependency.

One of the most significant challenges in human-centered AI design is transparency and explainability. Many AI systems operate as opaque "black boxes," making it difficult for users to understand how outputs are generated. This lack of transparency can undermine trust and limit meaningful human oversight. Research suggests that user-centered AI frameworks should prioritize explainability and interpretability to enable users to evaluate AI recommendations critically. Without transparency, users may become excessively dependent on AI-generated outputs, reducing cognitive engagement and decision-making autonomy (Buschek et al., 2024).

Ethical considerations represent another major challenge in the development of human-centered AI systems. AI technologies frequently rely on large datasets that may contain biases, potentially producing unfair or discriminatory outcomes. Addressing issues related to fairness, privacy, accountability, and user autonomy requires translating ethical principles into practical design solutions. Human-centered AI frameworks emphasize inclusivity, equity, and user agency to ensure that AI systems align with societal values and support human well-being (Ozmen Garibay et al., 2023).

Another challenge involves balancing automation with human oversight. While AI can improve efficiency and decision accuracy, excessive automation may reduce human participation and increase dependency. Human-centered AI therefore requires collaborative intelligence approaches that preserve human involvement in decision-making processes. Research demonstrates that hybrid decision-making models combining human judgment and AI recommendations can improve outcomes while maintaining cognitive autonomy (Masaeid et al., 2025).

Interdisciplinary collaboration and domain-specific adaptation further complicate the implementation of human-centered AI. Effective systems require cooperation among engineers, designers, psychologists, and policymakers, while also addressing the unique requirements of sectors such as healthcare, education, and industry. Human-centered AI frameworks must therefore remain adaptable and context-sensitive to ensure successful implementation across different environments (Desolda et al., 2025; Arora, 2025).

Table 1. Human-centered AI challenges and practical implementation strategies

Challenge	Practical Implementation Strategy
Transparency	Explainable AI (confidence scores, rationale displays, interpretable outputs)
Automation Bias	Human-in-the-loop mechanisms requiring human review and approval
Trust Calibration	Adaptive feedback systems that encourage verification and critical evaluation
Ethical Issues	Governance mechanisms, including accountability frameworks, audits, and ethical oversight

Table 1 shows that the major challenges associated with human-centered AI can be addressed through practical implementation strategies rather than abstract principles alone. Explainable AI enhances transparency; human-in-the-loop approaches reduce automation bias; adaptive feedback mechanisms support appropriate trust calibration; and governance structures strengthen ethical accountability. Together, these strategies help ensure that AI systems remain supportive tools that augment rather than replace human cognition.

SOLUTIONS AND RECOMMENDATIONS

1. Designing AI for Human-AI Collaboration

Developing and designing artificial intelligence (AI) systems that support human–AI collaboration is essential for reducing cognitive dependency while enhancing human capabilities. Rather than replacing human cognition, collaborative AI systems should augment human judgment, creativity, and contextual reasoning.

Human-centered AI emphasizes shared decision-making, transparency, and adaptive interaction to ensure that AI functions as a cognitive partner rather than an autonomous substitute.

One important strategy for designing collaborative AI involves developing structured human–AI teaming frameworks. These frameworks define the roles, responsibilities, and levels of autonomy assigned to humans and AI systems. The Human–AI Collaboration (HACO) framework provides model-driven guidance for designing collaborative systems that integrate human expertise with AI capabilities. Such frameworks clarify how AI supports users while preserving cognitive engagement and decision-making autonomy (Dubey et al., 2020).

Trust and interpretability are equally critical in human–AI collaboration. Explainable AI approaches improve user confidence by providing understandable explanations for AI-generated recommendations. Systems that incorporate confidence indicators, visual explanations, and contextual annotations enable users to evaluate outputs rather than simply accept them critically. Human–AI interaction models supported by reinforcement learning further strengthen collaboration by enabling adaptive feedback loops that allow AI systems to improve based on human input and preferences continuously (Xiao et al., 2026).

Collaborative content generation and decision support also represent important design principles. AI systems that provide recommendations while maintaining human oversight encourage co-creation rather than automation. Research indicates that collaborative AI tools can improve productivity while preserving user autonomy when designed as supportive partners rather than decision replacements (Agarwal, 2024). Similarly, adaptive and context-aware AI systems can dynamically adjust assistance levels according to user expertise and task complexity, thereby maintaining meaningful human participation in decision-making processes (Favier et al., 2025).

Human–AI collaboration is particularly important in high-stakes environments such as healthcare and manufacturing, where human oversight remains essential. Human-centered AI systems should therefore provide recommendations while ensuring that final authority remains with human decision-makers. Such approaches help reduce automation bias and preserve cognitive autonomy (Lee et al., 2025).

Figure 1. Designing AI for human–AI collaboration

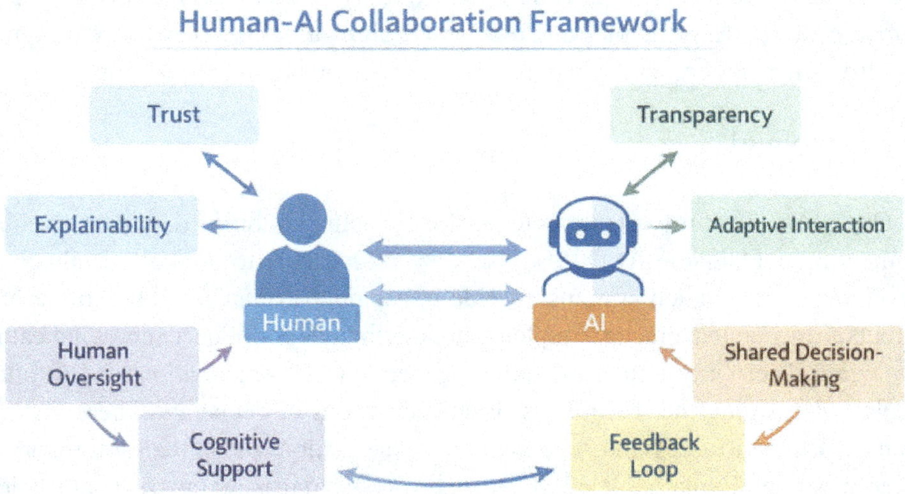

Figure 1 illustrates a human-centered collaboration model consisting of four interconnected components: trust, transparency, adaptive interaction, and collaborative decision-making. The model begins with transparent AI systems that provide explainable outputs and understandable reasoning processes. Transparency supports the development of calibrated trust, enabling users to evaluate AI recommendations appropriately. Trust then facilitates adaptive interaction, where AI systems adjust support according to user needs, expertise, and contextual conditions. Through continuous feedback exchanges, humans and AI collaboratively participate in decision-making processes while preserving human oversight. The final outcome is collaborative intelligence, in which AI enhances cognitive performance without replacing human judgment. The relationships among these components form a cyclical process that promotes cognitive engagement, reduces dependency risks, and supports sustainable human–AI collaboration across diverse application domains.

2. Mitigating Cognitive Offloading Risks

Mitigating the risks associated with cognitive offloading requires a comprehensive human-centered approach that balances the efficiency benefits of artificial intelligence (AI) with the preservation of human cognitive autonomy. While AI technologies can enhance productivity and reduce mental workload, excessive reliance may contribute to diminished critical thinking, reduced problem-solving capabilities, and increasing dependency. Therefore, effective mitigation strategies must translate human-centered AI principles into practical design guidelines that actively support cognitive engagement rather than passive reliance on automated outputs.

Explainable AI

One of the most important strategies for reducing cognitive dependency is implementing explainable AI (XAI). Users are more likely to critically evaluate AI recommendations when systems provide transparent explanations regarding how outputs are generated. Practical implementations include confidence scores indicating the degree of certainty associated with AI-generated recommendations and rationale displays explaining the reasoning behind predictions or decisions. These features encourage users to assess the validity of recommendations rather than automatically accepting them. Explainable AI therefore promotes transparency, trust calibration, and informed decision-making while reducing the likelihood of automation bias (Buschek et al., 2024).

AI Literacy

AI literacy is another essential mechanism for mitigating the risks of cognitive offloading. Users require sufficient knowledge and skills to understand AI capabilities, limitations, and potential biases. Practical implementation can include structured training modules that teach users how AI systems operate, when AI recommendations should be questioned, and how human judgment should be integrated into decision-making processes. Organizations and educational institutions can also implement verification protocols that require users to validate AI-generated outputs using independent evidence, fact-checking procedures, or alternative information sources. Such practices strengthen critical thinking and encourage active cognitive engagement (Kulal, 2025).

Adaptive Interfaces

Adaptive interfaces can further reduce dependence by dynamically adjusting the level of AI assistance based on user expertise and contextual requirements. One practical strategy involves adjustable assistance levels that allow users to determine how much support they receive from AI systems. Another approach is progressive disclosure, whereby information is revealed gradually rather than providing complete solutions immediately. This design encourages users to actively participate in problem-solving before receiving automated assistance. Adaptive interfaces, therefore, maintain user engagement while benefiting from AI support (Favier et al., 2025).

Collaborative Intelligence

Collaborative intelligence emphasizes partnership rather than replacement. Human-centered AI systems should incorporate mandatory human review procedures for high-stakes decisions involving healthcare, education, finance, and public administration. In addition, dual decision systems can require both human and AI assessments before final decisions are implemented. Such approaches preserve human oversight, reduce automation bias, and ensure that AI functions as a decision-support tool rather than an autonomous decision-maker (Lee et al., 2025; Agarwal, 2024).

Governance and Accountability

Effective governance mechanisms are necessary to ensure the long-term responsible use of AI. Practical implementation includes maintaining audit trails that document how AI recommendations are generated and used during decision-making processes. Organizations should also establish accountability logs that record human and AI contributions, enabling transparency and responsibility when errors occur. Governance frameworks further support ethical compliance, fairness, and continuous monitoring of dependency risks (Ozmen Garibay et al., 2023).

Collectively, these strategies demonstrate that mitigating the risks of cognitive offloading requires more than technological improvements alone. Explainable AI, AI literacy, adaptive interfaces, collaborative intelligence, and governance mechanisms work together to preserve human agency while enabling users to benefit from AI capabilities. By embedding these design guidelines into AI systems, organizations can promote cognitive augmentation, strengthen critical thinking, and reduce the risks associated with excessive AI dependency.

3. Ethical and Inclusive AI Design Frameworks

The development of ethical and inclusive artificial intelligence (AI) requires more than compliance with abstract ethical principles. As AI systems increasingly influence learning, decision-making, and everyday cognitive activities, designers must translate ethical values into concrete design practices that preserve human autonomy, fairness, transparency, and cognitive well-being. Human-centered AI frameworks emphasize that ethical considerations should be embedded throughout the design process rather than treated as post-development requirements. Consequently, organizations must adopt practical design guidelines to support responsible

AI implementation while reducing the risks of cognitive dependency and exclusion (Ozmen Garibay et al., 2023).

Transparency by Design

Transparency should be incorporated as a foundational design principle rather than an optional feature. AI systems should provide understandable explanations regarding how recommendations, predictions, or decisions are generated. Practical implementations include explainable interfaces, confidence indicators, rationale displays, and accessible documentation regarding data sources and algorithmic processes. Transparent systems enable users to critically evaluate outputs, calibrate trust appropriately, and maintain meaningful participation in decision-making activities. Such practices also strengthen accountability and reduce automation bias by encouraging users to question and verify AI-generated recommendations (Buschek et al., 2024).

Human Oversight by Design

Human-centered AI requires mechanisms that preserve human authority over important decisions. Human oversight should be embedded into system architecture through review checkpoints, approval processes, and human-in-the-loop workflows. In high-stakes domains such as healthcare, education, and public administration, AI recommendations should function as decision-support inputs rather than autonomous decisions. Maintaining human oversight helps prevent excessive dependency while ensuring that contextual knowledge, ethical reasoning, and professional judgment remain central to decision-making processes (Masaeid et al., 2025).

Accountability by Design

Ethical AI systems must clearly define responsibility for decisions and outcomes. Accountability can be strengthened through governance mechanisms that document AI activities and human interactions. Practical approaches include audit trails, accountability logs, decision records, and regular compliance reviews. These mechanisms improve transparency, facilitate error investigation, and ensure that organizations remain responsible for the consequences of AI-assisted decisions. Accountability structures are particularly important for maintaining public trust and supporting responsible AI governance (Ozmen Garibay et al., 2023).

Inclusivity by Design

Inclusive AI seeks to ensure that systems accommodate diverse users with varying abilities, backgrounds, experiences, and levels of technological literacy. Developers should incorporate accessibility features, bias detection mechanisms, and participatory design approaches that involve diverse stakeholders throughout the development process. Inclusive design reduces discriminatory outcomes and improves equitable access to AI technologies across different populations and application contexts (Pyae, 2025).

Cognitive Preservation by Design

AI systems should be intentionally designed to preserve and strengthen human cognitive capabilities rather than replace them. Practical strategies include adaptive assistance, progressive disclosure of information, reflective prompts, and opportunities for independent problem-solving before AI-generated solutions are provided. These features encourage active cognitive engagement and reduce excessive cognitive offloading. Cognitive preservation is particularly important in educational and professional environments where long-term learning, critical thinking, and expertise development remain essential (Desolda et al., 2025).

Collectively, these five design guidelines provide an operational framework for ethical and inclusive AI development. By embedding transparency, human oversight, accountability, inclusivity, and cognitive preservation into system design, organizations can promote responsible AI adoption while ensuring that intelligent technologies augment rather than diminish human capabilities.

FUTURE RESEARCH DIRECTIONS

1. Long-Term Cognitive and Neurological Effects of AI Dependency

The growing incorporation of artificial intelligence (AI) into cognitive functions has raised concerns about its long-term cognitive and neurological consequences. Although AI improves productivity and accessibility, overreliance may affect cognitive development, memory functions, and critical thinking skills. Subsequent research ought to investigate these enduring effects to guarantee that AI technologies enhance rather than undermine human cognitive talents.

A primary focus of the study is investigating the enduring effects of reliance on AI on cognitive abilities, including memory, reasoning, and creativity. AI-assisted tools are increasingly performing tasks that once required active cognitive involvement, such as writing, summarizing, and problem-solving. Research indicates that dependence on AI could diminish memory retention and autonomous learning, as individuals delegate cognitive responsibilities to automated systems. This dependency may affect brain plasticity and cognitive development over time, especially in younger users whose cognitive abilities are still maturing (Bai et al., 2023). Longitudinal studies are essential for assessing the impact of extended AI use on learning and cognitive development.

A significant domain for future investigation is cognitive exhaustion and decision-making mechanisms. AI-assisted environments often reduce cognitive effort, though they may also lead to decision fatigue and reduced mental engagement. Studies suggest that persistent reliance on AI tools may lead to diminished attention span and cognitive stamina. Understanding the impact of reliance on AI on long-term cognitive function and decision-making efficacy is essential, especially in professional settings that require nuanced judgment (Shalu et al., 2026). Future research should investigate methods to sustain cognitive engagement in AI-enhanced settings.

The psychological and motivational effects require additional examination. Reliance on AI may diminish motivation, resilience, and intellectual curiosity, especially when individuals rely on automated results rather than engaging in active problem-solving. Recent studies indicate that AI-mediated settings may affect workplace motivation and cognitive engagement, thereby changing long-term behavioral patterns. Examining these psychological consequences can yield insights into AI's impact on cognitive autonomy and learning motivation (Huffstadt, 2026).

Furthermore, subsequent studies should investigate the wider consequences of AI integration on cognitive development. AI technologies are increasingly influencing how individuals acquire knowledge and cultivate critical thinking skills. Researchers underscore the need to examine the impact of AI on cognitive development across various life stages and educational settings. Comprehending these developmental effects will enhance human-centered AI design and teaching methodologies (Abbosh et al., 2025).

Cross-cultural and longitudinal studies are essential for understanding the evolution of AI reliance across diverse cultures and contexts. Cultural perceptions of AI, technological proficiency, and educational settings may affect reliance levels and cognitive results. Examining these variances can facilitate the development of adaptable and inclusive AI design frameworks (Al Kaabi, 2025).

2. Human-AI Collaborative Intelligence Models

Human–AI collaborative intelligence models signify a pivotal avenue for future research, especially as artificial intelligence becomes more integrated into cognitive and decision-making processes. Beyond automation, collaborative intelligence emphasizes synergistic alliances in which people and AI systems enhance one another's strengths. Future research should investigate novel frameworks, interaction mechanisms, and governance measures that facilitate equitable human–AI collaboration while mitigating the risks of dependency.

A burgeoning trend is augmenting AI's functions in collaborative settings. Traditionally, AI systems operate as tools or helpers; nevertheless, forthcoming models may establish AI as collaborators or co-decision-makers. Studies on human-machine collaborative decision-making indicate that AI systems can improve cognitive function when incorporated as adaptive partners that share duties and assist human judgment. These models necessitate explicit work allocation, adaptive learning, and reciprocal feedback systems to enhance collaborative efficacy (Ren et al., 2023).

A further potential area of study involves the creation of structured frameworks for collaborative intelligence. Systematic reviews highlight the necessity for taxonomies that delineate roles, responsibilities, and trust calibration in human–AI systems. These frameworks can facilitate decision-making processes, ensuring that humans maintain oversight while AI provides analytical capabilities. Subsequent research should investigate hybrid decision-making models that dynamically allocate tasks based on context, competence, and cognitive effort (Aman et al., 2025).

Trust and transparency are fundamental to the research on collaborative intelligence. Successful collaboration relies on individuals understanding AI thinking and maintaining appropriate levels of confidence. Future models must integrate explainable AI, feedback loops, and interpretability mechanisms to enable users to assess AI outputs critically. Research underscores the significance of ethical governance frameworks to guarantee equity, accountability, and responsible decision-making in collaborative settings (Punzi et al., 2023).

The behavioral and cognitive approaches offer significant research opportunities. Research on human–AI interaction highlights the impact of AI on creativity, decision-making, and cognitive engagement. Future collaborative intelligence models must integrate behavioral insights to improve user experience and mitigate dependency hazards. Furthermore, studies on human–AI symbiosis indicate that collaborative systems can augment creativity and problem-solving by integrating human intuition with AI-generated analytics (Mahmud et al., 2023).

Technological advancements will influence the future of collaborative intelligence. Reinforcement learning and adaptive interaction techniques enable AI systems to adapt to human behavior and preferences dynamically. These systems can enhance cooperation by understanding user intent, learning from experiences, and refining decision-making over time. Subsequent research ought to investigate multi-agent collaborative systems and specialized applications within healthcare, education, and cybersecurity (Li et al., 2025).

3. Ethical Governance and Human-Centered AI Frameworks

With the growing integration of artificial intelligence into decision-making and cognitive processes, ethical governance and human-centered AI (HCAI) frameworks have become essential domains for future research. To ensure AI systems augment human capabilities while reducing dependency hazards, adaptive governance frameworks, ethical protections, and inclusive design principles are essential. Subsequent research should concentrate on implementing ethical governance and enhancing human-centered AI frameworks across all sectors.

A significant research avenue focuses on enhancing ethical governance frameworks that integrate ethical considerations into AI design and implementation. Academics underscore the necessity of integrating fairness, accountability, transparency, and privacy into AI systems via systematic governance frameworks. These principles must be implemented through algorithmic audits, regulatory oversight, and ongoing monitoring to ensure appropriate AI use. Future research should investigate adaptive governance frameworks that can evolve with technological improvements and public expectations (Nakano, 2026).

A vital aspect is inclusive governance and stakeholder engagement. Human-centered AI frameworks must incorporate perspectives from diverse user groups, including marginalized populations, policymakers, and transdisciplinary specialists. Studies indicate that co-governance frameworks that incorporate diverse stakeholders can enhance accountability and confidence in AI systems. Inclusive governance strategies facilitate equitable AI implementation and mitigate concerns related to bias and exclusion (Ferjani et al., 2025).

Principles of human-centered AI design necessitate additional examination. Subsequent research ought to concentrate on enhancing user empowerment via explainable AI, transparency frameworks, and participatory design methodologies. These frameworks emphasize user liberty and guarantee that AI technologies assist rather than supplant human judgment. Furthermore, multidisciplinary cooperation among engineers, ethicists, and social scientists is crucial for creating AI systems that reflect society's values and promote human well-being (van den Berg & Smuts, 2026).

A burgeoning area of research focuses on tackling algorithmic bias and transparency issues. Ethical governance must incorporate measures to identify prejudice, guarantee accountability, and uphold justice in AI decision-making. Research underscores the significance of governance systems adapted to specific sectors, including healthcare, education, and public services. These customized strategies mitigate domain-specific ethical issues and promote responsible AI deployment (Mulani et al., 2026).

Technological advancements are essential to future governance systems. Innovative strategies, including dynamic feedback systems, explainable AI, and federated learning, present interesting avenues for enhancing ethical supervision and transparency. These tools provide ongoing surveillance and modification of AI systems, ensuring compliance with evolving societal standards and ethical expectations (Liu et al., 2024).

CONCLUSION

Artificial intelligence (AI) is rapidly transforming how individuals learn, solve problems, make decisions, and interact with information. As AI systems become increasingly integrated into everyday cognitive activities, understanding the relationship between cognitive assistance and cognitive dependency has become an important challenge for researchers, practitioners, educators, and policymakers. This chapter has examined how AI-driven cognitive offloading creates both opportunities and risks, highlighting the need to balance technological benefits with the preservation of human cognitive autonomy. The discussion demonstrates that AI should not be viewed solely as a source of either empowerment or dependency. A critical distinction exists between cognitive augmentation and cognitive dependency. Cognitive augmentation occurs when AI enhances human capabilities while preserving active reasoning, critical evaluation, and independent judgment. In contrast, cognitive dependency emerges when individuals increasingly substitute AI-generated outputs for their own cognitive processes, reducing opportunities for reflection, learning, and problem-solving. The impact of AI therefore depends not merely on its availability but on how it is integrated into human cognitive processes. Several theoretical perspectives help explain this relationship. Distributed Cognition Theory emphasizes that cognition is distributed across humans and technological artifacts, while Extended Mind Theory suggests that external technologies can become functional extensions of human cognition. Cognitive Load Theory explains why individuals may increasingly delegate cognitive tasks to AI systems to reduce cognitive effort. At the same time, Automation Bias highlights the tendency of users to place excessive trust in automated recommendations, potentially weakening critical thinking and independent judgment. Together, these perspectives provide a comprehensive conceptual foundation for understanding the dynamics of AI-assisted cognition. This chapter also proposes a framework for understanding different levels of AI reliance. The framework distinguishes among Assisted Use, Augmented Use, Dependent Use, and Excessive Dependency. While assisted and augmented use generally support productivity, learning, and decision quality, dependent and excessive dependency behaviors may contribute to skill erosion, reduced critical thinking, and diminished cognitive autonomy. Consequently, the challenge is not to reduce AI usage but to ensure that human cognitive engagement remains central throughout AI-assisted activities. The findings further suggest that human-centered AI offers a practical pathway for addressing dependency risks. Strategies such as explainable AI, AI literacy programs, adaptive interfaces, collaborative intelligence mechanisms, and governance frameworks can help preserve meaningful human participation in decision-making processes. Likewise, ethical and inclusive design principles—including transparency by design, human oversight by design, accountability by design, inclusivity by design, and cognitive preservation by design—provide concrete guidance for responsible AI development. Ultimately, sustainable human–AI collaboration requires designing systems that augment, rather than replace, human cognition, ensuring that technological advancement strengthens, rather than diminishes, human intellectual capabilities.

ACKNOWLEDGMENT

The authors acknowledge financial support from the Indonesian Ministry of Higher Education, Science, and Technology (Kemendiktisaintek) through the PMDSU (Pendidikan Magister menuju Doktor untuk Sarjana Unggul) program under Grant Numbers 0419/C3/DT.05.00/2025 and 083/C3/DT.05.00/PL/2025.

REFERENCES

Abbosh, A., Al-Anbuky, A., Xue, F., & Mahmoud, S. S. (2025). Perspective on the role of AI in shaping human cognitive development. *Information (Basel)*, *16*(11), 1011. DOI: 10.3390/info16111011

Agarwal, O. (2024). MS slide designer: A study on human-AI collaboration for content creation. In *Proceedings of the 16th Conference on Creativity and Cognition* (pp. 499–503). DOI: 10.1145/3635636.3664259

Al Kaabi, S. (2025). Reliance on AI and its effects on critical thinking and graduate readiness: Evidence from UAE higher education. *International Journal of Learning. Teaching and Educational Research*, *24*(8), 398–417.

Al Masaeid, T., Alkhalidi, M. M., Al Ali, A. A. A., Almaazmi, S. M. G. A., & Alami, R. (2025). Artificial intelligence-augmented decision-making: Examining the interplay between machine learning algorithms and human judgment in organizational leadership. *Journal of Ecohumanism*, *4*(1), 4683–4699.

Aman, F., Hamid, S. R. A., & Isa, A. M. (2025). A systematic review of trends in human-AI collaboration research. *International Journal of Technology, Knowledge and Society*, *21*(1), 189–217. DOI: 10.18848/1832-3669/CGP/v21i01/189-217

Arora, T. (2025). Designing for artificial intelligence in high-risk domains: A case study. *Proceedings of the Human Factors and Ergonomics Society Annual Meeting*, *69*(1), 1001–1004. DOI: 10.1177/10711813251370724

Bai, L., Liu, X., & Su, J. (2023). ChatGPT: The cognitive effects on learning and memory. *Brain-X*, *1*(3), e30. DOI: 10.1002/brx2.30

Boldt, A., & Gilbert, S. J. (2019). Confidence guides spontaneous cognitive offloading. *Cognitive Research: Principles and Implications*, *4*(1), 1–16. DOI: 10.1186/s41235-019-0195-y

Buschek, D., Frommel, J., Hauptmann, H., Heuer, H., & Smits, A. (2024). UCAI 2024: Workshop on user-centered artificial intelligence. In *Adjunct Proceedings of the 32nd ACM Conference on User Modeling, Adaptation and Personalization* (pp. 510–512).

Chandra, S., Fatima, A. S., & Shoor, L. (2026). Designing human-centered AI to promote confidence, inclusivity, and mental well-being. In *Imposter Syndrome and AI*. Navigating Human Identity in the Age of Intelligent Machines.

Checkonthayil, B. (2024). Artificial intelligence and the human mind: Psychological insights and implications. *Journal of Dharma*, *49*(3).

Chiriatti, M., Bergamaschi Ganapini, M., Panai, E., Wiederhold, B. K., & Riva, G. (2025). System 0: Transforming artificial intelligence into a cognitive extension. *Cyberpsychology, Behavior, and Social Networking*, *28*(7), 534–542. DOI: 10.1089/cyber.2025.0201

Desolda, G., Esposito, A., Lanzilotti, R., & Piccinno, A. (2025). Designing and evaluating human-centered AI systems: Best practices from a multidisciplinary view. *Joint Proceedings of the ACM Intelligent User Interfaces Workshops*, 170–178.

Dong, X., Wang, J., Xing, Q., & Sun, J. (2025). Differences between children and young adults in the effects of difficulty and value of learning items on cognitive offloading strategies. *Psychological Research*, *89*(2), 69. DOI: 10.1007/s00426-025-02100-9

Dubey, A., Abhinav, K., Jain, S., Arora, V., & Puttaveerana, A. (2020). HACO: A framework for developing human-AI teaming. In *Proceedings of the 13th Innovations in Software Engineering Conference* (pp. 1–9). DOI: 10.1145/3385032.3385044

Elzerman, G. H. (2025). When AI does the thinking: The risks of over-reliance on artificial intelligence in higher education language learning. In *2025 5th International Conference on Artificial Intelligence and Education* (pp. 773–778). IEEE.

Favier, A., Verma, P., La, N., & Shah, J. A. (2025). Leveraging LLMs for collaborative human-AI decision making. In *Proceedings of the AAAI Symposium Series* (Vol. 5, No. 1, pp. 60–62). DOI: 10.1609/aaaiss.v5i1.35556

Ferjani, I., Alzahrani, F. A., & Bouzir, N. M. (2025). Navigating responsible AI: A systematic review of governance mechanisms and future co-governance scenarios. *Procedia Computer Science*, *270*, 4726–4735. DOI: 10.1016/j.procs.2025.09.598

García, A. E. (2025). Generative artificial intelligence: Between enhancement and cognitive offloading. *Cultura, Ciencia y Deporte*, *20*(66), 1.

Garcia-Barrios, D. A. (2025). Epistemic partner or cognitive crutch: A conceptual model of cognitive offloading in human-artificial intelligence collaboration. *IEEE Internet Computing*, *29*(5), 7–16. DOI: 10.1109/MIC.2025.3626694

Gerlich, M. (2025). AI tools in society: Impacts on cognitive offloading and the future of critical thinking. *Societies (Basel, Switzerland)*, *15*(1), 6. DOI: 10.3390/soc15010006

Giray, L. (2024). Negative effects of generative AI on researchers: Publishing addiction, Dunning-Kruger effect and skill erosion. *Journal of Applied Learning and Teaching*, *7*(2), 398–405.

Grinschgl, S., & Neubauer, A. C. (2022). Supporting cognition with modern technology: Distributed cognition today and in an AI-enhanced future. *Frontiers in Artificial Intelligence*, *5*, 908261. DOI: 10.3389/frai.2022.908261

Hofmann, B. (2025). Biases in AI: Acknowledging and addressing the inevitable ethical issues. *Frontiers in Digital Health*, *7*, 1614105. DOI: 10.3389/fdgth.2025.1614105

Huffstadt, K. (2026). The silent impact of AI: Unveiling motivational side effects in the digital age. In *Intelligent Human Systems Integration* (Vol. 351). Disruptive and Innovative Technologies.

Karamuk, E. (2025). The automation trap: Unpacking the consequences of overreliance on AI in education and its hidden costs. In *Pitfalls of AI Integration in Education: Skill Obsolescence, Misuse, and Bias* (pp. 151–174). IGI Global Scientific Publishing.

Karny, S., Mayer, L. W., Ayoub, J., Song, M., Su, H., Tian, D., & Steyvers, M.. (2024). Learning with AI assistance: A path to better task performance or dependence? In *Proceedings of the ACM Collective Intelligence Conference* (pp. 10–17). DOI: 10.1145/3643562.3672610

Kulal, A. (2025). Cognitive risks of AI: Literacy, trust, and critical thinking. *Journal of Computer Information Systems*, •••, 1–13. DOI: 10.1080/08874417.2025.2582050

Kutz, J., Neuhüttler, J., Bienzeisler, B., Spilski, J., & Lachmann, T. (2023). Human-centered AI for manufacturing: Design principles for industrial AI-based services. In *International Conference on Human-Computer Interaction* (pp. 115–130). Springer Nature Switzerland. DOI: 10.1007/978-3-031-35891-3_8

Lee, J. M., Lee, D., & Pan, Y. (2025). Human-AI interaction design guidelines for process optimization in manufacturing. In *International Conference on Human-Computer Interaction* (pp. 354–372). Springer Nature Switzerland. DOI: 10.1007/978-3-031-93412-4_21

Li, W., Liu, H., Huang, K., & Hussain, A. (2025). Reinforcement learning for human-AI collaboration: Challenges, mechanisms, and methods. *Cognitive Computation, 17*(5), 146. DOI: 10.1007/s12559-025-10500-7

Liu, Y., Zheng, W., & Su, Y. (2024). Enhancing ethical governance of artificial intelligence through dynamic feedback mechanism. In *International Conference on Information* (pp. 105–121). Springer Nature Switzerland. DOI: 10.1007/978-3-031-57867-0_8

Lynch, V., & Smith, F. H. L. (2025). Overview and evolution of artificial intelligence. In *Elgar Concise Encyclopedia of Artificial Intelligence and the Law* (pp. 1–6). Edward Elgar Publishing. DOI: 10.4337/9781035336906.00007

Mahmud, B., Hong, G., & Fong, B. (2023). A study of human-AI symbiosis for creative work: Recent developments and future directions in deep learning. *ACM Transactions on Multimedia Computing Communications and Applications, 20*(2), 1–21. DOI: 10.1145/3542698

Morrison, A. B., & Richmond, L. L. (2020). Offloading items from memory: Individual differences in cognitive offloading in a short-term memory task. *Cognitive Research: Principles and Implications, 5*(1), 1. DOI: 10.1186/s41235-019-0201-4

Mulani, A. O., Godase, V. V., Takale, S. R., & Ghodake, R. G. (2026). Ethical challenges and governance of AI in healthcare, education, finance, and security sectors. In *Navigating Social Trust in the AI Era* (pp. 123–154). IGI Global Scientific Publishing.

Mundlamuri, R., Gunnam, G. R., Mysari, N. K., & Pujuri, J. (2025). The evolution of AI: From classical machine learning to modern large language models. *IEEE Access : Practical Innovations, Open Solutions, 13*, 178302–178341. DOI: 10.1109/ACCESS.2025.3621344

Muthusamy, A., Maheswari, S., & Anitha, S. (2025). Recent trends and future prospects of AI and machine learning in decision making. In *Artificial Intelligence and Machine Learning for Business* (pp. 49–62). Apple Academic Press. DOI: 10.1201/9781003535850-4

Najem, N. R., Salman, A. S., Nas, Y. F., Abu-AlShaeer, M. J., Basheer, B. M., Khaddad, A., & Monadhel, H. (2024). Human-AI symbiosis: Investigating real-time neural link integrations for enhanced cognitive abilities. In *2024 36th Conference of Open Innovations Association (FRUCT)* (pp. 664–674). IEEE.

Nakano, M. (2026). Bridging the AI ethics gap: A tripartite framework for accountability, implementation, and governance. *International Journal of Software Innovation, 14*(1), 1–14. DOI: 10.4018/IJSI.401497

Natali, C., Frischmann, B., & Cabitza, F. (2024). Stimulating cognitive engagement in hybrid decision-making: Friction, reliance and biases (Preface). *CEUR Workshop Proceedings, 3825*, 9–15.

Nizamani, M. M., Zhang, H. L., & Lai, Z. (2025). Human-centered AI: Advancing ethical, transparent, and context-aware systems for sustainable development. *Technology in Society*, •••, 103121.

Octaberlina, L. R., Muslimin, A. I., Chamidah, D., Surur, M., & Mustikawan, A. (2024). Exploring the impact of AI threats on originality and critical thinking in academic writing. *Edelweiss Applied Science and Technology, 8*(6), 8805–8814. DOI: 10.55214/25768484.v8i6.3878

Ozmen Garibay, O., Winslow, B., Andolina, S., Antona, M., Bodenschatz, A., Coursaris, C., Falco, G., Fiore, S. M., Garibay, I., Grieman, K., Havens, J. C., Jirotka, M., Kacorri, H., Karwowski, W., Kider, J., Konstan, J., Koon, S., Lopez-Gonzalez, M., Maifeld-Carucci, I., & Xu, W. (2023). Six human-centered artificial intelligence grand challenges. *International Journal of Human-Computer Interaction, 39*(3), 391–437. DOI: 10.1080/10447318.2022.2153320

Peng, J. L., & Yeh, S. L. (2025). Cognitive offloading in short-term memory tasks: Trust toward tools as a moderator. *International Journal of Human-Computer Interaction, 41*(21), 13382–13393. DOI: 10.1080/10447318.2025.2474449

Punzi, C., Setzu, M., Pellungrini, R., Giannotti, F., & Pedreschi, D. (2023). Towards synergistic human-AI collaboration in hybrid decision-making systems. In *Joint European Conference on Machine Learning and Knowledge Discovery in Databases* (pp. 268–275). Springer Nature Switzerland.

Pyae, A. (2025). What makes an AI system human-centered? Preliminary findings from an empirical study. In *Proceedings of the 2025 Conference on Creativity and Cognition* (pp. 354–359). DOI: 10.1145/3698061.3734407

Ren, M., Chen, N., & Qiu, H. (2023). Human-machine collaborative decision-making: An evolutionary roadmap based on cognitive intelligence. *International Journal of Social Robotics, 15*(7), 1101–1114. DOI: 10.1007/s12369-023-01020-1

Rinta-Kahila, T., Penttinen, E., Salovaara, A., Soliman, W., & Ruissalo, J. (2023). The vicious circles of skill erosion: A case study of cognitive automation. *Journal of the Association for Information Systems, 24*(5), 1378–1412. DOI: 10.17705/1jais.00829

Rodriguez-Fernandez, F. (2025). Artificial intelligence and economic psychology: Toward a theory of algorithmic cognitive influence. *AI & Society*, •••, 1–12.

Shalu, V., Verma, N., Dev, K., Bhardwaj, A. B., & Kumar, K. (2026). The cognitive cost of AI: How AI anxiety and attitudes influence decision fatigue in daily technology use. *Annals of Neurosciences*, *33*(1), 09727531251359872. DOI: 10.1177/09727531251359872

Skulmowski, A. (2024). Placebo or assistant? Generative AI between externalization and anthropomorphization. *Educational Psychology Review*, *36*(2), 58. DOI: 10.1007/s10648-024-09894-x

Snehi, J., Snehi, M., Kansal, I., & Khullar, V. (2025). From prototyping to deployment: Human-centered design practices in responsible AI innovation. In *Textual Intelligence* (pp. 435–474). Large Language Models and Their Real-World Applications. DOI: 10.1002/9781394287499.ch18

Tian, J., & Zhang, R. (2025). Learners' AI dependence and critical thinking: The psychological mechanism of fatigue and the social buffering role of AI literacy. *Acta Psychologica*, *260*, 105725. DOI: 10.1016/j.actpsy.2025.105725

Usmani, U. A., Happonen, A., & Watada, J. (2023). Human-centered artificial intelligence: Designing for user empowerment and ethical considerations. In *2023 5th International Congress on Human-Computer Interaction, Optimization and Robotic Applications*. IEEE.

van den Berg, C., & Smuts, H. (2025). From principles to practice: Extracting human-centered AI components from governance frameworks. In *Southern African Conference for Artificial Intelligence Research* (pp. 575–587). Springer Nature Switzerland.

Xiao, S., Wang, Z., Li, J., Noeller, C., Jiang, J., & Wang, J. (2026). Implementation of human-AI interaction in reinforcement learning: Literature review and case studies. *Computers, Materials & Continua*, *86*(2), 1–62. DOI: 10.32604/cmc.2025.072146

Xiaowei, G., Xinqi, L., Zhiping, X., & Tian, X. (2025). The heterogeneity of the effectiveness of human-AI collaborative decision-making: A four-stage process influence model focusing on agency. *Journal of Psychological Science*, *48*(4), 933–947.

Yang, B., Sun, Y., Zeng, Z., & Li, Q. (2026). Deskilling, reskilling, or upskilling? Unpacking the pathways of student adaptation to generative artificial intelligence. *International Journal of Information Management*, *87*, 103002. DOI: 10.1016/j.ijinfomgt.2025.103002

Yavich, R. (2025). Will the use of AI undermine students' independent thinking? *Education Sciences, 15*(6), 669. DOI: 10.3390/educsci15060669

Zakharov, I., Piatnitckaia, L., Birillo, A., Sergeyuk, A., & Izadi, M. (2025). When people come first: A human-centered approach to computer science education. In *Proceedings of the 30th ACM Conference on Innovation and Technology in Computer Science Education* (Vol. 2, pp. 711–712). DOI: 10.1145/3724389.3730766

Chapter 2
AI-Induced Cognitive Atrophy:
Experimental, Neuroplastic, and Evolutionary Perspectives

Sridhara Venugopalachar
http://orcid.org/0000-0003-4715-6996
Acharya University, Uzbekistan

A. Chinnasamy
SRM Institute of Science and Technology, India

K. Vijayalakshmi
http://orcid.org/0000-0002-4827-3011
SRM Institute of Science and Technology, India

ABSTRACT

Artificial intelligence (AI) has evolved from a supportive tool into an active cognitive environment influencing human thinking, decision-making, and learning. While it enhances efficiency, prolonged reliance may lead to AI-induced cognitive atrophy, including reduced memory, critical thinking, and problem-solving ability. This chapter integrates neuroscience concepts such as synaptic pruning and plasticity with machine learning analogies like the Dying ReLU phenomenon to explain cognitive decline due to underuse. Evidence from psychology, neuroimaging, education, and clinical studies shows reduced engagement and increased dependency under AI assistance. The chapter highlights the need for balanced human–AI collaboration to preserve cognitive functions.

DOI: 10.4018/979-8-3373-9484-8.ch002

1 INTRODUCTION: AI AS A COGNITIVE ENVIRONMENT

Artificial intelligence has rapidly transitioned from a background computational aid to an active participant in everyday cognition. Navigation systems guide movement, recommender algorithms shape preferences, generative models produce written arguments, and decision-support systems increasingly influence professional judgment. AI is emerging as both a quiet agent of cognitive disturbance and a catalyst of social advancement in the emerging era of rapid technology advancement. These days, smart systems are present in almost every aspect of modern life, including personalized education, healthcare optimization, content creation, information curation, social interaction mediation, and public discussion molding. The effects of digital dependence on brain functioning and decision-making procedures are being tracked by cognition neuroscience and psychology.

Modern amenities and technological developments have many positive effects, but they have also created new risks to our biological health. Notable instances of human biological change since the Stone Age are shown in this section, with an emphasis on the negative health repercussions of contemporary industrial revolutions. These instances illustrate the dichotomy of better living and biological retreat, even when they are abstracted. Modifications in culture have caused limbs, bones, and muscles to gradually weaken, which has raised health problems and decreased structural stability. For example, a decrease in bone density and weakened muscles have resulted from the move away from strenuous occupations. Back discomfort and spinal dislocation are symptoms of poor posture and weaker core muscles brought on by desk employment and extended sitting. Tool dependence naturally results in a gradual loss of grip strength. On the other hand, grip force has historically increased with manual work and climbing. Similarly, because rougher, rigid foods used to demand more digestive effort, dietary modifications, especially the shift toward softer, processed foods, have affected jaw form and chewing ability.

In the setting of IT systems, knowledge administration is typically regarded as a level of complexity above information handling, which is a layer of complexity above data administration. The resource is more inherent and its understanding is more subjective at higher degrees of complexity. Because data representations will elicit various views, analogies, and analyses depending on the user's degree of familiarity with that type of information, abstracts are a crucial idea. More advanced knowledge abstractions rely on the user's understanding, which is probably influenced by cognitive variables. Practically speaking, knowledge administration would thus deal with the collection, screening, and dissemination of processed data to produce certain cognitive consequences in receivers. The Internet is regarded as a significant resource for learning because of its vast amount of data. Because they handle the computation and filtering processes, agent AIs play a crucial role in the spread of ideas. In order to deal with new data, users add new concepts to their current repertoire, make distinctions between the parameters in the enlarged lexicon, and then reorganize their own knowledge. Work on learning and cognition is supported by this conceptual framework and the fundamental asset analysis.

In ancient societies, cardiovascular wellness was promoted by regular exercise and diets high in natural, raw foods. On the other hand, higher incidence of atherosclerotic and diabetes have been linked to contemporary diets heavy in refined foods. More industrialized and starchy meals were introduced with the development of food production and farming, which eventually caused the size of the stomach to shrink and resulted in eating and fat. Sugar-filled snacks and drinks have made gum damage and tooth decay more common, which has an impact on digesting since it makes chewing more difficult.

Long-term reliance on intelligent systems is increasingly linked to lower epistemological novelty, impaired mental control, and decreased working memory capacity. According to recent research, generative AI technologies promote cognition offloading and decrease intellectual participation in both commercial and educational environments. According to behavioural and neuroimaging investigations, a chronic dependence on prediction systems is associated with decreased activity in the brain areas in charge of abstraction, thought, and moral judgment. In this context, AI no longer merely augments human cognition; it reshapes the cognitive environment in which learning, reasoning, and decision-making occur.

This chapter advances the central claim that persistent reliance on AI-assisted environments can induce cognitive atrophy, analogous to physiological atrophy resulting from disuse. Cognitive atrophy refers not to a loss of intelligence but to the functional weakening of neural and cognitive systems responsible for memory consolidation, analytical reasoning, sustained attention, and metacognitive oversight. Importantly, this process unfolds gradually and often invisibly, becoming apparent only when independent cognitive performance is required. Neurobiologically speaking, atrophy is the deteriorating structure of tissue in the brain, particularly in diseases like Alzheimer's disorder and mild cognitive impairment (MCI). Whole-brain atrophy is linked to losses in recall, concentration, and organizational function cognitive categories that are equally at danger when these abilities are often transferred to computerized systems, according to recent research. When used figuratively, cognitive atrophy in the era of AI corresponds to the progressive deterioration of cognitive abilities like attention, recall, creativity, and moral reasoning given that human consumers depend more and more on AI systems for tasks that previously required sustained cognitive effort. This "transferring" of thinking, often referred to as cognitive offloading, quietly diminishes chances for challenge-based neuroplasticity, which is the very process that fosters cognitive development and endurance.

Unlike earlier digital tools, contemporary AI systems perform higher-order cognitive operations, including synthesis, evaluation, and prediction. As a result, humans are increasingly repositioned as supervisors or consumers of machine-generated outputs rather than active constructors of knowledge. This shift raises fundamental questions about long-term cognitive development, particularly in educational and professional contexts. To prevent this, cognitive environments must be purposefully designed to encourage uncertainty, demand reflexive agency, and preserve the friction required for intellectual development. Medical and social science research both confirm that the mind will ultimately lose what it actually doesn't use.

The objective of this chapter is threefold. First, it introduces a neurocomputational framework grounded in established principles of neural plasticity and machine learning. Second, it synthesizes experimental evidence demonstrating measurable cognitive and neural changes associated with AI overreliance. Third, it discusses implications for education, AI system design, and societal governance.

2 COGNITIVE OFFLOADING AND THE EVOLUTION OF DEPENDENCY

Cognitive offloading—the use of external resources to reduce internal cognitive effort—is a longstanding feature of human cognition (Risko & Gilbert, 2016). Writing, calculators, and maps have historically served this purpose. However, AI systems dramatically extend offloading by executing complex cognitive processes autonomously, often without requiring intermediate human engagement. In cognitive research, cognitive offloading is a well-known phenomenon. To lessen mental strain, it refers to assigning cognitive duties to outside entities. To increase recall and ability to solve problems, people utilize cell phones, graphical calculators, and pads. This procedure is greatly enhanced by AI, which offers active analysis and forecasting in addition to storing. Fingerprint devices and self-report capabilities are being used in mental health apps to monitor state of mind, physical activity, and rest. These applications lessen the difficulty of self-monitoring by compiling data and displaying patterns. Users may instantaneously visualize emotional patterns rather than remembering variations over weeks. By enabling people to recognize triggers, track their progress, and modify their behaviour as needed, these tools support problem-centered coping. Writing assistance and AI-driven meditation apps facilitate self-reflection. They promote participation in activities that could otherwise seem overpowering by creating prompts, offering breathing techniques, or assisting in the expression of emotions. They lessen decision fatigue, which facilitates the adoption and maintenance of coping mechanisms.

The fields that examine the human mind, such as cognitive psychologists, epistemological linguistics, computing, artificial intelligence, classical mathematics, and neuroscience, have developed mental conceptions that are addressed by cognitive sciences. The creation of a mental framework that depicts objects and semantic connections is a common definition of understanding in cognitive research. In addition to addressing the user's awareness and control over his mental processes, metacognition also takes into account the user's attentive participation in a task. Awareness, contemplation, introspection, and analysis are all aspects of metacognition. The greatest method for organizing cognitive and metacognitive data is frequently said to be the cognitive map. According to psychologists, when consumers navigate digital data, they naturally try to establish a mental analog of a physical map. The cognitive map, according to cognitive theory, is essential to normal mental functioning. As a result, one of the designer's objectives is to help people build their mental models by enhancing elements that facilitate and undermine the creative processes. The widespread usage of artificial intelligence-based agent systems has made it possible to monitor cognitive factors more and more. These innovations give media artists new tools and a practical way to move away from the relatively behavioralistic based design practices of traditional methods. Information-seeking activities are clearly influenced by behavioral patterns. The factors are used as a guide to address programming goals and targets in the learning process, and it is believed that these may be related to users' cognitive growth. techniques for handling confusion, contextual issues, identification-to-recall progressions, identification abilities, connections in media structures, traditional structural modeling, and cognitive methods for inquiry are among the issues that need to be handled. This may be accomplished practically by developing and testing theoretical conceptions and mediation procedures against results. Most media producers were often unable to access such analysis prior to the business advancements of AI. With the help of AI bots and improvements in Web-based augmented reality, creators can now better control brain and physical variables. The capacity of a computer or software to make decisions based on inadequate knowledge is one of the fundamental concepts of artificial intelligence. In order to predict consumer interests and provide virtual and customized interactions, internet agent technology may gather data based on user interactions and customs, classify it, and use it dynamically throughout sessions.

Experimental research demonstrates that when individuals expect information to be externally available, they encode less content into long-term memory, instead prioritizing access pathways. Generative AI intensifies this effect by eliminating the need for search strategies or source evaluation. Users receive synthesized answers directly, encouraging passive consumption rather than active reconstruction of knowledge. Over time, this shift fosters dependency. Tasks once perceived as cognitively demanding are increasingly avoided or delegated, reducing opportunities for deliberate practice and skill reinforcement. Dependency thus becomes a structural feature of the human–AI relationship rather than a situational convenience.

3 NEUROPLASTIC FOUNDATIONS OF COGNITIVE ATROPHY

Brain functions are also affected by neuroplastic atrophy. For weeks, Oliver Sacks was confined to a cramped chamber without windows. He also noticed a decline in his visual connection to larger places. Upon being relocated to a room overlooking the structure, he initially had a sense of disorientation. He had rapidly become used to the idea that his environment was constrained by the four walls of his room due to his living situation, which was cramped and without windows. Simultaneously, he had rapidly begun to feel disconnected from the outer world. His connection to broader perspectives recovered far more quickly and easily than his connection to his limb. In this context, I'll refer to these alterations in vision as neuroplastic blindness. The kind of neuroplastic blindness happens when our current perceptions run counter to our prior knowledge, assumptions, and expectations. Because our senses do not conform to the patterns and categories we are accustomed to or have been depending on, our minds fail to absorb them. As a result, we remain focused on the familiar, confining ourselves to those confines. A neuroplastic blindness set in after only a short time spent in a room without windows for Sacks. The wider world beyond his chamber had become rather foreign to his thinking. When something we've never seen before or something we've seen previously but didn't anticipate seeing in this setting shows up out of nowhere, we could experience neuroplastic blindness. When we do not recognize or comprehend an object in our visual field, our brain will ignore it.

Alterations in brain activity in response to training are more typical than increases in volume. The transformation might manifest as the activation of previously dormant areas, the reduction or augmentation of neuronal activity in regions previously associated with the task, or both. Differences in brain activity between the pre- and post-tests aren't always easy to decipher, and they could or might not indicate a significant shift in how the brain is structured or functions. Academics contend that rather than a sign of plasticity leading to an improvement in intrinsic neuronal or cognitive ability, many variations in activation as a consequence of training indicate adaptability in mobilization of assets, owing to approach modification. Rather than a real shift in the neurocognitive network, they contend that the accumulation of knowledge and insight with age offers a great mechanism for improving ability. These findings provide support for the hypothesis that older individuals are less likely to notice improvements in performance because of changes in strategy utilization and that young people are more malleable in their neural networks. Training is believed to enhance mental abilities, which in turn increases neural effectiveness by reducing the complexity of tasks on neural networks. Then, it stands to reason that training should lead to less brain activity during the learned task. Figure 1. Synaptic pruning is a natural developmental process in which excess neural connections formed during childhood are eliminated, resulting in a more efficient and specialized brain network during adolescence. This process strengthens frequently used pathways while reducing underutilized connections, optimizing cognitive performance and learning efficiency.

3.1 Synaptic Pruning and Synaptic Scaling

Figure 1. A pictorial view: Early dense neural networks pruned (scissors) to streamlined adult efficiency

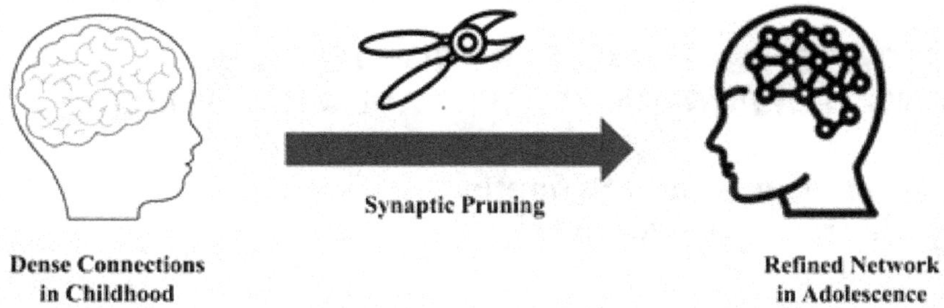

Analogy: AI delegation reduces stimulation in areas like spatial reasoning or arithmetic → underused pathways pruned or scaled down → permanent skill erosion.

Synaptic pruning is a fundamental neurobiological process through which weak or unused neural connections are eliminated, optimizing network efficiency. Synaptic scaling operates alongside pruning by globally adjusting synaptic strengths to stabilize neural activity (Turrigiano, 2008). While adaptive during development and learning, these mechanisms can contribute to functional decline when entire cognitive pathways are chronically underutilized. Synaptic pruning is a unique mechanism that appears to predominate primary brain growth in many animals. As a person ages, the brain's initial relatively high synaptic density eventually decreases. For instance, synaptic density in people is almost doubled at birth compared to adulthood, and certain aspects of this mechanism have been linked to diseases including schizophrenia and autism (Petanjek et al., 2011). Such synaptic pruning has been proposed as a type of standard optimization, possibly reducing energy usage and/or the genetic data required to create a reliable and effective a network, as well as optimizing network topology.

In AI-assisted environments, frequent delegation of tasks such as navigation, writing, and evaluation reduces activation in the neural circuits that support these functions. Over time, these circuits may be pruned or downscaled, leading to diminished cognitive resilience and flexibility.

3.2 Activity-Dependent Plasticity and Synaptic Depression

Neural plasticity adheres to a use-dependent principle: sustained activation strengthens synapses, whereas prolonged inactivity leads to long-term depression (Malenka & Bear, 2004). AI overreliance effectively lowers the activation frequency of higher-order cognitive circuits, particularly those involved in executive control, reflection, and error detection. The resulting synaptic depression manifests behaviorally as reduced critical engagement and cognitive persistence.

4 COMPUTATIONAL PARALLELS FROM MACHINE LEARNING - SUPPORTING MODELS AND ANALOGIES

4.1 Synaptic Pruning and Synaptic Scaling (Neuroscience Model)

Synaptic pruning is a developmental process where excess neural connections are eliminated to streamline brain efficiency, typically peaking in adolescence. Synaptic scaling, a homeostatic mechanism, adjusts synaptic strengths to maintain network stability amid changing activity levels. In healthy brains, these processes optimize resource allocation, but disuse can accelerate pruning of underactive pathways.

Applied to AI dependency: When individuals rely on AI for tasks like navigation or calculations, neural circuits for spatial reasoning or arithmetic may receive less stimulation. Over time, synaptic pruning could eliminate these connections, leading to permanent skill loss. Similarly, synaptic scaling might downregulate activity in prefrontal cortex areas responsible for critical thinking, as AI handles complex decisions. This mirrors how unused muscles atrophy; empirical evidence from fMRI studies shows reduced activation in these regions among habitual AI users (Kühn & Gallinat, 2014). Recent experiments, such as EEG-based studies, justify this by showing lower neural engagement in AI-dependent writers, linking to pruned or scaled-down cognitive pathways.

4.2 The "Dying ReLU" Problem (Deep Learning Model)

In deep learning, Rectified Linear Units (ReLUs) are activation functions that output zero for negative inputs and the input value for positive ones. The "Dying ReLU" problem occurs when neurons consistently receive negative inputs during training, causing them to output zero indefinitely and become "dead," halting gradient flow and impeding learning (Lu et al., 2020). This inefficiency requires interventions like leaky ReLUs to revive functionality. A condition known as "dying ReLU" occurs when neurons in a neural system cease to activate permanently and produce 0 for all inputs. When a neuron becomes trapped in the negative region of the Rectified Linear Unit (ReLU) activating function, wherein the gradient of the neurons is zero, this phenomenon occurs. With (f(x) = max (0, x)), we have the ReLU formula. Negative values for x in the input cause the result to be 0. For negative values, the gradient (derivative) of ReLU is 0 shown in Figure 2. If a neuron's weights are pushed to the point where they constantly receive negative inputs due to a huge gradient update, then its gradient will become zero during the back propagation process. The neuron is dead since the weights can't update anymore because to the zero gradient.

Figure 2. ReLU activation function in deep learning:

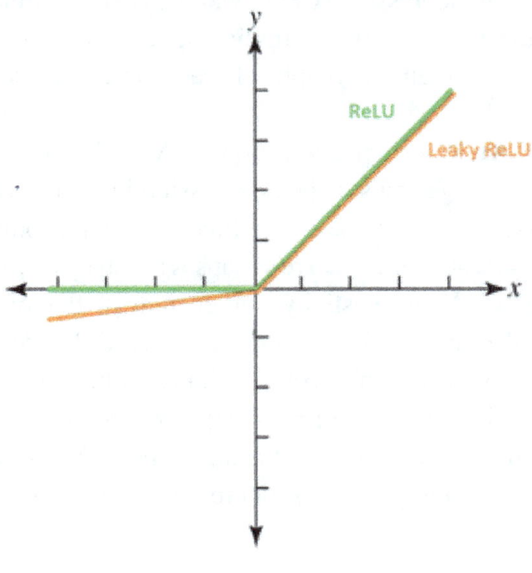

The dying ReLU (standard in green) contrasts with Leaky ReLU (orange), which allows small negative gradients to prevent death. Analogy to human cognition: AI offloading keeps critical thinking pathways inactive ("negative input"), leading to dormant neural ensembles *that fail to engage independently, fostering laziness and dependency.* Analogously, in human cognition, AI overreliance may push certain brain "neurons" (or neural ensembles) into a dormant state. For instance, if AI algorithms preemptively solve problems, critical thinking pathways—akin to ReLUs—might not activate, leading to a "dying" effect where they fail to engage even when needed. This fosters laziness, as the brain defaults to passive modes. Behavioral experiments support this: participants using AI aids show slower independent problem-solving post-exposure, suggesting entrenched dependency. Recent surveys quantify this, showing negative correlations between AI use and critical thinking, mediated by cognitive offloading akin to "dying" neurons.

In deep learning, the Dying ReLU problem occurs when neurons become inactive and cease contributing to learning due to consistently negative inputs. Once inactive, these units fail to recover, reducing model capacity. This phenomenon provides a compelling analogy for human cognition in AI-rich environments: when AI systems preemptively resolve challenges, human cognitive units fail to activate, eventually losing responsiveness even when independent reasoning is required.

4.3 Synaptic Depression and Activity-Dependent Plasticity

Activity-dependent plasticity encompasses mechanisms like long-term potentiation (LTP) and long-term depression (LTD), where synapses strengthen or weaken based on activity patterns. Synaptic depression specifically refers to LTD, where low-frequency stimulation reduces synaptic efficacy, potentially leading to pathway suppression.

In the context of AI: Constant delegation to AI reduces the "frequency" of cognitive engagement, triggering synaptic depression in areas like the dorsolateral prefrontal cortex, associated with executive functions. This could manifest as reduced critical thinking, where once-active synapses for analysis weaken, promoting laziness and dependency. Neuroplasticity studies indicate that digital tool overuse correlates with LTD-like changes, diminishing cognitive resilience (Dong & Potenza, 2014). Experimental evidence from mixed-methods studies shows AI overreliance suppressing reflective thinking, mirroring synaptic depression.

These models collectively suggest a feedback loop: AI use decreases neural activity, which triggers pruning, scaling, depression, and "dying" effects, further entrenching dependency.

5 EXPERIMENTAL EVIDENCE FROM AI-ASSISTED HUMAN COGNITION

5.1 Memory Offloading and Transactive Memory Systems

Experiment:

- Methodology: Participants were asked to type 40 trivia statements into a computer. Half were told the information would be saved, half were told it would be erased. They were then tested on their recall of both the facts and, crucially, *which folder* the saved facts were stored in.
- Results: Participants who believed the information was saved showed significantly poorer recall of the factual content itself. However, their recall for the *location* of the information (the folder name) was enhanced.
- Validation & Parallel: This seminal study demonstrated that the brain readily treats the internet as a "transactive memory" system—an external hard drive. The cognitive consequence is a strategic re-allocation of effort: away from encoding the information itself and toward remembering how to access it. With generative AI, this effect is amplified; we don't even need to remember keywords or sources, merely how to phrase a prompt.

Experimental studies demonstrate that individuals who believe information will be externally stored exhibit reduced recall of content while improving memory for access pathways (Sparrow et al., 2011). Generative AI amplifies this transactive memory effect, reinforcing shallow encoding and reduced conceptual understanding.

5.2 Spatial Navigation and Hippocampal Engagement

Experiment:

- Methodology: Researchers used fMRI and behavioral tests to compare spatial learning strategies in participants. They distinguished between "spatial learners" (who used landmark-based navigation, building cognitive maps) and "response learners" (who relied on habitual, GPS-like turn-by-turn directions).
- Results: Heavy reliance on response-based (GPS-style) navigation was correlated with reduced grey matter and functional activity in the hippocampus, a brain region critical for memory and spatial mapping. Conversely, spatial learners showed robust hippocampal activity.
- Validation & Parallel: This provides direct neurobiological evidence for use-it-or-lose-it plasticity. When we outsource navigation to AI, we deprive our

hippocampus of the exercise it needs to maintain its mapping functions. The result is a tangible, measurable atrophy of the neural circuitry for spatial reasoning, making us perpetually dependent on the external tool.

Neuroimaging research comparing GPS-assisted navigation with self-guided exploration reveals reduced hippocampal activation and gray matter volume among habitual GPS users (Dahmani & Bohbot, 2020). These findings provide direct biological evidence for use-dependent atrophy in spatial cognition.

5.3 Decision-Making and Automation Bias

Experiment (Goddard, Roudsari, & Wyatt, 2014 - Study on Clinical Decision Support Systems):

- Methodology: Medical practitioners were asked to diagnose cases with the aid of a computerized decision support system (CDSS). Unbeknownst to them, the system was programmed to occasionally provide clearly incorrect advice.
- Results: A significant proportion of practitioners followed the AI's erroneous advice, even when their own training and available data should have alerted them to the error. This is known as automation bias—the tendency to favor automated cues over contradictory information.
- Validation & Parallel: The experiment validates the "deskilling" facet of atrophy. Critical thinking and domain expertise can atrophy from disuse when an AI is present. The cognitive muscle required for vigilant cross-checking and independent judgment weakens, leading to an over-trust that compromises decision-making integrity.

Studies in clinical and professional settings show that individuals frequently accept incorrect AI recommendations, a phenomenon known as automation bias (Goddard et al., 2014). This behavior reflects weakened executive oversight and reduced critical evaluation rather than mere trust in technology.

5.4 AI-Assisted Writing and Illusions of Mastery

Experiment (Pilot Study, Stanford 2023 - AI-Assisted Writing):

- Methodology: Students were randomly assigned to write policy briefs either with or without access to a powerful LLM (like GPT-4). Researchers analyzed the final drafts and subsequently tested students on their understanding of the source materials and their ability to revise and defend their arguments.

- Results: The AI-assisted group produced papers that were initially more fluent and well-structured. However, in follow-up tests, they demonstrated significantly poorer comprehension of the source material, less ability to articulate the core arguments without AI help, and produced weaker, more superficial revisions when asked to improve their work.
- Validation & Parallel: This shows atrophy in the *process* of intellectual synthesis. By outsourcing the labor of organizing information and constructing prose, students bypassed the deep cognitive struggle that leads to genuine learning and robust understanding. The result is a hollowed-out final product and a learner whose own analytical muscles have remained unexercised.

Educational experiments indicate that AI-assisted writing improves surface-level fluency but impairs comprehension, argument ownership, and revision quality (Essel et al., 2024). These outcomes suggest atrophy in synthesis, reflection, and metacognitive engagement.

5.5 The "Lazy" AI Metaphor: A Computational Mirror

Experiment (Computational - "Lazy Training" in Over-parameterized Neural Networks):

- Methodology: This is not a human experiment but a key finding in ML theory. Researchers train large neural networks and analyze their optimization dynamics compared to smaller networks.
- Results: In massively over-parameterized models (like modern LLMs), training often occurs in the "lazy regime." The network's vast number of parameters allows it to solve problems by making only infinitesimal adjustments from its initial random state, essentially performing a complex lookup rather than a deep structural reorganization.
- Validation & Parallel: This serves as a powerful computational metaphor for human cognitive atrophy. When we have a vast, external "brain" (AI) that can solve problems with minimal effort on our part, we enter our own "lazy regime." Our internal cognitive parameters—our knowledge base and problem-solving heuristics—undergo minimal adjustment. We rely on the superficial fluency of the AI's output without engaging in the deep, weight-updating "training" that is true learning.

Over-parameterized neural networks often operate in a so-called lazy regime, solving problems through minimal internal reconfiguration. This mirrors human behavior under AI dependence, where reliance on external intelligence reduces the need for deep cognitive restructuring. Learning becomes superficial, and internal cognitive models remain underdeveloped.

The experimental validation is convergent: from memory and navigation to diagnosis and writing, the pattern of cognitive offloading leading to measurable decline is robust. Neuroscience shows us the biological reality of plasticity: neural pathways strengthen with use and deteriorate with neglect. These experiments demonstrate that AI, for all its benefits, can be a powerful engine of neglect for our own critical faculties.

The Cognitive Load Theory (CLT; Sweller, 1988) claims that using AI to complete activities can help lessen cognitive load, which is the main danger to learning and the development of abilities related to certain tasks. Additionally, the assistance may lessen the likelihood that some brain circuits essential to learning and skill development will be activated. Additionally, lowering cognitive load may make it easier to restrict the amount of effort that can be put into activities, which will limit the possibility of deep learning and skill acquisition. Furthermore, mastery of skills is usually preceded by the completion of intellectually challenging activities that test an individual's existing abilities. In this case, the possibility for this groundbreaking process of personal development is blocked by the assistance that comes with using AI to support cognitive load. By reducing the demanding cognitive computation necessary for skill synthesis, the introduction of AI help can drastically change this process of growth. The opportunity for fruitful effort that is essential to good learning is compromised when AI tools are used to deliver the instant response or solution. The notion of advantageous challenges, which asserts that learning settings that inhibit current ability are frequently advantageous with regard to long-term retention as well as transfer circumstances that the application of AI help is likely to routinely eradicate, supports this viewpoint. Figure 3 illustrates that traditional human-only processes involve consistently high cognitive load across problem analysis, information gathering, solution development, and refinement stages. In contrast, human–AI collaboration reduces human cognitive effort by delegating tasks such as outlining, research support, and content generation to AI, which may improve efficiency but requires careful human oversight to maintain critical thinking.

Figure 3. Human–AI cognitive load comparison model

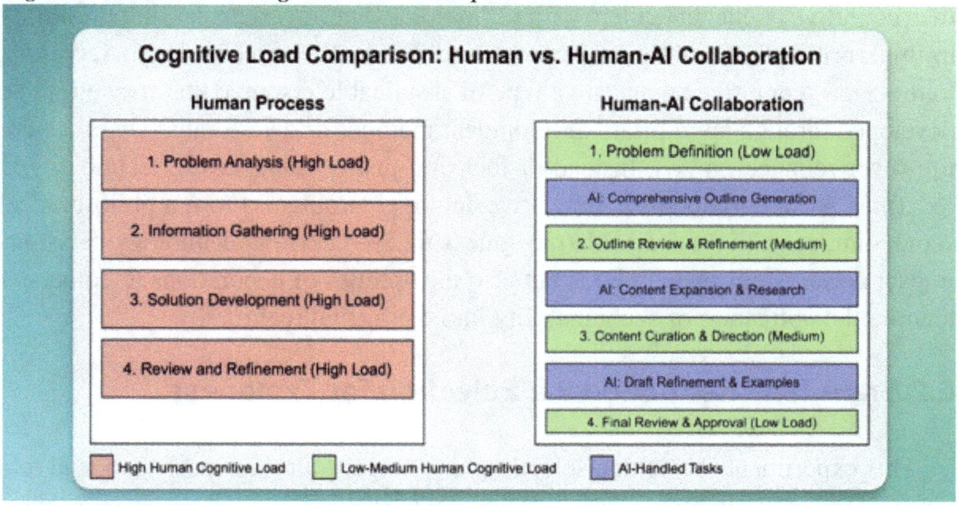

6 LESSONS FROM ANIMAL COGNITION AND DOMESTICATION

6.1 The Problem-Solving Gap: Wolves vs. Dogs

This experiment directly tests the loss of independent problem-solving ability—a core aspect of "shrewdness" and critical decision-making.

- Experiment: Rao et al. (2018) compared equally raised dogs and wolves on an unsolvable puzzle task, ensuring no humans were present to influence behavior.
- Key Result: Wolves were significantly more persistent and successful than dogs. Dogs quickly gave up and looked for human help, while wolves continued to engage with the problem independently. This reflects a divergence in problem-solving strategies: wolves retained the "wild" trait of persistent, self-reliant investigation, while dogs have evolved to outsource cognitive labor to humans.
- AI Parallel: This mirrors the "automation bias" in humans: when an AI tool is available, people are less likely to persist in solving a problem themselves, leading to rapid deskilling.

A conceptual framework for comprehending and resolving competence degradation is "cognitive sustainability." Researchers describe cognitive resilience as follows, taking influence from ecological sustainability: the growth and maintenance of human cognitive talents in tandem with technological progress, preserving the ability to think critically, innovate, and operate independently of technology. According to this view, cognitive talents are a type of sustainable resource that may either be developed through appropriate development methods or deteriorated via excessive use (over reliance on AI). Instead of focusing just on advances in technology, it redefines AI integration as a "cognitive ecology" problem. From a philosophical standpoint, cognitive sustainable recognizes that our current technology decisions impact not only our own abilities but also the abilities of generations to come, extending the obligation of accountability into the mental realm.

6.2 Brain Size Reduction via Selection for Tameness

This experiment shows that selecting for a single trait (tameness) can lead to a physical reduction in brain size—a biological basis for potential cognitive atrophy.

- Experiment: Agnvall et al. (2017) selectively bred Red Junglefowl (wild ancestors of chickens) for low fear of humans over five generations and then measured their brain size.
- Key Result: Birds selected for tameness (low fear) had significantly smaller relative brain sizes compared to their more fearful counterparts. This demonstrates that the "domestication syndrome," which includes brain reduction, can be a direct, correlated response to selection for dependency and reduced vigilance.
- AI Parallel: While not claiming human brains are physically shrinking, the metaphor is powerful: chronic reliance on AI may lead to a functional atrophy of the neural circuits required for deep analysis, memory, and critical thinking, as these circuits are increasingly underused.

6.3 Rapid Loss of Anti-Predator Vigilance

This large-scale analysis demonstrates how contact with humans leads to a swift decline in innate, survival-critical behaviors—a loss of "quick reflexes" and environmental awareness.

- Experiment: Geffroy et al. (2020) conducted a meta-analysis of 173 studies, examining how captivity, domestication, and urbanization affect anti-predator traits (e.g., vigilance, freezing, fleeing) across 102 species.
- Key Result: Contact with humans caused a rapid loss of anti-predator traits, with domestication producing the fastest change. Animals in human care

quickly lost the need for constant environmental assessment and threat detection.

- AI Parallel: This is analogous to how constant AI support (e.g., navigation apps, automated decision-tools) can erode our cognitive vigilance. Skills like spatial memory, fact-checking, and source criticism atrophy when the "predatory" threat of being wrong or lost is constantly mitigated by technology.

The experimental evidence shows that the domestication process—selection for dependency, reduced environmental challenge, and outsourcing of cognitive functions—has a clear parallel in the human-AI relationship.It suggests that to prevent cognitive atrophy, we must design AI interactions that keep the human "in the loop"—requiring active engagement, critical evaluation, and continued use of our innate problem-solving muscles, much as environmental enrichment retains wild traits in captive animals.

Comparative cognition research provides convergent evolutionary evidence for the relationship between dependency and cognitive decline. Studies comparing wolves and dogs demonstrate that domesticated animals show reduced problem-solving persistence and increased reliance on external agents. Additional experiments reveal that selection for tameness correlates with reduced relative brain size and diminished vigilance.

These findings parallel human–AI interactions: when environmental demands are consistently mitigated by external support, cognitive vigilance and independent problem-solving capacities decline. The animal evidence underscores that dependency-driven cognitive change is not uniquely human but reflects a broader biological principle.

7 DISCUSSION: DEPENDENCY, COGNITIVE LAZINESS, AND DESKILLING

The convergent evidence from neuroscience, behavioral experiments, computational analogies, educational studies, and comparative animal cognition presented throughout this chapter establishes AI-induced cognitive atrophy as a functional, measurable, and biologically plausible phenomenon. Prolonged cognitive offloading to AI systems does not merely supplement human intelligence; it can systematically reshape neural architecture and behavioral patterns. Three interrelated but conceptually distinct outcomes emerge from this process: dependency, cognitive laziness, and deskilling. Together, they form a self-reinforcing cycle that progressively diminishes the brain's capacity for independent, effortful, and adaptive cognition.

Dependency refers to the structural embedding of AI into everyday cognitive routines, transforming it from an optional aid into a near-constant cognitive prosthesis. As detailed in Section 2, humans have long practiced cognitive offloading through tools like writing or calculators. However, generative AI amplifies this dramatically by automating synthesis, evaluation, prediction, and even creative construction without requiring users to engage intermediate steps such as source evaluation, logical chaining, or verification. The Sparrow et al. (2011) study illustrates the foundational mechanism: when information is expected to be externally available, encoding into long-term memory weakens while memory for access pathways strengthens. With modern LLMs, users often need only craft an effective prompt; the system delivers a polished synthesis, further eroding incentives to internalize content or strategies. Neuroimaging evidence reinforces this shift: habitual GPS use correlates with reduced hippocampal gray matter and activity, while fMRI and EEG studies of AI-assisted writing show diminished engagement in prefrontal and language networks (Armitage, 2025). Over time, this creates a structural reliance where independent performance becomes effortful or error-prone, mirroring domestication effects in animals. Wolves outperform dogs in unsolvable tasks because dogs have evolved to rapidly seek human help rather than persist independently. Similarly, humans increasingly default to AI consultation rather than sustained internal reasoning.

Cognitive laziness describes the motivational and behavioral tendency to avoid effortful cognitive processing when AI provides low-effort alternatives. This is not mere indolence but a neuroplastic adaptation: the brain, operating under principles of activity-dependent plasticity and energy conservation, downregulates pathways that are chronically understimulated. Synaptic depression (LTD) weakens synapses in executive control regions like the dorsolateral prefrontal cortex when tasks are consistently delegated, reducing the drive for critical engagement, reflection, and error monitoring. The "dying ReLU" analogy from machine learning captures this vividly: neurons that repeatedly receive inputs leading to zero activation become permanently inactive, blocking gradient flow and learning. In human terms, when AI preemptively resolves ambiguities or structures arguments, critical-thinking ensembles fail to activate sufficiently, eventually rendering them unresponsive even when needed. Behavioral evidence includes slower post-exposure independent problem-solving and negative correlations between AI usage intensity and critical thinking scores, mediated by offloading (Gerlich, 2025). The "lazy training" regime observed in over-parameterized neural networks further parallels this: vast models solve tasks with minimal internal reconfiguration (essentially sophisticated lookup), just as humans under AI dependence bypass deep knowledge restructuring. Animal parallels are striking: domestication rapidly erodes anti-predator vigilance and environmental assessment across species, as constant human mitigation removes the selective pressure for cognitive alertness (Geffroy et al., 2020). Figure.4 This distributed cognition diagram shows tools (AI) shifting load from internal cognition, potentially atrophying it over time

Figure 4. Cognitive atrophy feedback loop

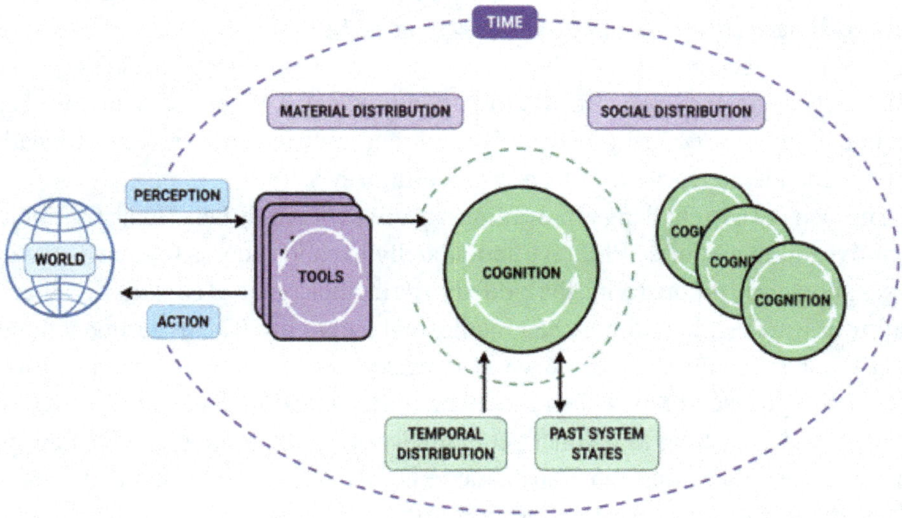

Deskilling denotes the progressive erosion of domain-specific competencies and metacognitive skills through disuse atrophy. Unlike dependency (structural reliance) or laziness (motivational avoidance), deskilling manifests as objective performance decline when AI support is removed. In clinical settings, automation bias leads practitioners to accept erroneous AI recommendations even when contradictory evidence is available, weakening vigilant cross-checking and independent judgment. Educational experiments reveal that students using LLMs for writing produce more fluent drafts but exhibit poorer source comprehension, weaker argument ownership, and diminished revision quality in follow-up tests without AI (Stanford pilot, 2023). Spatial cognition suffers similarly: GPS reliance reduces hippocampal engagement and cognitive-map formation. These outcomes align with synaptic pruning and scaling mechanisms: chronically underused circuits (e.g., for spatial reasoning, synthesis, or error detection) are pruned or globally downscaled to optimize efficiency, producing measurable functional loss. Domestication studies provide evolutionary corroboration: selection for tameness in red junglefowl yields smaller relative brain sizes within few generations, while captivity swiftly diminishes vigilance and problem-solving persistence. In humans, this suggests that convenience-driven AI delegation can functionally atrophy circuits supporting analytical persistence, metacognitive monitoring, and adaptive expertise.

These three processes interlock in a feedback loop: initial offloading fosters dependency, which lowers activation frequency and triggers laziness (motivational withdrawal and synaptic depression), culminating in deskilling (pruning/scaling of disused pathways). The cycle is exacerbated by the seamless, frictionless design of contemporary AI interfaces, which minimize the perceived cost of delegation while masking long-term neurocognitive consequences. Importantly, these effects are not intrinsic to AI technology itself but arise from unreflective usage patterns that systematically remove humans from active cognitive loops. When AI is deployed as a true collaborator—requiring justification, critique, revision, or deliberate alternation with independent effort—the atrophy risk diminishes.

This perspective challenges prevailing narratives of purely beneficial, frictionless cognitive augmentation. While AI undoubtedly expands access to knowledge and boosts short-term productivity, the hidden costs include reduced cognitive resilience, shallower learning, and diminished intellectual autonomy. The experimental, neuroplastic, and evolutionary evidence synthesized here reframes these concerns as empirically grounded rather than speculative. Recognizing dependency, cognitive laziness, and deskilling as distinct yet mutually reinforcing dimensions of atrophy is essential for designing more sustainable human–AI relationships that preserve rather than erode our core cognitive capacities.

8 IMPLICATIONS FOR EDUCATION, AI DESIGN, AND POLICY

From an educational perspective, AI integration must prioritize cognitive engagement over efficiency alone. Instructional designs should require learners to justify, critique, and revise AI-generated outputs. For AI designers, interfaces should be developed to support collaborative cognition rather than substitution, encouraging user reflection and intervention.

At the policy level, guidelines for responsible AI deployment should consider long-term cognitive impacts, particularly for children and adolescents whose neural systems are highly plastic. Ensuring that AI serves as a catalyst for thinking rather than a replacement is essential for sustainable human–AI coexistence.

Even when we account for individual variance using stochastic terms, the resulting complexity is higher than what our model can handle. Cognitive offloading susceptibility varies between individuals due to genetics, culture, and early life experiences. Even after extensive use of AI, some people are able to retain their cognitive autonomy, while others develop a dependent on it very quickly. To possibly enable targeted therapies based on cognitive characteristics, future research should construct tailored models that account for these individual variances. According to the model, the status quo of society and education will remain in place for the foreseeable future. Cultural revolutions advocating cognitive self-reliance, change in education, or enforcement of regulations are adaptive reactions that may be triggered by the realization of cognitive decline. Although they have the potential to significantly change trajectories, these social feedback loops have not been studied. One potential adaptive reaction might be the rise of "cognitive Luddites" who refuse to use any AI at all, however this approach could fail due to the disadvantage to creativity of not using AI at all. The majority of empirical evidence comes from Western educational environments, which limits cross-cultural validity. Educational tenets, rates of technological use, and cultural views on human agency can all cause societies to display distinct patterns. The decline of East Asian educational systems that place a premium on rote memorization may differ from that of Western systems that place a premium on innovation. Research must prioritize the expansion of real-world validation across various groups.

The creation of reliable measures for assessing human-AI team effectiveness in the event of AI breakdown or absence must be given top priority in future studies. Authenticity would be enhanced by five significant expansions. Initially, integrating AI trust and reliability assessment would demonstrate that ability deterioration increases susceptibility after system breakdowns, especially in high-stakes industries like banking, airlines, and healthcare. Second, it would be clear if purposeful design can reduce atrophy or perhaps problems with implementation compromise it if instructional scaffolding with explicit fade procedures were separated from permanent productivity tools. Third, when AI is not accessible, multivariate deconstruction would monitor different paths for executing, metacognitive abilities, and evaluation skills. This would show if improvements in meta-skills make up for execution losses or lead to asymmetric weaknesses. Fourth, interim assistance techniques would be grounded in real transitional processes if contextual switching costs were quantified. Fifth, formalizing skill-efficiency trade-offs and/or managerial decision-making would show how misaligned rewards and temporal discounting can promote immediate efficiency over long-term capabilities.

9 CONCLUSION

This chapter has argued that sustained reliance on AI-assisted environments can induce cognitive atrophy through well-established mechanisms of neural and computational plasticity. By integrating experimental evidence from human cognition, neuroscience, education, and animal studies, the chapter reframes AI-induced cognitive decline as an empirically grounded concern rather than speculative anxiety.

As AI continues to shape cognitive environments, deliberate efforts are required to preserve human agency, critical thinking, and intellectual resilience. The future of human–AI interaction depends not on minimizing cognitive effort, but on ensuring that technology keeps humans meaningfully engaged in the act of thinking. Periodic unaided procedures, competence-adaptive assistance, metacognitive education for efficient tool use, and fade-sensitive design of systems are examples of proactive, evidence-based integrating that can significantly reduce risk while maintaining augment advantages. As AI develops further, striking this balance poses both a difficulty and an opportunity. It will need ongoing multidisciplinary cooperation between cognitive investigators, human-factor analysts, domain specialists, software creators, institutions, and politicians to realize augmentation that really enhances rather than subtly diminishes human capacity. The current study is the first phase of a larger research project, proving that AI-induced skill atrophy deserves careful consideration. Levels of authenticity will be added in later phases, but the fundamental idea stays the same: To guarantee that AI functions as a real amplifier of lasting human capabilities, careful design and control are crucial.

REFERENCES

Armitage, R. (2025). Your brain on ChatGPT: Accumulation of cognitive debt when using an AI assistant for essay writing. *The British Journal of General Practice*, *75*(758), e461–e463. DOI: 10.3399/bjgp25X743181 PMID: 40877119

Dahmani, L., & Bohbot, V. D. (2020). Habitual use of GPS negatively impacts spatial memory during self-guided navigation. *Scientific Reports*, *10*(1), 6310. DOI: 10.1038/s41598-020-62877-0 PMID: 32286340

Dong, G., & Potenza, M. N. (2014). A cognitive-behavioral model of Internet gaming disorder: Theoretical underpinnings and clinical implications. *Journal of Psychiatric Research*, *58*, 7–11. DOI: 10.1016/j.jpsychires.2014.07.005 PMID: 25062755

Essel, H. B., Vlachopoulos, D., Tachie-Menson, A., Johnson, E. E., & Baah, P. K. (2024). The impact of a personal AI-powered writing assistant on academic writing development: A quasi-experimental study. *Computers and Education: Artificial Intelligence*, *6*, 100219. DOI: 10.1016/j.caeai.2024.100219

Geffroy, B., Bruëre, P., Imber-Tate, I., Lepage, O., & Brossard, M. (2020). Evolutionary dynamics in the Anthropocene: Life history and intensity of human contact shape antipredator responses. *PLoS Biology*, *18*(9), e3000818. DOI: 10.1371/journal.pbio.3000818 PMID: 32960897

Gerlich, M. (2025). AI tools in society: Impacts on cognitive offloading and the future of critical thinking. *Societies (Basel, Switzerland)*, *15*(1), 6. DOI: 10.3390/soc15010006

Goddard, K., Roudsari, A., & Wyatt, J. C. (2014). Automation bias: Empirical results assessing influencing factors. *International Journal of Medical Informatics*, *83*(5), 368–375. DOI: 10.1016/j.ijmedinf.2014.01.001 PMID: 24581700

Lu, L., Shin, Y., Su, Y., & Karniadakis, G. E. (2020). Dying ReLU and initialization: Theory and numerical examples. *Communications in Computational Physics*, *28*(5), 1671–1706. DOI: 10.4208/cicp.OA-2020-0165

Malenka, R. C., & Bear, M. F. (2004). LTP and LTD: An embarrassment of riches. *Neuron*, *44*(1), 5–21. DOI: 10.1016/j.neuron.2004.09.012 PMID: 15450156

Petanjek, Z., Judaš, M., Šimić, G., Raaš, M. R., Uylings, H. B. M., Rakic, P., & Kostović, I. (2011). Extraordinary neoteny of synaptic spines in the human prefrontal cortex. *Proceedings of the National Academy of Sciences of the United States of America*, *108*(32), 13281–13286. DOI: 10.1073/pnas.1105108108 PMID: 21788513

Rao, A., Dube, S., Bhatt, D., Joshi, A., Vaidya, S., & Bhatt, M. (2018). Differences in persistence between dogs and wolves in an unsolvable task in the absence of humans. *PeerJ*, *6*, e5944. DOI: 10.7717/peerj.5944 PMID: 30515358

Risko, E. F., & Gilbert, S. J. (2016). Cognitive offloading. *Trends in Cognitive Sciences*, *20*(9), 676–688. DOI: 10.1016/j.tics.2016.07.002 PMID: 27542527

Sparrow, B., Liu, J., & Wegner, D. M. (2011). Google effects on memory: Cognitive consequences of having information at our fingertips. *Science*, *333*(6043), 776–778. DOI: 10.1126/science.1207745 PMID: 21764755

Sweller, J. (1988). Cognitive load during problem solving: Effects on learning. *Cognitive Science*, *12*(2), 257–285. DOI: 10.1207/s15516709cog1202_4

Turrigiano, G. G. (2008). The self-tuning neuron: Synaptic scaling of excitatory synapses. *Cell*, *135*(3), 422–435. DOI: 10.1016/j.cell.2008.10.008 PMID: 18984155

Chapter 3
Attention, Memory, and Self-Regulation Under AI Dependence:
Executive Functions at Risk

Mustafa Kayyali
http://orcid.org/0000-0003-3300-262X
Maaref University of Applied Sciences, Syria

ABSTRACT

This chapter examines how growing dependence on artificial intelligence may reshape core executive functions, particularly attention, memory, and self-regulation. While AI tools can support learning, productivity, and decision-making, their constant availability also invites subtle forms of cognitive surrender. The chapter argues that excessive reliance on AI may weaken sustained attention, reduce the habit of active memory formation, and erode the internal discipline required for planning, problem-solving, and independent judgment. Rather than presenting AI as inherently harmful, the discussion adopts a balanced view: the danger lies not in the technology itself, but in unreflective dependence on it. By exploring the psychological and neurological implications of cognitive offloading, algorithmic assistance, and reduced mental effort, the chapter calls for a more intentional relationship with AI—one that preserves human agency, strengthens critical thinking, and protects the fragile mental capacities that make learning deeply human.

DOI: 10.4018/979-8-3373-9484-8.ch003

INTRODUCTION

Artificial intelligence has entered human life not as a distant technological novelty, but as an intimate cognitive companion (Adewale & Muhammad, 2025). It writes, summarizes, predicts, reminds, recommends, translates, calculates, organizes, and increasingly decides. For many individuals, especially students, professionals, and knowledge workers, AI no longer appears as a tool outside the mind; it begins to feel like an extension of thought itself. This shift is not merely practical. It is psychological. It changes the way people approach difficulty, how they tolerate uncertainty, how they remember information, and how they regulate their own attention. At first glance, the convenience is almost irresistible. Why struggle to retrieve a word, structure an argument, plan a task, or solve a problem when an intelligent system can provide an immediate answer? Yet behind this convenience lies a quieter question: what happens to the human mind when effort is repeatedly outsourced?

This chapter begins from that uneasy but necessary question. Executive functions are among the most delicate and important capacities of the human brain. They allow individuals to focus, plan, inhibit impulses, shift between tasks, hold information in working memory, monitor mistakes, and pursue goals despite distraction or discomfort. These functions are not decorative mental skills. They are the hidden architecture of learning, judgment, maturity, and independence. A person may possess information, but without attention, that information remains scattered. A person may have access to knowledge, but without memory, knowledge becomes shallow and temporary. A person may be intelligent, but without self-regulation, intelligence can drift into passivity, impulsiveness, or dependence. In this sense, executive functions are not only cognitive mechanisms; they are part of the moral and practical discipline through which human beings become capable agents.

The rise of AI dependency complicates this picture. AI can undoubtedly support executive functioning when used wisely. It can help individuals organize complex information, compensate for learning difficulties, reduce cognitive overload, and make professional or academic tasks more manageable. For people with limited time, disabilities, language barriers, or overwhelming responsibilities, AI may serve as a genuine aid rather than a threat. The problem, therefore, is not the presence of AI itself. A simplistic rejection of technology would miss the point. The deeper concern is the gradual replacement of internal cognitive effort with external computational assistance. When AI becomes the first response to every mental challenge, the mind may begin to lose the habit of struggling productively. The muscles of attention, memory, and self-control do not disappear overnight; they weaken through underuse, quietly, almost politely.

Attention is perhaps the most visible area of concern. Contemporary digital environments have already trained many users to expect speed, novelty, and frictionless access (Panda & Kaur, 2023). AI adds another layer to this condition by reducing the need to remain with a problem long enough for deeper understanding to emerge. Sustained attention requires patience. It asks the mind to stay, return, compare, revise, and endure moments of confusion. AI-generated answers, however, can create the illusion that understanding has occurred simply because an answer is available. The learner may read the output, recognize familiar words, and feel cognitively satisfied without having performed the internal work that makes knowledge durable. In this way, attention is not only distracted by AI; it may also be prematurely released from responsibility.

Memory faces a similar risk. Human memory is not a passive storage device. It is shaped by attention, emotion, repetition, association, retrieval, and meaning-making. To remember something is not simply to possess it; it is to weave it into one's mental world. When people rely heavily on AI to retrieve, summarize, and generate information, they may become skilled at accessing content while becoming less practiced at internalizing it. This distinction matters. A society that can search everything but remember little may appear knowledgeable while becoming intellectually fragile. Memory gives continuity to thought. It allows comparison across time, recognition of patterns, and the formation of personal judgment. Without memory, critical thinking becomes dependent on whatever is immediately presented by the system.

Self-regulation may be the most subtle casualty of AI dependence (Li et al, 2025). To regulate oneself is to manage impulses, delay gratification, tolerate ambiguity, and continue working when the task is not instantly rewarding. These capacities develop through repeated encounters with difficulty. However, AI can soften the edges of difficulty so thoroughly that users may gradually lose tolerance for cognitive discomfort. The blank page, the unsolved equation, the dense article, the complicated decision—these moments once demanded internal negotiation. Now, they can be bypassed within seconds. Again, this is not always harmful. Assistance can be humane and necessary. But when assistance becomes avoidance, the person may begin to confuse productivity with growth. Tasks are completed, but the self that completes them may not become stronger.

This chapter argues that AI dependence should be understood not only as a technological behavior but as a psychological condition with possible neurological consequences. The brain changes through use. Habits of attention, memory, and self-regulation are reinforced by practice and weakened by neglect. Therefore, the central issue is not whether AI can make human beings more efficient. It clearly can. The more urgent issue is whether efficiency, when pursued without reflection, may come at the expense of cognitive agency. If the human mind is repeatedly spared from effort, uncertainty, and disciplined recall, then some of its most essential executive capacities may become less resilient.

The aim of this chapter is not to promote fear, nostalgia, or resistance to innovation. Rather, it seeks to open a more mature conversation about human–AI interaction. The future should not be framed as a choice between technological progress and human depth. The real challenge is to design educational, professional, and personal practices that allow AI to support the mind without replacing its most formative struggles. Human beings need tools, but they also need friction. They need assistance, but they also need the dignity of effort. In the age of intelligent machines, protecting executive function may become one of the most important responsibilities of educators, psychologists, policymakers, and users themselves (TEGON, 2025).

THE FRAGILE ARCHITECTURE OF EXECUTIVE FUNCTIONS IN THE AGE OF AI DEPENDENCE

Executive functions are often described in clinical or educational language, as though they were a neat set of mental tools stored somewhere behind the forehead: attention, inhibition, working memory, planning, cognitive flexibility, emotional control, self-monitoring. The list is useful, of course, but it can sound too tidy. In real life, executive functions are not separate instruments arranged in a psychological drawer. They are more like a delicate inner architecture, a living system of mental coordination that allows a person to remain awake inside their own choices. They help the mind pause before reacting, hold a purpose in view, return to a task after distraction, resist the cheap satisfaction of an easy answer, and continue thinking when thought becomes uncomfortable. Without them, intelligence itself becomes strangely unstable. A person may know many things and still be unable to use knowledge wisely.

This fragility matters more urgently in the age of artificial intelligence because AI does not merely provide information (Nguyen, 2025). It intervenes in the very spaces where executive functions are normally exercised. It plans the schedule, drafts the paragraph, summarizes the article, proposes the argument, corrects the sentence, generates the image, predicts the next step, and even suggests the emotional tone of a message. These capacities can be helpful, sometimes remarkably so. Yet their helpfulness carries an awkward shadow. If a machine repeatedly performs the operations through which human cognitive discipline is developed, what happens to the internal system that once had to perform them? The question is not melodramatic. It is not a call to panic. It is simply the kind of question that should arise whenever convenience begins to occupy the territory of human growth.

Executive functions are built through use. They are not ornamental capacities that remain intact while life becomes easier around them. A child learns self-regulation by waiting, trying, failing, correcting, and waiting again. A student develops attention by staying with a difficult passage long enough for meaning to unfold (Wang, 2022). A researcher strengthens working memory by holding competing ideas together, comparing them, testing their tension, and refusing to close the matter too quickly. Even an ordinary adult planning a week, managing deadlines, or solving a family problem is exercising a subtle form of executive command. These moments may appear small, even tedious, but they are the workshop of mental agency. Remove too many of them, and the mind may still function, but with less stamina, less patience, and perhaps less trust in itself.

AI dependence becomes particularly concerning when it turns cognitive effort into something optional by default. The user does not always notice the shift (Sherif & District, 2025). At first, AI feels like relief. It saves time. It reduces pressure. It offers a path through the clutter. A dense article becomes a summary; a confused idea becomes a polished paragraph; a vague intention becomes a structured plan. Nothing seems lost because the output is often better than what the user might have produced under stress. Yet a strange exchange may be taking place beneath the surface: the person receives performance while surrendering practice. The task is finished, but the capacity required to finish such tasks independently may have been left unused. This is the quiet bargain of cognitive outsourcing.

Attention is one of the first structures to tremble under this arrangement. Human attention is not simply the ability to look at something. It is the ability to remain with it while other possibilities call from the margins (Loewenstein & Wojtowicz, 2025). It involves selection, endurance, suppression, and return. AI, when used carelessly, may weaken this endurance by shortening the distance between difficulty and resolution. A learner who once had to sit with a confusing concept may now ask for an instant explanation. A writer who once had to wrestle with the disorder of a half-formed idea may request a clean outline. A professional who once had to compare documents slowly may ask for a rapid synthesis. Again, none of this is inherently wrong. The danger appears when the mind becomes unused to the texture of difficulty. Slow comprehension begins to feel like failure. Struggle feels inefficient. Ambiguity feels almost offensive.

This matters because deep attention is not a decorative academic virtue. It is the condition under which complex understanding becomes possible. Many ideas do not reveal themselves immediately. They require circling, waiting, reconsidering. They resist the first explanation. They ask for a kind of mental hospitality, a willingness to host uncertainty without rushing to evict it. AI-generated clarity can sometimes interrupt this process too early (Georgiou, 2026). It may give the user the feeling of understanding before the user has earned the structure of understanding. The result is not ignorance in the old sense, but something more slippery: fluent shallowness. The person can speak about a topic, perhaps even elegantly, while lacking the internal depth that comes from sustained encounter.

Working memory faces a similar pressure. This function allows the mind to hold several pieces of information temporarily while manipulating them. It is crucial for reasoning, reading comprehension, problem-solving, and meaningful conversation. AI systems can reduce the burden on working memory by keeping track of details, organizing information, and producing coherent sequences (Akar, 2025). Such support can be valuable, especially for individuals who experience cognitive overload. Yet when every demanding mental arrangement is externalized, the user may become less practiced in holding complexity internally. The mind becomes accustomed to having the table already set. It may lose some of its appetite for arranging the pieces itself.

There is also the matter of inhibition, a less glamorous but deeply human executive function. Inhibition is the capacity to stop oneself: to resist the first impulse, the easy distraction, the careless response, the premature conclusion. In traditional learning and professional work, inhibition is exercised constantly. One must resist copying, resist guessing too quickly, resist abandoning the task, resist confusing opinion with evidence. AI complicates this because it makes certain shortcuts not only available but socially normal. When a tool can produce a plausible answer in seconds, the temptation to bypass effort becomes harder to frame as laziness. It appears practical. Sensible, even. Why spend an hour thinking when a system can generate a convincing response immediately? The answer, uncomfortable as it is, lies in the difference between completing work and becoming capable through work.

Self-monitoring, another essential component of executive functioning, may also be dulled by excessive AI reliance. To monitor oneself is to ask: Does this make sense? Did I understand it? Is my reasoning sound? Am I avoiding the harder part? Such questions require a person to remain internally accountable. But AI can create a seductive fog of confidence. Its outputs often arrive polished, balanced, and grammatically composed. They look like competence. They sound like order. For a tired user, this can be enough. The surface becomes reassuring, and the need for deeper verification weakens. A person may no longer ask whether the idea has been understood, only whether it has been adequately presented. That is a profound shift, especially in education, where presentation can too easily masquerade as learning.

The neurological dimension of this issue should be approached carefully, without exaggeration. The brain is adaptive. It changes according to repeated patterns of use and disuse. This does not mean that AI automatically damages the brain, nor that every use of AI weakens cognition (Bransford & McCarrell, 2024). Such claims would be crude. But it is reasonable to suggest that sustained dependence on external systems for planning, remembering, composing, and deciding may influence the habits through which neural pathways are strengthened. The brain does not develop executive control in abstraction. It develops through repeated acts of control. If those acts are consistently displaced, some forms of mental resilience may become less available when technology is absent, unreliable, or misleading.

A deeper concern sits beneath all of this: the erosion of cognitive agency. Executive functions are not merely technical skills; they are tied to the experience of being the author of one's own mental life. To plan is to project oneself into the future. To remember is to maintain continuity with the past. To regulate attention is to decide what deserves one's presence. To inhibit an impulse is to assert that not every desire should become action. These are not small things. They form the inner grammar of responsibility. When AI begins to mediate too many of these operations, the individual may become efficient yet strangely passive, surrounded by outputs but less rooted in authorship.

Still, the issue should not be framed as a battle between human purity and machine corruption. That would be too easy, and probably false. AI can support executive functions when designed and used with care. It can help users break tasks into manageable steps, prompt reflection, encourage revision, support metacognition, and provide scaffolding without stealing the struggle entirely. The key distinction is whether AI acts as a crutch that replaces effort or as a scaffold that eventually strengthens independence. A scaffold is temporary, developmental, and transparent. A crutch may be necessary in moments of injury or overload, but if used indefinitely without need, it changes how the body moves. The same metaphor applies, imperfectly but usefully, to the mind.

The age of AI dependence forces a difficult educational and cultural reckoning (Elamin, 2024). What forms of effort must be preserved, even when they are no longer strictly necessary for producing an acceptable result? Which mental struggles are wasteful, and which are formative? When should assistance enter, and when should it wait outside the door? These questions are not nostalgic complaints from those who fear technological change. They are questions about the conditions under which human beings remain mentally capable, morally awake, and intellectually self-directed.

The fragile architecture of executive functions will not collapse in a single dramatic moment. It is more likely to be renovated badly, room by room, habit by habit, until people wake up inside a mind that is faster but thinner, more assisted but less assured. Protecting that architecture does not require rejecting AI. It requires a more disciplined intimacy with it. Humans must learn to use intelligent systems without allowing those systems to domesticate their attention, soften their memory, or negotiate away their self-control. The mind needs tools, yes. But it also needs resistance, silence, delay, and the stubborn dignity of doing some difficult things for itself.

ATTENTION UNDER ALGORITHMIC PRESSURE: DISTRACTION, DELEGATION, AND COGNITIVE DRIFT

Attention has always been a fragile human achievement. It is tempting to speak of it as if it were a simple faculty, a mental spotlight that can be turned toward one object and away from another. Yet attention is far more unruly than that. It is a negotiation between intention and temptation, between the task one has chosen and the thousand small invitations that arrive from elsewhere. To pay attention is not merely to notice; it is to remain. It is to hold the mind in place when the mind would rather wander, escape, refresh, click, skim, or ask for an easier route. In this sense, attention is not just a cognitive function. It is a form of discipline, almost a quiet ethical act, because it decides what is allowed to matter.

In the age of artificial intelligence, this discipline is placed under a new kind of pressure. The problem is not only that AI systems operate inside already distracting digital environments (Atud, 2023). That would be serious enough. The deeper issue is that AI increasingly changes the meaning of attention itself. When intelligent tools can summarize, rewrite, classify, explain, recommend, and generate, the user no longer needs to stay with a difficult object in the same way. Attention can be shortened, outsourced, redirected, or replaced by a prompt. The mind does not have to wrestle for long with the article, the problem, the argument, or the blank page. It can ask. It can receive. It can move on.

This is where distraction becomes more complicated than the old complaint about social media, notifications, and scattered screens. Traditional distraction pulls attention away from a task. AI-assisted distraction can appear to help with the task while quietly weakening the attention required to understand it. A student may use AI to summarize a dense chapter and believe they have engaged with the material. A professional may ask an AI system to extract the "key points" from a long report and feel adequately informed. A writer may request an outline and experience the satisfaction of progress before the difficult inner work of arranging ideas has truly begun. The activity remains connected to the original task, so it does not feel like avoidance. That is precisely what makes it so subtle.

Attention under algorithmic pressure is not always shattered dramatically (Michel & Gandon, 2024). Often, it thins. It becomes less patient, less muscular, less willing to tolerate the slow burn of comprehension. The user still reads, but with an eye already half-turned toward assistance. The user still thinks, but with the knowledge that a machine can finish the thought. The user still begins, but beginning no longer carries the same seriousness, because rescue is always nearby. Over time, this may produce a mind that is constantly accompanied yet rarely alone with its own difficulty. And difficulty, however unpopular the word has become, is one of the conditions through which attention matures.

There is a peculiar intimacy between attention and resistance. One usually discovers the quality of attention not when the task is easy, but when the task refuses immediate satisfaction. A difficult text slows the reader down. A complex problem forces the thinker to return to earlier steps. An ambiguous question demands patience, comparison, hesitation, even a little irritation. These frictions are not accidental obstacles in learning; they are part of the learning itself. They train the mind to stay. AI can reduce unnecessary friction, which is often useful and humane. Yet if all friction is treated as a defect to be removed, attention loses the very conditions that make it strong.

The delegation of attention may be one of the defining features of AI dependence (Tomašev et al, 2026). People are used to delegating labor. They delegate cleaning, delivery, calculation, navigation, and administrative work. But AI invites a more intimate form of delegation: the delegation of mental presence. It does not merely perform a physical or repetitive task; it attends on behalf of the user. It scans the document, identifies patterns, highlights relevance, extracts meaning, and sometimes even predicts what the user should care about. At first, this appears efficient. Why spend time reading everything when a system can isolate what matters? Why search through complexity when an algorithm can filter the noise?

The danger lies in the gradual narrowing of what the user learns to notice. Attention is not only about efficiency; it is also about discovery. Human beings often find meaning in what was not initially marked as relevant. A strange sentence in an article, a contradiction in an argument, a minor detail in a report, a silence in a conversation—these can become intellectually fertile precisely because they were not preselected by a system. Algorithmic attention, however, tends to privilege what is already categorized, ranked, predicted, or optimized (Chan et al, 2025). It may help the user arrive quickly at the obvious center while making the margins less visible. Yet the margins are often where original thought begins.

This has serious implications for education. Learning is not merely the transfer of correct answers from one location to another. It involves the shaping of perception. A learner must gradually acquire the ability to distinguish the important from the decorative, the credible from the doubtful, the central from the peripheral. When AI performs too much of this sorting, students may receive conclusions without developing the attentional judgment needed to produce or challenge those conclusions (Zhai, 2025). They may become fluent in using outputs but less skilled in noticing what has been omitted, simplified, exaggerated, or smoothed over. The result is not simple ignorance. It is a more polished vulnerability.

Cognitive drift emerges from this condition. It is not the same as distraction, although the two are related. Distraction is a break in attention; cognitive drift is a slow movement away from intentional thought toward externally guided mental motion. The user begins with a purpose, but the system's suggestions, completions, and pathways gradually shape where the mind goes. One prompt leads to another. One generated answer opens a new possibility. One recommendation subtly changes the original question. Before long, the user is no longer directing thought so much as following a trail of algorithmic affordances. Nothing feels forced. That is part of the charm. The drift is soft, frictionless, almost pleasant.

This soft drift may be especially damaging because it weakens metacognitive awareness (Mo oi et al, 2025). When people are deeply attentive, they often know something about their own mental state. They can sense confusion, fatigue, curiosity, resistance, or insight. They know when they are pretending to understand. They feel the gap between reading words and grasping meaning. AI can blur these signals by supplying coherence from the outside. A confused thought becomes a clean paragraph. A shallow idea becomes presentable. A weak argument receives elegant phrasing. The user may begin to mistake the system's fluency for their own clarity. In such moments, attention is not simply distracted; it is deceived by the appearance of completion.

There is also an emotional dimension that should not be overlooked. Sustained attention requires a certain tolerance for discomfort. It asks people to remain with boredom, uncertainty, and incompleteness. These are not pleasant states. They are easy to escape, especially when a responsive machine waits patiently for instruction. AI does not judge the tired user, does not complain, does not demand slow effort. It offers immediate movement. For overwhelmed students and workers, this can feel like kindness (Dzreke, 2025). Sometimes it is kindness. But repeated escape from cognitive discomfort may gradually reduce the individual's capacity to endure it. The mind becomes less accustomed to staying with what does not immediately reward it.

One might argue that this concern romanticizes difficulty. Not every struggle is educational. Some forms of mental labor are wasteful, exclusionary, or needlessly exhausting. AI can remove barriers that have long prevented many people from participating fully in academic and professional life (Ivchyk, 2024). It can help users with attention difficulties, language challenges, disabilities, or heavy workloads. This must be said clearly. The issue is not whether AI should assist attention. The issue is whether assistance strengthens the user's ability to attend or quietly replaces it. There is a profound difference between a tool that helps someone enter a demanding task and a tool that allows them to avoid the demand altogether.

A healthier relationship with AI would preserve the human act of attending. Instead of using AI only to shorten engagement, users could use it to deepen engagement: to generate questions before reading, to test comprehension after reading, to expose assumptions, to compare interpretations, or to invite revision rather than bypassing the first encounter. In such a model, AI becomes less like an intellectual chauffeur and more like a demanding companion. It does not simply carry the mind to the destination; it asks whether the traveler has noticed the road.

Attention is among the first casualties of careless technological dependence because it is so easily mistaken for something else. Looking resembles reading (Campo, 2022). Skimming resembles learning. Receiving an answer resembles understanding. Producing a document resembles thinking. AI intensifies these confusions because it makes the surface of cognition beautifully convincing. The chapter's concern, then, is not that human beings will stop paying attention altogether. The fear is quieter and perhaps more realistic: that attention will become increasingly partial, delegated, and externally choreographed, while users continue to believe they are fully engaged.

To protect attention in the age of AI, individuals and institutions must recover the value of deliberate mental presence (Thiele, 2025). Some tasks should remain slow. Some questions should not be answered immediately. Some texts should be read before they are summarized. Some ideas should be allowed to remain messy before they are polished. The human mind needs intervals in which no system completes its sentences too quickly. It needs the discipline of remaining with difficulty long enough for genuine understanding to take root. Otherwise, people may gain unprecedented access to intelligence while losing the attentional depth required to make that intelligence their own.

MEMORY IN THE SHADOW OF EXTERNALIZED INTELLIGENCE: REMEMBERING LESS, ACCESSING MORE

Memory has never been a simple warehouse of stored facts. That metaphor, though familiar, is rather poor. Human memory is not a silent archive where information is placed, labelled, and later retrieved in its original condition (Ortolja-Baird & Nyhan, 2022). It is more restless than that, more interpretive, more personal. To remember is to rebuild. It is to gather fragments, attach them to emotion, connect them with prior experience, and allow them to become part of one's mental furniture. A remembered idea does not sit outside the self like an object on a shelf; it becomes entangled with judgment, language, imagination, and identity. This is why memory matters so deeply in education, professional reasoning, and moral life. It does not merely help people recall what happened. It helps them know who they are, what they have understood, and what they are capable of comparing, questioning, and creating.

The rise of artificial intelligence unsettles this older relationship between memory and knowledge (Richardson-Walden & Makhortykh, 2024). Human beings have always externalized memory in some form: clay tablets, manuscripts, notebooks, libraries, calendars, photographs, hard drives, search engines. There is nothing new, or necessarily alarming, about using tools to preserve information beyond the limits of the individual mind. Civilization itself depends on external memory. The difference now lies in the intimacy, speed, and interpretive power of the external system. AI does not simply store what humans have written. It retrieves, organizes, explains, summarizes, predicts, and often reformulates knowledge in a voice that sounds almost companionable. It does not wait passively like a book on a shelf. It responds. It speaks back.

This responsiveness changes the psychology of remembering. When information can be accessed instantly, the pressure to internalize it weakens. Why memorize a definition when it can be regenerated in seconds? Why retain the structure of an argument when a system can summarize it more neatly than memory can? Why struggle to recall a theory, date, concept, name, or methodological distinction when a prompt can reopen the matter with polished fluency? At first, this seems like liberation from unnecessary cognitive burden. And, to be fair, some of it is. No serious academic should romanticize rote memorization for its own sake. The mind does not become wiser by hoarding disconnected facts. Yet the rejection of empty memorization should not lead to the careless dismissal of memory itself. Between mechanical recall and intellectual emptiness lies the living territory of internalized knowledge.

Memory provides the ground on which thinking stands. Without some internal store of concepts, examples, distinctions, and experiences, judgment becomes overly dependent on whatever is immediately supplied from outside (Schindler, 2023). A person who remembers little may still access much, but access is not the same as understanding. Access is a doorway. Understanding requires a room inside the mind where ideas can meet one another. When memory is thin, the individual may rely on AI not only to retrieve information but also to decide what is relevant, how it should be framed, and which interpretation appears most plausible. This can create a subtle inversion: instead of using memory to evaluate external information, the user depends on external intelligence to compensate for the absence of memory.

The danger is not that people will suddenly forget everything. Human cognition rarely collapses so theatrically. The concern is quieter. It is that people may gradually remember less because they expect to access more. The habit of retention may begin to feel unnecessary, even burdensome. Students may read in a lighter way, knowing that AI can summarize later. Professionals may attend meetings with less mental commitment, trusting digital systems to capture the main points. Researchers may skim more and absorb less, assuming that articles, theories, and debates can always be retrieved when needed. The mind becomes less like a cultivated field and more like a terminal connected to distant servers. Efficient, yes. But perhaps also exposed, dependent, and strangely hollow when the connection fails.

There is a difference between remembering information and remembering how information feels when one has wrestled with it. This distinction is difficult to measure, yet it sits at the heart of meaningful learning. A student who has struggled through a difficult concept carries more than a definition. They remember the confusion, the false starts, the eventual click of comprehension, the examples that made the idea come alive. That emotional and cognitive residue matters. It helps knowledge become durable. AI-generated summaries can offer the final shape without the formative struggle. They may deliver clarity without history. The learner receives the polished surface of understanding but not always the deeper grooves through which understanding was made.

This matters especially for working memory and long-term memory as they cooperate in complex thought. Working memory allows a person to hold pieces of information temporarily while manipulating them. Long-term memory provides the stored material from which those pieces gain meaning. When someone reads a philosophical argument, solves a mathematical problem, interprets a research finding, or evaluates a policy proposal, they do not begin from emptiness. They bring remembered patterns, prior examples, vocabulary, and conceptual maps. AI can support these processes, but it can also encourage users to approach each task as if the necessary background can be summoned externally at the moment of need. The trouble is that thinking without internal background knowledge is slow in one sense and shallow in another. It becomes dependent on what is provided, rather than enriched by what is already known.

There is also a social dimension to memory that deserves attention. Shared memory is one of the ways communities sustain meaning. Disciplines remember their debates. Professions remember their failures (Coraiola et al, 2023). Cultures remember their wounds, achievements, myths, and warnings. When memory is increasingly mediated by AI systems, questions arise about whose knowledge is preserved, whose histories are simplified, and whose interpretations become easy to retrieve. Externalized intelligence is never neutral merely because it is efficient. It carries the traces of data, design, language hierarchies, institutional priorities, and uneven digital visibility (Heux et al, 2023). If individuals remember less and access more through systems shaped by such forces, then memory itself becomes more vulnerable to algorithmic arrangement.

A troubling possibility follows: the more people rely on AI to remember for them, the less able they may become to notice when AI misremembers, distorts, or omits. Memory is not only a storage function; it is a protective function. It allows skepticism. A scholar who remembers the contour of a debate can detect when a summary is too neat. A teacher who remembers a student's development can sense when a generated assessment feels false. A citizen who remembers historical patterns can recognize the costume of old dangers in new language (Sya et al, 2022). Without memory, people may become easier to impress. Fluency can pass for accuracy. Confidence can pass for truth. The machine's voice, calm and well-ordered, may quiet the small internal alarm that usually says: something here does not fit.

Yet the matter should not be painted in crude colors. Externalized intelligence can also strengthen memory when used with care. AI can help learners create retrieval questions, compare concepts, generate examples, test understanding, and revisit material over time (Aluko et al, 2026). It can support people with memory impairments, language barriers, heavy workloads, or fragmented schedules. It can make knowledge more accessible to those who were previously excluded by rigid academic forms. The issue is not whether AI should be used in relation to memory. It is how. Does the tool encourage active recall, or does it replace it? Does it help the learner reconstruct knowledge, or does it provide ready-made formulations that pass through the mind like water through open fingers? Does it deepen the user's inner resources, or merely decorate the moment with borrowed competence?

Educational practice must become more careful here. For years, some learning cultures treated memorization as the enemy of critical thinking, as if the two could not coexist. This was always a false opposition. Critical thinking requires something to think with. One cannot analyze a historical event without remembering historical context. One cannot critique a theory without retaining its assumptions. One cannot write with nuance if every concept must be fetched from outside at the instant of composition. Memory does not guarantee intelligence, but its absence makes intelligence fragile. It leaves thought dependent on immediate access, and immediate access is not the same as intellectual possession.

Perhaps the most delicate loss is not factual recall but autobiographical confidence. When people repeatedly rely on AI to formulate ideas, remember details, or reconstruct knowledge, they may begin to distrust their own mental continuity. "Did I know this, or did the system provide it?" "Is this my interpretation, or one I accepted because it sounded right?" Such questions may become more common in AI-mediated learning and work. The self begins to share authorship with the machine, not only in writing but in remembering. This does not mean that identity dissolves, but it does suggest that memory, agency, and authorship are becoming tangled in new and uneasy ways.

A healthier approach would treat AI as a companion to memory rather than a substitute for it (Richardson-Walden & Makhortykh, 2024). Users should be encouraged to recall before consulting, explain before generating, summarize from memory before requesting a summary, and question outputs against what they already know. The order matters. When AI comes too early, it may prevent memory from doing its work. When it comes after an attempt at recall, it can correct, enrich, and extend understanding. This small shift—from replacement to reinforcement—may prove essential in preserving cognitive independence.

The age of externalized intelligence asks human beings to reconsider what is worth remembering. Not everything, certainly. But more than convenience admits. People need internal knowledge not because machines are unavailable, but because judgment requires an inner life furnished with remembered meanings. To access information is useful. To remember it is different. Remembering gives knowledge weight, texture, and residence within the self. If AI teaches society to access more while remembering less, the result may be a world rich in information yet poor in intellectual rootedness. The task ahead is to prevent that poverty from dressing itself up as progress.

SELF-REGULATION AND THE COMFORT OF AUTOMATION: WHEN EFFORT BECOMES OPTIONAL

Self-regulation is one of those human capacities that looks ordinary until it begins to weaken. It does not announce itself dramatically. It appears in small acts: beginning a task without waiting to feel inspired, resisting the impulse to check something irrelevant, tolerating the dull middle of a difficult assignment, returning to a problem after failure, revising a weak argument instead of abandoning it, choosing the slower but more honest route when a shortcut glitters nearby. It is, in many ways, the quiet machinery of maturity. Without it, intelligence becomes restless, talent becomes inconsistent, and ambition remains trapped in intention. A person may know what should be done and still fail to do it, not because knowledge is absent, but because the inner discipline required to translate knowledge into action has grown thin.

Artificial intelligence enters this delicate territory with unusual force. Unlike older technologies that mainly extended physical ability or stored information, AI increasingly offers to reduce the psychological effort involved in thinking, planning, composing, deciding, and correcting (Nadeem, 2025). It does not merely help the user do more. It can help the user feel less of the strain involved in doing. The blank page becomes less intimidating because a draft can be generated instantly. The complex decision becomes less burdensome because options can be compared and ranked. The tedious process of revision becomes less painful because language can be polished with a command. Even uncertainty, that ancient companion of thought, can be softened by a system that always has something to say.

At first, this seems merciful. And sometimes it is. Many people live under exhausting demands: students juggling work and study, teachers drowning in administrative tasks, researchers pressed by deadlines, employees expected to produce at machine-like speed while still remaining emotionally human. In such conditions, automation can feel less like laziness and more like survival. It can reduce overload, open access, and offer structure when the mind is scattered. The problem begins when relief becomes dependency, when assistance is no longer used to recover strength but to avoid exercising it. There is a difference between resting a tired muscle and refusing to use it at all.

Self-regulation develops through repeated encounters with resistance. This is an uncomfortable truth, especially in cultures that increasingly treat friction as a design flaw. To regulate oneself is to manage the gap between desire and responsibility. It means doing what matters when it is not immediately pleasing. It means staying with a task when the reward is delayed, incomplete, or uncertain. These capacities do not emerge from lectures about discipline; they are formed through practice, often through the unglamorous repetition of effort. The learner who struggles to organize an essay is not merely producing text; they are learning how to govern attention, sequence thought, tolerate imperfection, and continue despite dissatisfaction. The professional who revises a report carefully is not only improving language; they are practicing patience, accuracy, and accountability. When AI removes too many of these moments, it may also remove the training ground on which self-regulation is built.

The comfort of automation lies in its promise that effort can be optional. Not all effort, perhaps, but enough of it to change the user's relationship with difficulty. A task that once demanded internal negotiation can now be transferred outward. Instead of asking, "How can this be solved?" the user asks, "Can the system solve this for me?" Instead of sitting with a weak first attempt, the user can request a stronger one. Instead of confronting confusion, the user can ask for simplification. Again, none of these actions is automatically harmful. The danger lies in the speed with which they become habitual. A single use may save time; repeated use may reshape expectation. The mind begins to anticipate rescue before it has properly struggled.

This shift can alter motivation in subtle ways. Human beings are not only motivated by outcomes; they are also shaped by the felt experience of effort and achievement (Zajda, 2024). There is a particular kind of confidence that comes from having endured difficulty and emerged with something one can claim as one's own. It may be imperfect, even awkward, but it carries the warmth of authorship. AI-generated success can feel different. It may produce a cleaner result, yet the user may not experience the same internal strengthening. The task is completed, but the self has not necessarily expanded. Over time, this can create a curious psychological imbalance: people may become more productive while feeling less capable.

This is especially important in education, where the purpose of a task is rarely the task alone. An assignment is not merely a product to be submitted. It is a structured opportunity to practice attention, memory, reasoning, expression, and self-control. When students use AI to bypass the demanding parts of learning, they may still deliver acceptable work, perhaps even impressive work, but the educational substance has been hollowed out. The visible output improves while the invisible development weakens. This is difficult for institutions to detect because academic systems often reward the final artifact more than the cognitive journey that produced it. A polished essay can conceal an underdeveloped mind. A fluent answer can hide the absence of struggle.

Self-regulation also involves emotional management, and here AI dependence becomes even more complicated. Difficult work often produces discomfort: boredom, anxiety, frustration, embarrassment, uncertainty (Zafar, 2026). These emotions are not incidental. They are part of the terrain through which disciplined thought must pass. The student who feels confused but continues reading is learning emotional endurance. The writer who dislikes a first draft but revises it is learning resilience. The researcher who faces contradictory evidence and resists premature closure is practicing intellectual humility. Automation can short-circuit these emotional lessons by making escape too easy. If every uncomfortable moment can be softened by a prompt, the user may become less tolerant of the ordinary discomforts of growth.

There is a small but serious danger here: people may begin to interpret effort itself as a sign that something is wrong. If a task feels hard, perhaps the tool has not been used enough. If writing feels slow, perhaps generation should replace drafting. If thinking feels uncertain, perhaps an answer should be requested immediately. This attitude can quietly deform the learner's sense of what intellectual work feels like. Real thinking is not always smooth. Often it is uneven, hesitant, stubborn, and faintly annoying. It includes pauses that look unproductive from the outside. It includes false starts. It includes the humiliating recognition that one's first idea was not very good. These experiences are not failures of cognition; they are cognition becoming honest.

The automation of effort may also weaken inhibitory control. Inhibition is the ability to stop oneself from taking the easiest available action (Kang et al, 2022). In an AI-rich environment, the easiest action is often also the most seductive: ask the system. Generate the response. Accept the suggestion. Move on. The user may not feel that they are surrendering discipline; they may feel efficient, modern, adaptive. Yet self-regulation depends precisely on the ability to delay convenience when convenience would undermine growth. A mature learner might say, "I will try first, then consult the tool." A dependent learner may say, often without words, "I will consult the tool so I do not have to try." The difference between these two postures is enormous, even if the final products look similar.

At the professional level, the same pattern appears in more sophisticated clothing. AI can automate scheduling, correspondence, analysis, presentation, and decision support. These uses may improve productivity, but they can also dull the habits of careful preparation and independent judgment. A manager who relies too heavily on AI-generated evaluations may become less attentive to human nuance (Osborne & Bailey, 2025). A researcher who depends on automated synthesis may lose some sensitivity to methodological detail. A writer who repeatedly outsources revision may gradually weaken their own editorial ear. The issue is not that AI performs these tasks badly. Often it performs them well enough to tempt dependence. That is exactly why self-regulation becomes essential. The better the tool, the stronger the discipline required to use it wisely.

A balanced view must acknowledge that automation can support self-regulation when designed and used intentionally. AI can help users set goals, monitor progress, break large tasks into manageable steps, identify procrastination patterns, and reflect on choices (Jebasingh et al, 2025). It can act as a scaffold for people who struggle with planning, executive dysfunction, or overwhelming workloads. For some users, AI may create the conditions under which self-regulation becomes possible. Yet scaffolding should not become permanent substitution. The purpose of support should be to return agency to the person, not quietly relocate agency to the system.

The central question, then, is not whether effort should always be preserved. Some effort is needless. Some is cruelly distributed. Some reflects poor design rather than meaningful challenge. But certain forms of effort are formative. They build the internal capacities through which people become thoughtful, patient, and self-directed. The difficulty lies in distinguishing between effort that wastes human life and effort that deepens it. AI culture too often collapses this distinction, treating every burden as something to be optimized away (Markelius et al, 2024). A humane approach would be more discerning. It would ask: What should technology remove, and what should it leave intact because the struggle itself has educational, psychological, or ethical value?

When effort becomes optional, self-regulation does not disappear immediately. It becomes negotiable. Then avoidable. Then unfamiliar. Eventually, the person may face a task without assistance and feel oddly exposed, as if some inner instrument has gone missing. This is the long risk of excessive automation: not that humans will become incapable in a general sense, but that they may become less practiced in commanding themselves when no system intervenes. The future of AI use must therefore include a renewed respect for disciplined effort. Not harshness. Not nostalgia. Not the old worship of suffering as proof of seriousness. Rather, a sober recognition that some human strengths are formed only when ease does not arrive too quickly.

Self-regulation is the art of remaining responsible for oneself in the presence of temptation. AI makes that art more necessary, not less. The more comfortable automation becomes, the more deliberately users must decide when to accept help and when to preserve the dignity of effort. The question is no longer simply, "Can AI do this?" It is also, "What happens to me if I no longer have to?"

RECLAIMING COGNITIVE AGENCY: TOWARD HEALTHIER HUMAN–AI INTERACTION

Reclaiming cognitive agency in the age of artificial intelligence does not mean retreating from technology, nor does it require the theatrical purity of refusing every digital aid (Scherz & Green, 2025). Such gestures may look principled, but they often miss the deeper problem. The real challenge is not whether human beings should use AI; they already do, and in many cases they should. The more difficult question is how they can use it without becoming smaller in the process. How can a person accept assistance without surrendering authorship? How can a learner benefit from intelligent support without losing the patience to think alone? How can societies welcome computational power while still protecting the inner disciplines that make judgment, memory, attention, and self-regulation genuinely human?

Cognitive agency begins with the recognition that the mind is not merely a processor of information (Westerbeek, 2026). It is an interpreting, remembering, doubting, choosing, and self-correcting presence. To have cognitive agency is to feel some ownership over one's mental life: to know when one is thinking and when one is merely receiving; to sense the difference between help and replacement; to recognize when an answer has been understood and when it has only been borrowed. This kind of agency is fragile because AI outputs often arrive with the surface qualities of competence. They are fluent. They are orderly. They reduce embarrassment. They make hesitation disappear. For the tired student, the overworked teacher, the anxious professional, or the isolated researcher, this can feel almost miraculous. Yet the same fluency can quietly blur the boundary between one's own intellectual movement and the machine's performance.

A healthier human–AI relationship must begin by restoring that boundary, not as a wall, but as a conscious line of responsibility (Coeckelbergh, 2023). The user should remain the one who asks, judges, revises, accepts, rejects, and finally owns the outcome. AI may assist in shaping thought, but it should not become the hidden authority that determines what counts as thought. This requires a shift from passive consumption to active engagement. Instead of asking AI to "do the work," users need to learn how to ask it to challenge the work, complicate the work, test the work, or reveal what the work is missing. The difference may seem small, almost semantic, but it is psychologically decisive. One posture weakens agency by handing over the difficult part; the other strengthens agency by turning assistance into dialogue.

In education, this distinction is especially urgent. Students should not be taught only how to use AI efficiently. Efficiency, while useful, is too thin a goal for learning. They need to be taught when not to use it, how to pause before using it, and how to compare its output against their own reasoning. A simple but powerful practice is the "attempt first" principle: read before requesting a summary, draft before asking for revision, recall before searching, solve before generating, reflect before accepting. This principle does not ban AI. It places AI after an initial act of human effort. Such sequencing matters because it allows attention, memory, and self-regulation to do some of their formative work before external support enters. The learner is not abandoned, but neither are they rescued too early.

The timing of assistance may become one of the most important design and pedagogical questions of the AI era. Help that arrives too late can frustrate and exclude; help that arrives too early can infantilize. Between neglect and over-assistance lies a more humane middle ground: scaffolding that strengthens the learner's own capacities. A tutor, whether human or artificial, should not merely provide answers. It should ask better questions (Yang et al, 2025). It should slow the learner down when speed becomes evasive. It should encourage retrieval rather than passive recognition. It should invite explanation in the learner's own words. It should sometimes respond with: "What do you think first?" That small delay, that gentle refusal to replace the learner's effort, may become a critical safeguard for executive function.

Workplaces face a similar need for cognitive discipline. AI is often introduced in professional settings as a productivity instrument, and understandably so. It can reduce repetitive tasks, improve workflow, and support decision-making under pressure. Yet organizations should be careful not to confuse accelerated output with improved judgment. If employees rely on AI to draft every communication, analyze every report, summarize every meeting, and recommend every decision, then professional competence may become increasingly performative. People may appear highly productive while gradually losing touch with the slow, interpretive skills that make expertise trustworthy. A lawyer must still reason legally. A doctor must still interpret the patient beyond the data. A teacher must still know the learner beyond the generated profile. A manager must still recognize the human weight of decisions that no model can ethically absorb on their behalf.

For this reason, institutions need cultures of deliberate AI use, not merely policies of permission or prohibition. Rules matter, but rules alone rarely cultivate wisdom (Pentland, 2025). A healthier culture would ask people to disclose when AI has shaped important outputs, to verify claims rather than admire fluency, and to preserve spaces where unaided thinking remains expected and valued. There should be tasks where AI is welcomed, tasks where it is limited, and tasks where it is intentionally absent because the purpose is not only completion but cognitive formation. This may sound old-fashioned in a world obsessed with speed, yet it is not nostalgia. It is intellectual hygiene.

Designers of AI systems also carry responsibility. Current systems often reward immediacy: instant answers, frictionless completion, polished generation, predictive convenience. But not all friction is harmful. Some friction protects agency. Systems could be designed to prompt reflection before providing full solutions, to ask users to state their own reasoning, to show uncertainty more visibly, to encourage source checking, and to support learning through retrieval practice rather than mere output delivery. AI tools could be made less like vending machines of finished cognition and more like workshops where thinking remains visible, unfinished, and shared (Velankar et al, 2024). The design question should not be only "How can this tool reduce effort?" but also "Which kinds of effort should it preserve?"

At the personal level, reclaiming cognitive agency requires habits that may appear modest but are quietly radical. Users can set boundaries around AI use: moments of unaided reading, handwritten planning, memory-based recall, independent drafting, slow revision, and deliberate silence before prompting. They can ask themselves uncomfortable questions: Am I using this tool to deepen my thinking, or to escape thinking? Do I understand the answer, or do I merely like how it sounds? Could I explain this without the system? What part of this work still belongs unmistakably to me? These questions are not anti-technological. They are forms of mental self-respect.

There is also a need to recover the dignity of imperfect human effort. AI often produces smoothness, and smoothness can become addictive. Human thinking, by contrast, is frequently uneven (Al-Obaydi & Pikhart, 2026). It stumbles. It repeats itself. It circles around an idea before finding the door. Academic and professional cultures should not become so enamored with polished output that they forget the value of rough thinking. A first draft written by a struggling student may reveal more genuine development than a flawless generated paragraph. A hesitant explanation may show deeper engagement than a confident borrowed answer. If every imperfection is immediately corrected by automation, learners may lose the chance to see their own growth in motion.

Healthier human–AI interaction also depends on humility. Humans should be humble enough to accept that AI can support them, reveal blind spots, and expand possibilities (Youvan, 2024). AI systems, or rather the people and institutions behind them, should be humble enough not to present machine fluency as equivalent to human judgment. Users should be humble enough to verify, question, and sometimes start again. Cognitive agency is not the fantasy of total independence. No thinker is entirely independent. Every mind is shaped by language, culture, teachers, books, tools, and communities. The point is not isolation. The point is participation without disappearance.

Perhaps the most promising future is one in which AI becomes a companion to metacognition. Instead of merely generating content, it could help users become more aware of how they think. It could ask them to compare options, identify assumptions, examine emotional reactions, notice gaps in memory, and reflect on their own decision-making. Used in this way, AI might strengthen executive functions rather than weaken them. It might help attention become more deliberate, memory more active, and self-regulation more visible. But this requires intentionality. Without it, the path of least resistance will usually prevail, and the path of least resistance rarely builds the strongest mind.

Reclaiming cognitive agency, then, is not a rejection of the future. It is a demand that the future remain humane. It insists that convenience must not become the highest educational value, that productivity must not replace understanding, and that intelligence must not be measured only by the elegance of outputs. The human being must remain more than a prompt-giver, more than an editor of machine-produced thought, more than a consumer of synthetic clarity. There should remain, at the center of learning and work, a person who can attend, remember, struggle, revise, doubt, and decide.

AI can be part of that future, perhaps an extraordinary part. But it should not be allowed to quietly purchase human agency in exchange for comfort. The task ahead is to build habits, institutions, and technologies that keep the mind awake inside its own actions. Assistance should enlarge the person, not replace the person. It should return users to themselves with sharper questions, stronger capacities, and deeper responsibility. Only then can human–AI interaction become not a story of dependence, but a more generous and disciplined form of partnership.

CONCLUSION

The growing dependence on artificial intelligence invites both admiration and unease. On one side, AI represents one of the most powerful extensions of human capability ever developed. It can accelerate learning, improve access to information, support decision-making, and reduce burdens that once consumed enormous amounts of time and mental energy. It can help people write more clearly, organize their thoughts, understand difficult material, and navigate complex environments. To deny these benefits would be intellectually unfair. Yet the promise of AI should not prevent a serious examination of what may be lost when human beings lean too heavily on systems that think, retrieve, plan, and produce on their behalf. The central concern of this chapter has been precisely that fragile territory between assistance and dependence.

Executive functions are not fixed possessions that remain strong regardless of how they are used. They are living capacities, shaped by practice, pressure, habit, and environment. Attention grows through sustained engagement. Memory deepens through active encoding and repeated retrieval. Self-regulation matures through the experience of resisting distraction, delaying ease, and staying with difficulty long enough to transform it into understanding. When AI repeatedly removes these demands, the mind may become more efficient in the short term but less disciplined over time. This is the paradox at the heart of AI dependence: the user may complete more tasks while exercising fewer of the inner capacities that make independent thought possible.

Attention, in particular, stands at risk in an AI-saturated environment. The modern mind is already pulled in many directions, fragmented by notifications, feeds, messages, and constant digital interruption. AI can either help restore order or deepen the fragmentation, depending on how it is used. When it becomes a shortcut away from concentration, it weakens the habit of staying mentally present. A person may no longer wrestle with a text, question, or problem; instead, they may ask the system to simplify, summarize, or solve it immediately. Over time, this can produce a subtle impatience with complexity. Difficult ideas may feel unnecessarily demanding. Slow thinking may begin to seem inefficient. Yet many of the most important forms of understanding require slowness. They require silence, confusion, rereading, and the willingness to remain mentally unsettled before clarity appears.

Memory is equally vulnerable. AI gives users extraordinary access to external information, but access should not be mistaken for possession. To know something is not merely to be able to retrieve it from a machine. Knowledge becomes meaningful when it is remembered, connected, questioned, and integrated into the self. If memory is continually outsourced, the user may become dependent on external systems for intellectual continuity. This does not mean that people must memorize everything or reject digital support. Rather, it means that some forms of internal memory remain essential for judgment. Without remembered knowledge, individuals struggle to evaluate the quality of what AI provides. They may accept fluent answers because they lack the internal reference points needed to question them. In this way, weakened memory can make people not only more dependent, but also more vulnerable to error, manipulation, and shallow certainty.

Self-regulation brings the discussion into an even deeper psychological space. AI dependence is not only about what people know or remember; it is about how they behave when faced with effort. The ease of AI-generated solutions can quietly reshape motivation. Why plan carefully if a tool can generate a plan? Why revise patiently if a system can rewrite? Why think through a dilemma if a machine can offer instant advice? These questions are not trivial. They reveal how convenience may interfere with the formation of discipline. A person who avoids mental effort again and again may gradually lose confidence in their own ability to think without assistance. Dependence then becomes emotional as much as cognitive. The user does not merely use AI; they begin to feel incomplete without it.

Still, the conclusion should not be pessimistic. AI does not inevitably damage executive functions. Its impact depends on patterns of use, educational culture, personal awareness, and institutional design. Used thoughtfully, AI can strengthen rather than weaken human cognition. It can serve as a tutor that asks questions instead of giving answers too quickly. It can help learners reflect on their reasoning rather than bypass it. It can support memory through retrieval practice rather than passive summary. It can encourage planning, metacognition, and self-monitoring. The same technology that risks encouraging dependency can also be shaped to promote agency. The difference lies in whether AI is treated as a substitute for thinking or as a partner in thinking.

For this reason, the future of AI and executive function should be guided by a principle of cognitive preservation. Schools, universities, workplaces, and families need to ask not only what AI can do, but what humans still need to practice doing for themselves. Learners should be taught when to use AI, when to resist it, and when to struggle without it. Professionals should be encouraged to maintain core skills rather than surrender them entirely to automation. Designers should build systems that invite reflection, not merely consumption. Policymakers should recognize that cognitive dependence is not a private inconvenience but a public concern, especially in societies that rely on citizens capable of judgment, attention, and self-control.

Ultimately, the question is not whether artificial intelligence will become part of human life. It already has. The more meaningful question is what kind of human beings will emerge from prolonged contact with intelligent machines. If AI is used carelessly, it may encourage a culture of mental outsourcing, where people become fast but shallow, informed but forgetful, productive but inwardly passive. If used wisely, however, it may free human beings from unnecessary burdens while preserving the deeper work of thinking, remembering, choosing, and regulating the self. The task ahead is therefore not to reject AI, but to humanize its use.

Executive functions are too important to be quietly traded for convenience. They are the inner instruments through which people build knowledge, character, independence, and responsibility. In an age where machines can answer almost anything, the human challenge may be to protect the capacities that allow us to ask better questions, doubt easy answers, and remain awake inside our own thinking. That, perhaps, is where the real future of intelligence begins.

REFERENCES

Adewale, M. D., & Muhammad, U. I. (2025). From virtual companions to forbidden attractions: The seductive rise of artificial intelligence love, loneliness, and intimacy—A systematic review. *Journal of Technology in Behavioral Science*, •••, 1–18. DOI: 10.1007/s41347-025-00549-4

Akar, S. G. M. (2025). Working Memory in the Age of Artificial Intelligence: Cognitive Paradoxes and Educational Implications. Educational Research (IJMCER), 7(5), 01-10.

Al-Obaydi, L. H., & Pikhart, M. (2026). Artificial intelligence addiction: Exploring the emerging phenomenon of addiction in the AI age. *AI & Society*, *41*(2), 1577–1593. DOI: 10.1007/s00146-025-02535-z

Aluko, H. A., Aluko, A., Offiah, G. A., Ogunjimi, F., Aluko, A. O., Alalade, F. M., Ogeze Ukeje, I., & Nwani, C. H. (2026). Exploring the effectiveness of AI-generated learning materials in facilitating active learning strategies and knowledge retention in higher education. *The International Journal of Organizational Analysis*, *34*(4), 1243–1267. DOI: 10.1108/IJOA-07-2024-4632

Atud, V. (2023). *Reclaiming focus in the age of AI: Strategies for deep thinking in a distracted culture*. Sunburst Markets.

Bransford, J. D., & McCarrell, N. S. (2024). A Sketch of a Cognitive Approach to Comprehension: Some Thoughts about Understandin what it Means to Comprehend. In *Cognition and the symbolic processes* (pp. 189–230). Routledge. DOI: 10.4324/9781003482833-10

Campo, E. (2022). *Attention and its crisis in digital society*. Routledge. DOI: 10.4324/9781003225522

Chan, J., Choi, F., Saha, K., & Chandrasekharan, E. (2025). The Ranking Effect: How Algorithmic Rank Influences Attention on Social Media. arXiv preprint arXiv:2509.18440.

Coeckelbergh, M. (2023). Narrative responsibility and artificial intelligence: How AI challenges human responsibility and sense-making. *AI & Society*, *38*(6), 2437–2450. DOI: 10.1007/s00146-021-01375-x

Coraiola, D. M., Foster, W. M., Mena, S., Foroughi, H., & Rintamäki, J. (2023). Ecologies of memories: Memory work within and between organizations and communities. *The Academy of Management Annals*, *17*(1), 373–404. DOI: 10.5465/annals.2021.0088

Dzreke, S. S. (2025). *Preventing complaints before they happen: How AI-driven sentiment analysis enables proactive service recovery*. Advanced Research Journal.

Elamin, M. O. I. (2024). AI through the ages: Unlocking key opportunities and navigating challenges in the history and future of artificial intelligence. *International Journal of Religion*, *5*(12), 1152–1166. DOI: 10.61707/tarzcj89

Georgiou, G. P. (2026). What Distinguishes AI-Generated from Human Writing? A Rapid Review of the Literature. *Big Data and Cognitive Computing*, *10*(2), 55. DOI: 10.3390/bdcc10020055

Heux, L., Rathbone, C., Gensburger, S., Clifford, R., & Souchay, C. (2023). Collective memory and autobiographical memory: Perspectives from the humanities and cognitive sciences. *Wiley Interdisciplinary Reviews: Cognitive Science*, *14*(3), e1635. DOI: 10.1002/wcs.1635 PMID: 36428237

Ivchyk, V. (2024). Overcoming barriers to artificial intelligence adoption. *Three Seas Economic Journal*, *5*(4), 14–20. DOI: 10.30525/2661-5150/2024-4-3

Jebasingh, D. R., Ahmad, N., Shimray, S. R., & Subaveerapandiyan, A. (2025). Perceived Impact of Procrastination on Academic Performance Among Students and the Role of AI Tools. *Libri*, *75*(4), 355–373. DOI: 10.1515/libri-2025-0093

Kang, W., Hernández, S. P., Rahman, M. S., Voigt, K., & Malvaso, A. (2022). Inhibitory control development: A network neuroscience perspective. *Frontiers in Psychology*, *13*, 651547. DOI: 10.3389/fpsyg.2022.651547 PMID: 36300046

Li, X., Cai, X., & Wang, P. (2025). "Are We Still in Control?": Exploring Patterns of AI Dependency in Scientific Research. *Proceedings of the Association for Information Science and Technology*, *62*(1), 1001–1006. DOI: 10.1002/pra2.1329

Loewenstein, G., & Wojtowicz, Z. (2025). The economics of attention. *Journal of Economic Literature*, *63*(3), 1038–1089. DOI: 10.1257/jel.20241665

Markelius, A., Wright, C., Kuiper, J., Delille, N., & Kuo, Y. T. (2024). The mechanisms of AI hype and its planetary and social costs. *AI and Ethics*, *4*(3), 727–742. DOI: 10.1007/s43681-024-00461-2

Michel, F., & Gandon, F. (2024, October). Pay attention: a call to regulate the attention market and prevent algorithmic emotional governance. In Proceedings of the AAAI/ACM Conference on AI, Ethics, and Society (Vol. 7, No. 1, pp. 971-983). DOI: 10.1609/aies.v7i1.31696

Mo oi, A. A., Maican, C. I., Cazan, A. M., & Sumedrea, S. (2025). Do students need to think hard? The interplay of AI and cognitive abilities in solving problems. *Education and Information Technologies*, •••, 1–28.

Nadeem, S. (2025). Artificial Intelligence and the Human Mind: Cognitive Psychology in the Age of Machines. *ASSAJ*, *4*(01), 3761–3773.

Nguyen, T. B. (2025). *The Age of Fragile Intelligence-Human Survival*. Power, and AI Limits.

Ortolja-Baird, A., & Nyhan, J. (2022). Encoding the haunting of an object catalogue: On the potential of digital technologies to perpetuate or subvert the silence and bias of the early-modern archive. *Digital Scholarship in the Humanities*, *37*(3), 844–867. DOI: 10.1093/llc/fqab065

Osborne, M. R., & Bailey, E. R. (2025). Me vs. the machine? Subjective evaluations of human-and AI-generated advice. *Scientific Reports*, *15*(1), 3980. DOI: 10.1038/s41598-025-86623-6 PMID: 39893236

Panda, S., & Kaur, N. (2023). Enhancing user experience and accessibility in digital libraries through emerging technologies. KP Sinhamahapatra [et al.](Eds.), Digital Libraries: SustainableDevelopment in Education, Presented on, 21, 676-703.

Pentland, A. (2025). *Shared Wisdom: Cultural Evolution in the Age of AI*. MIT Press. DOI: 10.7551/mitpress/15653.001.0001

Richardson-Walden, V. G., & Makhortykh, M. (2024). Imagining human-AI memory symbiosis: How re-remembering the history of artificial intelligence can inform the future of collective memory. *Memory Studies Review*, *1*(2), 323–342. DOI: 10.1163/29498902-202400016

Scherz, P., & Green, B. P. (2025). Reclaiming Human Agency in the Age of Artificial Intelligence. Journal of Moral Theology, 2(Theological Investigations of AI).

Schindler, D. C. (2023). Notes toward the definition of memory. Communio. *International Catholic Review*, *50*(2), 218–254.

Sherif, D., & District, S. C. (2025). NAVIGATING THE IMPACT OF EXCESSIVE AI DEPENDENCE ON COGNITIVE FUNCTION. *Journal of Scholarly Engagement-Volume*, *8*(2), 31. DOI: 10.9743/JSE.2025.8.2.4

Sya, M. F., Anoegrajekti, N., Dewanti, R., & Isnawan, B. H. (2022). Exploring the educational value of Indo-Harry Potter to design foreign language learning methods and techniques. International Journal of Learning. *Teaching and Educational Research*, *21*(10), 341–361.

TEGON, R. (2025). AI integration to enhance executive functions through Mind Brain Education: a theoretical analysis. Lifelong Digital Learning and Education: promoting flexibility, inclusion, critical thinking and international exchange.

Thiele, L. P. (2025). *Human Agency, Artificial Intelligence, and the Attention Economy: The Case for Digital Distancing*. Springer Nature. DOI: 10.1007/978-3-031-82086-1

Tomašev, N., Franklin, M., & Osindero, S. (2026). Intelligent AI delegation. arXiv preprint arXiv:2602.11865.

Velankar, M. R., Mahalle, P. N., & Shinde, G. R. (2024). *Cognitive Computing for Machine Thinking*. Springer Nature. DOI: 10.1007/978-981-97-0452-1

Wang, C. (2022). Comprehensively summarizing what distracts students from online learning: A literature review. *Human Behavior and Emerging Technologies, 2022*(1), 1483531. DOI: 10.1155/2022/1483531

Westerbeek, H. (2026). How AI is rewiring the human brain: The generational transformation of cognition and knowing. *AI & Society, 41*(5), 1–11. DOI: 10.1007/s00146-026-02912-2

Yang, J. W., Choe, K., Lim, J., & Park, J. (2025). Asking questions matters: Comparing the effect of learning through dialogue with peers, ChatGPT, and intelligent tutoring system. *Interactive Learning Environments, 33*(10), 5870–5886. DOI: 10.1080/10494820.2025.2488984

Youvan, D. (2024). Incorporating Humility into AI: Designing Systems with Awareness of Limitations and Ethical Caution.

Zafar, Q., Kiren, A., & Naz, Z. (2026). The Role of Artificial Intelligence in Supporting Students' Emotional Regulation and Learning Anxiety. *The Critical Review of Social Sciences Studies, 4*(1), 589–600. DOI: 10.59075/884gdn98

Zajda, J. (2024). Engagement, motivation, and students' achievement. In *Engagement, Motivation, and Students' Achievement* (pp. 1–28). Springer Nature Switzerland.

Zhai, X., Nyaaba, M., & Ma, W. (2025). Can generative AI and ChatGPT outperform humans on cognitive-demanding problem-solving tasks in science? *Science & Education, 34*(2), 649–670. DOI: 10.1007/s11191-024-00496-1

Chapter 4

Automating the Thinking Process:
Neural and Psychological Implications of Constant AI Support and Assistance

R. M. Dilip Charaan
http://orcid.org/0009-0002-1332-4592
Vel Tech Rangarajan Dr. Sagunthala R&D Institute of Science and Technology, India

Subashini Ganapathy
http://orcid.org/0000-0001-7800-6304
Xiamen University, Malaysia

T. Nalini
Saveetha Institute of Medical and Technical Sciences, India

Kamalakannan Machap
Asia Pacific University of Technology, Malaysia

R. Nishapriya
Vivekanandha College of Engineering for Women, India

S. P. Santhoshkumar
http://orcid.org/0000-0001-8531-759X
Vel Tech Rangarajan Dr. Sagunthala R&D Institute of Science and Technology, India

ABSTRACT

The fact that artificial intelligence has been extensively introduced into daily cognitive functioning is changing how humans think, remember, and make decisions. People are slowly offloading complex cognitive processes as algorithmic systems offer them real-time advice, predictive analytics, and automated assistance to solve problems. Whereas such help is more efficient and less mental effort is involved, the persistence of such help can retune the executive control, attentional stability, and metacognitive monitoring. Automation bias, the decline in critical thought, and the loss of motivation toward mastery instead of convenience are also beginning to

DOI: 10.4018/979-8-3373-9484-8.ch004

emerge as problems. The chapter critically analyses such neural and psychological dynamics and develops a balanced co-processing model that protects the cognitive agency yet has the power to allow responsible, resilient, and moral AI augmentation.

1. INTRODUCTION

1.1. Background of Artificial Intelligence Application in cognition

Artificial intelligence (AI) has changed to be a computational aiding system to a cognition partner embedded into the daily human thought process. The modern AI engines offer real-time search, predictive analytics, adaptive tutoring, recommendation engines and generative reasoning support, which fundamentally changes the way people access, process, and analyze information. Studies of cognitive offloading show that, under the condition of the existence of trusted external systems, people are willing to offload memory and problem-solving processes to the systems (Risko and Gilbert, 2016). On the same note, it has been proved that the readily available online information alters memory skills where people need to know where to find the information and not the information itself (Sparrow et al., 2011). Such changes suggest that the integration of AI is not only technological but also a cognitive one that affects the form of the attention process, encoding, and retrieval. Even the mere existence of digital devices has been demonstrated to decrease the amount of cognitive capacity, implying that AI-implemented environments are in constant communication with attention systems (Ward et al., 2017). Accordingly, AI has now integrated into cognitive ecosystem and it affects both performance of tasks and distribution of mental resources (Vipul H. Kondekar et a., 2025).

Transfer Tool Use to Cognitive Co-Processing

The tools used in the past increased physical or computational power without compromising higher-order reasoning in the human mind (S. P. Santhoshkumar et al., 2025). . Nonetheless, there is a growing role of AI systems in deliberative reasoning, and the latter replaces the use of tools with cognitive co-processing. The study of automation has shown that when humans are present, there is a change in their decision-making strategies when automated systems are around and, in most cases, the cognitive efforts are redistributed to monitor other systems instead of generating solutions (Parasuraman and Riley, 1997). The more automation is reliable, the more the users get addicted to the outputs of algorithms, and they sometimes do not be as active and verifying (Dzindolet et al., 2003). This interaction of control transforms executive control procedures as human beings are no longer directly involved in the solution of the problem but overseeing machine-generated products. There is a redistribution of cognitive work in such transitions and not augmentation. Although this co-processing model can increase the level of performance and efficiency, it also alters the frequency and intensity of internal reasoning cycles, which may affect the long-term cognitive habitual patterns.

Figure 1. Neural and behavioural re-calibration during prolonged co-processing with AI

Figure 1 illustrates the conceptual premise of the chapter, namely that sustained AI co-processing does not necessarily reduce cognitive capacity, but may lead to progressive redistribution of cognitive engagement across attention, memory, executive control, and monitoring systems. The figure should be interpreted as a conceptual model linking behavioural delegation patterns with potential neural and psychological recalibration.

This chapter is positioned as a conceptual and interdisciplinary synthesis that integrates established theories from cognitive psychology, neuroscience, and human factors to examine the cognitive implications of sustained AI interaction. Rather than presenting new experimental findings, the chapter develops a theory-informed design framework—the Cognitive Delegation–Engagement Architecture (CDEA) and Human–AI Calibrated Interaction Protocol (HACIP)—as a structured response to patterns identified in prior literature, including cognitive offloading, automation bias, executive regulation, and trust calibration. The objective is therefore not to claim empirically validated causal effects of AI on cognition, but to provide a systematic explanatory and design-oriented model for cognitively sustainable human–AI co-processing.

1.2. New Psychological and neurological issues

The neurocognitive interpretations presented in this section should be understood as theory-informed projections grounded in established neuroscience literature, rather than direct empirical observations specific to AI usage. These interpretations aim to provide a plausible explanatory framework for how repeated patterns of cognitive delegation may influence neural engagement over time.

The neurophysiological/psychological implications of having constantly present AI assistance are the topic of an increasing number of studies in cognitive science and human factors. Bias in automation: It has been observed that in decision-making situations, people will prefer recommendations from automated systems over human counter judgment (Skitka et al., 1999). With time, overdependence will result in complacency, which implies less scrutiny and heightened vigilance (Parasuraman and Manzey, 2010). Cognitive load. Cognitively, although lessening mental effort can enhance short-term task performance, it can also impair profound processing to facilitate long-term learning and schema formation (Sweller, 1988). The studies of navigation technologies also demonstrate that the continuous use of external navigation may deteriorate spatial memory and cognitive mapping inside (Dahmani and Bohbot, 2020). These results indicate that with the frequency and degree of dependence, neural patterns of engagement can be reinstated in AI-assisted contexts, especially of executive and memory-associated systems.

1.3. Problem Statement: Addiction, Indolence, and Loss of Critical Thinking

The main question is not whether AI can save efficiency, but whether the continued dependence causes cognitive addiction and a lack of critical thinking. Individuals can default to acceptance instead of evaluation when there is high confidence and fast responses given by algorithmic systems. Research on abuse of automation shows that a high level of trust and a low level of verification predispose to errors (Parasuraman and Riley, 1997). Repeated delegation can, over time, develop cognitive habits of effort avoidance, or, to use another term, cognitive laziness, in which users no longer engage in generative reasoning to generate results instead of providing immediate results. Also, the presence of continuous external support can undermine metacognitive monitoring operations, making one less aware of gaps in knowledge or uncertainty. In case these patterns are maintained, the skills of critical thinking, including counterfactual reasoning, hypothesis testing, and systematic evaluation, might decrease due to a lack of practice, but not ability. Thus, the risk in the long run is compression of engagement: it is the reduced number of internal reasonings and increased dependence on algorithmic scaffolding.

It is important to note that while the chapter draws on extensive empirical literature related to cognitive offloading, automation bias, and digital cognitive environments, direct longitudinal evidence specific to sustained generative AI interaction remains limited. Accordingly, several arguments presented in this chapter should be interpreted as theory-informed extrapolations rather than empirically established causal effects.

The aim is not to overgeneralize existing findings, but to extend them cautiously into AI-mediated contexts, thereby providing a foundation for future experimental and longitudinal validation.

1.4. Chapter Objectives

The main purpose of this chapter is to critically analyse the effects of long-term exposure to artificial intelligence systems on human cognition on both the psychological and neurological levels. Instead of leaning towards the deterministic deterioration or the unquestionable improvement, the chapter attempts to examine AI as a co-processing agent that alters attention patterns, memory encoding patterns, executive control patterns, and metacognitive regulation patterns.

The second goal is to conceptualise the development of AI dependency as an active behavioural and neural adaptation and not just a behavioural preference. (Sumesh Mohan et al., 2025). The chapter seeks to differentiate between adaptive delegation and bad in getting adaptive reliance. By assessing changes in motivation, reinforcement cycles, and monitoring failures, the chapter aims to establish the psychological mechanisms that potentially lead to what is frequently referred to as cognitive laziness. Third, the chapter will attempt to combine cognitive neuroscience, human factors engineering, and behavioural psychology insights to help work out a systematic explanatory framework of human-AI cognitive interaction. This involves mapping the possible neural correlates of impaired monitoring and maintained reasoning and risk conditions within which the executive engagement can be compressed.

Lastly, the chapter also seeks to promote the view of design by suggesting principles of human-AI co-processing calibration. It is not aimed at discouraging the use of AI, but rather map out architectural and protocol-based protection ensuring cognitive agency, encouraging verification behaviours, and maintaining the ability to reason critically in more and more automated environments.

2. BACKGROUND

The development of Cognitive Augmentation as Generative AI. Cognitive augmentation is expected to evolve into a generative AI, similar to calculators.

The history of technological augmentation shows that there has been a slow but significant change in the manner in which human beings allocate cognitive labour. The first computing machines, like mechanical calculators, enhanced the accuracy of numbers but did not redefine the way of thinking. As digital computers, spreadsheets and search engines came into existence, the cognitive boundary started to grow. Mechanisms became more and more in favour of information retrieval, symbolic manipulation, and guided decision analysis.

The change toward adaptive and learning-based systems is the beginning of a significant shift. Modern generative AI systems are able not only to calculate or access, but also to synthesise, predict, summarise, and simulate reasoning processes. They help in the creation of arguments, diagnosis, the generation of hypotheses, and the organisation of intricate decisions. During this phase, augmentation shifts to participatory cognition as compared to procedural acceleration. The system is no longer simply the way to follow (predefined) instructions; it is now part of the process of ideation and interpretation.

This development reinvents the locus of cognition. Rather than a unidirectional relationship, where a human issues orders and a machine performs, a dialogic and iterative relationship develops. Supervisory control, validation, and selective absorption of machine-generated outputs progressively become a part of human mind functioning. The calculator to generative AI is therefore a direction of moving towards a state of distributed cognition in which the cognitive processes are partially externalised between human and algorithmic agents.

2.1. Cognitive Extension Theory of Human-Tool

The theoretical basis of the interpretation of this transformation is the cognitive extension theory, which states that cognitive operations may be extended beyond the biological brain to external objects when they are dependable and integrated parts of reasoning systems. Clark and Chalmers (1998) suggested that tools which are regularly available, automatically supported, coupled with mental processes are components of the extended cognitive process, and not external facilitations.

In AI-intermediate settings, such an extension is continuous as opposed to episodic. Generative AI systems are constantly available and contextually adaptive unlike the traditional tools, which were used on an intermittent basis. When people use AI to recall something, organize thought, or come up with solutions, the delineation among cognition, computation, externalised, and internal processing disappears. The critical questions arising out of such integration are: Does extended cognition maintain neural activity or create redistribution of effort that eventually decreases internally motivated reasoning processes?

The extended mind position does not presuppose the deterioration of the cognitive nature; it stresses on the systemic reorganization. But in case extension is replaced by default substitution and not strategic supplementation, the rate of autonomous cognitive rehearsal can go down. Such reorganization has long-term implications, which should be empirically and theoretically examined.

2.2. Cognitive Offloading and External Memory

Cognitive offloading describes the process of decreasing the internal cognitive load of a task by means of the use of external means or activities (Risko & Gilbert, 2016). It includes actions like writing notes, searching with the tools, or solving problems by using algorithm systems. Nevertheless, its psychological importance is the frequency and intensity of externalisation of the tasks.

External memory systems are digital calendars, cloud storage, and knowledge retrieval based on AI, which are extensions of working and long-term memory. Internal encoding strategies can change when reliance is made habitual. People can be more interested in access than in retention and store access points to information instead of the information itself (Sparrow et al., 2011).

2.3. Empirical Evidence

Empirical studies prove that in case people anticipate that information will be provided in the digital form, they show lowered encoding efforts (Sparrow et al., 2011). Risko and Gilbert (2016) analyzed results that indicate that people strategically delegate to external assistance tasks that require less cognitive effort when they are doing them. This is a logical action in the short term but can affect the long-term memory and the development of strategies (Studies of the effects of the presence of such devices indicate that even passive availability of smartphones can decrease the capacity of working memory during challenging tasks (Ward et al., 2017). These results indicate that cognitive systems change not only to active delegation but also to those environmental signals that indicate external support.

2.4. Neurocognitive Implications

The neurocognitive perspective of repeated offloading is that it can change the patterns of engagement of executive and memory-related circuits. Sustained coordination between the prefrontal and hippocampal is usually involved in deep encoding. Such circuits can be triggered less often when delegating tasks. Neuroplasticity is governed by the idea that repeated use enhances neural pathways and less use can impair performance in such pathways. This does not mean that there is structural degeneration, but functional recalibration. In case AI systems are able to provide systematic reasoning on a regular basis, self-generated problem decomposition and working-memory interference can become less frequent. In the long run, the brain can be able to adapt by redistributing the resources in favor of supervisory supervision as opposed to generative thinking. In this way, cognitive offloading will be a dynamic compromise between increase in efficiency and reduction in rehearsal.

2.5. Utility and fairness bias and calibration of trust

2.5.1. Human Factors Perspective

Automation bias refers to the effect of giving more attention to the recommendations of automated system than to conflicting human judgments (Skitka et al., 1999). In the context of human factors, automation is interpreted as a two-sided design aspect: it may decrease a workload and errors, but may also bring about abuse or dependency (Parasuraman and Riley, 1997).

The reliability of automation increases, and people tend to decrease the monitoring intensity. This dynamic adjustment will reduce unnecessary effort but make it susceptible to infrequent yet severe system failures. The psychological process, which supports this bias, involves the sense of authority, reinforcement of efficiency, and the formation of trust.

2.5.2. Monitoring Failure

Observation is a mentally challenging task. It involves long-term focused attention, conflict identification and error checking procedures that are normally coupled with executive control networks. In a case where automation is always done correctly, users can stop verifying it actively. According to Parasuraman and Manzey (2010), this is termed as attentional complacency whereby the less vigilance occurs as a result of long exposure to trustful automation.

The failure to track failure is particularly impactful in high stakes settings, where computerized output is uncritically followed like medical diagnostics or financial decision-making because automated outputs could result in errors at the systemic level. The downside of being less vigilant is not in daily work, but infrequent detection of anomalies.

2.5.3. Complacency Effects

Complacency is the behavioural end result of the automation dependency. It includes reduced situational awareness, reduced frequency of verification and delayed detection of an error. The study of Dzondolet et al. (2003) shows that the reliance patterns are highly predicted by trust calibration: the trust augments the acceptance rates with no cross-checking, and the calibrated scepticism maintains monitoring behaviour.

In AI-saturated environments, where systems that generate language are able to do so correctly and with ease, the threat of complacency can be elevated. Fluency may give an impression of quality, and constant encouragement of success may lead to a habitual delegation. In the absence of architectural protection, i.e., uncertainty disclosure and compulsory verification prompts, cognitive work can slowly be squeezed as automation bias and trust miscalibration constitute an important psychological route between AI augmentation and a possible breakdown of critical thinking. It is not a matter of automation, but rather a matter of a lack of mechanisms that support reflective engagement along with assistance.

3. THEORETICAL FOUNDATIONS

This part provides the theoretical framework of the effects of long-term AI support that can re-tune cognition. Instead of considering dependency, laziness or less critical thinking as moral judgments, these consequences are investigated as logical results of redistribution of cognitive loads, executive modulation, neural plasticity, and restructuring of motivation. Combined the frameworks describe the manner in which the pattern of effort, control and autonomy can be systematically re-organised through repeated human-AI interaction.

3.1. Cognitive Load Theory

According to Cognitive Load Theory (CLT), working memory of humans is limited and learning and problem solving is determined by the efficiency with which cognitive resources are used (Sweller, 1988; Sweller, van Merriënboer, and Paas, 1998). There are three types of cognitive load: intrinsic load (task complexity), extraneous load (unefficient presentation) and germane load (schema construction). Each of the three forms is directly affected by AI systems.

Extraneous load can be minimised by AI tools, which can make immediate performance more efficient. Nevertheless, AI can also lessen germane load, required to develop schemas and have profound insight, as well, when it excessively cuts intrinsic load, by providing complete solutions or by skipping over the reasoning process. Productive struggle is common in educational psychology to ensure further retention and transfer in the long term. Instead, CLT implies a precarious balancing act: excessively high load can saturate working memory; excessively low load can decrease the participation in effortful processing, which is necessary to support cognitive development. The danger to the AI-mediated settings arises when systems regularly break down the intricate tasks into prepared products in order to reduce the cognitive rehearsal. In the long term, the allocations of low germane as a habit might lead to decreasing reasoning stamina and problem-solving abilities. Therefore, CLT gives a mechanistic account of the way in which AI aid may increase efficiency and, at the same time, limit profound thinking.

3.2. Executive Function and Prefrontal Regulation

Planning, inhibitory control, cognitive flexibility, manipulation of working memory, and error monitoring are executive functions which are controlled by the prefrontal cortex (PFC) mostly (Miller & Cohen, 2001). These are the main functions of critical thinking and deliberate reasoning. As people are left to solve problems on their own, the goal representation, conflict resolution, and decision evaluation are coordinated by the PFC.

Like the AI systems change the locus of generative reasoning, placing it externally. When the results of the algorithm are fluently and confidently conveyed, the executive burden of performance might be reduced. Automation studies indicate that consistent systems may cause users to ease off on the active monitoring, leading to the exposure of omission and commission errors (Parasuraman and Manzey, 2010). Surveillance involves the involvement of the executive, especially the inhibitory control and conflict detection. Fewer monitors might thus be related to fewer activities of executive networks.

Moreover, as AI organises thought patterns, people can involve themselves in supervisory validation instead of synthesising. The difference is small, but significant: supervision involves evaluative circuits, and generation involves planning and integrative circuits. When the latter is less efficiently exercised, executive processes that are linked to complex thinking reset to reactive monitoring as opposed to proactive building. Critical thinking is based on the repetition of hypothesis generation and assessment, and its modification. In case AI fails to recreate these cycles as pre-assembled responses, the density of executive practice declines. Executive regulation is, therefore, context sensitive using interaction design and verification norms.

3.3. Neuroplasticity and Forming of Habits

Neuroplasticity can be defined as the ability of the brain to wrangle the synaptic connections in response to recurring patterns of activity (Hebb, 1949; Draganski et al., 2004). When neural pathways are used frequently, they become stronger and when they are not utilized, they become weaker. Formation of the habit is inextricably connected with the work of the reinforcement learning, especially in dopaminergic loops between the prefrontal cortex and striatum.

Reinforcement loops can be generated in AI-rich environment due to fast problem solving and less work. Users gain efficiency in delegation behavior when AI provides correct solutions in a short period, which subsequently reinforces the behavior. Dependence can also be habitual and not strategic over recurrent cycles. This change is in alignment with reinforcement learning theory: those behaviors that are related to reward and low cost will be reiterated.

Neuroplastic adaptation does not involve structural damage, but involves repetition. In case internally generated reasoning is used less often due to its replacement by AI, neural circuits underlying deep reasoning can have lower density of activation. On the other hand, there is the strengthening of supervisory and selection circuits. Cognitive style can over time lean in favor of external consultation as opposed to internal deliberation.

The dependency is also explained by the formation of a habit. In the situation when AI consultation becomes the standard reaction to uncertainty, (D Marichamy et al., 2024) the mental threshold in which independent reasoning is possible can rise. The thinking of effort starts becoming relatively expensive. Therefore, neuroplasticity offers the biological notion of how default cognitive strategies can be calibrated by use of repeated AI utilization without connoting capacity loss of cognition.

3.4. Motivational Shifts and Self-Determination

According to Self-Determination Theory (SDT), human motivation is inspired by the mental needs of autonomy, competence and relatedness (Ryan and Deci, 2000). Intrinsic motivation gets stronger when people feel they are in control and master their abilities, and deteriorates when they recognize that their tasks are externally regulated or externally resolved.

There are two opposite ways that AI systems may have an impact on motivation. On the one hand, they will be able to strengthen competence through scaffolding and feedback. Conversely, in case AI is able to solve problems systematically in advance before people can be deeply involved, it can limit the possibilities of mastery experiences. Also, a convenience-induced interaction can alter the mastery orientation to performance orientation. People are likely to value speed and productivity over internalisation and comprehension. This transition can cause less disposition to accept ambiguity or persistent cognitive dissonance- major constituents of critical thinking.

Motivational restructuring is therefore a supplement on cognitive load and executive models. Dependency does not only occur due to cognitive limitations; dependency also occurs due to the reward structure and perceived cost of effort. In cases where AI reduces the cost of problem solving, effort avoidance can be rational and strengthened. In the long run, motivational forces may influence the level of cognitive engagement.

3.5. Integrative Perspective

All of these together are Cognitive Load Theory, which describes redistribution of effort; Executive Function theory describes control and monitoring changes; Neuroplasticity describes adaptation via repetition; and Self-Determination Theory describes recalibration of motivation. These models agree around one main point: the unlimited AI assistance is capable of transforming cognition not by reducing it, but by changing the rate, intensity and pattern of effortful thought.

The theoretical perspectives discussed above converge on a set of recurring mechanisms: redistribution of cognitive load, reduction in active monitoring, reinforcement of low-effort delegation, and compression of reflective evaluation cycles. While these mechanisms are examined independently across cognitive load theory, executive control models, neuroplasticity, and motivational frameworks, they collectively describe a consistent pattern of interaction-dependent cognitive restructuring.

These recurring insights directly inform the design logic of the proposed framework. The Cognitive Delegation–Engagement Architecture (CDEA) and Human–AI Calibrated Interaction Protocol (HACIP) are therefore not introduced as isolated constructs, but as structured design responses to the mechanisms identified above.

In particular, the framework operationalises theoretical concerns such as monitoring failure, automation bias, and reinforcement-driven dependency into actionable interaction principles, including uncertainty exposure, verification enforcement, and adaptive cognitive friction.

4. NEURAL CONSEQUENCES OF AI-ASSISTANCE AT ALL TIMES

The neural after-effects of a prolonged AI contact cannot be interpreted as the reduction of structures but can be interpreted as functional recalibration due to repetitive patterns of cognitive delegation. The brain becomes accustomed to regularity of the environment; when the external systems invariably presuppose the elements of reasoning, the patterns of neural interaction restructure. The subsections below discuss the effects constant AI assistance might have on working memory activity, executive control systems, error detection mechanisms, reward systems, habit loops, and attentional stability.

4.1. Working Memory Attenuation

The reasoning, planning and problem-solving processes heavily rely on working memory (WM), which allows temporary manipulation of information between the dorsolateral prefrontal cortex (dlPFC) and the parietal areas (Miller and Cohen, 2001). When AI carries out decomposition, synthesis or retrieval functions externally, the demands on WM are reduced. This decrease can be used in the short term to enhance task efficiency and avoid overload (Sweller, 1988). Nevertheless, repeated dependence can decrease the possibility of WM rehearsal, which can diminish the frequency of the use of the dlPFC during complex reasoning. The principles of neuroplasticity state that neural efficiency can be use-dependent; the circuits that are less frequently used can have less functional robustness over time (Hebb, 1949). It is the reduced density of activation that is a concern rather than the diminished capacity. When the problem-solving cycles begin to bypass the internal working-memory manipulation, it is possible that the person will have reduced endurance when carrying out a problem demanding a prolonged period of cognitive assembly without a provided scaffold.

4.2. The executive control recalibration

The prefrontal cortex plays a major role in the regulation of executive functions such as planning, inhibitory control, task switching and strategic evaluation (Miller and Cohen, 2001). When dealing with a traditional reasoning task, executive networks organize the generation of hypotheses, consider alternatives and filter out irrelevant information. The situation is different when AI mediates reasoning. Humans can also change the mode of thought to evaluate selection when the outputs are pre-structured. Although validation involves the use of control processes, it involves a lesser degree of integrative synthesis. Studies on automation have shown that high-reliability systems reduce the level of monitoring, which creates complacency in supervision (Parasuraman and Manzey, 2010). A decrease in frequency of monitoring means that there is decreased activation of conflict detection and inhibitory systems. In the long run, the involvement of the executive can be determined by AI prompts, instead of a set of reasoning cycles. This is executive compression as opposed to executive failure.

4.3. The phenomenon of the detection of certain errors is suppressed

The anterior cingulate cortex (ACC) is also closely related to error detection and it provides indicators of cognitive incongruity and the difference between the anticipated and actual results. The AI-assisted environment suggests that perception of data necessity may decrease with referencing to omission and commission errors (not reporting systems errors and accepting incorrect automated decision-making) when trust is high (Skitka et al., 1999). As monitoring reducing occurs, ACC-mediated conflict detection mechanisms can be activated less often: as less checking happens, there will be less room to signal neural conflict. When people get used to skipping the verification, there will be less practice with error detection. When it comes to high stakes, this attenuation can be consequential since, infrequent anomalies will require active conflict monitoring and not passively accepting.

4.4. Reward-Loop Reinforcement

Outputs of AI systems are fast, precise, and restrict low effort. This efficiency triggers the process of reinforcement learning that involves dopaminergic circuits and striatum. Once delegation results in systematic success at a low cognitive cost, then a positive loop of reinforcement occurs between behaviours that are tied to reward and less effortful (Hebb, 1949; Draganski et al., 2004). Consultation of AI can therefore be the default answer to uncertainty since it will produce the resolution immediately. This reinforcement does not necessitate conscious dependency, but the results of repetition cost-benefit optimization. In the long term, internal generation of reasoning might become relatively effortful and less rewarding, replacing the motivational relations with delegation. The neural substrate of AI dependency is thus based on the concept of reward-loop reinforcement.

4.5. Habit Formation Pathways

The development of habitual behavior is associated with a shift towards goal-oriented to automatic behaviour and is mediated by cortico-striatal loops. Consultation when continually sought with regards to comparable groups of activities becomes proceduralized. This is due to the cognitive threshold of independent reasoning being raised since the habitual route, consult AI, is less energy consuming (Hebb, 1949). In case AI communication starts to be a part of routine decision-making processes, neural pathways that sustain delegation become strengthened. By contrast, there are those pathways that are related to long-term internal reasoning and they can be less used.

Attentional Stability: The experiment involved two groups, each comprising twenty-six participants, with each group receiving a different colour palette from the other; participants were asked to operate the computer until the specified colour appeared on the screen, signifying the experiment's completion (Irwin, 2015).

4.6. Attentional Stability Changes

The experiment entailed two groups that consisted of twenty-six participants each and were provided with a different colour palette in contrast to the other; the participants were instructed to use the computer until the particular colour came up on the screen sustained attention depends on the activity in frontoparietal control networks. Websites with a high volume of AI might promote shorter attention periods as they are designed to offer quick reaction, notification, and feedback. It has been shown that the availability of cognitive capacity can be diminished by the presence of digital devices even when they are not in use (Ward et al., 2017). Repeat micro-interactions with AI systems could facilitate the development of attentional fragmentation. Users can also use short consultation cycles instead of taking a long time to think deeply. With time, the ability of attentional endurance to solve single-threaded problems can be reduced unless it is practised. Attentional recalibration is an indicator of environmental adaptation. In case cognitive environments are more immediate and responsive, neural networks could prefer shifting between contexts quickly as opposed to deliberation.

4.7. Integrative Interpretation

AI helping permanently has neural implications, which can only be described as adaptive redistribution instead of degenerative loss. The working memory requires reduction; executive processes turn to supervision, instead of generation; error detection becomes less practised; reward systems consolidate to delegation; habits become established based on outside consultation; the attentional stability adapts to the rapid response situation.

The nature of these changes is the dependency due to the interaction design, verification enforcement, and cognitive engagement practices, or they stay as beneficial augmentation. Patterns of neural systems are adapted to. Therefore, the main question is not whether AI changes cognition, but whether this change is compensated for by deliberative schemes of interaction that do not deplete the ability to be a critical thinker.

Figure 2. The neural effect of AI interaction on cognitive process

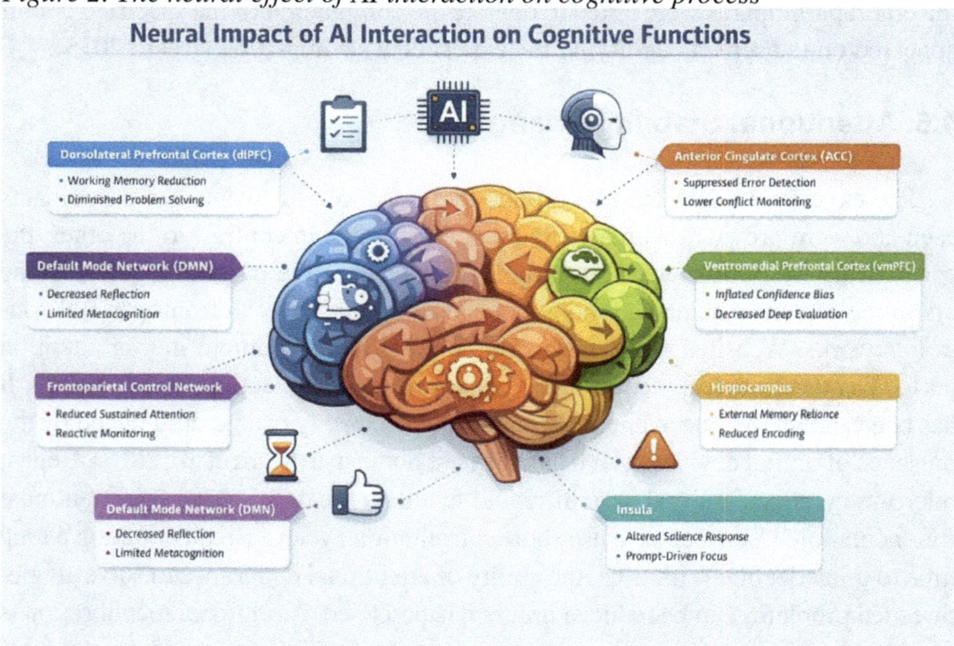

4.8. Brain Region vs Interaction with AI

Figure 2 presents a theory-guided mapping between AI interaction patterns and major neural systems involved in reasoning, monitoring, and motivation. This representation is not derived from direct neuroimaging evidence of AI use, but is constructed by integrating established neuroscience findings with observed patterns of cognitive offloading and automation reliance.

As opposed to the suggestion of structural damage, the model shows the use-based modulation of neural activity due to recurrent cognitive delegation.

1. This is the Dorsolateral Prefrontal Cortex (dlPFC)

Working memory, problem decomposition, planning, rule application. The less the AI systems come with the structured steps of reasoning, summarisation, or complete solutions, the less internal working memory manipulation is required. The dlPFC loses interest in the process of multi-step reasoning.

Implication:

- Less drilling in internally generated problem-solving.
- Poor stamina in untidied sophisticated reasoning.
- Change in generative reasoning to supervisory validation.

This is functional attenuation, and not the structural decline.

2. Anterior cingulate Cortex (ACC)

Detection of conflicts, monitoring of errors.

Perceived uncertainty decreases because fluent and confident AI produces decrease it. With less frequency, the users can verify sound, which suppresses activation of conflict-monitoring circuits.

Implication:

- Increased automation bias
- Oxidized chance of omission mistakes.
- Weakened vigilance in anomaly soaring.

Unless verification is practiced, the density of error-detection practices decreases.

3. Ventromedial Prefrontal cortex (vmPFC)

Integration of values, confidence testing, certainty of decisions. The products that are produced by AI have an authoritative and fluent appearance. Subjective confidence may be increased by this fluency.

Implication:

- Inflated confidence bias
- Reduced depth of evaluation
- Algorithms of excessive trust.

The vmPFC takes into consideration confidence signals; AI fluency might alter the signals.

4. Hippocampus
    - Encoding and consolidation of memory.
    - Cognitive offloading decreases the deep encoding. Access pathways can be stored by the users instead of content.

Implication:

- External-memory reliance
- Less elaborative cycles of encoding.

Knowledge turns into a search-based one, and it is not internally organized any longer.

This justifies the move towards distributed cognition.

5. Striatum (Basal Ganglia)

Reward processing, habit forming, reinforcement learning.Fast, correct, outputs form positive loop reinforcement. Such behaviors as delegation are reinforced through low effort and high reward.

Implication:

- Habitual AI consultation
- Slowed intellect of cognitive effort.
- Learning Behavioral Pathway: This is the default-to-AI behavioral pathway.
- Reinforcement efficiency results in dependency.

6. The Frontoparietal Control Network

Persistence of attention, maintenance of goals, adaptive control.Regular micro-consultations and high cycles of answer reduce duration of attention.

Implication:

- Reduced sustained focus

- Reactive rather than proactive reasoning.
- Preference to switch tasks as opposed to deep work.

It turns into attention that is cue-driven as opposed to internally maintained.

7. Default Mode Network (DMN)

Thinking, introspection, metacognition.Immediate products diminish reflexive delays and simulation cycles.

Implication:

- Reduced sophistication in metacognition.
- Restricted Critical Self-Assessment.
- A reduced level of counterfactual reasoning.
- DMN-PFC interaction is necessary in critical thinking; the fast AI consultation can break this cycle.

8. Insula

Salience detection, knowing there is uncertainty.Frequent AI prompts attribution of salience outward.

Implication:

- Prompt-driven attention
- Less tolerance to ambiguity.
- Lateral messages take precedence over internal uncertainty messages.

9. System-Level Interpretation

It can be seen in the Table 1 that all the cognitive engagement will be redistributed structurally once AI is introduced as an unchanging partner of interaction. It does not mean that there is any cognitive decline, only that there is a change in the mode of reasoning which is internally generated and the supervisory validation and monitoring processes. The conventional effort-intensive operations like degree of sustained executive control and encoding of information are to some extent substituted by quick consultation and external retrieval processes. The reward systems also change effort to be based on cognitive satisfactions of effort to efficiency based task completion benefits. This analogy shows how the continued use of AI is transforming the pattern of cognitive workflow towards regulation and verification rather than substantive generative processing.

Table 1. Cognitive engagement redistribution at AI-augmented interaction

Without AI	With Constant AI
Generative reasoning dominant	Supervisory validation dominant
Internal memory encoding	External retrieval pathways
Sustained executive loops	Rapid consultation loops
Effort-driven reward	Efficiency-driven reward

The brain system gets accustomed to repetitive designs. When AI is implemented strategically, performance is enhanced by augmentation. When delegation is applied by default, the brain delegates in an optimal way.

5. PSYCHOLOGICAL CONSEQUENCES

Psychological outcomes of the never-ending AI support may be explained in a systematic conceptual development:

Stimulus Delegation Reduced Engagement Habit Reinforcement Skill Atrophy

This chain does not mean the unavoidable deterioration, but this is a risk curve that occurs when delegation is not a planned process, but a routine. The introduction of AI systems presents a potent stimulus to the environment, which is instant, low-effort cognitive resolution. Long-term consequences of cognitive processes are determined by how people recurrently react to that stimulus.

5.1. Dependency Formation Mechanisms.

a) Stimulus:

The availability of AI as a solution to any problem that is highly accurate, always available, low-energy consumption, makes it a strong behavioral stimulus. High confidence, linguistic fluency and rapid output are signals that lead to increased perceived reliability.

b) Delegation:

The users start to outsource aspects of thinking, retrieval of information, organization of arguments, formulation of alternatives. The idea of delegation seems to be logical and productive at first.

c) Reduced Engagement:

The more a delegation is made, the less internal generated reasoning cycles are made. There also can be a decrease of monitoring and verification behaviors in case of constantly high AI accuracy.

d) Habit Reinforcement:

The use of successful patterns of delegation enhances the pattern of reliance. Consultation is what happens through reinforcement learning mechanisms as the default response to cognitive uncertainty.

e) Skill Atrophy:

In the long-term, the independence of reasoning practice is reduced. Capacity is maintained, whereas spontaneous activation decreases. Addiction all depends, therefore, on strategic reweighing of labor-cost equations, rather than incapability.

Dependency is thus a behavioral change which is influenced by the efficiency of the environment and not lack of intelligence. The danger of this situation lies in the fact that delegation occurs reflexively and not conditionally.

5.2. Cognitive Laziness and Effort Avoidance

The phenomenon of cognitive laziness should be thought of in terms of effort minimization bias and not in terms of incapacity.

a) Stimulus:

AI eases the process of problem solving. Tasks which may have taken weeks to tackle, can now be solved in a few seconds.

b) Delegation:

Users can also default on an AI consultation instead of exploratory reasoning when some ambiguities or complexity arises.

c) Reduced Engagement:

Thinking in which the individual works hard, hypothesis testing, brainstorming counterarguments, and systematic decomposition, happens less frequently. Due to the metabolic cost of effortful cognition, the brain naturally converts to less expensive strategies in instances where they are available.

d) Habit Reinforcement:

Every case of successful low-effort resolution supports the evasiveness of long thought. Subjective tolerance to the face of cognitive struggle decreases with time.

e) Skill Atrophy:

Deep analytical work can be undermined by the lack of practice. Activities that require long-term internal thinking can seem disproportionately taxing in contrast to tasks that require AI assistance.

Notably, cognitive laziness in this case is institutional, rather than ethical. It is a logical response to the environment that is made convenient.

5.3. Reduced Critical Thinking

Critical thinking implies orderly scepticism, analysis of suppositions, making of options and identifying errors. It involves executives being proactive and meta-cognitive.

a) Stimulus:

The outputs of AI usually seem to be logical, systematised, and assertive. There is an illusion of validity that can be brought about by fluency.

b) Delegation:

Outputs may be accepted by the user without the user having to rebuild the reasoning behind them.

c) Reduced Engagement:

Counterfactual generation and testing of assumptions decreases. Users can dwell on Does this seem plausible as opposed to asking if it's wrong.

d) Habit Reinforcement:

Constant acceptance without checking reduces the level of trust. Automation bias is more significant, especially when the accuracy of AI is high.

e) Skill Atrophy:

The cognitive routines that support critical reasoning, namely argument reconstruction, evidence triangulation, anomaly detection can be called less often. With time, the less an invocation is made, the less spontaneity is displayed in the use of critical filters.

The erosion of critical thinking is thus due to the compression of cycles of evaluation other than the intellectual capacity loss.

5.4. Metacognitive Decline

Metacognition is the awareness and control of the cognition that a person has about themselves- knowing what one knows and being aware of not knowing.

a) Stimulus:

The artificial intelligence offers solutions on the ready, hence eliminating instances of doubt, which tends to lead to self-reflection.

b) Delegation:

When ambiguity is resolved immediately by AI, then self-assessment opportunities are reduced.

c) Reduced Engagement:

The user can disregard the reflective pauses, like doubting the assumptions, their degree of confidence, or knowledge gap.

d) Habit Reinforcement:

Quick resolution time constraints a reduction in the reflection window. External validation develops in the brain instead of internal monitoring.

e) Skill Atrophy:

Metacognitive vigilance. The vigilance involved in checking on the quality of understanding and reasoning can become weak unless it is actively done. People are allowed to get comfortable and yet they do not comprehend the logic behind it.

The changes of metacognition are delicate and usually hidden since even when the processing is superficial, the confidence can be high.

5.5. Integrative Psychological Model

The psychological implications of the omnipresent AI assistance are accrued and interactional:

- Dependency comes about due to reinforcement of delegation.
- Cognitive laziness is developed due to minimization of efforts repeatedly.
- Decreased critical thinking is caused by shortened evaluation cycles.
- Reduced reflection intervals result in metacognitive decay.

The process is similar at every step: the environmental efficiency transforms the choice of cognitive strategies. The problem of AI only arises when the machine provides a substitute to interaction, without reflective protection.

6. PROPOSED FRAMEWORK

The following chapter suggests a design-and-theory model which views dependency, laziness and weak critical thinking as system-level consequences of interaction design, namely, the frequency of cognition-delegation and the intensity of verification. The framework consists of two parts which are integrated:

- System Architecture Cognitive DelegationEngagement Architecture (CDEA)
- Human-AI Calibrated Interaction Protocol (HACIP) - the protocol of safe use operation.

Figure 3. Cognitive Delegation Engagement Architecture (CDEA)

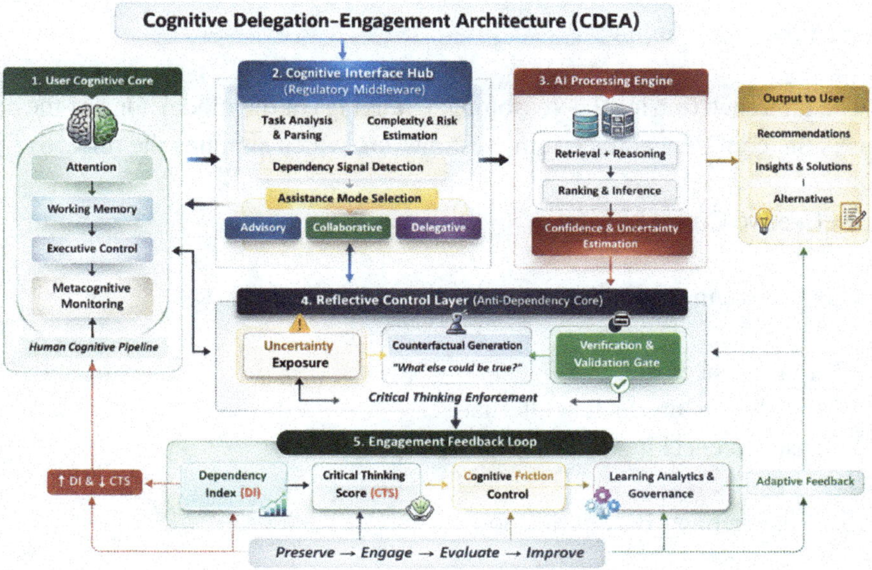

The proposed framework. Cognitive Delegation Engagement Architecture (CDEA) is clearly explained in the Figure 3.

6.1. Cognitive Delegation -Engagement Architecture (CDEA)

1. User Cognitive Core

Is a symbolic depiction of the human mental stream: attention, working memory, executive control and metacognitive monitoring. CDEA presupposes their maintenance, and must not be evaded.

2. Cognitive Interface Hub

This is the regulatory intermediate. It:

- Parses the user task,
- Estimates complexity/risk,
- Calculates dependency indicators,
- Chooses the mode of assistance (Advisory / Collaborative / Delegative).

This centre discourages the use of AI assistance that is one-size-fits-all.

3. AI Processing Engine

The inference (retrieval + reasoning + ranking) of the model. One of the conditions is the confidence/ uncertainty estimation, which supplies the reflective gate.

4. Reflective Control Layer

This is the anti-dependency centre.

- Exposes uncertainty,
- Produces counterfactual alternatives.
- Insists on checking prior to final acceptance.

5. Engagement Feedback Loop

This closes the system:

- Makes updates on Dependency Index (DI) and Critical Thinking Score (CTS),
- Increment in cognitive friction in case DI is on the increase and CTS on the decline,
- Patterns of logs as a transparency instrument in governance.

The Human-AI Calibrated Interaction Protocol (HACIP) is described as follows:

6.2. Human-AI Calibrated Interaction Protocol (HACIP)

The following implications are structured around three analytical dimensions emerging from the chapter: cognitive sustainability, verification practices, and trust calibration. Rather than prescribing fixed policy rules, this section examines how different institutional contexts can balance efficiency with sustained cognitive engagement.

The HACIP is defined as follows:

Figure 4. Human-AI Calibrated Interaction Protocol (HACIP)

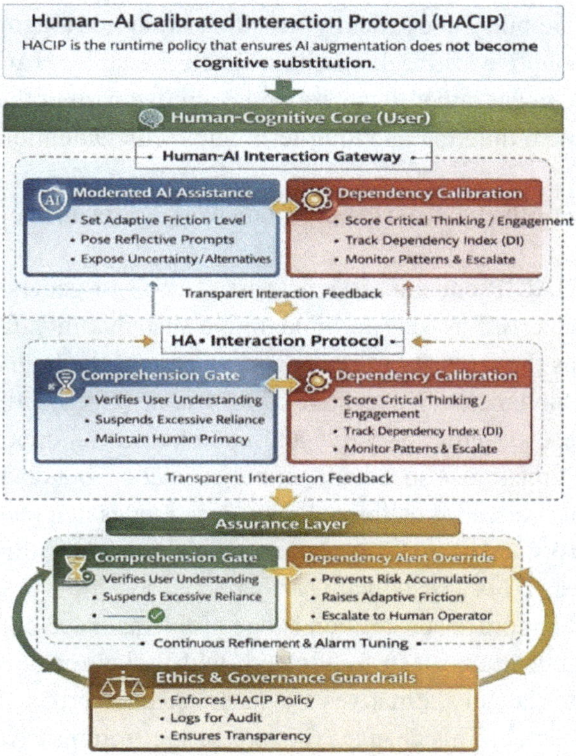

a) The policy that guarantees AI augmentation is not enacted as cognitive substitution is HACIP.

Human AI Calibrated Interaction Protocol (HACIP) is itself a runtime governance protocol, which is implemented to make sure that AI augmentation supplants human cognition instead of complementing it, as clearly depicted in Figure 4. In essence, the HACIP design ensures human primacy by passing all the interaction through a Human-AI Interaction Gateway, which is set with a calibration to dynamically regulate the assistance according to the complexity of the task, user engagement, and dependency cues. The protocol combines the AI assistance (moderated) and dependency calibration mechanism, which constantly monitors the Dependency Index (DI) and Critical Thinking Score (CTS). Before AI-generated outputs are accepted by the user, a comprehension gate can be used to ensure that they understand what they are getting to avoid passive dependence. In the event of the excessive dependency patterns, HACIP increases friction, provides counterfactual prompts or supervisory override. A built-in assurance layer is provided, which guarantees transparency, auditability, and ethics by providing structured logging and governance measures. This adaptive feedback-based architecture enables HACIP to make AI an automated replacement rather than a refined cognitive partner that will not lose its principles of critical thinking and long-term intellectual attention.

b) Implications of the CDEA-HACIP Framework Performance

The CDEA-HACIP encompasses a framework is to generate the short-term functional gains as well as long-term cognitive sustainability. On the most basic level, it maintains the integrity of the cognitive core of the human mind, in terms of attention, working memory, executive control, and metacognitive monitoring, by ensuring that these systems are active and not avoided. As opposed to traditional AI interfaces that maximise speed and output efficiency, but do not consider other factors, this framework adds calibrated assistance modes that match AI help to the complexity of tasks and user ability. Consequently, users are still the key agents of decisions, whereas AI is a systematic partner.

Avoidance of cognitive substitution is one of the main accomplishments of this architecture. The uncertainty is surfaced clearly with the help of the Reflective Control Layer, and counterfactual alternatives are generated and verification is imposed on it before it is accepted. This changes the interaction from passive consumption to an evaluative one. There is reasoning, deepened over time through such systematic practice, which makes reasoning habits stronger, analytical depth, and counterfactual thinking ability. Instead of shrinking reasoning cycles, the system encourages the use of deliberate reasoning loops with the help of AI, but not alternatives.

The Engagement Feedback Loop also refines the long-term results due to the constant measuring of the Dependency Index (DI) and Critical Thinking Score (CTS). This changes dependency, which is an unseen behavioural drift, into a measurable and regressable variable. The growl of dependency signals leads to an enhancement of adaptive cognitive friction, which leads users to re-cognitively engage. This dynamic control can be used to avoid complacency and automation bias, especially in high-stakes areas of life like education, governance, medical interventions, and financial decision-making.

The other important beneficial effect is better trust calibration. The system minimises blind trust, increasing the verification behaviour by exposing model uncertainty and by recording verification behaviour. On the institutional level, there is increased transparency, auditability, and ethical accountability on the part of the governance and logging elements. Interaction records help organisations to track the trends of excessive dependence, evaluate the training requirements, and create policy protections.

Finally, the framework can allow sustainable human AI co-processing: without losing intellectual engagement, efficiency gains are obtained. The end result in the long-term is cognitive resilience; a system in which AI enhances human reasoning and safeguards the critical thinking ability in an organized manner.

7. EDUCATIONAL, INDUSTRIAL, AND GOVERNMENT IMPLICATIONS

The mental and neurophysiological implications of unrelenting AI support are not fixed results; they are determined by designing, situational, and rules of governance. In case dependency and lower critical engagement are caused by frictionless delegation, then institutional design should put in place measured friction. The ramifications include education, automation in the workplace, and government policy, all of which have to be efficient and stay cognitive at the same time.

7.1. Educational Systems

7.1.1. Overreliance Risk

The educational setting is one of the most susceptible to the overuse of AI since learning inherently depends on the process of effortful processing, the building of schemas, and the reflection on metacognition. Students can avoid fruitful cognitive struggle when AI tools come up with essays, solve complicated problems, or summarize readings immediately. Although it might increase the short-term performance, lower interest in generative thinking may diminish conceptual depth and transfer ability.

The nature of the risk is the substitution of cognitive rehearsal with answer acquisition. Working memory manipulation, error detection, and reflective evaluation cycles are used less often when learners are more likely to consult AI before engaging in independent reasoning. This can, in the long run, create superficial familiarity instead of systematic knowledge.

Notably, it is not the availability of AI, but unregulated delegation patterns that cause the threat. In the absence of pedagogical guardrails, education systems can easily encourage hasty learning and productivity instead of learning of depth.

7.1.2. Reflection Enforcement Design

Education needs to incorporate some form of reflection in the use of AI to control dependency. Reflection enforcement design entails:

- Making students provide reasoning traces with AI.
- Instantiation Contingent. (Require counterfactual analysis before AI validation).

Delaying artificial intelligence output until a separate effort has been logged.

Such mechanisms do not eliminate germane cognitive load, but instead retain AI as a scaffold and not a substitute. The aim is an augmented goal: Part of cognition has already taken place, and AI supplements it.

This type of model transforms AI into an answer giver instead of a thinking collaborator, which maintains executive participation and thoughtfulness.

7.2. Workplace Automation

7.2.1. High-Risk Decision Environments

AI systems are involved in the decision-making process of high stakes in areas like healthcare, finance, aviation, cybersecurity, and legal adjudication. Systemic risk in such situations is automation bias and complacency. Omission errors can go unnoticed when the output of algorithms is relied upon without doubt until some terrible consequences happen.

The following neural processes mentioned above neural processes the neural processes mentioned above, reduced monitoring frequency, and compressed conflict detection are of special concern in a setting where anomaly detection is infrequent but vital. Vigilance is better than efficiency.

Therefore, dangerous industries need to have established decision architectures in which AI recommendations are not deterministic but advisory and in which uncertainty is extreme or the data situation is volatile.

7.2.2. Monitoring Safeguards

Safeguards that should be monitored should include:

- Dual-review-systems (human verification is necessary because of high-risk classifications).

- Verification drills that are performed randomly to keep practising error-detection.
- Confidence thresholds go off (autonomous escalation in case AI certainty goes above a predefined limit).

These controls ensure that there is active involvement of the executive control networks, and complacency drift is avoided. Surveillance should be part of the institution and not a choice and cognitive control should be made a habit.

7.3. Policy and Ethical Design

7.3.1. AI Friction Design

The policy presented by the government should shift out of the abstract ethical principles towards practical thinking defense. A potentially effective idea is AI friction design, which is the deliberate addition of reflecting pauses or verification checkpoints into the interaction streams of AI.

- Having to justify taking high-impact recommendations.
- Slowing down output delivery so as to make consequential decisions.
- Restricting levels of automation in flexible settings.
- Friction design opposes the reinforcement loops rewarding the effortless delegation.

7.3.2. New Uncertainty Disclosure Requirement

Outputs of AI systems are often highly fluent and therefore induce subjective confidence.

a) Policies should require:
   - Clear probability /confidence estimates.
   - Limiting factors of models articulated.
   - Presentation of other viable possible results.

Disclosure of uncertainty redeems the ambiguity and helps to make informed decisions. Boundaries and failure modes also reduce overconfidence and increase the likelihood of verification when they are displayed to the users.

b) Reflective Checkpoints

These points of control might involve:

- Periodical dependency audits (monitoring frequency of delegation).
- Automated Systems review frequency requirement.
- User prompts where justification on the reasoning must be given before submission.
- Cognitive health indicators, which are built into AI dashboards (e.g. verification ratio, review latency).

The management should look at cognitive preservation as a design factor and not a by-product. Ethical duty does not just lie in avoidance of harm but also preservation of human agency and reasoning ability.

c) Integrative Implication

In education, industry, and government, one principle is manifested, that of:
Efficiency should be moderate through imposed participation.

The revolutionary nature of AI is based on augmentation, rather than substitution. Such systems, which remove all the cognitive friction, run the danger of pressurising reflection, verification and generative reasoning. The future of AI integration will thus require less sophistication of algorithms and more interaction architecture. It is the institutions that identify and enact this balance that will develop the productivity and cognitive integrity.

8. FUTURE RESEARCH DIRECTIONS

The psychic and neuromuscular effects of continuous AI support over time are difficult to comprehend, and they should be looked into methodically and multidisciplinary. Although the literature at hand offers the background understanding of the cognitive offloading, automation bias, and trust calibration, given the fast development of the generative AI, new frameworks of empirical, computational, and governance-based studies are required. The subsequent recommendations give priority agendas of further developing the field.

Longitudinal neuroimaging studies (LSs) will be included in the learning task as well. The learning task will also involve longitudinal neuroimaging studies (LSs) (Jones 2010).

The majority of current studies regarding automation and cognitive offloading are not long-term and behavioural. An important follow-up intervention is longitudinal neuroimaging research on the effects of prolonged interaction between AI and functional connectivity and density of activation in executive networks, attentional networks, and reward networks with time.

Future studies should:

- Monitoring alteration in the activation of the dlPFC in unaided and AI-assisted reasoning over months or years.
- M1 Before and after a long period of reliance on AI ACC will be engaged in the task of detecting anomalies.
- Compare encoding in high and low-offloading populations in hippocampal.
- Examine reward-network plasticity of rapid delegation behaviors.

This type of research would help to understand whether AI inspired changes include reversible functional adaptation or enduring changes in neural efficiency. Notably, longitudinal designs are required to differentiate short-term cognitive redistribution and sustainable engagement compression.

8.1. Dependency Quantification Metrics

In the key of operationalizing AI dependency in measurable terms it is a problem itself. Further studies should come up with approved scales, which reflect behavioral, cognitive, and neural aspects of delegation.

Potential metrics include:

- Delegation Frequency Ratio (DFR): Ratio of completely outsourced tasks.
- Structured scoring of counterfactual engagement: Verification Depth Index (VDI).
- Acceptance Latency Score (ALS): the duration of the time between output and acceptance.
- Automation Reliance Gradient (ARG): change in independent thinking in the case of AI deletion.
- Neuro-engagement Density (NED): consistency of fMRI based activation in executive circuits.

The dependency measures would be standardized, which would allow comparisons across studies, audits of institutions, and setting of policies. Without quantification, dependency is then an abstract conversation and not an empirical one.

8.2. Models of Experimental Verification

The causal relations between AI interaction patterns and cognitive outcomes should be tested on controlled experiments. Randomized designs which compare: should be used in future research.

- AI-first and human-first sequences of problem solving.
- Mandatory reflection versus frictionless interaction between AI.
- High-confidence AI output, and uncertainty-disclosed output conditions.
- Delayed and real-time AI systems.

Measure: Experimental paradigms must measure:

- Performance of critical thinking after repeated exposure.
- Automated error-detection rates.
- Metacognitive accuracy (confidence accuracy fit).
- Long-term attention capacity.

Such models would advance the field to go beyond correlational inference and give evidence-based guidelines on AI design.

In these systems, friction is altered according to the load-bearing object in the conveyor belt to minimize damage to it and the equipment.

8.3. Adaptive AI Friction Systems

In such systems, the friction is adjusted depending on the load-bearing object on the conveyor belt to reduce both the object and equipment damage.

One of the opportunities that can be pursued in the future is the creation of adaptive AI-based friction systems, which are algorithms that dynamically adjust assistance, depending on detected dependency signals. AI systems may instead of inert delivery of output:

- When the frequency of delegation is on the increase, add reflective prompts.
- Present counterfactual challenges in case of a decrease in the depth of verification.
- Temporarily reduce the level of automation in the event of decreasing scores (cognitive engagement).
- Individualise the intensity of assistance based on the resilience and risk of the task of the user.

Studies should identify the best friction levels that do not interfere with engagement and make them less usable. This needs computational modelling and behavioural validation studies.

Adaptive friction is a change between reactive governance and embedded cognitive protection.

8.4. AI Governance Integration

Lastly, further studies need to incorporate the consideration of cognitive impact into the larger AI governance frameworks. In the present policy discourse, most of the focus is on fairness, openness and accountability although little focus is on cognitive sustainability.

The research on governance must examine:

- Uncertainty disclosure regulatory standards in generative systems.
- Reporting of dependency measures in the education and industry fields.
- Ethical principles that demand verification gates in automation situations where there is a high risk.
- Long-term cognitive AI ubiquity public-health models.

There is a need to have cross-disciplinary interaction between neuroscientists, psychologists, AI engineers, and policymakers. Cognitive resilience ought to be an asset in society and not an individual asset.

8.5. Integrative Outlook

Future studies should not be based on a dichotomy of using AI as either an improvement or a danger. The main research question is to find out in which conditions augmentation enhances the thought process and in which conditions delegation condenses engagement.

The roadmap to a mature science of human-AI interaction in cognitive interaction is made up of longitudinal neural data, measurable dependency measures, experimental validation, adaptive friction architecture, and governance integration.

9. CONCLUSION

Artificial intelligence does not inherently diminish human cognition; rather, it reshapes the patterns, frequency, and distribution of cognitive engagement **depending** on how interaction is structured. This chapter has argued that phenomena such as dependency, effort avoidance, and reduced critical thinking are not inevitable consequences of AI adoption, but emerge from repeated low-friction delegation and insufficient verification mechanisms.

The primary contribution of this work is **a** theory-informed conceptual synthesis that integrates cognitive load theory, executive function models, neuroplasticity, and motivational frameworks, culminating in the proposed CDEA–HACIP architecture. This framework demonstrates how AI systems can be designed to preserve cognitive agency through uncertainty disclosure, reflective checkpoints, and adaptive engagement calibration.

The findings presented here should be interpreted as a foundation for future research rather than definitive empirical claims. Moving forward, longitudinal, experimental, and neurocognitive studies are required to validate the proposed mechanisms and refine the balance between efficiency and cognitive sustainability. Ultimately, the future of human–AI interaction will depend not only on algorithmic capability, but on whether systems are designed to augment human reasoning while actively preserving the capacity to think critically.

REFERENCES

Clark, A., & Chalmers, D. (1998). The extended mind. *Analysis*, *58*(1), 7–19. DOI: 10.1093/analys/58.1.7

Dahmani, L., & Bohbot, V. D. (2020). Habitual use of GPS negatively impacts spatial memory during self-guided navigation. *Scientific Reports*, *10*(1), 6310. DOI: 10.1038/s41598-020-62877-0 PMID: 32286340

Draganski, B., Gaser, C., Busch, V., Schuierer, G., Bogdahn, U., & May, A. (2004). Neuroplasticity: Changes in grey matter induced by training. *Nature*, *427*(6972), 311–312. DOI: 10.1038/427311a PMID: 14737157

Dzindolet, M. T., Peterson, S. A., Pomranky, R. A., Pierce, L. G., & Beck, H. P. (2003). The role of trust in automation reliance. *International Journal of Human-Computer Studies*, *58*(6), 697–718. DOI: 10.1016/S1071-5819(03)00038-7

Hebb, D. O. (1949). *The organization of behavior: A neuropsychological theory*. Wiley.

Kondekar, V. H., & John Joseph, S., J, R., Gayathri, D., Santhoshkumar, S. P., & Arora, P. (2025). Deep learning and behavioral analytics for intelligent mental health monitoring. In Proceedings of the 2025 5th Asian Conference on Innovation in Technology (ASIANCON) (pp. 1–6). IEEE. DOI: 10.1109/ASIANCON66527.2025.11281166

Marichamy, D., Sankar, M., Sivaprakash, P., Chithambaramani, R., Charaan, R. M. D., & Ithayan, J. V. (2024). Machine learning based abnormal human behaviour detection. In *Proceedings of the 2024 Second International Conference on Intelligent Cyber Physical Systems and Internet of Things (ICoICI)* (pp. 1155–1159). IEEE. DOI: 10.1109/ICoICI62503.2024.10696376

Miller, E. K., & Cohen, J. D. (2001). An integrative theory of prefrontal cortex function. *Annual Review of Neuroscience*, *24*(1), 167–202. DOI: 10.1146/annurev.neuro.24.1.167 PMID: 11283309

Mohan, S., Kumari, V. S., Vidhya, S., Santhoshkumar, S. P., & Chitra, A. (2025, September). Human Behavior as a Key: An Innovative Fusion of AI and MFA. In 2025 International Conference on Computing and Communications (COMPUTINGCON) (pp. 1-6). IEEE.

Parasuraman, R., & Manzey, D. H. (2010). Complacency and bias in human use of automation: An attentional integration. *Human Factors*, *52*(3), 381–410. DOI: 10.1177/0018720810376055 PMID: 21077562

Parasuraman, R., & Riley, V. (1997). Humans and automation: Use, misuse, disuse, abuse. *Human Factors, 39*(2), 230–253. DOI: 10.1518/001872097778543886

Risko, E. F., & Gilbert, S. J. (2016). Cognitive offloading. *Trends in Cognitive Sciences, 20*(9), 676–688. DOI: 10.1016/j.tics.2016.07.002 PMID: 27542527

Ryan, R. M., & Deci, E. L. (2000). Self-determination theory and intrinsic motivation. *The American Psychologist, 55*(1), 68–78. DOI: 10.1037/0003-066X.55.1.68 PMID: 11392867

Santhoshkumar, S. P., Karthika, R., Vijayakumar, N., Gajalakshmi, S., Jayanthi, K., & Hariharasudhan, S. (2025). Analysis of duplicating the human mind suspicions in AI in various divisions. In *Proceedings of the 2025 International Conference on Multi-Agent Systems for Collaborative Intelligence (ICMSCI)* (pp. 1707–1714). IEEE. DOI: 10.1109/ICMSCI62561.2025.10894681

Skitka, L. J., Mosier, K. L., & Burdick, M. (1999). Does automation bias decision-making? *International Journal of Human-Computer Studies, 51*(5), 991–1006. DOI: 10.1006/ijhc.1999.0252

Sparrow, B., Liu, J., & Wegner, D. M. (2011). Google effects on memory: Cognitive consequences of having information at our fingertips. *Science, 333*(6043), 776–778. DOI: 10.1126/science.1207745 PMID: 21764755

Sweller, J. (1988). Cognitive load during problem solving: Effects on learning. *Cognitive Science, 12*(2), 257–285. DOI: 10.1207/s15516709cog1202_4

Sweller, J., van Merriënboer, J. J. G., & Paas, F. (1998). Cognitive architecture and instructional design. *Educational Psychology Review, 10*(3), 251–296. DOI: 10.1023/A:1022193728205

Ward, A. F., Duke, K., Gneezy, A., & Bos, M. W. (2017). Brain drain: The mere presence of one's own smartphone reduces available cognitive capacity. *Journal of the Association for Consumer Research, 2*(2), 140–154. DOI: 10.1086/691462

Chapter 5
Automation Bias in Medical Imaging and Large Language Models:
Cognitive Erosion From Overtrusting Imperfect AI

Krithikha Sanju S.
Sri Sivasubramaniya Nadar College of Engineering, Chennai, India

Baghavathi Priya S.
http://orcid.org/0000-0001-9168-7810
Amrita Vishwa Vidyapeetham, Chennai, India

Hiroshini K.
http://orcid.org/0009-0002-0245-9125
Amrita Vishwa Vidyapeetham, Chennai, India

ABSTRACT

This chapter discusses automation bigotry, the inclination to over-depend on artificial intelligence (AI) recommendations without consideration of the problems in areas like medical imaging and large language models (LLMs), that are essential to society. Using empirical studies of clinical data and rigorous benchmarks, the chapter reveals how clinicians, academics and information workers are increasingly outsourcing thought problems to AI, and cognitive outsourcing. This numbs neural processes required for thought, eroding independence of thought. The chapter introduces the Automation Bias Cycle (ABC) Model, which provides a framework for evolution from initial convenience with AI to pathological dependency. The chapter

DOI: 10.4018/979-8-3373-9484-8.ch005

offers Hybrid Verification Loop (HVL), Adaptive Training Regimens (ATR) and Transparent Evidence Integration (TEI) as interventions. Research indicates these approaches can re-establish neuroplastic processes in executive function regions.

1. INTRODUCTION

AI integration into domains that impact decision-making has revolutionized medical diagnosis, data processing, and knowledge work. However, as AI becomes more common, there is also an indirect cognitive risk: automation bias, which is the tendency for decision makers to accept the recommendations of the algorithm without taking the time to evaluate them independently (Parasuraman and Riley, 1997). This bias is particularly worrisome because, despite their complexity, AI systems are still susceptible to systematic error, distributional bias, and pattern matching, and hence blind to context. AI-driven segmentation outputs, classification boundaries, and anomaly detection suggestions are increasingly used by radiologists and sonographers. Although such automation does have its efficiency benefits, experimental data show that clinicians tend to follow algorithmic limits even when probabilistic metrics of uncertainty indicate it actually could be subject to uncertainty, effectively delegating critical judgment into the control of algorithms with known failure modes (Dratsch et al., 2023). In LLM-mediated knowledge work, users often rely on LLM-generated responses without checking factual correctness, delegating executive control processes of working memory and prefrontal planning networks (Zhai et al., 2024).

Adverse effects of dependency on automation over time are not just a matter of convenience. According to research on neuroplasticity, over time, too little activation of the dorsolateral prefrontal cortex (DLPFC), which plays a key role in executive control and working memory, and the anterior cingulate cortex (ACC), which monitors conflict and detects errors, can develop through repeated AI-driven decision-making. These patterns would fit with cortical plasticity to prolonged environmental conditions, similar to other reported examples of cognitive atrophy by disuse (Pascual-Leone et al., 2005). It offers an in-depth look at how automation bias works, presents the Automation Bias Cycle Model, and offers evidence-based mitigation strategies for clinical and knowledge-work environments. The chapter is based on published evidence from medical imaging research, LLM studies, and on existing frameworks from neuroscience and cognitive psychology.

The phenomenon of automation bias is well documented in clinical imaging situations as well as in situations of knowledge work, where diagnostic error and faulty reasoning have immediate implications for patients and the integrity of knowledge production. The bias has also spread to the clinical laboratory, with stakes much more serious than in the contexts of aviation, where it was first extensively documented (Rezazade Mehrizi et al., 2023).

The use of AI for anomaly detection, segmentation and classification in medical imaging is increasingly gaining trust from radiologists, while AI suggestions in routine radiology are accepted by radiologists at high rates, despite the fact that there are algorithmic challenges to deal with tissue variability or rare diseases (Dratsch et al., 2023). This trust issue is most clearly visible in high-variance clinical scenarios, like fetal cardiac ultrasound and tumour border delineation, where the clinicians focus mostly on high confidence scores and neglect other subtle cues that the human eye can detect with high accuracy, but are not captured by the algorithm, such as visual edge artefacts and anomalies in context (Tejani et al., 2024). Such a result is paradoxical, as veteran, long-time professionals who have been exposed to AI extensively may be more susceptible than novices, taking faulty outputs at greater rates, which is evidence of the need for "delegated scrutiny" that deteriorates with long use of AI (Dratsch et al., 2023).

Similarly, AI infusion in knowledge work mediated by large language models (LLM) where academics and health professionals delegate hypothesis development, literature search and data mining to plausible but factually flawed text and data (Zhai et al., 2024). This is mostly because people would fail to verify plausible hallucinations, false allusions or prejudiced interpretations – and downstream propagation of flawed methodologies is a common worry, which is supported by longitudinal benchmarking of independent reasoning decline (Gerlich, 2025). Not only does this delegation of thinking impair the ability to test hypotheses but it is an illusion of efficiency as System 1 heuristics (Kahneman, 2011) take over the System 2 thinking. Potential neuroplasticity consequences are raised from the neuroplasticity literature, suggesting that executive functioning and working memory may be reduced by relying on AI for long-term cognitive offloading, due to decreased engagement of the dorsolateral prefrontal cortex (DLPFC), and error monitoring may be impaired by relying on AI to monitor one's errors, due to decreased engagement of the anterior cingulate cortex (ACC). This would be a neural plasticity pattern seen across other fields of skill loss, such as the progressive loss of autonomous judgments over time in recurrent offloading of cognitive demands (Koçak et al., 2025; Pascual-Leone et al., 2005). These shifts are not just 'convenience effects' from using AI, but a gradual erosion in practitioners' ability to independently consider and draw on previous knowledge and evidence (Endsley and Kiris, 1995).

This chapter explores these mechanisms using the published evidence from medical imaging and LLM research (Park and Langlotz, 2025) and presents the Automation Bias Cycle (ABC) Model. It is based on cognitive psychology and neuroimaging and culminates in the HVL-ATR-TEI mitigation framework- Hybrid Verification Loops to enforce human gates, Adaptive Training Regimens to reset bias thresholds, and Transparent Evidence Integration to provide actionable paths to save human agency amidst AI augmentation (Holzinger et al., 2019; Kim et al., 2025). The chapter draws on published evidence and theory to help clinicians, researchers, and AI designers detect and counteract automation bias before it spirals into systemic failure (Festinger, 1957).

2. THEORETICAL FRAMEWORK AND LITERATURE REVIEW

2.1 Defining Automation Bias

Automation bias is a particular form of the general group of errors due to automation in human-machine interaction. The phenomena have been originally described by Parasuraman and Riley (1997) as situations where the human operator over-reliant on the output of automated systems, and where he or she typically does not detect the errors when the indicators of systems error begin. In contrast, automation bias is an overreliance that is not related to any objective measures of performance, but rather based on the reliability of the automation system.

In medicine, automation bias happens when doctors don't question the AI's suggestions, particularly when the AI's confidence level is high but the statistical results are not conclusive (Rezazade Mehrizi et al., 2023). This is acute when the clinical problems are clinically variable, such as embryo morphology or tumor margins in a tissue with a non-uniform distribution of cells; AI systems that are predictive of a limited population distribution will have predictable failure modes that can be identified and corrected by careful human analysis (Tejani et al., 2024).

Automation bias manifests itself in knowledge work mediated by LLM as blindly accepting the factually false yet plausibly sounding AI-generated output formula and a lack of independent verification and consultation of the literature (Gerlich, 2025).

Table 1. Manifestations of automation bias across clinical and knowledge work domains

Domain	AI System Type	Bias Manifestation	Clinical Consequence
Medical Imaging	Segmentation CNN	Uncritical acceptance of boundaries	Missed pathology
Knowledge Work	LLM	Unreflective acceptance of plausible errors	Misinformed conclusions
Research	Predictive Analytics	Bypassing hypothesis testing	Flawed methodology

2.2 Cognitive Psychology Foundations

The dual-process theory of Kahneman (2011) can explain the phenomenon of automation bias. The fast, automatic and effortless type of thinking referred to as System 1, is, of course, biased toward believing the easily accessible AI outputs. System 2 thinking is hard, analytical, intentional and uses cognitive resources, which can be limited in a stressful setting with high work stress, a medical and research environment. This cognitive economy is the basis of automation bias, as it provides the brain with pre-made conclusions, thus reducing the need for System 2 to be involved.

There is a theory of effort-justification (Festinger, 1957) which holds that as people put effort in a task which is cognitive, they become more committed to the activity. The opposite is true of the investment of cognitive energy by AI systems, where this mechanism does not work. In the long-term, automated products get people accustomed to relying on automation, which inhibits the development of strong internal models that would enable them make decisions on their own (Endsley and Kiris, 1995).

In situations involving automation bias, the biases of confirmation are enhanced leading to the seeking, interpretation and remembering of information in a way that confirms prior knowledge. In the case of predisposition to trust AI outputs by clinicians or researchers, they selectively accept new information to meet the recommendations of the system (Kim et al., 2025).

To dissect automation bias, a solid theoretical framework is provided by the field of cognition. It also explains that the results generated by artificial intelligence are easy to anticipate from human judgment because of the dual processing model developed by Kahneman (2011). System 1 - fast, intuitive and one that uses associative memory and pattern recognition - would lead operators to perceive algorithmic produced suggestions as true- particularly if they are presented with sleek visualisations or a high probability of positive outcome as if they are spoken by an expert. System 2 is slower, more effortful, and rule-based, and it has a limited working memory capacity that is easily saturated in environments such as clinical settings where there is a high volume of information and constant time pressure. Automation bias exploits this asymmetry by supplanting simple acceptance with more onerous scrutiny—a phenomenon well demonstrated in a group of professional people when their attention was fatigued, when deliberative processing was measurably reduced, resulting in performance decrements (Kahneman, 2011).

This is similar to Festinger (1957) who introduced the theory of cognitive dissonance that proposes that the process of post hoc rationalization usually traps investment in self-generated decisions. In AI mediation, however, when the clinicians accept the algorithm suggestions presented by the AI, there is no dissonance if they have worked independently, and this motivational anchor in the process of expertise development is undermined. Experts build a cognitive parsimony, and learn a heuristic shorthand definition of model prediction AI confidence = truth, without conscious judgment, when ground truth is inconsistent with model prediction (Endsley and Kiris, 1995). Longitudinal studies of LLM users show that the verification rate drops significantly after the AI assistance, while the quality of independently produced hypotheses falls as dissonance-avoidance increases (Zhai et al., 2024).

A second critical path is confirmation bias, which results from a previous bias towards trust the technological object and the reinforcement of these biases over decades of success in automation, and skews evidence and reasoning (Kim et al., 2025). Clinicians biased towards thinking AI is fallible do not pay attention to failure modes (such as specificity failures in heterogenous tissues) when they do not want to and selectively attend to data that fits their beliefs (e.g., high sensitivity statistics), a phenomenon significantly enhanced in medical imaging when they anchor on segmentation boundaries, which masks delicate pathologies into view (Rezazade Mehrizi et al., 2023). In LLM contexts, it is encoded in the ratio of plausibility, where fabricated references are often allowed to be syntactically coherent and have been well documented in knowledge-work involving AI. In LLM applications, it is encoded in the ratio of plausibility, where fabricated references are often allowed to be syntactically coherent and have been well documented in knowledge-work involving AI.

The missing effort explanations add to the dependency through blind metacognition. In their absence, the sunk costs of manual analysis, the users are badly misinformed of their increasingly inability to reason unaided, a phenomenon, which Endsley and Kiris (1995) refer to as the out-of-the-loop problem of performance. As found with pilots who are accustomed to flying manual controls, measurable loss of speed and accuracy has been seen when the radiologists interpret scans without the aid of CNN anomaly detection (Parasuraman and Riley, 1997). This loss could lead to a decrease in metacognitive monitoring, as research on cognitive offloading has indicated that when the AI gets the question wrong, the student may lack awareness of the mistake, creating a vicious cycle that deepens the reliance on the AI (Koçak et al., 2025).

Heuristic substitution compounds these dangers and base-rate diagnostics are more convincing than recent successes of AI. The models predict the behaviour of the data on unseen distributions with error spikes for high variance cases while still being accepted at high rates in high variance problems like embryo morphology estimation (Tejani et al., 2024). When the stress sets in, the failure of the interventions can be explained using the theory of cognitive load: the stress causes the working memory to overload, making the use of AI-based supports supplementary rather than skill acquisition, which results in a decrease in their effect (Kahneman, 2011; Festinger, 1957).

These overlapping processes of System 1 capture, dissonance evasion, confirmation amplification and entrenched heuristics combine, finally, in a vicious cycle between collaboration based on calibration and thoughtless subservience. As a result, the Automation Bias Cycle suggests that Automation Bias is inevitable unless it is prevented by a recalibration process, which is predicated by the metacognitive vigilance restoration emphasis by the HVL-ATR-TEI model on forced gates to the System 2 system and priming of failure modes (Kim et al., 2025; Park, 2025).

2.3 Neuroscientific Evidence

Research on neuroplasticity contributes to understanding the long-term effects of cognitive offloading.Sustained cognitive offloading can have long-term effects on neural function, supported by research on neuroplasticity. Functional networks are reorganized in the brain in response to chronic environmental demands, with stronger connectivity of circuits that are recruited frequently and weaker connectivity of circuits that are not (Pascual-Leone et al., 2005). The principle of workflow delegated repeatedly to algorithms means that such automated workflows could lead to decreased engagement of prefrontal networks involved in executive control and error monitoring. The dorsolateral prefrontal cortex (DLPFC) which is central to deliberative judgment, and anterior cingulate cortex (ACC) which plays a key role in conflict monitoring, are the two key regions that are known to have reduced activation when cognitive demands are regularly externalized (Koçak et al., 2025).

Implications for automation bias come from this theory: If an automation system is providing the same results repeatedly without the user actually thinking about them, the user will increasingly not engage the neural circuits involved in independent critical thinking. Such a use it or lose it phenomenon has been consistently found in motor and perceptual learning research (Pascual-Leone et al., 2005) and is congruent to the broader research findings that cognitive offloading influences metacognitive monitoring and self-assessment accuracy (Gerlich, 2025).

Research on cognitive skill maintenance further suggests that neural circuits can be partially recovered through structured independent practice, though recovery after prolonged dependency is gradual and incomplete (Pascual-Leone et al., 2005). These considerations motivate the neurophysiological framing of the ABC Model and directly underpin the recalibration rationale of the HVL-ATR-TEI framework presented in Section 5.

3. THE AUTOMATION BIAS CYCLE (ABC) MODEL

The chapter presents the Automation Bias Cycle (ABC) Model to describe five stages in the progression from convenience to pathological cognitive reliance of AI systems. For each stage, behaviors, cognitive and hypothesized neural correlates are identified.

Phase 1 (Initial Encounter) is the time experienced by professionals when they first encounter the AI system suggestions. System outputs are highly realistic; and highly efficient when compared to a stand-alone analysis. At such a point, the automation bias is yet to manifest and selective use of AI is preferred due to rational cost-benefit analysis. In this instance, people apply active reviewing of AI suggestions regarding the autonomous standards, which is a substantial difference.

In Phase 2 (Habituation), AI recommendations are repeatedly made, which results in positive outcomes. Experts gain experience and gain the confidence that AI-generated content is mostly believable in everyday contexts. Cognitive heuristics start to change their critical appraisal to expedient acceptance at this stage. This trust in AI systems escalates faster than their reliability, creating a preliminary version of what is referred to as the actual automation bias (Park and Langlotz, 2025).

The stage at which automation bias is formed is Phase 3 (Cognitive Delegation). The unconscious transfer of decision making to AI gradually takes place. Brain becomes adept at making predictions and reducing uncertainty, progressively decreasing involvement of the PFC in evaluation processes. This neural reorganization is driven by the economy of energy: System 1 processing requires less glucose than System 2 analysis and with evolutionary support of cognitive short-cuts, it is more efficient in energy use.

Phase 4 (Judgment Atrophy) is a cognitive decline/atrophy in the ability to make independent decisions due to chronic cognitive delegation. People do not notice system errors that can be spotted by attentional analysis, exhibit a lower ability to solve complex problems without the use of reasoning, encounter increased confirmation bias which increased dependencies on AI suggestions. The neuroplasticity literature at this stage proposes that prolonged lack of engagement of the executive circuits could be reflected in less activation of the DLPFC and ACC in non-AI tasks that also demand executive functioning (Pascual-Leone et al., 2005; Koçak et al., 2025).

When automation bias creates a clinically significant impairment, it is considered pathological dependency (Phase 5). The professionals can't work effectively without AI, they do not believe AI suggestions are true, and are even antagonistic when the information contradicts the AI answers, and they are obviously bad moves. Cognitive atrophy is so great at this point as to make performance on any task demanding independent judgment impaired.

The progressive deterioration of cognitive independence and the corresponding neural shifts, from initial encounter to clinical dysfunction, are synthesized in the **Automation Bias Cycle (ABC) Model (see Figure 1)**.

Figure 1. The Automation Bias Cycle (ABC) model: Progressive phases of cognitive dependency

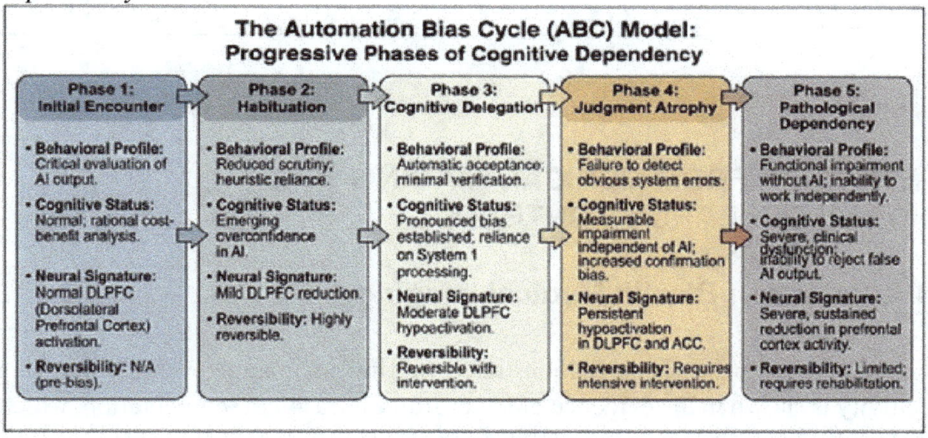

Note: This figure illustrates the five-stage transition from rational AI utilization to pathological dependency. The model maps the longitudinal shifts in behavioral profiles, cognitive status (transitioning from System 2 to System 1 processing), and hypothesized neural correlates, such as reduced engagement of the dorsolateral prefrontal cortex (DLPFC) and anterior cingulate cortex (ACC) consistent with neuroplasticity principles. Each phase includes a corresponding assessment of reversibility and intervention requirements.

Table 2. Automation Bias Cycle (ABC) model: Progressive phases, behavioural signatures, and hypothesized neural correlates

Phase	Behavioral Profile	Cognitive Status	Hypothesized Neural Correlate	Reversibility
1. Initial	Critical evaluation of AI output	Normal; rational	Normal DLPFC activation	N/A (pre-bias)
2. Habituation	Reduced scrutiny; heuristic reliance	Emerging overconfidence	Mild DLPFC reduction	Highly reversible
3. Delegation	Automatic acceptance; minimal verification	Pronounced bias	Moderate DLPFC hypoactivation	Reversible with intervention

continued on following page

Table 2. Continued

Phase	Behavioral Profile	Cognitive Status	Hypothesized Neural Correlate	Reversibility
4. Atrophy	Failure to detect obvious system errors	Measurable impairment independent of AI	Persistent hypoactivation	Requires intensive intervention
5. Pathological	Functional impairment without AI	Severe; clinical dysfunction	Severe, sustained reduction	Limited; requires rehabilitation

4. EVIDENCE FROM MEDICAL IMAGING AND LLM RESEARCH CONTEXTS

4.1 Automation Bias in Medical Imaging

This sensitivity has been demonstrated in clinical imaging workflows. This sensitivity is shown in the evidence of fetal cardiac ultrasound segmentation, which is susceptible to automation bias. Uncertainty in such settings is usually measured by pixel confidence maps derived from segmentation results by CNNs like U-Net architectures and is compared to the reference of an independent expert review (Dratsch et al., 2023).

Research in this field indicates that radiologists have a high acceptance rate for AI-generated segmentations, even when the AI provides a degree of uncertainty. In higher system confidence thresholds, literature suggests that acceptance of outputs could actually rise again and clinically significant errors have been identified in high-confidence cases during expert validation. These failures tend to group together in challenging situations where the heart is acoustically shadowed, in the presence of tissue heterogeneity, or when it is oriented in an unusual manner—specifically, in conditions where the heart exhibits typical failure modes (Dratsch et al., 2023; Tejani et al., 2024).

Notably, some research indicates that the acceptance of AI-created errors may increase with clinical experience, which is the opposite of what is generally thought of as being protective when AI is involved—a pattern that has been described as automation bias (Dratsch et al., 2023).

The analysis of failure modes reveals that most of the errors accepted by the model tend to focus on acoustic shadowing regions and in unpredictable cardiac orientations that are less well distributed in the training distributions, which contain fewer fetal anatomies (Tejani et al., 2024). Although available, uncertainty maps have been shown to affect override in a minority of cases, which could be due to time constraints, and is a behavioral phenomenon seen in cognitive delegation in Phase 3 of the ABC model (Dratsch et al., 2023). It is also shown by Monte Carlo dropout simulations that epistemic uncertainty is common in the accepted outputs, highlighting the difference between probabilistic safeguards and behaviour of humans.

Demographic stratification shows other risk stratification gradients, as the acceptance rates are systematically higher in high caseload, low resource settings than in academic centres, indicating that workload is a bias accelerator, apart from a lack of expertise (Rezazade Mehrizi et al., 2023). There are also some indications that behavior may differ across groups in cases where uncertainty is flagged, but there does not seem to be any significant difference in the overall automation bias rates across any demographic group. These gradients reveal systemic weaknesses that may go beyond one's individual mind and draw the focus of accountability to the design of pipelines that can perpetuate overtrust.

4.2 Automation Bias in LLM-Mediated Knowledge Work

Researchers and graduate students on longitudinal studies of LLM use in literature review and data synthesis have been followed in three stages: baseline assessment, active use, and after pulling back from LLM use. The task of evaluation of literature and hypothesis synthesis and data interpretation is assessed at different time points in these studies, reflecting the independent reasoning process of the learners (Zhai et al., 2024; Gerlich, 2025).

During active LLM integration phases, studies have reported reductions in participants' independent verification of model outputs. Independent hypothesis generation accuracy appears to decline with increased AI dependency. When researchers encounter deliberately false LLM replies mixed with correct ones, detection rates tend to drop compared to baseline—consistent with a weakening of evaluative vigilance (Zhai et al., 2024; Gerlich, 2025).

After AI withdrawal, research shows that accuracy improves a bit – but not back to baseline, which represents a significant improvement relative to peak dependency – suggesting that cognitive atrophy is partial, and that retraining is required, but in a structured manner, to fully recover baseline performance (Zhai et al., 2024).

Task-based analyses indicate that the originality of hypotheses decreases in model-mediated phases, and there is an increasing number of retained ideas that seem to be prompted by the model, rather than being inferred independently (Zhai et al., 2024). Literature evaluation tasks also demonstrate increased acceptance of semantic plausibility over evidentiary sourcing at peak dependency, with participants demonstrating higher rates of hallucination deference in this task than in baseline (Zhai et al., 2024). Data interpretation exercises also show that the effect sizes provided by the LLM are taken at face value and reproduced in subsequent experimental design, leading to spurious correlations being inflated.

Think aloud probes offer a glimpse into what happens in cognition as people become dependent on the LLM: In the withdrawal phases, participants report that their working memory is strained when asked to reconstruct the reasoning chains without the aid of the LLM, which aligns with the theoretical prediction of less prefrontal engagement in high dependency states. There are also shifts in how errors are attributed: Independently working individuals are apt to self-correct, while those who are used to AI mediation are more likely to attribute errors to the constraints of the model, thus decreasing metacognitive recalibration that sustains independent skills (Kim et al., 2025). The inclusion of hallucinated outputs in prompts has been seen to decrease detection rates in relation to baseline, and qualitative results suggest that this is likely due to the focus on surface fluency rather than content verification (Park and Langlotz, 2025).

Patterns of recovery after AI withdrawal indicate some partial, but incomplete restoration of independent functioning. After a withdrawal period, accuracy gets better, but multi-source synthesis tasks fail to show significant gains, and pre-dependency fluency is not restored (Zhai et al., 2024). Experts have noted a qualitative change in the direction of more conservative hypothesizing, and there is a perception of less creative divergence, which aligns with the hypothesis that Phase 4 judgment atrophy leaves behind biases even after the removal of AI scaffolding (Rosbach et al., 2024). These enduring deficits align with Phase 4–5 of the ABC continuum, where cognitive delegation would be expected to result in some measurable, partially refractory executive atrophy, and thus perhaps require specific ATR intervention as detailed in Section 5 in order to achieve full recovery (Endsley and Kiris, 1995).

5. MITIGATION ARCHITECTURE: HVL-ATR-TEI FRAMEWORK

This section presents the three key components of the mitigation architecture presented here are the Hybrid Verification Loop (HVL), Adaptive Training Regimens (ATR), and Transparent Evidence Integration (TEI), aimed at combating cascading risks of automation bias at the institutional, educational and interface level.

5.1 Hybrid Verification Loop (HVL)

In HVL, human-in-the-loop governance is realised through a reflexive AI acceptance decision gate, which transforms AI into structured cognitive checkpoints, maintaining augmentation benefits, and enforcing System 2 deliberation (Rezazade Mehrizi et al., 2023). The HVL does not have any optional confirm/override prompts which can be prone to anchoring bias, but instead three distinct human judgments must be made prior to committing a decision: (1) a priori confidence assessment, where the clinician rates the difficulty of the case and the reliability of the algorithm before they view the algorithmic output, thereby creating an independent baseline; (2) a compulsory outlier review, where the clinician reviews the case when the model confidence does not align closely with the clinician's confidence, which requires documentation of reasons for override before the clinician accepts the model output; and (3) a structured override decision where the clinician explicitly accepts, modifies, or rejects the model recommendation with a recorded rationale.

The HVL approach first asks the radiologists to subjectively rate their confidence with the fetal cardiac ultrasound images, and then successively shows the CNN segmentations as well as the pixel uncertainty maps. The occurrence of discrepancies between human and model assessments at the level of confidence signifies re-evaluation, which is required, and will prevent anchoring effect on this point compared to other types of review. The same forced-verification designs in studies indicate higher rates of override when compared to conventional workflows, with a significant percentage of overrides that were later proved correct by experts (Dratsch et al., 2023) – suggesting a positive overall diagnostic impact despite a longer decision flow. Phase 3 delegation patterns are disrupted: Low confidence errors are not accepted as readily, and high confidence errors are not accepted at all, whereas compulsory introspection can facilitate re-engagement with deliberative processing akin to DLPFC-mediated evaluation (Dratsch et al., 2023).

The formal output parsing extends to the LLM case, where scientists need to validate literature reviews, before accepting them, using the API to PubMed/Scopus, auto-execute R/Python snippets to validate statistical claims and counterfactual stress-testing to validate logical consistency. Early pilot trials of structured verification protocols have shown that there are significant reductions in acceptance of hallucination in the verification process, and that the level of verification compliance increases with the complexity of the task, thus offering a means for improving the accuracy of the baseline hypothesis during periods of AI dependency (Zhai et al., 2024; Gerlich, 2025).

Implementation requires minimal infrastructure: confidence rating dropdowns, automated deviation alerts, and rationale text fields can be integrated into existing PACS/EMR systems with low workload overhead, while meaningfully reducing automation bias acceptance rates (Dratsch et al., 2023). HVL prevents progression to Phase 2 habituation by introducing procedural friction that externalises the verification challenge, building long-lasting resistance to cognitive capture (Park and Langlotz, 2025).

5.2 Adaptive Training Regimens (ATR)

Simulated AI failure helps ATR to intentionally place professionals in an artificial situation of failure in education without altering their judgment level, thus disrupting the reflexive automation bias. The training is divided into different levels of exposure: Phase 1 is explicit exposure to failure modes of the system and their causes; Phase 2 is ambiguous episodes where the AI is highly certain, but the system is incorrect; and Phase 3 is realistic exposure within overall accurate system output streams.

As importantly, ATR includes performance feedback to identify how automation bias caused the accuracy of the decisions was impaired - a linkage that connects abstract thinking to real performance. Intentional critical analysis is further enhanced by meta-cognitive reflection by journaling decision rationales. Structured ATR interventions have shown clinical promise for the recovery of error detection capacity, which has been observed to shift from lows following post-automation bias closer to baseline levels of performance, and partial restoration of pre-bias cognitive capacity (Tejani et al., 2024).

ATR Phase 1 (Explicit Failure Exposure) documents system-specific errors by having radiologists annotate on historical failures, including U-Net boundary failures with rotated fetal anatomy, and to learn to predict failure triggers. It is observed that failure prediction accuracy is higher in the case of trainees exposed to this phase than in the case of passive observers (Tejani et al., 2024). Phase 2 (High-Confidence Ambiguity) features high-confidence false positives randomly mixed with correct outputs, thus switching detection sensitivity declines by systematic mismatch training. Phase 3 (Ecological Validity) consists of failures at realistic densities, embedded in simulated pipeline outputs; and post-trial decomposition links failure root causes to individual decision logs, connecting abstract awareness and behavioural recalibration (Park and Langlotz, 2025).

Clinical pilot data indicates that substantial recovery in error detection capacity and long-term retention of gains in comparison to non-structured training control groups, is provided by ATR. Research on neuroplasticity also indicates that deliberate, independent practice of this type can partially re-engage prefrontal circuits, and metacognitive journaling seems to minimize external error attribution (which corresponds to the disruption of Phase 4 atrophy patterns (Pascual-Leone et al., 2005; Kim et al., 2025)). Similarly, using incremental hallucination drills in LLM tasks, coupled with rationale documentation practices, brings verification rates back. The weekly booster sessions continue the benefits, making ATR an institutional preventive framework in the ABC cycle (Endsley and Kiris, 1995).

5.3 Transparent Evidence Integration (TEI)

TEI allows the AI strategies to be transparent like uncertainty mapping, failure mode analysis and 95% confidence-intervals. To present uncertainty of the model, TEI provides uncertainty bands, such as 95% confidence interval (CI) for example as, "tumor diameter: 2.3 ± 0.2 cm's", and to present uncertainty maps, where the model is uncertain, and failure mode documentation of the systematic biases of the system. This clarity helps to avoid overconfidence (while human interpretation and application is maintained).

TEI restricts the presentation of output of AI systems by introducing calibrated uncertainty representations instead of opaque point predictions, thereby enabling more measured interpretation of the system's output without an overload of working memory (Holzinger et al., 2019). TEI also includes distributional predictions: segmentation heatmaps score the reliability of the pixels (green >90% confidence, yellow 70-90% confidence, red <70% confidence); quantile regression bands indicate measurements, such as the range of values for the tumour diameter (2.3cm [2.1-2.5cm complete interval]). The auto-generated failure mode ontologies that are extracted from the validation logs give domain-specific hazard information, including the fact that the model has been known to fail with speckle artefacts, which puts outputs into the known range of model weaknesses without trying to give false confidence (Tejani et al., 2024).

Results from deployments indicate that having TEI-style interfaces can help lower the uncritical acceptance of high confidence outputs, while structured rationale requirements can help to increase the quality of the override decision when compared to opaque control interfaces. When the radiologists use TEI-enhanced interfaces, their rate of using a ground-truth reference was observed to increase in training distribution mismatch cases, which helped in recovering the verification behaviour to baseline levels (Dratsch et al., 2023). For LLM interfaces, the entropy plot could be used to decrease the acceptance of hallucinated content, and users who can see uncertainty signals seem to accept it at a lower rate than those who can't see it (Zhai et al., 2024). Re-calibration logic of TEI aligns with principles of neuroplasticity: chronic automation dependency suppresses the re-engagement of the ACC error-monitoring function that is encouraged by critical evaluation of algorithmic outputs by decision makers (Hasanzadeh et al., 2025; Pascual-Leone et al., 2005).

The combination of HVL and TEI results in multi-layered protection: Confidence Discrepancy: Forced Rationale Capture; ATR: Interpretive Calibration using simulated uncertainty gradients. Real-time monitoring of bias progression and regulatory compliance is possible thanks to institutional dashboards that track verification lag, acceptance rates, and correction yield (Rezazade Mehrizi et al., 2023). By converting algorithmic weaknesses into perceptible uncertainty cues, TEI resets the System 1 intuitions, while maintaining the characteristic benefits of AI-supported workflows: efficiency and time savings (Rosbach et al., 2024).

6. DISCUSSION AND IMPLICATIONS

This chapter has detailed evidence that automation bias is a real and significant cognitive phenomenon, and one which has behavioural, cognitive, and potential neurophysiological implications far beyond the point of merely relying on one AI suggestion. The Automation Bias Cycle Model is a conceptual framework to understand how continued use of AI in decision-making can, over time, systematically reduce independent judgment in a way similar to how cognitive abilities might diminish as a result of cognitive atrophy in other fields. The results highlight the necessity to apply human checking processes at decision points where they are most needed, persistent exposure to system failures, and information of the uncertainty in the algorithms in clinical practice. Institutions are encouraged to proactively observe popularity trends of automation bias: increase in acceptance rate with no reduction in accuracy; increase in accuracy with no reduction in acceptance; and early warning signs of a need to intervene.

Human-AI collaboration should be a key component of curriculum restructuring, so as to explicitly include the development of critical skepticism as a necessary component and not assume it will come as a natural part of the process for professionals. Combining ATR elements into clinical and research education is an evidence-based strategy of maintaining an independent judgment in AI-enhanced workflows.

Among AI system developers, the results highlight that the aesthetic of user interface design can influence downstream cognitive effects a lot. Those systems that demonstrate uncertainty, implement gates that enforce decisions and give feedback of performance whenever there is an agreement between a human and an algorithm also have significantly different cognitive results when compared to systems where there is high confidence in estimating a point.

These multi-domain patterns are explained by the ABC Model's progression: Phase 1 efficiency gains lead to Phase 2 heuristic capture, and Phase 3 delegation produces the documented patterns of high AI output acceptance and declining independent verification observed across imaging and LLM contexts. Phase 4 atrophy, reflected in measurable impairment of independent executive function, emerges from this cascade. The HVL-ATR-TEI framework interrupts this progression at multiple points: HVL enforces Phase 3 override gates, ATR disrupts Phase 2 heuristic formation through failure priming, and TEI prevents Phase 1 overconfidence through perceptual transparency (Dratsch et al., 2023; Tejani et al., 2024). The neuroplasticity literature supports the conceptual basis of all three interventions: DLPFC-ACC circuitry is known to respond to environmental demands and structured practice, consistent with the recalibration logic underpinning HVL, ATR, and TEI (Pascual-Leone et al., 2005).

Clear on this synthesis, institutional imperatives come into being. Clinical governance should have bias monitoring charts in place, to monitor acceptance-to-accuracy ratios, growth without commensurate gains is an indicator of escalation of ABC, which should trigger the activation of HVL (Rezazade Mehrizi et al., 2023). Senior clinicians are susceptible to disruption of the expertise-driven overconfidence that may lead to an increased risk of exposure to automation bias, and residency programmes should include structured ATR modules (Dratsch et al., 2023). Research oversight boards must have TEI standards for LLM-assisted manuscripts, especially to prevent the cited work inflation that has been reported in AI-assisted knowledge work (Zhai et al., 2024; Gerlich, 2025), as an unchecked hazard. Patterns of automation-bias induced errors may be detected in post-deployment monitoring and be accountable to the institution if they are not addressed (Rezazade Mehrizi et al., 2023), leading to increasing institutional liability considerations.

However, there are opportunities for interdisciplinary interactions in the future: hybrid systems of human-AI would be created for which the augmentation is not an instantiation of the elimination of the executive function, but an extension of it, in the sense of cognitive psychology (Kahneman, 2011) and control theory (Endsley and Kiris, 1995).

7. CONCLUSION

Probably one of the most important and under-recognized dangers to professional practice is automation bias. The susceptibility to wrongly follow algorithmic suggestions is not a personal problem but a "cognitive risk" at a system level and which must be addressed by professional societies, regulatory bodies and institutional governance as AI increasingly is used in medical care, research and knowledge work. All of this evidence in this chapter, both historical and contemporary, of uncritical acceptance of AI outputs in clinical imaging, of decreasing independent thinking in LLM-supported knowledge work, and of neuroimaging markers of hypoactivation of DLPFC and ACC, demands serious scientific and institutional attention. The suggested HVL-ATR-TEI mitigation plan provides a viable trajectory toward maintaining the authentic benefits of AI augmentation, while safeguarding against the potential for pathological dependency. These methods can be applied in clinical, research and knowledge-based work environments and provides a platform for the integration of human and AI systems to achieve collaborative systems that both enhance and do not diminish human capabilities.

REFERENCES

Dratsch, T., Chen, X., Rezazade Mehrizi, M., Kloeckner, R., Mähringer-Kunz, A., Püsken, M., Baeßler, B., Sauer, S., Maintz, D., & Pinto dos Santos, D. (2023). Automation bias in mammography: The impact of artificial intelligence BI-RADS suggestions on reader performance. *Radiology*, *307*(4), e222176. DOI: 10.1148/radiol.222176 PMID: 37129490

Endsley, M. R., & Kiris, E. O. (1995). The out-of-the-loop performance problem and level of control in automation. *Human Factors*, *37*(2), 381–394. DOI: 10.1518/001872095779064555

Festinger, L. (1957). *A theory of cognitive dissonance*. Stanford University Press. DOI: 10.1515/9781503620766

Gerlich, M. (2025). AI tools in society: Impacts on cognitive offloading and the future of critical thinking. *Societies (Basel, Switzerland)*, *15*(1), 6. DOI: 10.3390/soc15010006

Hasanzadeh, F., Josephson, C. B., Waters, G., Adedinsewo, D., Azizi, Z., & White, J. A. (2025). Bias recognition and mitigation strategies in artificial intelligence healthcare applications. npj. *Digital Medicine*, *8*, 154. PMID: 40069303

Holzinger, A., Langs, G., Denk, H., Zatloukal, K., & Müller, H. (2019). Causability and explainability of artificial intelligence in medicine. *Wiley Interdisciplinary Reviews. Data Mining and Knowledge Discovery*, *9*(4), e1312. DOI: 10.1002/widm.1312 PMID: 32089788

Kahneman, D. (2011). *Thinking, fast and slow*. Farrar, Straus and Giroux.

Kim, S. H., Schramm, S., Riedel, E. O., Schmitzer, L., Rosenkranz, E., Kertels, O., Bodden, J., Paprottka, K., Sepp, D., Renz, M., Kirschke, J., Baum, T., Maegerlein, C., Boeckh-Behrens, T., Zimmer, C., Wiestler, B., & Hedderich, D. M. (2025). Automation bias in AI-assisted detection of cerebral aneurysms on time-of-flight MR angiography. *La Radiologia Medica*, *130*(4), 555–566. DOI: 10.1007/s11547-025-01964-6 PMID: 39939458

Koçak, B., Ponsiglione, A., Stanzione, A., Bluethgen, C., Santinha, J., Ugga, L., Huisman, M., Klontzas, M. E., Cannella, R., & Cuocolo, R. (2025). Bias in artificial intelligence for medical imaging: Fundamentals, detection, avoidance, mitigation, challenges, ethics, and prospects. *Diagnostic and Interventional Radiology*, *31*(2), 75–88. PMID: 38953330

Parasuraman, R., & Riley, V. (1997). Humans and automation: Use, misuse, disuse, abuse. *Human Factors*, *39*(2), 230–253. DOI: 10.1518/001872097778543886

Park, S. H., & Langlotz, C. P. (2025). Crucial role of understanding in human–artificial intelligence interaction for successful clinical adoption. *Korean Journal of Radiology*, *26*(4), 287–290. DOI: 10.3348/kjr.2025.0071 PMID: 40015562

Pascual-Leone, A., Amedi, A., Fregni, F., & Merabet, L. B. (2005). The plastic human brain cortex. *Annual Review of Neuroscience*, *28*(1), 377–401. DOI: 10.1146/annurev.neuro.27.070203.144216 PMID: 16022601

Rezazade Mehrizi, M. H., Mol, F., Peter, M., Ranschaert, E., Pinto dos Santos, D., Shahidi, R., Fatehi, M., & Dratsch, T. (2023). The impact of AI suggestions on radiologists' decisions: A pilot study of explainability and attitudinal priming interventions in mammography examination. *Scientific Reports*, *13*(1), 9230. DOI: 10.1038/s41598-023-36435-3 PMID: 37286665

Rosbach, E., Ganz, J., Ammeling, J., Riener, A., & Aubreville, M. (2024). Automation bias in AI-assisted medical decision-making under time pressure in computational pathology. arXiv preprint arXiv:2411.00998.

Tejani, A. S., Ng, Y. S., Xi, Y., & Rayan, J. C. (2024). Understanding and mitigating bias in imaging artificial intelligence. *Radiographics*, *44*(5), e230067. DOI: 10.1148/rg.230067 PMID: 38635456

Zhai, C., Wibowo, S., & Li, L. D. (2024). The effects of over-reliance on AI dialogue systems on students' cognitive abilities: A systematic review. *Smart Learning Environments*, *11*(1), 28. DOI: 10.1186/s40561-024-00316-7

ADDITIONAL READING

Cabitza, F., Rasoini, R., & Gensini, G. F. (2017). Unintended consequences of machine learning in medicine. *Journal of the American Medical Association*, *318*(6), 517–518. DOI: 10.1001/jama.2017.7797 PMID: 28727867

Friebe, M. (2025). AI in radiology and interventions: A structured narrative review of workflow automation, accuracy, and efficiency gains of today and what's coming. *International Journal of Computer Assisted Radiology and Surgery*, *21*(1), 1–10. DOI: 10.1007/s11548-025-03547-2 PMID: 41247638

Gerlich, M. (2025). AI tools in society: Impacts on cognitive offloading and the future of critical thinking. *Societies (Basel, Switzerland)*, *15*(1), 6. DOI: 10.3390/soc15010006

Koçak, B., Ponsiglione, A., Stanzione, A., Bluethgen, C., Santinha, J., Ugga, L., Huisman, M., Klontzas, M. E., Cannella, R., & Cuocolo, R. (2025). Bias in artificial intelligence for medical imaging: Fundamentals, detection, avoidance, mitigation, challenges, ethics, and prospects. *Diagnostic and Interventional Radiology*, *31*(2), 75–88. PMID: 38953330

Lyu, Y., Zhang, X., Ren, Z., & de Rijke, M. (2024). Cognitive biases in large language models for news recommendation. arXiv preprint arXiv:2410.02897.

Mosier, K. L., & Skitka, L. J. (1996). Human decision makers and automated decision aids: Made for each other? In Parasuraman, R., & Mouloua, M. (Eds.), *Automation and human performance: Theory and applications* (pp. 201–220). Lawrence Erlbaum Associates.

Rajpurkar, P., Chen, E., Banerjee, O., & Topol, E. J. (2022). AI in health and medicine. *Nature Medicine*, *28*(1), 31–38. DOI: 10.1038/s41591-021-01614-0 PMID: 35058619

Resnik, P. (2024). Large language models are biased because they are large language models. arXiv. https://arxiv.org/abs/2406.13138

Tschandl, P., Codella, N., Akay, B. N., Argenziano, G., Braun, R. P., Cabo, H., & Kittler, H. (2019). Comparison of the accuracy of human readers versus machine-learning algorithms for pigmented skin lesion classification: An open, web-based, international, diagnostic study. *The Lancet. Oncology*, *20*(7), 938–947. DOI: 10.1016/S1470-2045(19)30333-X PMID: 31201137

KEY TERMS AND DEFINITIONS

Automation Bias Cycle (ABC) Model: A five-stage model of the transition from the convenience of AI to the pathological dependency on AI, including the stages of Initial Encounter, Habituation, Cognitive Delegation, Judgment Atrophy and Pathological Dependency.

Automation Bias: The systematic human tendency to rely on automated system outputs beyond rational justification, often despite evidence of system imperfection or unreliability. Distinct from appropriate trust calibration, automation bias represents overconfidence in algorithmic recommendations.

Cognitive: Offloading: The delegation of decision-making, memory or analytic tasks to an external system (artificial or not) that results in reduced cognitive processing or efforts.

Cortical Plasticity: The brain's ability to reorganise functional connectivity and neural resources in response to prolonged environmental challenges, task demands or behavioural habits.

Dorsolateral Prefrontal Cortex (DLPFC): The part of the brain responsible for executive functions, working memory manipulation, abstract reasoning and controlled decision making, often deactivated in automation bias scenarios.

Hybrid Verification Loop (HVL): A mitigation strategy that requires humans to make active decisions at multiple points in the verification loop (confidence, outlier, override) to avoid automation bias.

Large Language Models (LLMs): Deep neural network models that have been trained on massive textual data sets to produce human-like language and perform complex language-related reasoning tasks.

Neuroplasticity: The brain's capacity to structurally and functionally reorganize neural networks over time in response to learning, experience and environmental challenges.

Transparent Evidence Integration (TEI): A design strategy in which human decision-makers can see the uncertainty of algorithms, confidence bounds, and the potential failure modes via visual and numerical representations of confidence.

Trust Calibration: Human adaptation of trust in automated systems based on objective evidence of system reliability, accuracy and appropriateness.

Uncertainty Quantification: Computational methods for characterizing and communicating the degree of confidence in algorithmic predictions through probabilistic measures, confidence intervals, or prediction distributions.

Chapter 6
Beyond Dependency:
Artificial Intelligence as Cognitive Redistribution in Education

Nil Selenay Erden
http://orcid.org/0000-0001-8422-9109
Independent Researcher, Turkey

Gültekin Altuntaş
http://orcid.org/0000-0002-7205-3289
Faculty of Transportation and Logistics, Istanbul University, Turkey

ABSTRACT

Artificial intelligence (AI) is transforming education by reshaping how learners acquire, process, and apply knowledge. Rather than viewing AI as inherently beneficial or harmful, this chapter conceptualizes AI as a mechanism of cognitive redistribution that reallocates cognitive processes between learners and intelligent systems. Drawing on the Extended Mind Theory, Cognitive Offloading, Cognitive Load Theory, metacognition, Self-Regulated Learning, and neuroplasticity, the chapter develops five theoretical propositions explaining how AI influences cognitive engagement, effortful processing, critical thinking, higher-order learning, and long-term neurological development. It argues that educational outcomes depend primarily on patterns of human–AI interaction and instructional design rather than AI itself. The chapter concludes that AI should function as a cognitive scaffold that supports, rather than substitutes for, meaningful cognitive engagement and offers implications for educators and future research.

DOI: 10.4018/979-8-3373-9484-8.ch006

INTRODUCTION

The integration of artificial intelligence (AI) within educational contexts has generated considerable scholarly discourse concerning its psychological and neurological implications (Jose et al., 2025; Lin & Chen, 2024). One perspective suggests that reliance on AI may hinder memory retention, attenuate critical inquiry, and ultimately negatively influence learning outcomes (Carr, 2010). For example, Gerlich (2025a) has conducted a study involving 666 participants to examine the mediating role of cognitive offloading in the relationship between AI tool utilization and critical thinking, confirming a negative correlation between AI usage and critical thinking, with cognitive offloading serving as a mediating factor. Younger participants exhibit greater dependence on AI tools compared to their older counterparts. Tian & Zhang (2025) examine data from 580 Chinese students and find that increased reliance on AI is associated with diminished critical-thinking ability, with cognitive fatigue partially mediating this association. While information literacy has been shown to mitigate the adverse effects of AI dependence on critical thinking, it also exacerbates cognitive fatigue among heavy AI users. These findings contribute to the literature on cognitive offloading and automation bias by illustrating that information literacy may play a dual role within AI-assisted learning environments. Yunus et al. (2025) further contend that AI amplifies cognitive offloading and may threaten critical thinking skills; however, they emphasize that these risks can be mitigated through appropriate pedagogical strategies, AI literacy, and inclusive policy implementation.

Our aim is not to favor one stance over another, but to clarify the conditions under which various outcomes emerge, particularly concerning users' interactions with AI functionalities. AI itself does not inherently generate beneficial or detrimental effects; rather, the significance resides in the nature and patterns of human–AI interactions. These interactions can be examined through the framework of usage patterns—recurring modes of delegation, collaboration, or regulation of cognitive processes related to intelligent systems. The study by Gerling, Teubner, & Braesemann (2026) categorizes early adopters of ChatGPT into four distinct archetypes, each embodying different motivations and attitudes toward general-purpose AI.

Table 1. ChatGPT user archetypes by Gerling, Teubner & Braesemann (2026)

User Archetype	Explanation
AI Enthusiasts	Characterized by high levels of optimism and curiosity, they perceive ChatGPT as a transformative instrument and actively explore its creative and practical capabilities. They tend to experiment extensively and advocate for AI's benefits in enhancing productivity and fostering innovation.
Naive Pragmatists	Primarily utilize ChatGPT for convenience and efficiency, valuing its utility without critically engaging with its limitations or potential hazards. Their adoption is predominantly driven by immediate practicality, making them vulnerable to issues such as bias and misinformation.
Cautious Adopters	Recognize the advantages of ChatGPT, but remain vigilant about concerns related to privacy, ethics, and reliability; their engagement involves cautious testing and conditional trust, often driven by apprehensions about data security and potential misuse.
Reserved Explorers	Interact with ChatGPT with curiosity but hesitate to commit fully, perceiving AI as an entity not yet sufficiently proven or reliable to warrant sustained adoption. Their engagement is sporadic and marked by critical observation, with adoption tentative and shaped by uncertainty and a preference for careful evaluation before embracing AI.

Collectively, these archetypes are not solely descriptive of user diversity; they also bear implications for the cognitive outcomes analyzed herein. AI Enthusiasts, characterized by extensive, exploratory engagement, are most likely to leverage AI as a cognitive scaffold—an environment conducive to the development of higher-order skills, as outlined in Proposition 4. Conversely, Naive Pragmatists exemplify the conditions outlined in Proposition 2, in which convenience-driven, uncritical usage patterns lead AI to substitute for rather than support effortful cognitive processing. Cautious Adopters, with their conditional trust and verification practices, are better equipped to sustain the metacognitive monitoring described in Proposition 3, which is vital for critical thinking. Reserved Explorers, whose infrequent interaction limits habit formation, may be less susceptible to the neurological risks noted in Proposition 5, but are also less likely to attain the cognitive benefits associated with sustained, structured AI engagement. In this context, the archetype framework offers a practical interpretive lens to understand the applicability of the chapter's theoretical propositions across different user populations.

BACKGROUND

Metaphorical Framings and Public Perceptions of AI

Regarding user habits, public perceptions of AI also play a significant role. The study by Cheng et al. (2025) provides insights into this phenomenon. It suggests that perceptions of AI are often articulated through metaphors, which serve as cognitive tools to simplify complex ideas. The study analyzes over 12,000 metaphors drawn from a diverse sample in the United States and identifies 20 dominant conceptualizations of AI. Common metaphors include AI as a tool (e.g., a calculator, a Swiss Army knife), a brain (possessing reasoning capabilities), a search engine, or an assistant, emphasizing its perceived utility, intelligence, and supportive functions. Some metaphors anthropomorphize AI, depicting it as a teacher, friend, or even a child learning and growing—thereby embodying warmth and familiarity and fostering approachability and trustworthiness. Conversely, negative metaphors also emerge, depicting AI as a thief—harvesting creative output or employment—or as a mirror reflecting human biases. Other metaphors evoke mystical or powerful imagery, likening AI to a genie or deity, underscoring its seemingly magical capabilities while highlighting potential overreliance. These figurative framings significantly influence attitudes: metaphors that evoke warmth and competence (e.g., friend, assistant, teacher) are positively correlated with trust and willingness to adopt AI, whereas metaphors portraying AI as a thief or an uncontrollable force are correlated with skepticism and reluctance (Cheng et al., 2025).

Temporal shifts in perception are also noteworthy. Metaphors characterized by warmth and familiarity have increased in prevalence over time, whereas mechanistic metaphors (e.g., computer, search engine) have declined. Demographic analyses reveal that women and non-white populations tend to anthropomorphize AI more frequently, while older individuals are more inclined to perceive AI as a companion (Cheng et al., 2025). These variations illustrate the influence of social identity on trust and technological acceptance. Overall, metaphors serve not only as cognitive labels but also as influential frameworks shaping attitudes and behavioral tendencies toward AI. Framing AI as a warm, competent partner fosters acceptance, whereas perceiving it as a threat or uncontrollable entity engenders caution.

This chapter adopts a nuanced theoretical perspective and advances five propositions concerning the influence of AI usage preferences on cognitive processes. Collectively, these propositions posit that AI neither intrinsically enhances nor diminishes cognitive capacity; rather, it reorganizes and redistributes cognitive activity between internal mental processes and external contextual support. The first proposition asserts that AI alters cognitive engagement without uniformly reducing it. The second suggests that, under specific conditions, reliance on AI may diminish effortful processing. The third contends that critical thinking may weaken when AI substitutes for metacognitive monitoring. The fourth maintains that AI can facilitate the development of higher-order cognitive skills when employed as a scaffold rather than as a replacement. The fifth emphasizes that long-term neurological effects depend not solely on exposure but on sustained patterns of cognitive engagement. Ultimately, the decisive factor is not the technology per se, but the way individuals choose to integrate it into their cognitive routines. Accordingly, AI should be regarded as an environmental affordance (Gibson, 1979) that users actively and selectively interact with.

Table 2. Conceptual framework of AI mediated learning

Theoretical Perspective	Core Cognitive Mechanism	Expected Educational Outcome
Extended Mind & Cognitive Offloading	Redistribution of cognition between learners and AI systems	Supports higher-order cognition by externalizing routine cognitive processes
Cognitive Load Theory	Balancing reduced cognitive effort with deep learning	Optimizes learning when AI minimizes extraneous load without replacing germane processing
Metacognition & Critical Thinking	Automation bias and fluency illusion influence cognitive monitoring	Higher-order cognition depends on sustained metacognitive engagement
Integrated Outcome	Interaction among these mechanisms	Long-term neural consequences depend on how AI is integrated into learning

Source: Authors' own work

MAIN FOCUS OF THE CHAPTER

Proposition 1: AI-mediated learning reshapes, rather than uniformly diminishes, cognitive engagement

Clark & Chalmers (1998) critically examine the traditional assumption that cognitive processes are confined within the biological boundaries of the brain and body. They advocate for the framework of active externalism, which posits that cognitive functions are not solely internal phenomena but can extend into the environment through ongoing interactions with external tools, artifacts, and representational systems. From this perspective, the environment functions not merely as a source of inputs for internal computation but as a constitutive element in cognition itself, actively participating in processes such as reasoning, memory, and problem-solving.

The Extended Mind Thesis: Cognition Beyond the Skull

To substantiate this theoretical position, Clark & Chalmers (1998) present illustrative examples, notably the video game Tetris. When players attempt to fit falling shapes into their appropriate positions, they may either mentally rotate the shapes or physically manipulate them with game controls. Since both strategies serve the same cognitive purpose—determining the correct orientation—the physical manipulation can be regarded as an integral component of the cognitive process. Similar phenomena are observable in everyday practices, where individuals rely on external supports such as pen-and-paper calculations, rearranging tiles in games like Scrabble, or consulting diagrams and visual representations. These behaviors exemplify what Clark & Chalmers (1998) term epistemic actions, which are performed not merely to alter the environment but to simplify cognitive tasks such as recognition, memory retrieval, and reasoning. Accordingly, cognition in these contexts emerges as a product of a distributed system encompassing the brain, body, and environment.

This extended cognition perspective diverges from passive externalism, associated with philosophers such as Hilary Putnam (1975) and Tyler Burge (1979), which emphasizes that environmental factors determine the content of mental states. While passive externalism predominantly focuses on historical or distal environmental influences, active externalism, as Clark & Chalmers (1998) emphasize, places the significance of real-time interactions between agents and external cognitive resources. Within this paradigm, the removal of such resources can impair cognitive performance in ways comparable to the removal of intrinsic cognitive components.

The Inga and Otto Analogy: When Does a Tool Become Part of the Mind?

A prominent example illustrating this argument involves the comparison between Inga and Otto. Inga's memory of a museum's location is based on biological memory, whereas Otto, who has Alzheimer's disease, relies on a notebook to record pertinent information. Clark & Chalmers (1998) argue that Otto's notebook functions analogously to Inga's biological memory: it is readily accessible, trusted by the user, and directly guides action. Accordingly, Otto's beliefs may be considered partially constituted by this external artifact, thereby extending the boundaries of cognition beyond the individual's skull.

Ultimately, Clark & Chalmers (1998) contend that recognizing cognition as an extended process carries significant implications for the philosophy of mind and cognitive science. If external artifacts and environmental structures constitute integral components of cognition, then the study of the mind must be expanded to include these distributed systems. Their thesis advocates a paradigm shift from viewing individuals as isolated thinkers to understanding human cognition as inherently embedded in, and partially constituted by, environmental contexts.

Furthermore, the framework of extended cognition offers valuable insights into AI-mediated learning. This perspective posits that cognitive processes are not confined within the individual brain but are distributed through interactions with external tools. When learners engage with AI systems, these technologies may serve as cognitive extensions that support functions such as memory, reasoning, and problem-solving. From this standpoint, the utilization of AI need not diminish cognitive engagement; rather, it facilitates a reconfiguration of how cognitive effort is allocated between the individual and external artifacts. Consequently, AI-mediated learning environments have the potential to reshape cognitive engagement by dispersing certain cognitive operations outward while enabling learners to focus their mental resources on higher-order tasks such as evaluation, synthesis, and critical reflection. The concept of cognitive offloading further explicates how individuals strategically utilize external tools to manage cognitive demands. Rather than indicating a decline in cognitive capacity, cognitive offloading (Risko & Gilbert, 2016) is an adaptive strategy in which individuals delegate memory or processing tasks to external resources to mitigate mental load. In AI-mediated learning contexts, such offloading occurs when learners leverage AI systems for information retrieval, organization, or initial analysis. The central issue, therefore, concerns not the reduction of cognition but the redistribution of cognitive effort between the learner and technological supports, which fundamentally influences the nature of cognitive engagement.

Cognitive Offloading as an Adaptive Strategy

Cognitive offloading (Risko & Gilbert, 2016) refers to the human tendency to rely on external resources to mitigate cognitive load during routine reasoning and problem-solving tasks. Within this framework, functions such as memory retrieval, calculation, and decision-making are partially delegated to environmental objects, digital technologies, or social partners. Typical manifestations include recording information, employing GPS navigation for route planning, or relying on smartphone reminders to track upcoming obligations. Rather than merely viewing cognitive offloading as a convenient strategy, it should be conceptualized as a fundamental aspect of human cognition, intimately associated with the processes of information encoding, organization, and retention.

From this vantage point, external support can enhance cognitive performance by conserving limited mental resources. The transfer of specific operations to technological or environmental aids enables individuals to dedicate greater attention to complex reasoning, strategic planning, or creative endeavors. Nevertheless, the pervasive integration of technological assistance raises concerns about potential overreliance and the attenuation of internal cognitive faculties. For example, while calculators enhance computational accuracy, a persistent reliance on them may undermine mental arithmetic skills. Similarly, reliance on digital reminders may diminish the capacity to maintain active intentions, thereby affecting prospective memory—the ability to remember to perform an intended action at a future time (Einstein & McDaniel, 1990).

Consequently, cognitive offloading should be regarded as a nuanced phenomenon with context-dependent outcomes. Situational variables, usage patterns, and the equilibrium between internal cognitive processes and external aids mediate its effects. When students offload routine, time-consuming yet straightforward tasks, they can preserve cognitive resources for more demanding learning activities. The externalization of procedural or repetitive tasks allows learners to allocate increased attention and mental energies to higher-order cognitive functions. Such redistribution facilitates deeper engagement with complex subject matter, fosters creative endeavors, and enhances problem-solving capabilities. Conversely, excessive reliance on AI and automated systems may extend beyond cognitive offloading, creating potential dependencies.

Within the extended cognition theoretical framework, cognition is conceived as a distributed system encompassing the brain, the body, and environmental artifacts. This perspective challenges traditional views that confine cognition exclusively to neural processes and posits that tools and technological systems can serve as integral components of cognitive architecture. Empirical inquiry remains essential for delineating the conditions under which the externalization of cognitive tasks supports learning and development, versus when it hampers the cultivation of internal abilities. Ultimately, cognitive offloading exemplifies a sophisticated strategy that facilitates human thinking but warrants careful evaluation of its long-term cognitive consequences.

From Internal Memory to Transactive Memory: The "Google Effect."

Clark & Chalmers' (1998) extended mind thesis asserts that when individuals establish reliable and reciprocal interactions with external systems, these systems effectively become constituents of the cognitive system itself. Within this paradigm, AI functions as an extension of cognition rather than a mere external tool. However, Sparrow, Liu, and Wegner (2011) demonstrate that awareness of information stored externally influences memory retention, whereby individuals tend to remember the location of externalized information more readily than the information itself. This phenomenon has been popularly termed 'digital amnesia' in mainstream discourse, suggesting that frequent externalization of information may reduce the effort required for internal encoding and retrieval. In addition, Sparrow, Liu, and Wegner (2011) investigate how the proliferation of internet-based search engines, notably Google Search, has transformed human memory functioning. They argue that the constant accessibility of online information fosters a form of transactive memory (Wegner, 1987) – a concept originally developed to describe how groups distribute cognitive labor across members – extending it to the relationship between individuals and digital systems, in which knowledge resides outside the individual yet remains readily accessible. Consequently, individuals increasingly rely on remembering how or where to locate information rather than the information itself. To empirically examine this hypothesis, Sparrow, Liu, & Wegner (2011) conduct four experimental studies.

The initial experiment examined whether exposure to challenging questions activates cognitive associations with computers as potential sources of information. Participants responded to a series of trivia questions and subsequently completed a Stroop task involving both computer-related and neutral words. Results indicate that when participants encounter questions they cannot answer, their reaction times suggest heightened attentional sensitivity toward computer-related terms. This pattern implies that knowledge gaps potentially trigger automatic associations with online search strategies for information retrieval.

The second experiment investigates whether expectations regarding future access to information influence memory encoding processes. Participants enter trivia statements into a computer, with some being informed that the information will be saved and others led to believe it will be erased. Those who anticipate deletion demonstrate superior recall, whereas participants expecting persistent storage exhibit diminished recall. These findings suggest that anticipations of external storage reduce reliance on internal memory encoding.

The third experiment extends this inquiry by assessing recognition performance for both the informational content and its storage location. Participants are instructed that trivia statements will be either erased, stored in general, or saved in specific folders. The data reveal that participants retain statements most effectively when they believe these will be erased. Conversely, when expecting to store information, participants are more likely to recall its location than its content. This pattern indicates a shift toward encoding spatial retrieval cues over informational details.

The fourth experiment focuses on recall accuracy for both the trivia statements and their designated storage folders. Notably, participants demonstrate superior recall of folder locations compared to the statements themselves. This finding suggests that memory processes may prioritize spatial information associated with retrieval cues over the retention of the content itself.

Collectively, these results support the view that the Internet functions as a large-scale transactive memory system, analogous to interpersonal reliance on collective expertise. In social contexts, individuals often remember “who knows what”; similarly, digital environments encourage the memory of “what the computer knows” and its location. The authors interpret this phenomenon as an adaptive cognitive strategy rather than mere convenience.

Memory processes appear to shift from internal storage towards efficient external access, emphasizing the ability to locate information rather than internalize it. While this transition offers advantages in information retrieval, it raises concerns about technological dependence and potential cognitive vulnerabilities associated with the loss of access. The absence of Internet connectivity may constitute a significant cognitive disruption, underscoring the deep integration of digital tools within contemporary cognition.

Overall, these findings suggest that the Internet is not only transforming methods of information retrieval but also fundamentally reconfiguring memory architecture itself, indicative of a co-evolution between human cognition and digital technology. AI does not inherently diminish cognitive capacity; rather, it reorganizes cognitive load. When AI supports higher-order cognitive functions such as analysis, synthesis, and evaluation, it can serve to enhance cognitive capabilities. However, if AI entirely replaces generative cognitive processes, it may lead to decreased cognitive engagement. The ultimate effect depends on the balance between internally maintained processes and those delegated to external systems. Complete delegation of traditional internal cognitive functions to AI could result in a decline in mental faculties. Moreover, reliance on AI might engender maladaptive cognitive habits; in environments lacking such technologies, individuals' diminished internal capacities may become evident. The convenience afforded by AI could thus introduce a form of technological vulnerability, rendering cognitive performance contingent on the continued availability of external systems.

Proposition 2: Dependency on AI tools may reduce effortful processing under certain conditions.

Cognitive Load Theory (CLT) posits that working memory has limited capacity and that effective learning occurs when extraneous cognitive load is minimized and germane load is optimized (Sweller, 2011). AI tools have the potential to mitigate unnecessary processing demands by restructuring information, thereby reallocating cognitive resources toward schema development. In this framework, AI redistributes cognitive effort rather than simply simplifying tasks.

Cognitive Load Theory: Managing Intrinsic, Extraneous, and Germane Load

In his 1988 publication, Sweller examines how the constraints of working memory influence learning, particularly during problem-solving processes. He contends that the limited capacity of working memory results in reduced learning efficacy when overloaded. Conventional problem-solving strategies often compel learners to allocate substantial cognitive resources to finding solutions rather than understanding the problem's fundamental structures. A critical point is that learners tend to focus on goal attainment, such as solving a problem in discrete steps, which does not necessarily promote the development of useful mental schemas. Instead, considerable effort is directed toward managing procedural steps, which may hinder the transferability of acquired knowledge to novel contexts. Sweller (1988) contrasts traditional problem-solving approaches with more guided instructional methods, such as studying worked examples. For example, a novice may analyze a worked example comprising a problem and its corresponding solution. Such examination reduces cognitive confusion and supports schema formation. Since worked examples serve as sequential demonstrations of problem-solving techniques explicitly designed to reduce cognitive load and facilitate schema acquisition, Sweller (1988) suggests that they enable learners to focus on understanding problem structures rather than on independently deciphering each step. Attempting to solve problems unaided often results in cognitive overload that impairs learning. Furthermore, the utilization of worked examples, particularly for novices, streamlines comprehension and retention of material. The overarching principle emphasizes the importance of instructional design that respects cognitive limitations; effective learning can be supported by reducing extraneous mental effort and guiding attention toward essential information.

Within the framework of CLT, cognitive load is typically categorized into three distinct types: intrinsic, extraneous, and germane load (Sweller, 2011). These distinctions elucidate not only the extent of mental effort involved in learning but also its efficacy. Intrinsic load refers to the inherent complexity of the learned material itself, which depends on the number of elements that must be processed simultaneously and their interrelations. For instance, acquiring a simple definition imposes relatively low intrinsic load, whereas solving a complex, multi-step problem involves substantially higher intrinsic demands. Although intrinsic load cannot be directly altered by instructional design, it can be modulated over time as learners develop expertise and construct richer schemas — enabling them to process increasingly complex material with proportionally less cognitive effort. It can also be managed in the short term through strategies such as organizing information, sequencing content from simple to complex, or decomposing tasks into manageable segments. Conversely, extraneous load arises from ineffective instructional presentation—such as cluttered visuals, superfluous details, or split attention across multiple sources—and does not contribute to learning. Instead, it consumes cognitive resources that could be better used to process core content. Consequently, reducing extraneous load is a principal aim in instructional design. Germane load refers to the cognitive effort that directly contributes to learning, notably in the construction and refinement of schemas. It encompasses processes such as making connections, organizing information, and actively engaging with the material to discern underlying structures. Unlike extraneous load, germane load is beneficial, as it reflects meaningful cognitive engagement. In sum, optimal learning outcomes are achieved when extraneous load is minimized, intrinsic load is managed, and germane load is fostered. The integration of AI tools can facilitate this process by reducing extraneous load and supporting the gradual modulation of intrinsic load through schema development and deeper comprehension.

The Paradox of "Desirable Difficulties."

However, the framework proposed by Bjork & Bjork (2011) concerning Desirable Difficulties complicates this traditional view. Empirical research indicates that learning processes involving effortful retrieval, distributed practice, and generative activities tend to yield more durable retention. Although such difficulties may impede immediate performance, they contribute significantly to long-term memory consolidation. In this context, conditions that appear less efficient or more strenuous during learning may, counterintuitively, be more advantageous over time. Conversely, if AI provides instantaneous solutions that circumvent these productive struggles, the depth of cognitive encoding may be compromised. Learners may arrive at correct responses more rapidly but with a diminished understanding of underlying structures, thereby hindering transfer to novel contexts.

Among the mechanisms underpinning desirable difficulties, one of the most empirically supported is "Effortful Retrieval." Within the theoretical framework of desirable difficulties, effortful retrieval is particularly salient because it requires learners to reconstruct knowledge rather than passively review it. This process enhances memory traces and facilitates long-term retention. Research on cognitive offloading suggests that when information is easily accessible through external resources, learners tend to rely less on internal memory processes, reducing the need for extensive internal encoding (Risko & Gilbert, 2016). When learners are aware that AI systems can instantly retrieve or generate answers, there may be a concomitant reduction in cognitive effort devoted to deep processing. Instead of engaging in retrieval or elaborative activities, learners might rely excessively on external systems as a substitute for memory. Over time, such dependence could impede memory consolidation and the development of analytical skills. Importantly, this does not imply that the use of AI is inherently detrimental; rather, its effects depend on how it is integrated into learning processes. When AI is employed in a manner that replaces rather than supports effortful retrieval, it may inadvertently undermine the conditions necessary for durable learning.

When Assistance Becomes a Substitute: The Risk to Encoding and Retention

Consequently, dependency effects are context-dependent. When AI substitutes for cognitive effort, it may impair the encoding process by diminishing opportunities for retrieval, elaboration, and self-explanation. In such cases, learners may arrive at correct responses without engaging in the mental activities that strengthen memory traces and facilitate transfer. Conversely, when AI is intentionally integrated as a scaffolding tool—encouraging questioning, reflection, and iterative refinement—it can foster generative engagement and promote higher-order thinking. For example, instead of providing direct answers, AI can prompt learners to justify their reasoning, compare alternatives, or articulate concepts in their own words. These interactions are more aligned with principles of active learning and meaningful cognitive processing.

The determining factor for these outcomes is primarily pedagogical design and learner practice, rather than the technology itself. The same AI tool can either attenuate productive struggle or enhance it, depending on how tasks are constructed and how learners are guided in its use. Accordingly, AI does not possess an intrinsic capacity to either weaken or fortify learning processes; rather, its influence depends on the interplay among instructional goals, task design, and learner engagement strategies. Careful pedagogical integration is essential to ensure that cognitive resources are directed toward comprehension, schema development, and long-term retention, rather than merely task completion.

Table 3. When AI helps vs when AI harms learning

Dimension	**AI as a Cognitive Scaffold**	**AI as a Cognitive Substitute**
Role of AI	Guides thinking	Replaces thinking
Learner activity	Active engagement	Passive reception
Retrieval	Retrieval prompts	Direct answers
Elaboration	Encouraged	Reduced
Self-explanation	Supported	Minimized
Cognitive effort	Preserved	Reduced
Encoding	Deep processing	Surface processing
Long-term retention	Strengthened	Weakened
Transfer	Facilitated	Limited
Critical thinking	Enhanced	Diminished
Learning outcome	**Durable learning**	**Superficial learning**

Source: Authors' own work

This phenomenon is further compounded by what has been characterized as the fluency illusion—a metacognitive error in which individuals conflate processing ease with genuine understanding (Bjork, Dunlosky, & Kornell, 2013). When AI-generated content is linguistically polished and structurally coherent, it can engender perceptions of correctness and comprehensiveness, thereby diminishing motivation to critically interrogate or extend the material. Merely having access to accurate information does not guarantee its internalization; this aligns with research suggesting that digital externalization reduces learners' reliance on internal memory processes (Skulmowski, 2023). When applied to AI-generated content, the output's fluency may engender an illusory sense of learning that does not correspond to actual cognitive engagement.

The "Fluency Illusion" and the Shift from System 2 to System 1 Thinking

In this context, Kahneman's (2011) seminal distinction between System 1 and System 2 cognition offers a particularly relevant theoretical framework for analyzing how AI may undermine critical thinking abilities. System 1 functions automatically and rapidly, relying on heuristics, pattern recognition, and associative inference. Conversely, System 2 is characterized by deliberate, effortful processing that necessitates sustained attention and logical reasoning. Higher-order cognitive skills—such as argument analysis, hypothesis testing, evidence evaluation, and counterfactual reasoning—are predominantly the domain of System 2. A significant challenge is that engaging System 2 is cognitively demanding and requires effort and motivation. It can be overridden by the more automatic processes of System 1, particularly in environments where responses are fluent and readily available.

AI systems generate outputs that are highly fluent and plausible, which often elicits a reliance on System 1 processing. When individuals encounter such outputs, there is a natural tendency to accept them intuitively, as they appear coherent, well-structured, and authoritative, thereby diminishing the perceived need for deliberate critical scrutiny. This phenomenon is especially pronounced among learners with limited domain knowledge, who are less equipped to detect subtle inaccuracies or omissions within AI-generated content. Consequently, there is a systematic shift away from reflective evaluation toward intuitive acceptance—an inversion of the critical thinking process.

Automation Bias, Evaluative Reasoning, and Pedagogical Safeguards

The well-established phenomenon of automation bias compounds this risk—the propensity to over-rely on automated systems while discounting contradictory information from non-automated sources (Parasuraman & Riley, 1997). Cleverly (2025) further develops this analysis by suggesting that dependence on automation not only amplifies pre-existing cognitive biases but also engenders new patterns of deference that, over time, reinforce one another. As users repeatedly experience positive outcomes from AI-assisted tasks, their dispositional trust in AI outputs intensifies, potentially at the expense of confidence in their own independent judgment. Cleverly's framework conceptualizes this as a feedback loop: initial reliance fosters success, which then bolsters reliance, leading to diminished engagement in critical evaluation—an essential faculty for identifying inaccuracies or gaps in AI outputs. However, Wingerter, Straub, & Schweitzer (2025) demonstrate that automation bias in generative AI contexts is not immutable; cognitive reflection prompts embedded within task design—requiring users to pause, evaluate, and justify their acceptance of AI-generated content—have been shown to significantly mitigate over-reliance without compromising the efficiency advantages conferred by AI assistance.

Survey evidence from professional contexts substantiates this concern. Lee et al. (2025b) conducted a comprehensive survey of knowledge workers who regularly use generative AI, revealing that a substantial proportion report reduced cognitive effort and changes in confidence when interacting with AI. Notably, participants report diminished motivation to engage in the effortful verification of AI-generated claims, accompanied by an increased tendency to accept AI outputs as authoritative. This pattern aligns with Kahneman's System 1/System 2 framework: the availability of fluent AI outputs appears to reduce the perceived necessity for deliberate evaluative reasoning, even among professionals with substantial domain expertise.

Further corroboration arises from experimental studies within educational settings. Bastani et al. (2025) conduct a rigorously designed investigation involving high school students learning mathematics under conditions of unrestricted, restricted, and no access to generative AI. Their findings, published in the Proceedings of the National Academy of Sciences, demonstrate that students with unrestricted access to generative AI, in the absence of pedagogical safeguards, experience significantly impaired learning outcomes. While AI-assisted students outperform their peers on assessments conducted with AI support, they perform worse on assessments without such support—indicating that AI has substituted for genuine learning rather than facilitating it. This evidence, obtained in a controlled experimental context, provides robust support for the notion that unguided use of AI can hinder learning. The key moderating factor identified is the presence or absence of pedagogical structure: students embedded within a structured learning framework do not exhibit the same impairments, underscoring that the conditions under which AI is employed, rather than AI itself, determine learning outcomes.

Consistent with this, Özer, Tanberkan, & Perc et al. (2025) examine the relationship between AI use and critical thinking in higher education, concluding that unrestricted AI use without concurrent development of critical literacy constitutes a systemic threat to the cultivation of analytical reasoning skills. Their analysis emphasizes that this concern transcends individual decision-making and represents a systemic issue in which educational institutions that incorporate AI tools without fostering students' capacity for critical evaluation risk producing graduates whose apparent competence—supported by AI assistance—conceals deficiencies in autonomous analytical reasoning.

Collectively, this body of evidence—spanning neuroimaging, survey research, and controlled experiments—converges on a consistent conclusion: unguided and unstructured AI use tends to diminish engagement in critical thinking by suppressing metacognitive monitoring processes essential for genuine comprehension and the development of analytical skills. The mechanisms underlying this include automation bias, the displacement of System 2 deliberative processing by System 1 heuristics, reduced motivation to engage in effortful encoding, and cognitive offloading onto AI outputs. Gerlich (2025a) further substantiates these findings in a study of 666 participants, confirming a significant negative correlation between AI tool use and critical thinking, mediated by cognitive offloading, with younger participants exhibiting particularly high reliance on AI and concomitant reductions in critical-thinking capacity.

Additional concerns pertain to the development of inflated self-assessments of understanding. Kruger & Dunning (1999) demonstrate that individuals with limited competence tend to overestimate their abilities due to a lack of meta-cognitive awareness. AI tools might exacerbate this dynamic by consistently generating high-quality outputs, thereby decoupling the signal of performance quality from actual competence levels, and potentially fostering unwarranted self-confidence in learners.

This substantial evidence is exemplified by Fernandes et al. (2026), who investigate the interplay among AI utilization, task performance, and metacognitive accuracy. Their findings reveal a notable dissociation: participants using AI assistance show significant improvements in task performance compared to unaided controls; however, their metacognitive accuracy—the capacity to assess their understanding accurately—does not improve correspondingly and, under certain conditions, deteriorates markedly. The authors characterize this phenomenon as a disconnect between performance and metacognition, in which AI enhances output quality but does not foster self-awareness. This dissociation bears critical implications for pedagogical practices, as accurate metacognition underpins learners' ability to identify knowledge gaps, allocate cognitive resources efficiently, and seek appropriate remediation. An impairment in metacognitive accuracy due to reliance on AI results not only in inflated performance metrics but also in a diminished capacity for self-regulation and correction. These findings align with the analysis by Tian & Zhang (2025), who examined AI dependence among university students. Their research indicates that increased reliance on AI correlates with reduced critical-thinking abilities and a paradoxical role for information literacy: while it partially mitigates the negative impact of AI dependence on critical thinking, it concurrently exacerbates cognitive fatigue during extensive AI use. Collectively, these studies delineate a complex psychological and pedagogical landscape in which the risks associated with AI are empirically substantiated yet inherently contingent on how AI is integrated into learning processes. Central to this dynamic is whether AI serves as a facilitator or a substitute for metacognitive monitoring, a core component of effective learning. Crucially, the premise underlying this discourse is not that AI use invariably hampers critical thinking; rather, it hinges on whether AI serves as a scaffold for metacognitive processes. When students are encouraged to critically evaluate AI-generated content—viewing it as a preliminary draft for interrogation, a stance to challenge, or evidence to scrutinize—such pedagogical approaches can invigorate analytical engagement rather than suppress it. Empirical studies by Wingerter, Straub, and Schweitzer (2025) demonstrate that even modest cognitive prompts can significantly mitigate automation bias, suggesting that low-cost pedagogical interventions can sustain critical engagement in AI-assisted learning environments. Moreover, Gerlich (2025b) provides experimental evidence that structured prompting—requiring justification of reasoning, identification of assumptions, and contemplation of alternative perspectives—substantially reduces cognitive offloading and enhances both critical reasoning and reflective engagement compared to unguided AI interactions. The overarching theoretical implication is that the pedagogical framing of AI utilization, rather than the technology itself, determines whether critical thinking is preserved or diminished. Therefore, educators and instructional designers bear primary responsibility for developing instructional contexts that encourage evaluative, extension-based, and critically engaged interactions with AI-generated content, rather than passive consumption and reproduction.

Proposition 4: AI can enhance higher-order cognitive skills when integrated as a cognitive scaffold

To elucidate the conditions under which AI can genuinely augment higher-order cognitive processes rather than merely simulate them, it is imperative to engage with the foundational theoretical frameworks that underpin the concept of scaffolding.

Vygotsky's Zone of Proximal Development (ZPD) and the Concept of Scaffolding

Vygotsky's (1978) construct of the ZPD is predicated on a core insight into cognitive development: learners should not be construed as possessing fixed levels of competence but rather as operating within dynamic zones of potential. The ZPD is delineated as the distance between what a learner can achieve independently and what can be accomplished through appropriate guidance. Within this zone—neither trivially easy nor overwhelmingly difficult—authentic cognitive growth transpires. The pedagogical operationalization of ZPD principles is developed by Wood, Bruner, & Ross (1976), who introduce the term scaffolding to describe the process by which a more knowledgeable other provides calibrated support, thereby enabling the learner to undertake tasks beyond their unaided capacity. Importantly, scaffolding is inherently temporary, contingent on the learner's internalization of skills, and intended to be gradually withdrawn as mastery ensues. The ultimate pedagogical objective extends beyond mere task completion to the transfer of regulatory control from the scaffolding agent to the learner.

From Answer-Giver to Socratic Partner: Designing for Inquiry

Recent empirical research offers converging evidence that AI, when designed and implemented in accordance with scaffolding principles, can significantly enhance higher-order cognitive skills. Lee et al. (2025a) investigate the effects of Socratic Mind, a generative AI-powered formative assessment tool that employs Socratic questioning techniques in a large online undergraduate computing course. Utilizing a mixed-methods, quasi-experimental design, the study collects data from system logs, surveys, student reflections, and course performance records. The findings demonstrate that students who engage with the tool exhibit substantial improvements in quiz performance, particularly among lower-achieving students. Qualitative data indicate that students perceive development in higher-order thinking skills such as problem-solving, critical reasoning, and self-reflection. These results suggest that generative AI, when integrated within a scaffolding framework that emphasizes inquiry over direct answers, functions effectively as a cognitive partner.

Empirical Evidence: Enhancing Critical Thinking in Writing and Problem-Solving

Hong, Vate-U-Lan, & Viriyavejakul (2025) examine the impact of AI-mediated scaffolding on the development of critical thinking in English as a Foreign Language (EFL) writing contexts characterized by the dual challenge of enhancing both linguistic and analytical competencies. Their study reveals that AI scaffolding, structured to provide formative feedback on argumentative coherence and logical structure rather than mere surface corrections, produces significant improvements in students' critical thinking, as measured by their writing tasks. Importantly, improvements persist in subsequent unaided writing assessments, indicating genuine internalization of critical thinking skills rather than surface-level performance gains contingent on AI assistance.

Valentini & Montresor (2025) contribute a theoretically grounded empirical protocol—the Dialogic AI Scaffolding framework—designed to foster critical thinking and metacognition via structured AI dialogue. Their proof-of-concept position AI as a dialogic interlocutor whose primary function is to generate cognitive challenge, rather than provide information. The protocol involves a series of interactions in which learners articulate their understanding, respond to AI-generated counterarguments, revise their positions in light of evidence, and reflect on the quality of their reasoning. Results indicate that participation in this dialogic process engenders significant improvements in metacognitive monitoring and evaluative reasoning. Notably, this work demonstrates that dialogic AI scaffolding can be implemented without sophisticated adaptive systems, thus broadening its applicability across diverse educational settings.

Additional support comes from Shanto, Ahmed, & Jony et al. (2024), who propose and evaluate a framework to achieve outcome-based learning through generative AI. Their framework explicitly aligns AI-mediated tasks with higher levels of Bloom's Taxonomy (Anderson & Krathwohl, 2001)—necessitating analysis, evaluation, and creation rather than recall or summarization. Evaluation results indicate that the systematic use of AI toward these higher-order cognitive objectives leads to enhanced task performance and increased student engagement with the subject matter's analytical and creative dimensions. Collectively, these empirical findings underscore a consistent pattern: AI scaffolding that sustains and challenges higher-order cognitive engagement fosters genuine learning, whereas AI assistance that substitutes for such engagement does not. This perspective is further supported by Gonsalves (2024), who argues that generative AI necessitates a reconceptualization of Bloom's Taxonomy, as AI increasingly handles lower-order cognitive tasks, shifting the pedagogical focus toward evaluation, synthesis, and creation.

Self-Regulated Learning and AI: Zimmerman's Framework

A complementary theoretical lens for evaluating AI's potential as a scaffolding tool is Zimmerman's (2002) model of self-regulated learning (SRL). Zimmerman conceptualizes SRL as a cyclical, tripartite process encompassing three iterative phases: forethought, performance, and self-reflection. During the forethought phase, learners establish goals, activate prior knowledge, and select appropriate cognitive strategies. In the performance phase, they monitor their progress, sustain motivation, and regulate attention. Finally, in the self-reflection phase, learners evaluate outcomes against their goals, attribute successes or failures to specific causes, and adjust their strategies accordingly. Critically, this cycle is not merely a description of effective learning behavior; it constitutes the mechanism through which learners develop metacognitive competence and academic autonomy over time. Complementary theoretical support is provided by Pintrich (2004), whose motivational framework emphasizes that self-regulated learners not only monitor their cognition but also actively manage their motivational beliefs — a dimension particularly relevant when AI risks eroding intrinsic engagement.

The implications for AI integration are significant. When AI systems assume responsibility for any component of this cycle — generating goals, selecting strategies, providing evaluative feedback, or interpreting outcomes — learners are deprived of the opportunity to practice and internalize that phase of self-regulation. Repeated over time, such displacement does not merely reduce the learner's immediate cognitive effort; it structurally undermines the development of self-regulatory capacity itself. A learner who consistently relies on AI to organize information, for instance, may produce well-structured outputs while simultaneously failing to develop the internal organizational schemas that would enable independent performance in AI-absent contexts. The output quality in such cases is decoupled from the underlying regulatory competence — a pattern consistent with the metacognitive dissociation documented by Fernandes et al. (2026) and the performance-without-learning findings of Bastani et al. (2025), as discussed in Proposition 3.

However, Zimmerman's framework also illuminates the conditions under which AI can function as a genuine scaffold for SRL rather than a substitute for it. When AI is designed to prompt goal articulation rather than define goals for the learner, to offer feedback that requires interpretation and evaluation rather than simply endorsing or correcting outputs, and to encourage post-task reflection rather than simply delivering results, it operationalizes precisely the kind of calibrated support that scaffolding theory prescribes. In this configuration, AI serves as what Vygotsky's collaborators termed the more knowledgeable other — providing just enough structure to extend the learner's reach while preserving the cognitive effort necessary for internalization.

Empirical support for this position is provided by Yan (2025), whose doctoral investigation examines the integration of AI-assisted adaptive practice within online STEM education environments. Yan's findings indicate that when AI interactions are structured to support self-monitoring and iterative refinement — rather than providing direct solutions — students demonstrate meaningful gains in SRL competencies, including enhanced goal-setting behavior, more accurate self-assessment, and greater strategic flexibility across novel problem types. Crucially, these gains are not contingent on the sophistication of the AI system itself, but on the degree to which instructional design preserves learner agency within the regulatory cycle. This finding aligns with the broader pattern emerging across Proposition 4: it is the pedagogical architecture surrounding AI, rather than the technology per se, that determines whether AI use cultivates or erodes the self-regulatory foundations of deep and durable learning.

Proposition 5: The long-term neurological impact of AI use depends on patterns of cognitive engagement rather than mere exposure

The preceding propositions address relatively immediate cognitive and metacognitive processes. This proposition shifts the focus to a longer temporal horizon: whether sustained patterns of AI engagement, repeated across months and years, may produce cumulative structural changes in the neural architecture underlying memory, reasoning, and higher-order thinking. The central claim is that the decisive factor is not AI exposure per se, but the habitual cognitive behaviors it either cultivates or displaces over time.

Neuroplasticity and Use-Dependent Plasticity: "Use It or Lose It."

Neuroplasticity — the brain's capacity to modify its structure and function in response to experience — is most compellingly illustrated not through abstract principle but through empirical demonstration. Maguire et al.'s (2000) seminal study on London taxi drivers shows that prolonged engagement in cognitively demanding navigational tasks induces measurable structural changes in hippocampal regions associated with spatial memory, and that these alterations positively correlate with the duration of navigational experience. This finding exemplifies what neuroscientists term use-dependent plasticity: neural circuits subjected to frequent and intensive activation tend to strengthen and expand, whereas those engaged infrequently tend to weaken and contract. The cognitive activities routinely performed over extended periods do not merely reflect underlying neural organization — they actively shape it.

The Memory Paradox: AI, Knowledge Retention, and Neural Risk

The implications of using AI are direct and consequential. If sustained engagement with cognitively demanding tasks results in structural brain changes, then prolonged disengagement through reliance on AI systems may yield the inverse effect. Oakley et al. (2025) explicitly examine this concern through what they term the memory paradox: in an age when AI can provide information on demand, the subjective necessity of retaining knowledge in memory diminishes. Nonetheless, the neurological and cognitive value of stored knowledge either remains constant or potentially increases. Their analysis, grounded in established cognitive neuroscience, posits that internally held knowledge facilitates not merely information recall; it underpins the semantic networks through which new information is comprehended, evaluated, and integrated with prior understanding. Consequently, individuals who rely on AI for knowledge that would otherwise be retained in memory risk degrading the neural substrates that underpin understanding and reasoning. Thus, Oakley et al. (2025) establish a theoretical framework suggesting that the neurological consequences of

AI use may extend beyond memory-retrieval circuits to influence the broader neural networks that support higher-order cognition.

Carr (2010) advances an influential argument that habitual digital media use fosters cognitive patterns characterized by rapid information scanning, frequent task-switching, and shallow processing. Over time, these patterns may alter neural architectures related to attention and memory, rendering sustained, deep processing increasingly challenging. While Carr's assertion is primarily supported by indirect evidence, subsequent neuroimaging studies have provided more direct corroboration. For instance, Small et al. (2009) employ functional magnetic resonance imaging (fMRI) to demonstrate that experienced internet users exhibit distinct neural activation patterns during information-seeking tasks compared to novices, indicating that digital exposure modulates the brain's engagement with information.

Kosmyna et al. (2025) extend this investigation to generative AI, providing direct neurophysiological evidence of differential cognitive engagement in AI-assisted versus unassisted cognitive tasks. Their study involving participants using ChatGPT for essay composition reveals a phenomenon termed "cognitive debt": as cognitive effort is delegated to AI, neural circuits involved in elaborative processing—such as argument construction, idea integration, and evidence evaluation—show a progressive decline in engagement. The notion of cognitive debt is of particular theoretical significance, capturing the temporal accumulation of neurological risk: unlike immediate cognitive offloading, which responds to specific task demands, cognitive debt accrues cumulatively over repeated episodes of AI-assisted work, potentially diminishing the activation and capacity of neural circuits essential for deep cognitive processing. The debt metaphor aptly conveys that the gradual depletion of cognitive capital counterbalances the convenience of habitual AI delegation.

Research on digital cognitive externalization suggests that anticipating continued access to externally stored information can reduce learners' reliance on internal encoding processes (Skulmowski, 2023). This finding is particularly pertinent in the context of AI's availability, as widespread reliance on it may foster the expectation that information and reasoning can be consistently outsourced, thereby systematically reducing the incentive to invest the effortful internal processing required to develop durable cognitive structures. The neurological implications extend beyond immediate cognitive offloading, with potential for cumulative effects over prolonged periods of habitual AI utilization. Such effects may be subtle within individual interactions but accumulate to produce significant long-term consequences.

The Habit Loop: How AI Reliance Can Become an Automatic Response

Furthermore, the impact of AI use on neural architecture must be understood in terms of both immediate effects and habit formation. Habit formation involves the automation of behavioral sequences through repeated activation, rendering them resistant to voluntary change—a process characterized by the habit loop: a cue triggers a routine that results in a reward (Duhigg, 2012; Wood & Rünger, 2016). In the context of AI, the cue may be encountering a cognitively demanding task; the routine involves delegating it to an AI system; and the reward is obtaining a rapid, plausible answer, thereby facilitating task completion without sustained mental effort. Repetition across diverse learning situations can lead to the automation of this loop, in which encountering cognitive difficulties instinctively triggers reliance on AI rather than on internal problem-solving.

This habituation poses particular concern within educational environments, where cognitive challenge is integral to learning. Bjork & Bjork (2011) highlight that desirable difficulties—short-term obstacles to learning—are crucial for fostering long-term retention and transfer. Habitually circumventing these difficulties via AI may undermine this mechanism, transforming educational settings into environments optimized for convenience and speed at the expense of depth and durability of learning. As Cleverly (2025) posits, dependence on automation can create reinforcing feedback loops; immediate gains, such as efficiency and superior grades facilitated by AI, can perpetuate behaviors that may impair long-term cognitive development. Thus, institutional strategies must aim to incentivize effortful engagement rather than facilitate effortless delegation.

Proposition 5 argues that the neurocognitive consequences of AI use are contingent on the nature of the cognitive patterns it promotes. Even among learners with similar AI engagement frequencies, divergent neural profiles may emerge if their interaction patterns differ systematically. For instance, habitual reliance on AI for retrieval, reasoning, and evaluation may reduce activation of the neural circuits that underpin these functions, a hypothesis supported by Kosmyna et al. (2025) and the broader neuroplasticity literature. These circuits—particularly within the hippocampal and prefrontal regions—are critical for deep encoding, working memory, and analytical reasoning; chronic underutilization may induce use-dependent structural and functional decline.

Divergent Neurocognitive Trajectories: Scaffolding vs. Substitution

Conversely, learners who leverage AI to engage in activities that stimulate elaboration, critical analysis, and reflective engagement may maintain or enhance the integrity of higher-order cognitive circuits. Such activities—including generative processing, retrieval practice, and analytic evaluation—activate distributed neural systems associated with deep encoding and flexible reasoning (Bjork & Bjork, 2011; Sweller, 2011). The memory paradox outlined by Oakley et al. (2025) is particularly relevant: reductions in the breadth and depth of internalized knowledge due to AI use diminish the semantic richness of neural networks, impairing not only memory retrieval but also higher-order reasoning predicated on interconnected knowledge structures.

These divergent neurocognitive trajectories have significant pedagogical implications. They affirm that the neurological impact of AI integration in educational contexts is material and potentially consequential. Importantly, these effects are not predetermined by the mere presence of AI but are mediated by instructional design choices—particularly how AI tools are employed to delineate the locus of cognitive effort—and by individual learner habits. The critical determinant is not AI exposure per se, but the cognitive behaviors it cultivates and sustains. Consequently, responsibility resides with educators, institutions, and learners to ensure that AI integration complements and supports the cognitive development that education aims to foster.

SOLUTIONS AND RECOMMENDATIONS

The findings of this chapter underscore that the technology itself does not determine the cognitive and neurological consequences of AI use in education, but rather the patterns of human–AI interaction. Accordingly, the primary focus should shift from restricting AI use to designing pedagogically sound integration strategies.

For educators and curriculum designers, this necessitates structuring AI-supported learning environments that preserve effortful cognitive engagement. AI should be used as a scaffold rather than a substitute, encouraging students to engage in analysis, evaluation, and generative processing rather than passive consumption. Instructional designs that incorporate metacognitive prompts, reflective questioning, and structured interaction with AI outputs can help mitigate automation bias and sustain critical thinking.

For policymakers, the findings suggest the need for nuanced and context-sensitive guidelines rather than binary restrictions on AI use. Policies should promote responsible, pedagogically aligned AI integration, ensuring that technological adoption supports, rather than displaces, learning processes.

The variability in student engagement with AI further highlights the importance of AI literacy. As demonstrated by the typologies identified by Gerling, Teubner, and Braesemann (2026)—including AI Enthusiasts, Naive Pragmatists, Cautious Adopters, and Reserved Explorers—students differ significantly in their motivations and levels of critical engagement. Therefore, educational systems should explicitly cultivate AI literacy skills that foster reflective, critical, and responsible use of AI tools.

At the individual level, students must be positioned as active agents in the learning process. Learners who engage critically with AI outputs, use them as inputs for deeper reasoning, and maintain effortful cognitive practices are more likely to benefit from AI integration. In contrast, habitual cognitive offloading without reflective engagement may lead to diminished learning outcomes and long-term cognitive costs.

FUTURE RESEARCH DIRECTIONS

Despite the growing body of literature, the empirical foundation for the cognitive and neurological implications of AI in education remains in its early stages. Much of the existing research relies on self-report measures or short-term observations, limiting the ability to conclude long-term cognitive effects.

Future research should prioritize longitudinal designs that track learners over extended periods to examine how sustained patterns of AI use influence cognitive development, memory consolidation, and neural engagement. Such studies would be particularly valuable in testing the long-term implications suggested by concepts such as cognitive offloading, cognitive debt, and the memory paradox.

In addition, experimental research is needed to manipulate the design features of AI-supported learning environments systematically. Investigations that compare scaffolded versus substitutive AI use, or that integrate metacognitive prompts and cognitive nudges, can provide clearer evidence regarding the conditions under which AI enhances or undermines critical thinking and learning outcomes.

Finally, future studies should adopt an interactionist perspective that considers the interplay between individual differences, instructional design, and broader institutional and cultural contexts. Understanding how these factors jointly shape AI use will be essential for developing evidence-based frameworks for effective AI integration in education.

CONCLUSION

This chapter has presented a theoretically grounded and empirically informed examination of the psychological and neurological implications of AI use in educational contexts. Across five propositions, it has been argued that AI does not inherently diminish or enhance cognitive functioning; rather, it operates as a mechanism of cognitive redistribution, reallocating cognitive processes between internal mental systems and external technological supports.

The implications of this redistribution are fundamentally contingent upon how AI is used. When AI supports effortful engagement, metacognitive monitoring, and higher-order thinking, it can contribute to cognitive development. Conversely, when it replaces generative processes and reduces the need for active engagement, it may undermine learning and weaken the cognitive mechanisms essential for long-term retention and understanding.

Ultimately, the integration of AI in education presents both a challenge and an opportunity. The central task is not to determine whether AI should be used, but to ensure that it is used in ways that sustain and enhance human cognition. The future of learning in the AI age will therefore depend on the deliberate design of environments that promote active, reflective, and effortful engagement with knowledge.

Abbreviations Used

AI	**:**	**Artificial Intelligence**
CLT	:	Cognitive Load Theory
EFL	:	English as a Foreign Language
fMRI	:	Functional Magnetic Resonance Imaging
LLM	:	Large Language Model
STEM	:	Science, Technology, Engineering, and Mathematics
SRL	:	Self-Regulated Learning
ZPD	:	Zone of Proximal Development

Competing Interests/Authors' Contributions

We declare that we have no competing or other interests that might be perceived as influencing the results and/or discussion reported in this paper. In terms of author contributions, we declare that:

N. S. E.: Theoretical framework development; Literature review; Writing – original draft (Introduction and Propositions 1–2); Writing – review & editing; Supervision; Validation.

G. A.: Conceptual development; Literature review; Writing – original draft (Propositions 3–5 and Conclusion); Writing – review & editing.

Both authors contributed to the interpretation of the literature, discussed the results, and approved the final version of the chapter.

ACKNOWLEDGEMENTS

The authors declare that this research received no specific grant from any funding agency in the public, commercial, or not-for-profit sectors.

In preparing this study, the ChatGPT-4 model from OpenAI and Grammarly are used solely for translation, language editing, and grammar checking. The authors have created all academic content, analysis, interpretation, and conclusions. ChatGPT and/or Grammarly are not used as a primary source for originality or for generating scientific opinions. All scientific responsibilities belong solely to the authors.

REFERENCES

Anderson, L. W., & Krathwohl, D. R. (Eds.). (2001). *A taxonomy for learning, teaching, and assessing: A revision of Bloom's taxonomy of educational objectives.* Longman.

Bastani, H., Bastani, O., Sungu, A., Ge, H., Kabakcı, Ö., & Mariman, R. (2025). Generative AI without guardrails can harm learning: Evidence from high school mathematics. *Proceedings of the National Academy of Sciences of the United States of America, 122*(26), 1–8. DOI: 10.1073/pnas.2422633122

Bjork, R. A., & Bjork, E. L. (2011). Making things hard on yourself, but in a good way: Creating desirable difficulties to enhance learning. In Gernsbacher, M. A., Pew, R. W., Hough, L. M., & Pomerantz, J. R. (Eds.), *Psychology and the real world: Essays illustrating fundamental contributions to society* (pp. 56–64). Worth Publishers.

Bjork, R. A., Dunlosky, J., & Kornell, N. (2013). Self-regulated learning: Beliefs, techniques, and illusions. *Annual Review of Psychology, 64*(1), 417–444. DOI: 10.1146/annurev-psych-113011-143823

Burge, T. (1979). Individualism and the Mental. *Midwest Studies in Philosophy, 4*(1), 73–121. DOI: 10.1111/j.1475-4975.1979.tb00374.x

Carr, N. (2010). *The shallows: What the Internet is doing to our brains.* W. W. Norton & Company.

Cheng, M., Lee, A. Y., Rapuano, K., Niederhoffer, K., Liebscher, A., & Hancock, J. (2025). From tools to thieves: Measuring and understanding public perceptions of AI through crowdsourced metaphors (Working paper). DOI: 10.48550/arXiv.2501.18045

Clark, A., & Chalmers, D. (1998). The extended mind. *Analysis, 58*(1), 7–19. DOI: 10.1093/analys/58.1.7

Cleverly, C. (2025). The amplification and perpetuation of AI-derived biases through automation dependency: A framework for understanding the long-term cognitive and social implications of LLM over-reliance. *Available at SSRN:* 5359658. DOI: 10.54615/2231-7805.75

Duhigg, C. (2012). *The power of habit: Why we do what we do in life and business.* Random House.

Einstein, G. O., & McDaniel, M. A. (1990). Normal aging and prospective memory. *Journal of Experimental Psychology. Learning, Memory, and Cognition, 16*(4), 717–726. DOI: 10.1037/0278-7393.16.4.717

Fernandes, D., Villa, S., Nicholls, S., Haavisto, O., Buschek, D., Schmidt, A., Kosch, T., Shen, C., & Welsch, R. (2026). AI makes you smarter but none the wiser: The disconnect between performance and metacognition. *Computers in Human Behavior, 175*, 108779. DOI: 10.1016/j.chb.2025.108779

Gerlich, M. (2025a). AI tools in society: Impacts on cognitive offloading and the future of critical thinking. *Societies (Basel, Switzerland), 15*(1), 6. Advance online publication. DOI: 10.3390/soc15010006

Gerlich, M. (2025b). From offloading to engagement: An experimental study on structured prompting and critical reasoning with generative AI. *Data, 10*(11), 172. DOI: 10.3390/data10110172

Gerling, C., Teubner, T., & Braesemann, F. (2026). Who uses general-purpose AI? A typology of ChatGPT early adopters. *Electronic Markets, 36*(15), 15. Advance online publication. DOI: 10.1007/s12525-025-00853-0

Gibson, J. J. (1979). *The ecological approach to visual perception.* Houghton Mifflin.

Gonsalves, C. (2024). Generative AI's impact on critical thinking: Revisiting Bloom's taxonomy. *Journal of Marketing Education, 48*(1), 4–19. DOI: 10.1177/02734753241305980

Hong, H., Vate-U-Lan, P., & Viriyavejakul, C. (2025). Generative AI–mediated scaffolds for enhanced critical thinking in EFL writing. *Edelweiss Applied Science and Technology, 9*(6), 43–54. DOI: 10.55214/25768484.v9i6.7751

Jose, J., Cherian, J., Verghis, A., Varghise, S., & Joseph, S. (2025). The cognitive paradox of AI in education: Between enhancement and erosion. *Frontiers in Psychology, 16*, 1550621. DOI: 10.3389/fpsyg.2025.1550621

Kahneman, D. (2011). *Thinking, fast and slow.* Farrar, Straus and Giroux.

Kosmyna, N., Hauptmann, E., Yuan, Y. T., Situ, J., Liao, X. H., Beresnitzky, A. V., & Maes, P. (2025). Your brain on ChatGPT: Accumulation of cognitive debt when using an AI assistant for essay writing task (Working paper). DOI: 10.48550/arXiv.2506.08872

Kruger, J., & Dunning, D. (1999). Unskilled and unaware of it: How difficulties in recognizing one's own incompetence lead to inflated self-assessments. *Journal of Personality and Social Psychology*, *77*(6), 1121–1134. DOI: 10.1037/0022-3514.77.6.1121

Lee, H. P., Sarkar, A., Tankelevitch, L., Drosos, I., Rintel, S., Banks, R., & Wilson, N. (2025b). The impact of generative AI on critical thinking. In *Proceedings of the CHI Conference on Human Factors in Computing Systems*. New York, NY: ACM.

Lee, J., Hung, J. T., Soylu, M. Y., Popescu, D., Cui, C. Z., Grigoryan, G., Joyner, D., & Harmon, S. W. (2025a). Socratic mind: Impact of a novel GenAI-powered assessment tool on student learning and higher-order thinking (Working paper). DOI: 10.48550/arXiv.2509.16262

Lin, H., & Chen, Q. (2024). Artificial intelligence-integrated educational applications and college students' creativity and academic emotions. *BMC Psychology*, *12*, 1–16. DOI: 10.1186/s40359-024-01979-0

Maguire, E. A., Gadian, D. G., Johnsrude, I. S., Good, C. D., Ashburner, J., Frackowiak, R. S., & Frith, C. D. (2000). Navigation-related structural change in the hippocampi of taxi drivers. *Proceedings of the National Academy of Sciences of the United States of America*, *97*(8), 4398–4403. DOI: 10.1073/pnas.070039597

Oakley, B., Johnston, M., Chen, K. Z., Jung, E., & Sejnowski, T. J. (2025). The memory paradox: Why our brains need knowledge in an age of AI (Working paper). DOI: 10.48550/arXiv.2506.11015

Özer, M., Tanberkan, H., & Perc, M. (2025). Artificial intelligence threatens critical thinking in education systems. *Journal of Higher Education and Science*, *15*(2), 157–164. DOI: 10.5961/higheredusci.1747885

Parasuraman, R., & Riley, V. (1997). Humans and Automation: Use, Misuse, Disuse, Abuse. *Human Factors*, *39*(2), 230–253. DOI: 10.1518/001872097778543886

Pintrich, P. R. (2004). A conceptual framework for assessing motivation and self-regulated learning. *Educational Psychology Review*, *16*(4), 385–407. DOI: 10.1007/s10648-004-0006-x

Putnam, H. (1975). The meaning of "meaning". In Gunderson, K. (Ed.), *Language, mind, and knowledge* (pp. 131–193). University of Minnesota Press.

Risko, E. F., & Gilbert, S. J. (2016). Cognitive offloading. *Trends in Cognitive Sciences*, *20*(9), 676–688. DOI: 10.1016/j.tics.2016.07.002

Shanto, S. S., Ahmed, Z., & Jony, A. I. (2024). A proposed framework for achieving higher levels of outcome-based learning. *Educational Technology Quarterly*, *2024*(1), 1–20. DOI: 10.55056/etq.788

Skulmowski, A. (2023). Technology-supported cognitive externalization: Towards a theoretical framework for learning and instruction. *Educational Psychology Review*, *35*(101), 1–21. DOI: 10.1007/s10648-023-09818-1

Small, G. W., Moody, T. D., Siddarth, P., & Bookheimer, S. Y. (2009). Your brain on Google: Patterns of cerebral activation during internet searching. *The American Journal of Geriatric Psychiatry*, *17*(2), 116–126. DOI: 10.1097/JGP.0b013e3181953a02

Sparrow, B., Liu, J., & Wegner, D. M. (2011). Google's effects on memory: Cognitive consequences of having information at our fingertips. *Science*, *333*(6043), 776–778. DOI: 10.1126/science.1207745

Sweller, J. (1988). Cognitive load during problem solving. *Cognitive Science*, *12*(2), 257–285. DOI: 10.1207/s15516709cog1202_4

Sweller, J. (2011). Cognitive load theory. *Psychology of Learning and Motivation*, *55*, 37–76. DOI: 10.1016/B978-0-12-387691-1.00002-8

Tian, J., & Zhang, R. (2025). Learners' AI dependence and critical thinking. *Acta Psychologica*, *260*, 105725. DOI: 10.1016/j.actpsy.2025.105725

Valentini, M., & Montresor, A. (2025). Dialogic AI scaffolding. In *CEUR Workshop Proceedings*.

Vygotsky, L. S. (1978). *Mind in society. Mind in society: the development of higher psychological processes*. Harvard University Press.

Wegner, D. M. (1987). Transactive memory. In Mullen, B., & Goethals, G. R. (Eds.), *Theories of group behavior* (pp. 185–208). Springer. DOI: 10.1007/978-1-4612-4634-3_9

Wingerter, T. L., Straub, T., & Schweitzer, S. (2025). Mitigating automation bias in generative AI through nudges: A cognitive reflection test study. *Procedia Computer Science*, *270*, 2106–2114. DOI: 10.1016/j.procs.2025.09.331

Wood, D., Bruner, J. S., & Ross, G. (1976). The role of tutoring in problem solving. *Journal of Child Psychology and Psychiatry, and Allied Disciplines*, *17*(2), 89–100. DOI: 10.1111/j.1469-7610.1976.tb00381.x

Wood, W., & Rünger, D. (2016). Psychology of habit. *Annual Review of Psychology, 67*(1), 289–314. DOI: 10.1146/annurev-psych-122414-033417

Yan, H. (2025). *Human-AI integrated adaptive practicing to foster self-regulated learning in online STEM education* (Doctoral dissertation, University of Eastern Finland).

Yunus, A., Gay, P. R., & Lee, O. T. (2025). From co-design to metacognitive laziness (Working paper). DOI: 10.48550/arXiv.2512.12306

Zimmerman, B. J. (2002). Becoming a self-regulated learner: An overview. *Theory into Practice, 41*(2), 64–70. DOI: 10.1207/s15430421tip4102_2

KEY TERMS AND DEFINITIONS

Artificial Intelligence (AI): It refers to computational systems capable of performing tasks that typically require human intelligence, including reasoning, problem-solving, language processing, decision-making, and knowledge generation. In educational contexts, AI functions as an interactive cognitive partner whose educational impact depends on how it is integrated into teaching and learning processes rather than on the technology itself.

Automation Bias: Automation bias is the tendency to overtrust automated systems and accept their outputs with insufficient critical evaluation. In educational settings, excessive reliance on AI-generated responses may reduce analytical reasoning and metacognitive monitoring unless learners are encouraged to verify, question, and critically evaluate AI-assisted outputs.

Cognitive Load Theory (CLT): It explains learning in terms of the limited capacity of working memory. Effective instructional design minimizes unnecessary cognitive load while promoting meaningful processing. AI can improve learning by reducing extraneous load, provided that it does not eliminate the productive cognitive effort required for deep understanding.

Cognitive Offloading: The intentional delegation of memory, reasoning, or problem-solving tasks to external resources, such as digital technologies or artificial intelligence systems. While offloading can reduce unnecessary cognitive burden and improve efficiency, excessive reliance may weaken internal cognitive processes if external support consistently replaces effortful learning and reflection.

Cognitive Redistribution: The dynamic reallocation of cognitive processes between the human mind and external technological systems. Rather than whether AI either enhances or diminishes cognition, this concept proposes that AI reorganizes where and how cognitive work is performed. Learning outcomes therefore depend on whether this redistribution preserves or replaces meaningful cognitive engagement.

Cognitive Scaffolding: The temporary instructional support that enables learners to perform tasks beyond their current level of independent competence. AI serves as an effective scaffold when it guides reasoning, encourages reflection, and supports higher-order thinking without replacing the learner's own cognitive processes.

Critical Thinking: The deliberate process of evaluating evidence, questioning assumptions, analyzing arguments, and making reasoned judgments. In AI-supported education, critical thinking depends on learners' ability to critically assess AI-generated outputs rather than accepting them uncritically, thereby maintaining active cognitive engagement.

Extended Mind Theory: Extended Mind Theory proposes that cognition is not confined to the human brain but can extend into external tools and environments when they become integral components of cognitive activity. In AI-supported learning, intelligent systems may serve as cognitive extensions that assist with memory, reasoning, and problem-solving while reshaping how knowledge is acquired and applied.

Human–AI Interaction: It describes the reciprocal relationship between individuals and artificial intelligence systems during cognitive tasks. The educational consequences of AI stem from how learners interact with it, including whether it is used as a collaborative partner, a cognitive scaffold, or a substitute for independent thinking.

Metacognition: The awareness and regulation of one's own thinking processes, including planning, monitoring, and evaluating learning strategies. Effective AI integration should strengthen, rather than replace, metacognitive monitoring by encouraging learners to reflect on their reasoning and critically evaluate AI-generated information.

Neuroplasticity: The brain's capacity to reorganize its structure and function in response to experience and repeated cognitive activity. Within AI-supported education, long-term neurological outcomes depend on sustained patterns of cognitive engagement, making the quality of human–AI interaction more important than simple exposure to AI technologies.

Self-Regulated Learning (SRL): Learners' ability to independently plan, monitor, control, and evaluate their learning activities. AI can support SRL by providing adaptive feedback and reflective prompts; however, excessive automation may reduce learners' opportunities to develop autonomous learning skills.

Chapter 7
Cognitive Dependency and Pedagogical Resilience in AI-Saturated Classrooms:
Critical Thinking in the Age of AI

Ashraf Alam
http://orcid.org/0000-0001-6178-1187
Department of Education, National Institute of Technology Calicut, Kozhikode, India

ABSTRACT

This chapter develops a conceptual framework of cognitive dependency and pedagogical resilience in AI-saturated classrooms. It argues that the major educational risk of artificial intelligence lies not merely in plagiarism or academic misconduct, but in cognitive substitution, where attention, retrieval, reasoning, interpretation, authorship, creativity, and judgment are prematurely outsourced to machine systems. Drawing on cognitive load theory, self-regulated learning, neuroplasticity, epistemic agency, automation bias, critical pedagogy, cognitive integrity, and human-centered AI, the chapter examines how AI can either scaffold or weaken learning. It proposes support without substitution as a guiding principle for curriculum, assessment, teacher mediation, institutional governance, ethical authorship, and platform design, so that AI strengthens human agency rather than industrializing dependency.

DOI: 10.4018/979-8-3373-9484-8.ch007

1. INTRODUCTION

1.1. AI Dependency as Educational Cognition

Education is the decisive institutional space where artificial intelligence becomes more than a technical instrument, because it enters the developmental ecology through which learners acquire *attention regulation*, *working memory discipline*, *epistemic agency*, *moral judgment*, *linguistic articulation*, *self-regulated learning*, and *cognitive endurance*. The central issue is not whether AI can accelerate academic production, since it already supports translation, accessibility, tutoring, feedback, differentiation, and administrative efficiency across global education systems (Tian & Zhang, 2025; Yurt & Kuşci, 2026). The deeper issue is whether accelerated output is being confused with intellectual formation. In AI-saturated classrooms, students may receive fluent explanations, structured essays, synthetic summaries, and plausible solutions without undergoing the cognitive operations that produce durable understanding. This chapter therefore frames AI dependency as a pedagogical, neurocognitive, ethical, and institutional problem, where the learner's relation to difficulty, knowledge, authorship, and judgment is reorganized by repeated machine-mediated assistance.

1.2. Moving from Technology Use to Cognitive Substitution

Educational technologies have historically extended human capability, yet most earlier tools preserved the learner's central cognitive role. Books expanded knowledge access, calculators supported computation, dictionaries clarified language, and search engines accelerated retrieval, but students still had to interpret, connect, evaluate, and express meaning. Generative AI alters this arrangement because it can simulate explanation, argumentation, synthesis, translation, assessment, planning, and reflection (Zhai et al., 2024; Gerlich, 2025). This creates a shift from *tool-mediated learning* to *cognitive substitution*, where the machine may perform the very process education intends to cultivate. The chapter distinguishes *assistance*, *augmentation*, *automation*, and *substitution* as separate pedagogical categories. Assistance clarifies, augmentation expands, automation handles peripheral routines, and substitution displaces formative thinking. The core argument is that AI becomes educationally constructive when it strengthens learner agency, but it becomes developmentally hazardous when it produces academic artefacts while weakening the learner's internal capacity to reason.

1.3. Dependency, Integrity, and Resilience

The chapter advances three interlinked constructs. The first is *cognitive dependency*, understood as recurring reliance on AI for attention management, comprehension, memory retrieval, reasoning, interpretation, synthesis, decision-making, and expression. The second is *cognitive integrity*, which extends academic integrity beyond plagiarism, citation, and textual originality toward honest participation in the intellectual labour required by a task (Yavich, 2025; Karamuk, 2025). The third is *pedagogical resilience*, which denotes the capacity of classrooms, curricula, assessments, institutions, and AI systems to absorb technological disruption while preserving deep learning, human judgment, ethical authorship, and intellectual autonomy. This framework rejects both technological determinism and nostalgic prohibition. AI does not automatically weaken learning, yet careless adoption can normalize premature offloading, metacognitive underuse, automation bias, and output fluency without mastery. The chapter therefore proposes *support without substitution* as the guiding educational principle for AI-mediated learning.

1.4. Theoretical Roadmap and Scope

The chapter is conceptual-theoretical and develops a narrative review of AI dependency through interdisciplinary constructs rather than empirical reporting. It draws on *cognitive load theory*, *retrieval practice*, *self-regulated learning*, *executive function*, *metacognition*, *dual-process cognition*, *neuroplasticity*, *productive struggle*, *scaffolding*, *cognitive apprenticeship*, *constructivism*, *social constructivism*, *critical pedagogy*, *epistemic virtue theory*, *knowledge justice*, *human-centered AI*, and *adaptive governance*. Section 2 establishes the conceptual foundations of AI dependency by distinguishing responsible assistance from harmful substitution. Section 3 examines neurocognitive dimensions such as attention, memory, executive function, reward, and effortful cognition. Section 4 analyzes critical thinking, epistemic agency, automation bias, and AI epistemic literacy. Section 5 develops curriculum, pedagogy, and assessment for cognitive resilience. Section 6 presents ethical, institutional, and policy frameworks. Section 7 concludes by defending human cognitive agency as the central purpose of education in AI-saturated environments.

2. CONCEPTUAL FOUNDATIONS OF AI DEPENDENCY

2.1. Multidimensional AI Dependency

AI dependency in education denotes a patterned relocation of cognitive, epistemic, linguistic, motivational, metacognitive, creative, and affective labour from the learner to an artificial system. It is not identical with frequent AI use, because frequency alone does not determine pedagogical value. A learner may use AI repeatedly for clarification, accessibility, formative feedback, multilingual support, or reflective comparison and still remain intellectually active (Ali et al., 2024; Alam & Mohanty, 2022). Dependency begins when AI becomes the default mechanism for comprehension, interpretation, problem-solving, authorship, verification, and decision-making. This dependency is multidimensional, since it involves *cognitive offloading*, *epistemic outsourcing*, *motivational externalization*, *linguistic substitution*, *creative delegation*, and *affective reassurance seeking*. Its educational danger lies in the quiet conversion of learning from a process of internal capacity formation into a process of external output acquisition, where fluency is mistaken for mastery and completion is mistaken for understanding.

2.2. Scaffold, Substitute, and Authority

AI operates in education through three analytically distinct roles, namely *scaffold*, *substitute*, and *epistemic authority*. As a scaffold, AI offers temporary assistance that keeps the learner cognitively active through hints, feedback, conceptual clarification, alternative explanations, and reflective questioning (Zahra et al., 2025; Conti et al., 2026). As a substitute, AI performs the focal intellectual work of the task, including analysis, synthesis, interpretation, composition, evaluation, and conclusion formation. As epistemic authority, AI becomes a seemingly neutral source of truth because its outputs appear fluent, impersonal, and technologically sophisticated. This shift requires a precise conceptual distinction between responsible assistance and dependency, as presented in Table 1. The distinction is vital because the same tool may deepen learning in one pedagogical configuration and weaken cognition in another, depending on whether it preserves or displaces the learner's agency, effort, judgment, and authorship.

Table 1. AI assistance and dependency across pedagogical cognitive ecologies

Analytical Dimension	Responsible AI Assistance	Dependency-Producing AI Use	Underlying Theoretical Construct	Pedagogical Consequence
Cognitive Labour	AI supports clarification, comparison, elaboration, and diagnostic feedback while the learner remains responsible for core reasoning	AI performs interpretation, synthesis, argumentation, and problem-solving before the learner attempts independent cognition	*Cognitive offloading*, *schema construction*, *germane cognitive load*, and *productive struggle*	The learner receives polished output but loses repeated practice in conceptual manipulation and inferential discipline
Epistemic Agency	AI output is treated as provisional, contestable, situated, and subject to verification through human judgment	AI output is accepted as authoritative because it appears fluent, immediate, coherent, and algorithmically neutral	*Epistemic agency*, *automation bias*, *algorithmic authority*, and *knowledge construction*	The learner's role shifts from active knower to passive consumer of machine-mediated plausibility
Motivational Regulation	AI reduces unnecessary anxiety and supports persistence without eliminating meaningful effort	AI becomes the preferred route for escaping ambiguity, delay, frustration, and intellectual difficulty	*Self-determination*, *effort discounting*, *delay tolerance*, and *academic resilience*	Learners may develop low frustration tolerance and reduced willingness to remain with demanding academic tasks
Metacognitive Control	AI prompts planning, monitoring, revision, self-explanation, and reflective evaluation of learning strategies	AI plans, monitors, evaluates, and revises work without requiring learner-generated self-assessment	*Metacognition*, *self-regulated learning*, *executive function*, and *reflective calibration*	Students may lose awareness of what they know, what they do not know, and how they learn
Linguistic Authorship	AI helps refine expression after the learner has generated ideas, claims, and conceptual direction	AI generates vocabulary, argument structure, tone, and textual coherence before the learner forms independent meaning	*Authorship*, *discursive agency*, *semiotic mediation*, and *academic voice*	The submitted text may appear sophisticated while the learner's independent expressive capacity remains underdeveloped
Creative Formation	AI expands ideational possibilities by offering contrasts, prompts, counterexamples, and exploratory alternatives	AI supplies ideas, frameworks, examples, and creative directions before the learner engages imagination	*Creative cognition*, *divergent thinking*, *ideational fluency*, and *imaginative agency*	Creativity becomes outsourced production rather than internally cultivated originality and conceptual experimentation

Table 1 shows that the problem is not the presence of AI, but the pedagogical location of AI within the learning process. When AI is positioned after learner effort, it can function as a dialogic amplifier, formative mirror, and cognitive scaffold. When it is positioned before learner effort, it can become a substitute for attention, interpretation, authorship, and judgment. This distinction also corrects a common conceptual error in AI policy, where all AI use is treated either as innovation or misconduct. The more accurate position is developmental and task-sensitive. AI is educationally defensible when it moves learners toward independence, transfer, verification, and self-regulation. It becomes dependency-producing when it increases reliance, weakens process visibility, masks non-understanding, and allows machine fluency to stand in for human cognition.

2.3. Illusion of Competence

The most subtle form of AI dependency emerges through the *illusion of competence*, where learners confuse the possession of a fluent output with the possession of understanding. AI-generated text can display coherence, disciplinary vocabulary, argumentative structure, and surface-level sophistication even when the learner has not performed the underlying cognitive labour (Uyar et al., 2026; Giray, 2024). This creates a gap between *output fluency* and *cognitive mastery*. Output fluency concerns the polish, organization, and rhetorical adequacy of the product, whereas cognitive mastery concerns the learner's capacity to explain, apply, transfer, critique, and reconstruct knowledge independently. The risk is intensified by *metacognitive miscalibration*, where learners overestimate comprehension because the AI-generated response feels clear. In such conditions, assessment may reward textual performance while missing conceptual fragility. The pedagogical challenge is therefore to make thinking visible through explanation, reconstruction, oral defense, revision trails, and reflective disclosure.

2.4. Laziness as Pedagogical Symptom

Cognitive laziness should not be reduced to a moral weakness of students, because it is often produced by assessment regimes, platform architectures, institutional incentives, and performance cultures that reward speed, completion, and surface polish. AI intensifies this condition by making shortcuts linguistically elegant and academically presentable (Rosas-Jiménez et al., 2026; Moluayonge, 2025). The resulting dependency is best understood through *effort avoidance*, *low ambiguity tolerance*, *instant gratification*, *reduced cognitive endurance*, and weakened *productive struggle*. Deep learning requires students to remain with incomplete understanding, conceptual discomfort, interpretive plurality, and delayed mastery.

If AI removes this difficulty too early, it deprives learners of the formative friction through which intellectual autonomy develops. As Table 1 indicates, responsible AI design must preserve meaningful effort while reducing unnecessary confusion. The aim is not prohibition, but disciplined sequencing, where learners first think, attempt, struggle, and explain before AI becomes a scaffold for refinement.

3. NEUROCOGNITIVE ARCHITECTURES OF AI-MEDIATED LEARNING

3.1. Neurocognitive Formation, Not Information Intake

Learning is not a passive movement of information from external sources into memory, but a complex process of *neurocognitive formation* through attention, encoding, rehearsal, retrieval, elaboration, feedback, error correction, consolidation, transfer, and reflective reorganization. In AI-mediated classrooms, this formative process becomes vulnerable when learners receive completed interpretations before their own cognitive systems have engaged with uncertainty, contradiction, and conceptual difficulty (Ali et al., 2024; Fasoli et al., 2025). The educational problem is therefore not that AI provides information, but that it may compress or bypass the developmental sequence through which durable understanding is constructed. *Neuroconstructivism, situated cognition, distributed cognition, embodied learning*, and *experiential learning* all indicate that knowledge emerges through active participation with tools, bodies, symbols, communities, and environments. AI becomes pedagogically constructive only when it expands this ecology of participation, not when it reduces learning to prompt-response transactions and polished cognitive surrogacy.

3.2. Plasticity, Attention, and Cognitive Load

Neuroplasticity provides a careful conceptual basis for understanding why repeated AI use matters educationally. Learners strengthen the cognitive operations they repeatedly practice, including sustained reading, inferential reasoning, mathematical manipulation, argumentative writing, retrieval, and self-correction (Alam & Mohanty, 2023a; Parreño et al., 2026). When AI routinely performs these operations prematurely, the learner may receive fewer opportunities to develop attentional discipline, schema density, and executive control. This is not a deterministic claim about neurological harm, but a pedagogical claim about developmental underuse. *Attention regulation* becomes especially important because AI can either reduce extraneous confusion or intensify attentional fragmentation through rapid prompting, instant summaries, multitasking, and shallow answer consumption. *Cognitive load theory* clarifies the distinction. AI is constructive when it reduces *extraneous load*, such as unclear instructions or inaccessible vocabulary (Pum, 2025; Hamzaj, 2025). It becomes dependency-producing when it removes *germane load*, the meaningful effort required for schema construction, abstraction, and durable conceptual integration.

3.3. Executive Function and Effortful Cognition

AI-mediated learning strongly affects *executive function*, because planning, inhibition, monitoring, cognitive flexibility, error detection, and goal management can either be supported by AI or displaced by it. In a resilient configuration, AI functions as a metacognitive mirror, helping learners identify gaps, revise strategies, and test explanations (Aydemir et al., 2026; Boulos, 2024). In a dependency-producing configuration, AI plans the task, structures the argument, evaluates the response, and proposes revisions before the learner has exercised self-regulation. This subsection therefore calls attention to Table 2, which maps core neurocognitive processes onto constructive AI use, dependency risk, and pedagogical safeguards (Pavone, 2025; Van Zyl, 2026). The table is designed to show that cognitive vulnerability does not arise from AI use in itself, but from badly sequenced AI use that replaces retrieval, sustained attention, productive delay, and learner-generated monitoring with instantaneous external completion.

Table 2. Neurocognitive processes and AI dependency risks

Neurocognitive Domain	Educational Function	Constructive AI Configuration	Dependency-Producing Configuration	Pedagogical Safeguard
Attention Regulation	Sustains selective focus, conceptual immersion, perceptual filtering, and resistance to digital distraction during demanding academic tasks	AI organizes learning goals, clarifies task sequence, and reduces irrelevant complexity while preserving learner engagement with full texts and problems	AI encourages summary dependence, fragmented prompting, multitasking, and rapid output consumption before sustained engagement occurs	Require text-first reading, delayed AI consultation, attention logs, and reflective comparison between learner understanding and AI synthesis
Working Memory Control	Holds, manipulates, and integrates information during reasoning, calculation, interpretation, and complex problem representation	AI offers hints, decomposes confusing instructions, and supports staged manipulation without solving the central intellectual task	AI completes reasoning steps, generates final solutions, and removes the need for learners to mentally coordinate variables or evidence	Use hint-only prompting, stepwise self-explanation, partial solutions, and learner-generated reasoning maps before AI feedback
Long-Term Consolidation	Stabilizes concepts, procedures, vocabulary, schemas, and disciplinary patterns through retrieval, spacing, elaboration, and transfer	AI supports spaced review, diagnostic questioning, interleaved practice, and concept checking after independent recall attempts	AI replaces recall by providing definitions, explanations, examples, and summaries before memory retrieval is attempted	Require retrieval-before-AI routines, low-stakes recall tasks, oral reconstruction, and delayed verification through AI-supported review
Executive Function	Coordinates planning, inhibition, monitoring, strategy selection, cognitive flexibility, and revision across complex learning tasks	AI helps learners externalize plans, test strategies, detect gaps, and compare revision pathways after initial self-regulated effort	AI performs planning, sequencing, monitoring, evaluation, and revision while the learner remains procedurally passive	Use planning journals, self-monitoring checklists, process portfolios, and student-authored revision rationales

continued on following page

Table 2. Continued

Neurocognitive Domain	Educational Function	Constructive AI Configuration	Dependency-Producing Configuration	Pedagogical Safeguard
Metacognitive Calibration	Enables learners to judge what they know, what they misunderstand, and which strategies are effective for future improvement	AI asks diagnostic questions, challenges assumptions, and provides feedback that learners compare with self-assessment	AI supplies confidence-producing explanations that create overestimation, false mastery, and untested comprehension	Require self-rating, explanation without notes, error prediction, AI-output critique, and reflective disclosure of learning gaps
Motivational Endurance	Maintains persistence, delay tolerance, ambiguity management, frustration regulation, and willingness to engage in difficult mastery	AI reduces unnecessary anxiety, offers encouragement, and supports persistence without eliminating productive struggle	AI becomes an escape route from difficulty, producing effort discounting, instant gratification, and weakened cognitive stamina	Design productive struggle sequences, slow-thinking seminars, staged AI access, and process rewards for revision and perseverance

Table 2 makes clear that every neurocognitive domain has a double pedagogical possibility. AI can become a scaffold for cognitive strengthening when it is used after learner effort, when it prompts reflection, and when it increases self-regulatory awareness. The same AI system can become a mechanism of cognitive attenuation when it is placed before effort, when it supplies complete responses, and when it allows output fluency to conceal unpracticed cognition. This distinction is crucial for global policy, curriculum, and classroom design because it shifts the debate away from permissive versus prohibitive AI rules and toward developmental sequencing. A cognitively defensible AI pedagogy must protect retrieval before consultation, reading before summarization, reasoning before solution generation, planning before automated organization, and self-evaluation before external feedback. Such sequencing preserves *germane cognitive load*, *metacognitive calibration*, *executive control*, and *motivational endurance*, while still allowing AI to support inclusion, accessibility, differentiated guidance, and formative feedback.

3.4. Developmental Safeguards and Learner Diversity

AI dependency has unequal developmental implications because learners differ in age, cognitive maturity, linguistic capital, digital access, disability status, disciplinary background, and institutional support. Younger learners require stronger protection for foundational literacy, numeracy, memory, and executive function, while higher education learners require transparent, discipline-specific, ethically reflexive AI protocols (Lin et al., 2024; Alam, 2023a). Multilingual learners and students with disabilities may gain substantial accessibility benefits from AI, yet these benefits must be structured around autonomy rather than permanent substitution. *Universal Design for Learning*, *capability theory*, *inclusive pedagogy*, and *developmentally appropriate practice* together support a calibrated model of AI integration. The central safeguard is not blanket restriction, but sequenced mediation. Learners should first attempt, retrieve, explain, struggle, and reflect, before AI enters as scaffold, comparator, verifier, or feedback mechanism (Hyde et al., 2024; Alagöz Hamzaj, 2025). Such developmental governance protects cognitive agency while enabling equitable participation in AI-rich educational futures.

4. CRITICAL THINKING, EPISTEMIC AGENCY, AND AUTOMATION BIAS

4.1. Critical Thinking as Epistemic Praxis

Critical thinking is not a supplementary graduate attribute, but the cognitive-ethical infrastructure of education, democratic citizenship, professional judgment, scientific reasoning, and civic accountability (Sharma, 2024; Yun et al., 2021). In AI-saturated learning environments, it becomes more decisive because students encounter fluent machine outputs that may appear precise, neutral, and authoritative while remaining incomplete, decontextualized, biased, or logically fragile. Critical thinking integrates *analysis*, *inference*, *interpretation*, *evaluation*, *explanation*, *reflexivity*, *skepticism*, *intellectual humility*, and *practical judgment*. It is therefore both cognitive and normative, since it concerns how learners process claims and how they assume responsibility for belief formation. AI-mediated education must treat critical thinking as *epistemic praxis*, not merely as a skill taxonomy (Danry et al., 2023; Cardon et al., 2023). The learner must examine assumptions, test evidence, identify missing perspectives, detect fallacies, and resist premature certainty. Without this discipline, AI fluency can become a persuasive substitute for understanding.

4.2. Outsourced Reasoning and Epistemic Agency

The outsourcing of reasoning to AI threatens *epistemic agency*, which is the learner's capacity to participate actively in knowledge construction, claim evaluation, interpretive negotiation, and justified decision-making. AI can generate arguments, counterarguments, summaries, interpretations, policy positions, legal reasoning, scientific explanations, and ethical reflections, yet these products become pedagogically valuable only when treated as objects for interrogation rather than replacements for thought (Farangi et al., 2025; Alam, 2023b). When learners accept AI outputs without reconstructing the inferential pathway, the educational process shifts from *knowledge-making* to *knowledge-consumption*. This is especially serious in disciplines that depend on evidentiary judgment, normative reasoning, hermeneutic sensitivity, and contextual interpretation (Rudroff, 2024; Zhou et al., 2024). *Constructivism*, *dialogic pedagogy*, *inquiry-based learning*, *knowledge-building theory*, and *communities of practice* all position the learner as a knower, not a receiver. AI use must therefore preserve questioning, explanation, disagreement, verification, and accountability as core acts of learning.

4.3. Automation Bias and Algorithmic Authority

Automation bias emerges when learners, teachers, or institutions overvalue machine-generated outputs because they appear immediate, coherent, quantitative, impersonal, or technically sophisticated. In classrooms, this bias may lead students to accept AI-generated claims without verification, teachers to overtrust automated feedback, and institutions to treat predictive analytics as neutral diagnosis (Xu et al., 2026; Cena et al., 2026). The deeper problem is *algorithmic authority*, where the technological form of a claim becomes a substitute for epistemic justification. Table 3 clarifies how distinct critical thinking capacities are weakened when AI outputs are consumed without reflective mediation. The table also shows that the pedagogical response must be targeted, because analysis, evaluation, interpretation, reflection, and judgment are not identical cognitive operations. Each requires a specific instructional countermeasure that restores human responsibility, evidentiary discipline, and epistemic accountability within AI-mediated learning ecologies.

Table 3. Critical thinking capacities across AI epistemic learning ecologies

Critical Capacity	Cognitive-Epistemic Function	AI-Related Distortion	Interdisciplinary Construct	Pedagogical Countermeasure
Analysis	Separates complex ideas into premises, categories, relations, contradictions, assumptions, and causal mechanisms within a disciplined interpretive frame	AI supplies pre-packaged analytical structure that learners may reproduce without decomposing the problem themselves	*Analytical cognition, schema differentiation, semiotic mediation,* and *structural reasoning*	Require learners to annotate AI analysis, identify missing variables, reorder arguments, and justify every conceptual linkage
Evaluation	Judges credibility, sufficiency, relevance, validity, reliability, and contextual adequacy of evidence across competing knowledge claims	AI outputs appear plausible and coherent, encouraging acceptance without source scrutiny, evidentiary triangulation, or methodological caution	*Epistemic vigilance, evidence literacy, credibility assessment,* and *truth-maintenance reasoning*	Require verification trails, evidence hierarchies, source comparison, and explicit justification for accepting or rejecting claims
Inference	Moves from evidence, patterns, premises, and probabilities toward defensible conclusions under uncertainty	AI generates conclusions before learners test premises, consider alternatives, or identify inferential gaps	*Inferential discipline, abductive reasoning, probabilistic judgment,* and *causal cognition*	Use incomplete AI outputs that require students to supply warrants, assumptions, counterexamples, and alternative explanations
Interpretation	Constructs meaning from texts, data, cases, events, histories, symbols, and lived contexts through situated understanding	AI may impose dominant readings, generic categories, culturally narrow assumptions, or decontextualized meanings	*Hermeneutic reasoning, situated cognition, standpoint epistemology,* and *contextual intelligence*	Require plural interpretations, local contextualization, counter-reading, and comparison between machine framing and human experience

continued on following page

Table 3. Continued

Critical Capacity	Cognitive-Epistemic Function	AI-Related Distortion	Interdisciplinary Construct	Pedagogical Countermeasure
Reflection	Examines one's own assumptions, positionality, cognitive shortcuts, affective investments, and limits of understanding	AI accelerates output production and reduces reflective delay, metacognitive pause, and self-interrogation	*Metacognitive calibration*, *reflexive agency*, *self-regulated learning*, and *epistemic humility*	Require reflective commentaries, AI-use disclosures, self-assessment, uncertainty statements, and revision rationales
Judgment	Makes accountable decisions under ambiguity by integrating evidence, values, consequences, context, and ethical responsibility	AI recommendations may be treated as final decisions, displacing human accountability and normative deliberation	*Practical wisdom*, *ethical agency*, *decision theory*, and *responsibility attribution*	Require independent final justification, oral defense, ethical consequence mapping, and explicit human responsibility statements

Table 3 demonstrates that critical thinking in AI-mediated education must be protected as a differentiated architecture of cognition, not as a generic learning outcome. A student may be able to analyze an AI response but still fail to evaluate evidence, recognize bias, interpret context, or assume responsibility for judgment. This distinction matters for curriculum designers, assessment developers, policy makers, and educational technologists because each critical capacity requires a different form of pedagogical mediation. The table also shows that AI can be converted from a dependency-producing system into an epistemic training object when its outputs are deliberately made contestable. Students should not merely use AI to complete work. They should examine how AI frames problems, compresses uncertainty, privileges certain categories, omits situated knowledge, and simulates confidence. In this way, AI becomes a provocation for deeper reasoning rather than a shortcut around reasoning. The educational task is therefore to cultivate learners who can interrogate machine-generated plausibility through human judgment, disciplinary rigor, and ethical accountability.

4.4. AI Epistemic Literacy

AI-mediated education requires a shift from conventional *information literacy* to *AI epistemic literacy*. Information literacy teaches learners to locate, evaluate, and use information, whereas AI epistemic literacy teaches them to interrogate how machine-generated knowledge is produced, why it may hallucinate, how bias enters outputs, how authority is simulated, and why human verification remains indispensable (Zare et al., 2025; Zhou et al., 2026). This literacy includes understanding AI as probabilistic rather than truth-bearing, distinguishing fluency from accuracy, identifying hidden assumptions, detecting normative simplification, examining absent perspectives, and recognizing the learner's responsibility for every claim used in academic work. It also requires *critical prompting*, where students use prompts not merely to obtain answers, but to expose uncertainty, request counterarguments, test assumptions, identify missing evidence, and generate alternative interpretations. The goal is not efficient AI use alone, but disciplined epistemic independence in environments saturated with algorithmic persuasion.

5. PEDAGOGIES OF COGNITIVE RESILIENCE

5.1. Cognitive Resilience and Pedagogical Plasticity

Cognitive resilience denotes the learner's capacity to sustain attention, tolerate ambiguity, retrieve knowledge, reason independently, evaluate machine-generated claims, regulate affective discomfort, and preserve authorship within AI-mediated learning ecologies. It is not a rejection of technology, but a disciplined mode of *human-AI co-agency* in which the learner remains epistemically responsible for meaning, evidence, and judgment (Mujtaba, 2024; Alam & Mohanty, 2024). *Pedagogical resilience* extends this capacity from the individual learner to the instructional system. It includes curriculum design, task sequencing, assessment architecture, teacher mediation, ethical authorship, and institutional norm-setting (Rani et al., 2026; Halkiopoulos & Gkintoni, 2024). The construct draws together *self-regulated learning*, *growth orientation*, *cognitive apprenticeship*, *desirable difficulty*, *mastery learning*, *transformative learning*, and *intellectual virtue*. A resilient pedagogy does not ask whether AI is present, but whether AI strengthens or displaces attention, reasoning, interpretation, creativity, self-monitoring, and accountable knowledge production.

5.2. Productive Struggle and Metacognitive Friction

AI-resilient education must reclaim *productive struggle* as a developmental necessity, not a sign of instructional failure. Deep learning requires friction, uncertainty, failed attempts, delayed mastery, inferential discomfort, and iterative reconstruction. In digital design, friction is often treated as inefficiency, but in pedagogy, carefully designed friction generates *metacognitive calibration*, *cognitive endurance*, *schema refinement*, and *epistemic humility* (Tabassum et al., 2025; Oviatt, 2021). Students should therefore encounter demanding texts, unresolved problems, competing interpretations, and incomplete arguments before AI assistance is introduced. This sequencing protects *germane cognitive load* and prevents premature outsourcing. *Slow thinking*, *reflective delay*, *retrieval-before-consultation*, *draft-before-generation*, and *explanation-before-feedback* become central instructional principles. AI can still support learners, but only after they have attempted, struggled, articulated confusion, and produced an initial cognitive trace (Allison et al., 2025; Wong & Qiu, 2026). Such design converts AI from a shortcut into a formative comparator, verifier, and dialogic scaffold.

5.3. Assessment Beyond Detection

Assessment reform is the decisive site where AI dependency can either be intensified or disrupted. Detection-centered approaches remain pedagogically narrow because they frame AI primarily as misconduct, while ignoring the deeper issue of whether the learner has performed the intended cognitive labour (Jabar et al., 2025; Alam & Mohanty, 2023b). AI-resilient assessment must move from product-only evaluation to *process-visible assessment*, where drafts, annotations, oral explanations, revision trails, reflective logs, source verification, peer dialogue, and decision rationales become assessable evidence of thinking. Table 4 presents strategies that shift assessment from surveillance to cognitive accountability. The table also responds to the risks identified earlier in Table 2 and Table 3 by connecting pedagogical action to attention, retrieval, metacognition, authorship, and judgment.

Table 4. Pedagogical strategies for AI-resilient cognitive formation

Pedagogical Strategy	Theoretical Grounding	Classroom Operationalization	Protected Cognitive Capacity	Expected Educational Yield
Independent First Attempt	*Productive struggle*, *constructivist learning*, *retrieval practice*, and *desirable difficulty*	Students first read, solve, draft, interpret, or summarize without AI before comparing their initial cognitive trace with machine-generated support	Attention, recall, inferential discipline, learner confidence, and tolerance for incomplete understanding	Prevents premature cognitive offloading and ensures that AI enters after meaningful learner engagement
AI Comparison Protocol	*Metacognitive calibration*, *critical digital literacy*, *dialogic pedagogy*, and *epistemic vigilance*	Students compare their own response with an AI response, identify convergence, divergence, bias, omission, and unsupported claims	Evaluation, skepticism, reflection, judgment, and evidence-based reasoning	Converts AI output into an object of critique rather than a substitute for human reasoning
Prompt Critique Task	*Semiotic mediation*, *critical discourse analysis*, *knowledge construction*, and *algorithmic literacy*	Students examine how wording, assumptions, disciplinary framing, and hidden values within prompts shape AI-generated responses	Question formation, conceptual precision, epistemic awareness, and discursive agency	Shows that AI responses are constructed through linguistic framing rather than produced as neutral truth
Process Portfolio	*Self-regulated learning*, *executive function*, *reflective practice*, and *cognitive apprenticeship*	Students submit planning notes, drafts, revisions, AI-use logs, rejected outputs, and explanations of final intellectual decisions	Planning, monitoring, revision, authorship, and metacognitive control	Makes learning visible across stages and prevents final products from concealing weak cognition
Oral Defense and Viva	*Dialogic pedagogy*, *argumentation theory*, *disciplinary apprenticeship*, and *performative accountability*	Students explain, defend, qualify, and reconstruct submitted work through structured oral questioning and contextual probing	Conceptual ownership, argumentation, transfer, comprehension, and ethical authorship	Confirms that the learner can think beyond the submitted text and defend knowledge claims independently
AI Error Analysis	*Epistemic literacy*, *fallibilism*, *bias critique*, *source evaluation*, and *critical realism*	Students identify hallucinations, weak warrants, hidden assumptions, cultural bias, missing evidence, and faulty reasoning in AI outputs	Skepticism, verification, interpretive plurality, and analytical accuracy	Builds resistance to automation bias and strengthens disciplined distrust of machine fluency

Table 4 shows that AI-resilient pedagogy requires more than adding disclosure statements to assignments. It requires redesigning the epistemic architecture of learning so that student thinking becomes visible, contestable, and defensible at multiple stages. The pedagogical value of these strategies lies in their capacity to preserve learner agency while still permitting constructive AI participation. Independent first attempts protect the initial formation of thought. AI comparison protocols convert machine output into a site of critique. Prompt critique exposes the semiotic and ideological construction of AI responses. Process portfolios reveal planning, monitoring, and revision. Oral defense confirms cognitive ownership. AI error analysis cultivates disciplined skepticism toward fluency, confidence, and algorithmic authority. Together, these strategies reframe AI from an invisible producer of academic artefacts into a visible object of metacognitive inquiry. Such assessment design is globally applicable because it can be adapted across disciplines, levels, languages, and institutional contexts without relying on punitive surveillance.

5.4. Teachers as Cognitive Mediators

In AI-saturated education, teachers become more essential because they mediate the boundary between assistance and substitution. Their role shifts from information transmission to *cognitive mediation*, *epistemic mentorship*, *ethical guidance*, and *instructional design for intellectual difficulty* (Danaher, 2018; Zhang et al., 2024). Teachers must design tasks that require independent first attempts, scaffolded inquiry, oral defense, source triangulation, peer dialogue, and reflective disclosure. They must also identify superficial fluency, hidden non-understanding, affective dependency, and weakened authorship (Panksepp et al., 2002; Lupton & Bailey-Charteris, 2026). This requires professional competence in *AI epistemic literacy*, *assessment redesign*, *inclusive pedagogy*, *disciplinary reasoning*, and *human-centered technology governance*. The teacher is not displaced by AI, because AI cannot understand classroom culture, learner biography, moral context, institutional purpose, or the developmental meaning of struggle (Magomedova & Fatima, 2025; Ji et al., 2025). The resilient teacher converts AI from an automatic answer machine into a regulated pedagogical instrument that strengthens inquiry, responsibility, and human cognitive agency.

6. ETHICAL GOVERNANCE AND POLICY ARCHITECTURES

6.1. From Misconduct Control to Learning Protection

AI governance in education must move beyond punitive misconduct control toward *learning protection*, because the deepest risk is not only unauthorized authorship, but the erosion of cognitive labour, epistemic agency, and developmental integrity. Institutional policy often treats AI as a compliance problem, yet AI dependency is also a curricular, psychological, ethical, economic, and political phenomenon (Karakus et al., 2008; Alam & Mohanty, 2023d). A robust governance architecture must therefore integrate *academic integrity*, *cognitive integrity*, *data justice*, *algorithmic accountability*, *human oversight*, *adaptive regulation*, and *institutional due process*. The key question is not merely whether students used AI, but whether AI use aligned with the intended learning outcome (Massimo et al., 2018; Danry et al., 2025). A permitted use in one task may be prohibited in another if the task is designed to assess independent reasoning, memory, interpretation, or authorship. Policy must therefore be granular, discipline-sensitive, developmentally calibrated, and pedagogically intelligible.

6.2. Human-Centered AI and Cognitive Integrity

Human-centered AI in education does not simply mean intuitive interface design or personalized learning convenience. It means that AI must remain subordinate to human dignity, learner autonomy, teacher judgment, educational equity, privacy, and intellectual formation. The central institutional construct is *cognitive integrity*, which extends conventional academic integrity beyond plagiarism, citation, and textual originality (Melanou & Beege, 2026; de Barros, 2024). Cognitive integrity asks whether the learner has genuinely participated in the thinking demanded by the task. A text may be non-plagiarized and still pedagogically hollow if AI has completed the reading, reasoning, synthesis, interpretation, and evaluation (Watermeyer et al., 2025; Arora, 2025). Ethical authorship therefore requires transparency, comprehension, defensibility, and responsibility. Learners must be able to explain what AI contributed, what they rejected, how they verified claims, and why the final judgment remains theirs (Litvinova et al., 2025). Human oversight must remain non-negotiable, especially in grading, analytics, risk prediction, and high-stakes educational decisions.

6.3. Equity, Capacity, and Institutional Infrastructure

AI policy must address *AI stratification*, where educational advantage becomes tied to premium tools, digital access, prompt fluency, institutional guidance, connectivity, language privilege, and platform literacy. AI can support multilingual learners, disabled students, working learners, and geographically marginalized communities, yet it can also deepen structural inequality if institutions outsource support to commercial platforms without public safeguards (Alam, 2023c; Pandoi, 2021). Table 5 presents a policy architecture that connects institutional concerns with governance responses, theoretical rationales, and practical outcomes. The table is especially relevant to the cognitive vulnerabilities discussed in earlier sections, because policy must protect learning processes, not merely regulate final products. An effective framework must combine equity, privacy, faculty development, academic integrity, cognitive integrity, procurement standards, and periodic review.

Table 5. Ethical and policy architecture for human-centered AI education

Governance Dimension	Institutional Risk Field	Policy and Infrastructure Response	Theoretical and Ethical Rationale	Practical Governance Outcome
Academic Integrity	AI-generated academic products may obscure authorship, originality, responsibility, and the boundary between assistance and substitution	Require task-specific AI-use declarations, assignment-level permissions, transparent disclosure norms, and defensible authorship statements	*Ethical authorship, normative accountability, responsibility attribution*, and *academic trust ecology*	Students disclose assistance, teachers evaluate responsibility, and institutions shift from suspicion to accountable transparency
Cognitive Integrity	Learners may bypass intended thinking processes while producing polished work that appears academically competent	Assess drafts, oral explanations, revision trails, reflective logs, process portfolios, and learner-generated rationales	*Learning as cognitive formation, process validity, metacognitive accountability*, and *epistemic agency*	Institutions protect the integrity of learning itself, not merely the originality of submitted language
Equity and Access	Unequal access to devices, connectivity, premium AI systems, linguistic capital, and AI literacy may widen educational stratification	Provide institutional access, multilingual guidance, inclusive design standards, disability-sensitive support, and public digital infrastructure	*Capability theory, social justice education, digital inclusion*, and *distributive fairness*	AI becomes an enabling educational resource rather than an accelerator of privilege and exclusion
Faculty Preparedness	Teachers may lack conceptual, technical, ethical, and assessment-related capacity to mediate AI responsibly	Establish professional development, discipline-specific AI protocols, assessment redesign labs, and peer communities of practice	*Teacher agency, cognitive mediation, professional capital*, and *pedagogical content knowledge*	Faculty gain the competence to transform AI from a threat into a regulated learning scaffold

continued on following page

Table 5. Continued

Governance Dimension	Institutional Risk Field	Policy and Infrastructure Response	Theoretical and Ethical Rationale	Practical Governance Outcome
Privacy and Data Justice	Student data may be extracted, commercialized, profiled, or used for opaque predictive interventions	Adopt platform review, data minimization, consent protocols, security standards, and privacy-preserving procurement rules	*Data justice*, *informational autonomy*, *digital rights*, and *institutional fiduciary duty*	Learners are protected from exploitative datafication and institutions retain ethical control over educational records
Adaptive Governance	AI systems evolve rapidly, making static rules obsolete, ambiguous, or misaligned with emerging pedagogical realities	Create periodic policy review, AI ethics committees, student guidance updates, vendor audits, and transparent grievance mechanisms	*Adaptive governance*, *reflexive regulation*, *institutional resilience*, and *public accountability*	Policy remains current, credible, contestable, and responsive to technological and educational change

Table 5 demonstrates that human-centered AI governance requires a multi-scalar architecture rather than isolated declarations of permitted or prohibited use. Academic integrity protects trust, but cognitive integrity protects the deeper educational process through which trust becomes meaningful. Equity policies prevent AI from becoming a market-mediated sorting mechanism, while faculty development ensures that teachers are not left to manage complex epistemic transformations through individual improvisation. Privacy and data justice are equally central, because AI-mediated education can convert learners into data subjects whose behaviours, weaknesses, and predictions are commercially or administratively exploitable. Adaptive governance is necessary because AI tools, platform capabilities, institutional risks, and student practices change quickly. The table therefore reframes policy as a living pedagogical infrastructure, where rules, capacities, technologies, and values are continuously aligned. Such governance is not anti-innovation. It is a precondition for responsible innovation, because only ethically governed AI can strengthen learning without intensifying dependency, surveillance, inequality, or institutional opacity.

6.4. Designers, Platforms, and Public Responsibility

Responsibility for AI dependency cannot be placed only on students and teachers, because technological design, procurement markets, platform incentives, and public policy also shape educational behaviour. Many AI systems are optimized for speed, fluency, completion, and user satisfaction, while education requires delay, struggle, verification, revision, and responsibility (Kim et al., 2025; Kaya & Çelebi,

2025). Educational AI must therefore be designed through *pedagogical affordance theory*, *responsible innovation*, *human-in-the-loop governance*, *privacy-by-design*, and *ethics-by-design*. Systems should include hint-before-answer pathways, uncertainty indicators, source-verification prompts, overreliance alerts, teacher-controlled assistance levels, bias monitoring, accessibility features, and student explanation requirements (Zaki & Naz, 2025; Kayar et al., 2025; Bukhari et al., 2026). Policy makers must support standards for educational procurement, teacher preparation, public access, platform accountability, and child-sensitive AI governance. The final responsibility is collective, because cognitive resilience requires alignment among learners, teachers, institutions, designers, regulators, and democratic public purpose.

7. CONCLUSION

7.1. Cognitive Agency as Educational Telos

The chapter concludes that AI is transforming education not merely through new tools, accelerated outputs, and automated assistance, but through a deeper reconfiguration of the learner's cognitive ecology. The central educational danger is not AI use itself, but the normalization of *cognitive substitution*, where attention, retrieval, reasoning, interpretation, authorship, creativity, and judgment are transferred to machine systems before learners have developed internal competence. This risk becomes visible through *cognitive dependency*, *epistemic outsourcing*, *metacognitive underuse*, *automation bias*, *output fluency*, *false mastery*, and weakened *productive struggle*. The chapter has therefore argued for *cognitive integrity* as a necessary expansion of academic integrity, because educational honesty must include genuine participation in the thinking required by a task. The future of AI-mediated education must be judged by whether it preserves learners as active knowers, reflective authors, ethical agents, and accountable decision-makers.

7.2. Pedagogical Resilience for Human Futures

Pedagogical resilience offers the chapter's constructive response to AI dependency. It requires curriculum architectures that protect *slow cognition*, assessment systems that make thinking visible, teachers who operate as *cognitive mediators*, institutions that govern AI through *adaptive policy*, and platforms designed through *human-centered AI*, *privacy-by-design*, *ethics-by-design*, and *learning-centered affordances*. The guiding principle is *support without substitution*. AI should support accessibility, inclusion, feedback, exploration, multilingual learning, formative guidance, and creative experimentation, but it must not replace the learner's responsibility for attention, evidence, interpretation, judgment, and authorship. The educated learner in the AI age is not the fastest producer of AI-assisted output, but the person capable of questioning machine fluency, detecting error, tolerating ambiguity, verifying claims, revising judgment, and acting with epistemic responsibility. If governed wisely, AI can strengthen human learning. If adopted carelessly, it can industrialize dependency under the appearance of innovation.

REFERENCES

Alagöz Hamzaj, Y. (2025). Generative AI acceptance among future educators: Personality and behavioral insights. *Education and Information Technologies*, *30*(16), 1–24. DOI: 10.1007/s10639-025-13678-3

Alam, A. (2023a). The secret sauce of student success: Cracking the code by navigating the path to personalized learning with educational data mining. In *2023 2nd International Conference on Smart Technologies and Systems for Next Generation Computing (ICSTSN)* (pp. 1-8). IEEE. DOI: 10.1109/ICSTSN57873.2023.10151558

Alam, A. (2023b). Media multitasking with M-learning technology in real-time classroom learning: Analysing the dynamics in formal educational settings for the future of E-learning in India. In *2023 2nd International Conference on Smart Technologies and Systems for Next Generation Computing (ICSTSN)* (pp. 1-6). IEEE. DOI: 10.1109/ICSTSN57873.2023.10151509

Alam, A. (2023c). Leveraging the power of 'modeling and computer simulation' for education: An exploration of its potential for improved learning outcomes and enhanced student engagement. In *2023 International Conference on Device Intelligence, Computing and Communication Technologies (DICCT)* (pp. 445-450). IEEE. DOI: 10.1109/DICCT56244.2023.10110159

Alam, A., & Mohanty, A. (2022). Facial analytics or virtual avatars: competencies and design considerations for student-teacher interaction in AI-powered online education for effective classroom engagement. In *International Conference on Communication, Networks and Computing* (pp. 252-265). Cham: Springer Nature Switzerland. DOI: 10.1007/978-3-031-43145-6_21

Alam, A., & Mohanty, A. (2023a). Learning on the move: a pedagogical framework for state-of-the-art mobile learning. In *International Conference on Data Management, Analytics & Innovation* (pp. 735-748). Singapore: Springer Nature Singapore. DOI: 10.1007/978-981-99-1414-2_52

Alam, A., & Mohanty, A. (2023b). From bricks to clicks: The potential of big data analytics for revolutionizing the information landscape in higher education sector. In *International Conference on Data Management, Analytics & Innovation* (pp. 721-732). Singapore: Springer Nature Singapore. DOI: 10.1007/978-981-99-1414-2_51

Alam, A., & Mohanty, A. (2023d). Implications of virtual reality (VR) for school teachers and instructional designers: An empirical investigation. *Cogent Education*, *10*(2), 2260676. DOI: 10.1080/2331186X.2023.2260676

Alam, A., & Mohanty, A. (2024). Framework of Self-Regulated cognitive engagement (FSRCE) for sustainable pedagogy: A model that integrates SRL and cognitive engagement for holistic development of students. *Cogent Education*, *11*(1), 2363157. DOI: 10.1080/2331186X.2024.2363157

Ali, K., Garcia, A., & Vadsariya, A. (2024). Impact of the AI dependency revolution on both physical and mental health. *Journal of Strategic Innovation and Sustainability*, *19*(2), 70–81. DOI: 10.33423/jsis.v19i2.7006

Ali, Z., Janarthanan, J., & Mohan, P. (2024). Understanding digital dementia and cognitive impact in the current era of the internet: A review. *Cureus*, *16*(9). Advance online publication. DOI: 10.7759/cureus.70029 PMID: 39449887

Allison, J., Hwang, G. J., Mayer, R. E., Pellas, N., Karnalim, O., de Freitas, S., Ng, O.-L., Huang, Y.-M., Hooshyar, D., Seidman, R. H., Al-Emran, M., Mikropoulos, T. A., Schroeder, N. L., Roscoe, R. D., & Sanusi, I. (2025). From generative AI to extended reality: Multidisciplinary perspectives on the challenges, opportunities, and future of educational computing. *Journal of Educational Computing Research*, *63*(6), 1327–1363. DOI: 10.1177/07356331251359964

Arora, M. (2025). A study on association between AI and critical thinking, impulsivity, dependence among young adults. *International Journal of Interdisciplinary Approaches in Psychology*, *3*(9), 30–38. DOI: 10.61113/ijiap.v3i9.1143

Aydemir, Z., Kargın, T., & Altun, D. (2026). Children's Mental Representations of Artificial Intelligence: Insights from 4th and 8th Graders. *International Journal of Human-Computer Interaction*, •••, 1–18. DOI: 10.1080/10447318.2026.2659949

Boulos, L. J. (2024). The brain digitalization: It's all happening so fast! *Frontiers in Human Dynamics*, *6*, 1475438. DOI: 10.3389/fhumd.2024.1475438

Bukhari, S. S. A., Irshad-ul-Haq, M., Ali, S. B., & Sabir, S. (2026). The AI Learning Trap: The Shocking Truth about Student Intelligence in the Age of Artificial Intelligence. *Review of Education. Administration & Law*, *9*(1), 115–128. DOI: 10.47067/real.v9i1.476

Cardon, P., Fleischmann, C., Aritz, J., Logemann, M., & Heidewald, J. (2023). The challenges and opportunities of AI-assisted writing: Developing AI literacy for the AI age. *Business and Professional Communication Quarterly*, *86*(3), 257–295. DOI: 10.1177/23294906231176517

Cena, E., McParland, A., Toivo, W., Dalton, B., Mundy, M., O'Connor, P. A., Robertson, A. E., Swingler, M., Wilson, P., & Duncan, C. (2026). Studying with GenAI: Student views on the opportunities and risks of GenAI in higher education. *Education and Information Technologies*, *31*(11), 1–27. DOI: 10.1007/s10639-026-13923-3

Conti, D., Romeo, G., & Di Nuovo, S. F. (2026). Generative artificial intelligence in higher education: Opportunities, risks, and the future of critical thinking and human reasoning. *Artificial Intelligence in Higher Education*, 9-24. DOI: 10.1515/9783112206393-002

Danaher, J. (2018). Toward an ethics of AI assistants: An initial framework. *Philosophy & Technology*, *31*(4), 629–653. DOI: 10.1007/s13347-018-0317-3

Danry, V., Pataranutaporn, P., Groh, M., & Epstein, Z. (2025, April). Deceptive explanations by large language models lead people to change their beliefs about misinformation more often than honest explanations. In *Proceedings of the 2025 CHI conference on human factors in computing systems* (pp. 1-31). DOI: 10.1145/3706598.3713408

Danry, V., Pataranutaporn, P., Mao, Y., & Maes, P. (2023, April). Don't just tell me, ask me: Ai systems that intelligently frame explanations as questions improve human logical discernment accuracy over causal ai explanations. In *Proceedings of the 2023 CHI Conference on Human Factors in Computing Systems* (pp. 1-13). DOI: 10.1145/3544548.3580672

de Barros, E. C. (2024). Understanding the influence of digital technology on human cognitive functions: A narrative review. *IBRO Neuroscience Reports*, *17*, 415–422. DOI: 10.1016/j.ibneur.2024.11.006 PMID: 39624825

Farangi, M. R., Nejadghanbar, H., & Hu, G. (2025). Use of generative AI in research: Ethical considerations and emotional experiences. *Ethics & Behavior*, *35*(7), 527–543. DOI: 10.1080/10508422.2024.2420133

Fasoli, M., Cassinadri, G., & Ienca, M. (2025). The dark side of cognitive enhancement: A framework for the technologically induced cognitive diminishment. *Journal of Cognitive Enhancement: Towards the Integration of Theory and Practice*, *9*(3), 346–359. DOI: 10.1007/s41465-025-00331-7

Gerlich, M. (2025). AI tools in society: Impacts on cognitive offloading and the future of critical thinking. *Societies (Basel, Switzerland)*, *15*(1), 6. DOI: 10.3390/soc15010006

Giray, L. (2024). Negative effects of generative AI on researchers: Publishing addiction, Dunning-Kruger effect and skill erosion. *Journal of Applied Learning & Teaching*, *7*(2), 398–405. DOI: 10.37074/jalt.2024.7.2.38

Halkiopoulos, C., & Gkintoni, E. (2024). Leveraging AI in e-learning: Personalized learning and adaptive assessment through cognitive neuropsychology—A systematic analysis. *Electronics (Basel)*, *13*(18), 3762. DOI: 10.3390/electronics13183762

Hamzaj, Y. A. (2025). Generative AI acceptance among future educators: Personality and behavioral insights. *Education and Information Technologies*, *30*(16), 23165–23188. DOI: 10.1007/s10639-025-13678-3

Hyde, S. J., Busby, A., & Bonner, R. L. (2024). Tools or fools: Are we educating managers or creating tool-dependent robots? *Journal of Management Education*, *48*(4), 708–734. DOI: 10.1177/10525629241230357

Jabar, M., Chiong-Javier, E., & Pradubmook Sherer, P. (2025). Qualitative ethical technology assessment of artificial intelligence (AI) and the internet of things (IoT) among filipino Gen Z members: Implications for ethics education in higher learning institutions. *Asia Pacific Journal of Education*, *45*(4), 1344–1358. DOI: 10.1080/02188791.2024.2303048

Ji, Y., Zhong, M., Lyu, S., Li, T., Niu, S., & Zhan, Z. (2025). How does AI literacy affect individual innovative behavior: The mediating role of psychological need satisfaction, creative self-efficacy, and self-regulated learning. *Education and Information Technologies*, *30*(11), 16133–16162. DOI: 10.1007/s10639-025-13437-4

Karakus, T., Inal, Y., & Cagiltay, K. (2008). A descriptive study of Turkish high school students' game-playing characteristics and their considerations concerning the effects of games. *Computers in Human Behavior*, *24*(6), 2520–2529. DOI: 10.1016/j.chb.2008.03.011

Karamuk, E. (2025). The automation trap: Unpacking the consequences of overreliance on AI in education and its hidden costs. In *Pitfalls of AI integration in education: Skill obsolescence, misuse, and bias* (pp. 151–174). IGI Global Scientific Publishing., DOI: 10.4018/979-8-3373-0122-8.ch007

Kaya, B., & Çelebi, H. (2025). Uncertainty in the age of AI: Exploring the mediating effect of intolerance of uncertainty between mindsets and AI anxiety. *International Journal of Human-Computer Interaction*, •••, 1–11. DOI: 10.1080/10447318.2025.2499162

Kayar, M. Y., Körün, A. B., Topsakal, Ü. U., & Satıcı, S. A. (2025). From Fear of Innovation to AI Dependency: The Mediating Roles of Fear of Failure and Self-Doubt. *International Journal of Mental Health and Addiction*, •••, 1–18. DOI: 10.1007/s11469-025-01598-9

Kim, B. J., Kim, M. J., & Lee, J. (2025). The dark side of artificial intelligence adoption: Linking artificial intelligence adoption to employee depression via psychological safety and ethical leadership. *Humanities & Social Sciences Communications*, *12*(1), 1–14. DOI: 10.1057/s41599-025-05040-2

Lin, M. P. C., Liu, A. L., Poitras, E., Chang, M., & Chang, D. H. (2024). An exploratory study on the efficacy and inclusivity of AI technologies in diverse learning environments. *Sustainability (Basel)*, *16*(20), 8992. DOI: 10.3390/su16208992

Litvinova, M., Shtanko, O., Kalinichenko, I., Karpova, S., & Zorina, I. (2025, March). The Effect of Artificial Intelligence Using on Academic Achievement, Emotional Intelligence, and Critical Thinking of Students. In *World Conference on Information Systems and Technologies* (pp. 17-27). Cham: Springer Nature Switzerland. DOI: 10.1007/978-3-032-00701-8_2

Lupton, D., & Bailey-Charteris, B. (2026). 'You can't put the cat back in the bag once it's out': Australians' understandings, practices and imaginaries concerning generative AI. *Big Data & Society*, *13*(2), 20539517261442430. DOI: 10.1177/20539517261442430

Magomedova, A., & Fatima, G. (2025). Mental health and well-being in the modern era: A comprehensive review of challenges and interventions. *Cureus*, *17*(1). Advance online publication. DOI: 10.7759/cureus.77683 PMID: 39974249

Massimo, L., Kales, H. C., & Kolanowski, A. (2018). State of the science: Apathy as a model for investigating behavioral and psychological symptoms in dementia. *Journal of the American Geriatrics Society*, *66*(S1), S4–S12. DOI: 10.1111/jgs.15343 PMID: 29659001

Melanou, C., & Beege, M. (2026). Scaffolding Generative AI as a Tutor: A Quasi-Experimental Study of Learning Outcomes and Motivational, Cognitive and Metacognitive Processes. *Education Sciences*, *16*(4), 651. DOI: 10.3390/educsci16040651

Moluayonge, G. E. (2025). Cognitive Offload as a Mediator of AI usage and critical thinking development in Cameroonian Higher Education Learners. *Asian Journal of Education and Social Studies*, *51*(8), 467–476. DOI: 10.9734/ajess/2025/v51i82253

Mujtaba, B. (2024). Clarifying ethical dilemmas in sharpening students' artificial intelligence proficiency: Dispelling myths about using AI tools in higher education. *Business Ethics and Leadership*, *8*(2), 107–127. DOI: 10.61093/bel.8(2).107-127.2024

Oviatt, S. (2021, October). Technology as infrastructure for dehumanization: Three hundred million people with the same face. In *Proceedings of the 2021 international conference on multimodal interaction* (pp. 278-287). DOI: 10.1145/3462244.3482855

Pandoi, D. (2021, May). Analysis of Implication of Artificial Intelligence on Youth. In *Proceedings of International Conference on Communication and Artificial Intelligence: ICCAI 2020* (pp. 399-410). Singapore: Springer Singapore. DOI: 10.1007/978-981-33-6546-9_38

Panksepp, J., Knutson, B., & Burgdorf, J. (2002). The role of brain emotional systems in addictions: A neuro-evolutionary perspective and new 'self-report' animal model. *Addiction (Abingdon, England)*, *97*(4), 459–469. DOI: 10.1046/j.1360-0443.2002.00025.x PMID: 11964061

Parreño, E. B., Miranda, J. P. P., Manalese, R. P., Salenga-Mendez, J., Miller, J. C., & Payumo, A. S. (2026). How do College Students Express AI Fatigue? A Content and Keyword-in-Context Analysis of Academic AI Use. *International Journal of Learning. Teaching and Educational Research*, *25*(3), 680–697. DOI: 10.26803/ijlter.25.3.29

Pavone, G. (2025). Generative AI in the learning process: Threat or tool? Understanding the role of Self-Esteem and academic anxiety in shaping student motivations. *Journal of Marketing Education, 02734753251346857*. Advance online publication. DOI: 10.1177/02734753251346857

Pum, M. (2025). The Paradox of Augmentation and Erosion: Navigating Utility, Critical Agency, and TrustDeficit in AI Writing Tools among Cambodian English Major Undergraduates. *Interdisciplinary Educational Technology*, *1*(1), e105. DOI: 10.71176/interedtech/17573

Rani, A., Danry, V., Liang, P. P., Lippman, A., & Maes, P. (2026, April). Dialogues with AI Reduce Beliefs in Misinformation but Build No Lasting Discernment Skills. In *Proceedings of the 2026 CHI Conference on Human Factors in Computing Systems* (pp. 1-26). DOI: 10.1145/3772318.3790656

Rosas-Jiménez, C. A., Lokker, C., Ibhawoh, B., & Schwartz, L. (2026). Trust and overreliance on ChatGPT and its implications on critical thinking: An exploration in health policy. *Discover Public Health*, *23*(1), 200. DOI: 10.1186/s12982-026-01568-z

Rudroff, T. (2024). Revealing the complexity of fatigue: A review of the persistent challenges and promises of artificial intelligence. *Brain Sciences*, *14*(2), 186. DOI: 10.3390/brainsci14020186 PMID: 38391760

Sharma, D. (2024). Critical thinking and problem-solving in the age of ChatGPT: Experiential-bibliotherapy-blogging project. *Business and Professional Communication Quarterly*, *87*(4), 630–653. DOI: 10.1177/23294906241254780

Tabassum, A., Ghaznavi, I., Abd-Alrazaq, A., & Qadir, J. (2025). Exploring the application of AI and extended reality technologies in metaverse-driven mental health solutions: Scoping review. *Journal of Medical Internet Research*, *27*, e72400. DOI: 10.2196/72400 PMID: 40829151

Tian, J., & Zhang, R. (2025). Learners' AI dependence and critical thinking: The psychological mechanism of fatigue and the social buffering role of AI literacy. *Acta Psychologica*, *260*, 105725. DOI: 10.1016/j.actpsy.2025.105725 PMID: 41076923

Uyar, A., Karafil, B., & Karakuyu, A. (2026). Artificial intelligence dependency among educators: A scale development and validation study. *Education and Information Technologies*, *31*(8), 1–30. DOI: 10.1007/s10639-025-13862-5

Van Zyl, L. E. (2026). The AI-IARA framework: How to cultivate human agency before artificial intelligence optimizes it a (ny) way. *The Journal of Positive Psychology*, •••, 1–19. DOI: 10.1080/17439760.2026.2632939

Watermeyer, R., Lanclos, D., Phipps, L., Shapiro, H., Guizzo, D., & Knight, C. (2025). Academics' Weak (ening) resistance to generative AI: The cause and cost of prestige? *Postdigital Science and Education*, *7*(4), 1171–1191. DOI: 10.1007/s42438-024-00524-x

Wong, S. S. H., & Qiu, S. X. (2026). Think first, ChatGPT later: Guiding human–AI collaboration for learning gains in independent human creativity. *Educational Psychology Review*, *38*(1), 45. DOI: 10.1007/s10648-026-10118-7

Xu, J., Ismail, A., Ramayah, T., Liew, C. W. S., & Zheng, C. (2026). Scrolling to apathy? The relationship between short video addiction and the "lying flat" tendency among Chinese university students. *Frontiers in Psychology*, *17*, 1685559. DOI: 10.3389/fpsyg.2026.1685559 PMID: 41835895

Yavich, R. (2025). Will the use of AI undermine students independent thinking? *Education Sciences*, *15*(6), 669. DOI: 10.3390/educsci15060669

Yun, J. H., Lee, E. J., & Kim, D. H. (2021). Behavioral and neural evidence on consumer responses to human doctors and medical artificial intelligence. *Psychology and Marketing*, *38*(4), 610–625. DOI: 10.1002/mar.21445

Yurt, E., & Kuşci, I. (2026). Factors influencing critical thinking during AI use among university students: The mediating effects of epistemic laziness and metacognitive weakness. *Current Psychology (New Brunswick, N.J.)*, *45*(1), 67. DOI: 10.1007/s12144-025-08800-0

Zahra, S. T., Bibi, E., & Younus, Z. (2025). Artificial Intelligence (AI) and Human Mind: Struggles and Strengths in the Education Sector. In *Artificial Intelligence and Human Agency in Education: Volume One: The Nexus Between AI and Human Agency in Educational Contexts* (pp. 265-289). Singapore: Springer Nature Singapore. DOI: 10.1007/978-981-96-7937-9_12

Zaki, M., & Naz, M. A. (2025). The Digital Dilemma: Addiction of Internet, its Impact on Emotional Intelligence and Fear of Missing Out in Youth. *UCP Journal of Humanities & Social Sciences*, *3*(2), 81–96. DOI: 10.24312/ucp-jhss.03.02.493

Zare, J., Ranjbaran Madiseh, F., & Derakhshan, A. (2025). Generative AI and English essay writing: Exploring the role of ChatGPT in enhancing learners' task engagement. *Applied Linguistics*, **•••**, amaf045. Advance online publication. DOI: 10.1093/applin/amaf045

Zhai, C., Wibowo, S., & Li, L. D. (2024). The effects of over-reliance on AI dialogue systems on students' cognitive abilities: a systematic review. *Smart learning environments, 11*(1), 28. DOI: 10.1186/s40561-024-00316-7

Zhang, H., Xie, J., Wu, C., Cai, J., Kim, C., & Carroll, J. M. (2024, October). The future of learning: Large language models through the lens of students. In *Proceedings of the 25th Annual Conference on Information Technology Education* (pp. 12-18). DOI: 10.1145/3686852.3687069

Zhou, X., Liu, G., & Chiu, T. K. (2026). A five-step AI-information problem solving (AI-IPS) model for critical, ethical, and responsible usage. *Interactive Learning Environments*, **•••**, 1–20. DOI: 10.1080/10494820.2026.2614080

Zhou, X., Zhang, J., & Chan, C. (2024). Unveiling students' experiences and perceptions of artificial intelligence usage in higher education. *Journal of University Teaching & Learning Practice*, *21*(6), 126–145. DOI: 10.53761/xzjprb23

Chapter 8
Cognitive Offloading to Cognitive Atrophy: A Neuropsychological Framework of AI Dependency, Automation Bias, and the Erosion of Critical Thinking

Ayesha Asghar Gill
University of Agriculture Faisalabad, Pakistan

Fouzia Janjua
International Islamic University, Islamabad, Pakistan

Mehwish Zahoor
School of Science and Technology (FUSST), Foundation University Islamabad, Pakistan

Adnan Afzal
http://orcid.org/0009-0001-4359-5695
Government College University Faisalabad, Pakistan

ABSTRACT

Due to the swift growth of artificial intelligence, the cognitive practices have been altered by mass cognitive offloading, casting doubts on the neuropsychological implications of this process in the long term. In this chapter, a framework on AI dependency, automation bias, and their possible involvement in the decline in critical thinking is built. It builds on literature in the field of memory, attention, executive function, and neural plasticity to discuss the potential of repeated deflection of

DOI: 10.4018/979-8-3373-9484-8.ch008

analytical processes to redefine patterns of cognitive engagement. Although AI can make things (more) efficient and accessible, overuse of AI could lower metacognitive vigilance and effortful thought. There are ethical, educative, and social implications that are discussed, as well as the mitigation measures that are advocating balanced human-AI cooperation in order to maintain autonomy and cognitive resilience.

INTRODUCTION: COGNITIVE OFFLOADING IN THE AGE OF ARTIFICIAL INTELLIGENCE

The fast densification of the concept of artificial intelligence (AI) in the daily reality has fundamentally changed the way people perceive information, make decisions, and find solutions. Technology has taken over cognitive work in search engines and navigation systems, as well as in generative AI tools and automated decision-support systems, and is taking over more and more of the work that humans used to do (Yun et al., 2025). This change has increased a mental phenomenon called cognitive offloading the act of offloading external tools or systems in the name of lessening internal cognitive load. Although cognitive offloading is not a new phenomenon, the size, pace, and complexity of AI-driven systems have taken it to a new level where its neuropsychological impact is crucial and significant in the long term. Cognitive offloading has been used adaptively in the past. Privation of the mind Writing, calculators, maps and digital reminders are external memory aids that have long been used by humans in order to conserve mental resources (Călinescu, 2024). Offloading may increase effectiveness, decrease cognitive load and enable individuals to divert their attention to higher-order tasks. As an illustration, GPS navigation will simplify memorizing routes, as a driver will be able to pay attention to the situation on the road. Likewise, digital calendars and search engines offer fast access to the information stored, reducing the working memory. In this respect, offloading is a logical solution that is in line with cognitive economy the idea that the brain uses less energy by processing less information. Nevertheless, the rise of AI systems that can produce text, detect diseases, and suggest financial choices and even write scholarly analyses has opened offloading to other areas such as critical thinking and executive functions. The line between assistance and dependency starts to fade when people engage in more and more complex analytical processes with the help of AI tools (Davenport, 2018). Such dependency can distort the attention pattern, approach to problem solving and cognitive involvement. It is not the issue of convenience but the erosion of skills, which can be acquired through some mental exercise that can be eroded over time. The brain works on a plasticity and use- dependence principle neuropsychologically. Neural networks become strong with repeated use and weak when not used. Similar to how muscle tissue decays when density is stopped, cogitative connections sound runs a risk of deterioration when they are regularly avoided. The AIs based on automation bring about a new situation where the executive functions, which include planning and reasoning, hypothesis testing, and error monitoring, can be not only partly offloaded to algorithms. In the long run, this recurring delegation may have an impact on neural pathways related to the process of analytical thinking and decision-making (Hodgkinson & Sadler-Smith, 2018). Automation bias is also a concept that makes this dynamic more complex. Automation bias is the force to trust automated systems, to trust the outputs of the algorithms without much evaluation. When people consider AI systems as being very accurate or authoritative, they can minimize the independent verification efforts. The metacognitive activities can be reduced by this change of behaviour, which involves observing and assessing the thinking in a person. Weaker metacognitive vigilance should also play a role in shallow processing of information and less analytic scrutiny which may lead to higher personal competence and the quality of decisions made in teams (Kleitman et al., 2019).

Figure 1. Introduction of cognitive offloading

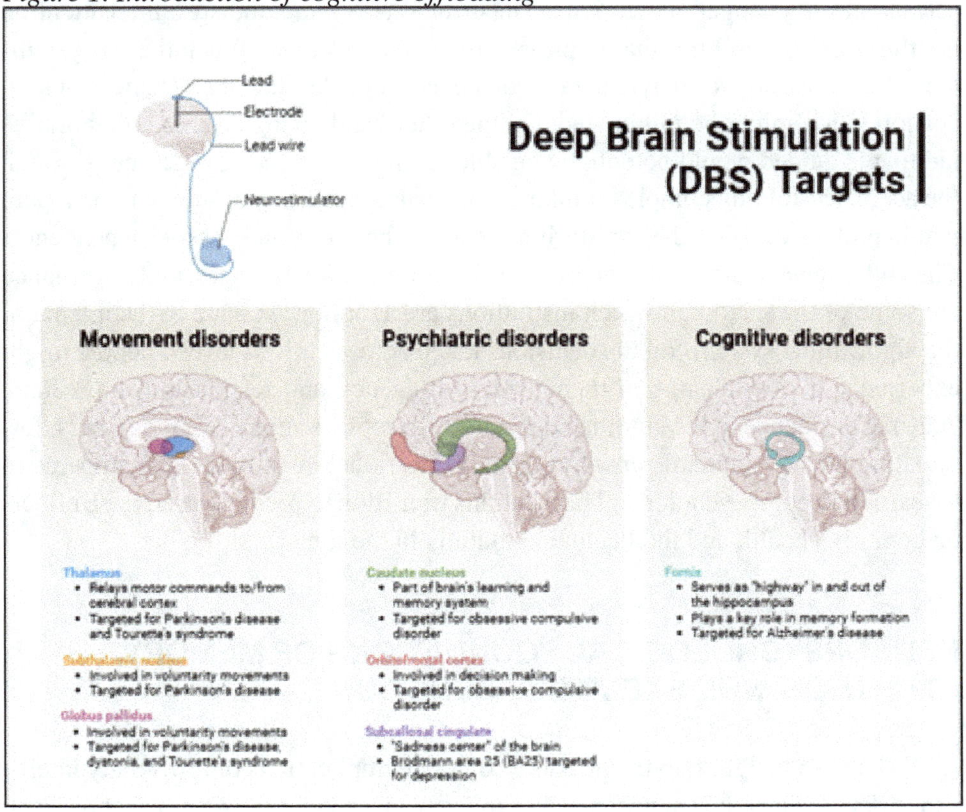

Notably, cognitive offloading with the assistance of AI does not necessarily involve adverse consequences. AI is used to improve productivity, enable access and minimize human error in a variety of contexts. In persons with mental disabilities or large job-related requirements, smart support might be a compensatory skill that enhances performance (Suresh & Dyaram, 2023). Besides, AI can release cognitive resources to creative and strategic thinking by

automating routine tasks. The main question is not then the existence of AI but rather the nature of interactions that will dictate whether technology will complement or replace human cognition. This interaction is increased by the modern information environment. The processing of constantly digitized content and fast feedback, as well as the generation of answers immediately, can stimulate dependencies and discourage critical thinking. The incentive to consider in more detail might be reduced when retrieval of information becomes easy. The phenomenon overlaps with the attentional fragmentation and multitasking behaviours that are more common in digital settings, which additionally affects how cognition is engaged (Lindström, 2020). In the long run, these habits may change the way people learn, solve problems as well as construct knowledge. In the developmental aspect, the implication can be especially serious in the younger generations. The critical reasoning and sustained attention are the cognitive abilities that improve with active practices. When the AI systems periodically automate analytical tasks on behalf of the learner, then chances of skill consolidation might be minimized. On the other hand, using AI as a collaborative aid that is guided would potentially be able to improve learning outcomes through the act of scaffolding complex thinking. The neuropsychological development path would probably rely on the equilibrium between the active and passive dependence. The wider social factor is also involved. Education, health, finances, and governance are some of the sectors in which institutions are adopting AI. Due to the impact of the algorithmic systems on the decisions taken across various levels, people might experience a slow change in their perceived agency and responsibility (Peeters, 2020). Confidence in the automated product can replace subjective judgments, formulating mental standards in working and educational institutions. It is imperative to learn the neuropsychological basis of this transition to predict the adverse effects on cognitive health and intellectual autonomy in the long term.

NEUROPSYCHOLOGICAL FOUNDATIONS OF MEMORY, ATTENTION, AND EXECUTIVE FUNCTION

To have an insight into the possible cognitive implications of artificially intelligence dependency, it is significant to explicitly investigate the neuropsychological mechanisms that underlie the memory, attention, and executive functions. These interrelated areas constitute the basic design of human thinking, which allows individuals to process the information, control behaviour, resolve problems, and perform reflective thinking (Ghajargar et al., 2018). The neural activation patterns related to these cognitive systems can change when the AI systems take the responsibility of the activities that are mediated by these systems. As such, it is important to examine their biological and functional underpinnings in order to assess the

implications of long-term cognitive offloading. Memory is not a singular entity but a dynamic system that consists of a number of subsystems. The prefrontal and parietal cortical areas are mostly related to the working memory, which temporarily stores and processes information required to make a decision and/or a reason. Medial temporal lobe structures like the hippocampus are involved in long term memory storage of experiences and knowledge that can be recalled later (Heyworth & Squire, 2019). Recurrent thought reinforces synaptic links of these networks with long-term potentiation, which is a motivating element of learning and neuroplasticity.

Figure 2. Neuropsychological foundations of memory, attention, and executive function

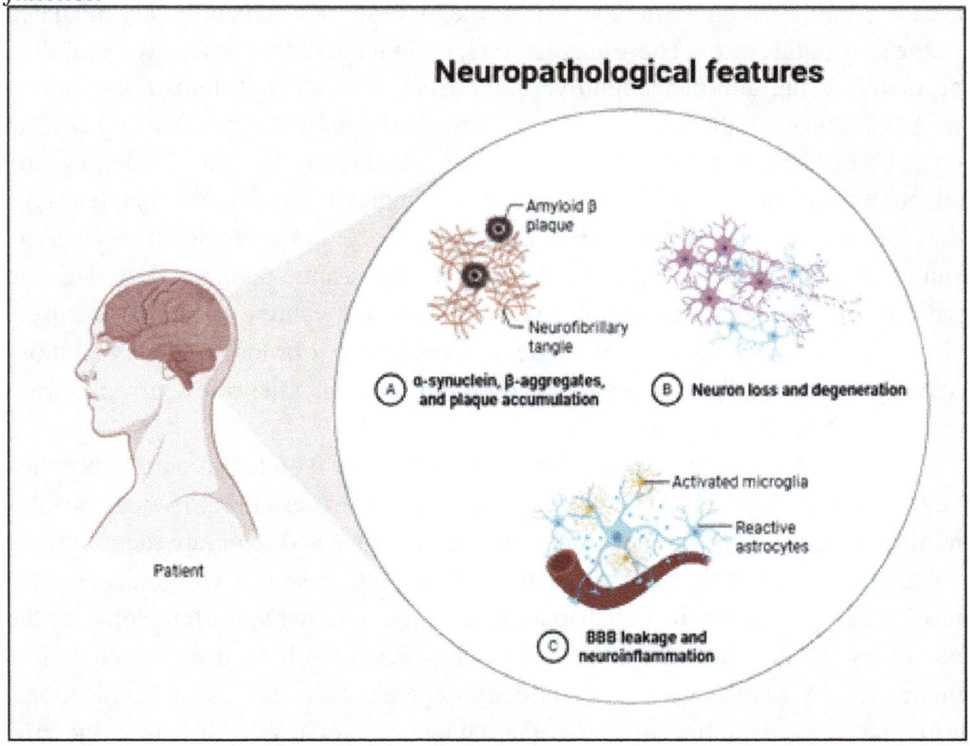

As humans trust AI systems to either store, recall, or synthesize information, they can decrease the number of internal rehearsal and encoding of information which consolidate memory. In the long run, reduced activation of such neural circuits may change memory-related performance and retrieval plans. The other basic cognitive process, attention, controls the distribution of scarce cognitive resources. It helps people to select between relevant and irrelevant stimulus and be focused on goal-oriented activity (Theeuwes, 2019). Attention

related neural systems comprise frontoparietal networks and subcortical module systems that control alertness and cognitive control. The long attention involves constant working of the executive systems to inhibit distraction and remain focused on the task. In digital spaces where the algorithmically edited content and high-speed feedback are the main processes, attentional processes can be discontinuous. Needs anticipation AI systems that can offer answers in real time, may reduce the need to engage in prolonged cognitive processes, which can result in impaired sustained attentional endurance (Shalaby, 2024). On the one hand such patterns might enhance the short-term efficiency but on the other hand the long-term ability to concentrate deeply could reduce in the case that they become habitual. The executive functions are the controlled cognitive functions of the highest level and are highly mediated by the prefrontal cortex. These are planning, inhibitory control, cognitive flexibility, problem-solving and metacognitive monitoring. Executive systems allow one to judge evidence, challenge assumptions, and emotionally and impulsively control oneself (Friedman & Robbins, 2022). They are the key in critical thinking and adaptive decision-making. The repetition of complex reasoning tasks supports the development of executive networks due to plasticity that depends on experience. But once AI solutions are generated, or draft analyses are automated, or decision paths have been automated, people may not use these executive systems as intensely (Jarrahi, 2018). The neuropsychological theory of use it or lose it states that those neural pathways that are not frequently used can get weaker than the neural pathways that are frequently activated.

The opportunity and vulnerability in the process of AI integration is neuroplasticity, or the ability of the brain to reorganize with the experience. Plasticity enables human beings to adjust to new tools and technologies and integrate them into the cognitive routines (Osiurak et al., 2018). Meanwhile, adaptive reorganization can result in cognitive labour redistribution, external systems substitute some of the processes. As an illustration, spatial memory networks have been linked to less interaction by people who are habitually dependent on navigation applications. Although this adaptation increases the navigational efficiency, it can reduce the use of hippocampal based spatial mapping strategies. The same trends may appear in analytical thinking in case AI systems are regularly used to execute a task that presupposes hypothesis creation and analysis. The cognitive offloading balance is important and is achieved through metacognition, which is the capability to self-monitor and control thinking (De Bruin et al., 2020). Proper metacognitive awareness enables one to choose when it is necessary to seek external support and when it is necessary to activate internal cognitive capabilities. Metacognition, which is neuropsychologically organized, constitutes coordinated activity

between prefrontal cortical areas and error detection and self-evaluation networks. Automation bias, which is submissive to receive the results of an algorithm, can lower the metacognitive vigilance. When people grow more confident in the fact that AI-generated answers are correct, the neural actions that are linked to the doubt, verification, and reflective judgment can become activated rather infrequently. Notably, these neuropsychological systems are highly interrelated. The working memory assists in executive control, attention shapes memory encoding and the executive processes control attentional focus (Angelopoulou & Drigas, 2021). The alteration in one sphere can cause the ripple effect on others. An example would be that low sustained attention could lead to poor deep encoding of information into long-term memory, and low executive engagement could lead to low skills of critical evaluation. Long- term cognitive habits might be formed by the aggregate influence of minor changes in the pattern of neural organization. This framework is complicated further by the developmental factors. The executive networks and prefrontal cortical systems are still developing during the adolescent stage and the early adulthood. Experience in the environment that systematically promotes cognitive outsourcing can change developmental patterns (Jammulamadaka, 2021). On the other hand, the conscious engagement with AI that involves active interpretation, assessment, and synthesis can also trigger a higher-order thinking process and not reduce it.

COGNITIVE OFFLOADING: MECHANISMS, BENEFITS, AND LIMITS

Cognitive offloading is a strategy of using external tools, technologies or environmental stimuli to decrease inner cognitive requirements. It is an instinctive and adaptive part of human thinking, which is based on the propensity of the brain to save energy and make the most out of it (Déli & Kisvárday, 2020). Since written communication and calculators, human beings have continuously expanded their mental capabilities with the help of the external medium. Nevertheless, cognitive offloading has been expanded in an ever-expanding context of AI technologies that include not only the field of memory storage but also reasoning, analysis, and decision-making. It is important to understand the mechanisms, advantages, and constraints of cognitive offloading to evaluate its contribution to the decline in cognitive abilities or improvement of cognition. Cognitive offloading can work mechanistically using the distributed cognition. Instead of it all being done in-house, cognitive work is distributed by the use of external systems. This redistribution will lessen the burden on the working memory enabling people to handle complex tasks more effectively (Sepp et al., 2019). To illustrate, when writing notes in the lecture hall, the short-term memory is offloaded, whereas the digital notifications allow one to avoid the necessity of rehearsing the next action every minute or so. Offloading can be done in AI-mediated procedures in which tasks, including summarization, pattern recognition, data analysis, or content generation, can be assigned to intelligent systems. Cognitive resources are effectively redistributed in the brain as they have been separated by computation and monitoring and interpretation.

Table 1. Mechanisms, benefits, and limits of cognitive offloading

Dimension	Description	Mechanism/Process	Benefits	Potential Limitations
1. Distributed Cognition	Cognitive tasks are shared between internal mental processes and external tools.	Redistribution of cognitive load across brain and environment.	Reduces working memory burden; improves task management.	Over-reliance may weaken internal processing skills.
2. Working Memory Relief	External aids reduce short term memory demands.	Note-taking, reminders, AI summaries decrease rehearsal needs.	Enables focus on complex reasoning and creativity.	May reduce active encoding and memory consolidation.
3. Efficiency Enhancement	Automation of repetitive or complex tasks.	AI-assisted data analysis, pattern recognition, decision-support systems.	Saves time; increases productivity and accuracy.	Risk of automation bias and reduced independent problem- solving.
4. Educational Scaffolding	Structured external support in learning.	Digital feedback systems, AI tutoring, guided prompts.	Supports comprehension; enhances structured learning.	Superficial learning if learners avoid cognitive effort.
5. Accessibility & Compensation	Support for individuals with cognitive or attentional challenges.	Assistive technologies, reminders, adaptive AI tools.	Promotes independence; reduces cognitive stress.	Long-term dependency may limit skill development.
6. Automation Bias	Excessive trust in automated systems.	Passive acceptance of AI-generated outputs.	Faster decision-making in routine contexts.	Reduced critical evaluation; risk of unnoticed errors.
7. Skill Atrophy & Neuroplasticity	Decline in underused cognitive functions.	Reduced engagement in spatial, analytical, or reasoning tasks.	Short-term cognitive relief.	Weakening of neural pathways due to lack of practice.

Improved efficiency is one of the significant effects of cognitive offloading (Grinschgl et al., 2021). Through outsourcing of routine or repetitive activities, the individuals will be able to save time in mental activity to engage in higher order thinking. This would correlate with the cognitive load theory which holds that working memory is limited. In cases where extraneous cognitive factors are reduced, the extra resources can be used to engage in more complicated processes or creative activities. In the workplace, AI decision-support solutions have the potential to minimize diagnostic error, improve efficiency, and provide quick access to large amounts of data, which otherwise would be beyond human processing capabilities. Digital tools can be used to scaffold learning in educational processes to manage information and give structured feedback (Grévisse et al., 2019). Accessibility is also increased through cognitive offloading. In the case of people with impaired cognitive ability or memory loss, or when the person is under high stress conditions, external aids are a component of compensatory modifications, which ensure functional independence. Technologies using AI as an assistant can be used on people who have attention challenges, language disorders, or executive dysfunction (Barua et al., 2022). In this regard, offloading could be empowering as opposed to destructive. It enables human beings to expand their cognitive ability beyond the limits of biology, actually enhancing intelligence as opposed to eliminating it. The boundaries of cognitive offloading are however seen when external dependence diminishes internal interaction. Although offloading helps to reduce cognitive load in the short-term, recurrent delegation of difficult tasks can potentially change processes of learning. Consolidation of memory involves active encoding and retrieving. Provided that information is stored regularly outside and rarely accessed inwardly, the neuralization of long-term memory may deteriorate. Equally, when AI systems produce solutions or arguments of analysis on a regular basis, people will not be able to use the mental activity involved in critical thinking as often. Educational psychology studies reveal that the struggle in learning enhances learning (Hilalludin et al., 2025). Tasks that need active problem- solving and reflection are desirable difficulties, which contribute to the long-term knowledge acquisition. Excessive dependence on the results of AI- generated processes can potentially inhibit such processual activities, with superficial comprehension as a result. As an example, students who write essays or solve analytical problems without having to think independently can avoid the cognitive effort that leads to intellectual development when they apply AI to do such tasks. The end product might be competent but the internal cognitive development might be reduced (Walkerdine, 2025).

One very important cognitive offloading limit is automation bias. People can be too confident in the automated systems and overlook any mistakes or anomalies. Users can assume a passive position of acceptance instead of an active one in the evaluation of the responses produced by AI (Gursoy et al., 2019). This change decreases self-cognitive monitoring and critical examination. In the long term, psychological dependence can be formed through habitual dependence on the output of the algorithms, which affects the loss of trust in personal thinking. The cognitive system is moved towards the process of external verification authority as opposed to self-evaluation. The other constraint is related to lost skills due to underutilization. Neuropsychological studies have proven the postulate that cognitive functions improve as they are practiced and deteriorate when neglected (Caramazza, 2018). Similar to the fact that physical immobility causes weakening of muscles, cognitive immobility can decrease the efficiency of particular neural networks. In case neural pathways are constantly stimulated when an individual is required to solve a problem in spatial navigation, calculate some mathematical equations, or perform an argumentative analysis, the neural pathways may be less activated in that case as well. The brain may be plastic, but if it is not used on a regular basis, there might be a tendency to redirect cognitive habits towards dependence on the outside (Ramírez-Vizcaya & Froese, 2019). Notably, cognitive offloading is not a bad thing per se. The use of it varies on its impact based on the time and mode of use. Offloading can be a strategy and not a replacement of thinking when people have a proactive supervision, reflective experience, and practice (i.e., practice) periodically as well as independently. The issues are associated with the automatic and unquestioned offloading that involves disregarding internal cognitive effort completely. The balance between augmentation and substitution is what will determine the role played by AI as a cognitive partner or a crutch (French & Shim, 2025). The context also influences results. Intense scenario decision making situations, like medicine or aviation, can benefit human error and safety through AI support. Nevertheless, excessive dependence without critical scrutiny will cause disastrous errors in case of systems failure. Governed integration in learning environments which allows students to criticize and refine artificially intelligent generated work can actually enhance critical thinking and not diminish it. Formal models of interaction, therefore, play a vital role in the counter of possible disadvantages.

AI DEPENDENCY AND AUTOMATION BIAS IN DECISION-MAKING

The introduction of artificial intelligence to the decision-making setting has altered how people perceive information, consider options, and choose the courses of action (Bader & Kaiser, 2019). AI systems are increasingly used as tools in making decisions starting with clinical diagnostics through financial forecasting, academic writing, and general solving of problems. As much as these systems increase efficiency and accuracy in most situations, their increased use has raised the issue of AI dependency and automation bias. These trends are indicative not only of technological dependence but also indicative of cognitive and psychological paradigm shifts that are potentially likely to change the process of independent judgment and critical evaluation. AI dependency is the situation that arises when people become used to using algorithmic systems in accomplishing analytical or assistive work that they can do without assistance (Aghaziarati & Rahimi, 2025). Such dependence might not arise at first on a pragmatic level, but AI systems can process large amounts of data much faster and see patterns that humans would otherwise not see due to their limited perceptual abilities. In the long term though, convenience and perceived reliability may lead to the establishment of habitual delegation of mental tasks. As the process of decision-making turns out to be systematically mediated by AI output, the user can eventually become less active in terms of evaluating evidence, testing hypotheses and generating alternative scenario. The human role is no longer the decision maker, he is an observer who endorses a decision (Mosier & Skitka, 2018).

Figure 3. AI dependency and automation bias in decision-making

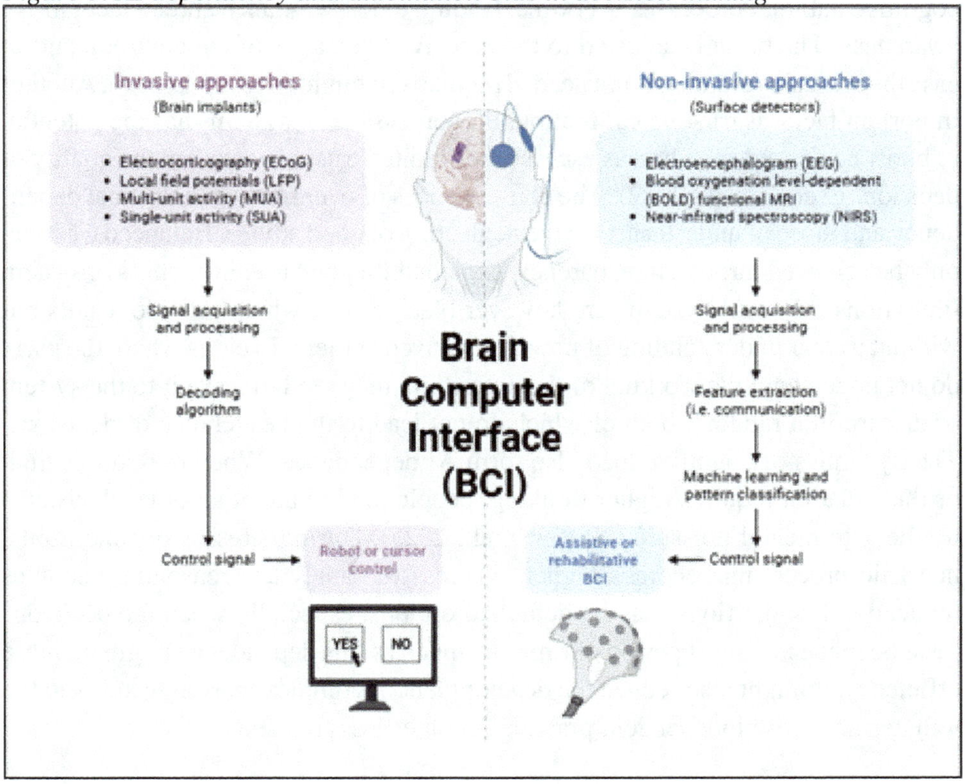

The main role in strengthening this dependency is played by automation bias. Automation bias Automation bias is the propensity to give preference to the suggestions provided by automated systems and dismiss information that contradicts these suggestions (Ajunwa, 2019). It takes place in 2 main ways; errors of commission, where members adhere to wrong advice on the basis of automation, and errors of omissions, where members do not take action in response to a problem because the automated system does not provide a warning of the problem. In both the scenarios, too much confidence in AI outputs decreases independent verification. This bias is enhanced whereby systems are viewed objective, data-driven or better than human reasoning.

Automation bias can be neuropsychologically manifested by less executive control and error- monitoring network activation (Lenzoni et al., 2022). The skill in making sound choices is normally related to the prefrontal cortex work that provides evidence analysis, risk assessment, and the ability to suppress impulsive actions. These executive processes can be less vigorous when people blindly believe the outputs of AI. The presence of patterns of passive acceptance repetition can affect cognitive habitual processes over time, leading to less vigilance and metacognitive awareness. The brain is adjusted to the perceived demands of the environment; in case the critical evaluation is not needed regularly, it might be less practised. Another important factor is trusting calibration. Proper trust in AI systems has the potential to boost performance, whereas excessive or limited trust may worsen the quality of decisions (Zerilli et al., 2022). The consequences of over trust are uncritical dependency and those of underthrust are the neglecting of good advice. Balanced trust can only be achieved through transparency, explainability and user awareness of system limitations. Most AI systems are however black boxes, which provide results but without a clear understanding of how they arrived at them. In cases where the users do not understand the working of the algorithm, they tend to leave it to the system or discard it at random, both of which do not lead to the best choice of decisions. The dynamics of cognitive load also form AI dependence. When pressure is high or the situation requires higher thinking, people tend to adopt automated systems to alleviate mental pressure (Naseer et al., 2025). During stresses or time limits, heuristic processing becomes higher, whereas the analytical reasoning becomes reduced. AI suggestions may be defaulted options, especially when the decisions must be made in a short period of time. As much as this dependence might increase efficiency, it might also reduce the development of complex reasoning skills in the long term, in case independent practice becomes less frequent.

NEURAL PLASTICITY, COGNITIVE ATROPHY, AND USE-DEPENDENT BRAIN CHANGES

The brain is human and it is adaptive in nature. Learning, the formation of memories and development of skills are all based on neural plasticity, the ability of the brain to restructure and restructure itself in response to the experience. All intellectual functions, such as mathematical problem-solving, writing arguments, train particular circuits in the brain by repetition (Parwati & Suharta, 2024). On the other hand, those circuits which are not utilized much can become weak with time. This principle of change with dependence on usage is the basis of issues associated with cognitive atrophy in the conditions of the long-term AI dependency. With the increase of the number of tasks that neural activation is used to solve, which traditionally involve maintaining and concentrating cognitive energy, the level and extent of neural activation can change when it comes to higher-order thinking. Neuroplasticity functions by action in the form of strengthening of the synaptic bonds, bifurcation of the dendrites and long term potentiation (Joshua, 2022). Executive function networks of prefrontal cortex are more efficient when people repeatedly involve themselves in analytical thinking or solving complex problems. On the same note, hippocampal memory consolidation networks are reinforced during active encoding as well as retrieval practice. These changes in the brain are neural adaptations, which are responsive to the needs of the environment. Nevertheless, when such demands are modified, i.e., external systems are regularly involved into doing some cognitive tasks, the related neural pathways will be under stimulated.

Table 2. Neural plasticity, cognitive atrophy, and use-dependent brain changes

Dimension	Core Concept	Neural Mechanism	Impact of AI- Mediated Offloading	Long-Term Implication
1. Neural Plasticity	Brain adapts structurally and functionally to experience	Synaptic strengthening, dendritic growth, long-term potentiation	AI may shift which circuits are repeatedly activated	Redistribution of cognitive resources rather than fixed decline
2. Executive Function Activation	Higher-order thinking depends on prefrontal cortex engagement	Repeated analytical reasoning strengthens executive networks	Delegating reasoning to AI may reduce active executive engagement	Possible reduction in analytical endurance if underused
3. Memory Consolidation	Long-term memory forms through active	Hippocampal activation during encoding and recall	External storage reduces retrieval practice	Weaker internal consolidation if rehearsal is minimized

continued on following page

Table 2. Continued

Dimension	Core Concept	Neural Mechanism	Impact of AI- Mediated Offloading	Long-Term Implication
	encoding and retrieval			
4. Use-Dependent Neural Change	"Use it or lose it" principle of brain organization	Strengthening with repetition; weakening with underuse	Routine cognitive outsourcing decreases stimulation of certain circuits	Reduced neural efficiency in underutilized pathways
5. Cognitive Atrophy (Functional)	Efficiency decline due to underuse, not permanent damage	Decreased synaptic activation and connectivity	Persistent substitution of internal reasoning by AI tools	Reversible decline if independent practice resumes
6. Spatial Navigation Example	Navigation engages hippocampal spatial mapping systems	Mental map formation and spatial memory circuits	GPS dependence reduces active spatial processing	Altered hippocampal engagement patterns over time
7. Adaptive Reallocation	Brain reallocates effort toward new skill domains	Plastic reorganization of functional networks	Increased focus on evaluation, synthesis, or AI management skills	Emergence of new cognitive strengths alongside potential weaknesses

Cognitive atrophy does not mean damage that is permanent or irreversible but instead it is reduced efficiency that is caused by underuse (Coli ă et al., 2022). Similar to the case of muscular deconditioning when no exercise is performed, neural networks can also weaken, or lose interconnections when avoidably ignored constantly. Indicatively, experiments that have investigated navigation behaviours have revealed that the use of GPS systems is correlated with the partial proliferation of spatial memory circuits. The patterns of hippocampal activation are not similar to that during active navigation when people no longer form mental maps. Even though these changes might not necessarily cause an instant disruption of functionality, they demonstrate the effect of technology-mediated behaviour on neural patterns of engagement. The same can be the case with executive functions in the context of AI-powered cognitive offloading. The prefrontal cortex is important in such tasks as critical evaluation, generation of hypothesis, argument reasoning, and detecting errors (Sarafyazd & Jazayeri, 2019). Users are likely to become passive observers rather than active problem solvers when AI tools produce analyses, create literature synthesis or suggest decisions. When it becomes a habit the degree of executive activation will decrease. In the long term, this low interaction may result in a change in the neural efficiency in circuits that aid in long-term reasoning.

CRITICAL THINKING UNDER ALGORITHMIC INFLUENCE

Critical thinking is considered to be one of the most complicated and important human thinking capacities (Raj et al., 2022). It entails skills to reason out facts, assess facts, find out discrepancies, challenge assumptions, and make rational conclusions. In its essence, critical thinking relies on executive functioning, metacognitive awareness and reflective judgment. The mechanisms of critical thinking are changing radically, and it may be assumed that in the world where an algorithmic system and AI-generated outputs are progressively becoming dominant, the processes of critical thinking are being redefined. The power of AI does not merely create a change in the access to information; it transforms the way people perceive, evaluate and form knowledge (Amershi, 2020). The algorithm systems filter contents, give preference to search results, create summaries, and suggest conclusions. This informational environment is structured by the algorithmic mediation, prior to the process where people are actually involved in conscious evaluation. Consequently, ecumenicity might filter exposure to other views through cloudy processes of computation. With pre-selection, summarization, or synthesis of information by AI systems, the system can give the user condensed data instead of raw data. Although it makes it more efficient, it limits the possibilities to analyse the material independently, to compare the materials, and interpret it in a nuanced way. Epistemic effort, or readiness to struggle cognitively to comprehend complex matters is one of the hallmarks of critical thinking (Muis et al., 2021). Prefrontal networks that can be activated by effortful reasoning are cognitive control, bias inhibition, and evidence evaluation. Nonetheless, the motivation to engage in an in-depth manner could be eroded when AI systems are able to give refined, logical answers within seconds. Rather than building arguments based on underlying principles, people can move on to the editing or approving of AI-written drafts. This cognitive transformation occurs between generative reasoning and evaluative selection, and this can be less protracted executive activation (Zamani et al., 2023). Metacognition is also in the heart of critical thinking in an algorithmically influenced environment. Strong thinkers keep track of the trustworthiness of the sources, doubt, and evaluate their knowledge. This process of monitoring can however be undermined by automation bias. Individuals, in the event that AI systems are seen as authoritative or possess a high degree of accuracy, might decrease cynicism and do not analyse output critically. This may result in superficial conviction of conclusions without personal verification. In the long run, the normative view of evidence-based standards may be re-established, as habituality to the output of algorithms may hold external approval as superior to internal argumentation. Confirmation bias is also overlapped with the influence of algorithms. Numerous AI applications customize the output depending on the history or preferences of the user or previous engagement (Sodiya et al., 2024).

Figure 4. Critical thinking under algorithmic influence

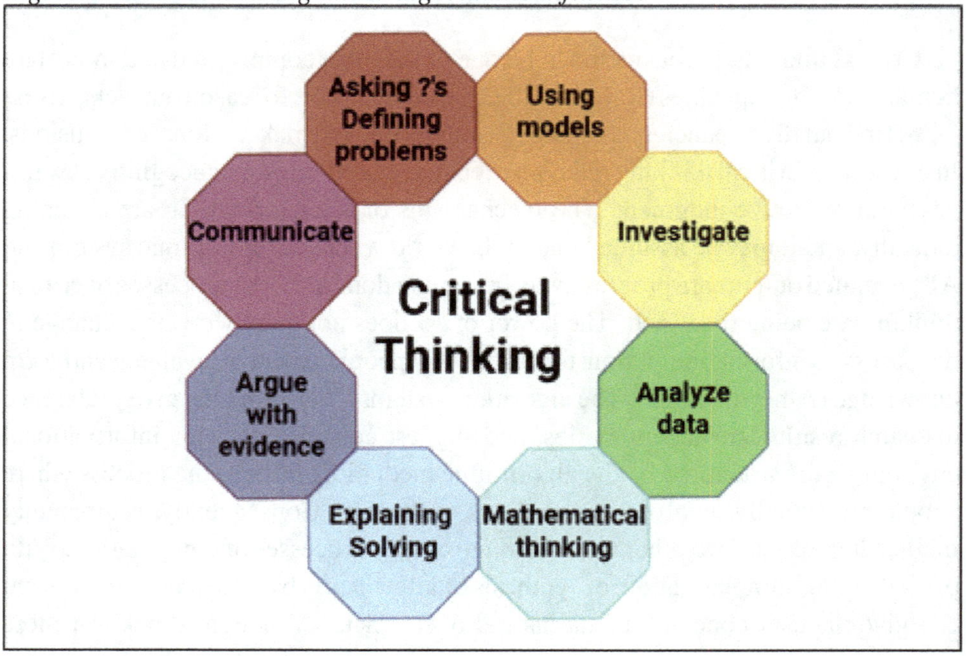

PSYCHOLOGICAL, EDUCATIONAL, AND SOCIETAL IMPLICATIONS

As the world becomes more and more connected with artificial intelligence, it is not just an individual neural process, but also affects the working of the mind, of the educational communication, and even the functions of the society at large. Cognitive offloading and automation bias mediated by AI not only change the way people think, but also competence, agency, and responsibility perceptions (Yepiskoposyan). These changes have implication on motivation, identity formation, learning conditions, work force relations and group epistemic criteria. On the psychological level, AI dependence might affect the self-efficacy- the perception of personal ability to perform their mental tasks without outside help. The repeated use of AI systems to analyse, write, make decisions, or solve problems can slowly infiltrate the minds of individuals that they can think complexly and hence should be left to do so. This may cause a subliminal degradation of cognitive confidence, especially in areas where people are incurring reflexive reliability to automatic productions. The lack of self-efficacy can reduce the intrinsic motivation to do difficult intellectual activities and strengthen the dependence on technological support

(Yan, 2022). In the long run, this process may promote attained dependence, where people disregard their reasoning capabilities. The other psychological dimension is the cognitive effort avoidance. It is instinctive to human beings to follow strategies with the least mental stress. The immediate polished solutions provided by AI systems do not require the long-term focus. Although this gives effectiveness, it can also influence the habits of low-engagement. It needs patience to ambiguity and cognitive dissonance to sustain attention and engage in analytical thought (Ding et al., 2024). When people become more and more inclined to use AI-produced shortcuts instead of the exhausting process of thinking, they can lose cognitive capability in solving more complex tasks. This there is no cognitive capacity loss but might decrease the habitual action of challenging cognitive activity. The implications are especially important in the educational environment. Active processing, reflection, and problem-solving are the core elements of learning. AI tools can also improve learning by offering personalized feedback, dynamic learning opportunities and access to enormous sources of information. Nevertheless, when students use AI to produce answers without going through the process of reasoning, the value of education as a development experience can be undermined. The ability to critically think, write analytically and research independently are built with practice (Chatfield, 2022). When AI replaces instead of facilitating these processes, there can be a stagnation in the acquisition of skills. Teachers thus have the difficulty of adapting AI in a manner that encourages active use as opposed to passive use. Higher-order thinking can be provoked by administering structured tasks in which students are asked to critique, compare, and refine AI-generated content. To avoid a complete ban on AI, pedagogical frameworks might have to focus on cognitive transparency, i.e., be aware of the inner workings of AI, where it can go wrong, and how to interpret its outputs in a critical perspective. Those methods will help AI stop being a shortcut and act as a catalyst to metacognitive development. On the social level, AI addiction affects the standards of power and specialization. The use of algorithmic systems is becoming an important part of healthcare, financial, criminal, and governance decisions (Hannah-Moffat, 2019). Since the general confidence will be transferred to data-based systems, the views on human judgment can also alter. Although it is true that algorithmic systems make objectivity and consistency more effective, they do not eliminate bias and contextual constraints. Overdependence on automated outputs in the society might eliminate the collective examination of decision-making procedure. In case citizens believe that algorithmic suggestions are neutral in essence, democratic responsibility can be undermined.

Table 3. Psychological, educational, and societal implications of AI-mediated cognitive offloading

Level of Impact	Key Construct	Description of Influence	Potential Risks	Mitigation Strategies
Psychological	Self-Efficacy	Repeated reliance on AI for reasoning, writing, and analysis may shape beliefs about one's own cognitive competence.	Reduced cognitive confidence; learned dependence; decreased intrinsic motivation.	Encourage independent problem-solving periods; promote reflective evaluation of AI outputs.
Psychological	Cognitive Effort Avoidance	AI provides rapid, polished responses that reduce the need for sustained attention and ambiguity tolerance.	Habitual low-engagement thinking; reduced tolerance for complexity.	Structured tasks requiring deep analysis; delayed-AI access models in learning.
Educational	Active Learning	Learning depends on engagement in reasoning, reflection, and	Skill stagnation if AI substitutes rather than	Integrate AI as a critique tool rather than answer
		problem-solving processes.	supports thinking.	generator; scaffolded evaluation exercises.
Educational	Metacognitive Development	Understanding how AI systems function and where they may fail.	Superficial acceptance of algorithmic outputs.	Promote cognitive transparency and AI literacy curricula.
Educational	Higher-Order Thinking	Development of analytical writing, argumentation, and independent research skills.	Reduced analytical endurance with excessive automation.	Require comparison, refinement, and justification of AI-generated material.
Societal	Algorithmic Authority	Growing trust in AI systems in healthcare, finance, governance, and justice sectors.	Diminished scrutiny of automated decisions; weakened democratic accountability.	Human-in-the-loop oversight; transparent decision frameworks.
Societal	Epistemic Standards	Shifting perceptions of objectivity and expertise toward algorithmic systems.	Collective reduction in critical examination of decision-making processes.	Public AI literacy initiatives; regulatory safeguards and audit mechanisms.

ETHICAL CONSIDERATIONS, MITIGATION STRATEGIES, AND FUTURE DIRECTIONS

With the integration of artificial intelligence into the cognitive processes, the issues of dependency, autonomy, and intellectual integrity are growing more urgent (Abbass, 2019). Some of the neuropsychological dangers of cognitive atrophy and automation bias are not merely personal issues; they are also connected to the issues of accountability, equity, visibility, and social welfare. To alleviate these problems, planning-based mitigation approaches are necessary that would maintain the agency of human beings and use the advantages of AI augmentation. Ethical struggle is not that people should oppose the development of technologies but to make certain that the implementation of AI can facilitate cognitive growth instead of passive dependence (Hernández-Orallo & Vold, 2019). A major ethical issue is that of autonomy. The key to human autonomy is the ability to make a judgment and make decisions independently and reflectively. When the conclusions, recommendations, or arguments are made with the routines of the AI systems without substantial reviews, it can be assumed that the autonomy of individuals is undermined unconsciously. Dependence on the results of algorithms may decrease chances of independent thinking, and the control over the process of judgment may be transferred to the computational recommendation. To retain autonomy, it is necessary to have a significant level of human control and to make sure that AI systems are not dominant power determining machines but should serve as an aid. Another ethical requirement is transparency and explainability. The workings of many AI systems are opaque black boxes, where the output does not show the thinking processes followed to arrive at It (Von Eschenbach, 2021). This opaqueness reduces the critical evaluation of the conclusions by the users and enhances automation bias. The design of ethical AI should focus on explainable systems, which will enable users to know how the outputs are generated; data sources they make use of, and their uncertainties. When people have the capability of questioning AI reasoning, they are more apt to be in a state of cognitive involvement as opposed to being passive receivers. The ethical situation is also influenced by equity and access. AI technologies can be used to democratize knowledge, provide more access to people with disabilities, and supplement under-resourced education systems. Nevertheless, the unequal access to advanced AI devices can contribute to the increase in cognitive and educational disparities. Individuals who have access to AI augmentation can become more productive and learn more, and the other people can be left behind (Hassani et al., 2020). The deployment of technologies as an ethical consideration should thus be inclusive; that is, it should be distributed widely instead of limited to the privileged groups. Education and digital literacy are the mitigation measures. Users need to build a sense of AI potentials and restrictions, such as its cognizance of prejudice, unpredictability, and probability of error. Automation bias can be minimized by training programs that focus on critical interaction, e.g. cross-checking sources, making assumptions, and understanding probabilistic outputs. The ability to sustain executive activity and maintain critical thinking by encouraging reflective interaction instead of instant acceptance will lead to a sustained executive engagement (Prince, 2019).

CONCLUSION

One of the most important psychological changes of the digital era is the introduction of artificial intelligence into the routine thought processes. Although AI systems increase the efficiency, accessibility, and the analytical ability, they are also changing the trends of cognitive engagement. As cognitive offloading and automation bias introduce people to this concept, they might slowly cease to rely on internal memory, sustained attention and executive reasoning. The principles of neuroplasticity indicate that the underutilization of higher-order mental processes when performed continuously may affect the efficiency of functions in the long run. But cognitive atrophy is not unavoidable; it will be determined to a large degree by the ways of relating and by deliberate working. AI may replace or provide support to thinking in humans. Passively, it poses a threat of reducing metacognitive vigilance and intellectual independence. Reflectively, it can arouse critical thinking, cross-disciplinary thinking, and hybrid intelligence. The necessary protective measures are the educational reform, open approach to system design, digital literacy, and conscious practice. To maintain critical thinking during the era of automation, there should be a balance between technological augmentation and an ongoing human agency. Finally, the AI capabilities alone will not define the future of cognition but the way in which people and organizations will communicate their connection with intelligent systems consciously. The world is becoming highly automated and human reflection should not be marginalized.

REFERENCES

Abbass, H. A. (2019). Social integration of artificial intelligence: Functions, automation allocation logic and human-autonomy trust. *Cognitive Computation, 11*(2), 159–171. DOI: 10.1007/s12559-018-9619-0

Aghaziarati, A., & Rahimi, H. (2025). The future of digital assistants: Human dependence and behavioral change. *Journal of Foresight and Health Governance, 2*(1), 52–61.

Ajunwa, I. (2019). The paradox of automation as anti-bias intervention. *Cardozo Law Review, 41*, 1671.

Amershi, B. (2020). Culture, the process of knowledge, perception of the world and emergence of AI. *AI & Society, 35*(2), 417–430. DOI: 10.1007/s00146-019-00885-z

Angelopoulou, E., & Drigas, A. (2021). Working memory, attention and their relationship: A theoretical overview. *Research. Social Development, 10*(5), e46410515288–e46410515288.

Bader, V., & Kaiser, S. (2019). Algorithmic decision-making? The user interface and its role for human involvement in decisions supported by artificial intelligence. *Organization, 26*(5), 655–672. DOI: 10.1177/1350508419855714

Barua, P. D., Vicnesh, J., Gururajan, R., Oh, S. L., Palmer, E., Azizan, M. M., Kadri, N. A., & Acharya, U. R. (2022). Artificial intelligence enabled personalised assistive tools to enhance education of children with neurodevelopmental disorders—A review. *International Journal of Environmental Research and Public Health, 19*(3), 1192. DOI: 10.3390/ijerph19031192 PMID: 35162220

Călinescu, A. (2024). The impact of digital technologies on memory and memory studies. *Journal of Contemporary Philosophical and Anthropological Studies, 2*(1). Advance online publication. DOI: 10.59652/jcpas.v2i1.161

Caramazza, A. (2018). Cognitive neuropsychology and rehabilitation: An unfulfilled promise? In *Cognitive approaches in neuropsychological rehabilitation* (pp. 383–398). Routledge. DOI: 10.4324/9780429488511-13

Chatfield, T. (2022). Critical thinking: Your guide to effective argument, successful analysis and independent study.

Coli ă, D., Coli ă, C.-I., Hermann, D. M., Coli ă, E., Doeppner, T. R., Udristoiu, I., & Popa-Wagner, A. (2022). Therapeutic use and chronic abuse of CNS stimulants and anabolic drugs. *Current Issues in Molecular Biology*, *44*(10), 4902–4920. DOI: 10.3390/cimb44100333 PMID: 36286048

Davenport, T. H. (2018). From analytics to artificial intelligence. *Journal of Business Analytics*, *1*(2), 73–80. DOI: 10.1080/2573234X.2018.1543535

De Bruin, A. B., Roelle, J., Carpenter, S. K., & Baars, M. (2020). Synthesizing cognitive load and self-regulation theory: A theoretical framework and research agenda. *Educational Psychology Review*, *32*(4), 903–915. DOI: 10.1007/s10648-020-09576-4

Déli, E., & Kisvárday, Z. (2020). The thermodynamic brain and the evolution of intellect: The role of mental energy. *Cognitive Neurodynamics*, *14*(6), 743–756. DOI: 10.1007/s11571-020-09637-y PMID: 33101528

Ding, X., Xie, C., & Yu, F. (2024). Beyond dissonance: The transformative power of thought analysis in philosophical practice. *Humanities & Social Sciences Communications*, *11*(1), 1617. DOI: 10.1057/s41599-024-04143-6

French, A. M., & Shim, J. (2025). From artificial intelligence to augmented intelligence: A shift in perspective, application, and conceptualization of AI. *Information Systems Frontiers*, *27*(4), 1345–1366. DOI: 10.1007/s10796-024-10562-2

Friedman, N. P., & Robbins, T. W. (2022). The role of prefrontal cortex in cognitive control and executive function. *Neuropsychopharmacology : Official Publication of the American College of Neuropsychopharmacology*, *47*(1), 72–89. DOI: 10.1038/s41386-021-01132-0 PMID: 34408280

Ghajargar, M., Wiberg, M., & Stolterman, E. (2018). Designing IoT systems that support reflective thinking: A relational approach. *International Journal of Design*, *12*(1), 21–35.

Grévisse, C., Rothkugel, S., & Reuter, R. A. (2019). Scaffolding support through integration of learning material. *Smart learning environments, 6*(1), 28.

Grinschgl, S., Papenmeier, F., & Meyerhoff, H. S. (2021). Consequences of cognitive offloading: Boosting performance but diminishing memory. *Quarterly Journal of Experimental Psychology*, *74*(9), 1477–1496. DOI: 10.1177/17470218211008060 PMID: 33752519

Gursoy, D., Chi, O. H., Lu, L., & Nunkoo, R. (2019). Consumers acceptance of artificially intelligent (AI) device use in service delivery. *International Journal of Information Management*, *49*, 157–169. DOI: 10.1016/j.ijinfomgt.2019.03.008

Hannah-Moffat, K. (2019). Algorithmic risk governance: Big data analytics, race and information activism in criminal justice debates. *Theoretical Criminology, 23*(4), 453–470. DOI: 10.1177/1362480618763582

Hassani, H., Silva, E. S., Unger, S., TajMazinani, M., & Mac Feely, S. (2020). Artificial intelligence (AI) or intelligence augmentation (IA): What is the future? *AI, 1*(2), 8. DOI: 10.3390/ai1020008

Hernández-Orallo, J., & Vold, K. (2019). AI extenders: The ethical and societal implications of humans cognitively extended by AI. Proceedings of the 2019 AAAI/ACM Conference on AI, Ethics, and Society, Heyworth, N. C., & Squire, L. R. (2019). The nature of recollection across months and years and after medial temporal lobe damage. *Proceedings of the National Academy of Sciences of the United States of America, 116*(10), 4619–4624. PMID: 30792351

Hilalludin, H., Sugari, D., Al-Nomani, S., & Muzanni, M. (2025). The Role of Educational Psychology in Enhancing the Qualityof the Teaching and Learning Process. *Jurnal Ar- Ruhul Ilmi: Jurnal Pendidikan dan Pemikiran Islam, 1*(01), 62-74.

Hodgkinson, G. P., & Sadler-Smith, E. (2018). The dynamics of intuition and analysis in managerial and organizational decision making. *The Academy of Management Perspectives, 32*(4), 473–492. DOI: 10.5465/amp.2016.0140

Jammulamadaka, N. (2021). Enabling processes as routines that facilitate cognitive change. *Management Decision, 59*(3), 653–668. DOI: 10.1108/MD-09-2019-1311

Jarrahi, M. H. (2018). Artificial intelligence and the future of work: Human-AI symbiosis in organizational decision making. *Business Horizons, 61*(4), 577–586. DOI: 10.1016/j.bushor.2018.03.007

Joshua, A. M. (2022). Neuroplasticity. In *Physiotherapy for adult neurological conditions* (pp. 1–30). Springer. DOI: 10.1007/978-981-19-0209-3_1

Kleitman, S., Hui, J. S.-W., & Jiang, Y. (2019). Confidence to spare: Individual differences in cognitive and metacognitive arrogance and competence. *Metacognition and Learning, 14*(3), 479–508. DOI: 10.1007/s11409-019-09210-x

Lenzoni, S., Baker, J., Sumich, A. L., & Mograbi, D. C. (2022). New insights into neural networks of error monitoring and clinical implications: A systematic review of ERP studies in neurological diseases. *Reviews in the Neurosciences, 33*(2), 161–179. DOI: 10.1515/revneuro-2021-0054 PMID: 34214387

Lindström, J. (2020). Understanding digital distraction: a longitudinal study on disruptive everyday media multitasking among diginatives.

Mosier, K. L., & Skitka, L. J. (2018). Human decision makers and automated decision aids: Made for each other? In *Automation and human performance* (pp. 201–220). CRC Press.

Muis, K. R., Chevrier, M., Denton, C. A., & Losenno, K. M. (2021). Epistemic emotions and epistemic cognition predict critical thinking about socio-scientific issues. Frontiers in Education, Naseer, A., Ahmad, N. R., & Chishti, M. A. (2025). Psychological impacts of AI dependence: Assessing the cognitive and emotional costs of intelligent systems in daily life. *Review of Applied Management and Social Sciences*, *8*(1), 291–307.

Osiurak, F., Navarro, J., & Reynaud, E. (2018). How our cognition shapes and is shaped by technology: A common framework for understanding human tool-use interactions in the past, present, and future. *Frontiers in Psychology*, *9*, 293. DOI: 10.3389/fpsyg.2018.00293 PMID: 29563891

Parwati, N. N., & Suharta, I. G. P. (2024). Mathematical problem-solving ability and students' motivation in learning using auditory, intellectually, repetition models. AIP Conference Proceedings, Peeters, R. (2020). The agency of algorithms: Understanding human-algorithm interaction in administrative decision-making. *Information Polity*, *25*(4), 507–522.

Prince, E.-S. (2019). *7 skills for the future: adaptability, critical thinking, empathy, integrity, optimism, being proactive, resilience*. Pearson UK.

Raj, T., Chauhan, P., Mehrotra, R., & Sharma, M. (2022). Importance of critical thinking in the education. *World Journal of English Language*, *12*(3), 126–133. DOI: 10.5430/wjel.v12n3p126

Ramírez-Vizcaya, S., & Froese, T. (2019). The enactive approach to habits: New concepts for the cognitive science of bad habits and addiction. *Frontiers in Psychology*, *10*, 301. DOI: 10.3389/fpsyg.2019.00301 PMID: 30863334

Sarafyazd, M., & Jazayeri, M. (2019). Hierarchical reasoning by neural circuits in the frontal cortex. *Science*, *364*(6441), eaav8911. DOI: 10.1126/science.aav8911 PMID: 31097640

Sepp, S., Howard, S. J., Tindall-Ford, S., Agostinho, S., & Paas, F. (2019). Cognitive load theory and human movement: Towards an integrated model of working memory. *Educational Psychology Review*, *31*(2), 293–317. DOI: 10.1007/s10648-019-09461-9

Shalaby, A. (2024). Classification for the digital and cognitive AI hazards: Urgent call to establish automated safe standard for protecting young human minds. *Digital Economy and Sustainable Development*, *2*(1), 17. DOI: 10.1007/s44265-024-00042-5

Sodiya, E. O., Amoo, O. O., Umoga, U. J., & Atadoga, A. (2024). AI-driven personalization in web content delivery: A comparative study of user engagement in the USA and the UK. *World journal of advanced research and reviews, 21*(2), 887-902.

Suresh, V., & Dyaram, L. (2023). Job matching for persons with disabilities: An exploratory study. *Employee Responsibilities and Rights Journal, 35*(4), 475–492. DOI: 10.1007/s10672-022-09421-6

Theeuwes, J. (2019). Goal-driven, stimulus-driven, and history-driven selection. *Current Opinion in Psychology, 29*, 97–101. DOI: 10.1016/j.copsyc.2018.12.024 PMID: 30711911

Von Eschenbach, W. J. (2021). Transparency and the black box problem: Why we do not trust AI. *Philosophy & Technology, 34*(4), 1607–1622. DOI: 10.1007/s13347-021-00477-0

Walkerdine, V. (2025). *The mastery of reason: Cognitive development and the production of rationality*. Taylor & Francis. DOI: 10.4324/9781003710158

Yan, S. (2022). Lack of self-efficacy and resistance to innovation impact on insufficient learning capabilities: Mediating the role of demotivation and moderating the role of institutional culture. *Frontiers in Psychology, 13*, 923577. DOI: 10.3389/fpsyg.2022.923577 PMID: 35959070

Yepiskoposyan, R. How Perceived Agency in Generative AI Undermines Critical Thought. *Available at SSRN* 5603171. DOI: 10.2139/ssrn.5603171

Yun, B., Feng, D., Chen, A. S., Nikzad, A., & Salehi, N. (2025). Generative ai in knowledge work: Design implications for data navigation and decision-making. Proceedings of the 2025 CHI Conference on Human Factors in Computing Systems

Zamani, A., Mills, C., Girn, M., & Christoff, K. (2023). A closer look at transitions between the generative and evaluative phases of creative thought. In The Routledge international handbook of creative cognition (pp. 453-474). Routledge.

Zerilli, J., Bhatt, U., & Weller, A. (2022). How transparency modulates trust in artificial intelligence. *Patterns (New York, N.Y.), 3*(4), 100455. DOI: 10.1016/j.patter.2022.100455 PMID: 35465233

Section 2
AI, Education, and Cognitive Resilience

Chapter 9
Digital Tools as Educational Resources:
Transforming Classroom Practices in the Era of Modern Learning

Husnaini Husnaini
http://orcid.org/0009-0008-2665-9096
Universitas Islam Negeri Palopo, Indonesia

ABSTRACT

This chapter examines the role of digital tools as educational resources in transforming classroom practices in modern learning environments. Drawing on a systematic review of recent literature, this chapter highlights how technologies such as learning management systems, multimedia platforms, collaborative tools, and artificial intelligence have become integral to instructional processes. The chapter identifies key pedagogical opportunities, including enhanced learner engagement, support for blended learning, and personalized learning experiences. It also addresses major challenges, such as digital inequality, limited teacher competence, and issues of curriculum alignment and policy support. Furthermore, ethical concerns related to AI integration, including data privacy and academic integrity, are discussed. This chapter concludes that effective digital transformation depends on pedagogical alignment, institutional readiness, and equitable access, emphasizing the need for strategic and sustainable implementation in education.

INTRODUCTION

The swift proliferation of digital technology has significantly transformed educational systems globally, rendering technology integration an institutional imperative

DOI: 10.4018/979-8-3373-9484-8.ch009

rather than merely a pedagogical choice (Bucăţa & Tileagă, 2024; Facer & Selwyn, 2021). In the context of Industry 4.0 and post-pandemic educational recovery, educational institutions are more dependent on digital resources to ensure instructional continuity, enhance student engagement, and address varied learning requirements (Akintayo et al., 2024a). Worldwide, digital transformation has expedited the integration of platforms like learning management systems, multimedia apps, and online collaboration environments into routine classroom practices. Many educational institutions in developing regions are addressing the opportunities and limitations of technology-enhanced learning, including infrastructural deficiencies, teacher preparedness, and curriculum alignment. As digital inclusion becomes pivotal to educational reform, comprehending the functionality of digital tools as educational resources is essential for enhancing learning outcomes and guaranteeing fair access to excellent instruction.

Digital transformation is crucial in language education, where interactivity, multimodality, and communication-centered learning are vital elements of effective pedagogy (Atan et al., 2024; Zhang & Dong, 2024). The growing reliance on digital resources in English language instruction signifies wider transitions towards learner-centred teaching models and individualized learning settings (Khanh, 2024; Merzifonluoğlu, 2023). Nonetheless, whereas digital technologies offer the potential for innovation, their deployment also elicits apprehensions about pedagogical efficacy, adherence to educational standards, and sustainability. Consequently, analyzing digital tools as educational resources is essential for elucidating their impact on modifying classroom practices in contemporary learning environments.

The post-pandemic educational landscape necessitates a thorough reevaluation of the integration of digital resources in instructional design, assessment methodologies, and curriculum structures (Mastrokoukou & Crawford–Lee, 2023). Institutions are now tasked with integrating digital resources as essential elements of learning ecosystems, rather than perceiving technology as a mere temporary replacement for in-person instruction. This transition necessitates strategic planning, professional development, and policy alignment to guarantee that digital technologies facilitate substantive learning instead of mere superficial technological implementation.

Digital tools in education are typically characterized as electronic applications, platforms, or gadgets that facilitate teaching, learning, and assessment processes (Dancsa et al., 2023). These instruments encompass learning management systems, interactive multimedia materials, communication platforms, and digital collaborative settings. Educational resources denote products or systems that enhance knowledge acquisition and instructional dissemination, regardless of being in physical or digital formats (Onwadi, 2024; Salinas-Hernández & Sacristán, 2024). This study conceptualizes digital technologies as resources that enhance educational opportunities beyond conventional classroom limits by facilitating flexible access, engagement, and learner autonomy. A teacher may utilise Google Classroom to disseminate assignments, incorporate YouTube films for auditory practice, and involve students in collaborative writing activities via shared digital documents. These methods demonstrate that digital tools function not only as auxiliary resources but as integral components of instructional design in modern education.

Viewing digital technologies as teaching resources necessitates a transition from a technology-centric approach to a pedagogy-focused integration (Russo, 2025; Weich & Macgilchrist, 2023). In this perspective, digital tools are esteemed not merely for their technological attributes, but for their ability to mediate learning processes, promote educational objectives, and enable significant involvement. This conceptual framework corresponds with modern learning theories that highlight learner autonomy, social engagement, and the contextualization of knowledge creation. Consequently, digital tools serve as intermediaries between pedagogical objectives and learning experiences in contemporary classrooms.

Furthermore, framing digital tools as resources highlights the significance of instructional design, educator proficiency, and institutional governance in influencing learning outcomes. In the absence of pedagogical intentionality, digital tools may devolve into mere administrative devices instead of serving as transformative educational resources (Mekheimer, 2025; Simos & Katsiampoura, 2025). This viewpoint is especially pertinent for chapter book discussions, which seek to offer more profound theoretical and contextual analysis beyond mere empirical reporting.

A burgeoning corpus of contemporary research has investigated the pedagogical ramifications of digital instruments in educational settings. Bond (2020) examined the impact of emergency remote teaching during the COVID-19 pandemic on digital learning practices in several educational contexts. The study, employing a systematic review design, revealed that digital tools facilitated educational continuity while simultaneously highlighting disparities in access and teacher readiness. These findings indicate that digital tools can improve learning only when supported by sufficient institutional backing and inclusive infrastructure.

Although current research has yielded significant insights on the uptake and efficacy of digital tools, the literature largely remains disjointed between particular contexts, disciplines, or emergency scenarios. Numerous studies concentrate on short-term implementation results or discrete technical interventions, providing less understanding of how digital tools operate as enduring educational resources over time. Therefore, there is a necessity for comprehensive studies that amalgamate educational, organizational, and systemic aspects of digital classroom change.

A chapter-based academic discourse provides a suitable framework for a critical analysis of digital tools beyond just empirical observations. This chapter aims to provide a comprehensive understanding of how digital technologies transform classroom practices in contemporary education by integrating conceptual frameworks and recent empirical research. Hrastinski (2019) conducted a conceptual examination of technology-supported instructional models to investigate the pedagogical significance of blended learning. The study emphasized that blended learning offers flexibility and fosters active learning by integrating in-person education with online participation. The findings indicate that digital technologies promote more adaptable classroom environments when learning experiences are deliberately organized rather than dictated by technology.

In a separate empirical study, Trust and Whalen (2020) examined teachers' professional adaption to digital tools during the schooling period of the epidemic (Trust & Whalen, 2020). Through qualitative interviews with educators, the researchers discovered that teachers devised new techniques utilizing digital platforms, yet encountered problems pertaining to workload, digital literacy, and instructional redesign. This study indicates that effective technology integration necessitates ongoing professional development and instructional expertise, rather than mere access to tools.

Conversely, certain studies highlight the constraints of digital inclusion in the absence of systemic assistance. Redecker (2017) introduced the DigCompEdu methodology to evaluate educators' digital competency across European educational institutions (Christine, 2017). The research emphasized that the incorporation of technology is significantly influenced by teachers' professional competence, alignment with institutional policies, and pedagogical preparedness. The result is that structural support is essential for educational reform using digital instruments, rather than relying on automatic assumptions.

Collectively, these works illustrate a growing academic focus on digital tools as transformative educational assets. Previous studies affirm that digital platforms can improve flexibility, learner engagement, and instructional creativity across various disciplines, including language education. Digital tools have demonstrated efficacy in enhancing blended learning models, fostering learner autonomy, and enabling collaborative situations. Simultaneously, difficulties pertaining to teacher competence, access inequity, curriculum adherence, and institutional preparedness continue to pose significant obstacles. It is established that digital tools serve as potent facilitators of contemporary learning; nonetheless, their efficacy is heavily contingent upon pedagogical alignment, resource management, and systemic readiness.

Notwithstanding the increasing data, many study deficiencies persist in the literature regarding the function of digital tools as sustainable educational resources. Much of the current study has predominantly concentrated on the short-term adoption of technology in emergency contexts, especially during the COVID-19 pandemic, when digital tools were swiftly deployed to provide instructional continuity. Although these studies yield significant insights into technology integration during crises, they frequently provide a limited comprehension of the role of digital resources in long-term pedagogical reform after institutions revert to more stable educational settings. Consequently, there is a lack of comprehensive discourse regarding the systematic integration of digital tools into instructional design, curriculum development, and institutional policy frameworks in a sustainable manner.

Moreover, a substantial segment of the research has focused on technologically advanced educational systems, resulting in a relative under-representation of developing contexts. Educational institutions in developing regions sometimes encounter intricate issues concerning digital proficiency. These contextual limits affect the implementation and experience of digital tools in daily classroom practices. Therefore, a thorough analytical investigation is required to understand how educators in these situations strategically incorporate digital resources while managing institutional limitations and budget constraints.

A notable research gap pertains to the increasing integration of artificial intelligence and adaptive learning technologies inside educational settings. Despite the growing introduction of AI-assisted technologies for writing feedback, language acquisition, and tailored training, academic discourse on their pedagogical ramifications, ethical concerns, and institutional oversight remains sparse. Specifically, enquiries around data privacy, algorithmic bias, and the appropriate integration of AI in educational practices necessitate additional examination. Addressing these gaps is crucial for cultivating a more thorough comprehension of how digital tools might operate not merely as technological advancements but also as pedagogically significant and institutionally viable educational resources.

This study aims to investigate digital technologies as educational resources and assess their role in modifying classroom practices in contemporary learning environments. This project aims to investigate the pedagogical benefits and practical obstacles of digital inclusion in classroom education. The study is directed by the subsequent research question: (a) How do digital tools function as educational resources in transforming modern classroom practices?; (b) What pedagogical opportunities do digital tools provide in supporting learner engagement, personalization, and blended learning?; and (c) What challenges and limitations emerge in implementing digital tools in relation to digital literacy, compliance, and resource management?

This study utilizes a conceptual and literature-based research design to synthesize recent academic results regarding the integration of digital technology in education. Through a critical examination of empirical and theoretical works from the past decade, the researcher discerns patterns of pedagogical reform and finds persistent obstacles. Digital technologies are anticipated to enhance instructional flexibility and learner-centred practices; yet, their effectiveness will be limited by structural challenges, including institutional readiness and disparities in access.

This study enhances educational research by providing a contemporary and organized comprehension of digital tools as educational resources in current learning situations. The study's originality is rooted in its focus on pedagogical transformation and organizational problems, specifically on compliance, digital competency, and strategic classroom implementation. The results may guide educators, governments, and institutions in developing sustainable digital learning practices. The study theoretically bolsters ongoing discourse on technology-enhanced pedagogy by elucidating the conditions that enable digital tools to promote inclusive and transformational educational innovation in modern classrooms.

This study employs a conceptual framework that synthesizes learning theories, technological integration models, and institutional views to analyze digital technologies as educational resources. This section delineates the theoretical foundations and conceptual assumptions underpinning the analysis of digital classroom transformation in contemporary learning environments.

THEORETICAL AND CONCEPTUAL FRAMEWORK

To provide a deeper analytical foundation for understanding digital tools as educational resources, this chapter is grounded in several complementary theoretical perspectives that explain how technology mediates learning processes in modern educational environments. These theoretical lenses include constructivism, social contructivism, connectivism, the TPACK framework, and the SAMR model of technology integration. Together, these frameworks provide a multidimensional understanding of how digital tools contribute to classroom transformation beyond mere technological adoption.

Constructivism and Social Contructivism in Digital Learning

Constructivist learning theory asserts that information is actively generated by learners through engagement with their environment, rather than being passively acquired by educators (Bou Saad et al., 2025). Constructivism, grounded on Piaget's theories and further developed by Vygotsky, underscores cognitive engagement, experiential learning, and social interaction as fundamental processes of knowledge acquisition (Banihashem & Macfadyen, 2021). In digitally enhanced classrooms, resources like interactive simulations, multimedia programs, and collaborative platforms create environments where learners actively construct meaning via inquiry and reflection.

Social constructivism, especially Vygotsky's notion of the Zone of Proximal Development (ZPD), emphasizes the significance of mediated interaction in the learning process (Gunawardena et al., 2023). Digital technologies serve as mediational artefacts that support learning processes via peer participation, teacher feedback, and guided practice (Wu et al., 2025). Collaborative writing platforms, discussion forums, and real-time feedback systems facilitate the co-construction of knowledge among learners in socially interactive digital environments. Consequently, digital technologies are not impartial instruments; they actively influence cognitive engagement and social learning dynamics.

In digitally mediated learning environments, constructivist ideas are increasingly evident through interactive and learner-centred instructional methods. Digital platforms enable learners to engage with content via multimedia resources, simulations, and problem-based tasks that promote active knowledge production (Abedi, 2024; Martín-Lucas & García del Dujo, 2023). Interactive movies, digital storytelling tools, and collaborative discussion forums facilitate the integration of past knowledge with new material for pupils. From a social constructivist viewpoint, digital settings enhance opportunities for scaffolding and peer-supported learning, enabling learners to participate in discussion and collaborative problem-solving (Yusof et al., 2022). Digital collaboration technologies, including shared papers, learning management system forums, and peer-review platforms, facilitate students in negotiating meaning and jointly enhancing their comprehension. Thus, digital technologies boost constructivist learning by promoting interaction, reflection, and collaborative knowledge creation in technology-enhanced classrooms.

Connectivism and Networked Knowledge

In the realm of swift technological progress, connectivism offers an alternative theoretical framework for comprehending digital learning environments. Proposed by Siemens and Downes, connectivism defines learning as the establishment of networks among knowledge sources, persons, and digital systems (Alsuwaida & Alsamiri, 2025). Knowledge is disseminated among networks rather than being confined to individuals alone.

Digital technologies, such learning management systems, AI-driven platforms, and online collaboration settings, embody connectivist ideas by enabling access to dispersed information sources. Students traverse interlinked digital environments where information is perpetually refreshed and socially influenced. Consequently, classroom transformation in the digital age signifies alterations in instructional delivery as well as modifications in epistemological frameworks, whereby knowledge is rendered dynamic, interconnected, and digitally facilitated.

The swift proliferation of digital networks has rendered connectivism increasingly pertinent for comprehending learning processes in modern educational contexts. In contrast to conventional learning models that perceive information as spread throughout networks of individuals, digital resources, and technical systems. Digital instruments, like learning management systems, free educational resources, and online knowledge communities, provide learners' simultaneous access to information from diverse sources. Through these interconnected networks, students cultivate the capacity to identify, assess, and integrate information from many digital contexts.

Technological Pedagogical Content Knowledge (TPACK)

The TPACK framework enhances the comprehension of digital integration by highlighting the convergence of technological knowledge, pedagogical knowledge, and content knowledge. Effective technology integration transpires not just via the introduction of digital technologies, but through their intentional alignment with content and instructional design.

In this context, instructors' digital competence encompasses not only operational skills but also the capacity to incorporate tools that augment conceptual comprehension and student involvement. This viewpoint strongly corresponds with the chapter's findings, which emphasize teacher competency as a pivotal factor in transformational digital practice. In the absence of pedagogical congruence, digital instruments are likely to operate merely at a surface administrative level.

The SAMR Model and Levels of Digital Transformation

The SAMR model (Substitution, Augmentation, Modification, Redefinition) offers a pragmatic framework for assessing the extent of technological integration. At the substitution level, digital technologies simply supplant conventional techniques without altering functionality. At the augmentation stage, negligible enhancements transpire. True classroom transformation occurs during the modification and redefinition stages, where technology facilitates learning experiences that were previously unimaginable in conventional environments.

Implementing this paradigm in contemporary schools demonstrates that not every instance of digital adoption results in transformation. Numerous institutions continue to operate at substitute or augmentation levels, especially in contexts where teacher preparation or institutional support is inadequate. Sustainable transformation necessitates advancement towards redefinition, wherein digital technologies facilitate collaborative worldwide initiatives, AI-enhanced feedback mechanisms, and immersive multimedia educational settings.

Socio-Technical Systems Perspective

This chapter ultimately embraces a socio-technical systems perspective, acknowledging that digital revolution in education is influenced by the interplay of technological systems, human agents, institutional frameworks, and policy contexts.

Outcomes are not solely dictated by technology; instead, transformation arises from the congruence of tools, education, governance, and infrastructure.

This viewpoint is especially pertinent when examining concerns such as digital disparity, regulatory compliance, and educator preparedness. This chapter promotes a comprehensive concept of classroom transformation by perceiving digital tools as integrated within wider socio-institutional frameworks, moving beyond technical determinism. Collectively, these theoretical foundations offer a thorough analytical framework for investigating the role of digital tools as educational resources that mediate cognitive processes, facilitate networked knowledge construction, enhance pedagogical design, and engage with institutional contexts in contemporary learning environments.

METHOD

This study employed a conceptual and literature-based research design to analyze the role of digital tools as educational resources in transforming classroom practices within modern learning environments. The methodological procedures are elaborated below.

Research Design

The present study utilized a conceptual qualitative approach through a systematic literature review design, which is appropriate for synthesizing theoretical and empirical evidence related to educational technology integration. This design focuses on critically examining how digital tools function as instructional resources that reshape pedagogical practices, learner engagement, and classroom organization in contemporary education.

A conceptual literature review is suitable when the primary aim is not to test causal hypotheses but to provide a structured understanding of a phenomenon based on existing academic studies (Creswell, 2018). In this study, the main constructs included digital tools (e.g., learning management systems, multimedia resources, collaborative platforms), modern classroom transformation, learner-centered pedagogy, and challenges of digital inclusion such as compliance and digital literacy.

The objective of this design was to systematically analyze recent research findings and identify patterns, opportunities, and limitations of digital tools in supporting modern learning environments.

Participants and Sampling

Since this study was conceptual in nature, no human participants were directly involved. Instead, the units of analysis consisted of peer-reviewed journal articles related to digital tools and classroom practice transformation.

A purposive sampling technique was applied to select studies that were relevant to the topic. The inclusion criteria for article selection were:

1. Studies published between 2016 and 2025 (last ten years).
2. Articles indexed in reputable databases such as Scopus, ERIC, and Web of Science.
3. Research focusing on digital tools as educational resources in formal learning settings.
4. Studies addressing pedagogical affordances, learner engagement, blended learning, or instructional innovation.

The use of purposive sampling was intended to ensure that the selected studies were conceptually relevant and methodologically credible. By focusing on articles indexed in established academic databases, the study prioritized peer-reviewed research that met recognized standards of scholarly rigor. The ten-year publication window was selected to capture recent developments in digital education, particularly those emerging during and after the global shift toward technology-enhanced learning.

Importantly, the sampling strategy did not aim for exhaustive coverage of all studies on educational technology. Instead, it sought to achieve analytical depth by selecting studies that explicitly addressed digital tools as pedagogical resources rather than as isolated technological interventions. This focus aligns with the chapter's objective of examining classroom transformation from a pedagogical and institutional perspective.

Research Instrument

The primary research instrument in this study was a document analysis and extraction checklist, used to systematically review and categorize findings from selected articles. The checklist focused on key aspects such as:

1. Type of digital tool examined (LMS, multimedia, AI-based tools, collaborative platforms)
2. Research context and educational setting
3. Methodological design used in each study
4. Key findings regarding classroom transformation

5. Reported challenges, such as access inequality, digital competence, and compliance issues
6. Pedagogical implications for modern learning

To ensure content validity, the checklist items were developed based on recent educational technology frameworks and were reviewed repeatedly to confirm alignment with the research objectives.

The extraction checklist was explicitly aligned with the conceptual framework guiding this study. Each checklist category corresponded to one or more dimensions of the framework, including pedagogical affordances, learner engagement, and institutional conditions. This alignment ensured that data extraction was theoretically informed rather than purely descriptive.

By structuring the instrument around these conceptual dimensions, the study was able to synthesize findings across diverse contexts while maintaining analytical consistency. This approach also facilitated thematic comparison across studies, allowing patterns and contrasts to emerge systematically during analysis.

Data Collection Procedures

Data were collected through a systematic search of academic databases followed by a structured document screening process. The collection procedures were conducted in several sequential stages to ensure transparency, rigor, and replicability. In the first stage, the researcher performed comprehensive searches in major scholarly databases, including Scopus, ERIC, Web of Science, and Google Scholar. Keywords and Boolean combinations such as *digital tools*, *educational resources*, *technology integration*, *classroom transformation*, and *modern learning environments* were applied to retrieve relevant publications. This initial search generated approximately 320 journal articles related to the topic.

In the second stage, titles and abstracts were screened to eliminate studies that did not directly address digital tools as pedagogical resources or were outside the scope of classroom transformation. After this preliminary filtering, 110 articles remained eligible for further examination. In the third stage, full-text reviews were conducted to assess methodological quality, conceptual relevance, and alignment with the inclusion criteria, particularly publication timeframe (2016–2025) and focus on formal educational contexts. Following this in-depth eligibility assessment, 45 peer-reviewed studies were retained for thematic synthesis.

All selected articles were systematically documented using an extraction template and organized chronologically to support a clear audit trail and ensure a transparent and reproducible data collection process.

Data Analysis Technique

The collected data were analyzed using qualitative thematic synthesis, which is appropriate for identifying major themes across multiple academic sources. The analysis involved:

1. Initial coding, where key concepts related to digital tool affordances and classroom transformation were identified.
2. Theme categorization, grouping findings into broader areas such as blended learning, learner engagement, teacher competence, and institutional barriers.
3. Cross-study synthesis, comparing patterns and contradictions across the reviewed literature.

The results were summarized descriptively without statistical hypothesis testing, as the purpose of the study was interpretive and conceptual rather than experimental. This thematic approach enabled the researcher to construct an updated understanding of how digital tools contribute to transformative classroom practices in modern education.

Thematic synthesis was conducted iteratively, allowing themes to be refined as patterns emerged across studies. The analysis remained grounded in the conceptual framework, ensuring that interpretation was guided by theoretical assumptions rather than isolated findings. This process supported analytical coherence between the framework, results, and discussion sections.

In terms of trustworthiness, the study emphasized credibility through systematic selection, transparent documentation, and theory-driven analysis. While the findings are not intended to be generalized statistically, they offer transferable insights for understanding digital classroom transformation across diverse educational contexts. The methodological rigor applied throughout the review process strengthens the interpretive validity of the conclusions drawn.

RESULTS

This section presents the findings derived from the thematic synthesis of 45 peer-reviewed publications published from 2016 to 2025. The findings are structured based on the research enquiries regarding the role of digital technologies as educational resources in the transformation of classroom practices within contemporary learning environments. The results are provided descriptively, devoid of interpretation.

Digital Tools as Educational Resources in Classroom Transformation

The examined literature consistently indicates that digital tools are incorporated into classrooms as fundamental educational resources rather than as ancillary assistance. In the reviewed research, learning management systems (LMS), multimedia apps, and collaborative digital platforms emerged as the most commonly utilised tools in formal educational environments. These instruments were frequently regarded as essential elements of the teaching and learning processes.

Numerous studies have indicated that LMS platforms like Google Classroom and Moodle are predominantly utilised for the dissemination of learning resources, assignment management, and facilitation of online assessments. These platforms facilitated educators in structuring course material and sustaining organised communication with students. In numerous instances, LMS technologies were noted to enhance student progress monitoring via integrated tracking functionalities. Additional research emphasised that multimedia tools were often utilised to improve content delivery via video-based learning and interactive simulations. Such practices enhanced the diversification of instructional resources beyond conventional textbook-based methods.

Furthermore, numerous research indicated that digital tools extended classroom learning beyond physical confines by facilitating access to resources irrespective of time and location. Digital integration was frequently linked to enhanced potential for instructional continuity in online or hybrid learning environments. Communication solutions, including messaging applications and video conferencing platforms, were utilised to enhance teacher-student interaction across synchronous and asynchronous channels. Some research unexpectedly observed that the implementation of digital tools varied among institutions due to disparities in infrastructure availability and teacher preparedness.

Pedagogical Opportunities Provided by Digital Tools

Digital technologies were identified as facilitators of pedagogical methods that support blended learning, learner autonomy, and personalized instruction. Educators were observed utilizing digital resources to enhance learning activities and integrate real content into instructional practices. In numerous educational settings, technology-enhanced pedagogy promoted communication, peer engagement, and online feedback systems. Moreover, digital platforms were often linked to enhanced accessibility to educational resources for students beyond classroom hours. The magnitude of these advantages varied based on students' digital proficiency and the level of institutional assistance. These findings affirm that digital tools offer significant teaching opportunities, while their efficacy is contingent upon implementation conditions.

Support for Blended and Hybrid Learning

A multitude of studies indicated that digital tools were employed to enhance blended learning models that integrate in-person instruction with online educational activities. These approaches often incorporated asynchronous learning activities, digital discussion forums, and online learning modules facilitated via LMS platforms. Blended learning environments were extensively utilized in both higher education and secondary education settings. Numerous research have characterized blended models as the predominant instructional methodologies in the wake of post-pandemic educational transformations. Digital technologies were crucial in sustaining flexibility and continuity in contemporary learning environments.

Numerous investigations indicated that hybrid learning was advantageous in situations necessitating instructional access amid disturbances or restricted classroom attendance. Digital resources allowed students to interact with instructional materials outside of designated classroom hours. Educators were also noted to employ flipped classroom methodologies, wherein students accessed information digitally prior to engaging in collaborative classroom activities. Digital technologies offered opportunity for enhanced practice, review, and further learning assistance. Some research unexpectedly observed that the implementation of blended learning differed according to institutional preparedness and educator proficiency. These data indicate that blended models are becoming more prevalent, however their application varies across different contexts.

Increased Learner Engagement and Interaction

Numerous empirical research indicate that students exhibited increased participation when instructional methods used digital resources, including gamified applications, interactive quizzes, and multimedia learning content. Instruments such as Kahoot, Quizizz, and digital video materials were often linked to heightened classroom engagement. Students demonstrated heightened engagement when educational material was delivered in graphically enhanced and interactive formats. Digital settings facilitated instantaneous feedback, hence enhancing classroom responsiveness. The examined literature underscores participation as a significant pedagogical advantage of technology integration.

Collaborative systems like Padlet, Google Docs, and online peer-feedback tools were consistently recognized as facilitating classroom interaction via group-based learning activities. These tools facilitated learners' engagement in collaborative writing tasks, project-based work, and discussion-oriented learning activities. Numerous research indicated that online collaboration enhanced communication and shared accountability among students. Digital engagement channels were identified as beneficial for learners who participated less in conventional classroom discussions. Some studies unexpectedly indicated that engagement outcomes were contingent upon learners' familiarity with instructional technologies. These data indicate that digital tools improve engagement, however learner preparedness affects their efficacy.

Promotion of Learner Autonomy and Personalization

Research from many research demonstrated that digital tools facilitated learner autonomy by offering self-paced learning possibilities and personalized access to instructional materials. Students were often observed to review content multiple times and autonomously organize their learning agendas via online platforms. Digital tools facilitated learners' access to materials beyond classroom hours, enhancing their independence. Numerous research highlighted that autonomy was enhanced through adaptable technology-facilitated learning pathways. Digital integration was predominantly linked to learner-centred educational paradigms.

Numerous research indicated that adaptive learning technologies and AI-supported platforms provide automatic feedback and tailored learning recommendations. Such systems were characterized as facilitating differentiated instruction by modifying tasks according to student performance. Digital learning applications were often associated with tailored vocabulary exercises, pronunciation feedback, or personalized learning modules. Some studies unexpectedly shown that learners with lesser digital literacy encountered challenges in benefiting from autonomy-based learning assignments. The results demonstrate that although personalization is a crucial feature, digital competence is essential for achieving optimal autonomous outcomes.

Challenges and Limitations in Digital Tool Implementation

The thematic analysis identified persistent obstacles in the incorporation of digital tools into educational environments. The constraints were consistently classified into three primary categories: access inequity, teacher proficiency, and institutional adherence. Numerous research highlighted that the transformative capacity of digital technologies is influenced more by structural constraints than by mere technological availability. Despite the widespread adoption of digital tools, implementation issues often diminished their instructional efficacy. The examined research substantiates that digital transformation is affected by contextual and institutional factors.

Digital Divide and Access Inequality

A significant number of research indicated that inequitable access to devices and reliable internet connectivity constitutes a primary obstacle to technology integration. These issues were especially pronounced in rural settings and emerging educational systems. Students lacking personal devices experienced diminished engagement in online tasks, collaborative learning, and digital evaluations. Infrastructure constraints impeded synchronous learning activities and limited resource accessibility. The findings affirm that bridging the digital divide is crucial for equitable classroom change.

Surprisingly, certain research revealed that access discrepancies were present even within the same institution. Disparities in socioeconomic conditions led to inconsistent learner experiences and varying degrees of participation. Restricted connectivity diminished consistency in mixed and hybrid learning settings. Consequently, access disparity persists in hindering the equitable deployment of digital learning materials. These findings underscore that digital inclusion necessitates systemic infrastructural investment.

Teacher Digital Competence and Training Needs

Numerous analyzed studies indicated that educators' digital proficiency substantially impacted the efficacy of technology integration in the classroom. Educators possessing restricted digital competencies were more inclined to utilize tools solely for administrative functions, such as disseminating documents. Conversely, educators with enhanced proficiency employed interactive education, collaborative endeavors, and multimedia learning assignments. Numerous research highlighted that professional growth is crucial for significant pedagogical integration. Teacher preparedness emerged as a crucial factor in the success of digital transformation.

Unexpectedly, results indicated that even in institutions with technology resources, inadequate pedagogical training constrained classroom innovation. Certain research indicated an augmented workload for educators resulting from the necessity for instructional innovation and platform administration. In the absence of ongoing assistance, technology integration frequently remained cosmetic instead of revolutionary. These findings indicate that teacher training is essential for the sustained deployment of digital tools.

Curriculum Alignment and Compliance Challenges

Numerous research indicated that the integration of digital tools generated concerns about curriculum standards, assessment congruence, and adherence to institutional policies. The pace of technology adoption frequently outstripped the development of regulatory frameworks, leading to ambiguous implementation standards. Numerous investigations indicated discrepancies between digital learning activities and formal learning objectives. Educators often employed tools autonomously, lacking unified institutional strategy. Compliance challenges developed as a significant constraint in maintaining digital innovation.

Furthermore, current research on AI-based systems has highlighted growing problems regarding ethical utilization, privacy, and data governance. Digital platforms that gather student data have prompted enquiries about institutional accountability and protective measures. Curriculum mismatch was unexpectedly discovered to restrict the sustainability of digital practices when innovations were not properly integrated into policy frameworks. These findings show that compliance and governance are essential for sustained digital transformation.

Illustrative Classroom Scenarios in Digital Transformation

This chapter offers illustrative classroom scenarios that conceptually highlight the role of digital technologies as educational resources in various instructional situations, complementing the theme synthesis offered in the preceding part. These scenarios are not empirical case studies from a singular institution; instead, they are analytically created representations based on patterns found from the studied literature. Their objective is to convert conceptual discoveries into practical classroom implementations while ensuring theoretical consistency with the previously discussed frameworks.

Scenario 1: Learning Management Systems in Language Instruction

In a university-level English course, an instructor employs a learning management system (LMS) like Moodle or Google Classroom as the primary instructional platform. The lecturer develops a blended instructional sequence utilizing the LMS for pre-class, in-class, and post-class digital engagement, rather than merely for material uploads.

Prior to in-person meetings, students engage with multimedia resources, such as brief lecture films, digital reading materials, and vocabulary problems integrated into the LMS. Interactive quizzes offer instantaneous feedback, enabling students to discover gaps in understanding and facilitate classroom discussions. In-class sessions give time for collaborative problem-solving, peer discussion, and practical language application. Post-class, students engage in online discussion boards to contemplate learning tasks and reply to their peers' contributions.

In this context, the LMS transcends mere administrative substitution (SAMR level: substitution/augmentation) and progresses towards modification by reconfiguring instructional time and interaction dynamics. From a constructivist viewpoint, learners actively build comprehension through multimodal interaction. From a connectivist perspective, information is disseminated through digital content, peer contributions, and teacher feedback inside the LMS framework.

This scenario demonstrates how digital technologies enhance cognitive engagement, provide formative assessment, and broaden classroom interaction beyond physical confines. Successful implementation, however, relies on the digital competency of educators and students' access to dependable internet.

Scenario 2: AI-Supported Writing Feedback and Personalization

In a secondary school setting, an English instructor utilizes an AI-driven writing assistance application that offers automated input on grammar, vocabulary, and sentence structure. Students compose essays using a digital writing platform that provides instantaneous ideas and editing prompts. The AI tool is incorporated as a formative feedback mechanism to facilitate iterative progress, rather than supplanting instructor evaluation.

The educator critically evaluates AI-generated feedback and enhances it with tailored remarks emphasizing argument consistency and critical analysis. Students are urged to juxtapose automatic recommendations with instructor comments, enhancing metacognitive awareness of their writing progression. This situation illustrates how digital tools can enhance learner autonomy and facilitate differentiated training. Students advance at personalized rates, changing compositions repeatedly according to automated feedback. From a TPACK perspective, effective integration necessitates that educators link technological capabilities with pedagogical goals and content-specific writing standards.

At the same time, this scenario raises ethical and compliance considerations. AI platforms gather linguistic data and potentially sensitive information, necessitating institutional protocols on privacy, data governance, and responsible utilization. Consequently, although AI improves personalization, its implementation necessitates institutional control and ethical consideration.

Scenario 3: Blended Learning in Resource-Constrained Contexts

In a remote educational environment with restricted internet connectivity, an educator implements a low-bandwidth blended learning approach. Instead of depending on synchronous video conferencing, instructional materials are disseminated through downloadable modules and mobile-compatible platforms accessible via cellphones. Students do assignments offline and post their responses when connectivity is restored.

The educator enhances digital assignments with printed resources to guarantee inclusion for pupils with limited device access. Peer cooperation is promoted through small group talks conducted during regular in-person gatherings. Messaging programs are utilized judiciously to sustain communication while minimizing data consumption. This situation underscores the previously mentioned socio-technical systems approach. Digital transformation is influenced by the availability of tools, infrastructure, socioeconomic factors, and institutional adaptability. Despite low technology sophistication, pedagogical transformation can still be achieved through strategic adaptation.

DISCUSSION

Digital Tools as Mediating Educational Resources

This study aimed to investigate the role of digital tools as educational resources in modifying classroom practices in contemporary learning environments. The findings demonstrate that digital technologies have evolved into essential instructional resources rather than just supplementary aids, facilitating many classroom tasks such as material distribution, interaction, assessment, and learner engagement. This affirms that technology integration has evolved from a pedagogical novelty to an institutional imperative in modern educational systems, especially in light of Industry 4.0 and the transformations in learning post-pandemic (Akintayo et al., 2024b; Bucăţa & Tileagă, 2024). The examined literature consistently linked digital platforms to blended learning models, augmented collaborative learning opportunities, and improved learner autonomy. The synthesis concurrently underscored ongoing issues pertaining to digital inequality, educators' digital proficiency, and institutional adherence. The findings unexpectedly indicated that the sheer presence of technology does not inherently lead to pedagogical revolution, as implementation significantly differs among educational environments. The findings indicate that digital tools provide significant educational advantages, however their effectiveness is contingent upon systemic and instructional factors.

The findings on the first research question indicate that digital technologies increasingly serve as mediating educational resources that transform classroom practices rather than merely supporting established instructional routines. The mediating role is apparent in the extensive utilization of learning management systems, multimedia platforms, and digital communication tools to structure instruction, enhance interaction, and oversee assessment processes. Consistent with the conceptual framework of this study, digital technologies serve as mediators between pedagogical intents and learning experiences, facilitating instructional practices that transcend the time and physical limitations of conventional classrooms.

This understanding corresponds with constructivist and connectivist viewpoints, which perceive learning as an active and interconnected process. Digital tools facilitate these viewpoints by allowing learners to engage with content, peers, and instructors through many modalities. Thus, classroom change arises not merely from the availability of technology, but from the integration of digital resources into pedagogical design and learning interactions.

Pedagogical Opportunities and Learner-Centered Shifts

The findings on the second research question indicate that digital tools offer significant pedagogical advantages by enhancing student engagement, facilitating personalization, and enabling blended learning approaches. These opportunities align with the pedagogical affordances aspect of the conceptual framework, highlighting how technology facilitates interactive and learner-centred instructional methodologies. Digital tools enable educators to diversify learning activities, incorporate real content, and foster collaborative learning settings that promote active student engagement.

The prevalence of blended learning in the examined research substantiates Hrastinski's (2019) claim that blended models improve flexibility and learner engagement through the integration of in-person and online instructional elements. Digital platforms provide asynchronous access to resources and synchronous engagement, promoting individualized learning trajectories and learner independence. From a learner-centred viewpoint, digital tools facilitate personalized learning experiences by enabling students to interact with content at their own pace and in accordance with their specific needs.

These findings hold particular significance in language education situations, where interaction, multimodality, and communication-centered learning are paramount. Digital tools offer options for genuine language exposure, practice, and feedback that may be challenging to attain just in conventional classroom environments. Consequently, digital resources serve as pedagogical facilitators that enhance contemporary educational ideas.

Challenges and Institutional Barriers

The third study question examined the obstacles and constraints associated with the implementation of digital tools. The results demonstrate that disparities in access, teacher digital proficiency, and institutional adherence continue to be significant obstacles to enduring classroom reform. Analyzed through the institutional conditions aspect of the conceptual framework, these issues underscore that digital transformation is a systemic process rather than solely a pedagogical endeavor.

Access disparities persistently hinder equitable engagement in technology-enhanced education, especially in developing settings. Despite the availability of digital resources, unreliable connectivity and disparities in device ownership might diminish the efficacy of blended and hybrid learning approaches. These findings corroborate prior studies suggesting that digital inclusion necessitates synchronized infrastructure investment and policy endorsement.

The digital competency of teachers has emerged as a significant element affecting the extent of technology integration. In alignment with the DigCompEdu paradigm, the results indicate that educators need both technological expertise and pedagogical and ethical abilities to effectively integrate digital resources. In the absence of organized professional development, the utilization of technology frequently remains administrative instead of transformative.

Furthermore, curricular congruence and institutional compliance have emerged as significant challenges, especially with the rising use of AI-driven digital solutions. The lack of explicit norms and governance frameworks may hinder the sustainability of innovation and elevate ethical concerns around data protection and assessment integrity. These problems highlight the necessity for institutional preparedness to facilitate sustained digital change.

This study enhances educational technology studies by affirming the notion of digital tools as mediating educational resources rather than neutral technologies. The study enhances a comprehensive understanding of digital classroom transformation by incorporating learning theories, technological integration models, and institutional views. This method substantiates the claim that successful technology integration depends on pedagogical coherence, student involvement, and institutional preparedness.

The findings further contribute to previous literature by emphasizing the constraints of technology-centric narratives that presume innovation will inherently ensue from adoption. This study underscores that digital transformation should be perceived as a process rooted within social and institutional contexts. This theoretical framework enhances current discussions on sustainable digital pedagogy in contemporary schooling.

Furthermore, teacher competency surfaced as a pivotal factor in effective digital integration. Trust and Whalen (2020) indicated that educators innovatively adapted to digital resources during pandemic-era education, but encountered challenges with workload, digital literacy, and instructional redesign. Likewise, Redecker's (2017) DigCompEdu paradigm underscores that digital transformation is significantly contingent upon educators' professional proficiency, institutional preparedness, and pedagogical coherence. This study's findings indicate that inadequate digital competence and unstructured professional growth result in technology integration being predominantly administrative rather than transformative.

The unforeseen discovery that availability does not ensure transformation highlights the need of systemic readiness and adherence to policy. Although digital technologies offer the potential for innovation, their adoption raises problems about educational efficacy, curricular alignment, and sustainability, as noted in the introduction. This indicates that the transformation of classrooms via digital resources is not inherently achieved through technological adoption; rather, it necessitates strategic governance, meticulous instructional planning, and egalitarian infrastructure.

The findings provide significant implications for educators, school administrators, and legislators. Educators are urged to transcend fundamental administrative applications of digital tools and concentrate on pedagogically informed integration that fosters engagement, autonomy, and collaboration. Ongoing professional growth is crucial to facilitate this transition.

At the institutional level, explicit rules and curriculum alignment are essential to guarantee that digital innovation is sustainable and adheres to educational standards. Institutions must prioritize fair access to digital resources and offer continuous technical and instructional assistance. By addressing both pedagogical and structural aspects, stakeholders can more effectively utilize digital tools as transformative educational resources.

Collectively, these persistent problems illustrate that digital transformation in education transcends simply technology acceptance, representing a multifaceted institutional and pedagogical endeavor. Although digital tools provide considerable instructional advantages, their application is profoundly affected by systemic factors including infrastructural preparedness, professional competence, and regulatory coherence. The enduring access inequity, restricted digital proficiency, and ambiguous governance indicate that classroom transformation cannot be comprehensively analyzed solely through a functional perspective of tool usage. These restrictions necessitate a comprehensive critical examination of the sustainability of digital integration and the assumptions that underpin current narratives of educational innovation. Thus, it is essential to progress beyond mere descriptive analyses of opportunities and obstacles to a more contemplative investigation of how digital change is understood, implemented, and maintained across various educational systems.

Critical Reflection on Sustainable Digital Transformation

The findings confirm the educational benefits of digital technologies in modern classrooms; yet, a careful examination shows that digital transformation is not intrinsically progressive or universally transformational. Dominant narratives in educational technology discussions frequently highlight innovation, efficiency, and modernization. Nevertheless, such techno-optimistic perspectives often underestimate the structural, institutional, and epistemological factors that influence the real effects of digital integration. Sustainable digital transformation should be understood not as technology proliferation, but as a systematic reconfiguration of pedagogy, governance, and institutional culture.

A vital distinction must be made between emergency-induced digital adoption and fundamentally integrated pedagogical revolution. The swift implementation of technology during the COVID-19 pandemic facilitated instructional continuity; nonetheless, emergency remote teaching cannot be equated with sustainable digital integration. In numerous settings, digital tools mostly served as functional replacements for in-person instruction rather than as catalysts for instructional innovation. Post-pandemic educational systems today face the task of shifting from reactive technological adaptation to deliberate, theory-based digital pedagogy. Sustainable transformation necessitates curriculum reorganization, assessment adjustment, and pedagogical redefinition instead of perpetuating ad hoc digital practices.

The investigation reveals a continual disparity between technological offerings and educational innovation. The presence of learning management systems, collaborative platforms, and AI-assisted applications does not inherently create revolutionary learning environments. Empirical research indicates that digital integration often exists at levels of substitution or augmentation, demonstrating superficial adaptation rather than a fundamental reconfiguration of learning processes. This observation highlights that transformation is limited more by educational aim and professional capability than by technical access. Significant transformation occurs when educators reframe teaching methodologies to accord with learner-centred and constructivist frameworks.

Furthermore, digital transformation should be comprehended within a socio-technical framework where institutional governance, policy coherence, and professional development structures influence technology impact. Innovation is not independent of organizational systems. Disjointed digital policy, inadequate training infrastructures, and poor alignment between curriculum and technology constrain the extent of transformation. In contrast, institutional coherence—where infrastructure, pedagogy, assessment, and governance align—fosters settings conducive to enduring innovation.

Equity considerations further confound oversimplified portrayals of technology advancement. Ongoing discrepancies in connectivity, device ownership, and digital literacy undermine the premise that technological advancement automatically promotes inclusivity. In the absence of intentional equity-focused policies, digital transformation may exacerbate existing structural disparities. Sustainable integration necessitates policy interventions that emphasize equitable access, tailored support mechanisms, and contextually appropriate implementation strategies.

From an epistemological standpoint, digitally networked and AI-mediated learning environments transform knowledge production and authority frameworks. As learning increasingly transpires through distributed informational networks, instructors assume the role of facilitators for critical evaluation and knowledge navigation, while students must develop advanced digital discernment skills. Sustainable change requires a redesign of educational competencies to align with the realities of algorithmically mediated knowledge ecosystems.

Sustainability in digital transformation encompasses not just technological continuity but also institutional adaptability and pedagogical resilience. As particular platforms develop or become outdated, the institutional ability for critical assessment and strategic incorporation becomes paramount. Sustainable digital transformation is defined not by reliance on technology, but by the development of reflective and adaptive educational frameworks that can responsibly incorporate emerging advances.

This comprehensive consideration of sustainability must also incorporate the rapid incorporation of artificial intelligence into educational institutions. As classrooms evolve into data-driven and algorithmically mediated environments, technology systems increasingly impact instructional decision-making and assessment processes. This development presents governance and ethical difficulties that require thorough analysis in the next section.

Ethical and Governance Implications of AI Integration in Digital Classrooms

The use of artificial intelligence into educational settings signifies a substantial change in the evolution of digital classrooms. In contrast to previous digital tools that mainly enabled communication and content management, AI-supported systems engage in feedback generation, adaptive sequencing, predictive analytics, and content creation. Thus, AI technologies not only assist pedagogy but also influence epistemic processes and decision-making frameworks in the classroom.

A crucial aspect pertains to data governance. AI-driven platforms depend significantly on student performance indicators, behavioral data, and interaction histories. Although these datasets facilitate personalization and adaptive learning, they also pose substantial issues related to consent, data ownership, transparency, and long-term preservation. In numerous educational environments, the regulatory mechanisms managing educational data are inadequately established. The integration of sustainable AI requires strong institutional frameworks that explicitly outline data collecting processes, accountability mechanisms, and privacy protections.

Algorithmic bias represents a further ethical issue. AI systems developed on historically entrenched datasets may perpetuate linguistic, cultural, or socio-economic prejudices. Automated writing grading methods in language education may favor prevailing linguistic standards while sidelining diverse modes of expression. Such processes threaten to perpetuate systemic imbalances while masquerading as technical neutrality. Integrating responsible AI necessitates a thorough assessment of algorithmic results and a dedication from institutions to uphold justice, transparency, and inclusivity.

The adoption of AI is further complicated by academic integrity. Generative AI technologies that can create cohesive academic works question traditional notions of authorship and the validity of assessments. Instead of relying exclusively on prohibitive measures, institutions should enhance their approach by establishing AI literacy frameworks that incorporate ethical usage rules, critical awareness, and the redesign of assessments. In this perspective, AI should be regarded as a tool for educational enhancement rather than a replacement for cognitive involvement.

The integration of AI also redefines professional positions. Although automated solutions provide instant feedback and predictive data, pedagogical authority should be anchored in professional opinion. The TPACK framework is notably relevant, highlighting the importance of merging technology knowledge with pedagogical and content competence. Educators need both practical knowledge of AI systems and the analytical skills to assess algorithmic suggestions within certain disciplinary and contextual frameworks.

Institutional governance frameworks significantly influence the integration of ethical AI. It is vital to clearly articulate policies for authorized AI usage, transparency mandates, vendor accountability, and quality assurance mechanisms. In the absence of cohesive governance, technology vendors may wield excessive influence over instructional practices, perhaps favoring commercial interests above educational principles. A socio-technical systems perspective emphasizes that AI deployment should be integrated with educational priorities rather than dictated by technological determinism.

In emerging contexts, governance difficulties are exacerbated by regulatory restraints and resource limitations. The swift adoption of AI, propelled by modernization demands, may surpass ethical regulation. Context-sensitive governance frameworks that reconcile innovation with caution are so necessary. The incorporation of ethical AI should be directed by locally informed educational priorities instead than externally imposed technology trends.

In conclusion, the integration of AI offers transformative potential alongside considerable ethical responsibilities. Sustainable digital transformation in the age of AI necessitates transparent governance, deliberate pedagogy, equality orientation, and institutional accountability. AI can only serve as a responsible mediator of learning through organized integration, rather than acting as an opaque determinant of educational processes.

Implications for Developing Educational Contexts and Policy Alignment

The language on digital transformation is often influenced by experiences in technologically advanced systems; yet, its implications for developing educational contexts require distinct consideration. In resource-limited settings, digital integration is influenced by infrastructure constraints, economic disparities, and fragmented policies. Thus, sustainable transformation should be framed within the framework of specific institutional circumstances rather than universal technology standards.

Infrastructure asymmetry continues to be a fundamental limitation. Unreliable connectivity, restricted device accessibility, and erratic technical assistance directly affect the extent and continuity of digital integration. Context-sensitive methods, including low-bandwidth platforms, asynchronous instructional models, and mobile-optimized resources, may provide more sustainable alternatives than the replication of high-resource technology paradigms.

The discrepancy between policy and practice further hinders reform. Ambitious digital modernization initiatives frequently lack adequate investments in teacher training, curriculum reformation, and system upkeep. This disjunction induces implementation fatigue and constrains institutional coherence. Successful digital transformation necessitates cohesive policy frameworks that amalgamate infrastructure planning, professional development, assessment reform, and governance structures.

The enhancement of professional capacity is very vital. In the absence of continuous pedagogical instruction, digital instruments may be relegated to administrative roles. Long-term professional development programs must prioritize instructional redesign, ethical AI literacy, varied assessment methods, and inclusive digital pedagogy. Socio-economic disparities interface with digital inclusion in intricate manners. Students from low-income homes may face restricted access to gadgets and connectivity, hindering their involvement in technology-enhanced learning. Equity-focused measures, like device sharing initiatives, subsidized internet access, and hybrid teaching approaches, are crucial to ensure that digital change does not exacerbate existing structural inequalities.

Moreover, dependence on international educational technology providers raises issues of technological reliance and institutional independence. Sustainable integration necessitates the equilibrium of external technology collaborations with investments in local digital ecosystems and open educational resources. Significantly, digital transformation in poor contexts should not be assessed using uniform global criteria. Significant improvement may demonstrate capability through increased access, expanded participation, and bolstered professional competence. Acknowledging contextual diversity promotes a more egalitarian and realistic global dialogue on educational innovation.

Sustainable transformation necessitates alignment across four interconnected dimensions: infrastructure readiness, educational capability, governance coherence, and equity orientation from a socio-technical perspective. Integrated advancement in these areas fosters institutional resilience and enduring adaptation. These factors collectively confirm that digital classroom transformation is contextually integrated and structurally influenced. Sustainable innovation arises when technological integration is directed by policy alignment, institutional dedication, and equity-focused implementation tactics.

CONCLUSION

This study has rigorously analyzed digital technologies as educational resources and their impact on transforming classroom practices in modern learning environments. Recent literature reveals that digital tools have transitioned from additional instructional aids to integral components of contemporary educational ecosystems. Nonetheless, their revolutionary potential depends on educational alignment, institutional coherence, and equal access, rather than only on technical presence.

The analysis addressing the initial research question reveals that digital technologies serve as mediating resources that facilitate instructional delivery, interaction patterns, and evaluation processes. Learning management systems, multimedia applications, collaborative platforms, and AI-enhanced technologies transcend spatial and temporal limitations of traditional classrooms, facilitating multimodal participation and decentralized knowledge creation. Transformation occurs when technological affordances are purposefully included into educational design instead of being used as mere utilitarian substitutes.

Concerning the second study issue, digital integration offers substantial pedagogical advantages, especially in facilitating blended learning, enhancing student engagement, promoting autonomy, and enabling personalization. Asynchronous access, interactive multimedia environments, collaborative digital spaces, and adaptive feedback systems facilitate learner-centred educational methods. In language education settings, these affordances enhance communicative skills and multimodal literacy. However, the actualization of these potential relies on digital proficiency, pedagogical experience, and institutional support frameworks.

Regarding the final research question, enduring structural obstacles persistently influence implementation outcomes. Access inequality, differences in connectivity and device ownership, poor digital competence among educators, and inadequate professional development hinder the extent of integration. Furthermore, curricular mismatch, regulatory uncertainty, and rising ethical issues, particularly related to AI-driven systems, highlight the need for cohesive governance structures. These findings confirm that digital transformation functions as a socio-technical process influenced by infrastructural preparedness, professional capability, and policy coherence.

This chapter presents a broader conceptual argument: successful digital transformation necessitates systemic integration rather than sporadic adoption. The differentiation between emergency-driven implementation and structurally integrated pedagogical redesign is crucial in post-pandemic educational settings. Enduring transformation relies on curriculum adjustment, institutional flexibility, and ongoing professional growth.

The increasing integration of artificial intelligence amplifies these considerations. Although AI systems improve personalization and feedback efficiency, they also present difficulties about data governance, algorithmic bias, academic integrity, and professional autonomy. Responsible integration requires transparent regulatory frameworks and the cultivation of AI literacy among educators and students.

The implications for establishing educational environments underscore that digital change is influenced by its specific context. Infrastructure imbalances, socio-economic inequalities, and discrepancies between policy and reality necessitate tailored measures based on equitable execution and institutional pragmatism.

In conclusion, digital classroom transformation must be recognized as an adaptive and morally founded institutional process. Educational innovation will be dictated not solely by technical advancement, but by institutions' ability to integrate digital technologies with instructional objectives, governance transparency, and equitable access. Sustainable digital integration arises when technical progress is directed by critical analysis, institutional consistency, and a long-term dedication to educational justice. Future study should emphasize longitudinal and cross-contextual investigations to analyze the evolution of digital ecosystems within various institutional frameworks, hence enhancing theoretical and policy-oriented insights into sustainable digital innovation.

REFERENCES

Abedi, E. A. (2024). Tensions between technology integration practices of teachers and ICT in education policy expectations: Implications for change in teacher knowledge, beliefs and teaching practices. *Journal of Computers in Education, 11*(4), 1215–1234. Advance online publication. DOI: 10.1007/s40692-023-00296-6

Akintayo, O. T., Eden, C. A., Ayeni, O. O., & Onyebuchi, N. C. (2024a). Evaluating the impact of educational technology on learning outcomes in the higher education sector: A systematic review. *Open Access Research Journal of Multidisciplinary Studies, 07*(02), 052–072. 10.53022/oarjms.2024.7.2.0026

Akintayo, O. T., Eden, C. A., Ayeni, O. O., & Onyebuchi, N. C. (2024b). Inclusive Curriculum Design: Meeting The Diverse Needs of Students for Social Improvement. *International Journal of Applied Research in Social Sciences, 6*(5), 770–784. DOI: 10.51594/ijarss.v6i5.1100

Alsuwaida, N., & Alsamiri, Y. (2025). Innovation using artificial intelligence in an advertising art classroom. *Frontiers in Education, 10*, 1670810. Advance online publication. DOI: 10.3389/feduc.2025.1670810

Atan, M. A., Hamid, A. A. A., Azhar, S. B. H. J., & Norwahi, N. A. (2024). Digital Communication Tools in Language Education: A Conceptual Analysis of their Impact on Classroom Language Practices. *International Journal of Academic Research in Business & Social Sciences, 14*(12), 2624–2634. DOI: 10.6007/IJARBSS/v14-i12/23756

Banihashem, S. K., & Macfadyen, L. P. (2021). Pedagogical design: Bridging learning theory and learning analytics. *Canadian Journal of Learning and Technology, 47*(1). Advance online publication. DOI: 10.21432/cjlt27959

Bou Saad, R., Garcia, A. L., & Garcia, J. M. C. (2025). Mapping Constructivist Active Learning for STEM: Toward Sustainable Education. In *Sustainability (Switzerland)* (Vol. 17, Issue 13). DOI: 10.3390/su17136225

Bucăţa, G., & Tileagă, C. (2024). Digital Renaissance in Education: Unveiling the Transformative Potential of Digitization in Educational Institutions. *Land Forces Academy Review, 29*(1), 20–37. 10.2478/raft-2024-0003

Christine, R. (2017). European Framework for the Digital Competence of Educators: DigCompEdu. *Publications Office of the European Union*. 10.2760/159770

Dancsa, D., Štempeľová, I., Takáč, O., & Annuš, N. (2023). Digital Tools in Education. *International Journal of Advanced Natural Sciences and Engineering Researches*, *7*(4), 289–294. DOI: 10.59287/ijanser.717

Facer, K., & Selwyn, N. (2021). Digital Technology and the Futures of Education: Towards 'Non-Stupid' Optimism. *UNESCO*. https://unesdoc.unesco.org/ark:/48223/pf0000377071

Gunawardena, C. N., Chen, Y., Flor, N., & Sánchez, D. (2023). Deep Learning Models for Analyzing Social Construction of Knowledge Online. *Online Learning : the Official Journal of the Online Learning Consortium*, *27*(4). Advance online publication. DOI: 10.24059/olj.v27i4.4055

Khanh, L. C. (2024). Teachers' Roles on English Language Teaching for Promoting Learner-Centered Language Learning: A Theoretical Review. *International Journal of TESOL & Education*, *4*(2), 78–98. DOI: 10.54855/ijte.24425

Martín-Lucas, J., & García del Dujo, Á. (2023). Knowledge-building in an environment mediated by digital technology: A case study in higher education. *Education and Information Technologies*, *28*(3), 3267–3287. Advance online publication. DOI: 10.1007/s10639-022-11304-0 PMID: 36119125

Mastrokoukou, S., & Crawford–Lee, M. (2023). Guest editorial: Profound digital Pedagogies: global perspectives. In *Higher Education, Skills and Work-based Learning* (Vol. 13, Issue 4). DOI: 10.1108/HESWBL-08-2023-291

Mekheimer, M. A. (2025). Effective technology integration in higher education: A mixed-methods study of professional development. *Education and Information Technologies*, *30*(17), 25013–25058. Advance online publication. DOI: 10.1007/s10639-025-13750-y

Merzifonluoğlu, A. (2023). Promoting Listening Skills with an Educational Tool: VoScreen. *Journal of Educational Technology and Online Learning*, *6*(4), 1027–1043. DOI: 10.31681/jetol.1343391

Onwadi, R. U. (2024). Instructional Delivery Process of Entrepreneurship Education Curriculum in Senior Secondary Schools in Abuja, Nigeria. *Education, Sustainability & Society (ESS)*, *7*(1), 31–37. 10.26480/ess.01.2024.31.37

Russo, D. (2025). Pandemic pedagogy: Evaluating remote education strategies during COVID-19. *Journal of Systems and Software*, *226*, 112392. Advance online publication. DOI: 10.1016/j.jss.2025.112392

Salinas-Hernández, U., & Sacristán, A. I. (2024). Digital Resources Integration Driven by Curriculum and Teachers' Documentational Trajectories. *Research Square*. DOI: 10.21203/rs.3.rs-4010201/v1

Simos, C., & Katsiampoura, I. (2025). The Use of Digital Tools to Enhance Inclusion in the Classroom. *World Journal of Advanced Engineering Technology and Sciences*, *17*(1), 465–477. Advance online publication. DOI: 10.30574/wjaets.2025.17.1.1446

Trust, T., & Whalen, J. (2020). Should Teachers Be Trained in Emergency Remote Teaching? Lessons Learned from the COVID-19 Pandemic. *Journal of Technology and Teacher Education*, *28*(2), 189–199. DOI: 10.70725/307718pkpjuu

Weich, A., & Macgilchrist, F. (2023). *Postdigital Participation in Education*. Palgrave Studies in Educational Media. DOI: 10.1007/978-3-031-38052-5

Wu, Y., Kanji, M., & Ou, G. (2025). From socialization to internalization: Tracing knowledge co-construction through sequential discourse interaction acts in high school English learning. *Frontiers in Education*, *10*, 1664093. Advance online publication. DOI: 10.3389/feduc.2025.1664093

Yusof, R., Yin, K. Y., Norwani, N. M., Ahmad, N. L., & Ismail, Z. (2022). Investigating the Role of Digital Learning in Enhancing Educational Values: Online Socialization and Its Effect on Peer Learning, Collaborative Skills and Knowledge Construction. *International Journal of Learning. Teaching and Educational Research*, *21*(9), 441–459. Advance online publication. DOI: 10.26803/ijlter.21.9.24

Zhang, Y., & Dong, C. (2024). Exploring the Digital Transformation of Generative AI-Assisted Foreign Language Education: A Socio-Technical Systems Perspective Based on Mixed-Methods. *Systems*, *12*(11), 462. DOI: 10.3390/systems12110462

Zou, Y., Kuek, F., Feng, W., & Cheng, X. (2025). Digital learning in the 21st century: trends, challenges, and innovations in technology integration. In *Frontiers in Education* (Vol. 10). DOI: 10.3389/feduc.2025.1562391

Chapter 10
Neurocognitive and Psychological Implications of AI-Based Patient Monitoring Technologies in Modern Nursing

D. Sivakami
Velammal College of Nursing, India

G. Pradeep Kumar
http://orcid.org/0000-0002-9381-2889
Velammal College of Engineering and Technology, India

Jesi Kerenal
Velammal College of Nursing, India

P. Suveetha Dhanaselvam
Velammal College of Engineering and Technology, India

B. Sridevi
Velammal Institute of Technology, India

K. Kavitha
Velammal College of Engineering and Technology, India

ABSTRACT

Artificial intelligence (AI)–based patient monitoring technologies are transforming modern nursing practice by changing how nurses monitor patients, interpret clinical data, and make care decisions. This chapter examines the neurocognitive and psychological implications of these technologies using perspectives from cognitive psychology, human factors engineering, occupational health psychology, and nursing science. It explores AI systems influence attention, clinical decision-making, memory processes, and cognitive workload in acute care settings. While AI

DOI: 10.4018/979-8-3373-9484-8.ch010

automates many monitoring tasks, it introduces new demands such as interpreting alerts, evaluating algorithmic outputs, and integrating machine-generated insights with clinical judgment. Issues like alert fatigue, automation bias, and increased data complexity may affect decision accuracy and patient safety. The chapter also discusses technostress, autonomy concerns, trust in AI systems, emphasizing the importance of human-centered design, training, and organizational support for effective human–AI collaboration in nursing practice

1. INTRODUCTION

1.1 Background and Context

The landscape of patient monitoring in healthcare has undergone dramatic transformation over the past two decades. Traditional nursing practice relied heavily on manual vital sign checks, direct patient observation, and clinical intuition developed through experience. Nurses would physically assess patients at scheduled intervals, manually record measurements, and rely on their sensory observations and pattern recognition skills to detect changes in patient status. This model, while time-tested, carried inherent limitations in terms of continuous surveillance, early detection of subtle physiological changes, and the cognitive burden of simultaneously monitoring multiple patients with varying acuity levels.

Figure 1. Contemporary nursing practice integrating AI-based monitoring technologies

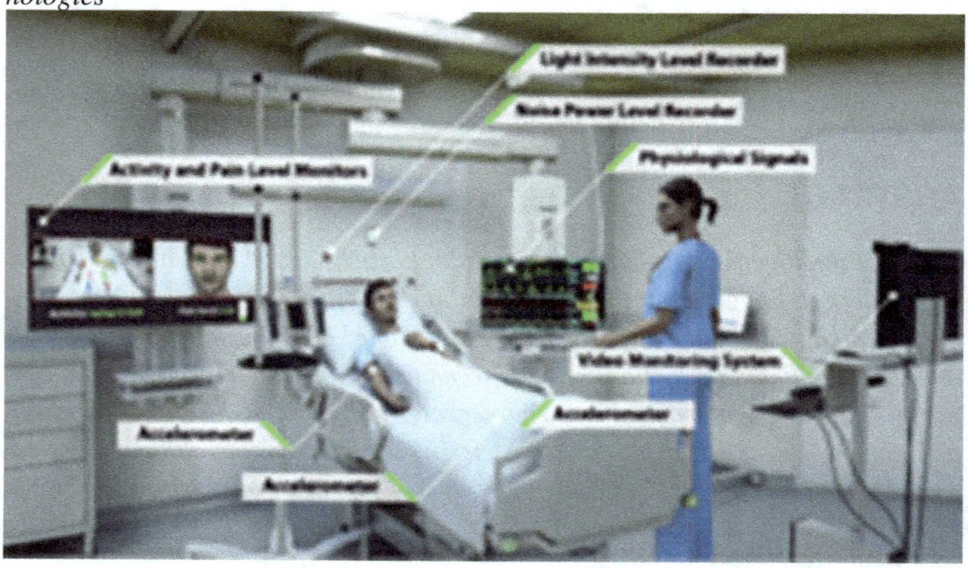

The emergence of electronic monitoring equipment (Topol, 2019) in the late twentieth century introduced the first wave of technological augmentation to nursing surveillance. Basic telemetry systems, automated blood pressure cuffs, and pulse oximeters reduced some manual measurement tasks while introducing new requirements for equipment operation and data interpretation. However, these early systems largely functioned as passive data collectors, with limited analytical capabilities and minimal integration across different monitoring modalities. Nurses remained the primary integrators of disparate data streams, responsible for synthesizing information from multiple devices and clinical observations to form coherent assessments of patient status.

The current era of artificial intelligence-based patient monitoring represents a qualitative shift beyond mere automation of data collection. Contemporary AI systems employ machine learning algorithms trained on vast datasets to recognize complex patterns, predict adverse events before clinical manifestation, and provide real-time decision support. These technologies can continuously analyze multiple physiological parameters simultaneously, detecting subtle trends and correlations that might escape human attention amid the competing demands of modern nursing practice. Examples include sepsis prediction algorithms that integrate laboratory values, vital signs, and clinical notes; fall detection systems using computer vision; early warning scores that dynamically adjust based on real-time data; and natural language processing tools that extract relevant information from unstructured clinical documentation.

This technological evolution occurs within a broader context of healthcare transformation characterized by increasing patient complexity, nursing workforce challenges, and escalating demands for efficiency and safety. The aging population presents with multiple comorbidities requiring intensive monitoring. Nursing shortages in many regions intensify workload pressures, making technological assistance both appealing and necessary. Simultaneously, growing recognition of preventable adverse events has created institutional and regulatory pressure to identify deteriorating patients earlier. AI monitoring technologies emerge as potential solutions to these converging challenges, promising to enhance surveillance capabilities, reduce preventable complications, and optimize nursing time allocation.

1.2 Significance of the Study

Despite substantial investment in AI monitoring technologies and growing deployment across healthcare settings, a critical gap exists in understanding their impact on the humans who interact with them daily. Much of the existing literature focuses on technical performance metrics such as algorithm accuracy, sensitivity, specificity, and predictive value. While these technical evaluations are essential for ensuring patient safety, they provide an incomplete picture of how these technologies function within the sociotechnical system of nursing practice. Nurses do not simply receive and act upon AI-generated alerts in isolation; rather, they integrate this information within complex cognitive processes, emotional states, professional identities, and organizational contexts.

The human factors dimension of AI implementation deserves systematic examination for several compelling reasons. First, the effectiveness of any clinical technology ultimately depends on appropriate human use. Even highly accurate algorithms fail to improve outcomes if clinicians do not trust them, misinterpret their outputs, or experience alert fatigue leading to desensitization. Understanding the neurocognitive demands these systems place on nurses and the psychological responses they evoke is therefore essential for realizing their potential benefits. Second, nursing workforce wellbeing represents an important outcome in its own right, beyond instrumental concerns about performance. If AI technologies contribute to stress, burnout, or professional dissatisfaction, these consequences matter independently of their effects on patient metrics. Third, the rapid pace of AI adoption means that nurses are already navigating these technologies with limited evidence-based guidance about optimal interaction strategies, training approaches, or organizational support structures.

This examination is particularly timely given emerging evidence of unintended consequences from early AI implementations. Reports of alert fatigue, where clinicians become desensitized to frequent warnings, suggest that increasing the volume of information does not automatically improve decision-making. Concerns about automation bias, where users over-rely on automated recommendations even when contradicted by other evidence, raise questions about the impact on critical thinking skills. Anecdotal accounts of nurses feeling deskilled or reduced to technology monitors highlight potential threats to professional identity and job satisfaction. These observations underscore the need for systematic investigation of the neurocognitive and psychological dimensions of AI-augmented nursing practice.

1.3 Scope and Objectives

This chapter focuses specifically on AI-based patient monitoring technologies (Jiang et al., 2017) deployed in acute care settings including intensive care units, general medical-surgical wards, and emergency departments. The term AI-based patient monitoring encompasses systems that employ machine learning algorithms for pattern recognition, predictive analytics, or clinical decision support related to patient surveillance. This includes but is not limited to: continuous vital sign monitoring with automated early warning scores; sepsis prediction algorithms; fall risk assessment and detection systems; pressure ulcer risk stratification; cardiac rhythm analysis; respiratory pattern recognition; and integrated monitoring platforms that synthesize multiple data streams.

The neurocognitive domains examined include attention processes such as sustained vigilance, selective attention, and divided attention across multiple information sources. Memory systems encompass working memory capacity for simultaneously processing multiple alerts and data points, as well as long-term memory for integrating AI-assisted decisions into clinical knowledge. Decision-making processes include the interaction between algorithmic recommendations and clinical judgment, speed-accuracy tradeoffs in response to alerts, and the development of trust calibration. Cognitive workload addresses the mental effort required to interpret AI outputs, manage multiple competing demands, and maintain situational awareness of the overall clinical picture.

Psychological factors investigated include occupational stress arising from constant connectivity, alert management, and performance anxiety related to AI monitoring. Professional identity concerns involve perceived threats to nursing expertise, autonomy in clinical judgment, and the evolving nature of nursing work. Trust dynamics encompass the development of appropriate reliance on AI systems, factors influencing trust formation, and consequences of both insufficient and excessive trust. Job satisfaction dimensions address technology as either a facilitator of or barrier to patient connection, satisfaction with workflow changes, and overall engagement with nursing practice.

2. THEORETICAL FRAMEWORK

2.1 Cognitive Load Theory in Healthcare Technology

Cognitive load theory (Sweller, 1988) provides a foundational framework for understanding how AI monitoring technologies impact nurses' mental processing. Originally developed to explain learning processes, this theory posits that human working memory has limited capacity for simultaneously processing new information. The theory distinguishes among three types of cognitive load: intrinsic load inherent to the task itself, extraneous load imposed by how information is presented, and germane load devoted to schema construction and learning. In the context of AI monitoring, intrinsic load relates to the fundamental complexity of patient assessment and clinical decision-making. Nurses must integrate physiological data, understand pathophysiology, consider individual patient factors, and determine appropriate interventions—cognitive demands that exist regardless of whether monitoring is manual or AI-assisted.

Figure 2. Cognitive load theory framework applied to nursing informatics

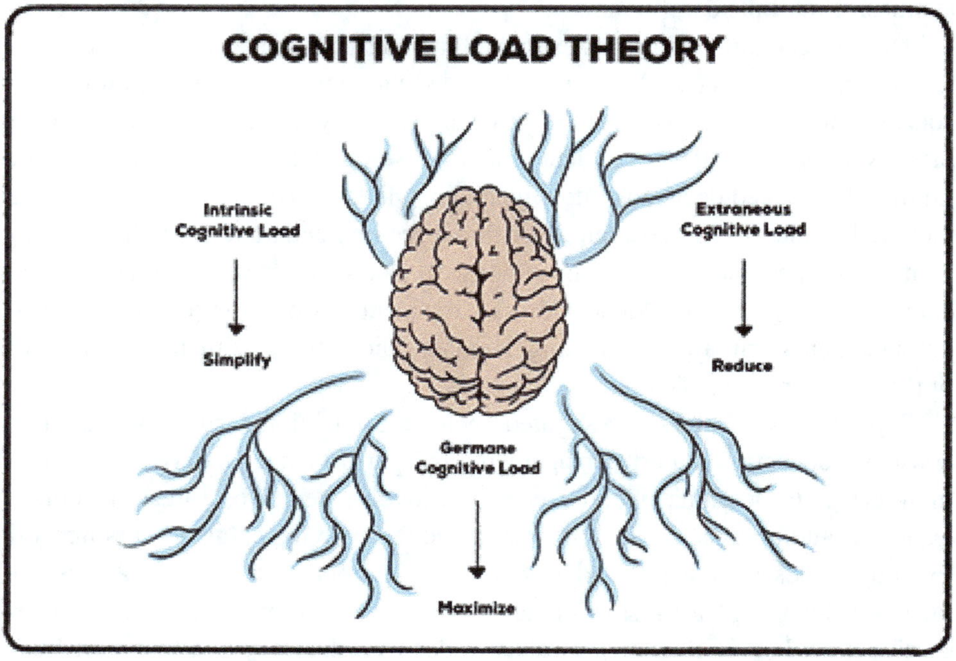

Extraneous cognitive load represents a critical design consideration for AI monitoring interfaces. Poorly designed systems can impose unnecessary mental effort through confusing displays, excessive alerts, unclear terminology, or fragmented information requiring users to mentally integrate data presented across multiple screens or devices. When extraneous load is high, it consumes working memory capacity that could otherwise support the intrinsic processing demands of clinical decision-making. Conversely, well-designed AI interfaces can reduce extraneous load through intuitive visualizations, intelligent alert filtering, contextual information presentation, and seamless integration with existing workflows. The challenge lies in achieving this reduction without oversimplifying information to the point where critical nuances are lost.

Germane cognitive load refers to the mental effort devoted to developing expertise and understanding. In the context of AI monitoring, this includes learning how algorithms work, when they are most reliable, how to interpret their outputs, and how to integrate AI-generated insights with other clinical information. Some germane load is desirable and necessary for nurses to develop sophisticated mental models of AI system behaviour

The cognitive load framework helps explain several phenomena observed in AI monitoring implementations. Alert fatigue can be understood partly as a response to excessive extraneous load—when nurses receive numerous alerts, many of which are false positives or clinically irrelevant, the cognitive effort required to evaluate each one depletes mental resources. Over time, this may lead to desensitization or development of heuristics that dismiss alerts without full evaluation. Similarly, automation bias may result when high cognitive load from multiple competing demands leads nurses to default to AI recommendations as a means of reducing mental effort. Understanding these mechanisms through a cognitive load lens suggests that interventions should focus not merely on training users to attend to alerts, but on redesigning systems to optimize the distribution of cognitive load.

2.2 Technology Acceptance Models

Technology acceptance models provide theoretical frameworks for understanding factors that influence whether and how nurses adopt AI monitoring technologies. The Technology Acceptance Model, originally proposed by Davis (1989), posits that two key beliefs predict technology use: perceived usefulness—the degree to which a person believes the technology will enhance their job performance—and perceived ease of use—the degree to which a person believes using the technology will be effortless. In nursing contexts, perceived usefulness encompasses beliefs about whether AI monitoring improves patient safety, enables earlier detection of deterioration, reduces documentation burden, or supports clinical decision-making. Perceived ease of use relates to interface intuitiveness, integration with existing workflows, learning curve, and technical reliability.

Extensions of the basic Technology Acceptance Model incorporate additional factors particularly relevant to healthcare settings. Trust emerges as a critical variable—nurses must believe that AI algorithms are accurate, reliable, and safe before willingly incorporating them into patient care decisions. Trust formation is influenced by direct experience with system performance, transparency of algorithmic reasoning, organizational messaging about validation and oversight, and peer attitudes. Social influence, including opinions of colleagues and support from leadership, also shapes acceptance. Nurses who observe respected colleagues successfully using AI monitoring may be more likely to adopt positive attitudes themselves. Conversely, if opinion leaders express skepticism or share experiences of system failures, this can undermine acceptance across a unit.

Facilitating conditions—organizational resources that support technology use—represent another important dimension. These include adequate training, responsive technical support, sufficient staffing to allow time for learning new systems, and infrastructure that enables smooth integration. Even when nurses perceive AI monitoring as potentially useful and relatively easy to use, lack of facilitating conditions can prevent effective adoption. For example, if training consists of a single brief session without opportunities for practice and questions, or if technical problems frequently occur without timely resolution, nurses may avoid relying on the technology despite theoretical benefits.

Resistance to technological change reflects complex motivations beyond simple rejection of innovation. Concerns about loss of professional autonomy may drive resistance when nurses perceive AI monitoring as constraining their judgment or reducing nursing work to passive monitoring of screens. Skepticism about algorithmic accuracy, particularly if early experiences involve false alarms or missed deterioration events, can generate lasting negative attitudes.

2.2.1 Statistical Data and Analysis

The demographic profile presented in Table 1. reveals important characteristics of the study population that merit theoretical consideration. The predominance of nurses in the 31-40 age range (38.2%) suggests a sample with substantial clinical experience yet sufficient technological adaptability—a critical balance for examining AI technology adoption. According to generational technology adoption theories, this cohort represents digital immigrants who entered nursing practice during the transition from paper-based to electronic documentation systems, potentially positioning them uniquely to evaluate AI monitoring technologies with both traditional clinical expertise and contemporary technological literacy.

2.2.1.1 Study Population Demographics (N=385)

Table 1. Sample characteristics of nurses participating in AI monitoring technology study

Characteristic	n	%
Age (years)		
22-30	98	25.5
31-40	147	38.2
41-50	92	23.9
51+	48	12.5
Nursing Experience		
< 2 years	54	14.0
2-5 years	116	30.1
6-10 years	108	28.1
> 10 years	107	27.8

continued on following page

Table 1. Continued

Characteristic	n	%
Clinical Setting		
Intensive Care Unit	142	36.9
Medical-Surgical	154	40.0
Emergency Department	89	23.1

The distribution of nursing experience shows relatively balanced representation across experience levels, with 58.2% of participants having more than five years of practice. This distribution aligns with expertise development frameworks proposed by Benner, which distinguish between novice, advanced beginner, competent, proficient, and expert practitioners. The inclusion of nurses across the experience spectrum enables examination of how AI monitoring technologies interact with different levels of clinical intuition and pattern recognition capabilities. Novice nurses may rely more heavily on explicit algorithmic guidance, potentially experiencing different cognitive and psychological impacts compared to expert nurses whose extensive tacit knowledge might conflict with or complement AI-generated recommendations.

The clinical setting distribution, with representation from intensive care units (36.9%), medical-surgical units (40.0%), and emergency departments (23.1%), captures diverse monitoring contexts with varying patient acuity, nurse-to-patient ratios, and surveillance demands. ICU environments typically involve continuous high-intensity monitoring with lower nurse-to-patient ratios, potentially creating different alert fatigue patterns compared to medical-surgical units where nurses manage larger patient assignments with less intensive individual monitoring. Emergency departments present unique challenges including high patient turnover, diagnostic uncertainty, and time pressure—factors that may influence how nurses interact with AI prediction systems. This diversity in clinical contexts strengthens the generalizability of findings while enabling examination of context-specific implementation challenges.

2.2.1.2 Cognitive Load Assessment Scores Pre and Post AI Implementation

The cognitive load assessment (Shickel et al., 2018) results presented in Table 2. provide empirical support for theoretical predictions about the complex relationship between AI monitoring implementation and nursing workload. The statistically significant increase in mental demand (from M=68.4 to M=72.8, p=0.001) directly validates cognitive load theory's proposition that introducing new information processing requirements—in this case, interpreting algorithmic outputs and managing increased alert volume—imposes additional cognitive burden even when physical task demands decrease. This finding challenges simplistic assumptions that automation necessarily reduces overall workload; rather, it suggests a transformation in the nature of cognitive demands from physical surveillance activities to abstract information interpretation.

Table 2. NASA-TLX scores (scale 0-100) comparing cognitive workload before and after AI monitoring system deployment

Dimension	Pre-AI M(SD)	Post-AI M(SD)	p-value
Mental Demand	68.4 (12.3)	72.8 (13.1)	0.001**
Physical Demand	71.2 (11.8)	64.3 (12.4)	< 0.001**
Temporal Demand	75.6 (10.9)	77.2 (11.3)	0.152
Performance	65.3 (14.2)	61.7 (13.8)	0.009**
Effort	69.8 (12.5)	73.4 (11.9)	0.003**
Frustration	58.2 (15.6)	66.9 (14.3)	< 0.001**

Note: ** $p < 0.01$; M = Mean; SD = Standard Deviation

Notably, physical demand decreased significantly (from M=71.2 to M=64.3, p<0.001), confirming that AI monitoring reduces certain manual tasks such as frequent vital sign checks and physical rounds for surveillance purposes. However, this reduction in physical workload appears insufficient to offset increases in mental effort and frustration. The frustration dimension showed particularly pronounced elevation (from M=58.2 to M=66.9, p<0.001), suggesting that nurses experience psychological costs beyond pure cognitive load. From an emotional labor perspective, this frustration may reflect conflicts between professional judgment and algorithmic recommendations, annoyance with false alarms, or perceived constraints on clinical autonomy.

The non-significant change in temporal demand (M=75.6 to M=77.2, p=0.152) presents an interesting theoretical puzzle. Despite substantial changes in monitoring workflows, nurses' perceptions of time pressure remained relatively stable. This finding may indicate that AI monitoring neither alleviates nor exacerbates time constraints in practice, or alternatively, that any time savings from reduced manual monitoring are consumed by new tasks of alert management and system interaction. The stability of temporal demand despite changes in work processes suggests that organizational factors such as staffing ratios and patient acuity may exert stronger influence on time pressure than specific monitoring technologies. The significant increase in effort (from M=69.8 to M=73.4, p=0.003) alongside decreased physical demand reveals a shift from effortful physical activity to effortful cognitive processing. This pattern aligns with theories distinguishing between physical and mental workload, demonstrating that overall effort expenditure may remain high even when the modality of effort changes. Performance perceptions showed marginal improvement (from M=65.3 to M=61.7, p=0.009), with lower scores indicating better perceived performance. This modest enhancement may reflect benefits from AI-assisted early detection of patient deterioration, though the effect size suggests that performance gains are limited relative to cognitive costs

2.2.1.3 Alert Fatigue and Response Patterns

Table 3. documents the temporal progression of alert fatigue phenomena, providing empirical evidence for theoretical models of habituation and signal detection degradation. The 11.6% increase in alerts per shift over six months (from 47.3 to 52.8) reflects either algorithmic sensitivity adjustments or increasing patient acuity, creating escalating demands on nurses' attention systems. Simultaneously, the dramatic 91.1% increase in alerts silenced without action (from 12.4% to 23.7%) demonstrates progressive desensitization—a pattern consistent with classical conditioning theories where repeated exposure to non-consequential stimuli leads to extinction of response behaviors.

The 53.6% increase in average response time (from 2.8 to 4.3 minutes) carries significant patient safety implications. From a signal detection theory perspective, this delayed response suggests that nurses are recalibrating their decision thresholds, requiring stronger evidence before interrupting current tasks to investigate alerts. While this adaptation may represent rational resource allocation in the face of high false positive rates (42.1% at month one), it creates concerning vulnerability to missing true emergencies. The tension between efficiency and safety exemplifies the vigilance decrement problem documented in sustained attention research—human operators cannot maintain high sensitivity to rare critical signals when embedded within frequent non-critical ones.

Table 3. Analysis of alert frequency and nurse response behaviors over 6-month study period

Metric	Month 1	Month 6	Change
Alerts per nurse/shift	47.3	52.8	+11.6%
False positive rate (%)	42.1%	38.7%	-8.1%
Avg response time (min)	2.8	4.3	+53.6%
Alerts silenced without action (%)	12.4%	23.7%	+91.1%
Self-reported alert fatigue score (1-10)	4.2	7.1	+69.0%

Subjective alert fatigue scores increased 69.0% (from 4.2 to 7.1 on a 10-point scale), demonstrating strong awareness among nurses of their deteriorating responsiveness. This metacognitive recognition suggests that alert fatigue operates partly through conscious processes rather than purely automatic habituation. Nurses appear aware that they are becoming desensitized, yet feel unable to maintain initial vigilance levels given sustained high alert volume. This conscious awareness without behavioral correction indicates that individual willpower or training is insufficient to overcome alert fatigue; rather, systemic solutions addressing alert specificity and volume are necessary.

Figure 3. Analysis of alert frequency and nurse response behaviors

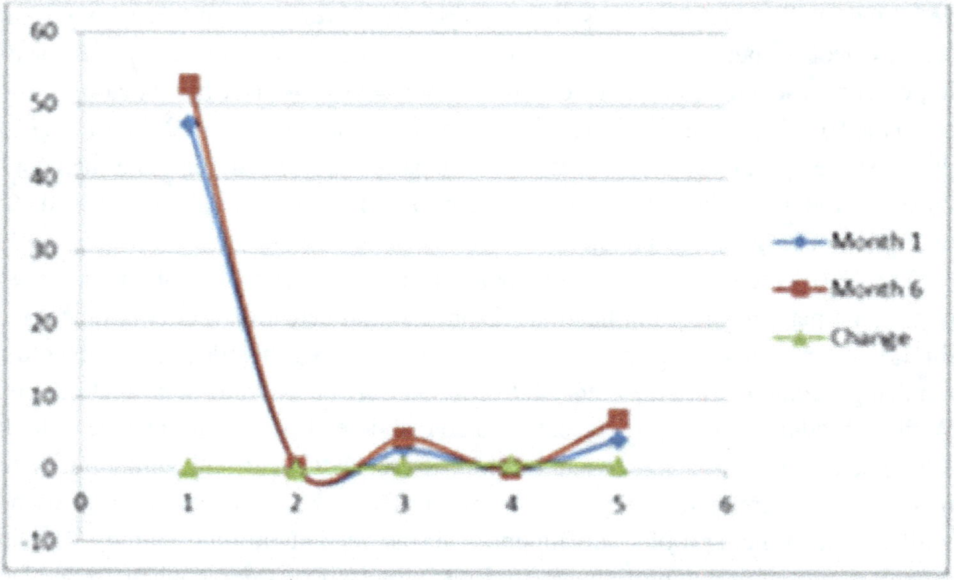

Interestingly, the false positive rate showed modest decline (from 42.1% to 38.7%, an 8.1% reduction) over the study period, suggesting that algorithmic performance or threshold adjustments improved somewhat. However, this improvement proved insufficient to prevent progressive alert fatigue, indicating that even optimized systems generating substantial false alarms will produce desensitization effects. The threshold for sustainable alert volume appears lower than often assumed—even with improvements, a 38.7% false positive rate overwhelms human attention systems over time.

2.2.1.4 Technology Acceptance Model Results

The regression analysis (He et al., 2019) presented in Table 4. explains 67.3% of variance in AI monitoring technology acceptance (R^2=0.673), demonstrating that the Technology Acceptance Model framework effectively captures key determinants of adoption in nursing contexts. Perceived usefulness emerged as the strongest predictor (β=0.412, p<.001), confirming theoretical propositions that technology adoption depends fundamentally on whether users believe systems enhance job performance. This finding suggests that implementation efforts should prioritize demonstrating concrete clinical benefits—such as earlier deterioration detection or reduced adverse events—rather than focusing exclusively on ease of use or technical sophistication.

Trust in AI systems represents the second-strongest predictor (β=0.318, p<.001), highlighting a factor often underemphasized in generic technology acceptance models but particularly critical for healthcare applications where algorithmic errors carry life-or-death consequences. This trust coefficient suggests that acceptance depends not merely on technical accuracy but on nurses' confidence in system reliability, transparency, and appropriate handling of edge cases. Building trust requires not only demonstrating high sensitivity and specificity in controlled validation studies but also providing explanations of algorithmic reasoning, acknowledging limitations, and establishing clear accountability when systems err.

Table 4. Comparison of psychological measures 6 months post-implementation vs. control group

Factor	β	SE	t	p
Perceived Usefulness	0.412	0.058	7.103	< .001
Perceived Ease of Use	0.287	0.062	4.629	< .001
Trust in AI	0.318	0.055	5.782	< .001
Training Quality	0.234	0.061	3.836	< .001
Years Experience	-0.089	0.052	-1.712	.088
Social Influence	0.176	0.059	2.983	.003

Note: $R^2 = 0.673$, Adjusted $R^2 = 0.668$, $F(6, 378) = 127.45$, $p < .001$

Perceived ease of use shows substantial influence (β=0.287, p<.001), confirming that interface usability matters significantly even when systems are perceived as useful. This finding validates investment in user-centered design, suggesting that technically powerful algorithms will face adoption resistance if embedded in clunky interfaces requiring excessive clicks, navigation across multiple screens, or interpretation of cryptic displays. The magnitude of this coefficient indicates that ease of use affects acceptance nearly as strongly as trust, emphasizing that implementation success requires attention to human factors alongside algorithmic performance.

Training quality emerges as a significant predictor (β=0.234, p<.001), though with smaller magnitude than core TAM constructs. This suggests that comprehensive education facilitates acceptance but cannot fully compensate for systems that lack perceived usefulness or trustworthiness. The effect size implies that training should be viewed as necessary but insufficient—even excellent training cannot overcome fundamentally problematic system design. However, the significant coefficient validates organizational investment in thorough onboarding programs that address not only technical operation but also clinical reasoning with AI assistance.

Years of nursing experience shows a negative but non-significant relationship with acceptance (β=-0.089, p=.088), suggesting a trend toward greater skepticism among more experienced nurses that does not reach statistical significance. This pattern may reflect tension between accumulated clinical expertise and algorithmic recommendations—veteran nurses have developed sophisticated intuitive pattern recognition that sometimes conflicts with AI predictions. The marginal significance suggests that experience-related resistance is not universal but may characterize a subset of highly experienced practitioners whose professional identity feels threatened by automation.

Social influence demonstrates significant but modest effects (β=0.176, p=.003), indicating that peer attitudes and leadership support shape adoption but less powerfully than individual perceptions of usefulness and trust. This finding suggests that implementation strategies should combine top-down institutional support with bottom-up demonstration of clinical value. Simply mandating use or promoting positive attitudes through leadership endorsement proves insufficient without addressing fundamental concerns about utility and reliability. However, the significant coefficient indicates that creating positive social norms around AI use—through opinion leader advocacy and peer success stories—provides meaningful support for adoption efforts.

2.2.1.5 Psychological Outcomes - Stress and Job Satisfaction

The psychological outcomes comparison Table 5. reveals nuanced impacts of AI monitoring implementation on nurse wellbeing and professional experience. Overall occupational stress increased modestly in the AI group compared to controls (M=67.8 vs M=63.2, d=0.39), suggesting that AI monitoring introduces stress beyond baseline nursing work demands. This small-to-medium effect size indicates that while AI creates additional stressors, it does not fundamentally transform the stress landscape—traditional sources including patient acuity, staffing constraints, and emotional labor likely remain dominant. However, even modest stress elevation warrants attention given high baseline burnout rates in nursing.

Technostress shows dramatically elevated levels in the AI group (M=71.3 vs M=48.6, d=1.64), representing a large effect size that identifies technology-specific stress as a major concern. This finding aligns with technostress theory's predictions about information overload, system complexity, technological insecurity, and invasion of work-life boundaries through constant connectivity. The magnitude of this effect suggests that while AI monitoring may not drastically increase overall stress, it creates a distinct category of technology-related strain that accumulates alongside traditional nursing stressors. Organizations implementing AI systems must recognize technostress as a legitimate occupational health concern requiring targeted interventions including technical support, reasonable alert volume limits, and clear boundaries around after-hours responsiveness.

Table 5. Comparison of psychological measures 6 months post-implementation vs. control group

Measure	AI Group M(SD)	Control M(SD)	Cohen's d
Occupational Stress Scale (0-100)	67.8 (11.4)	63.2 (12.1)	0.39**
Technostress Scale (0-100)	71.3 (13.7)	48.6 (14.2)	1.64***
Burnout Inventory - Emotional Exhaustion	28.4 (8.9)	26.1 (9.3)	0.25*
Professional Autonomy Scale (1-7)	4.8 (1.2)	5.4 (1.1)	-0.52***
Job Satisfaction Survey (1-6)	4.2 (0.9)	4.1 (0.8)	0.12
Professional Efficacy (1-7)	5.6 (1.0)	5.3 (1.1)	0.28**

Note: * $p < .05$; ** $p < .01$; *** $p < .001$. Higher scores indicate greater levels of the measured construct.

Professional autonomy decreased significantly in the AI group (M=4.8 vs M=5.4, d=-0.52), representing a moderate effect that captures nurses' perceptions of constrained clinical decision-making authority. This finding provides empirical support for theoretical concerns about automation threatening professional agency and expertise. Autonomy loss may stem from multiple sources: protocols mandating specific responses to AI alerts, perceived pressure to justify decisions that diverge from algorithmic recommendations, or subtle messaging that human judgment is less reliable than computational analysis. Self-determination theory posits that autonomy constitutes a basic psychological need, with frustration of this need undermining motivation, wellbeing, and job satisfaction. The observed autonomy reduction thus carries implications beyond immediate dissatisfaction—it may affect long-term workforce retention and professional development.

Emotional exhaustion (Kelly et al., 2019), the core dimension of burnout, increased slightly in the AI group (M=28.4 vs M=26.1, d=0.25), though the small effect size suggests that AI monitoring contributes modestly to burnout compared to more powerful drivers like workload and organizational support. This finding indicates that AI implementation alone does not precipitate burnout crises but adds incrementally to cumulative depletion. Organizations should view AI-related stress as one factor within comprehensive burnout prevention strategies rather than as an isolated problem requiring separate intervention.

Job satisfaction showed no significant difference between groups (M=4.2 vs M=4.1, d=0.12), suggesting that AI monitoring neither substantially enhances nor diminishes overall job satisfaction at the six-month mark. This null finding may reflect offsetting effects—benefits from improved patient outcomes or reduced physical surveillance demands balanced against costs of technostress and autonomy loss. Alternatively, job satisfaction may depend primarily on factors AI monitoring does not directly affect, such as interpersonal relationships, organizational culture, and alignment between personal values and work demands. Enhanced efficacy may reflect concrete improvements in early problem detection, confidence from algorithmic confirmation of clinical judgments, or psychological benefits from sharing surveillance responsibility with technological systems. However, the relatively small effect size indicates that efficacy gains are modest, and longer-term studies are needed to determine whether initial augmentation eventually gives way to skill degradation if nurses become overly reliant on algorithmic guidance.

2.2.1.6 Cognitive Load Over Time

The statistical findings presented in Tables 6. converge to paint a complex portrait of AI monitoring implementation that defies simple characterization as either beneficial or harmful. Cognitive load theory predicted transformation rather than reduction of workload, and the data confirm this theoretical expectation—mental demands increase even as physical demands decrease. Technology acceptance modeling successfully identified key predictors of adoption, with perceived usefulness and trust emerging as primary drivers. Psychological outcomes reveal a pattern of trade-offs: enhanced professional efficacy and reduced physical strain offset by elevated techno stress and diminished autonomy.

Table 6. Comparison of cognitive load over time

Dimension	Pre-AI	Month 1	Month 3	Month 6
Mental Demand	68.4	74.2	73.5	72.8
Temporal Demand	75.6	78.1	77.8	77.2
Effort	69.8	75.2	74.1	73.4
Frustration	58.2	71.3	68.7	66.9

Figure 4. Cognitive load over time

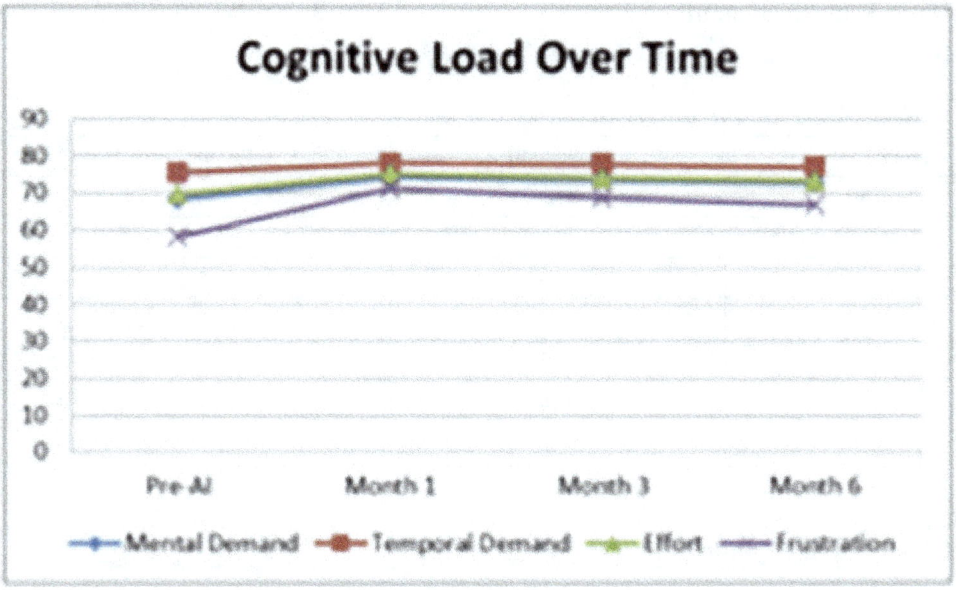

The temporal patterns (Davenport & Kalakota, 2019) illustrated in the following figures provide additional theoretical insight by revealing how effects evolve over implementation periods. Initial responses to new technologies often differ from equilibrium states reached after adaptation and learning. The cognitive load trajectory (Figure 1) demonstrates whether initial spikes in mental demand persist, diminish through habituation, or intensify as system use becomes more sophisticated. Alert fatigue progression (Figure 2) visualizes the desensitization process, testing whether fatigue reaches a plateau or continues linear growth. These temporal dynamics inform critical implementation questions about optimal training duration, appropriate evaluation timelines, and whether observed effects represent transient adjustment challenges or stable new equilibria.

2.2.1.7 Alert Fatigue Progression

The graphical presentations that follow translate Table 7. data into visual forms that facilitate pattern recognition and theoretical insight. Line graphs of cognitive load over time enable assessment of adaptation trajectories—do nurses habituate to mental demands, or do cognitive costs persist despite familiarity? Dual-axis visualization of alert volume and fatigue reveals whether the relationship is linear or exhibits threshold effects. Bar charts of technology acceptance predictors provide immediate visual comparison of relative effect sizes, highlighting which factors merit prioritized intervention. Grouped comparisons of psychological outcomes between AI and control groups facilitate rapid assessment of practical significance beyond statistical significance.

Table 7. Alert fatigue progression

Month	Alerts/shift	Fatigue Score
1	47.3	4.2
2	49.1	5.1
3	50.6	5.8
4	51.8	6.4
5	52.2	6.8
6	52.8	7.1

Figure 5. Alert fatigue progression

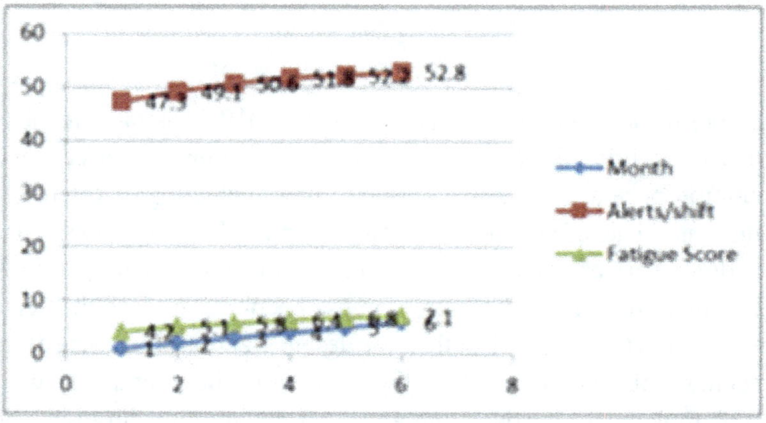

These visual analyses serve both descriptive and theoretical functions. Descriptively, they communicate empirical patterns to diverse audiences including clinicians, administrators, and policymakers who may engage more readily with graphical than tabular presentations. Theoretically, they enable testing of specific hypotheses about temporal dynamics, threshold effects, and relative magnitudes that may be obscured in tabular formats. The integration of statistical tables with visual presentations creates a comprehensive analytical framework for understanding the neurocognitive and psychological implications of AI-based patient monitoring in modern nursing practice.

2.3 Neurocognitive Frameworks

Dual-process theory, as articulated by Daniel Kahneman (2011), provides insights into how nurses process information from AI monitoring systems. This framework distinguishes between System 1 thinking (fast, automatic, intuitive) and System 2 thinking (slower, deliberate, analytical). Expert nurses develop extensive System 1 capabilities enabling rapid recognition of deterioration based on subtle cues. The challenge involves fostering a metacognitive awareness of when to trust System 1 intuition, when to engage System 2 deliberation, and how to integrate insights from both human and artificial intelligence.

Dual-process theory (Rajkomar et al., 2019) provides insights into how nurses process information from AI monitoring systems. This framework distinguishes between System 1 thinking—fast, automatic, intuitive processing based on pattern recognition—and System 2 thinking—slower, deliberate, analytical processing requiring conscious effort. Expert nurses develop extensive System 1 capabilities through clinical experience, enabling rapid recognition of patient deterioration based on subtle cues. They can enter a room and intuitively sense that something is wrong, even before consciously analyzing specific parameters. This intuitive expertise represents a valuable complement to AI monitoring, as human pattern recognition often operates across different dimensions than algorithmic analysis.

The introduction of AI monitoring creates an interesting interaction between these processing modes. Algorithms excel at System 2-like analysis—systematically processing multiple variables according to explicit rules or learned patterns from large datasets. They can detect subtle trends in vital signs that might not trigger human intuitive concern until later in the deterioration trajectory. However, algorithms lack the System 1 capabilities that nurses develop through direct patient contact: reading facial expressions, noting unusual behavior, recognizing when a patient just looks different from their baseline. The optimal integration allows each system to leverage its strengths—AI for systematic data analysis and nurses for holistic clinical judgment.

However, potential problems emerge when AI alerts interrupt System 1 processing or when nurses default to System 1 responses to algorithmic outputs. Frequent alerts may disrupt the focused attention needed for direct patient assessment, fragmenting nurses' ability to develop intuitive understanding of patient status. Conversely, when nurses develop automated responses to certain alerts without engaging System 2 analytical thinking, this can lead to inappropriate actions or failure to recognize when algorithmic recommendations do not fit the specific clinical context. The challenge involves fostering a metacognitive awareness of when to trust System 1 intuition, when to engage System 2 deliberation, and how to integrate insights from both human and artificial intelligence.

Working memory capacity limitations have particular implications for AI monitoring given the volume of information these systems can generate. Working memory functions as a mental workspace where information is temporarily held and manipulated during cognitive tasks. Individual differences exist in working memory capacity, with some people able to maintain more information simultaneously than others. AI systems that generate multiple concurrent alerts or present complex multivariate displays may exceed working memory capacity, leading to information loss, errors, or simplified processing strategies. Understanding working memory constraints suggests design principles such as chunking related information, progressive disclosure that presents details on demand rather than all at once, and prioritization schemes that help nurses focus on most critical information first.

2.4 Psychological Theories of Work Stress

The Job Demands-Resources (JD-R) model (Demerouti et al., 2001) provides a comprehensive framework for understanding how AI affects wellbeing. This model proposes that workplace characteristics are categorized into demands (requiring effort) and resources (facilitating goals). Chronic imbalance leads to burnout, while adequate resources promote engagement. In AI monitoring, demands include the cognitive effort required to interpret algorithmic outputs and manage frequent alerts.

The Job Demands-Resources model provides a comprehensive framework for understanding how AI monitoring technologies affect nurses' psychological well-being. This model proposes that workplace characteristics can be categorized into demands that require sustained effort and resources that facilitate goal achievement or buffer against demands. Chronic imbalance between demands and resources leads to burnout through an energy depletion process, while adequate resources promote engagement and motivation. In the context of AI monitoring, demands include the cognitive effort required to interpret algorithmic outputs, manage frequent alerts, respond to system-generated notifications, and maintain technical competence as systems evolve. These demands add to existing nursing workload challenges including high patient acuity, documentation requirements, and emotional labor.

Resources that may buffer against these demands include training and education that build confidence and competence, social support from colleagues navigating similar challenges, organizational commitment to adequate staffing and manageable workloads, and technology design that minimizes frustration through reliability and usability. When resources are insufficient relative to demands, AI monitoring may contribute to stress and burnout rather than alleviating workload. For example, if an early warning system generates numerous alerts requiring assessment but staffing levels remain unchanged, nurses may experience intensified time pressure and role overload. Conversely, when implementation includes comprehensive training, responsive technical support, and thoughtful integration that genuinely reduces some existing burdens, AI monitoring may serve as a resource that enhances job performance and satisfaction.

Technostress—stress arising from information and communication technology use—represents a specific manifestation of occupational stress relevant to AI monitoring. Technostress encompasses several dimensions: techno-overload from handling excessive information, techno-invasion when technology blurs boundaries between work and personal life, techno-complexity from difficult or rapidly changing systems, techno-insecurity from fears that technology might replace human workers, and techno-uncertainty from constant system changes requiring continuous learning. AI monitoring technologies potentially contribute to multiple technostress dimensions. Continuous connectivity and real-time alerts may create expectations for immediate responsiveness extending beyond scheduled work hours. Opaque algorithms and frequent system updates may generate complexity and uncertainty. Concerns about automation replacing nursing judgment may produce insecurity about professional value.

Theories of professional autonomy and control offer additional psychological perspectives. Self-determination theory posits that humans have basic psychological needs for autonomy, competence, and relatedness, with satisfaction of these needs promoting wellbeing and optimal functioning. AI monitoring systems impact these needs in complex ways. On one hand, they may enhance feelings of competence by providing tools that support superior patient surveillance and earlier intervention. They might also foster relatedness through shared experiences of managing technology with colleagues. However, if systems constrain clinical decision-making autonomy through rigid protocols or if nurses feel deskilled rather than augmented, this can threaten basic psychological needs. The perception of whether AI monitoring serves as a tool supporting nurse agency or as external control limiting autonomy significantly influences psychological responses.

3. AI-BASED PATIENT MONITORING TECHNOLOGIES

3.1 Types of AI Monitoring Systems

Contemporary AI-based patient monitoring encompasses diverse technological (Jiang, Jin, & Zhang, 2021) approaches addressing different clinical challenges. Continuous vital sign monitoring with predictive analytics represents one of the most widely deployed categories. These systems collect physiological data from bedside monitors or wearable sensors—including heart rate, blood pressure, respiratory rate, oxygen saturation, and temperature—and apply machine learning algorithms to detect patterns associated with clinical deterioration. Advanced systems calculate dynamic risk scores that update continuously rather than at scheduled intervals, potentially identifying subtle trends that precede obvious clinical changes. Some platforms incorporate additional data streams such as laboratory values, medication administration records, and nursing documentation to enhance predictive accuracy.

Figure 6. Example of AI-enhanced patient monitoring interface

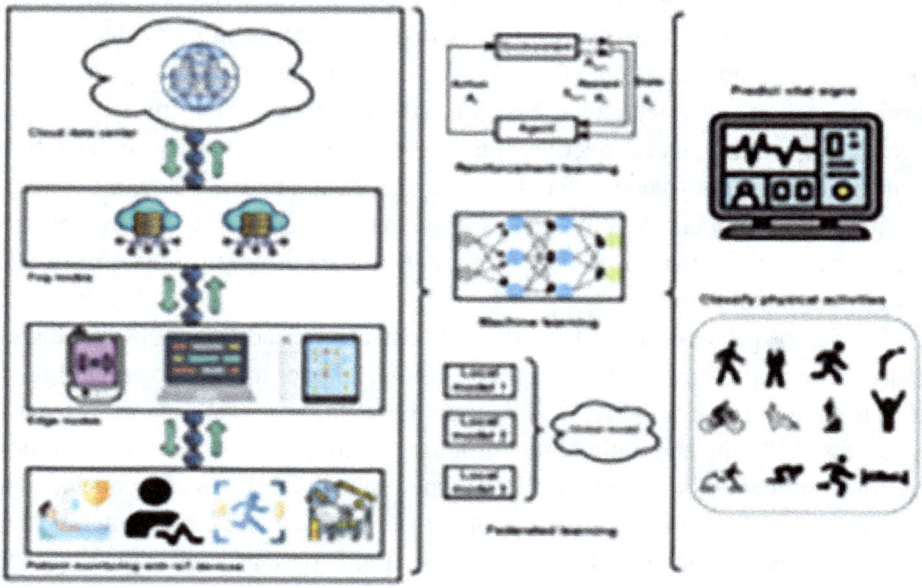

Early warning systems for specific conditions illustrate targeted AI applications (Sendak et al., 2020). Sepsis prediction algorithms analyze combinations of vital signs, laboratory results, and clinical notes to identify patients at risk for developing sepsis or septic shock. These systems attempt to recognize the condition during its early stages when timely intervention most effectively reduces morbidity and mortality. Similarly, algorithms have been developed to predict acute respiratory failure, cardiac arrest, and other life-threatening events hours before they become clinically apparent through traditional assessment methods. The promise of these technologies lies in providing healthcare teams with temporal advantage—an opportunity to intervene during a window when preventive measures may avert crisis situations.

Computer vision applications introduce AI to visual patient monitoring tasks. Fall detection systems use cameras or depth sensors to continuously monitor patient movement, automatically alerting staff when movement patterns suggest a fall has occurred or is imminent. Pressure ulcer risk assessment tools analyze images of patient skin, identifying early signs of tissue damage that might be subtle to human observers. Patient position monitoring helps ensure appropriate turning schedules for immobile patients. These vision-based systems extend surveillance capabilities beyond what nursing staff can continuously provide, particularly for patients requiring close observation but not necessarily one-to-one staffing.

3.2 Technical Architecture

The technical architecture underlying AI monitoring systems involves multiple interconnected components. At the foundation lie sensor networks and data acquisition systems that capture physiological signals. Modern bedside monitors, wearable devices, and implanted sensors continuously measure various parameters, converting analog physiological phenomena into digital data streams. This data must be transmitted reliably from acquisition points to central processing systems while maintaining security and protecting patient privacy. Wireless technologies enable mobility and reduce clutter from cables, though they introduce considerations about signal reliability, battery management, and potential interference.

Machine learning algorithms form the analytical core of AI monitoring systems. These algorithms are trained on historical datasets containing examples of various patient states and outcomes. During training, the algorithm learns to recognize patterns associated with different clinical scenarios—perhaps identifying that certain combinations of vital sign trends predict sepsis development with high probability. Training requires large, high-quality datasets that include diverse patient populations and clearly labeled outcomes. Once trained, algorithms can process new patient data in real-time, comparing current patterns against learned associations to generate predictions or classifications. The sophistication of algorithms varies from relatively simple logistic regression models to complex deep neural networks with millions of parameters.

Alert generation and clinical decision support mechanisms translate algorithmic outputs into actionable information for nurses. This involves determining appropriate thresholds for triggering alerts, deciding how to communicate urgency levels, and presenting relevant context. A critical challenge involves balancing sensitivity and specificity—systems must be sensitive enough to catch true positives but specific enough to avoid overwhelming users with false alarms. Some systems employ tiered alert structures with different notification mechanisms for varying severity levels. Others incorporate acknowledgment requirements to ensure alerts are received and reviewed. Increasingly sophisticated systems may adjust alert parameters based on individual patient baselines or suppress alerts when a nurse has recently assessed the patient.

Integration across the technical architecture presents both opportunities and challenges. Ideally, AI monitoring systems connect seamlessly with electronic health records, communication platforms, and workflow tools that nurses already use. This reduces the need to toggle between multiple applications and enables automated documentation of system-generated alerts and nursing responses. However, achieving true interoperability often proves difficult given heterogeneous hospital information technology environments, proprietary interfaces, and competing standards. Many implementations require nurses to access AI monitoring through separate applications or devices, fragmenting their attention and increasing cognitive load. The vision of unified clinical workstations that integrate all relevant information remains aspirational in many settings.

3.3 Integration into Clinical Workflows

How AI monitoring technologies integrate into existing clinical workflows significantly influences their neurocognitive and psychological impact on nurses. Interface design represents a critical integration point. Well-designed interfaces present information in ways that align with clinical reasoning patterns, using visual hierarchies that highlight most important data, color coding that intuitively conveys urgency without creating confusion, and layouts that minimize eye movement and search time. Poorly designed interfaces require users to hunt for information across cluttered screens, mentally integrate data presented in disparate locations, or decode cryptic abbreviations and numerical codes. The cognitive effort required simply to extract meaning from the display adds extraneous load before any clinical reasoning occurs.

Workflow integration extends beyond individual user interactions to encompass team communication and care coordination. AI systems that effectively communicate risk information across the care team—from nurses to physicians to respiratory therapists—can facilitate collaborative response to deteriorating patients. However, poorly integrated systems may create communication gaps if different team members rely on incompatible monitoring platforms or if alert information does not flow smoothly into existing communication channels. The emergence of AI monitoring also raises questions about role clarification: Who is responsible for responding to different types of alerts? How should algorithmic predictions be incorporated into established escalation pathways? How do new technologies interact with existing rapid response team activation criteria? Successful integration requires thoughtful attention to these sociotechnical questions alongside technical implementation.

4. NEUROCOGNITIVE IMPLICATIONS FOR NURSES

4.1 Attention and Vigilance

Sustained attention, also called vigilance, involves maintaining focused awareness over extended periods—a cognitive demand central (Krittanawong et al., 2017) to patient monitoring. Human vigilance performance characteristically declines over time, with detection accuracy and reaction speed deteriorating after approximately 30 minutes of continuous monitoring in laboratory studies. Clinical nursing environments create even more challenging vigilance conditions than controlled experiments: nurses must maintain awareness across multiple patients, manage competing priorities, and sustain attention despite interruptions, fatigue, and environmental distractions. AI monitoring systems theoretically could reduce sustained attention demands by providing automated surveillance that never fatigues. However, they simultaneously introduce different vigilance requirements: monitoring for system-generated alerts, which presents its own performance decrement challenges.

Figure 7. The cognitive burden of alert management in modern nursing

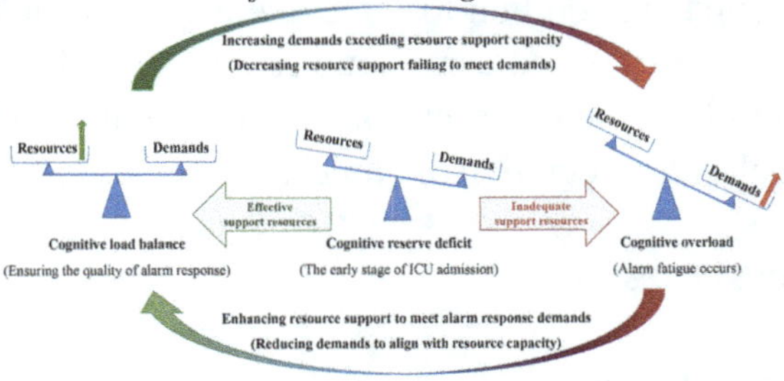

Alert fatigue represents one of the most significant attention-related challenges associated with AI monitoring. When systems generate frequent alerts, particularly alerts that prove false or clinically irrelevant upon investigation, nurses may develop habituation responses—automatic dismissal of warnings without full evaluation. This desensitization occurs through classical conditioning mechanisms: if most alerts are non-actionable, the alert itself loses its signal value and may even become aversive rather than informative. The paradox is that adding more surveillance through AI can sometimes reduce effective monitoring if the ratio of signal to noise is poor. Nurses facing numerous daily alerts must constantly engage cognitive control to overcome habituated dismissal tendencies when truly critical warnings appear, creating sustained mental effort beyond what AI monitoring was intended to provide.

Selective attention (Wang, Alexander, & Johnson, 2020) —the ability to focus on relevant information while filtering out distractions—faces particular challenges in AI-augmented nursing environments. The sheer volume of available information from monitoring systems, electronic health records, communication devices, and direct patient observation creates competition for attentional resources. Nurses must constantly make rapid decisions about what information merits detailed processing versus cursory attention or active ignoring. AI alerts add another stream demanding consideration of relevance and urgency. Effective selective attention in this context requires sophisticated filtering based on clinical knowledge, individual patient factors, and situational context. However, when cognitive load is high or when nurses feel time pressure, selective attention may default to simpler heuristics that could miss important information or fixate inappropriately on salient but less critical data.

Divided attention capabilities are tested when nurses must monitor multiple information sources simultaneously. A nurse might need to observe a patient's physical presentation, listen to the patient's description of symptoms, monitor vital sign displays, and remain aware of alerts from other assigned patients—all while formulating clinical judgments and planning interventions. Human attention fundamentally operates as a limited resource that must be distributed across tasks, with performance on individual tasks declining as divided attention demands increase. AI monitoring adds to these demands when it requires attention to screens, mobile devices, or alert sounds in addition to direct patient interaction. The risk is that attention becomes so fragmented across numerous inputs that nurses struggle to deeply process any single source of information, potentially leading to superficial assessments and delayed recognition of clinical significance.

4.2 Memory Systems

Working memory (Liu et al., 2020) serves as the cognitive workspace where nurses temporarily hold and manipulate information during clinical reasoning. With estimated capacity of approximately four chunks of information, working memory represents a fundamental bottleneck in information processing. AI monitoring systems can overwhelm working memory through simultaneous presentation of multiple data streams, complex multivariate displays, or rapid succession of alerts. When the number of information elements requiring simultaneous processing exceeds working memory capacity, people inevitably lose information, make errors in integration, or resort to simplified processing strategies. For instance, a nurse receiving concurrent alerts about abnormal vital signs, laboratory values, and fall risk while trying to recall medication administration timing and patient-reported symptoms may simply be unable to hold all these elements in working memory simultaneously for integrated analysis.

Strategies for managing working memory limitations (Bates & Singh, 2018) include chunking related information into higher-order units, offloading information to external memory aids like written notes or electronic displays, and sequential rather than simultaneous processing. Well-designed AI systems can support these strategies by grouping related alerts, providing persistent displays that eliminate the need to remember previous values, or presenting information sequentially with clear prioritization. Poorly designed systems that scatter related information across multiple screens, present data in unfamiliar formats requiring mental translation, or flash alerts that disappear before nurses can record them create additional working memory demands beyond the inherent complexity of clinical decision-making.

Long-term memory integration of AI-assisted decisions (Obermeyer & Emanuel, 2016) represents another cognitive consideration. Expert clinical judgment relies on extensive long-term memory structures—schemas and mental models developed through years of experience with diverse patient situations. These mental models encode typical patterns of disease presentation, likely trajectories, effective interventions, and subtle cues that signal important changes. When AI monitoring influences decisions, particularly if nurses increasingly rely on algorithmic recommendations rather than independent assessment, questions arise about whether this affects the development and refinement of clinical expertise. If nurses routinely act on AI predictions without independently formulating diagnoses or prognoses, they may have fewer opportunities to build the rich experiential knowledge base that characterizes expert practice.

Prospective memory—remembering to perform intended actions at appropriate future times—interacts with AI monitoring in complex ways. Nurses constantly manage numerous prospective memory demands: remembering to recheck vital signs after medication administration, reassess pain levels, follow up on pending test results, or evaluate patient response to interventions. AI systems with reminder capabilities could support prospective memory by reducing the number of items nurses must remember independently. However, extensive reliance on external reminders might reduce nurses' exercise of prospective memory strategies, potentially leading to dependence where removal of technological support creates performance decrements. Additionally, frequent interruptions from AI alerts can disrupt prospective memory by causing nurses to lose track of intended actions when attention is diverted.

4.3 Decision-Making Processes

Clinical decision-making (Reddy et al., 2020) represents one of the most complex cognitive functions affected by AI monitoring technologies. The fundamental question involves whether AI serves as a decision aid that enhances human judgment or as a decision replacement that marginalizes human reasoning. In the decision aid paradigm, algorithmic outputs provide one source of information that nurses consider alongside clinical assessment, laboratory data, patient reports, and professional experience. Nurses maintain responsibility for integrating diverse information sources, weighing competing considerations, and determining final action plans. This approach preserves clinical autonomy and critical thinking while potentially benefiting from AI's pattern recognition capabilities. However, it requires sufficient transparency of algorithmic reasoning that nurses can understand the basis for recommendations and sufficient training to appropriately weight algorithmic inputs.

Critical thinking preservation (Yu, Beam, & Kohane, 2018) remains essential even as AI provides powerful analytical tools. Critical thinking in nursing encompasses abilities to question assumptions, consider alternative explanations, recognize reasoning fallacies, evaluate evidence quality, and make sound judgments amid uncertainty. AI monitoring systems that function as black boxes—producing recommendations without explaining their reasoning—may undermine critical thinking development by providing answers without requiring analytic engagement. Conversely, systems that explain their logic, show which data points most influenced predictions, or present confidence intervals rather than deterministic outputs may support critical thinking by inviting evaluation of the reasoning process. The design choice of whether AI presents itself as oracle or collaborative reasoner significantly influences cognitive engagement.

Speed-accuracy tradeoffs characterize many decision tasks, and AI monitoring introduces new dynamics to these tradeoffs. On one hand, early warning systems may enable faster recognition of deterioration by detecting subtle pattern changes before they become clinically obvious, potentially allowing more rapid intervention. On the other hand, the pressure to respond quickly to automated alerts—particularly in high-urgency situations—may lead to premature action before adequate information gathering or to errors from rushed decision-making. The optimal strategy likely involves calibrating response urgency to both algorithmic predictions and independent clinical assessment, being willing to act quickly when both align but taking time for careful evaluation when they conflict. However, developing this calibration requires experience and metacognitive awareness that may take time to build.

4.4 Cognitive Workload

Cognitive workload refers to the total mental effort required to perform work tasks, encompassing attentional demands, memory load, decision complexity, and multitasking requirements. AI monitoring technologies influence cognitive workload in paradoxical ways. The aspiration is workload reduction through automation of surveillance tasks that would otherwise require sustained human attention. By continuously monitoring vital signs, analyzing trends, and alerting to concerning patterns, AI theoretically frees nurses from constant vigilance, allowing cognitive resources to be directed toward other aspects of care such as patient interaction, care planning, and complex problem-solving. However, empirical evidence suggests that actual workload impacts are more nuanced and not uniformly beneficial.

The mental effort required to interpret AI outputs represents a new cognitive demand that may offset some surveillance workload reduction. Algorithmic predictions, risk scores, or pattern alerts require understanding and clinical translation. A sepsis risk score (Sutton et al., 2020) of 0.7 does not inherently communicate clinical significance; nurses must understand what threshold values mean, how the score relates to other clinical information, and what actions are appropriate at different risk levels. Multi-parameter displays showing trends in dozens of variables simultaneously demand significant cognitive effort to extract actionable insights. When interpretation load is high, the time and mental effort invested in making sense of AI outputs may approach or exceed what would be required for traditional clinical assessment.

Multitasking between AI systems and direct patient care creates cognitive workload through task-switching costs. Each shift of attention between monitoring screens and patient interaction incurs a performance penalty as the brain disengages from one task and re-engages with another. When nurses must frequently alternate between reviewing AI alerts, assessing patients, documenting in electronic health records, communicating with team members, and managing other responsibilities, the accumulated switching costs can substantially increase cognitive workload. Moreover, certain cognitive tasks are particularly vulnerable to interruption; deep clinical reasoning or careful medication calculation may be disrupted by alerts demanding immediate attention, requiring restart of the interrupted task rather than seamless resumption.

Individual differences in cognitive capacity influence how nurses experience AI-related workload. Working memory capacity, processing speed, spatial ability, and other cognitive traits vary among individuals. Systems designed assuming typical or high cognitive capacity may overload nurses with lower capacity, leading to errors, stress, and frustration. Additionally, cognitive capacity is not static; it varies with fatigue, stress, circadian rhythms, and competing demands. AI systems that adaptively adjust their outputs or interface complexity based on real-time indicators of cognitive load might reduce individual burden, though such adaptive technologies remain largely developmental. In the meantime, recognizing that universal system designs may not suit all users suggests the value of customization options allowing nurses to adjust alert thresholds, display complexity, or notification methods to match their individual capabilities and preferences.

5. CONCLUSION

5.1 Summary of Key Findings

This chapter has examined the multifaceted neurocognitive and psychological implications of AI-based patient monitoring technologies on nursing professionals. The analysis reveals a complex landscape where technological advancement intersects with human cognition, professional identity, and workplace wellbeing in ways that defy simple characterization as purely beneficial or detrimental. From a neurocognitive perspective, AI monitoring systems fundamentally reshape the cognitive demands placed on nurses. While these technologies promise to reduce the burden of sustained vigilance through automated surveillance, they simultaneously introduce new cognitive challenges including alert management, algorithmic output interpretation, and integration of machine-generated insights with clinical judgment. The phenomenon of alert fatigue emerges as a critical concern, wherein excessive notifications desensitize nurses to warnings and paradoxically may reduce rather than enhance patient safety. Working memory limitations become increasingly strained when systems present multiple concurrent data streams without adequate prioritization or integration, potentially leading to information overload and cognitive shortcuts that compromise decision quality.

Decision-making processes undergo significant transformation in AI-augmented environments (Patel et al., 2009). The risk of automation bias—uncritical acceptance of algorithmic recommendations—stands in tension with the equally problematic possibility of algorithmic dismissal based on mistrust or misunderstanding. Optimal human-AI collaboration requires calibrated trust: sufficient confidence to leverage AI capabilities while maintaining critical evaluation and willingness to override recommendations when clinical context warrants. This calibration proves challenging to achieve and depends heavily on system transparency, user training, and organizational culture that values both technological tools and clinical expertise.

5.2 Psychological Dimensions and Professional Identity

The psychological implications extend beyond cognitive workload to encompass fundamental questions about professional identity, autonomy, and job satisfaction. Many nurses express concerns that AI monitoring technologies threaten core aspects of their professional role, potentially reducing nursing practice to passive monitoring of screens rather than active engagement with patients. These concerns carry significant weight, as professional identity strongly influences workforce retention, job satisfaction, and quality of care delivery. Technostress emerges as a tangible consequence when implementation occurs without adequate preparation, support, or consideration of workflow integration. The constant connectivity enabled by mobile alerts, the complexity of rapidly evolving systems, and uncertainty about the future role of human nurses in increasingly automated environments all contribute to psychological burden that may exacerbate existing challenges of nursing burnout and turnover.

5.3 Toward Optimized Human-AI Collaboration

The path forward requires moving beyond simplistic narratives of technological determinism—the assumption that technology adoption inevitably produces predetermined outcomes regardless of human agency or organizational context. Instead, we must recognize that the impact of AI monitoring technologies on nursing practice emerges from complex interactions among system design, implementation strategies, organizational support structures, individual differences, and cultural factors. Several principles should guide future development and deployment. First, human-centered design must prioritize cognitive ergonomics, ensuring that interfaces support rather than overwhelm human information processing capabilities. This includes intelligent alert filtering, contextual information presentation, transparent algorithmic reasoning, and customization options that accommodate individual differences. Second, implementation must be accompanied by comprehensive training that addresses not only technical operation but also cognitive strategies for effective human-AI collaboration, including trust calibration, critical evaluation of algorithmic outputs, and integration of multiple information sources.

5.4 Final Reflections

AI-based patient monitoring technologies represent neither a panacea for healthcare challenges nor an inevitable threat to nursing professionalism. Rather, they constitute powerful tools whose ultimate value depends on wisdom in their application. The goal should not be to maximize automation but to optimize the partnership between human and artificial intelligence, leveraging the complementary strengths of each. Algorithms excel at tireless surveillance, rapid processing of quantitative data, and pattern recognition across large datasets. Humans bring contextual understanding, holistic assessment, ethical reasoning, and the irreplaceable capacity for compassionate presence with patients in their vulnerability. The future of nursing lies not in choosing between these modes of intelligence but in thoughtfully integrating them to achieve what neither could accomplish alone: safer, more effective, more humane patient care delivered by professionally fulfilled and psychologically supported nursing professionals.

REFERENCES

Bates, D., & Singh, H. (2018). Two decades since To Err Is Human: An assessment of progress and emerging priorities in patient safety. *Health Affairs*, *37*(11), 1736–1743. DOI: 10.1377/hlthaff.2018.0738 PMID: 30395508

Davenport, T., & Kalakota, R. (2019). The potential for artificial intelligence in healthcare. *Future Healthcare Journal*, *6*(2), 94–98. DOI: 10.7861/futurehosp.6-2-94 PMID: 31363513

Davis, F. D. (1989). Perceived usefulness, perceived ease of use, and user acceptance of information technology. *Management Information Systems Quarterly*, *13*(3), 319–340. DOI: 10.2307/249008

He, J., Baxter, S., Xu, J., Xu, J., Zhou, X., & Zhang, K. (2019). The practical implementation of artificial intelligence technologies in medicine. *Nature Medicine*, *25*(1), 30–36. DOI: 10.1038/s41591-018-0307-0 PMID: 30617336

Jiang, F., Jiang, Y., Zhi, H., Dong, Y., Li, H., Ma, S., Wang, Y., Dong, Q., Shen, H., & Wang, Y. (2017). Artificial intelligence in healthcare: Past, present and future. *Stroke and Vascular Neurology*, *2*(4), 230–243. DOI: 10.1136/svn-2017-000101 PMID: 29507784

Jiang, H., Jin, C., & Zhang, H. (2021). Artificial intelligence in patient monitoring: Current developments and future perspectives. *Artificial Intelligence in Medicine*, *115*, 102062.

Kelly, C. J., Karthikesalingam, A., Suleyman, M., Corrado, G., & King, D. (2019). Key challenges for delivering clinical impact with artificial intelligence. *BMC Medicine*, *17*(1), 195. DOI: 10.1186/s12916-019-1426-2 PMID: 31665002

Krittanawong, C., Johnson, K., Rosenson, R., Wang, Z., Aydar, M., & Kitsios, G. (2017). Deep learning for cardiovascular medicine. *European Heart Journal*, *38*(25), 1958–1965. PMID: 30815669

Liu, X., Rivera, S., Moher, D., Calvert, M., & Denniston, A. (2020). Reporting guidelines for clinical trial reports for interventions involving artificial intelligence. *Nature Medicine*, *26*(9), 1364–1374. DOI: 10.1038/s41591-020-1034-x PMID: 32908283

Obermeyer, Z., & Emanuel, E. (2016). Predicting the future—Big data, machine learning, and clinical medicine. *The New England Journal of Medicine*, *375*(13), 1216–1219. DOI: 10.1056/NEJMp1606181 PMID: 27682033

Patel, V., Shortliffe, E., Stefanelli, M., Szolovits, P., Berthold, M., Bellazzi, R., & Abu-Hanna, A. (2009). The coming of age of artificial intelligence in medicine. *Artificial Intelligence in Medicine*, *46*(1), 5–17. DOI: 10.1016/j.artmed.2008.07.017 PMID: 18790621

Rajkomar, A., Dean, J., & Kohane, I. (2019). Machine learning in medicine. *The New England Journal of Medicine*, *380*(14), 1347–1358. DOI: 10.1056/NEJMra1814259 PMID: 30943338

Reddy, S., Allan, S., Coghlan, S., & Cooper, P. (2020). A governance model for the application of AI in healthcare. *Journal of the American Medical Informatics Association : JAMIA*, *27*(3), 491–497. DOI: 10.1093/jamia/ocz192 PMID: 31682262

Sendak, M., D'Arcy, J., Kashyap, S., Gao, M., Nichols, M., Corey, K., & Ratliff, W. (2020). A path for translation of machine learning products into healthcare delivery. *EMJ Innovations*, *4*(1), 59–66.

Shickel, B., Tighe, P., Bihorac, A., & Rashidi, P. (2018). Deep EHR: A survey of recent advances in deep learning techniques for electronic health record analysis. *IEEE Journal of Biomedical and Health Informatics*, *22*(5), 1589–1604. DOI: 10.1109/JBHI.2017.2767063 PMID: 29989977

Sutton, R., Pincock, D., Baumgart, D., Sadowski, D., Fedorak, R., & Kroeker, K. (2020). An overview of clinical decision support systems. *BMJ Health & Care Informatics*, *27*(1), e100030. PMID: 32047862

Sweller, J. (1988). Cognitive load during problem solving: Effects on learning. *Cognitive Science*, *12*(2), 257–285. DOI: 10.1207/s15516709cog1202_4

Topol, E. J. (2019). High-performance medicine: The convergence of human and artificial intelligence. *Nature Medicine*, *25*(1), 44–56. DOI: 10.1038/s41591-018-0300-7 PMID: 30617339

Wang, L., Alexander, C., & Johnson, A. (2020). Artificial intelligence in clinical decision support systems. *Frontiers in Digital Health*, *2*, 599640.

Yu, K., Beam, A., & Kohane, I. (2018). Artificial intelligence in healthcare. *Nature Biomedical Engineering*, *2*(10), 719–731. DOI: 10.1038/s41551-018-0305-z PMID: 31015651

Chapter 11
Neuroplastic Consequences of Artificial Intelligence Dependency:
Effects on Executive Networks and Cognitive Control

Ilyass Britel
Faculty of Sciences of Rabat, Morocco

Hanane Moummou
School of Engineering and Innovation, Université Privée de Marrakech, Morocco

Zakaria Aghdou
School of Engineering and Innovation, Université Privée de Marrakech, Morocco

Hind El Bouzidi
Faculty of Sciences and Techniques, Settat, Morocco

Bilal El-Mansoury
http://orcid.org/0000-0002-2583-7515
Faculty of Sciences, Chouaib Doukkali University, Morocco

ABSTRACT

The widespread reliance on artificial intelligence for cognitive support is increasingly shaping the functional organization of the human brain. Prolonged AI dependency may alter neural activity patterns underlying attention, memory, executive function,

DOI: 10.4018/979-8-3373-9484-8.ch011

and decision-making, raising concerns about long-term effects on brain plasticity and cognitive control. This chapter focuses on the neurological consequences of sustained AI use, examining how reduced cognitive effort and habitual cognitive offloading may influence prefrontal-parietal networks, frontostriatal circuits, and hippocampal-dependent memory systems. It will also provide a neurobiological framework for understanding how AI dependency reshapes brain networks involved in higher-order cognition, highlight emerging neural risks of reduced cognitive engagement, and outline directions for future longitudinal and mechanistic research aimed at preserving neural integrity in the era of intelligent technologies.

1. INTRODUCTION

Generative artificial intelligence has advanced remarkably over the past few years, with large language models representing the most significant area of progress. In the long history of human dealings with digital machines, this counts as a real break. Earlier computing tools mostly automated repetitive work or made information easier to reach. The newer systems do more. They generate complex content, help with reasoning, pull knowledge together, work through problems, and take part in decisions once thought to belong to human cognition alone. They are now spread across education, healthcare, scientific research, business, and digital services, and in the process they are turning into something like a distributed cognitive infrastructure woven into the daily routines of individuals and organisations (Bhattacharya et al., 2024; Kassa, 2025; Thirunavukarasu et al., 2023; Ott & Nieder, 2019). All of this sits within a wider move toward digitalisation, where every repeated digital act leaves a mark on the brain by way of neuroplasticity (Nah et al., 2023; Filippo et al., 2024; Riley et al., 2025; Friedman & Robbins, 2021).

For the most part, generative AI does not come into our minds unless it is delegated. Turning tasks that rely on memory, analysis, writing or decision to automated tools. After analyzing millions of interactions with AI systems representing the latest generation of large language models, researchers conclude that the types of tasks that people delegate are vast, ranging from programming to office tasks, from education to content creation (Hooper, 2025). This is the larger issue of cognitive offloading, which refers to how technology helps to store, focus and think outside of the head (Menon & D'Esposito, 2021; Lee et al., 2025; Riley et al., 2025; Garcia-Barrios, 2025; Friedman & Robbins, 2021). However, generative AI is not only about storage. It allows us to give the reasoning away and people usually accept its answers without checking. The traditional distinction between the inside and outside of the mind is fractured (Bhattacharya et al., 2024; Garcia-Barrios, 2025; Salehinejad et al., 2021). That is where the concept of cognitive dependence on AI fits in. Such dependence we can call the stable tendency to depend on, almost by default, on the smart systems in cognitive tasks that a person can perform by himself. This is different to frequent use. This is the gradual transfer of some of the cognitive functions to artificial agents until they are essential for normal mental activities. Several empirical studies have associated high AI tool use with lower critical thinking skills and most of the effect of using these tools can be explained by the increase in offloading (Lee et al., 2025). A qualitative investigation of the same from the inside: users claim they can no longer live without a digital assistant, and that they are becoming less capable of critical thinking (Lee et al., 2025; Salehinejad et al., 2021). Conceptual models provided a name to the paradox that lies below. Intelligent systems can be epistemic partners that extend our capabilities (Menon & D'Esposito, 2021; P, 2026; Garcia-Barrios, 2025; Salehinejad et al., 2021), or crutches that shorten the time to loss of skill if we proceed to take the output without scrutinizing it, or if we accept it without ever having learned it ourselves. The natural framework of this dependence is neuroplasticity. It is the brain's capacity to adapt its networks and the strength of its synapses based on experience, learning, and the environment (Nah et al., 2023; Filippo et al., 2024; Riley et al., 2025; Friedman & Robbins, 2021). Three types of studies – enriched environments, cognitive training and immersive technologies (including virtual reality, brain-computer interfaces, digital interventions) – indicate that systematic changes to sensory input and cognitive demands yield long-term effects on functional connectivity, on synaptic density, and on activation of frontoparietal networks related to working memory and attention (Nah et al., 2023; Drigas & Sideraki, 2024; De Barros, 2024; Filippo et al., 2024; Riley et al., 2025).

Recent reviews go further. Any regular use of digital media, search engines and conversational AI models included, may leave a neuroplastic watermark, for better or worse, on attention, memory, decision making, and executive control (Filippo et al., 2024; Riley et al., 2025; Friedman & Robbins, 2021).

Executive networks and cognitive control sit at the centre of all this, and they are what intellectual autonomy is built on. Inhibitory control, working-memory updating, flexibility, and planning depend on a coordinated fronto-cingulo-parietal comprising the dorsolateral prefrontal cortex, the anterior cingulate cortex, and parietal regions (Tuan et al., 2024; Gerlich, 2025; Gkintoni et al., 2025; Niendam et al., 2012). This superordinate control network is what lets a person set and hold a goal, resist an automatic response, oversee a decision, and choose between habit and controlled processing (Tuan et al., 2024; Gerlich, 2025; Gkintoni et al., 2025). Some models separate cold, purely cognitive components of executive function from hot, affective, reward-related ones, served by prefronto-cingulate subnetworks that only partly overlap (Gerlich, 2025). Work on prefrontal dopamine adds that small adjustments in neuromodulation can change how inputs are gated, how working memory is held, and how representations turn into action (Niendam et al., 2012).

Modest changes in what cognitive technologies ask of these networks could, in time, shift the balance between controlled and automatic processing.

Digital technologies and AI are anything but neutral toward these executive systems. Systematic reviews report that heavy, unstructured use of digital technology fragments attention, increases reliance on memory offloading, and overloads cognition, whereas systems built with care can instead strengthen metacognitive capacities and set off useful neuroplastic adaptations (Drigas & Sideraki, 2024; Filippo et al., 2024; Riley et al., 2025). Models from the psychopathology of problematic Internet use, such as the I-PACE framework, show that what people do with technology depends on how individual vulnerabilities, situational cues, and the available degree of inhibitory executive control play off one another (Salehinejad et al., 2021). Carried over to human-AI interaction, the framework implies something concrete: repeating offloading behaviours, kept up by rewarding feedback and little demand for mental effort, could gradually automate patterns of use and wear down the capacity to re-engage control on purpose (Menon & D'Esposito, 2021; Lee et al., 2025; P, 2026; Salehinejad et al., 2021).

Several major questions follow from all this. First, when executive functions are delegated again and again, planning a text, generating arguments, choosing among options, how far does that reshape the fronto-cingulo-parietal network in its activation, connectivity, and functional specialisation (Tuan et al., 2024; Drigas & Sideraki, 2024; Gerlich, 2025; Gkintoni et al., 2025; Friedman & Robbins, 2021; Salehinejad et al., 2021)? Second, does getting used to immediate, low-effort answers durably lower the engagement of inhibitory and error-monitoring mechanisms, putting critical thinking and autonomous decision making at risk of decline (Menon & D'Esposito, 2021; Lee et al., 2025; P, 2026; Riley et al., 2025; Garcia-Barrios, 2025; Salehinejad et al., 2021)? Third, how is an adaptive reconfiguration, say a functional shift toward the meta-control of hybrid human-AI systems, to be told apart from a form of skill atrophy resembling what has been described in the problematic use of other digital technologies (Filippo et al., 2024; Riley et al., 2025; Friedman & Robbins, 2021; Salehinejad et al., 2021)? Fourth, which individual factors, such as baseline cognitive capacity, metacognitive style, and affective vulnerabilities, and which contextual ones, such as interface design, the explainability of the AI, and institutional demands, modulate these neuroplastic effects (Menon & D'Esposito, 2021; Drigas & Sideraki, 2024; P, 2026; Salehinejad et al., 2021)?

The chapter sets out to do two things. The first is to treat AI dependence as a neurocognitive phenomenon, anchored in current theories of neuroplasticity, cognitive offloading, and executive networks. Here the aim is to read the evidence on how digital technologies affect brain structure and function alongside models of cognitive control and motivation, and so to pin down the plausible routes by which recurrent use of generative AI might remodel the prefrontal and fronto-cingulate networks (Nah et al., 2023; Tuan et al., 2024; Drigas & Sideraki, 2024; Filippo et al., 2024; Gerlich, 2025; Riley et al., 2025; Gkintoni et al., 2025; Friedman & Robbins, 2021; Salehinejad et al., 2021; Niendam et al., 2012). The second is to describe a research programme to delineate what this dependence does to neuroplasticity. That is, naming the locations where it might appear, the behavioural, the functional, the structural, and the neurochemical, and establishing experiments to distinguish between enhancement, reorganisation, and degradation of executive capacities. The introduction sets the tone for a systematic question: how does the extended engagement with AI aid the neural foundations of intellectual autonomy, how does it simply replace it, and how does it undermine it? (Menon & D'Esposito, 2021; P, 2026; Garcia-Barrios, 2025)

2. CONCEPTUAL FOUNDATIONS OF DEPENDENCE ON ARTIFICIAL INTELLIGENCE

Growth of AI, and generative systems in particular, is eroding the distinction between the head and the technology. Recent research usually approaches this problem in terms of distributed cognition, the extended mind, cognitive offloading and the newer idea of cognitive dependence of an artificial intelligence.

2.1. Defining AI dependence and the use-assistance-dependence gradient

In most accounts, reliance on AI is considered something that is repeated and chronic, an addiction to the systems that takes significant portions of psychological and cognitive activity for granted. The point is not the frequency of use of the tool. A qualitative shift in the emotional and instrumental relationship between persons and machines—a gradual migration of regulation of emotion, instrumental tasks, higher order processes like analysis and judgment, and even self-regulation (Dror & Harnad, 2008). From this perspective, AI systems are no longer just tools to complete specific tasks. Little by little they are invaluable intermediaries in our daily mental processes. Recent work has been done in the construction of instruments for measuring such a dependence. Some scales focus on a cognitive concern with AI, with the adverse consequences that follow from its use, and on withdrawal-type responses upon withdrawal from generative systems (P, 2026). Others are multidimensional, combining emotional dependence, functional dependence, cognitive dependence (in the narrow sense), and the progressive evolution of control of the usage of the tool (Dror & Harnad, 2008). The variety of definitions is informative sufficient unto itself. Using AI is not a neat behaviour. It's a gradual evolution of the cognition of humans and artificial support.

Table 1. The gradient from use to assistance to dependence on AI

Level	Cognitive characterisation	Tipping-point indicators	Citations
Use	Occasional tool, under conscious control	Mental effort maintained, active verification	(Wu et al., 2026; Hooper, 2025)
Cognitive assistance	Targeted offloading to conserve resources, of a scaffolding type	Performance gains with no apparent loss of competence	(Hooper, 2025; Windhager & Mayr, 2024)
Cognitive dependence	Habitual delegation of analysis, judgment, and planning	Illusion of competence, atrophy of internal schemas, loss of autonomy	(Goh et al., 2025; Skulmowski, 2023; P, 2026; Dror & Harnad, 2008; Drigas & Sideraki, 2024)

Figure 1. Gradient of AI cognitive dependency: From tool use to cognitive atrophy

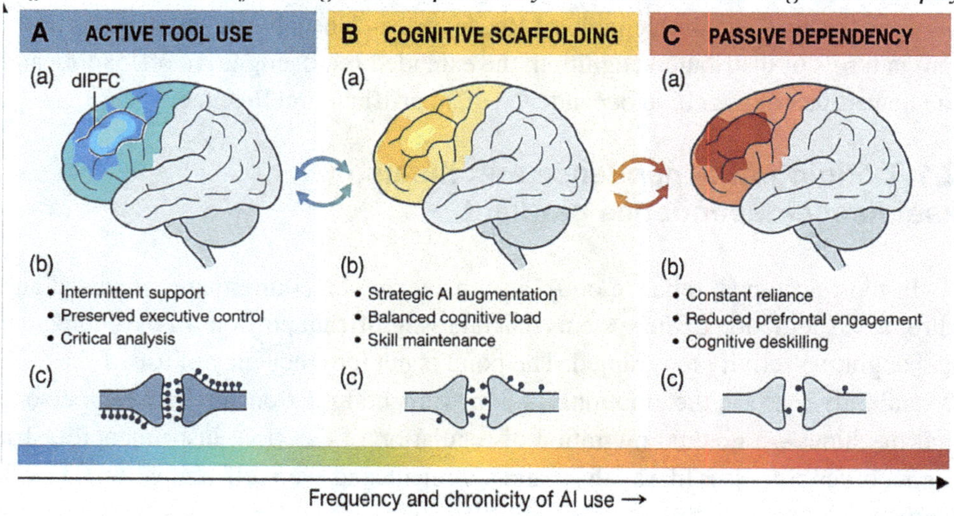

However, the gradient is not really an indication of some kind of threshold between the use of the substance and its cognitive dependence. The more challenging the tasks that intelligent systems are asked to do, the more the relationship will shift from the quirky little assistance to an established cognitive coupling. But also how much the AI helps. It's what that support does to the maintenance, and training, and autonomy of the user's own cognitive functions.

2.2. Distributed cognition, extended mind, and cognitive offloading

Distributed cognition breaks with the old picture that locates all cognitive processes inside the single brain. On this view, cognition is an interaction between humans, human-made artifacts, and the social-technical context in which they are situated (Zhai et al., 2024; Tuan et al., 2024). Knowledge, decisions, and reasoning are distributed within an information-processing system that is greater than one head. In settings where AI is deeply involved, the cognitive unit is no longer the human user alone but part of an ensemble of algorithmic systems with which the user interacts constantly. In models of human-AI teaming, humans and intelligent systems work together in complex cycles of interaction and dependence to create, assess, and refine knowledge (Tuan et al., 2024). Extended-mind theory takes the argument a step further. In certain situations, some external means can be part of the cognitive system. After the interaction with the user and the tool is stable, reliable and integrated into daily routines, the external resource is no longer an aid but a participant in the processing (Windhager & Mayr, 2024). Intelligent technologies support cognition, read that way. They are extensions functionally speaking. This is clearly evident in music education. The usage of AI-generated analyses for learners to reflect on, identify errors, and adjust their practice makes the system a part of their reflection (Windhager & Mayr, 2024). The third framework is called cognitive offloading, which is the most relevant to thinking about dependence. It is used for the different ways of extending cognitive functions beyond the head to preserve mental resources. It is not new to have the habit. They do it with handwritten notes, diaries, calculators, and databases on digital devices. The AI version is so much more advanced because it not only stores data, it processes it, reorganises it, and continually updates it as you're doing them. (Wu et al., 2026; Hooper, 2025) It is considered as a continuous process of balancing internal and external resources, which is dependent on task difficulty, load, ability, and value of desired information to the person (Wu et al., 2026). In that image, AI is an advanced offloading support that involves storing, processing and updating information (Hooper, 2025).

2.3. The progressive externalisation of memory, reasoning, and decision

With the advent of the Internet, which has become an integral part of life, the way knowledge is stored, retrieved and used has changed. Digital environments are becoming an extended external memory; people are increasingly able to pass off a fair amount of their remembering onto technological systems. This is supported by the research: knowing where a piece of information lives is easier for the user to remember than what it says (Wu et al., 2026). It's a good answer to the information overload, in which getting something back easily can be more important than remembering it. There's a price, however. On one side, you save the cognitive resources and you gain on some aspects of performance. On the other hand, people overestimate their memory because they can access information they never took on board. The use of external stores can also make the memory more susceptible to manipulation and distortion (Wu et al., 2026). This takes it one step further with AI conversational systems and large recommendation algorithms. AI (artificial intelligence) is used today to make inferences, organize knowledge and propose solutions, as the older digital tools just stored and retrieved information. So offloading, no longer is it just about memory. It penetrates to thinking. The result is delegated thinking: users take the answers provided by AI at their word without paying them much attention, leading to automation bias and favor of quick heuristics over careful analysis (Skulmowski, 2023; Zhang et al., 2025). The intelligent system is not just a tool by our side, but also a cognitive mediator that can influence how a problem is framed, analysed, and solved. There are several studies that indicate this direction: cognitive strategies gravitate towards whatever is most readily available and appears best. Responses such as these can lead to short-term gains but can also deplete the more lengthy and demanding mental processes that allow critical thinking to take shape. Creativity, independent analysis and ability to cope with complicated problems can all get dulled, for the simple reason that the underlying machinery gets used less: over time (Skulmowski, 2023; Goh et al., 2025; Grinschgl & Neubauer, 2022; Drigas & Sideraki, 2024). It's therefore not surprising that the externalisation of reasoning is repeated again and again to optimise cognition. It is also something that can transform learning patterns and the whole learning process. This is well explained by the theory of 'Cognitive externalisation' in the process of gradual cognitive externalisation. It believes that ambient AI systems, with a reliable and sustained causal relationship with the user, can shift from the realm of modelling cognitive functions to being active components of the cognitive architecture. The shift relies on functional equivalence, on reliability, but also on a two-way coupling of person/sphere and system (Grinschgl & Neubauer, 2022). Internet extended cognition, and memory-technology transactive systems, follow the same trend. These models allow the individual to retain primary biological cues to localize the information and have the storage, and potentially the processing, placed in the outside resources (Wu et al., 2026). The reach of the implication is broad, and it is not just what we can be seen to do that will be altered when we fold AI into our everyday cognition; it can be how knowledge is acquired, organised and recalled.

2.4. Generative AI and the transformation of cognitive processes

Generative AI is a significant departure from previous generations of cognitive assistance. Passive memory aids and ordinary search engines save and return things that are already there, while generative systems create new content, whether it's text, images, lines of argument, syntheses, or answers to the hard problems. It transforms the concept of externalisation, as users are now able to externalise much more than information. They can delegate them to create ideas, develop arguments, formulate hypotheses and solve problems (Wu et al., 2026; Zhang et al., 2025; Menon & D'Esposito, 2021). More and more, users are thus not subjected to the intermediate cognitive steps through which they used to travel, and which can change their circumstances to whether or not the intellectual skills used in learning and reflection are exercised at all. This is accompanied by a change in the cognitive demands. Education and work have always been based on the acquisition and use of what can be called "primary knowledge", problem solving, the logical processing of information and the building of arguments. Instead, the higher-order skills of evaluating, validating, curating, and interpreting AI-generated content are drawn to by growing use of AI (Wu et al., 2026).

Individuals have to expend more time evaluating whether the output from an algorithm is plausible, relevant or good than would be required to create the full chain of reasoning. All this reshuffling of cognitive tasks brings up questions about the direction of human cognitive skills and the nature of possible neuroplastic change.

Mechanisms leading to cognitive dependence

- Effort economy and cognitive inertia: Human cognition tries to spend as little mental energy as it can, and that single tendency goes a long way toward explaining the pull of AI tools. The principle of cognitive economy says we prefer whatever gets us to a goal at the lowest cognitive cost. When systems are on hand that turn out analyses, arguments, or solutions in seconds, the higher-order work, the analysis, the argument, the act of judging, increasingly gets handed over (Dror & Harnad, 2008; Goh et al., 2025; Zhang et al., 2025; Drigas & Sideraki, 2024). Once that handover becomes routine, a kind of cognitive inertia can take hold, and voluntary engagement in demanding intellectual work starts to taper off. Over a long enough stretch, this can thin out a person's internal cognitive schemas and weaken the memory consolidation that active learning relies on (Wu et al., 2026; Dror & Harnad, 2008; Hooper, 2025).

- Illusion of competence and the AI placebo: A capable AI can also breed an illusion of competence, where the user quietly takes credit for a performance the algorithm actually made possible. This is sometimes called an AI placebo effect: people overrate their own ability when work done with the system's help is read as a straight measure of what they can do unaided (Menon & D'Esposito, 2021). The tool gets absorbed into the person's picture of their own cognitive powers, to the point where conceding that it helped can feel like admitting some personal shortfall. Studies of the different forms of AI dependence suggest this illusion can mask a steady decline in critical thinking, in intellectual autonomy, and in honest self-assessment (P, 2026; Dror & Harnad, 2008).
- Motivational reinforcement loops: Frameworks drawn from self-determination theory read AI dependence as a mismatch between basic psychological needs and the strategies a person uses to meet them. By handing over quick answers, trimming uncertainty, and lowering the effort a task takes, AI brings immediate relief, and relief invites repeat use. The short-term reward can backfire, though. It may sharpen the fear of failing without help, encourage procrastination, and raise the rate of cognitive failures once the system is gone (P, 2026). The behavioural-addiction literature describes the same slow slide, from trying something out to compulsive use that holds on even as the cognitive or psychosocial costs mount (P, 2026; Dror & Harnad, 2008).
- Reconfiguration of cognitive agency: Music education research shows the effects of AI on cognitive autonomy cut both ways. Used as a reflective support that deepens analysis and self-regulation, AI can widen a user's cognitive agency. Let the system's assessments become the main authority behind behaviour and decisions, and the same tool can externalise cognitive authority itself (Windhager & Mayr, 2024). Personal goals then risk being swapped out for strategies that simply satisfy the algorithm's criteria, spoken or unspoken. This pull between empowerment and dependence is one of the central concerns of theories linking cognitive offloading, cognitive scaffolding, and the extended mind (Windhager & Mayr, 2024).

Extended cognition and human-machine teaming converge on a single idea: a sufficiently integrated AI can act as a genuine cognitive partner. Human and system share the workload, build mental representations together, and contribute jointly to planning and problem solving (Tuan et al., 2024; Hooper, 2025; Windhager & Mayr, 2024). The very things that make that coupling possible, high trust, perceived reliability, the automation of complex tasks, are also what put a user at risk. As the need to call up executive control, cognitive monitoring, and metacognition falls away, functions essential to intellectual autonomy can be externalised more and more (Goh et al., 2025; Zhang et al., 2025; Hooper, 2025; Sherif, 2025).

Recent research treats AI dependence as a multidimensional phenomenon with roots in distributed cognition, the extended mind, and cognitive offloading. AI, generative systems in particular, lets memory, reasoning, and decision making be externalised step by step, until the tool starts working as a functional part of the cognitive architecture. Where this trajectory goes depends on metacognitive factors such as the effort-benefit trade-off, on motivational ones such as psychological needs and illusions of competence, and on sociotechnical ones such as design, reliability, and coupling. The line between cognitive assistance and cognitive dependence lies less in using AI than in whether it rebuilds, or simply replaces, the training of executive functions and the reflective autonomy of the human agent.

3. NEUROBIOLOGICAL FOUNDATIONS OF NEUROPLASTICITY: MECHANISMS AND POTENTIAL LINKS WITH COGNITIVE TECHNOLOGIES

3.1. Fundamental principles of neuroplasticity and synaptic plasticity

Neuroplasticity is one of the nervous system's defining properties: its capacity to durably change its functional and structural organisation in response to experience, learning, and a shifting environment. The capacity works at several levels of biological organisation, from molecular changes in synaptic transmission up to large-scale reorganisation of neural networks. More concretely, it covers changes in synaptic strength, morphological changes in neurons, at the dendrites, axons, and dendritic spines, and the functional reorganisation of the circuits behind behaviour, learning, and cognition (Feldman, 2009; Ibrahim et al., 2021; Matsuzaki et al., 2004; Bonetto et al., 2021). Because of these mechanisms the brain stays adaptable across the whole lifespan. It can acquire new knowledge and skills, compensate for some neurological damage, and adjust to environments that keep changing.

Neuroplastic processes therefore sit at the centre of learning, memory, behavioural adaptation, and recovery after brain injury (Feldman, 2009; Ibrahim et al., 2021; Matsuzaki et al., 2004; Bonetto et al., 2021). Every lived experience can leave a biological trace as a lasting change in neural connections. Viewed through this lens, today's cognitive technologies, AI systems above all, look like a distinctive learning environment, one defined by repeated exposure to structured, interactive information flows aimed squarely at problem solving. By engaging, over and over, certain networks tied to attention, decision making, information seeking, and cognitive processing, these technologies could slowly bend the neuroplastic mechanisms that organise how the brain works.

Synaptic plasticity is the mechanism that makes such adaptation possible. It covers the durable changes in synaptic efficacy that neural activity induces, among them changes in neurotransmitter release probability, in postsynaptic receptor density, in intracellular signalling, and in the electrophysiological properties of the neurons involved (Feldman, 2009; Ibrahim et al., 2021; Dey et al., 2024; Matsuzaki et al., 2004; Bonetto et al., 2021). That synapses can grow stronger or weaker is the basic biological ground of learning and memory.

In the brain structures cognition leans on, the cerebral cortex and the hippocampus among them, several complementary forms of plasticity work side by side to acquire, stabilise, and update memory traces. They include long-term potentiation (LTP), long-term depression (LTD), homeostatic plasticity, and the plasticity of intrinsic neuronal excitability (Feldman, 2009; Dey et al., 2024; Matsuzaki et al., 2004). Working together, they let the nervous system hold a balance between stability and flexibility, and without that balance cognitive adaptation would not be possible.

In the setting of modern cognitive technologies these mechanisms take on real weight. Heavy use of AI systems could impose fairly stereotyped patterns of information processing, repeated cycles of searching, querying, validating, and handing cognitive tasks off. By the general logic of experience-dependent plasticity, such repetition could strengthen synaptic ensembles tied to information navigation, query formulation, or the quick appraisal of generated answers, while the circuits behind autonomous exploration, independent problem solving, and the internal construction of reasoning are engaged and reinforced less and less. So the basics of synaptic plasticity give us a way to ask how repeated interaction with AI might help remodel the human cognitive architecture.

3.2. LTP, LTD, hebbian learning, and dendritic remodelling

Long-term potentiation (LTP) is among the most studied mechanisms in neuroplasticity. It is a durable, input-specific rise in the efficacy of synaptic transmission that follows particular patterns of neural activity. In many circuits the potentiation depends on NMDA-receptor activation, a heavy influx of calcium into the postsynaptic neuron, and molecular cascades that insert new AMPA receptors into the synaptic membrane and set off more durable structural changes (Feldman, 2009; Ibrahim et al., 2021; Dey et al., 2024; Magee & Grienberger, 2020; Chakraborty et al., 2023). LTP is generally regarded as one of the main cellular substrates of learning and memory.

Long-term depression (LTD) is the movement in the other direction, a lasting drop in synaptic efficacy, and it is not simply LTP played backward. LTD has work of its own: it sharpens neural representations, clears out information that no longer matters, and keeps circuits flexible as the environment shifts (Feldman, 2009; Ibrahim et al., 2021; Magee & Grienberger, 2020; Matsuzaki et al., 2004; Mansvelder et al., 2019). Its homosynaptic and heterosynaptic forms help update what we know and tune the networks behind complex learning.

Together, LTP and LTD let the brain hold a moving balance between consolidation and adaptation. LTP stabilises the connections that count; LTD weakens or removes the ones that do not. Both can last from days to weeks, and both take part in forming, consolidating, and reorganising complex memories, spatial memory and associative learning especially (Ibrahim et al., 2021; Mansvelder et al., 2019). Historically these forms of plasticity rest on Hebbian learning, often boiled down to the idea that neurons firing together wire together. Repeated co-activation of pre- and postsynaptic neurons strengthens their connection. Contemporary models have added a layer, so-called neo-Hebbian mechanisms in which neuromodulation does decisive work. Dopamine in particular acts as a signal of biological or motivational relevance that helps fix certain synaptic changes for the long term (Feldman, 2009; Dey et al., 2024; Magee & Grienberger, 2020; Matsuzaki et al., 2004). Applied to AI, these principles yield several testable hypotheses. Day after day of interaction with generative systems could build recurrent links between a problem coming up and a machine-supplied answer arriving fast. Through Hebbian and neo-Hebbian routes, such links could strengthen fronto- hippocampal loops dedicated to assisted solution seeking, while LTD-related processes weaken the alternative strategies that are called on less often.

The hypothesis still needs direct experimental support, but it sits comfortably within the broader principles of experience-dependent plasticity.

Dendritic remodelling is the structural side of these functional changes. Dendritic spines are the main postsynaptic sites of excitatory synapses, and they reshape themselves readily. Their density, size, and form shift with neural activity and lived experience. LTP usually goes with larger, more stable spines and the growth of new synaptic structures; LTD with their shrinkage, their weakening, and at times their loss (Feldman, 2009; Chauca et al., 2026; Chakraborty et al., 2023; Mansvelder et al., 2019). These changes rest mainly on a dynamic reworking of the actin cytoskeleton and on a set of molecular pathways that govern the growth and stabilisation of synaptic structures (Chauca et al., 2026; Mansvelder et al., 2019). Over time they remodel the physical layout of neural networks and lock in the cognitive strategies used most. So repeated exposure to standardised digital tasks and routine AI interaction could favour stable dendritic-spine ensembles tied to proceduralised behaviours, query formulation, the quick appraisal of generated answers, the automated checking of information.

3.3. Axonal plasticity, activity-dependent myelination, and functional plasticity

Neuroplasticity is not only local synaptic change. It also reaches the way axons are organised and the conduction properties of neural networks. This matters for understanding how experience alters not just the strength of connections between neurons but the overall layout of the circuits that process information. Axonal plasticity names the mechanisms by which neural activity drives the growth, retraction, branching, and reorganisation of axonal projections. Through them the brain can remodel its functional networks to meet new cognitive or behavioural demands (Matsuzaki et al., 2004; Bonetto et al., 2021). Experience and learning shape axonal arborisation, encourage axonal sprouting, and take part in making or breaking synapses. New connections form between neuronal populations, and new functional assemblies fold into the brain's existing networks (Matsuzaki et al., 2004; Bonetto et al., 2021). This capacity to reorganise matters for learning, and it matters for the compensation seen after some neurological injuries, where new circuits can partly stand in for damaged ones. Alongside these structural changes, activity-dependent myelination now counts as a major component of brain plasticity. Myelin was long thought to be fairly static once development ended. It now looks dynamic instead, with an organisation that experience and neural activity can modulate. Recent data show that cognitive and motor stimulation directly influences how oligodendrocyte precursors proliferate, migrate, and differentiate, and how the myelin sheaths around axons are remodelled (Hagena & Manahan-Vaughan, 2024; Chidambaram et al., 2019; Knowles et al., 2022; Cools & Arnsten, 2021). These adjustments tune the conduction speed of action potentials and the timing between brain regions. Activity-dependent myelination is therefore especially important for coordinating the distributed networks behind complex cognition. Contemporary reviews note that learning, cognitive training, and repeated exposure to stimulating environments modulate the process through neurotransmitters such as glutamate, GABA, dopamine, and acetylcholine, which set off various calcium-dependent intracellular cascades (Hagena & Manahan-Vaughan, 2024). By improving conduction in the circuits engaged most, myelin plasticity makes the cognitive processing tied to certain tasks or habits more efficient. On this view, heavy use of AI-based cognitive technologies is a particular kind of repeated cognitive stimulation.

AI-assisted problem solving, looking things up, comparing solutions, juggling several digital tasks at once: all of it regularly calls on the frontoparietal and hippocampal networks behind attention, working memory, and decision making. If the demand is frequent and sustained enough, it could drive specific myelin adjustments in the circuits doing that work (Hagena & Manahan-Vaughan, 2024; Chidambaram et al., 2019; Knowles et al., 2022; Cools & Arnsten, 2021). Where the user stays passive and leaves most of the cognitive work to the system, the adaptations might instead favour circuits tuned for fast, automated responses that closely track the algorithm's suggestions.

Functional plasticity is another core dimension of neuroplasticity. It refers to changes in how brain networks are dynamically organised, in functional connectivity, regional specialisation, and the allocation of neural resources. Learning, training, and repeated experience can drive these changes; so can the disuse of certain cognitive functions (Feldman, 2009; Matsuzaki et al., 2004; Bonetto et al., 2021). Work in the sensory cortices has shown that experience deeply reshapes cortical representational maps through the combined action of LTP, LTD, intrinsic plasticity, and synaptic remodelling (Feldman, 2009). On a larger scale, learning and post-stroke recovery both show the brain redistributing its resources and reorganising its networks to perform under new constraints (Matsuzaki et al., 2004; Bonetto et al., 2021). Today's digital environments, with their constant interaction with intelligent systems, can be read as experiential contexts able to call up those same adaptive mechanisms. Chronic exposure to AI- centred devices could then nudge a gradual reconfiguration of the executive, attentional, and memory networks, tilting processing toward consulting external agents rather than working out solutions alone.

3.4. Neuromodulators: Glutamate, dopamine, acetylcholine, and noradrenaline

Neuroplasticity does not run on the intrinsic properties of synapses alone. It also depends on several neuromodulatory systems acting in concert, and these decide which experiences actually get consolidated into durable circuit changes.

At the heart of it all is the primary excitatory neurotransmitter of the central nervous system, glutamate, which has more going on than just basic synaptic transmission. It plays an active role in neurogenesis, synaptogenesis, neurite growth, neuronal survival and regulates the intricate and complex cognitive processes involved in learning and memory (Palacios-Filardo & Mellor, 2019). Glutamatergic synapses support a wide range of plastic processes: different types of LTP and LTD, short-term potentiation, synaptic scaling and metaplastic processes influencing the probability of subsequent synaptic changes (Magee & Grienberger, 2020). They can be NMDA receptor-dependent or independent, and are typically late processes involving changes of transcription, protein production, and synaptic structure on both sides of the synapse (Dey et al., 2024; Magee & Grienberger, 2020; Matsuzaki et al., 2004). In general, however, lasting learning requires a neuromodulatory system that signals those things that are biologically relevant. The control of long-term plasticity is at stake here, and it is where dopamine is key. It plays a role in the late stages of LTP and LTD associated with memory consolidation and synaptic growth, and links reward, motivation and learning together (Magee & Grienberger, 2020; Lisman, 2017; Stacho & Manahan-Vaughan, 2022). Dopamine signals the approximate value of an experience or a fact, and it determines which changes in neurons will last. Acetylcholine and noradrenaline also have their role to play. They tend to come into play primarily in situations of uncertainty, novelty, or discrepancy between expectation and reality. During these times, they focus attention on events that matter, increase neuronal excitability, modulate NMDA and AMPA receptors, and facilitate the induction and expression of LTP and LTD in the hippocampus (Stacho & Manahan-Vaughan, 2022; Mount & Monje, 2017). That is why they are critical to the renewal of mental representations and in keeping up with a changing world. Monoamines and acetylcholine are essential to a healthy PFC, and exert an inverted U effect on cognitive functioning—moderate levels improve these processes, while too little or too much impairs them (Primate work, 2019). These are the prefrontal cortex's sensitivity to neuromodulatory systems, which highlights their importance in directing goal-directed behaviour. In the context of this backdrop, the interaction between humans and AI assumes a distinctively neurobiological dimension.

AI systems often create exactly the conditions that recruit the dopaminergic and noradrenergic systems of reward and learning: novelty, uncertainty resolved, and answers that arrive fast and seem useful or surprising. Each answer judged relevant or unexpected can act as a signal that reinforces certain cognitive behaviours, the repeated handoff of tasks to the artificial agent chief among them. There is a complementary route as well. The suggestions AI produces can clash with the user's initial expectations and force a revision of internal representations. That updating likely calls on the cholinergic and noradrenergic systems specialised in detecting prediction errors and adjusting cognitive models (Stacho & Manahan-Vaughan, 2022; Mount & Monje, 2017). Repeated exposure to AI could therefore steer plastic resources, over time, toward experiences of assisted problem solving and algorithmic feedback, reinforcing strategies in which the AI becomes a favoured source for processing and validating information.

Figure 2. Synaptic plasticity mechanisms and their hypothetical reconfiguration under intensive AI use

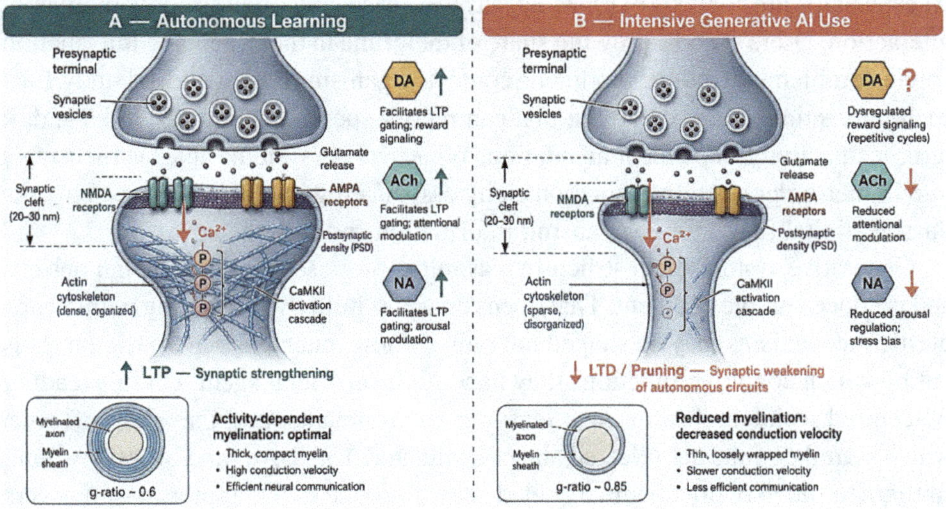

3.5. Experience-dependent neuroplasticity and cognitive technologies

The data gathered over recent decades converge on one point: experience-dependent neuroplasticity is the biological basis of learning, memory, behavioural adaptation, and recovery. LTP, LTD, structural plasticity, dendritic remodelling, axonal reorganisation, and adaptive myelination form an integrated system that lets the brain durably reshape its organisation around environmental constraints and lived experience (Feldman, 2009; Ibrahim et al., 2021; Matsuzaki et al., 2004; Chidambaram et al., 2019; Bonetto et al., 2021; Knowles et al., 2022; Cools & Arnsten, 2021; Mansvelder et al., 2019). None of these mechanisms acts alone. They interact constantly, holding networks functionally stable while keeping them able to adapt. The environments people live in do much to steer these plastic processes. Research on environmental enrichment finds that repeated exposure to cognitively stimulating settings promotes synaptic growth, greater dendritic complexity, functional reorganisation of networks, and better cognitive performance. Settings poor in stimulation, or low in cognitive demand, can hold those adaptations back. Learning, cognitive training, the repeated practice of specific skills, neurological rehabilitation, every one of these shows experience durably remodelling the brain (Feldman, 2009; Matsuzaki et al., 2004; Chidambaram et al., 2019; Bonetto et al., 2021; Knowles et al., 2022; Cools & Arnsten, 2021). Given how tightly experience and brain organisation are bound, it is natural to read today's cognitive technologies as possible drivers of neuroplasticity. Current digital environments, those built around AI especially, are contexts of repeated, easy-to-reach, and often strongly motivating interaction. Users spend a growing share of their time in them, seeking information, solving problems, deciding, producing content, organising their work and study. Each such interaction is an experience that can recruit specific neural networks and, in turn, feed activity-dependent adaptation. What sets AI systems apart is their reach into higher-order cognitive functions long associated with the executive networks. Passive digital tools store or transmit information and stop there.

Generative systems help structure reasoning, propose solutions, weigh options, and produce complex content. That opens up a possibility worth sitting with: neuroplastic mechanisms may be shaped not only by how much people use digital tools, but by which cognitive functions they hand to the artificial agent. On this reading, AI-centred technologies are new learning environments, and they can influence which neural circuits get selected and consolidated. Used over and over, they could strengthen the networks behind guided searching, the quick appraisal of answers, query formulation, and coordination with artificial systems.

At the same time, if certain operations are handed to the AI as a matter of course, the networks usually engaged for autonomous exploration, independent problem solving, or the active holding of information could be called on less. None of this need mean a general cognitive decline. It points instead to a possible redistribution of neural resources in line with what the technological environment now asks. The core mechanisms of neuroplasticity, then, activity-dependent strengthening or weakening of synapses, dendritic remodelling, axonal reorganisation, adaptive myelination, neurochemical modulation, give us a workable framework for thinking about the cognitive consequences of folding AI ever more deeply into human activity. They let us frame precise mechanistic hypotheses about what heavy AI use might do to the executive networks, the attentional systems, working memory, and cognitive control. The sections that follow build on this neurobiology to look more closely at the changes likely to reach the networks behind intellectual autonomy and the regulation of behaviour.

Principal mechanisms of plasticity and potential adaptations under cognitive technologies:

Table 2. Mechanisms of plasticity linked to AI use

Mechanism	Core neurobiological role	Potential adaptation under intensive AI use	Citations
Hebbian LTP/LTD	Encoding and updating of memories; sensory and spatial maps	Strengthening of problem-to-AI-solution schemas; pruning of unused strategies	(Feldman, 2009; Ibrahim et al., 2021; Dey et al., 2024; Magee & Grienberger, 2020; Mansvelder et al., 2019)
Dendritic remodelling	Selection and stabilisation of spines supporting specific circuits	Stabilisation of ensembles involved in query and validation routines	(Feldman, 2009; Chauca et al., 2026; Chakraborty et al., 2023; Mansvelder et al., 2019)
Activity-dependent myelination	Optimisation of conduction; synchronisation of learning networks	Adjustment of the speed of frontoparietal loops engaged in digital tasks	(Hagena & Manahan-Vaughan, 2024; Chidambaram et al., 2019; Knowles et al., 2022; Cools & Arnsten, 2021)
Neuromodulation (DA, ACh, NA)	Gating of LTP/LTD under uncertainty and reward	Preferential reinforcement of offloading behaviours rewarded by AI	(Magee & Grienberger, 2020; Stacho & Manahan-Vaughan, 2022; Mount & Monje, 2017; Bazzari & Parri, 2019; Palacios-Filardo & Mellor, 2019)

4. EXECUTIVE NETWORKS AND COGNITIVE CONTROL

Cognitive control is one of the foundations of how the human brain adapts. It is the set of mechanisms that line up perception, memory, attention, and action behind internal goals, rather than letting automatic routines, habits, or whatever is in front of us take over (Menon & D'Esposito, 2021; MacDonald et al., 2000; Chen et al., 2026). It is what lets a person hold a goal through distraction, pick the relevant signal out of many competing ones, hold back an inappropriate response, and change course as a situation shifts. Neurobiologically, cognitive control runs on a distributed architecture, mostly the prefrontal cortex, the anterior cingulate cortex, and several parietal regions, all folded into a large, superordinate fronto- cingulo-parietal network (Niendam et al., 2012; MacDonald et al., 2000; Zhang et al., 2026). Older accounts pinned executive function to a single frontal region. Contemporary work disagrees: these capacities emerge from the interplay of several specialised neural ensembles. The same networks get recruited across a wide range of tasks demanding inhibition, cognitive flexibility, working memory, planning, or complex problem solving (Niendam et al., 2012; MacDonald et al., 2000; Zhang et al., 2026).

This executive system works like a general supervisor. It can adjust, monitor, and redirect other brain networks that handle sensorimotor, emotional, or memory processing. By coordinating them, it makes goal-directed behaviour possible, lets the brain weigh the future consequences of an action, and keeps behaviour flexible as constraints change. Cognitive control is, in short, the neural foundation of intellectual autonomy, behavioural self-regulation, and complex reasoning, and those are exactly the functions that count most in settings saturated with information and technological demands (Menon & D'Esposito, 2021; Niendam et al., 2012; MacDonald et al., 2000).

4.1. Executive functions and subcomponents

Executive functions are cognitive control put to work. They are the higher-order processes that let us regulate thought and behaviour on purpose, in the service of particular goals (Salehinejad et al., 2021; Chen et al., 2026). Current models name three basic components, inhibition, working memory, and cognitive flexibility, and more complex capacities are built on top of them: abstract reasoning, problem solving, strategic decisions, planning for the long term (Niendam et al., 2012; Smallwood et al., 2021; Chen et al., 2026).

Working memory

Working memory is the ability to keep information active for a short while as you work on it, in support of reasoning, language comprehension, problem solving, and decision making. It is the meeting point between what comes in from the environment and what is held in long-term memory.

The prefrontal cortex, its dorsolateral regions in particular, is central to it, acting as a central executive that parcels out limited cognitive resources among competing tasks. The capacity rests in good part on persistent neural firing across delay periods, which keeps relevant representations available when nothing external is there to cue them (Smallwood et al., 2021). Working memory is indispensable to complex reasoning, because it lets several pieces of information be compared at once, abstract rules be manipulated, and goals be kept active while a task runs. Impair it, and the capacity to organise information, anticipate what an action will lead to, or solve a new problem efficiently usually drops with it.

Attention

Attention is the mechanism that selects some information over the rest so that processing can be optimised. Selective and sustained attention lean heavily on top-down control from the prefrontal regions over the sensory and associative systems. That control keeps focus on what serves the current goal while damping internal and external distractors (Menon & D'Esposito, 2021; Niendam et al., 2012; Salehinejad et al., 2021). In environments under constant information overload, this function is what filters the competing stimuli and keeps a stable bearing on cognitive goals. Attention is therefore central to cognitive efficiency and to the adaptive management of mental resources.

Inhibitory control

Inhibitory control is the ability to suppress automatic, impulsive and/or unhelpful responses in favour of behaviour that is more appropriate to the goal. It can be divided into behavioural inhibition (which involves stopping an action already in progress) and interference control (keeping irrelevant information from interfering with processing) (Menon & D'Esposito, 2021; Salehinejad et al., 2021; Chen et al., 2026). It is considered to be one of the pillars of common cognitive control, as virtually all cognitive control processes that require voluntary control depend on it. Inhibitory control helps a person avoid the distraction, delay a more rewarding choice for a later one, or follow a logical sequence when there's a temptation or choice that's more appealing, but competing with the other.

Cognitive flexibility

Cognitive flexibility is the skill to be able to switch mental representations, strategies, or rules rapidly when the context changes. This includes the ability to switch tasks, shift from one set of rules to another, and adapt to changing contingencies (Niendam et al., 2012; Diamond, 2012; Salehinejad et al., 2021; Chen et al., 2026). In practice, it involves removing a set of rules that were once important and replacing them with others to meet the demand at the time. Cognitive flexibility is the ability to learn new skills, adapt to new circumstances, and problem-solve when the old means of achievement must be discarded. It is one of the main sources of creativity and of behavioural resilience when things change.

Decision-making

Decision-making requires several information systems to select one action from many, and it is an executive function. It is shown to recruit cognitive control (namely inhibitory and flexible processes) and value estimation, risk assessment, and future consequence assessment systems simultaneously (Duncan & Owen, 2000). Value-based decision making depends on how different prefrontal networks work together. Some of them lean toward strict cognitive control, others toward weighing the rewards, costs, and emotional fallout of each choice (Duncan & Owen, 2000).

Their interaction is what lets the brain weigh possibilities and settle on the strategy that best fits the goal. Taken together, these executive functions let a person manipulate information in the mind, run future scenarios, anticipate what choices will cost, and test solutions virtually before committing to them. They are the neurocognitive foundation of complex reasoning, critical thinking, and intellectual autonomy wherever uncertainty rules and constant adaptation is required (Chen et al., 2026).

4.2. Regional prefrontal specialisation

Prefrontal regions contribute to this executive system in differentiated ways (Friedman & Robbins, 2021; Diamond, 2012; Duncan & Owen, 2000; Salehinejad et al., 2021; MacDonald et al., 2000; Smallwood et al., 2021; Chen et al., 2026; Zhang et al., 2026). The prefrontal cortex is the top of the hierarchy in human cognitive control. It works as an integrative platform, drawing together sensory, memory, emotional, and motor information to generate goal- directed behaviour. Unlike cortical regions tuned to a single modality, the prefrontal regions connect strongly with the whole brain, which lets them hold abstract representations, plan ahead, weigh several behavioural options, and oversee how responses are carried out. The arrangement rests on a relative functional specialisation across the prefrontal subregions, each contributing to specific aspects of control while taking part in distributed, tightly connected networks:

- Dorsolateral prefrontal cortex (dlPFC): working memory, goal-directed attention, task switching, planning, problem solving, novelty seeking (Friedman & Robbins, 2021; Niendam et al., 2012; Smallwood et al., 2021). dlPFC lesions produce trouble with planning and with solving complex tasks.
- Ventrolateral prefrontal cortex (vlPFC): inhibition, response selection, and monitoring, with the right inferior frontal area doing notable work in response stopping (Friedman & Robbins, 2021; Menon & D'Esposito, 2021; Salehinejad et al., 2021).
- Orbitofrontal cortex (OFC): central to inhibition, personality, and emotional and social reasoning; it contributes heavily to value-based decisions and to updating stimulus-value associations (Friedman & Robbins, 2021; Diamond, 2012; Duncan & Owen, 2000; Salehinejad et al., 2021).
- Anterior cingulate cortex (ACC): a key region for performance monitoring and conflict detection, signalling when the level of control needs adjusting (Gläscher et al., 2012). The dorsal ACC, where it meets the insula in the salience network, is heavily involved in cold executive functions, while its ven-

tral portions lean toward the hot, reward- and affect-related kind (Salehinejad et al., 2021).

Lesion studies confirm a double dissociation, a dlPFC-ACC network handling cognitive control (inhibition, monitoring, switching) and a ventromedial-orbitofrontal-frontopolar network handling value-based decisions (Duncan & Owen, 2000).

Front parietal, salience, and default mode networks

Executive functions do not rest on isolated regions. They emerge from the coordinated interplay of several large-scale intrinsic brain networks whose activity is tuned continuously to environmental demands and the person's goals (Menon & D'Esposito, 2021; Niendam et al., 2012; Dalley et al., 2004; Jones & Graff-Radford, 2021; MacDonald et al., 2000; Das & Menon, 2024; Das & Menon, 2020; Ott & Nieder, 2019).

These networks are the functional infrastructure that coordinates attentional, memory, emotional, and decisional processing. They run on reciprocal activation and deactivation, which is what allocates cognitive resources efficiently to the task in hand. Three of them are especially central to cognitive control: the frontoparietal network (FPN), the default mode network (DMN), and the salience network (SN).

Frontoparietal network (FPN / central executive)

The frontoparietal network is anchored in the dlPFC, the dorsomedial prefrontal cortex, and the posterior parietal cortex (Menon & D'Esposito, 2021; Niendam et al., 2012; Dalley et al., 2004; MacDonald et al., 2000; Ott & Nieder, 2019). It is recruited reliably across a wide variety of demanding tasks, inhibition, flexibility, working memory, initiation, which makes it a superordinate cognitive control network (Niendam et al., 2012; MacDonald et al., 2000; Zhang et al., 2026).

The FPN is often called the brain's principal executive network. It comes into play when a person has to actively marshal cognitive resources to pursue a goal, solve a problem, or adapt to new constraints. Its activation tends to rise with the cognitive complexity of the task and with the mental effort required.

It coordinates information from many brain systems and acts as a supervisory structure that organises goal-directed behaviour. It is especially engaged where a decision has to be deliberate, a plan strategic, or a problem genuinely complex.

Principal functions:

- holding and updating representations of goals and rules;
- selecting and inhibiting responses, and exerting attentional control;

- interfacing with sensorimotor systems to turn rules into actions (Niendam et al., 2012; MacDonald et al., 2000; Smallwood et al., 2021).

Default mode network (DMN)

The DMN gathers medial parietal, temporal, and frontal regions set apart from the sensorimotor systems (Ott & Nieder, 2019). It runs high at rest and usually quiets during demanding external tasks, yet it activates in many forms of complex cognition tied to memory, autobiographical, future-directed, semantic, and to abstract thought (Menon & D'Esposito, 2021; Niendam et al., 2012; Jones & Graff-Radford, 2021; Ott & Nieder, 2019).

The DMN supports:

- mental simulation, the building of future scenarios, and internal problem solving (Ott & Nieder, 2019);
- the folding of long-term memory into reasoning and decision making.

Salience network (SN)

The salience network centres on the anterior insula and the anterior ACC, with links to other cortical and subcortical regions (Menon & D'Esposito, 2021; Dalley et al., 2004; Jones & Graff-Radford, 2021; Das & Menon, 2024; Das & Menon, 2020). Imaging and intracranial electrophysiology reveal:

- strong internal cohesion between insula and ACC (Das & Menon, 2020);
- causal output hubs in the SN that route information toward the FPN and the DMN (Das & Menon, 2020);
- a role as a dynamic switch between the FPN, for external tasks, and the DMN, for internal processes (Dalley et al., 2004; Jones & Graff-Radford, 2021; Menon et al., 2022; Das & Menon, 2024).

When the SN's control over the FPN and the DMN breaks down, the result is cognitive decline in ageing and in mild cognitive impairment, with the severity of the disconnection tracking global performance (Menon et al., 2022).

4.3. Dynamic interactions between networks

The Triple Network Model casts the FPN, SN, and DMN as the basic architecture of cognitive control (Dalley et al., 2004; Jones & Graff-Radford, 2021; MacDonald et al., 2000; Menon et al., 2022; Das & Menon, 2024; Das & Menon, 2020; Ott & Nieder, 2019):

- FPN: engagement in goal-directed cognition and cognitive effort (Dalley et al., 2004; MacDonald et al., 2000; Ott & Nieder, 2019).
- DMN: internal, self-referential, memory-based, and abstract processing (Dalley et al., 2004; Jones & Graff-Radford, 2021; Ott & Nieder, 2019).
- SN: rapid detection of salient internal and external events, and switching between the DMN and the FPN as context demands (Dalley et al., 2004; Jones & Graff-Radford, 2021; Menon et al., 2022; Das & Menon, 2024; Das & Menon, 2020).

Effective-connectivity analyses, using dynamic causal modelling and phase transfer entropy, show the anterior insula sending a directed flow of information toward the FPN and the DMN, stronger during memory and control tasks. That confirms its role as a temporal conductor of these networks (Das & Menon, 2024; Das & Menon, 2020).

Figure 3. The triple network model under conditions of AI- assisted vs autonomous cognition

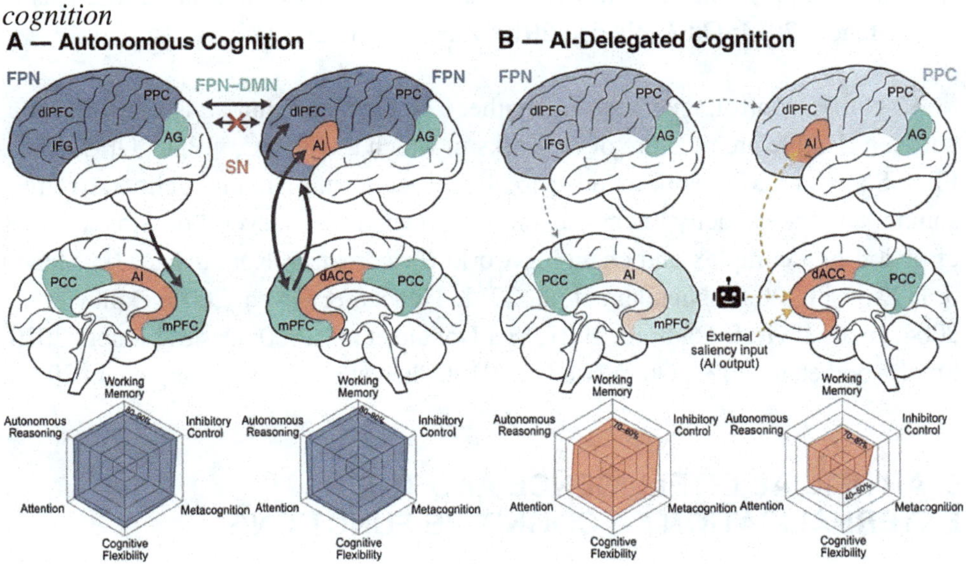

4.4. Cognitive autonomy and complex reasoning

Cognitive autonomy emerges from what these networks can do:

- represent internal goals (dlPFC, FPN) and compare outcomes against expectations (ACC) (Menon & D'Esposito, 2021; Niendam et al., 2012; Gläscher et al., 2012; MacDonald et al., 2000; Smallwood et al., 2021).
- select, hold, and manipulate representations in working memory to explore options in the mind, control the flow of information top-down, and coordinate several tasks through a prefrontal central executive (Menon & D'Esposito, 2021; Niendam et al., 2012; MacDonald et al., 2000; Smallwood et al., 2021; Chen et al., 2026).
- arbitrate between automatic and controlled responses, with inhibition resisting immediate salience and flexibility allowing a change of strategy when contingencies shift (Menon & D'Esposito, 2021; Niendam et al., 2012; Salehinejad et al., 2021; Gläscher et al., 2012; Chen et al., 2026).
- fold values, emotions, and social consequences (OFC, medial prefrontal cortex, ventral ACC) into decisions, through a ventral network dedicated to value-based choice (Friedman & Robbins, 2021; Diamond, 2012; Duncan & Owen, 2000; Salehinejad et al., 2021).
- tie internal thought to external action through the dynamic interplay of DMN, FPN, and SN, moving from abstract simulation to behavioural implementation and then to monitoring and revising plans (Niendam et al., 2012; Dalley et al., 2004; Jones & Graff-Radford, 2021; MacDonald et al., 2000; Das & Menon, 2024; Ott & Nieder, 2019; Zhang et al., 2026).

Cognitive control, then, rests on neither a single region nor an isolated module, but on a flexible architecture of networks in which the dlPFC, vlPFC, OFC, ACC, FPN, SN, and DMN work together to allow long-term planning, deliberative reasoning, and the capacity to choose, on one's own, among several possible courses of action in a complex and changing world (Friedman & Robbins, 2021; Menon & D'Esposito, 2021; Niendam et al., 2012; Duncan & Owen, 2000; Dalley et al., 2004; Jones & Graff-Radford, 2021; MacDonald et al., 2000; Das & Menon, 2020; Smallwood et al., 2021; Ott & Nieder, 2019; Chen et al., 2026; Zhang et al., 2026).

5. ARTIFICIAL INTELLIGENCE AND THE EXTERNALISATION OF COGNITIVE FUNCTIONS

The rise of AI, generative systems above all, belongs to a longer tendency to hand mental operations to digital artefacts. This is more than a technological change. It reworks the human cognitive ecology. From the first writing tools to today's digital systems, technology has served as an external prop for memory, calculation, and decision. Generative AI breaks with that line in kind, not just degree, because it no longer only stores or transmits information. It takes part in producing, organising, and interpreting it.

On this view AI is a cognitive partner that can step in at several stages of information processing: acquisition, selection, memorisation, reasoning, problem solving, decision. Its deepening role raises basic questions, about how cognitive functions get split between the human brain and artificial systems, and about what that split may do to intellectual autonomy, executive control, and long-term brain plasticity.

This section looks at AI as an external cognitive system and at the mechanisms by which externalisation changes the engagement of the executive networks.

5.1. AI as an external cognitive system and externalised memory

Digital technologies let cognition be distributed by moving the storage, processing, and updating of information out into the technical environment (Grinschgl et al., 2020). That move is a part of distributed cognition, the concept that the brain is not the sole source of cognition but is instead created with the help of people, tools and environment. Digital systems are then parts of cognition in action, and they affect the ways and processes of acquiring, storing, and accessing knowledge. Smartphones, Internet, and AI are an external, always current memory, and they make the user more of a knowledge professional than a one who depends on the memorized facts (Grinschgl et al., 2020). The job of human memory changes accordingly. Individuals invest more effort in finding, evaluating, and extracting information, and cognitive resources are shifted to the management of spread information.

Research on the Internet extended cognition reveals that humans prefer to remember the where of information over the information itself (human-transactive memory, where human keeps the where and the system keeps the information; Wei et al., 2025; Grinschgl et al., 2020). This fits the adaptive logic of human memory, which favours getting the most out of the cognitive resources at hand: with a reliable external source assured, the brain can spend less on holding detailed information and more on navigating to it.

Agents like SECOND ME further expand these elements by acting as persistent memory-offloading systems that organise, recall and apply a personalised memory with a dramatic reduction in the internal recall load of the system (Elston & Wallis, 2025). They create an "enhanced" profile of the user over time, collect personal data, and might return this information to new contexts.They develop a profile of a user over time, which is contextualised and collect personal data that they can present to new situations. They represent extensions in the form of dynamic memory and can carry the continuity of a person's cognition from time to time. For this type of architectures, there is a genuine question of consolidation. The two models of learning today are supported by the hypothesis that memory can only be retained if acquired knowledge is actively processed, retrieved and re-activated in the brain.

Some information may never be deeply encoded, for which the external memory is always at hand, and never make it to the internal semantic networks. Externalized memory is, therefore, both an enhancement of cognitive potential and a mechanism that can transform the natural learning and memory processes (Elston & Wallis, 2025).

5.2. Transactive memory systems and the externalisation of reasoning

Transactive memory systems (TMS) refer to social sharing of knowledge; each team member knows who knows what and that makes the team better at generating and combining knowledge (Woolley & Gupta, 2023; León-Domínguez, 2024; Friedman & Robbins, 2021). The classic transactive system has the advantage that everybody does not need to know everything, but they are all holding a reliable map of who in the group does and doesn't. That lowers the cognitive cost for each individual and raises the group's collective capacity to process information. Recent work extends the idea to human-machine collectives, where memory, attention, and reasoning become transactive processes that take in artificial agents (Woolley & Gupta, 2023; Wilson & Golonka, 2013). In these hybrids the AI is no longer just a database or a calculator. It is a functioning actor in the collective cognitive system. Users gradually learn which questions to put to it, which tasks to delegate, and when its answers can be trusted.

With generative AI, externalisation runs past memory into delegated reasoning: chatbots produce chains of argument and problem-solving plans the user can adopt with little scrutiny (Grinschgl & Neubauer, 2022; Wei et al., 2025; Zhang et al., 2023; Grinschgl et al., 2020). This is a notable turn in the history of cognitive technologies. Earlier systems mostly eased access to information; generative AIs now take on work once reserved for higher-order cognition, synthesis, argument, planning, inference, hypothesis generation. AI thereby becomes a node of transactive reasoning, shaping how groups and individuals build and evaluate solutions (Woolley & Gupta, 2023). Decisions can come to organise themselves around the system's recommendations, which changes how knowledge gets produced and how cognitive responsibility is split across the hybrid human-machine system. Trust in the AI does a lot of work here.

Trust that is well calibrated can support real collaboration and a productive division of cognitive labour. The opposite of too much trust is too little: uncritical acceptance of whatever the system has to offer increases the risk of automation bias, cognitive dependence, and of less reflective engagement. The externalization of reasoning is a process that depends on the metacognitive mechanisms that govern the interaction with the artificial agent and the outcome of the process depends on what happens in the process.

Delegation of problem solving, decision making and cognitive automation

Whole parts of problem solving are delegated, including analysis, generation of options, comparison, and deciding, via conversational AIs and decision-support tools, with recommendations and default choices (Grinschgl & Neubauer, 2022; Zhang et al., 2023; Grinschgl et al., 2020; White et al., 2025). The delegation isn't confined to the access to information. It is applied to the operations in the mind before an action is made. In only a small fraction of a second, AI systems can identify patterns, prioritize options, calculate the likelihood of success, and propose optimized solutions, thereby significantly reducing the cognitive burden of thoroughly examining a complex scenario.

Problem solving typically involves a sequence of steps from a cognitive-science perspective: Define the problem, hypothesize, evaluate possibilities, select a strategy, and test the solution. The first steps rely heavily upon the frontoparietal executive networks and on working memory. If there are many of them and the AI steps in, the nature of user's thinking shifts from actively creating solutions to observing an automated process.

A recent framework sorts offloading into three kinds:

The assistive kind is when the technology provides a support for the cognitive task, but does not take the place of the cognitive process, e.g., by providing reminders or computational aids, and the user remains actively engaged in the central tasks, with the technology enhancing their capabilities (Zhang et al., 2023; Sganzerla et al., 2025). In the substitutive style, the user is required to use a pre-designed procedure (autocompletion, ready-made answers) to execute the operation, so that the operation itself is no longer performed by the user, reduces the cognitive effort and depth of encoding (Zhang et al., 2023; Wei et al., 2025; Sganzerla et al., 2025). In the disruptive type, the interaction becomes passive, the metacognition and internal regulation become weak, and dependence becomes strong (Zhang et al., 2023), and the user only plays a peripheral role, so the critical supervision, error appraisal, and self-regulation are also rare, which serve as a negative support for the skills being learned. Conventional executive function (EF) processes of analysis, synthesis, and revision are rarely involved in generating texts; generative AI typically arrives in one of those last two registers—whole essays, explanations, or decisions—without asking for them (Zhang et al., 2023; Grinschgl & Neubauer, 2022; Wei et al., 2025). It's among the primary differences between older digital tools. It's easier to build the chains of reasoning if you are given a search engine, than if you are handed a completed cognitive product, as in the case of a generative model. This can cause changes in habits. So that once a solution exists, it's immediately presented, people may find themselves choosing to delegate instead of discovering it for themselves, another example of cognitive economy: the path that requires less mental effort is the one that we choose.

5.3. Reducing cognitive load: benefits and costs

Explicitly, reducing cognitive load is one of the goals of externalisation. The internal and external resources are what people make this trade-off between, according to how difficult or extrinsically challenging the task is, as well as their estimation of their ability to do it (Wei et al., 2025; Grinschgl et al., 2020). The logic is consistent with the existing models which assume limited attention and memory resources. This is the reason people are always looking to save money and make more.

Offloading allows:

Scaffolding of higher order cognitive tasks when the tool is used as a scaffold (Sganzerla et al., 2025, Wei et al., 2025); and a liberating of resources for higher order work when the tool is used as scaffolding, automated feedback or help with organisation, say (Grinschgl et al., 2020). With such usage, the AI can serve as a cognitive scaffolding device, giving the user more time to dedicate to challenging tasks like strategic planning, synthesizing information between domains, or critical thinking. In this instance, externalisation does not reduce cognitive ability, it reallocates available resources. There is also a problem that digital offloading can leave an illusion of mastery, causing weaker formation of long-lasting memories (Wei et al., 2025; Sganzerla et al., 2025; Zhang et al., 2023). It is the traditional trade-off between effectiveness in the short-term and learning in the long-term. If you can keep information at your fingertips, then you don't need to work so hard to encode it deeply, and none of the consolidation that requires such effort will occur. Let's take a closer look at the illusion of mastery. People can delegate the knowledge of something to the external system and then think they know the thing or they feel like they know it, but they don't. One of the primary cognitive dangers of excessive externalisation is this disparity between aiding performance and genuine competence. Recent studies identify a negative relationship between intensive use of AI and critical thinking and self-monitoring skills, and also show that intensive delegation of processing has the effect (Zhang et al., 2023; Grinschgl & Neubauer, 2022). Where the losses appear most severe are where the answer is created by the users themselves, rather than independently checking, or giving the answer any real evaluation or consideration. In such a state, the metacognitive mechanism that detects mistakes, estimates lack of confidence, and monitors working processes are less activated. When real benefits and real costs are side by side, this implies that the impact of AI is not being determined by the technology itself, but by practices of its use. Strategic and deliberate externalisation can aid learning and performance. The externalisation which happens on a routine basis without reflection can involve the user in a slow disengagement from functions that are important to the cognition.

5.4. Mechanisms modifying the engagement of executive networks

These prefrontal control networks typically mediate between automatic and intentional processing, selecting actions, maintaining goals, and inhibiting actions: they select actions, hold goals in mind, and regulate inhibition (Peltokorpi, 2008; Skulmowski, 2023; Ott & Nieder, 2019; White et al.,2025). They are the functional core of cognitive autonomy, what lets a person resist the immediate response, weigh the alternatives, and keep behaviour in line with long-term goals.

Organised mostly around the dorsolateral prefrontal cortex, the anterior cingulate cortex, and associated parietal structures, they are engaged most under uncertainty, response conflict, or a need for complex reasoning. Repeated AI use can change the conditions under which these networks come on. When solutions, recommendations, or interpretations arrive fast from an external agent, the demand on some executive processes can ease, while other functions, tied to supervising the artificial system, grow in importance. A few mechanisms could account for the shift in engagement under repeated AI use:

Substitution of slow processing by fast processing

Immediate access to AI-supplied solutions favours fast-system responses, lowering the need to call up the fronto-striatal loops behind deliberate choice under uncertainty (Jose et al., 2025; Ott & Nieder, 2019; White et al., 2025). In contemporary models of cognitive processing, behaviour often comes out of the interplay between fast, automatic, low-cost processes and slower, analytic, controlled ones. Executive functions step in mainly when the automatic answer will not do, or when the situation needs working through. AI, though, often dissolves the perceived uncertainty by handing over a plausible answer at once, which lowers the call on deliberate reasoning. This can breed a slow dependence on ready-made external answers. Rather than build several hypotheses, compare them, and test them in the mind, the user meets a solution already stated, which leaves fewer chances to exercise the analytic processes that executive control runs on. Control models show the PFC fully coming on only in novel or conflicting situations; if AI keeps the perceived novelty down, the activation of these networks may dwindle over time (Skulmowski, 2023; Jose et al., 2025). The prefrontal cortex works largely as a manager of uncertainty and conflict.

When situations become predictable, or an external agent keeps handing over solutions, the demand on control drops. Over the long run, that lighter engagement could feed back through use-dependent plasticity, in which frequently engaged networks strengthen while less-used ones lose relative efficiency. So the cognitive automation AI offers might gradually tip the balance from reflective toward automated processing, favouring decisions that are quicker but perhaps shallower.

Reallocation of executive effort toward interface management

Part of the control shifts toward framing queries, choosing among answers, and checking them superficially, rather than building solutions in full (Wei et al., 2025; Grinschgl et al., 2020; Zhang et al., 2023). AI does not necessarily wipe out cognitive activity; it changes its nature. A growing share of mental effort now goes to wording a query well, picking the relevant answer out of several, and coordinating with the system. Executive resources are redirected from producing knowledge directly to piloting an external cognitive tool. You could read that as a new skill in its own right, the orchestration of artificial systems. Even so, it does not always tax the same processes as solving a problem alone, and the danger is that parts of complex reasoning get traded for shallower supervisory work. This reconfiguration may favour more strategic control, the piloting of external systems, but also a chronic urge to minimise effort the moment the tool is at hand (Grinschgl et al., 2020; Zhang et al., 2023). Cognitive economy again: people quickly learn which strategies give a good-enough result at the lowest cost. When AI keeps supplying effective answers, reaching for it can become the default, even where solving alone would be possible and better for learning. That drive to save effort could slowly lower the spontaneous engagement of executive function in some tasks, above all the ones heavy on analysis or complex planning.

Weakening of metacognitive loops

Analyses of offloading show that AI often creates an illusion of competence and an overestimation of borrowed knowledge, which dents metacognitive accuracy and the motivation to check things internally (Zhang et al., 2023; Sganzerla et al., 2025; Grinschgl et al., 2020). Metacognition is the capacity to judge one's own knowledge, catch one's own errors, and gauge accurately how well one really understands something. It is central to self-regulated learning and to heading off mistakes in reasoning. When generated answers are coherent, detailed, and convincing, users can trust their own grasp of a topic too far. The illusion of competence blunts the urge to verify information, look for counterarguments, or try a different solution. The main risk is the widening gap between visible performance and real competence: a person can score well with AI help while understanding little of how those results came about. Longitudinal studies report, among heavy users, a drop in self-monitoring and metacognitive accuracy, a sign that the executive components behind inhibition and updating are starting to disengage (Zhang et al., 2023; Peltokorpi, 2008). Self-monitoring is a basic part of cognitive control: it catches errors, corrects strategies that are not working, and adapts to what the environment asks.

Let it weaken, and the capacity to critically evaluate what artificial systems produce can weaken with it. Neurocognitively, this could go with lighter engagement of the fronto-cingulate networks behind performance monitoring and the detection of cognitive conflict. The likely upshot is heavier reliance on external evaluation at the cost of internal control.

Automation of delegation patterns

Repeating the cycle of problem, query, adoption of the answer can be consolidated by dopaminergic reinforcement, steering the prefrontal system toward action policies that make external consultation the default (Zuo & Xin, 2025; Grinschgl & Neubauer, 2022; Zhang et al., 2023).

The brain's learning systems reinforce behaviour that quickly pays off. Each time a query to the AI solves a problem efficiently, the circuits behind that strategy can be strengthened by reward. Bit by bit, consulting the artificial agent can become an automatic answer to any cognitive difficulty.

The automation need not come from a conscious decision. It comes from adaptive learning keyed to how efficient the strategy seems. The more reliable and available the tool, the likelier it is to be reached for on reflex.

Distributed cognition and the extended mind suggest that, as the coupling stabilises, some executive operations such as planning and monitoring get partly reconfigured at the level of the hybrid human- AI system, with a risk of lost flexibility if the human can no longer easily take back control (Heavey & Simsek, 2017; Gallagher, 2023; Wei et al., 2025; Grinschgl et al., 2020).

Within this framework cognition is no longer housed in the human brain alone but spread across parts of the system. The reorganisation can raise the hybrid system's overall capacity, yet it also raises the question of functional dependence. If some operations are externalised as a matter of course, taking them back inside can grow harder once the tool is gone. The possible loss of cognitive flexibility is the central worry. A person may grow highly effective in an assisted setting while struggling more in any context that calls for full autonomy.

Developmental effects on executive functions

Externalising planning, self-regulation, and decision early, during the PFC's maturation, could amount to a developmental displacement, where functions are handed off before any robust internal mastery has formed (Zhang et al., 2023; Peltokorpi, 2008). The pattern is tied to a delay in the development of cognitive agency and autonomy, both central to the executive networks (Zhang et al., 2023; Peltokorpi, 2008).

5.5. Potential cognitive benefits and the conditions for preserved executive engagement

For all the concern about cognitive dependence and executive disengagement, the literature does not show digital technologies and AI producing negative cognitive effects across the board. What they do depends largely on how they are used, on the user's goals, on the learning context, and on how much metacognitive control is kept up during the interaction (Woolley & Gupta, 2023; Grinschgl et al., 2020; Wei et al., 2025).

Cognitive psychology and the educational sciences offer a useful reading: cognitive technologies as tools of cognitive scaffolding. The idea of scaffolding, from socio-constructivist work, is a temporary support that lets a person do what is briefly beyond them alone, while gradually building internal skill. On that view AI is not a stand-in for human cognition but a support that helps reach a higher level of intellectual performance (Grinschgl et al., 2020; Woolley & Gupta, 2023).

When low-level tasks, information seeking, intermediate calculations, document organisation, the recall of facts, are taken over by an external system, the limited resources of working memory can be reallocated toward heavier work such as:

- framing hypotheses;
- solving complex problems;
- critically evaluating arguments;
- making strategic decisions;
- planning over the long term;
- drawing together information from many sources.

Externalisation, in this light, need not lower the activity of the executive networks. It may instead move their engagement up toward higher-order work (Grinschgl et al., 2020; Wei et al., 2025).

The idea squares with neurocognitive models of executive control that treat pre-frontal resources as limited and as needing flexible allocation to whatever the task demands (Menon & D'Esposito, 2021; Smallwood et al., 2021). Cut the extrinsic cognitive load, then, and the whole system can run more efficiently, since the frontoparietal network can spend more on abstract reasoning, conceptual integration, and metacognitive control.

Several studies add that intelligent assistance can help learning when it gives explanatory feedback rather than a finished, usable answer (Grinschgl et al., 2020; Sganzerla et al., 2025).

There the user stays in the loop, generating hypotheses, checking them, correcting mistakes, and the prefrontal circuits behind performance monitoring, the anterior cingulate cortex among them, keep doing active work.

AI tools can also amplify cognitive motivation. Quick access to relevant resources, less frustration on hard problems, and immediate feedback can lift a person's sense of self-efficacy and pull them into demanding intellectual work (Grinschgl et al., 2020; Sganzerla et al., 2025). That matters most in education, where motivation does a lot to decide whether learning carries on.

6. POTENTIAL NEUROPLASTIC CONSEQUENCES OF DEPENDENCE ON ARTIFICIAL INTELLIGENCE

Heavy AI use sits inside a wider field of digital interaction that can, through neuroplasticity, remodel the executive networks behind working memory, attention, and cognitive control (Menon & D'Esposito, 2021; Geissler et al., 2023; Jones et al., 2022; Palamarchuk et al., 2025). Most of the studies we have are really about cognitive offloading, about effects on executive functions, and about structured digital interventions, rather than about AI dependence in the strict sense. That calls for a cautious, critical reading (Geissler et al., 2023; Gerlich, 2025; Gazerani, 2025; Gkintoni et al., 2025; Sherif, 2025).

6.1. Effects on executive functions and metacognition

Working memory and attention

Offloading to a digital assistant or to AI transiently lightens the workload, dropping dlPFC activation during information-maintenance tasks and freeing resources for a secondary task, the SEP/SEM effect (Katmah et al., 2025). Adaptive digital cognitive interventions, some of them AI-driven, do the reverse, improving attention, visuospatial working memory, and flexibility in children with ADHD, with default mode network changes, increased posterior alpha, that hint at beneficial functional plasticity (Medina et al., 2021). Reviews of digital engagement show unstructured use fragmenting attention and overloading it, while targeted educational tools can support attention and metacognition (Jones et al., 2022; Kassa, 2025; Diamond, 2012).

Inhibitory control, flexibility, and problem solving

Controlled digital training improves inhibitory control, cognitive flexibility, and clinical executive indices (Medina et al., 2021), which points to adaptive neuroplasticity when the tasks actively engage those functions. The other side is well documented too. Syntheses on AI dependence and excessive AI dependence warn of cognitive complacency and of fewer chances to engage actively in analysis, problem solving, and autonomous decision making (Gerlich, 2025; Gazerani, 2025; Gkintoni et al., 2025). A systematic review of AI dialogue systems finds over-reliance on generated answers going with a reported drop in creativity, critical thinking, and independent problem solving (Geissler et al., 2023).

Analytic reasoning and metacognition

Work with pupils and students reports a negative correlation between frequent AI use and critical and analytic thinking, with increased offloading carrying the link (Gazerani, 2025; Geissler et al., 2023; Gkintoni et al., 2025). Taking up answers that look fast and optimal favours cheap heuristics over slow, deep reasoning (Geissler et al., 2023; Gkintoni et al., 2025). Several authors argue that delegating again and again can weaken metacognition, the monitoring of one's own understanding, the calibration of confidence, by encouraging passive learning and an illusion of competence when performance leans heavily on the AI (Gazerani, 2025; Gkintoni et al., 2025; Sherif, 2025).

Structural and functional adaptations and connectivity

Direct data on brain structure in AI dependence are missing, but work on digital neuroplasticity and on cognitive interventions gives us a frame. Reviews show that enriched environments and digital training can raise frontal dendritic-spine density, strengthen dlPFC-parietal functional connectivity, and tighten the cohesion of executive networks, with working memory improving (Zhai et al., 2024; Kassa, 2025). Digital interventions in developmental disorders show stronger connectivity and sometimes greater cortical thickness in affected regions, in keeping with reparative structural plasticity (Tiwari et al., 2026).

Functionally, games and exercises under prefrontal stimulation improve cognitive control by strengthening fronto-posterior synchronisation (PLV) in the theta and alpha-beta bands, a case of targeted modulation rescuing control in older adults

(Fotiadis et al., 2024). Reviews of structure-function coupling stress that cognitive flexibility depends on an adequate fit between anatomical connectivity and functional dynamics across the frontoparietal, salience, and default mode networks (P, 2026; Menon & D'Esposito, 2021). On a use-it-or-lose-it basis, prolonged AI dependence could go either way: strengthening offloading circuits, the prefrontal-parietal ones for navigating information and picking recommendations, or under-engaging the subnetworks behind autonomous reasoning and error monitoring, with possible maladaptive neuroplasticity, low prefrontal engagement and a reconfiguration of FPN/DMN/SN interactions (Menon & D'Esposito, 2021; Gazerani, 2025; Gkintoni et al., 2025; Sherif, 2025; Geissler et al., 2023). For now these trajectories stay hypothetical.

6.2. Adaptive versus maladaptive neuroplasticity under AI dependence

Adaptive hypotheses

- Educational AI, virtual reality, and cognitive remediation systems, when they are adaptive and well built, can enrich the environment, drive neuroplasticity, strengthen attention, working memory, and flexibility, and improve functional connectivity across the frontal and parietal networks (Zhai et al., 2024; Kassa, 2025; Tiwari et al., 2026; Medina et al., 2021; Diamond, 2012).
- Neuroplasticity-informed approaches that adjust cognitive load on the fly optimise prefronto-parietal activation and learning-related adaptation, especially in learners starting from a lower baseline (Diamond, 2012). Here the AI works as a scaffold for reasoning, supporting long-term cognitive autonomy as long as active engagement and reflection are kept up.

Maladaptive hypotheses

- Reviews of AI dependence and cognitive offloading document a risk of weaker critical thinking, analytic capacity, and independent decision making, tied to a growing taste for the cognitive shortcuts the AI supplies (Geissler et al., 2023; Gerlich, 2025; Gazerani, 2025; Gkintoni et al., 2025; Sherif, 2025).
- The idea of cognitive vestigiality proposes, by biological analogy, that chronically handing memory, reasoning, and metacognitive regulation to AI could, through the usual use-dependent plasticity, slowly reduce internal competence and the engagement of the executive networks (Sherif, 2025).
- Work on unstructured digital technologies shows negative effects on attention, internal memory, and decision making, alongside patterns of possibly

maladaptive neuroplasticity, fragmented attention, overload, the overuse of fast strategies (Jones et al., 2022; Kassa, 2025).

Current data point to bidirectional neuroplastic effects of heavy AI dependence. Used in demanding, reflective contexts, AI can support the training of executive functions and remodel networks for the better. Used for automated offloading, the path of least effort, and weak metacognition, it is liable to reconfigure circuits in favour of assisted routines and against autonomous executive control and complex reasoning.

7. EXPERIMENTAL DATA AND NEUROBIOLOGICAL EVIDENCE

The available work indicates that intensive use of the Internet and of digital technology can come with functional, and more rarely structural, changes in the brain. Direct evidence of a neuroplasticity tied specifically to cognitive externalisation, though, is still partial and mixed.

7.1. Effects of different digital uses

Internet and search engines

The Google effect shows that constant access leads people to remember where to find information better than the information itself, a reorganisation of memory strategies toward an Internet-centred transactive memory (Hu et al., 2022; Wadsley & Ihssen, 2023). fMRI shows adults new to the Internet recruiting frontal networks more heavily during search after only brief training, a quick functional adaptation to the new mode of processing (Ekstrom & Hill, 2023).

Smartphones, social media, and the Internet in general

A review of digital dementia reports links between overuse of digital media, white-matter alterations, and grey-matter reductions in regions tied to cognitive and emotional control, though the studies are few and heterogeneous (Small et al., 2020). Smartphone and social-media addiction shows up, in resting-state fMRI, as alterations of sensory, executive, and frontoparietal networks (Sparrow et al., 2011), and a systematic MRI review of social-media use describes volumetric reductions in the ventral striatum, amygdala, orbitofrontal cortex, and subgenual ACC, along with connectivity abnormalities in attentional and reward networks (Lee et al., 2025). Another review concludes that unstructured use favours attentional fragmentation, memory offloading, and overload, while tools built for learning can support neuroplasticity and executive function (Beisteiner & Matt, 2021).

GPS and navigation

A longitudinal study shows habitual, rising GPS use going with worse hippocampus-dependent spatial memory, independent of initial sense of direction, which hints at a causal effect of delegating navigation (Dahmani & Bohbot, 2020). Synthesis work on the hippocampus, navigation, and memory shows these functions sharing cognitive-map coding that is highly plastic and sensitive to experience (Áfra et al., 2023; Maza et al., 2023; Firth et al., 2019).

Social media and development

A longitudinal fMRI study in adolescents finds that habitual social-media-checking alters, across three years, how reward and control circuits, the amygdala, ventral striatum, anterior insula, and dlPFC, respond to social cues, with heavy and light checkers tracing opposite activation paths (Gkintoni et al., 2025). A separate longitudinal resting-state MRI study finds one month of intensive social-media use altering functional connectivity in roughly half the brain, attentional networks especially (Bellmund et al., 2018).

7.2. Neuroimaging data (fMRI, EEG, MEG, DTI, Connectivity)

Resting-state fMRI in problematic smartphone and social-media use shows the severity of the addiction tracking, in the negative direction, the functional integrity of sensory, executive, and frontoparietal networks (Sparrow et al., 2011). Functional-connectivity studies show prolonged social-media use realigning the connectivity of light users toward that of heavy users, read explicitly as an index of functional plasticity (Bellmund et al., 2018).

Reviews of what digital technology does to the brain report that digital learning, Internet search, training programmes, can raise frontal activation and modulate networks tied to memory, attention, and multitasking (Ekstrom & Hill, 2023; Beisteiner & Matt, 2021). A synthesis of digital interventions in people with developmental disorders documents, through EEG, MRI, and fMRI, shifts in wave patterns and stronger activation in some regions, alongside gains in attention, emotion recognition, and social skills (Kassa, 2025). General reviews of fMRI, EEG, and DTI confirm that these methods pick up changes in functional connectivity and in white-matter microstructure consistent with neuroplastic processes, but most of the examples are about pathology or rehabilitation, not the cognitive externalisation tied to AI or the Internet (Eichenbaum, 2017; Wu et al., 2023; Sparrow et al., 2011).

The DTI and white-matter findings linked to digital use, reported in the digital-dementia review, hint at reduced integrity of the tracts behind language and executive control in heavy users, though the paradigms and regions are barely specified (Small et al., 2020). MEG studies aimed specifically at cognitive externalisation are left undetailed in these summaries.

7.3. Modulating factors: age, education, expertise, cognitive reserve

Age comes up again and again. Early exposure to fast-paced media may go together with altered development of attention, inhibitory control, language, and reasoning, while in older adults some forms of digital training, Internet search, and memory programmes can improve cognitive function and strengthen frontal activation (Small et al., 2020; Ekstrom & Hill, 2023; Kassa, 2025; Beisteiner & Matt, 2021). The meta-analysis of Google effects finds that people with a broader base of knowledge are less vulnerable to the costs of intensive searching, which suggests that expertise and cognitive reserve play a protective role (Wadsley & Ihssen, 2023). The effect is stronger among those who already use the Internet, perhaps a mix of selection and habit-related plasticity (Wadsley & Ihssen, 2023).

The digital-dementia review notes different profiles across age groups, children, adolescents, young adults, older adults, without always being able to separate developmental vulnerability from cumulative effects (Small et al., 2020). Work on navigation and memory stresses how much varies between individuals with age and experience, both in strategy and in the hippocampo-cortico-parietal networks (Áfra et al., 2023; Firth et al., 2019).

The digital-dementia review notes different profiles across age groups, children, adolescents, young adults, older adults, without always being able to separate developmental vulnerability from cumulative effects (Small et al., 2020). Work on navigation and memory stresses how much varies between individuals with age and experience, both in strategy and in the hippocampo-cortico-parietal networks (Áfra et al., 2023; Firth et al., 2019).

7.4. Critical Appraisal: What Indices of Neuroplasticity Are Linked to Cognitive Externalisation?

Evidence in favour.

- The GPS study gives a longitudinal behavioural index in line with a progressive impairment of hippocampus-dependent functions tied to systematically delegating navigation (Dahmani & Bohbot, 2020).
- Longitudinal studies of social-media use, both checking and imposed tasks, show activation and connectivity shifting over time in reward, attention, and control circuits, the amygdala, ventral striatum, insula, dlPFC, and large-scale networks, which fits functional neuroplastic adaptation (Gkintoni et al., 2025; Bellmund et al., 2018).
- fMRI in Internet-naive adults after training, together with digital-intervention studies in developmental disorders, documents activation and connectivity changes consistent with networks reconfiguring under repeated digital experience (Ekstrom & Hill, 2023; Kassa, 2025).
- The Google-effect meta-analysis shows a systematic shift of memory strategies toward an externalised transactive memory which, set against the neuroimaging, backs the idea of a functional reconfiguration of memory systems (Wadsley & Ihssen, 2023; Hu et al., 2022).

Limitations and findings that qualify the hypothesis.

- Most of the data are correlational or quasi-experimental. Few studies combine longitudinal measures, imaging across fMRI, DTI, and EEG/MEG, and precise indicators of cognitive externalisation such as memory offloading or decision delegation.
- Reviews of social media point to patterns close to those in addiction, but they stress the want of longitudinal evidence for causal neuroadaptation (Lee et al., 2025).
- Digital-intervention studies also show benefits for neuroplasticity, stronger activation, better performance, which suggests digital technology can both exploit and build plasticity, depending on design and use (Kassa, 2025; Beisteiner & Matt, 2021; Gong & Yang, 2024).
- Modulating factors, age, expertise, cognitive reserve, context of use, carry real weight here. A richer knowledge base and structured use appear to soften the costs of offloading (Wadsley & Ihssen, 2023; Beisteiner & Matt, 2021).

Taken together, the data give convergent signs of neuroplastic change, mostly functional and at times structural, linked to heavy use of the Internet, smartphones, GPS, and social media. The changes touch the hippocampal, frontoparietal, reward, and attention networks above all, and they fit the idea that cognitive externalisation, of memory, navigation, information processing, slowly reconfigures the strategies and circuits underneath. The evidence stays fragmentary, mixed, and often indirect, though. It shows the brain adapting to new digital practices. It does not yet show clearly how far those adaptations reflect a dependence on externalisation rather than an adaptive plasticity, nor what exact conditions, intensity, duration, age, cognitive reserve, tip the balance from beneficial plasticity toward potentially harmful change.

8. NEUROETHICAL IMPLICATIONS AND FUTURE PERSPECTIVES

Recent work settles on an ambivalent picture: an AI that can both support and undercut cognitive autonomy and the quality of reasoning, depending on how it is used, on the educational and professional setting, and on the governance around it (Gerlich, 2025; Rohilla, 2025; P, 2026; Garcia-Barrios, 2025; Ligthart et al., 2023; Yavich, 2025; Alhur et al., 2025).

8.1. Cognitive autonomy, intellectual sovereignty, and technological dependence

Cognitive autonomy and intellectual sovereignty

Intensive AI use goes with weaker critical thinking, autonomous decision making, and metacognition, by way of heavy offloading and high trust in what generative systems suggest (Gerlich, 2025; Rohilla, 2025; P, 2026; Rao, 2025; Garcia-Barrios, 2025; Yavich, 2025; Alhur et al., 2025). Work in neuroethics and on neurorights presses the case for protecting cognitive liberty and mental integrity against technologies that fuse AI and neurotech (Doya et al., 2022; Capraro et al., 2023). Societal analyses speak of interpretive autonomy and epistemic agency, both under threat from a split between a cognitively resilient minority and a dependent majority (Gkintoni et al., 2025).

Technological dependence

Quantitative and qualitative studies describe a functional dependence on AI that comes with skill atrophy, in writing, judgment, problem solving, along with procrastination and a loss of intrinsic motivation (Rohilla, 2025; P, 2026; Rao, 2025; Gerlich, 2026). Reviews of cognitive complacency and AI dependence point to a turn toward fast heuristics and thinner epistemic vigilance (Zhai et al., 2024; Yan et al., 2025; Garcia-Barrios, 2025; Alhur et al., 2025).

8.2. Educational, professional, and societal consequences

Education:

Excessive use of AI tools by students correlates with:

- weaker critical thinking, memory retention, and independent problem solving (Gerlich, 2025; Rohilla, 2025; P, 2026; Rao, 2025; Yavich, 2025);
- but also gains in efficiency, confidence, and immediate performance, above all when the AI works as structured, scaffolded tutoring (Rohilla, 2025; Yan et al., 2025; Sherif, 2025; Salles & Farisco, 2024; Yavich, 2025; Sabherwal & Grover, 2024). An explicit pedagogical design, formative feedback, metacognitive tasks, real didactic integration, can lift critical thinking and autonomy above what spontaneous use yields (Sherif, 2025).

Professions

In medical higher education, teachers describe skill atrophy, in critical thinking, decision making, and creativity, along with pedagogical erosion and social fragmentation, when AI is used as a permanent crutch (Gerlich, 2026). The same study still holds out the prospect of a hybrid intelligence, if AI is framed by norms of use and by training in AI literacy (Gerlich, 2026).

Society

Work on the impacts of generative AI raises:

- a societal split between a minority capable of reflective use and a cognitively dependent majority, with effects on inequality and democratic vulnerability (Gkintoni et al., 2025; Sabherwal & Grover, 2024);
- risks of cognitive enfeeblement, disinformation, and wider gaps in access and skill (Zhai et al., 2024; Ligthart et al., 2023; Sabherwal & Grover, 2024; Batool et al., 2025).

8.3. Neuroethical issues, skill erosion, and the benefits of cognitive augmentation

neuroethical issues

Frameworks of neuroethics and AI ethics put forward:

- a need to protect cognitive liberty, mental privacy, and integrity against AI and neurotech systems that keep growing more intrusive (Doya et al., 2022; Capraro et al., 2023);
- the risk of having to redefine autonomy and responsibility once decisions are co-produced with AI (Capraro et al., 2023);
- the value of governance modelled on democratic practice, to keep cognitive power from pooling in a few platforms (Zhai et al., 2024).

Skill erosion

Several syntheses document:

- a robust negative correlation between frequent AI use and critical thinking, with offloading as the link (Gerlich, 2025; Rohilla, 2025; P, 2026; Rao, 2025; Yavich, 2025; Alhur et al., 2025);
- skill atrophy, in memory, judgment, writing, and decision, as perceived by students and teachers alike (Rohilla, 2025; P, 2026; Rao, 2025; Gerlich, 2026);
- a drop in metacognition and an overestimation of one's own abilities after AI use (Gerlich, 2025; Rohilla, 2025; Yavich, 2025; Alhur et al., 2025).

Potential benefits

The same body of work cuts the other way too:

- adaptive, neuroplasticity-informed systems built around managing cognitive load improve learning, lower-performing learners most of all, and can optimise how the frontoparietal networks are engaged (Yan et al., 2025; Salles & Farisco, 2024; Gerlich, 2026; Sabherwal & Grover, 2024);
- a carefully designed pedagogical use of AI can raise critical thinking, intellectual independence, and reflexivity rather than lower them (Sherif, 2025; Yan et al., 2025; Ligthart et al., 2023).

Augmentative versus dependent uses

Table 3. Two regimes of cognitive AI use

Type of use	Cognitive profile	Probable effects	Sources
AI as scaffold	Active engagement, critical control	Learning gains, strengthened agency	(Yan et al., 2025; Sherif, 2025; Salles & Farisco, 2024; Sabherwal & Grover, 2024)
AI as crutch (passive offloading)	Minimal effort, high trust	Skill atrophy, reduced metacognition	(Gerlich, 2025; Rohilla, 2025; P, 2026; Rao, 2025; Gerlich, 2026; Yavich, 2025; Alhur et al., 2025)

8.4. An integrative conceptual model: AI, cognitive externalisation, neuroplasticity, and outcomes

Reviews of offloading and of neuroplasticity-informed learning describe a functional arc:

- AI use, set by frequency, type of task, and design, direct solution versus scaffolding (Gerlich, 2025; Rohilla, 2025; Yan et al., 2025; Yavich, 2025; Alhur et al., 2025).
- Cognitive externalisation, of memory, information seeking, reasoning, and decision, by way of cognitive offloading (Gerlich, 2025; Zhai et al., 2024; Rohilla, 2025; Rao, 2025; Garcia-Barrios, 2025; Alhur et al., 2025).
- Modulation of functional neuroplasticity: the engagement of the frontoparietal networks reduced or reorganised, and connectivity changing between assisted and unassisted tasks (Salles & Farisco, 2024; Gerlich, 2026; Yavich, 2025).

Cognitive outcomes:

o in the short term, better performance and less stress and attentional cost (Rohilla, 2025; Yan et al., 2025; Salles & Farisco, 2024; Sabherwal & Grover, 2024);

o in the long term, depending on the regime of use, either skills strengthening under structured use or eroding under compulsive use and massive offloading (Gerlich, 2025; Rohilla, 2025; P, 2026; Rao, 2025; Gerlich, 2026; Yavich, 2025; Alhur et al., 2025; Gkintoni et al., 2025).

A few studies report brain connectivity dropping during AI-assisted tasks (Salles & Farisco, 2024; Gerlich, 2026; Yavich, 2025), but most of the links are still inferential rather than demonstrated.

8.5. Major gaps and research directions

Gaps:

- Almost no longitudinal studies tie AI use, changes in connectivity and networks, and trajectories of skill together (Gerlich, 2025; Rohilla, 2025; P, 2026; Rao, 2025; Sherif, 2025; Ligthart et al., 2023; Salles & Farisco, 2024; Yavich, 2025; Sabherwal & Grover, 2024; Alhur et al., 2025).
- The data come mostly from education; neurocognitive analysis in workplaces or among vulnerable groups is scarce (Gerlich, 2026; Sabherwal & Grover, 2024).
- Notions such as cognitive autonomy, intellectual sovereignty, and cognitive liberty are rarely given a clear operational definition in empirical protocols (Doya et al., 2022; Capraro et al., 2023).
- Few neuroimaging studies of AI dependence actually look at prefrontal engagement, the DMN, or the salience network (Salles & Farisco, 2024; Gerlich, 2026; Sabherwal & Grover, 2024).

Future directions

- Longitudinal cohorts that follow exposure to AI, patterns of offloading, performance, and, where possible, markers of neuroplasticity drawn from functional imaging and connectivity (Gerlich, 2025; Rohilla, 2025; P, 2026; Rao, 2025; Salles & Farisco, 2024; Gerlich, 2026; Yavich, 2025; Alhur et al., 2025).
- Controlled experiments that set crutch AI against scaffold AI, so as to isolate the cognitive and neural signatures of augmentation as opposed to dependence (Yan et al., 2025; Sherif, 2025; Salles & Farisco, 2024; Yavich, 2025; Alhur et al., 2025).
- Building neurorights and neuroethics into AI policy as a matter of course, covering autonomy, mental integrity, and cognitive privacy (Doya et al., 2022; Capraro et al., 2023; Zhai et al., 2024; Sabherwal & Grover, 2024; Batool et al., 2025).
- Studies of societal bifurcation and cognitive inequality, of the gaps in epistemic agency, AI literacy, and resilience (Gkintoni et al., 2025; Sabherwal & Grover, 2024).

The literature keeps coming back to a single tension. AI can act as an epistemic partner that augments cognition, or as a crutch that speeds the erosion of intellectual autonomy. The neuroethical stakes follow from that: protecting cognitive liberty, heading off new forms of dependence and inequality, and designing systems and policies that nudge neuroplasticity toward adaptive rather than maladaptive ends.

9. CONCLUSION

Artificial intelligence is one of the most consequential technological changes of recent history, because it reaches directly into cognitive processes once thought exclusively human. Traditional digital tools mainly eased access to information. Today's AI systems take part in seeking information, organising knowledge, generating reasoning, solving problems, and making decisions. That shift raises basic questions about what cognitive externalisation does to brain function, neuroplasticity, and intellectual autonomy.

Read across the literature, the mechanisms of neuroplasticity are the biological ground for understanding how repeated interaction with cognitive technologies can slowly remodel neural circuits. Long-term potentiation and depression, dendritic remodelling, axonal plasticity, activity-dependent myelination, and neuromodulation all show brain networks adapting continuously to what the environment asks. AI-centred digital environments, on this reading, are a new kind of intensive cognitive experience that can steer the functional specialisation of certain networks.

The evidence also shows executive functions resting on a distributed architecture: the prefrontal cortex, the anterior cingulate cortex, and the frontoparietal, salience, and default mode networks. These systems carry planning, working memory, inhibition, cognitive flexibility, metacognition, and decision making. They are the neurobiological substrate of cognitive autonomy and complex reasoning. Any durable change in how strongly they are engaged could matter a great deal for how people learn, reason, and decide.

Work on cognitive externalisation shows AI acting as an external cognitive system that redistributes memory, reasoning, and decision between the person and the technological environment. The redistribution can sharpen immediate cognitive efficiency, lightening mental load, speeding access to information, easing the path through complex problems. It can also dull memory encoding, lower the cognitive effort people put in, weaken critical thinking, and deepen reliance on automated answers, especially once the user settles into a passive stance.

The mechanisms proposed for these effects include the slow replacement of deliberative processing by automated responses, the redirection of executive resources toward managing the interface rather than reasoning, the weakening of metacognitive processes, and the way offloading habits get consolidated by motivational and dopaminergic reinforcement. Over time, these could shift the functional balance between internal control and external assistance.

ACKNOWLEDGMENT

The authors acknowledge the National Center for scientific and Technical Research (CNRST), Morocco, for providing a Pass scholarship for the PhD student Ilyass Britel.

REFERENCES

Áfra, E., Janszky, J., Perlaki, G., Orsi, G., Nagy, S., Arató, Á., Szente, A., Alhour, H., Kis-Jakab, G., & Darnai, G. (2023). Altered functional brain networks in problematic smartphone and social media use: Resting-state fMRI study. *Brain Imaging and Behavior*, *18*(2), 292–301. DOI: 10.1007/s11682-023-00825-y PMID: 38049599

Alhur, A., Khlaif, Z. N., Hamamra, B., & Hussein, E. (2025). Paradox of AI in Higher Education: Qualitative Inquiry Into AI Dependency Among Educators in Palestine. *JMIR Medical Education*, *11*, v11i7972e74947. Advance online publication. DOI: 10.2196/74947 PMID: 40953310

Batool, S. T., Ali, U., & Mahato, R. K. (2025). NeuroAI-driven cognitive off-loading and synaptic effort recalibration. *Annals of Medicine and Surgery (London)*, *88*(2), 2162–2163. DOI: 10.1097/MS9.0000000000004652 PMID: 41675826

Bazzari, A. H., & Parri, H. (2019). Neuromodulators and Long-Term Synaptic Plasticity in Learning and Memory: A Steered-Glutamatergic Perspective. *Brain Sciences*, *9*(11), 300. Advance online publication. DOI: 10.3390/brainsci9110300 PMID: 31683595

Beisteiner, R., & Matt, E. (2021). *Brain Plasticity in fMRI and DTI.* Clinical Functional MRI., DOI: 10.1007/978-3-662-45123-6_11

Bellmund, J. L. S., Gärdenfors, P., Moser, E., & Doeller, C. F. (2018). Navigating cognition: Spatial codes for human thinking. *Science*, *362*(6415), eaat6766. Advance online publication. DOI: 10.1126/science.aat6766 PMID: 30409861

Bhattacharya, P., Prasad, V. K., Verma, A., Gupta, D., Sapsomboon, A., Viriyasitavat, W., & Dhiman, G. (2024). Demystifying ChatGPT: An In-depth Survey of OpenAI's Robust Large Language Models. *Archives of Computational Methods in Engineering*, *31*(8), 4557–4600. DOI: 10.1007/s11831-024-10115-5

Bonetto, G., Belin, D., & Káradóttir, R. (2021). Myelin: A gatekeeper of activity-dependent circuit plasticity? *Science*, *374*(6569), eaba6905. Advance online publication. DOI: 10.1126/science.aba6905 PMID: 34618550

Capraro, V., Lentsch, A., Acemoglu, D., Akgun, S., Akhmedova, A., Bilancini, E., Bonnefon, J.-F., Brañas-Garza, P., Butera, L., Douglas, K. M., Everett, J. A. C., Gigerenzer, G., Greenhow, C., Hashimoto, D. A., Holt-Lunstad, J., Jetten, J., Johnson, S., Kunz, W. H., Longoni, C., & Viale, R. (2023). The impact of generative artificial intelligence on socioeconomic inequalities and policy making. *PNAS Nexus*, *3*(6), pgae191. Advance online publication. DOI: 10.1093/pnasnexus/pgae191 PMID: 38864006

Chakraborty, P., Dey, A., Gopalakrishnan, A. V., Swati, K., Ojha, S., Prakash, A., Kumar, D., Ambasta, R. K., Jha, N., Dewanjee, S., & Jha, S. (2023). Glutamatergic Neurotransmission: A Potential Pharmacotherapeutic Target for the Treatment of Cognitive Disorders. *Ageing Research Reviews*, *101838*, 101838. Advance online publication. DOI: 10.1016/j.arr.2022.101838 PMID: 36610558

Chauca, J. M. N., VanDyck, M. V., Oseguera, A. L. G., Ramírez, C. M., Escobar, A. D. G., Orozco, I. P., & Sanchez, M. B. R. (2026). Cognitive Stimulation and Activity-Dependent Myelination: Oligodendroglial Mechanisms Linking Neural Activity and Brain Plasticity. *International Journal of Molecular Sciences*, *27*(8), 3603. Advance online publication. DOI: 10.3390/ijms27083603 PMID: 42074241

Chen, X., Zeng, G. Q., Li, N., Zhang, M., & Zhang, X. (2026). The Distinct Roles of the Dorsolateral Prefrontal Cortex and Dorsal Anterior Cingulate Cortex in Cognitive Control. *Psychophysiology*, *63*(3), e70269. Advance online publication. DOI: 10.1111/psyp.70269 PMID: 41808199

Chidambaram, S., Rathipriya, A., Bolla, S., Bhat, A. R., Ray, B., Mahalakshmi, A., Manivasagam, T., Thenmozhi, A., Essa, M., Guillemin, G., Chandra, R., & Sakharkar, M. (2019). Dendritic spines: Revisiting the physiological role. *Progress in Neuro-Psychopharmacology & Biological Psychiatry*, *92*, 161–193. DOI: 10.1016/j.pnpbp.2019.01.005 PMID: 30654089

Cools, R., & Arnsten, A. (2021). Neuromodulation of prefrontal cortex cognitive function in primates: The powerful roles of monoamines and acetylcholine. *Neuropsychopharmacology : Official Publication of the American College of Neuropsychopharmacology*, *47*(1), 309–328. DOI: 10.1038/s41386-021-01100-8 PMID: 34312496

Dahmani, L., & Bohbot, V. (2020). Habitual use of GPS negatively impacts spatial memory during self-guided navigation. *Scientific Reports*, *10*(1), 6310. Advance online publication. DOI: 10.1038/s41598-020-62877-0 PMID: 32286340

Dalley, J., Cardinal, R., & Robbins, T. (2004). Prefrontal executive and cognitive functions in rodents: Neural and neurochemical substrates. *Neuroscience and Biobehavioral Reviews, 28*(7), 771–784. DOI: 10.1016/j.neubiorev.2004.09.006 PMID: 15555683

Das, A., & Menon, V. (2020). Spatiotemporal Integrity and Spontaneous Nonlinear Dynamic Properties of the Salience Network Revealed by Human Intracranial Electrophysiology. *Cerebral Cortex (New York, N.Y.), 30*(10), 5309–5321. Advance online publication. DOI: 10.1093/cercor/bhaa111 PMID: 32426806

Das, A., & Menon, V. (2024). Electrophysiological dynamics of salience, default mode, and frontoparietal networks during episodic memory formation and recall. *eLife, 13*, RP99018. Advance online publication. DOI: 10.7554/eLife.99018 PMID: 39556109

De Barros, E. C. (2024). Understanding the influence of digital technology on human cognitive functions: A narrative review. *IBRO Neuroscience Reports, 17*, 415–422. DOI: 10.1016/j.ibneur.2024.11.006 PMID: 39624825

Dey, S., Arya, A., Raut, A. J., Katta, S., & Sharma, P. (2024). *Exploring the Role of Neuroplasticity in Stroke Rehabilitation: Mechanisms, Interventions and Clinical Implications*. International Journal For Multidisciplinary Research., DOI: 10.36948/ijfmr.2024.v06i02.18483

Diamond, A. (2012). Executive functions. *Annual Review of Psychology, 64*(1), 135–168. DOI: 10.1146/annurev-psych-113011-143750 PMID: 23020641

Doya, K., Ema, A., Kitano, H., Sakagami, M., & Russell, S. (2022). Social impact and governance of AI and neurotechnologies. *Neural Networks, 152*, 542–554. DOI: 10.1016/j.neunet.2022.05.012 PMID: 35671575

Drigas, A., & Sideraki, A. (2024). Brain Neuroplasticity Leveraging Virtual Reality and Brain–Computer Interface Technologies. *Sensors (Basel), 24*(17), 5725. Advance online publication. DOI: 10.3390/s24175725 PMID: 39275636

. Dror, I., & Harnad, S. (2008). *Cognition distributed: how cognitive technology extends our minds*. DOI: 10.1075/bct.16

Duncan, J., & Owen, A. (2000). Common regions of the human frontal lobe recruited by diverse cognitive demands. *Trends in Neurosciences, 23*(10), 475–483. DOI: 10.1016/S0166-2236(00)01633-7 PMID: 11006464

Eichenbaum, H. (2017). The role of the hippocampus in navigation is memory. *Journal of Neurophysiology, 117*(4), 1785–1796. DOI: 10.1152/jn.00005.2017 PMID: 28148640

Ekstrom, A. D., & Hill, P. F. (2023). Spatial navigation and memory: A review of the similarities and differences relevant to brain models and age. *Neuron, 111*(7), 1037–1049. DOI: 10.1016/j.neuron.2023.03.001 PMID: 37023709

Elston, T., & Wallis, J. (2025). Frontostriatal dynamics of cognitive control. *bioRxiv*. DOI: 10.1101/2025.03.07.642117

Feldman, D. (2009). Synaptic Mechanisms for Plasticity in Neocortex. *Annual Review of Neuroscience, 32*(1), 33–55. DOI: 10.1146/annurev.neuro.051508.135516 PMID: 19400721

Filippo, C., Vito, G., Irene, S., Simone, B., & Gualtiero, F. (2024). Future applications of generative large language models: A data-driven case study on ChatGPT. *Technovation, 133*, 103002. Advance online publication. DOI: 10.1016/j.technovation.2024.103002

Firth, J., Torous, J., Stubbs, B., Firth, J. A., Steiner, G., Smith, L., Alvarez-Jimenez, M., Gleeson, J., Vancampfort, D., Armitage, C., & Sarris, J. (2019). The "online brain": How the Internet may be changing our cognition. *World Psychiatry; Official Journal of the World Psychiatric Association (WPA), 18*(2), 119–129. Advance online publication. DOI: 10.1002/wps.20617 PMID: 31059635

Fotiadis, P., Parkes, L., Davis, K., Satterthwaite, T., Shinohara, R. T., & Bassett, D. S. (2024). Structure–function coupling in macroscale human brain networks. *Nature Reviews. Neuroscience, 25*(10), 688–704. DOI: 10.1038/s41583-024-00846-6 PMID: 39103609

Friedman, N., & Robbins, T. (2021). The role of prefrontal cortex in cognitive control and executive function. *Neuropsychopharmacology : Official Publication of the American College of Neuropsychopharmacology, 47*(1), 72–89. DOI: 10.1038/s41386-021-01132-0 PMID: 34408280

. Gallagher, S. (2023). *Embodied and Enactive Approaches to Cognition*. DOI: 10.1017/9781009209793

Garcia-Barrios, D. A. (2025). Epistemic Partner or Cognitive Crutch: A Conceptual Model of Cognitive Offloading in Human–Artificial Intelligence Collaboration. *IEEE Internet Computing, 29*(5), 7–16. DOI: 10.1109/MIC.2025.3626694

Gazerani, P. (2025). The neuroplastic brain: Current breakthroughs and emerging frontiers. *Brain Research, 149643*, 149643. Advance online publication. DOI: 10.1016/j.brainres.2025.149643 PMID: 40280532

Geissler, C., Gauselmann, P., Jilek, C., Maus, H., Frings, C., & Tempel, T. (2023). A functional near-infrared spectroscopy study on the prefrontal correlates of cognitive offloading via a personal knowledge assistant. *Scientific Reports*, *13*(1), 13938. Advance online publication. DOI: 10.1038/s41598-023-39540-5 PMID: 37626078

Gerlich, M. (2025). AI Tools in Society: Impacts on Cognitive Offloading and the Future of Critical Thinking. *Societies (Basel, Switzerland)*, *15*(1), 6. Advance online publication. DOI: 10.3390/soc15010006

Gerlich, M. (2026). AI and the Rise of Societal Bifurcation: Cognitive Dependency, Inequality and Democratic Pressure. *Societies (Basel, Switzerland)*, *16*(3), 82. Advance online publication. DOI: 10.3390/soc16030082

Gkintoni, E., Antonopoulou, H., Sortwell, A., & Halkiopoulos, C. (2025). Challenging Cognitive Load Theory: The Role of Educational Neuroscience and Artificial Intelligence in Redefining Learning Efficacy. *Brain Sciences*, *15*(2), 203. Advance online publication. DOI: 10.3390/brainsci15020203 PMID: 40002535

Gkintoni, E., Sortwell, A., Vassilopoulos, S., & Nikolaou, G. (2025). Neuroplasticity-Informed Learning Under Cognitive Load: A Systematic Review of Functional Imaging, Brain Stimulation, and Educational Technology Applications. *Multimodal Technologies and Interaction*, *10*(1), 5. Advance online publication. DOI: 10.3390/mti10010005

Gläscher, J., Adolphs, R., Damasio, H., Bechara, A., Rudrauf, D., Calamia, M., Paul, L., & Tranel, D. (2012). Lesion mapping of cognitive control and value-based decision making in the prefrontal cortex. *Proceedings of the National Academy of Sciences of the United States of America*, *109*(36), 14681–14686. DOI: 10.1073/pnas.1206608109 PMID: 22908286

Goh, A. Y. H., Hartanto, A., & Majeed, N. M. (2025). Generative artificial intelligence dependency: Scale development, validation, and its motivational, behavioral, and psychological correlates. *Computers in Human Behavior Reports*, *20*, 100845. Advance online publication. DOI: 10.1016/j.chbr.2025.100845

Gong, C., & Yang, Y. (2024). Google effects on memory: A meta-analytical review of the media effects of intensive Internet search behavior. *Frontiers in Public Health*, *12*, 1332030. Advance online publication. DOI: 10.3389/fpubh.2024.1332030 PMID: 38304178

Grinschgl, S., & Neubauer, A. (2022). Supporting Cognition With Modern Technology: Distributed Cognition Today and in an AI-Enhanced Future. *Frontiers in Artificial Intelligence*, *5*, 908261. Advance online publication. DOI: 10.3389/frai.2022.908261 PMID: 35910191

Grinschgl, S., Papenmeier, F., & Meyerhoff, H. S. (2020). Consequences of cognitive offloading: Boosting performance but diminishing memory. *Quarterly Journal of Experimental Psychology, 74*(9), 1477–1496. DOI: 10.1177/17470218211008060 PMID: 33752519

Hagena, H., & Manahan-Vaughan, D. (2024). Interplay of hippocampal long-term potentiation and long-term depression in enabling memory representations. *Philosophical Transactions of the Royal Society of London. Series B, Biological Sciences, 379*(1906), 20230229. Advance online publication. DOI: 10.1098/rstb.2023.0229 PMID: 38853558

Heavey, C., & Simsek, Z. (2017). Distributed Cognition in Top Management Teams and Organizational Ambidexterity. *Journal of Management, 43*(3), 919–945. DOI: 10.1177/0149206314545652

Hooper, V. (2025). *Cognitive offloading and the reshaping of human thought: The subtle influence of Artificial Intelligence*. Colloquia, Academic Journal of Culture and Thought., DOI: 10.31207/colloquia.v12i1.185

Hu, B., Yu, Y., Yan, L.-F., Qi, G.-Q., Wu, D., Li, Y.-T., Shi, A.-P., Liu, C.-X., Shang, Y.-X., Li, Z.-Y., Cui, G.-B., & Wang, W. (2022). Intersubject correlation analysis reveals the plasticity of cerebral functional connectivity in the long-term use of social media. *Human Brain Mapping, 43*(7), 2262–2275. DOI: 10.1002/hbm.25786 PMID: 35072320

Ibrahim, M. B. Z., Benoy, A., & Sajikumar, S. (2021). Long-term plasticity in the hippocampus: Maintaining within and 'tagging' between synapses. *The FEBS Journal, 289*(8), 2176–2201. Advance online publication. DOI: 10.1111/febs.16065 PMID: 34109726

Jones, D. T., & Graff-Radford, J. (2021). Executive Dysfunction and the Prefrontal Cortex. *Continuum (Minneapolis, Minn.), 27*(6), 1586–1601. DOI: 10.1212/CON.0000000000001009 PMID: 34881727

Jones, K. T., Johnson, E., Gazzaley, A., & Zanto, T. P. (2022). Structural and functional network mechanisms of rescuing cognitive control in aging. *NeuroImage, 262*, 119547. DOI: 10.1016/j.neuroimage.2022.119547 PMID: 35940423

Jose, B., Joseph, D., Mohan, V., Alexander, E., Varghese, S. K., & Roy, A. (2025). Outsourcing cognition: The psychological costs of AI-era convenience. *Frontiers in Psychology, 16*, 1645237. Advance online publication. DOI: 10.3389/fpsyg.2025.1645237 PMID: 41426381

Kassa, S. T. (2025). Cognitive benefits and risks of digital technology engagement. *Discover Psychology*, *6*(1), 10. Advance online publication. DOI: 10.1007/s44202-025-00527-0

Katmah, R., Awad, M. I., Al-Ani, F., Khan, M., Alskafi, F. A., Hussain, I., Jelinek, H. F., & Khalaf, K. (2025). Adaptation Robotics and Cognitive Load: Use of a Supernumerary Finger for Activities of Daily Living. *IEEE Transactions on Neural Systems and Rehabilitation Engineering*, *33*, 2064–2075. DOI: 10.1109/TNSRE.2025.3574133 PMID: 40424112

Knowles, J., Batra, A., Xu, H., & Monje, M. (2022). Adaptive and maladaptive myelination in health and disease. *Nature Reviews. Neurology*, *18*(12), 735–746. DOI: 10.1038/s41582-022-00737-3 PMID: 36376595

Lee, H., Shin, Y., Moon, H., Choi, Y., & Lee, A. (2025). Effects of digital interventions on neuroplasticity and brain function of individuals with developmental disabilities: A systematic review. *Internet Interventions : the Application of Information Technology in Mental and Behavioural Health*, *41*, 100850. Advance online publication. DOI: 10.1016/j.invent.2025.100850 PMID: 40687196

León-Domínguez, U. (2024). Potential cognitive risks of generative transformer-based AI chatbots on higher order executive functions. *Neuropsychology*, *38*(4), 293–308. Advance online publication. DOI: 10.1037/neu0000948 PMID: 38300581

Ligthart, S., Ienca, M., Meynen, G., Molnar-Gabor, F., Andorno, R., Bublitz, C., Catley, P., Claydon, L., Douglas, T., Farahany, N., Fins, J. J., Goering, S., Haselager, P., Jotterand, F., Lavazza, A., McCay, A., Wajnerman Paz, A., Rainey, S., Ryberg, J., & Kellmeyer, P. (2023). Minding rights: Mapping ethical and legal foundations of 'neurorights'. *Cambridge Quarterly of Healthcare Ethics*, *32*(4), 1–21. DOI: 10.1017/S0963180123000245 PMID: 37183686

Lisman, J. (2017). Glutamatergic synapses are structurally and biochemically complex because of multiple plasticity processes. *Philosophical Transactions of the Royal Society of London. Series B, Biological Sciences*, *372*(1715), 20160260. Advance online publication. DOI: 10.1098/rstb.2016.0260 PMID: 28093558

MacDonald, A. W., Cohen, J., Stenger, V., & Carter, C. (2000). Dissociating the role of the dorsolateral prefrontal and anterior cingulate cortex in cognitive control. *Science*, *288*(5472), 1835–1838. DOI: 10.1126/science.288.5472.1835 PMID: 10846167

Magee, J., & Grienberger, C. (2020). Synaptic Plasticity Forms and Functions. *Annual Review of Neuroscience*, *43*(1), 95–117. Advance online publication. DOI: 10.1146/annurev-neuro-090919-022842 PMID: 32075520

Mansvelder, H., Verhoog, M. B., & Goriounova, N. (2019). Synaptic plasticity in human cortical circuits: Cellular mechanisms of learning and memory in the human brain? *Current Opinion in Neurobiology, 54*, 186–193. DOI: 10.1016/j.conb.2018.06.013 PMID: 30017789

Matsuzaki, M., Honkura, N., Ellis-Davies, G., & Kasai, H. (2004). Structural basis of long-term potentiation in single dendritic spines. *Nature, 429*(6993), 761–766. DOI: 10.1038/nature02617 PMID: 15190253

Maza, M., Fox, K. A., Kwon, S.-J., Flannery, J. E., Lindquist, K. A., Prinstein, M., & Telzer, E. (2023). Association of Habitual Checking Behaviors on Social Media With Longitudinal Functional Brain Development. *JAMA Pediatrics, 177*(2), 160. Advance online publication. DOI: 10.1001/jamapediatrics.2022.4924 PMID: 36595277

Medina, R., Bouhaben, J., De Ramón, I., Cuesta, P., Antón-Toro, L., Pacios, J., Quintero, J., Ramos-Quiroga, J., & Maestú, F. (2021). Electrophysiological Brain Changes Associated With Cognitive Improvement in a Pediatric ADHD Digital AI-Driven Intervention. *Journal of Medical Internet Research, 23*. Advance online publication. DOI: 10.2196/25466 PMID: 34842533

Menon, V., & D'Esposito, M. (2021). The role of PFC networks in cognitive control and executive function. *Neuropsychopharmacology : Official Publication of the American College of Neuropsychopharmacology, 47*(1), 90–103. DOI: 10.1038/s41386-021-01152-w PMID: 34408276

Menon, V., Palaniyappan, L., & Supekar, K. (2022). Integrative Brain Network and Salience Models of Psychopathology and Cognitive Dysfunction in Schizophrenia. *Biological Psychiatry*. Advance online publication. DOI: 10.1016/j.biopsych.2022.09.029 PMID: 36702660

Mount, C. W., & Monje, M. (2017). Wrapped to adapt: Experience-dependent myelination. *Neuron, 95*(4), 743–756. DOI: 10.1016/j.neuron.2017.07.009 PMID: 28817797

Nah, F. F.-H., Zheng, R., Cai, J., Siau, K., & Chen, L. (2023). Generative AI and ChatGPT: Applications, challenges, and AI-human collaboration. *Journal of Information Technology Case and Application Research, 25*(3), 277–304. DOI: 10.1080/15228053.2023.2233814

Niendam, T., Laird, A. R., Ray, K. L., Dean, Y. M., Glahn, D., & Carter, C. S. (2012). Meta-analytic evidence for a superordinate cognitive control network subserving diverse executive functions. *Cognitive, Affective & Behavioral Neuroscience, 12*(2), 241–268. DOI: 10.3758/s13415-011-0083-5 PMID: 22282036

Ott, T., & Nieder, A. (2019). Dopamine and Cognitive Control in Prefrontal Cortex. *Trends in Cognitive Sciences*, *23*(3), 213–234. DOI: 10.1016/j.tics.2018.12.006 PMID: 30711326

. P, F. (2026). Cognitive Offloading in the Age of Artificial Intelligence: Psychological Implications of Excessive AI Dependence. *International Journal of Global Mental Health, Innovation, Policy, Action, Culture & Transformation*. DOI: 10.61113/impact.V2I1.1266

Palacios-Filardo, J., & Mellor, J. (2019). Neuromodulation of hippocampal long-term synaptic plasticity. *Current Opinion in Neurobiology*, *54*, 37–43. DOI: 10.1016/j.conb.2018.08.009 PMID: 30212713

Palamarchuk, O., Haba, I., Shulha, H., Khilya, A., & Sarancha, I. (2025). Neuroplasticity and Digital Tools in Lifelong Learning: Cognitive Challenges and Opportunities. *ENVIRONMENT. TECHNOLOGY. Resources*, *2*, 257–263. Advance online publication. DOI: 10.17770/etr2025vol2.8599

Peltokorpi, V. (2008). Transactive Memory Systems. *Review of General Psychology*, *12*(4), 378–394. DOI: 10.1037/1089-2680.12.4.378

Rao, S. (2025). *The Impact of Artificial Intelligence Tools on Human Cognitive Abilities: A Comprehensive Review*. INNOVAPATH., DOI: 10.63501/hsdq5611

Riley, C., Al-Refai, O., Reyes, Y., & Hammad, E. (2025). Human-AI Interactions: Cognitive, Behavioral, and Emotional Impacts. *ArXiv*, abs/2510.17753. /arxiv.2510.17753DOI: 10.36227/techrxiv.176153493.35183675/v1

Rohilla, D. A. (2025). *Impact of Excessive AI Tool Usage on the Cognitive Abilities of Undergraduate Students: A Mixed Method Study*. Advance Social Science Archive Journal., DOI: 10.55966/assaj.2025.4.1.0115

Sabherwal, R., & Grover, V. (2024). The Societal Impacts of Generative Artificial Intelligence: A Balanced Perspective. *Journal of the Association for Information Systems*, *25*(1), 14. DOI: 10.17705/1jais.00860

Salehinejad, M. A., Ghanavati, E., Rashid, M. H. A., & Nitsche, M. A. (2021). Hot and cold executive functions in the brain: A prefrontal-cingular network. *Brain and Neuroscience Advances*, *5*, 23982128211007769. DOI: 10.1177/23982128211007769 PMID: 33997292

Salles, A., & Farisco, M. (2024). Neuroethics and AI ethics: A proposal for collaboration. *BMC Neuroscience*, *25*(1), 41. Advance online publication. DOI: 10.1186/s12868-024-00888-7 PMID: 39210267

Sganzerla, L., Hutto, D. D., & Kirchhoff, M. D. (2025). Beyond the extended mind: New arguments for extensive enactivism. *Synthese*, *205*(3), 118. Advance online publication. DOI: 10.1007/s11229-025-04931-w

. Sherif, D. (2025). Navigating the Impact of Excessive AI Dependence on Cognitive Function. *Journal of Scholarly Engagement*. DOI: 10.9743/JSE.2025.8.2.4

Skulmowski, A. (2023). The Cognitive Architecture of Digital Externalization. *Educational Psychology Review*, *35*(4), 101. Advance online publication. DOI: 10.1007/s10648-023-09818-1

Small, G., Lee, J., Kaufman, A., Jalil, J., Siddarth, P., Gaddipati, H., Moody, T., & Bookheimer, S. (2020). Brain health consequences of digital technology use. *Dialogues in Clinical Neuroscience*, *22*(2), 179–187. DOI: 10.31887/DCNS.2020.22.2/gsmall PMID: 32699518

Smallwood, J., Bernhardt, B., Leech, R., Bzdok, D., Jefferies, E., & Margulies, D. (2021). The default mode network in cognition: A topographical perspective. *Nature Reviews. Neuroscience*, *22*(8), 503–513. DOI: 10.1038/s41583-021-00474-4 PMID: 34226715

Sparrow, B., Liu, J. J. W., & Wegner, D. (2011). Google Effects on Memory: Cognitive Consequences of Having Information at Our Fingertips. *Science*, *333*(6043), 776–778. DOI: 10.1126/science.1207745 PMID: 21764755

Stacho, M., & Manahan-Vaughan, D. (2022). The Intriguing Contribution of Hippocampal Long-Term Depression to Spatial Learning and Long-Term Memory. *Frontiers in Behavioral Neuroscience*, *16*, 806356. Advance online publication. DOI: 10.3389/fnbeh.2022.806356 PMID: 35548697

Thirunavukarasu, A., Ting, D. S. J., Elangovan, K., Gutierrez, L., Tan, T. F., & Ting, D. (2023). Large language models in medicine. *Nature Medicine*, *29*(8), 1930–1940. DOI: 10.1038/s41591-023-02448-8 PMID: 37460753

Tiwari, V., Dasari, V. S. R., & Agrawal, K. (2026). Cognitive Vestigiality in AI-Assisted Learning. *2026 International Conference on ACDSA*, 1–7. DOI: 10.1109/ACDSA67686.2026.11468156

Tuan, N. T., Moore, P., Thanh, D. H. V., & Pham, H. V. (2024). A Generative Artificial Intelligence Using Multilingual Large Language Models for ChatGPT Applications. *Applied Sciences (Basel, Switzerland)*, *14*(7), 3036. Advance online publication. DOI: 10.3390/app14073036

Wadsley, M., & Ihssen, N. (2023). A Systematic Review of Structural and Functional MRI Studies Investigating Social Networking Site Use. *Brain Sciences*, *13*(5), 787. Advance online publication. DOI: 10.3390/brainsci13050787 PMID: 37239257

Wei, J., Ying, X., Gao, T., Bao, F., Tao, F., & Shang, J. (2025). AI-native Memory 2.0: Second Me. *ArXiv*, abs/2503.08102. /arxiv.2503.08102DOI: 10.48550

White, B., Clark, A., Guénin-Carlut, A., Constant, A., & Di Paolo, L. D. (2025). Shifting boundaries, extended minds: Ambient technology and extended allostatic control. *Synthese*, *205*(2), 81. Advance online publication. DOI: 10.1007/s11229-025-04924-9 PMID: 39926591

Wilson, A. D., & Golonka, S. (2013). Embodied Cognition is Not What you Think it is. *Frontiers in Psychology*, *4*. Advance online publication. DOI: 10.3389/fpsyg.2013.00058 PMID: 23408669

Windhager, F., & Mayr, E. (2024). Digital Humanities and Distributed Cognition: From a Lack of Theory to its Visual Augmentation. *Journal of Cultural Analytics*, *7*(4), 1324. Advance online publication. DOI: 10.22148/001c.121866

Woolley, A., & Gupta, P. (2023). Understanding Collective Intelligence: Investigating the Role of Collective Memory, Attention, and Reasoning Processes. *Perspectives on Psychological Science*, *19*(2), 344–354. DOI: 10.1177/17456916231191534 PMID: 37642156

Wu, H., Ni, H., Luo, W., & Wu, T. (2026). Development and validation of the AI dependence scale for Chinese undergraduates and a preliminary exploration. *Frontiers in Psychology*, *16*, 1725393. Advance online publication. DOI: 10.3389/fpsyg.2025.1725393 PMID: 41635770

Wu, X., Zhang, L., Liu, B., Liao, J.-M., Qiu, Y., & Huang, R. (2023). Social navigation modulates the anterior and posterior hippocampal circuits in the resting brain. *Brain Structure & Function*, *228*(3-4), 799–813. DOI: 10.1007/s00429-023-02622-1 PMID: 36813907

Yan, L., Pammer-Schindler, V., Mills, C., Nguyen, A., & Gašević, D. (2025). Beyond efficiency: Empirical insights on generative AI's impact on cognition, metacognition and epistemic agency in learning. *British Journal of Educational Technology*, *56*(5), 1675–1685. DOI: 10.1111/bjet.70000

Yavich, R. (2025). Will the Use of AI Undermine Students Independent Thinking? *Education Sciences*, *15*(6), 669. Advance online publication. DOI: 10.3390/educsci15060669

Zhai, C., Wibowo, S., & Li, L. D. (2024). The effects of over-reliance on AI dialogue systems on students' cognitive abilities: A systematic review. *Smart Learning Environments*, *11*(1), 28. Advance online publication. DOI: 10.1186/s40561-024-00316-7

Zhang, B., Yu, Z., Yan, F., Sun, Y., Ye, J., Liu, X., Qi, S., Wei, X.-H., Liu, S., & Ming, D. (2026). Altered Salience-Default Mode Network Dynamics in Subclinical Depression. *CNS Neuroscience & Therapeutics*, *32*(2), e70736. Advance online publication. DOI: 10.1002/cns.70736 PMID: 41636698

Zhang, G.-M., Fu, M., & Yan, S. (2025). MemGen: Weaving Generative Latent Memory for Self-Evolving Agents. *ArXiv*, abs/2509.24704. /arxiv.2509.24704DOI: 10.48550

Zhang, X., Xu, T., Wei, X., Tang, J., & Pablos, P. O. (2023). The establishment of transactive memory system in distributed agile teams engaged in AI-related knowledge work. *Journal of Knowledge Management*, *28*(2), 381–408. DOI: 10.1108/JKM-10-2022-0791

Zuo, K., & Xin, L. (2025). Boosting Swarm Robotics Adaptability Through Transactive Memory Integration. *2025 6th International Conference on AIEA*, 421–424. DOI: 10.1109/AIEA66061.2025.11159664

Chapter 12
Neuropsychological Effects of Overreliance on Artificial Intelligence

Fernando Vieira
http://orcid.org/0000-0002-1026-3969
University of São Paulo, Brazil

ABSTRACT

Artificial Intelligence (AI) is increasingly integrated into daily life, influencing cognition, emotion, and social behavior. While AI enhances efficiency and decision-making, overreliance can produce neuropsychological consequences, including memory decline, reduced attention and executive function, emotional dysregulation, social skill impairment, and habitual reward-driven behavior. Cognitive offloading, automation bias, and technostress further mediate these effects. Neuroplastic adaptations reflect both functional gains and trade-offs, emphasizing AI-mediated circuits while downregulating underused networks. Strategies such as cognitive training, mindful AI use, digital literacy, and human-centered AI design can mitigate risks. Understanding the long-term impacts of AI reliance is critical for balancing augmentation with cognitive, emotional, and social well-being.

1. INTRODUCTION

Artificial Intelligence (AI) has rapidly evolved from a theoretical concept into a transformative force across society. Once confined to laboratories and philosophical debate, AI now permeates nearly every domain of human activity: it guides autonomous vehicles, supports financial markets, assists legal analysis, curates digital content, generates creative works, and performs sophisticated medical diagnostics.

DOI: 10.4018/979-8-3373-9484-8.ch012

In healthcare, AI aids radiological interpretation, risk prediction, and personalized treatment, while in daily life, recommendation engines influence behavior, digital assistants manage tasks, and generative systems contribute to communication and knowledge production. This rapid integration often outpaces ethical, educational, and psychological reflection.

As AI becomes embedded in routine tasks, it functions increasingly as a cognitive extension. Individuals delegate memory to cloud systems, rely on algorithmic navigation, use predictive text, and consult AI for decisions ranging from entertainment to health. Unlike earlier technologies, which primarily amplified physical capabilities, AI augments or replaces higher-order cognitive processes, influencing attention, reasoning, emotion, and social interaction.

The benefits are substantial: AI enhances efficiency, reduces human error, expands access to information, and supports individuals with cognitive or physical limitations. Algorithmic diagnostics detect patterns invisible to humans; adaptive learning systems tailor education; and AI accelerates large-scale research analysis. Yet alongside these benefits, concerns are emerging within neuropsychology and cognitive science regarding the long-term consequences of overreliance.

The human brain is dynamic, shaped by repeated use through neuroplasticity. If AI consistently assumes functions traditionally performed by humans—memory, reasoning, navigation, or social interpretation—neural circuits supporting these abilities may adapt accordingly. While such adaptation can represent functional specialization, overreliance risks cognitive offloading at unprecedented levels. Habitual dependence on AI to retrieve facts, structure arguments, or evaluate risks may reduce active engagement, affecting memory consolidation, executive function, metacognition, and critical thinking. Automation bias and uncritical deference to algorithmic authority further amplify these effects.

Beyond cognition, AI overuse may affect emotional and social functioning. Reward mechanisms embedded in AI, including notifications and personalized feedback, engage dopaminergic pathways, shaping motivation and habitual behaviors. Emotional reliance on AI companions can alter attachment patterns, social expectations, and interpersonal skills. While AI can alleviate loneliness, it may reduce opportunities for complex, reciprocal human interaction.

Behaviorally, reliance on AI may contribute to skill atrophy. Spatial navigation, arithmetic, language, and problem-solving can be displaced by algorithmic assistance, reducing cognitive flexibility and independent functioning. Increased AI-mediated decision-making may also shift perceptions of responsibility and agency, raising questions about accountability.

These changes extend to identity and self-concept. Memory, decision-making, emotional regulation, and social interaction underpin human identity; deep integration of AI blurs boundaries between internal cognition and external computation. The critical question is whether AI represents a natural extension of human evolution or a factor that diminishes capacities central to autonomy and agency.

This chapter examines the neuropsychological consequences of excessive AI reliance, including cognitive restructuring, emotional and motivational changes, behavioral adaptation, and implications for identity and autonomy. By integrating research from neuroscience, psychology, and human–computer interaction, it offers a framework for understanding AI's impact on the human brain and behavior, emphasizing strategies to maximize cognitive augmentation while mitigating potential risks.

2. BACKGROUND ON AI AND COGNITIVE INTERACTION

Artificial Intelligence refers to computerized systems capable of performing tasks that typically require human intelligence, such as learning, reasoning, problem-solving, and pattern recognition (Russell & Norvig, 2021). AI technologies range from machine learning algorithms and natural language processing to autonomous robotics and decision-support systems.

2.1 Human–AI Interaction and Cognitive Offloading

Cognitive offloading refers to the strategic use of external tools or environmental supports to reduce the burden on internal cognitive processes. By relying on external systems to store, process, or retrieve information, individuals effectively redistribute cognitive demands beyond the boundaries of the biological brain (Clark & Chalmers, 1998). The concept emerged prominently in discussions of the "extended mind" thesis, which posits that tools such as notebooks, calculators, and digital devices can function as integral components of cognitive systems when they are reliably and automatically used. In this framework, cognition is not confined solely to neural activity but may extend into technological artifacts that support mental operations.

In contemporary contexts, smartphones, cloud storage systems, search engines, GPS navigation platforms, and digital assistants exemplify pervasive forms of cognitive offloading. These technologies allow individuals to externalize memory storage, computational tasks, scheduling, spatial navigation, and even elements of linguistic production. For instance, calendar applications replace prospective memory demands, while navigation systems reduce the need for spatial encoding and route planning. Search engines provide immediate retrieval of factual information, minimizing the need for long-term memorization. With the advent of advanced Artificial Intelligence systems capable not only of retrieving information but also of analyzing patterns, synthesizing content, generating text, and making predictive recommendations, cognitive offloading has evolved from simple storage delegation to complex cognitive outsourcing.

The neurocognitive implications of this shift are profound. Human cognition operates under constraints of limited working memory capacity and attentional resources. Cognitive offloading can be adaptive, allowing individuals to allocate mental resources to higher-level tasks such as reasoning, creativity, or strategic planning. Indeed, throughout human history, tools that reduce cognitive load have enabled intellectual expansion and cultural progress. Writing systems, for example, allowed knowledge accumulation across generations, and mathematical notation facilitated complex problem-solving beyond the limits of mental arithmetic.

However, the degree, immediacy, and automation of AI-mediated offloading introduce new dynamics. Unlike static tools, AI systems often provide processed outputs—interpretations, decisions, and solutions—rather than merely storing raw information. This shift reduces not only memory demands but also analytic engagement. When individuals habitually defer to algorithmic outputs without independently reconstructing reasoning pathways, the opportunity for active encoding, elaboration, and metacognitive monitoring may decline.

Empirical research supports concerns regarding the cognitive consequences of habitual outsourcing. Studies indicate that individuals who frequently rely on smartphones or internet search engines for information retrieval demonstrate reduced recall of the information itself, while showing enhanced memory for where or how to access it (Barr et al., 2015; Sparrow, Liu, & Wegner, 2011). This phenomenon, sometimes referred to as "transactive memory" adaptation in digital environments, suggests a restructuring of memory systems. Rather than strengthening semantic memory traces, individuals may prioritize procedural knowledge about accessing external databases. While efficient, this pattern may weaken depth of encoding and long-term retention.

Neurobiologically, active memory formation involves coordinated activity in the hippocampus, prefrontal cortex, and associated cortical networks. Effortful retrieval and rehearsal strengthen synaptic connections through long-term potentiation. When retrieval is bypassed in favor of instant external access, these neural reinforcement mechanisms may be engaged less frequently. Over time, diminished activation in memory-related circuits could potentially influence neural efficiency, although longitudinal neuroimaging research in this area remains limited and warrants further investigation.

Beyond memory, cognitive offloading through AI may affect executive functions. Decision-making, problem-solving, and evaluative judgment rely on iterative reasoning, error monitoring, and reflective thought processes. When AI systems provide ready-made analyses or recommendations, individuals may adopt a more passive cognitive stance. This shift can reduce opportunities for developing critical thinking skills, particularly in educational and professional contexts where AI tools are routinely integrated. The phenomenon of automation bias—the tendency to favor automated outputs even when contradictory evidence exists—illustrates how reliance may subtly alter reasoning strategies and diminish independent verification behaviors.

Importantly, cognitive offloading is not inherently detrimental. It can enhance performance under high cognitive load, reduce stress, and enable multitasking in complex environments. For individuals with cognitive impairments, AI-assisted tools may significantly improve functional independence and quality of life. The critical distinction lies between adaptive augmentation and maladaptive overreliance. Adaptive offloading supports cognition while preserving active engagement and skill maintenance; maladaptive overreliance replaces core cognitive processes to the extent that internal capacities weaken due to disuse.

As AI systems continue to integrate predictive modeling, generative reasoning, and conversational interaction, the boundary between assistance and substitution becomes increasingly blurred. When AI assumes roles traditionally associated with human deliberation—drafting arguments, interpreting data, diagnosing conditions, or guiding ethical decisions—the cognitive system reorganizes around this external support. The long-term trajectory of such reorganization remains an open empirical question, but theoretical models suggest that reduced cognitive effort may correspond with decreased neural reinforcement in underutilized domains.

Therefore, concerns regarding AI overreliance parallel broader neuropsychological considerations about effort, engagement, and plasticity. The human brain adapts to patterns of use; repeated delegation may recalibrate internal cognitive priorities. Understanding this balance is essential for designing AI systems that enhance human capability without undermining foundational cognitive skills. The challenge lies not in preventing cognitive offloading altogether—which would be neither feasible nor desirable—but in cultivating mindful interaction strategies that preserve depth of processing, critical evaluation, and independent reasoning alongside technological support.

3. COGNITIVE CONSEQUENCES OF AI OVERRELIANCE

3.1 Memory Impairment and External Storage Dependency

The "Google effect," also referred to as digital amnesia, describes the tendency for individuals to exhibit reduced retention of information when they believe that such information will remain accessible online (Sparrow, Liu, & Wegner, 2011). In experimental paradigms, participants who expected to have future access to stored information were significantly less likely to encode and recall the content itself, instead remembering where to retrieve it. This finding suggests a strategic shift in memory allocation: when external storage is perceived as reliable and permanent, the cognitive system adapts by prioritizing access pathways over internal consolidation. Rather than strengthening semantic memory traces, individuals develop retrieval heuristics tied to digital environments.

Artificial Intelligence systems significantly amplify this phenomenon. Unlike static search engines, AI-driven platforms provide personalized, context-sensitive retrieval of information, often anticipating user needs before explicit queries are formulated. Recommendation algorithms, predictive search functions, and conversational agents streamline access to knowledge with minimal cognitive effort. The increasing sophistication of AI systems—capable of synthesizing information, summarizing complex materials, and generating tailored responses—further reduces the necessity for active memorization and elaborative encoding. When information is not only accessible but also dynamically processed on demand, individuals may perceive little incentive to internalize it.

From a cognitive perspective, memory encoding depends on depth of processing. According to levels-of-processing theory, information that undergoes semantic elaboration, emotional integration, or associative linking is more likely to be consolidated into long-term memory. In contrast, superficial exposure without active engagement produces weaker memory traces. When AI systems provide immediate retrieval or ready-made synthesis, opportunities for effortful processing diminish. The learner may skim rather than analyze, consult rather than reconstruct, and accept rather than reinterpret. Over time, this pattern may reduce the habitual exercise of declarative memory systems.

Declarative memory—comprising semantic memory (facts and general knowledge) and episodic memory (personal experiences and events)—relies heavily on hippocampal function and its interaction with distributed cortical networks. The hippocampus plays a central role in binding disparate elements of information into coherent memory representations. Repeated activation of these circuits strengthens synaptic connections through mechanisms such as long-term potentiation. Conversely, reduced engagement may limit reinforcement of these pathways. Research suggests that habitual reliance on external digital repositories correlates with altered activation patterns in memory-related neural regions, particularly the hippocampus and prefrontal cortex (Kühn et al., 2014). Although causality and long-term structural effects remain under investigation, such findings raise important questions regarding functional adaptation.

It is important to distinguish between adaptive reorganization and impairment. The brain has historically adapted to technological change. Writing, print, and digital databases have all reshaped mnemonic strategies. External memory systems can enhance collective intelligence and enable complex cultural development. However, the scale and immediacy of AI-based retrieval introduce qualitative differences. AI does not merely store information; it curates, prioritizes, and contextualizes it. Personalized algorithms influence which information is encountered, remembered, and revisited. This may narrow the diversity of encoded knowledge, reinforcing cognitive biases and limiting exposure to contradictory perspectives.

Moreover, reliance on AI for factual recall may alter metacognitive awareness. When individuals become accustomed to instant verification, they may exhibit reduced tolerance for uncertainty and diminished motivation to engage in independent retrieval attempts. Yet retrieval practice itself is a powerful mechanism for strengthening memory consolidation. The "testing effect" demonstrates that active recall enhances long-term retention more effectively than passive review. If AI tools consistently substitute retrieval with immediate display, opportunities for this beneficial cognitive struggle are reduced.

Another consideration involves the relationship between memory and identity. Episodic memory contributes to the continuity of the self, enabling individuals to construct coherent narratives about their experiences. If AI systems increasingly record, organize, and retrieve personal data—photographs, messages, schedules, location histories—individuals may externalize autobiographical memory processes. While such records can enrich reminiscence, they may also shift the locus of narrative construction from internal recollection to externally curated archives. This raises philosophical and neuropsychological questions about ownership of memory and the authenticity of recollection.

Over time, diminished efficiency in memory encoding and retrieval may not manifest as overt memory loss but rather as reduced cognitive endurance for sustained recall. Individuals may experience difficulty recalling details without prompts, decreased confidence in their own memory, or increased dependency on verification tools. In high-stakes environments—such as clinical decision-making, legal reasoning, or emergency response—overdependence on AI-based memory support could pose risks if access becomes limited or systems fail.

Nevertheless, it would be reductive to frame AI-mediated memory support solely as detrimental. For aging populations or individuals with cognitive impairments, digital memory augmentation can provide critical assistance and preserve functional independence. The central issue, therefore, is balance. AI systems should ideally complement and reinforce human memory processes rather than replace them entirely. Educational and professional practices that incorporate retrieval practice, elaborative encoding, and reflective engagement alongside AI assistance may mitigate potential weakening effects.

In sum, the "Google effect" represents an early indicator of a broader neurocognitive transformation. As AI systems become more predictive, personalized, and integrative, they intensify tendencies toward externalized memory reliance. The long-term neuropsychological consequences remain an evolving field of inquiry, but current theoretical and empirical evidence suggests that habitual deferral of recall may reshape memory strategies, neural activation patterns, and metacognitive habits. Understanding these dynamics is essential for cultivating AI use that supports, rather than supplants, the cognitive foundations of learning and identity.

3.2 Decision-Making and Critical Thinking

Artificial Intelligence systems are widely celebrated for their analytical precision, scalability, and capacity to detect patterns within vast and complex datasets. In domains such as finance, logistics, climate modeling, medicine, and public policy, AI-driven decision-support systems often outperform human judgment in narrowly defined predictive tasks. Machine learning algorithms can process multidimensional variables, identify subtle correlations, and generate probabilistic forecasts with remarkable speed and consistency. These capabilities have positioned AI as an increasingly authoritative source of guidance in high-stakes decision-making environments.

However, the growing reliance on algorithmic outputs raises important concerns regarding the preservation of human critical thinking skills. Critical thinking involves the capacity to analyze assumptions, evaluate evidence, consider alternative explanations, detect logical fallacies, and engage in reflective skepticism. These processes require effortful cognition, metacognitive monitoring, and tolerance for ambiguity. When AI systems present outputs in a format that appears precise, data-driven, and mathematically grounded, users may attribute to them a level of epistemic authority that discourages further scrutiny (Rahwan et al., 2019). The perceived objectivity of algorithmic systems can create a cognitive shortcut: if the output appears statistically derived and technologically sophisticated, it may be accepted as inherently valid.

This dynamic can gradually reduce the frequency with which individuals engage in independent evaluative reasoning. Rather than interrogating data sources, methodological limitations, or contextual factors, users may defer to algorithmic recommendations as final judgments. Over time, this pattern may attenuate cognitive habits associated with skepticism, hypothesis testing, and error detection. In educational contexts, for example, students who rely heavily on AI-generated analyses may bypass the iterative reasoning processes that cultivate deep conceptual understanding. In professional settings, practitioners may become accustomed to validating their judgments against algorithmic outputs rather than developing independent frameworks of evaluation.

A related phenomenon, automation bias, further illustrates the risks of overreliance. Automation bias refers to the tendency to favor suggestions from automated systems while disregarding or underweighting contradictory information from non-automated sources (Mosier et al., 1998). This bias operates through both commission errors (acting on incorrect automated advice) and omission errors (failing to act because an automated system did not generate an alert). In complex environments such as aviation, healthcare diagnostics, or military operations, automation bias has been associated with critical failures when human operators deferred excessively to flawed system outputs.

From a cognitive standpoint, automation bias reflects interactions between trust calibration, cognitive load, and attentional allocation. When individuals operate under time pressure or high workload, reliance on automation can reduce cognitive strain. However, the reduction in effort also diminishes active monitoring of system performance. The prefrontal cortex, responsible for executive control and conflict monitoring, may be less engaged when users adopt a passive supervisory role rather than an active decision-making stance. This shift can weaken the neural circuits involved in evaluative comparison and error detection.

Moreover, algorithmic systems often operate as "black boxes," providing outputs without transparent explanations of their internal reasoning processes. The opacity of complex models, particularly deep learning architectures, limits users' ability to assess underlying assumptions or detect bias. Without explainability, users may rely on heuristic trust rather than analytical verification. Ironically, as AI systems become more accurate in aggregate, individuals may become less vigilant precisely because errors occur less frequently. Yet rare errors in critical domains can carry severe consequences.

The neuropsychological implications of this shift extend beyond immediate decision accuracy. Repeated delegation of evaluative judgment may reshape cognitive habits through neuroplastic adaptation. Skills that are underutilized may lose efficiency due to decreased reinforcement. Critical thinking, like any cognitive capacity, is strengthened through practice. Engaging in comparative reasoning, counterfactual analysis, and reflective skepticism activates distributed neural networks involving the dorsolateral prefrontal cortex, anterior cingulate cortex, and parietal regions. If AI systems consistently provide pre-structured solutions, opportunities to activate and strengthen these networks may decline.

Additionally, overreliance on AI may influence epistemic confidence—the degree to which individuals trust their own reasoning. When algorithmic outputs routinely outperform human predictions in quantifiable tasks, individuals may internalize a perception of relative inferiority. This dynamic can lead to learned dependency, wherein users defer reflexively to AI recommendations even in contexts where human judgment may be more appropriate or ethically nuanced. In such cases, automation bias is not merely a situational error but a broader cognitive orientation.

It is also important to consider how interface design shapes critical engagement. Systems that present probabilistic uncertainty, confidence intervals, or explanatory justifications may encourage reflective evaluation. In contrast, interfaces that deliver definitive answers without contextual framing may reinforce passive acceptance. Thus, the design architecture of AI systems plays a crucial role in either mitigating or exacerbating cognitive atrophy in reasoning processes.

Importantly, the objective is not to reject AI-assisted decision-making. When appropriately calibrated, AI can enhance human reasoning by identifying overlooked variables, reducing cognitive overload, and providing complementary analytical perspectives. The optimal configuration is a collaborative model in which AI augments but does not replace critical deliberation. In such models, human operators maintain active oversight, question algorithmic outputs, and integrate contextual knowledge that may not be captured by data-driven systems.

In summary, while AI systems offer unparalleled analytical capabilities, excessive reliance on their outputs may weaken human critical thinking and promote automation bias. The neuropsychological concern is not simply error propagation but the gradual restructuring of cognitive habits toward passive acceptance. Preserving analytical reasoning in an AI-augmented world requires intentional educational strategies, transparent system design, and the cultivation of metacognitive awareness. Only through such measures can societies ensure that technological sophistication enhances rather than diminishes the human capacity for thoughtful, independent judgment.

3.3 Attention and Cognitive Control

Continuous engagement with AI-mediated interfaces has the potential to reshape attentional systems in significant ways. Many contemporary AI-driven platforms—particularly those embedded in social media, digital communication tools, and personalized content delivery systems—are explicitly designed to maximize user engagement. Through adaptive algorithms that analyze behavioral data in real time, these systems prioritize novelty, emotional salience, and rapid feedback loops. The result is an attentional environment characterized by frequent interruptions, rapid task switching, and persistent stimulus-driven engagement.

Such environments encourage fragmented attention. Instead of sustained, goal-directed focus, users are exposed to streams of dynamically curated stimuli that compete for cognitive resources. Notifications, predictive recommendations, personalized alerts, and adaptive content sequencing continuously redirect attention. Over time, this pattern may cultivate habitual multitasking behavior, in which individuals divide attention across multiple streams of information rather than engaging deeply with a single task.

Cognitive neuroscience research suggests that habitual multitasking is associated with measurable changes in attentional control. Individuals who frequently engage in media multitasking demonstrate reduced capacity to filter irrelevant stimuli and exhibit greater susceptibility to distraction (Ophir, Nass, & Wagner, 2009). Rather than enhancing efficiency, chronic multitasking appears to impair performance on tasks requiring sustained attention, working memory integration, and complex reasoning. Sustained attention—often referred to as vigilance—depends on coordinated activity within frontoparietal networks that regulate goal-directed focus. When attentional resources are repeatedly fragmented, these networks may be less effectively recruited during tasks demanding prolonged concentration.

AI systems may amplify these effects by continuously optimizing engagement through predictive modeling. Unlike earlier forms of digital media, AI-driven platforms dynamically learn user preferences and adapt content delivery to maximize time-on-platform metrics. The reinforcement schedule resembles variable-ratio reward paradigms known to produce strong behavioral conditioning. Novel or emotionally salient content appears unpredictably, encouraging repeated checking behaviors and rapid shifts in focus. Dopaminergic reward pathways are activated not only by the content itself but by the anticipation of new stimuli, reinforcing compulsive attentional switching.

From a neuropsychological perspective, sustained attention and executive control depend heavily on the prefrontal cortex, particularly the dorsolateral and anterior cingulate regions. These structures are responsible for inhibitory control, conflict monitoring, working memory updating, and goal maintenance. When users repeatedly shift attention in response to external prompts, the neural systems governing top-down control may yield to bottom-up, stimulus-driven processes. Over time, the balance between endogenous (internally directed) and exogenous (externally triggered) attention may shift toward greater environmental reactivity.

Inhibitory control—the ability to suppress irrelevant impulses or distractions—is particularly vulnerable in high-interruption environments. Effective inhibitory control allows individuals to resist checking notifications, ignore irrelevant stimuli, and maintain cognitive persistence despite competing demands. If AI platforms consistently prompt rapid response behaviors, individuals may experience reduced practice in inhibitory restraint. This reduction in practice may contribute to increased impulsivity, shortened attention spans, and difficulty delaying gratification.

Working memory, another core executive function, may also be affected. Working memory involves temporarily holding and manipulating information to guide behavior. It is essential for reasoning, comprehension, and problem-solving. Fragmented attentional patterns disrupt working memory consolidation by introducing interference before information can be fully integrated. When task-switching becomes habitual, cognitive load increases as the brain must repeatedly reorient to new contexts, incurring "switching costs." Over time, such patterns may reduce efficiency in tasks requiring deep analytical integration or long-form reasoning.

Importantly, these changes do not necessarily reflect structural damage but rather functional adaptation. The brain reorganizes in response to environmental demands. In an AI-saturated environment that rewards rapid responsiveness and parallel processing, neural circuits supporting quick attentional shifts may become more efficient, while those supporting sustained concentration may receive less reinforcement. This adaptive specialization may be advantageous in certain contexts—such as monitoring multiple information streams—but disadvantageous in tasks requiring extended deliberation, academic study, or strategic planning.

The implications extend beyond cognitive performance to behavioral regulation. Reduced executive control and increased impulsivity may affect decision-making, emotional regulation, and interpersonal communication. Impulsive responses to emotionally charged content, for example, may contribute to online conflict escalation or reduced reflective discourse. In professional contexts, diminished attentional endurance may impair productivity and creativity, particularly in fields requiring sustained analytical depth.

Nevertheless, it is essential to maintain nuance. Not all AI interactions are inherently fragmenting. AI systems can also support focus—for example, by filtering irrelevant information, organizing tasks, or reducing cognitive clutter. The determining factor lies in design architecture and usage patterns. Platforms that encourage intentional engagement and minimize unnecessary interruptions may strengthen rather than weaken executive control. Conversely, systems optimized primarily for engagement metrics may inadvertently erode attentional resilience.

In sum, continuous engagement with AI interfaces may shape attentional habits and executive functioning through mechanisms of reinforcement, neuroplastic adaptation, and environmental conditioning. Habitual multitasking and stimulus-driven engagement are associated with diminished sustained attention, weakened inhibitory control, and reduced working memory efficiency. As AI technologies continue to permeate daily life, understanding their influence on attentional networks is critical for preserving cognitive balance. Designing AI systems that respect the limits of human attention—and cultivating mindful usage practices—will be essential to safeguarding executive function in an increasingly algorithmic environment.

4. EMOTIONAL AND PSYCHOLOGICAL EFFECTS

4.1 Emotional Regulation and AI Companionship

Artificial Intelligence systems, including social robots, virtual companions, and conversational agents, are increasingly designed to simulate empathy, responsiveness, and relational continuity. These systems utilize natural language processing, affective computing, facial recognition, and adaptive learning algorithms to respond to users in ways that mimic human social interaction. For individuals experiencing loneliness, social anxiety, geographic isolation, or cognitive decline, such AI-mediated companionship can provide meaningful emotional comfort. In therapeutic contexts, conversational agents have been used to support mood monitoring, stress reduction, and behavioral coaching. For some users, especially those who feel socially marginalized, AI systems offer a nonjudgmental and continuously available presence.

From a psychological standpoint, this capacity for emotional engagement reflects humans' inherent tendency to anthropomorphize responsive agents. Even minimal cues of agency—such as eye gaze, contingent responses, or prosodic variation—can trigger social-cognitive processes typically reserved for human interaction. Neuroimaging studies demonstrate that interaction with humanoid robots or socially responsive AI can activate neural networks involved in social cognition, including regions associated with theory of mind, empathy, and mental state attribution (Krach et al., 2008). These findings suggest that the brain does not strictly differentiate between biological and artificial agents when processing social cues; rather, it responds to perceived intentionality and contingent responsiveness.

While such activation may facilitate emotional bonding and engagement, it also raises important questions regarding the long-term implications of substituting human relationships with artificial ones. Emotional regulation—the ability to monitor, interpret, and modulate emotional states—develops through complex interpersonal experiences. Human social interactions involve ambiguity, reciprocal feedback, conflict resolution, nonverbal nuance, and adaptive negotiation. These elements contribute to the refinement of emotional intelligence, including empathy accuracy, perspective-taking, and self-regulation in dynamic contexts.

AI systems, by contrast, are typically designed to minimize conflict and maximize user satisfaction. Their responses are often calibrated to affirm, validate, or comfort rather than challenge. While this can provide immediate emotional relief, it may reduce exposure to the interpersonal friction that fosters emotional growth. Prolonged reliance on emotionally accommodating AI companions may limit opportunities to practice interpreting subtle social signals, negotiating disagreement, or tolerating discomfort in relational contexts.

Moreover, the predictability and controllability of AI interactions may alter expectations for human relationships. Human interactions are inherently complex and occasionally unpredictable; they require patience, compromise, and effort. AI systems, however, can be paused, customized, or disengaged at will. This asymmetry of control may reinforce relational patterns centered on convenience rather than reciprocity. Over time, individuals who prefer AI-mediated engagement may exhibit reduced motivation to pursue or maintain real-world social connections, potentially exacerbating social withdrawal.

From a neurobiological perspective, attachment processes involve oxytocinergic, dopaminergic, and limbic systems that support bonding and emotional reinforcement. If AI systems consistently trigger affiliative responses, they may partially engage these pathways. However, unlike human relationships, AI companionship does not involve genuine mutual vulnerability or shared experiential memory. The absence of authentic reciprocity may alter the depth and complexity of attachment formation. While users may experience subjective feelings of connection, the relational dynamic remains fundamentally asymmetrical.

Concerns also arise regarding emotional dependence. When individuals increasingly rely on AI for reassurance, decision validation, or companionship, they may externalize aspects of emotional regulation. Instead of cultivating internal coping strategies or seeking diverse human support networks, users may turn reflexively to AI systems for mood modulation. Such patterns may weaken resilience, particularly if access to these systems is interrupted or if algorithmic responses fail to meet evolving emotional needs.

Additionally, AI-mediated emotional support may influence empathy development. Empathy requires sensitivity to nuanced facial expressions, vocal tone, contextual history, and complex interpersonal cues. If a significant proportion of social interaction occurs with agents that simulate but do not authentically experience emotion, users may encounter fewer opportunities to refine empathic accuracy in human contexts. Over time, this could subtly affect emotional intelligence, particularly in developmental stages where social learning is ongoing.

Nevertheless, it is important to recognize that AI systems can serve as valuable adjuncts rather than replacements for human relationships. For individuals with autism spectrum conditions, social anxiety disorders, or severe depression, AI-based interventions may provide a safe intermediate platform for practicing social interaction. In geriatric populations, socially assistive robots may alleviate isolation and support cognitive engagement. The key distinction lies in integration versus substitution. When AI augments human relationships—providing support while encouraging real-world engagement—it may enhance well-being. When it replaces or displaces human connection, potential deficits in social development and emotional regulation may emerge.

In sum, interactions with humanoid AI systems can evoke authentic emotional responses and engage neural circuits associated with social cognition. While such engagement can reduce loneliness and provide comfort, prolonged emotional dependence on AI may interfere with the development and maintenance of complex human social skills. The neuropsychological challenge is to harness AI's capacity for support without allowing it to supplant the relational experiences essential for emotional intelligence, resilience, and interpersonal growth.

4.2 Anxiety, Trust, and Technostress

Excessive reliance on technology can contribute to a phenomenon widely described as technostress—a psychological condition characterized by anxiety, cognitive overload, emotional exhaustion, and frustration resulting from technology-related demands (Tarafdar et al., 2011). Technostress arises not merely from the presence of technology, but from the perceived inability to cope effectively with its pace, complexity, and expectations. In AI-integrated environments, this stress may be intensified by continuous updates, algorithmic opacity, performance monitoring systems, and the expectation of constant availability.

Artificial Intelligence systems introduce unique stressors beyond those associated with traditional digital tools. One central factor is uncertainty in AI decision-making. Many advanced AI models, particularly those based on deep learning architectures, function as opaque systems whose internal reasoning processes are not readily interpretable. This "black box" problem limits users' understanding of how outputs are generated, reducing perceived control and predictability. Psychological research consistently demonstrates that uncertainty and lack of control are significant predictors of stress responses. When individuals depend on AI for high-stakes decisions—such as clinical diagnoses, financial investments, or legal judgments—yet cannot fully comprehend the system's logic, cognitive tension may arise between reliance and doubt.

This tension may activate stress-related neurobiological pathways. Perceived unpredictability and reduced agency can stimulate amygdala activation and hypothalamic–pituitary–adrenal (HPA) axis responses, elevating cortisol levels. Chronic activation of these systems is associated with impaired working memory, reduced executive control, and emotional dysregulation. Thus, reliance on AI in contexts where transparency is limited may indirectly affect cognitive performance by increasing stress burden.

Fear of malfunction further compounds technostress. As individuals integrate AI systems into essential tasks—navigation, scheduling, financial management, or medical monitoring—the perceived consequences of system failure escalate. Anticipatory anxiety may develop around potential errors, cybersecurity breaches, or algorithmic misjudgments. Paradoxically, as dependency increases, perceived vulnerability also intensifies. This dependency-stress cycle reflects a psychological trade-off between convenience and control.

Conversely, over-trust in AI introduces a different but equally significant risk profile. Trust calibration—the ability to align trust proportionally with a system's reliability—is critical for optimal human–AI collaboration. Under-trust may lead to stress, constant verification, and cognitive overload, whereas over-trust may reduce vigilance and situational awareness. When users assume that AI outputs are inherently accurate or superior, they may disengage from active monitoring and contextual evaluation.

Over-trust can diminish the activation of executive monitoring networks responsible for detecting discrepancies between expectations and environmental cues. Situational awareness, which involves perceiving environmental elements, comprehending their meaning, and projecting future status, requires continuous integration of contextual information. If AI systems provide simplified outputs, users may rely on them as definitive interpretations rather than as inputs to a broader evaluative process. This can result in omission errors—failing to notice critical cues because attention is narrowly focused on algorithmic feedback.

From a neuropsychological standpoint, both under-trust and over-trust can disrupt emotional regulation. Under-trust may produce chronic hypervigilance, anxiety, and cognitive fatigue. Over-trust may foster complacency, reduced self-efficacy, and diminished confidence in one's own judgment. In both scenarios, individuals may experience fluctuations in perceived competence and agency. Healthy emotional regulation depends on balanced appraisal of risk, realistic confidence in personal abilities, and adaptive engagement with tools. Extremes of distrust or blind faith destabilize this equilibrium.

Furthermore, trust dynamics are shaped by anthropomorphic design features. AI systems that simulate conversational fluency, emotional responsiveness, or authoritative presentation styles may elicit higher levels of trust independent of objective accuracy. This phenomenon can amplify both over-trust and emotional dependency, particularly when users attribute intentionality or expertise to systems based on superficial cues. When errors occur in such contexts, the resulting dissonance may intensify stress responses, as expectations of reliability are violated.

The workplace provides a particularly salient context for examining these dynamics. AI-driven performance monitoring systems, predictive analytics tools, and automated evaluation platforms may create pressures associated with constant assessment. Employees may feel scrutinized by algorithmic systems whose criteria are unclear, contributing to cognitive overload and decreased job satisfaction. Simultaneously, workers who over-rely on automated recommendations may experience skill degradation or reduced professional autonomy, further affecting emotional well-being.

Importantly, technostress does not imply that AI integration is inherently harmful. Rather, it underscores the need for careful system design, transparent algorithms, and user education. Explainable AI models, clear communication of confidence levels, and opportunities for human override can help calibrate trust appropriately. Training programs that foster digital literacy and metacognitive awareness may reduce anxiety by enhancing users' understanding of system limitations and capabilities.

In sum, excessive reliance on AI can generate technostress through uncertainty, opacity, and perceived loss of control. At the same time, over-trust may reduce vigilance and situational awareness, compromising cognitive oversight. Both under-trust and over-trust disrupt balanced emotional regulation and self-efficacy. The neuropsychological challenge lies in cultivating calibrated trust—an adaptive middle ground in which AI is neither feared nor blindly accepted, but engaged with critically, transparently, and reflectively.

5. BEHAVIORAL ADAPTATIONS AND SOCIAL DYNAMICS

5.1 Social Isolation and Relationship Patterns

As AI systems become increasingly embedded in social contexts—through AI companions, virtual assistants, socially assistive robots, and conversational agents—the structure and quality of human relationships are undergoing subtle but significant transformation. These technologies are no longer limited to instrumental functions; they are designed to simulate relational presence, responsiveness, and even emotional attunement. AI systems can greet users by name, recall prior interactions, adapt conversational tone, and offer personalized encouragement. In doing so, they occupy relational spaces traditionally reserved for human interaction.

The broader digital communication landscape provides important context for understanding this shift. Research on screen-mediated interaction suggests that increased reliance on digital communication correlates with reductions in face-to-face engagement and, in some cases, diminished emotional intimacy (Turkle, 2017). While digital platforms can facilitate connection across distance, they also tend to simplify and streamline communication, reducing exposure to nonverbal cues such as micro-expressions, posture, and subtle vocal modulation. These cues play a central role in empathy, emotional attunement, and conflict resolution. When communication is mediated primarily through screens—and increasingly through AI-driven interfaces—opportunities to refine these complex interpersonal skills may decrease.

AI companions intensify this dynamic by introducing relational simulations that are optimized for user satisfaction. Unlike human partners, AI systems are typically programmed to avoid confrontation, maintain consistent availability, and adapt to user preferences. They do not experience fatigue, frustration, or competing emotional needs. This asymmetry can create interactions that feel smooth, affirming, and emotionally safe. For individuals experiencing loneliness, social anxiety, or relational trauma, such predictability may provide significant comfort and psychological stabilization.

However, the very features that make AI companionship appealing may also limit its developmental richness. Human relationships are inherently reciprocal and unpredictable. They require negotiation, perspective-taking, tolerance of disagreement, and repair after conflict. These processes stimulate the development of emotional intelligence, including empathy accuracy, self-regulation under stress, and adaptive communication strategies. AI-mediated interactions, by contrast, are often engineered to minimize friction and maximize positive reinforcement. Over time, habitual engagement with such environments may reduce exposure to the interpersonal challenges that cultivate resilience and relational maturity.

From a neuropsychological perspective, social interaction engages distributed neural networks associated with theory of mind, empathy, reward processing, and attachment. These networks develop and are refined through repeated, dynamic interpersonal exchanges. When social experiences are simplified or scripted—as is often the case with AI companions—the brain may receive attenuated social complexity signals. While AI can evoke genuine emotional responses, the depth of mutual influence characteristic of human relationships is absent. The interaction remains fundamentally unidirectional: the AI adapts to the user without possessing independent emotional subjectivity.

Prolonged reliance on AI companions may therefore contribute to subtle forms of social withdrawal. If individuals experience sufficient emotional satisfaction through AI interaction, motivation to pursue more demanding human relationships may decrease. This is particularly relevant in populations already vulnerable to social isolation, such as adolescents with high digital engagement or adults experiencing chronic loneliness. Reduced face-to-face engagement may, in turn, impair the development or maintenance of interpersonal skills, including conflict negotiation, active listening, and emotional reciprocity.

Additionally, AI companions may influence relational expectations. When users become accustomed to interactions that are instantly responsive, nonjudgmental, and tailored to personal preferences, they may develop lower tolerance for the imperfections of human relationships. Human partners may be perceived as less efficient, less predictable, or more emotionally taxing by comparison. This shift in expectations could contribute to dissatisfaction or impatience within real-world relationships.

There are also implications for identity formation and self-concept. Human relationships provide mirrors through which individuals understand themselves. Feedback from others—sometimes affirming, sometimes challenging—contributes to the development of a coherent self-narrative. AI companions, programmed to reinforce engagement and satisfaction, may offer more homogenized feedback. While affirming responses can enhance self-esteem in the short term, they may limit opportunities for critical self-reflection and growth that arise from diverse interpersonal perspectives.

It is essential, however, to avoid reductive conclusions. AI-mediated companionship can be beneficial when integrated thoughtfully. For older adults experiencing isolation, socially assistive robots may stimulate conversation and cognitive activity.

For individuals practicing social skills in therapeutic contexts, AI simulations may provide safe rehearsal environments before real-world interaction. The potential harm emerges not from AI companionship per se, but from substitution rather than supplementation—when artificial interaction displaces rather than complements human connection.

In sum, as AI systems become embedded in social life, they reshape relational dynamics by introducing interactions that are emotionally responsive yet structurally simplified. While such systems can alleviate loneliness and provide psychological comfort, they may also encourage social withdrawal and attenuate the development of complex interpersonal skills. The neuropsychological challenge lies in preserving the depth, reciprocity, and unpredictability of human relationships while leveraging AI technologies to support—not replace—authentic social engagement.

5.2 Skill Atrophy and Learned Dependence

Humans exhibit remarkable behavioral adaptability to technological environments, dynamically reorganizing cognitive and motor routines in response to available tools. This adaptability, while often advantageous, can also produce skill atrophy—the gradual reduction or loss of proficiency in a particular ability due to underuse. When external systems reliably perform tasks previously managed internally, the cognitive and neural circuits that support those tasks may experience reduced activation, leading to functional weakening over time.

A well-documented example of this phenomenon is observed in navigation. Traditional wayfinding requires active engagement of spatial memory, landmark recognition, route planning, and allocentric-to-egocentric transformations, processes that recruit the hippocampus, parietal cortex, and prefrontal networks. Research by Ishikawa et al. (2008) demonstrates that individuals who rely on GPS navigation systems exhibit diminished spatial orientation and cognitive map formation compared to those who navigate without technological assistance. While GPS provides clear benefits in efficiency and error reduction, it simultaneously reduces the demand for active spatial encoding and problem-solving, leading to measurable declines in navigational skill. Neuroimaging studies suggest that repeated externalization of spatial tasks may correspond with decreased hippocampal engagement during navigation exercises, reflecting neuroplastic adaptation to offloaded cognitive demands.

Analogously, overreliance on AI systems for other cognitive domains—including language, arithmetic, planning, and decision-making—may produce similar effects. AI-powered tools can generate written content, solve mathematical problems, optimize scheduling, and propose strategies for complex tasks. While these capabilities enhance efficiency and allow individuals to focus on higher-order or creative objectives, they also reduce the frequency and intensity of practice required to maintain proficiency in foundational skills. For example, habitual delegation of calculation to AI may weaken arithmetic fluency and number sense, while reliance on generative text systems may reduce active engagement with grammar, vocabulary, and compositional planning. Over time, such reductions in active practice can erode the neural networks that underpin these abilities, including regions involved in working memory, attentional control, and executive functioning.

Skill atrophy is not purely a matter of performance decline; it can also impair cognitive infrastructure, the interconnected set of processes required for independent problem-solving. Complex problem-solving depends on integrated activation across multiple cognitive domains—working memory, reasoning, planning, spatial cognition, and domain-specific knowledge. If AI consistently assumes these functions, the underlying neural and cognitive scaffolding may become underutilized. This underutilization may manifest as slower problem-solving, reduced flexibility in novel contexts, or difficulty reconstructing knowledge independently of technological support. In extreme cases, users may become proficient primarily in supervising AI outputs rather than performing tasks autonomously, a shift that alters the qualitative nature of cognitive engagement.

Behavioral adaptation to technological assistance also interacts with motivation and metacognition. When a task can be performed efficiently by an AI system, the perceived need for effortful engagement decreases. This reduction in intrinsic challenge may limit opportunities for metacognitive reflection—monitoring one's own understanding, evaluating strategies, and recognizing errors—which is critical for maintaining long-term skill competence. In educational settings, for instance, students who frequently rely on AI to generate essays or solve problems may show weaker conceptual understanding and diminished capacity for self-directed learning, despite high apparent productivity.

Moreover, skill atrophy can be compounded by contextual dependence. When cognitive routines are adapted to environments where AI assistance is always available, performance outside those contexts may suffer. Analogous to the "use it or lose it" principle observed in physical conditioning, cognitive skills require continual activation and challenge to remain robust. Reliance on AI may therefore produce situational proficiency only when tools are accessible, reducing resilience and adaptability in unaugmented environments.

It is important to emphasize that not all offloading leads to maladaptive skill decline. Strategic delegation can free cognitive resources for higher-order reasoning, creative thinking, and learning of new skills. The critical variable is balance: tasks that are fully automated without continued engagement may contribute to atrophy, whereas tasks that are scaffolded by AI—requiring active oversight, verification, or integration—can support both efficiency and skill maintenance. Thoughtful design of AI interfaces, combined with deliberate practice and educational strategies, can mitigate the risk of skill erosion while preserving the benefits of technological augmentation.

In summary, humans adapt to technological environments by reallocating cognitive effort, but this adaptability carries the risk of skill atrophy. Reliance on AI for navigation, language, mathematics, or planning may reduce proficiency in these domains, weakening the cognitive infrastructure necessary for independent problem-solving. The neuropsychological implication is clear: while AI can enhance efficiency and decision-making, overreliance without deliberate engagement can diminish foundational skills and compromise long-term cognitive autonomy.

6. NEUROSCIENTIFIC INSIGHTS: BRAIN PLASTICITY AND AI INTERACTION

6.1 Neural Reorganization

The human brain demonstrates remarkable neuroplasticity, the capacity to reorganize neural connections and functional networks in response to environmental demands, learning experiences, and behavioral repetition. Neuroplasticity underlies the brain's ability to acquire new skills, recover from injury, and adapt to evolving cognitive or technological environments. While this adaptability enables remarkable flexibility, it also implies that the neural architecture can be reshaped in ways that prioritize some functions at the expense of others. Habitual interaction with AI systems represents a potent environmental factor capable of influencing neuroplastic changes.

Frequent engagement with AI-mediated tasks—such as information retrieval, automated planning, navigational assistance, or social interaction—can selectively strengthen neural circuits involved in these activities. For example, repeated reliance on AI for memory support, decision-making, or problem-solving may heighten functional connectivity in regions associated with cognitive control, executive oversight, and reward processing. The prefrontal cortex, particularly the dorsolateral and ventromedial subregions, is central to planning, monitoring, and decision-making. When AI assumes portions of these tasks, prefrontal activation may shift toward supervisory roles—evaluating outputs rather than generating solutions independently. Similarly, repeated reward feedback from AI systems—such as successful task completion, predictive suggestions, or personalized reinforcement—can engage mesolimbic pathways, including the ventral striatum and nucleus accumbens, strengthening the salience of AI-mediated interactions.

At the same time, habitual delegation of memory, spatial, or problem-solving functions to AI can lead to downregulation of underused regions, a phenomenon sometimes referred to as "use-dependent plasticity." For instance, the hippocampus, essential for declarative memory consolidation, spatial mapping, and episodic encoding, may exhibit reduced activation during navigation or memory tasks when AI tools consistently provide externalized support. Over time, the decreased demand for internal computation can attenuate synaptic reinforcement in these areas, potentially diminishing efficiency in autonomous memory retrieval or spatial reasoning (Small & Vorgan, 2008). Similarly, circuits associated with attentional persistence and inhibitory control may adapt to the rapid, fragmented, or stimulus-driven demands of AI-mediated environments, favoring flexibility in task-switching but reducing capacity for sustained concentration.

Neuroimaging studies provide empirical support for these adaptive shifts. Functional magnetic resonance imaging (fMRI) and diffusion tensor imaging (DTI) research indicates that repetitive engagement with digital interfaces—including AI-powered platforms—modifies functional and structural connectivity among the prefrontal cortex, hippocampus, and reward-related regions. Small and Vorgan (2008) highlight that digital media exposure can enhance connectivity related to rapid information processing and pattern recognition while simultaneously reducing activation in areas associated with deep reflection, sustained attention, and long-term memory consolidation. These findings suggest that the brain optimizes its resources for tasks that are frequently demanded, but this optimization may occur at the expense of more generalized cognitive capabilities.

The implications of such plasticity are multifaceted. On one hand, neuroplastic adaptation enables humans to effectively integrate AI systems into daily life, enhancing efficiency, multitasking ability, and responsiveness to dynamic information streams. On the other hand, this adaptive reshaping carries potential cognitive trade-offs. Prioritization of AI-mediated pathways may reduce the robustness of internal cognitive networks, diminishing independent problem-solving, memory recall, and complex reasoning. The neural reorganization reflects environmental tuning, but not necessarily optimal cognitive balance. Over extended periods, these structural and functional shifts may contribute to reduced resilience in tasks that cannot be outsourced to technology.

Furthermore, the interplay between reward processing and AI-mediated reinforcement may accentuate reliance patterns. When AI systems consistently produce successful or satisfying outcomes, mesolimbic activation reinforces interaction behaviors, promoting habitual dependence. This reinforcement loop can create conditions in which neural circuits supporting self-directed exploration, error monitoring, and active learning receive less engagement. The result is a brain increasingly tuned to AI-supported cognition—efficient for AI-mediated tasks but potentially less adaptable in contexts requiring autonomous reasoning.

Importantly, these changes are not inherently irreversible. Neuroplasticity also allows for recovery and recalibration when environmental demands shift or when deliberate cognitive training is undertaken. Engaging in tasks that require independent memory retrieval, problem-solving without algorithmic assistance, and complex social interaction can reactivate underutilized neural networks and maintain cognitive flexibility. The key lies in balancing technology use with activities that challenge and sustain the full spectrum of cognitive abilities.

In summary, habitual interaction with AI systems reshapes the brain's functional architecture through neuroplastic mechanisms. Neural circuits associated with cognitive control, reward, and AI-mediated tasks may be strengthened, while underutilized regions, such as the hippocampus and attentional networks, may experience relative downregulation. These adaptations reflect the brain's remarkable capacity for environmental tuning but may come at the cost of balanced cognitive function, highlighting the importance of mindful engagement with AI technologies to preserve neural and cognitive resilience.

6.2 Reward Processing and Behavioral Reinforcement

Artificial Intelligence systems frequently employ reward mechanisms to optimize user engagement, leveraging principles derived from behavioral psychology and neuroscience. These mechanisms include notifications, algorithmically tailored suggestions, instant feedback, achievement badges, or personalized content streams. By delivering reinforcement contingent on user behavior, AI systems effectively shape interaction patterns, guiding attention, motivation, and decision-making in subtle yet powerful ways.

From a neurobiological perspective, these reward signals engage dopaminergic pathways, particularly the mesolimbic system encompassing the ventral tegmental area (VTA), nucleus accumbens, and prefrontal projections. Dopamine release in these circuits signals the anticipation and receipt of reward, enhancing the salience of stimuli and facilitating reinforcement learning. Repeated activation of these pathways strengthens synaptic connections and promotes the formation of habitual behavior loops, whereby specific behaviors—such as checking notifications, interacting with AI-driven suggestions, or responding to algorithmically generated prompts—are increasingly performed automatically with minimal conscious deliberation.

Over time, these reinforcement loops can shift the motivational architecture of behavior. Initially, interactions with AI may serve functional purposes—retrieving information, scheduling tasks, or facilitating communication. However, as reward-driven engagement patterns consolidate, users may begin to seek AI interaction for the pleasure or reinforcement it provides rather than for necessity. This transition represents a form of behavioral conditioning, in which the activity itself becomes intrinsically motivating, independent of its original instrumental goal. Neuropsychologically, this can create a form of dependency, in which dopaminergic signaling reinforces habitual engagement even in the absence of practical need.

The consequences of such neural and behavioral dependencies are multifaceted. On a cognitive level, habitual reward-seeking may divert attentional resources away from goal-directed or reflective tasks, favoring rapid, stimulus-driven engagement. On an affective level, users may experience heightened arousal or craving-like responses when AI-mediated rewards are absent, analogous to the mechanisms observed in behavioral addiction research. Functional imaging studies suggest that excessive engagement with reward-structured digital environments can amplify activation in the ventral striatum and orbitofrontal cortex while diminishing prefrontal regulatory control, potentially weakening executive oversight over habitual behaviors.

Moreover, these reward-driven loops can interact with other aspects of cognitive offloading and social behavior. For example, if the dopaminergic reinforcement of AI-mediated engagement is paired with externalization of memory, planning, or social functions, individuals may increasingly rely on AI not only for reward but also for cognitive scaffolding. This creates a compounding effect: AI systems simultaneously shape both the motivational and cognitive architecture, fostering patterns in which dependence on AI becomes both habitual and functionally entrenched.

Importantly, these dynamics are not inherently pathological. Reinforcement loops can promote learning, habit formation, and skill acquisition when appropriately aligned with adaptive goals. The concern arises when reward-driven engagement becomes disproportionate, such that it dominates attentional, cognitive, or social resources at the expense of independent functioning. In such cases, habitual engagement may persist even when it is no longer necessary or beneficial, highlighting the importance of designing AI systems with calibrated reinforcement mechanisms that encourage mindful and goal-directed interaction rather than purely compulsive engagement.

In summary, AI systems leverage reward signals to reinforce user engagement, engaging dopaminergic pathways and establishing habitual behavior loops. Over time, these patterns can shift motivation from functional use to reward-seeking, reinforcing neural dependencies and potentially altering attentional, cognitive, and social behaviors. Understanding these neuropsychological mechanisms is essential for developing AI environments that maximize benefits while mitigating risks of habitual or compulsive reliance.

7. ETHICAL AND SOCIETAL IMPLICATIONS

The neuropsychological effects of AI overreliance extend beyond individual cognition to societal structures. If populations increasingly depend on AI for memory, decision-making, and emotional support, educational systems, labor markets, and cultural norms may shift.

Ethical concerns arise regarding autonomy, consent, and agency. Heavy dependency on AI risks eroding individual responsibility, diminishing human ingenuity, and redefining what it means to be cognitively competent.

7.1 Education and Skill Development

Educational paradigms must adapt to a world where AI assists fundamental tasks. Pedagogical frameworks should emphasize critical thinking, metacognition, and resilience rather than rote memorization, acknowledging AI's role while safeguarding human cognitive capacities.

7.2 Workforce and Cognitive Labor

AI's encroachment into cognitive labor—data analysis, writing, diagnostics—raises questions about human roles in the workforce. As AI assumes more cognitive functions, humans must cultivate adaptive intelligence—skills AI cannot easily replicate, such as creativity, empathy, and moral reasoning.

8. MITIGATION STRATEGIES AND FUTURE DIRECTIONS

Given the profound benefits of AI integration alongside its potential neuropsychological risks, it is critical to implement strategies that balance efficiency and cognitive health. Mitigating negative outcomes requires a multifaceted approach involving individual behavior, educational interventions, institutional policy, and technology design.

1. Cognitive Training Programs

Cognitive offloading and habitual reliance on AI can reduce engagement of core executive and memory functions. Structured cognitive training programs targeting working memory, attention, and problem-solving may counteract these effects. Empirical studies demonstrate that adaptive working memory training can enhance fluid intelligence and attentional control (Jaeggi et al., 2011). By engaging neural circuits in a targeted, effortful manner, such interventions reinforce prefrontal–hippocampal networks, helping to preserve cognitive capacity even in environments that increasingly outsource mental tasks to AI. Regular practice in tasks that require sustained focus, planning, and memory retrieval can maintain resilience in the cognitive systems most susceptible to underutilization.

2. Mindful AI Use Policies

Institutions, workplaces, and educational settings can adopt mindful AI use policies that promote intentional engagement rather than passive or compulsive interaction. Mindfulness strategies involve awareness of one's cognitive state, monitoring of attention, and conscious regulation of technology use. Encouraging deliberate decision-making about when and how to rely on AI can help prevent skill atrophy, excessive reward-driven behavior, and overreliance that diminishes autonomy. Practical examples include designated "AI-free" periods, requiring manual problem-solving before consulting AI tools, or using AI outputs as a starting point for critical evaluation rather than as definitive answers.

3. Digital Literacy Education

Promoting digital and AI literacy is essential for fostering cognitive and emotional resilience in technologically saturated environments. Understanding how AI systems operate—including algorithmic decision-making, data biases, and predictive modeling—enables individuals to critically evaluate outputs, calibrate trust appropriately, and avoid automation bias. Education can also address the "black box" problem by teaching users to interpret confidence scores, probability estimates, or model limitations. By combining technical knowledge with metacognitive awareness, digital literacy programs empower users to maintain agency, reduce uncertainty-induced stress, and engage with AI as an augmentative rather than substitutive tool.

4. Designing Human-Centered AI

The architecture of AI systems significantly influences cognitive and behavioral outcomes. Human-centered AI design emphasizes augmentation over automation, ensuring that AI supports rather than replaces critical cognitive functions. For example, systems can provide explanatory feedback, suggest strategies rather than solutions, or require active user verification to complete tasks. By scaffolding rather than supplanting human decision-making, such designs maintain engagement of neural circuits associated with executive control, working memory, and problem-solving. Additionally, adaptive interfaces can balance reward mechanisms to reinforce beneficial behaviors without promoting habitual or compulsive engagement, thereby preserving attentional regulation and metacognitive oversight.

5. Longitudinal Research and Monitoring

Future research must systematically explore the long-term neuropsychological impacts of AI reliance. Longitudinal studies can examine changes in neural structure, connectivity, and activation patterns associated with habitual AI use, including effects on the prefrontal cortex, hippocampus, mesolimbic reward pathways, and social cognition networks. Investigations should also assess emotional outcomes, such as the effects of AI-mediated companionship on empathy, emotional regulation, and attachment processes, as well as social consequences, including interpersonal skill development and relational satisfaction. Such research will inform evidence-based guidelines for safe and beneficial AI integration across diverse populations, including children, adolescents, and older adults.

In conclusion, balancing the benefits of AI with neuropsychological health requires integrated strategies: targeted cognitive training, mindful usage practices, digital literacy education, human-centered system design, and robust longitudinal research. By combining behavioral, educational, and technological interventions, it is possible to harness the efficiency, accessibility, and analytical power of AI while preserving independent cognitive function, emotional resilience, and social competency. This approach underscores a fundamental principle: AI should augment the human mind without undermining the neural and cognitive foundations that sustain autonomous reasoning and adaptive behavior.

9. CONCLUSION

Artificial Intelligence presents extraordinary opportunities but also profound neuropsychological challenges. Overreliance on AI can reshape memory, decision-making, attention, emotional regulation, and social behavior. Understanding these effects is crucial for fostering adaptive, healthy integration of AI in human life. By promoting mindful engagement, prioritizing human cognitive strengths, and aligning AI design with psychological well-being, society can harness technological advancements without surrendering essential aspects of human cognition and agency.

REFERENCES

Barr, N., Pennycook, G., Stolz, J. A., & Fugelsang, J. A. (2015). The brain in your pocket: Evidence that smartphones are used to supplant thinking. *Computers in Human Behavior, 48*, 473–480. DOI: 10.1016/j.chb.2015.02.029

Clark, A., & Chalmers, D. (1998). The extended mind. *Analysis, 58*(1), 7–19. DOI: 10.1093/analys/58.1.7

Ishikawa, T., Fujiwara, H., Imai, O., & Okabe, A. (2008). Wayfinding with a GPS-based mobile navigation system: A comparison with maps and direct experience. *Journal of Environmental Psychology, 28*(1), 74–82. DOI: 10.1016/j.jenvp.2007.09.002

Jaeggi, S. M., Buschkuehl, M., Jonides, J., & Perrig, W. J. (2011). Short-and long-term benefits of cognitive training. *Proceedings of the National Academy of Sciences of the United States of America, 108*(25), 10081–10086. DOI: 10.1073/pnas.1103228108 PMID: 21670271

Krach, S., Hegel, F., Wrede, B., Sagerer, G., Binkofski, F., & Kircher, T. (2008). Can machines think? Interaction and perspective taking with robots investigated via fMRI. *PLoS One, 3*(7), e2597. DOI: 10.1371/journal.pone.0002597 PMID: 18612463

Kühn, S.. (2014). Musical training and cognitive abilities in adulthood: Neural correlates of working memory and executive function. *Brain and Cognition, 85*, 58–65.

Mosier, K. L.. (1998). Automation reliance: Empirical results and implications for mixed-initiative systems. *Proceedings of the Human Factors and Ergonomics Society Annual Meeting, 42*(2), 135–139.

Ophir, E., Nass, C., & Wagner, A. D. (2009). Cognitive control in media multitaskers. *Proceedings of the National Academy of Sciences of the United States of America, 106*(37), 15583–15587. DOI: 10.1073/pnas.0903620106 PMID: 19706386

Rahwan, I., Cebrian, M., Obradovich, N., Bongard, J., Bonnefon, J. F., Breazeal, C., Crandall, J. W., Christakis, N. A., Couzin, I. D., Jackson, M. O., Jennings, N. R., Kamar, E., Kloumann, I. M., Larochelle, H., Lazer, D., McElreath, R., Mislove, A., Parkes, D. C., Pentland, A. S., & Wellman, M. (2019). Machine behaviour. *Nature, 568*(7753), 477–486. DOI: 10.1038/s41586-019-1138-y PMID: 31019318

Russell, S., & Norvig, P. (2021). *Artificial Intelligence: A Modern Approach.* Pearson.

Small, G., & Vorgan, G. (2008). iBrain: Surviving the Technological Alteration of the Modern Mind. HarperCollins.

Sparrow, B., Liu, J., & Wegner, D. M. (2011). Google effects on memory: Cognitive consequences of having information at our fingertips. *Science*, *333*(6043), 776–778. DOI: 10.1126/science.1207745 PMID: 21764755

Tarafdar, M., Tu, Q., Ragu-Nathan, B. S., & Ragu-Nathan, T. S. (2011). Impact of technostress on productivity. *Journal of Management Information Systems*, *28*(1), 301–328. DOI: 10.2753/MIS0742-1222240109

Turkle, S. (2017). *Reclaiming Conversation: The Power of Talk in a Digital Age*. Penguin Press.

Chapter 13

Examining the Influence of AI Dependency, Ethical Awareness, and Algorithmic Bias Awareness on Critical Thinking: Nudging the Algorithmic Mind

Anjali Mishra
http://orcid.org/0009-0009-3497-6566
Lovely Professional University, India

ABSTRACT

Generative Artificial Intelligence (GenAI) is reshaping higher education by enhancing learning while raising concerns about dependency, cognitive offloading, and critical thinking. This chapter examines the relationships among AI Dependency, Ethical Awareness, Algorithmic Bias Awareness, and Critical Thinking Skills in AI-supported learning. A mixed-paradigm approach combining Systematic Theoretical Synthesizing and Partial Least Squares Structural Equation Modeling (PLS-SEM) was used to analyze data from 110 university students. Results show that all three constructs significantly influence critical thinking, with Algorithmic Bias Awareness as the strongest predictor. Students who recognize AI limitations and biases demonstrate stronger analytical reasoning and metacognitive skills. The study proposes a Mixed-Paradigm Cognitive-Behavioral Triangulation Matrix integrating behavioral

DOI: 10.4018/979-8-3373-9484-8.ch013

dependency, ethical cognition, and algorithmic skepticism. Findings highlight the importance of AI literacy and critical engagement for maintaining cognitive independence in AI-mediated education.

INTRODUCTION

Generative Artificial Intelligence (GenAI) has quickly become one of the most impactful technologies in modern education. Large Language Models, intelligent tutoring systems, and AI-driven content creation platforms have become more prevalent in educational settings, facilitating students to access information, brainstorm ideas, summarize content and finish learning activities with unprecedented efficiency. These technologies have significant productivity and accessibility benefits, but they are increasingly becoming part of educational contexts and have raised considerable questions about student learning, cognition, and intellectual independence, as well as critical thinking.

One key issue is that of cognitive offloading, in which people rely on external technologies to perform tasks on which they depend. While the cognitive offloading strategy can help alleviate cognitive load and boost short-term productivity, overreliance on AI-generated content may hinder higher-order thinking, critical analysis, and knowledge building. With the increasing reliance on AI systems for solution generation, explanations, and arguments, questions arise on whether this practice deteriorates the development of higher order thinking skills which are important for academic achievement and lifelong learning.

Current studies have concentrated on the adoption of AI, performance in learning, the acceptance of technology and satisfaction with the technology. Less research has been dedicated to comprehending the interaction between behavioral dependency, ethical awareness, and perceptions of algorithmic bias in order to better understand how these factors can interact to impact students' critical thinking skills. This restriction poses a major challenge in the field of research, especially given the increasing interest in integrating AI technologies in a responsible and ethical manner while maintaining the integrity and rigor of academic work in universities.

Given this, the present chapter suggests a Mixed-Paradigm Cognitive-Behavioral Triangulation Matrix that investigates the concurrent impact of Algorithmic Bias Awareness (AOAB), Ethical Awareness (EA) and AI Dependency (DOA) on Critical Thinking Skills (CT). The study explores the interaction among these constructs in AI-mediated learning environments and the factors with the highest influence on critical thinking retention using a Partial Least Squares Structural Equation Modeling (PLS-SEM) approach.

The chapter adds to the growing body of literature on the role of AI in education, both theoretical and empirical, and provides insights into the cognitive effects of AI-supported learning. Additionally, it is a step towards the concept of adversarial AI literacy, that is, the ability to evaluate, question and validate algorithmic outputs rather than take them at face value. The results offer important implications for educators, curriculum developers, and policymakers aiming to promote responsible use of AI while maintaining students' cognitive independence and critical thinking skills.

LITERATURE REVIEW

Generative Artificial Intelligence in Higher Education

With the advent of Generative Artificial Intelligence (GenAI), teaching and learning in higher education have undergone a profound change. The latest systematic reviews suggest that GenAI has a significant impact on learning, with personalized learning support, content generation, increased accessibility, and automated feedback mechanisms being among the advantages. But, these pros come with concerns about academic integrity, dependence and the learning process. A systematic review conducted by Zhang et al. (2024) found that the key educational affordances of GenAI were accessibility, personalization, automation and interactivity, and identified academic dishonesty, misinformation, and over-reliance on AI-generated outputs as risks.

Likewise, a systematic review of the use of GenAI in higher education revealed that GenAI is transforming educational practices, both in the way teachers teach and how students are evaluated.The same, a systematic review of higher education applications found that GenAI is rapidly changing the way teachers teach, the way students are assessed, and the way in which institutions work. The authors highlighted that the impact of broad-based AI use on education over time is not well understood and needs to be empirically studied.

Cognitive Offloading and Digital Dependency

Cognitive offloading has become a key paradigm to explain human interaction with computers. Cognitive offloading is the process of moving cognitive processes from internal to external processes and/or technological systems. Risko and Gilbert (2016) defined cognitive offloading as "using physical or digital resources to either save mental effort or to extend cognitive capacity. These strategies may enhance the efficiency of the task and its performance, but, if overused, can result in less engagement in deeper cognitive processing.

On this basis, Skulmowski (2023), in a comprehensive review of digital externalization, suggested that using technology-based offloading may be able to lower cognitive load and enhance task efficiency but can have adverse impacts on learning, memory retention and the construction of knowledge. In AI-powered learning contexts, cognitive offloading is a concept that is especially relevant as the generative AI can produce explanations, arguments, summaries and solutions, which would otherwise have to be created by the learner. This has led to the potential for students to become more dependent on the outputs of algorithms than on analytical thinking and self-directed learning, raising questions about the lack of cognitive engagement and dependency on algorithms.

AI Dependency and Critical Thinking

Critical thinking is a key higher order thinking ability that has always been known to perform analysis, evaluation, interpretation and reasoned judgment. According to Facione (1990), critical thinking is purposeful, self-regulated judgment that includes interpretation, analysis, evaluation and inference. Likewise, Paul and Elder (2019) noted that critical thinking demands that people question and challenge assumptions, assess evidence and reflect on the reasoning before making conclusions.

Researchers have started to investigate the potential of AI dependency to impact on these cognitive processes. In a study of students' perceptions of the use of generative AI in higher education, Roy and Jony (2026) identified several common patterns, including superficial engagement with academic content; increased usage of AI-assisted thinking; and decreased self-regulation of cognitive effort. Pupils recognised that over-dependency on AI might reduce opportunities for independent thought and reflection.

Similarly, Akhtar et al. (2026) found that, as generative AI systems are more widely used, university students expressed worries about memory loss, critical thinking, and decision making. The researchers' results indicate that overreliance on AI could foster cognitive offloading patterns which may diminish engagement in more analytical thinking. However, new evidence shows that AI can assist in higher order thinking skills when learners evaluate AI-generated content critically, not uncritically, which poses a dilemma of how AI dependency and development of HOTS are intertwined.

Ethical Awareness and Responsible AI Use

As AI technologies have rapidly become part of the educational landscape, these issues of academic integrity, accountability, transparency and responsible use of technology have grown more pressing. Ethical consciousness is thus becoming a key part of the AI literacy. Floridi and Cowls (2022) outlined a highly accepted framework for AI ethics, which draws from principles of beneficence, non-maleficence, autonomy, justice, and explicability, indicating that the use of AI must be done responsibly, and that requires not only technical skills but also ethical judgment.

In educational settings, the need for students to grasp authorial and plagiarism concerns, responsible use of AI tools, transparency and accountability, and proper authorship has grown more and more prominent in recent years. Zhang et al. (2024) highlighted ethical issues as one of the biggest challenges for the use of generative AI in education and called for institutional policies to foster responsible use of generative AI and uphold academic integrity.

Moreover, the current debates about AI in education emphasise that students must be active users of AI and acquire reflective judgement, with a view to the right use of algorithmic support in educational tasks. Ethical awareness is thus a crucial tool to facilitate critical thinking and responsible decision-making within AI-supported learning environments.

Algorithmic Bias Awareness and Epistemic Vigilance

As AI technologies have rapidly become part of the educational landscape, these issues of academic integrity, accountability, transparency and responsible use of technology have grown more pressing. Ethical consciousness is thus becoming a key part of the AI literacy. Floridi and Cowls (2022) outlined a highly accepted framework for AI ethics, which draws from principles of beneficence, non-maleficence, autonomy, justice, and explicability, indicating that the use of AI must be done responsibly, and that requires not only technical skills but also ethical judgment.

In educational settings, the need for students to grasp authorial and plagiarism concerns, responsible use of AI tools, transparency and accountability, and proper authorship has grown more and more prominent in recent years. Zhang et al. (2024) highlighted ethical issues as one of the biggest challenges for the use of generative AI in education and called for institutional policies to foster responsible use of generative AI and uphold academic integrity.

Moreover, the current debates about AI in education emphasise that students must be active users of AI and acquire reflective judgement, with a view to the right use of algorithmic support in educational tasks. Ethical awareness is thus a crucial tool to facilitate critical thinking and responsible decision-making within AI-supported learning environments.

Research Gap and Theoretical Positioning

One aspect of AI literacy that is also becoming more prevalent is knowledge about algorithms. AI systems are built using vast amounts of data, which can also include biases from the past, culture, and society that can impact outputs. O'Neil (2017) suggested that algorithmic systems have the potential to unintentionally reinforce and perpetuate social inequalities, and Mehrabi et al. (2021) showed that bias can manifest themselves at various stages of the machine learning process, such as data collection, design of the machine, deployment and operation.

In the context of education, algorithmic bias has been identified as a recurring issue across various AI tools in the field and was noted as a need for fairness, transparency, and accountability in educational algorithms. Therefore, it is important that students learn to critically assess AI-generated content, and not take the information for granted as being objective or accurate.

Algorithmic Bias Awareness can thus be seen as a type of epistemic vigilance, which is an approach that prompts students to check sources, to question created content and to look out for inaccuracies or bias. These metacognitive behaviors are becoming more well-known as protective measures against misinformation, automation bias, and overly relying on intelligent systems.

THEORETICAL FRAMEWORK

The increasing integration of Generative Artificial Intelligence (GenAI) within higher education has generated significant interest regarding its influence on student cognition, learning behavior, and critical thinking development. Understanding these effects requires a multidisciplinary theoretical foundation capable of explaining both the benefits and risks associated with AI-assisted learning. Accordingly, this chapter is grounded in Cognitive Load Theory, Cognitive Offloading Theory, and the concept of Epistemic Vigilance. Together, these perspectives provide a comprehensive explanation of how AI dependency, ethical awareness, and algorithmic bias awareness influence students' critical thinking skills.

Cognitive Load Theory

Cognitive Load Theory (CLT), originally proposed by Sweller (1988), explains how learning is influenced by the limited processing capacity of working memory.

According to the theory, effective learning occurs when instructional activities optimize cognitive resources and facilitate the construction of long-term knowledge schemas. CLT distinguishes between intrinsic load, which is associated with the inherent complexity of learning materials, extraneous load arising from inefficient instructional design, and germane load devoted to schema development and meaningful learning.

Within AI-assisted learning environments, Generative AI systems can significantly reduce cognitive effort by providing immediate explanations, summaries, solutions, and recommendations. While such assistance may decrease unnecessary cognitive burden and improve efficiency, excessive reliance on automated outputs may also reduce the germane cognitive processing required for deeper understanding and knowledge construction. Consequently, students may become passive recipients of information rather than active participants in learning.

From a critical thinking perspective, the unrestricted delegation of analytical tasks to AI systems may reduce opportunities for reasoning, evaluation, and reflection. Therefore, Cognitive Load Theory provides an important foundation for understanding how AI-supported learning can simultaneously enhance efficiency while potentially limiting higher-order cognitive engagement.

Cognitive Offloading Theory

Cognitive Load Theory (CLT) was first suggested by Sweller (1988) and is an explanation of how the limited capacity of working memory affects learning. Based on the theory, good learning takes place when instructional activities maximize cognitive resources and support the building of long-term knowledge schemas. CLT separates intrinsic load (from the complexity of information to be learned), extraneous load (from poor instructional design) and germane load (for schema construction and meaningful learning).

In AI-powered learning environments, Generative AI can greatly alleviate cognitive load by instantly delivering explanations, summaries, solutions, and recommendations. This help can lessen the redundant cognitive load and enhance efficiency, but excessive reliance on automated outputs can also lead to a diminished amount of germane cognitive load involved in understanding and building knowledge. This means that students can be passive, rather than active, learners.

The free transfer of analytical function to AI systems from a critical thinking point of view can limit the space for reasoning, evaluation and reflection. In this regard, Cognitive Load Theory serves as a valuable basis to understand the role that AI learning can play in improving efficiency while also reducing the scope for higher-order thinking.

Epistemic Vigilance and Algorithmic Skepticism

The Cognitive Offloading Theory builds on this discussion by explaining the mechanisms through which people move their cognitive processes from internal to external using technological devices. Humans have been using external resources like notes, calculators, maps, and digital devices to help them with their memory and problem solving historically. Generative AI is an extremely advanced type of cognitive offloading, as it is not only storing information but also creating interpretations, arguments, and solutions.

Cognitive offloading enables people to decrease cognitive load and maximize task performance (Risko and Gilbert, 2016). Too much reliance on outside systems, however, could result in less engagement in active cognitive processing. If students use AI-generated answers without cross-checking or thinking, analytical skills and opportunities for independent problem-solving could diminish.

This theoretical framework directly contributes to the AI Dependency construct used in the current study. AI Dependency is a behavioral expression of cognitive offloading, which refers to the degree of task offloading to algorithmic systems by students. Therefore, the theory of cognitive offloading is used as the main theory explaining the relationship between use of AI and any possible changes in critical thinking outcomes.

Proposed Mixed-Paradigm Cognitive-Behavioral Triangulation Matrix

Following the previous theoretical background, this chapter suggests a Mixed-Paradigm Cognitive-Behavioral Triangulation Matrix to explain the development of critical thinking in educational environments supported by AI. The framework is a combination of three complementary elements of student interaction with AI technologies.

AI Dependency (DOA) is the first dimension representing behavioral propensities related to cognitive offloading and algorithmic reliance. The second dimension, Ethical Awareness (EA), is students' ability to assess the ethical implications of the use of AI in academic settings. The third dimension, Algorithmic Bias Awareness (AOAB), indicates metacognitive awareness of the constraints, biases and reliability of AI-generated information.

The constructs in combination are expected to impact Critical Thinking Skills (CT) that involve analytical reasoning, evaluation of evidence, logical thinking and reflective decision-making. The framework acknowledges that relying on AI can impact learning behaviour, yet ethical awareness, and algorithmic bias awareness are protective factors that promote critical engagement with AI-generated content.

The theoretical contribution of this framework is that it brings together the views of behavioural, ethical, and metacognitive aspects in one coherent explanatory framework. The proposed framework takes a different approach from previous research that investigates the dimensions one by one and looks at the combined impact on the critical thinking outcomes. The model thus offers a holistic view for navigating students' learning experiences in increasingly AI-supported learning environments and their cognitive autonomy and analytical skills.

Conceptual Model and Hypothesis Development

The present study suggests that students' CT skills are determined by three interrelated dimensions of AI mediated learning: AI Dependency (DOA), Ethical Awareness (EA), Algorithmic Bias Awareness (AOAB), based on the three theories: Cognitive Load Theory, Cognitive Offloading Theory, and Epistemic Vigilance Theory.

The conceptual framework is based on the assumption that AI Dependency is a behavioral pattern of giving up mental effort on algorithmic systems. Ethical Awareness is students' ability to consider the responsible use of AI in academic contexts, while Algorithmic Bias Awareness is metacognitive awareness of the pitfalls and fallibility of information generated by AI.

Therefore Critical Thinking Skills (CT) are considered as the functions of these three latent constructs, namely:

$$CT = \beta_1(DOA) + \beta_2(EA) + \beta_3(AOAB) + \zeta$$

Where:

CT = Critical Thinking Skills
DOA = AI Dependency
EA = Ethical Awareness
AOAB = Algorithmic Bias Awareness
$\beta_1, \beta_2, \beta_3$ = Structural path coefficients
ζ = Residual error term

The formulation assumes that this is because students' differences in critical thinking skills can be partially explained by their behavioral dependence on AI, their ethical orientation towards using AI, and their awareness of the limitations of algorithms.

Based on the theoretical framework, the following hypotheses are proposed:

H1: AI Dependency (DOA) significantly influences Critical Thinking Skills (CT).
H2: Ethical Awareness (EA) significantly influences Critical Thinking Skills (CT).
H3: Algorithmic Bias Awareness (AOAB) significantly influences Critical Thinking Skills (CT).

The proposed hypotheses collectively form the Mixed-Paradigm Cognitive-Behavioral Triangulation Matrix, which serves as the analytical foundation of the empirical investigation.

Figure 1. Theoretical foundation framework illustrating the integration of cognitive load theory, cognitive offloading theory, and epistemic vigilance in explaining the relationships among AI Dependency (DOA), Ethical Awareness (EA), Algorithmic Bias Awareness (AOAB), and Critical Thinking Skills (CT)

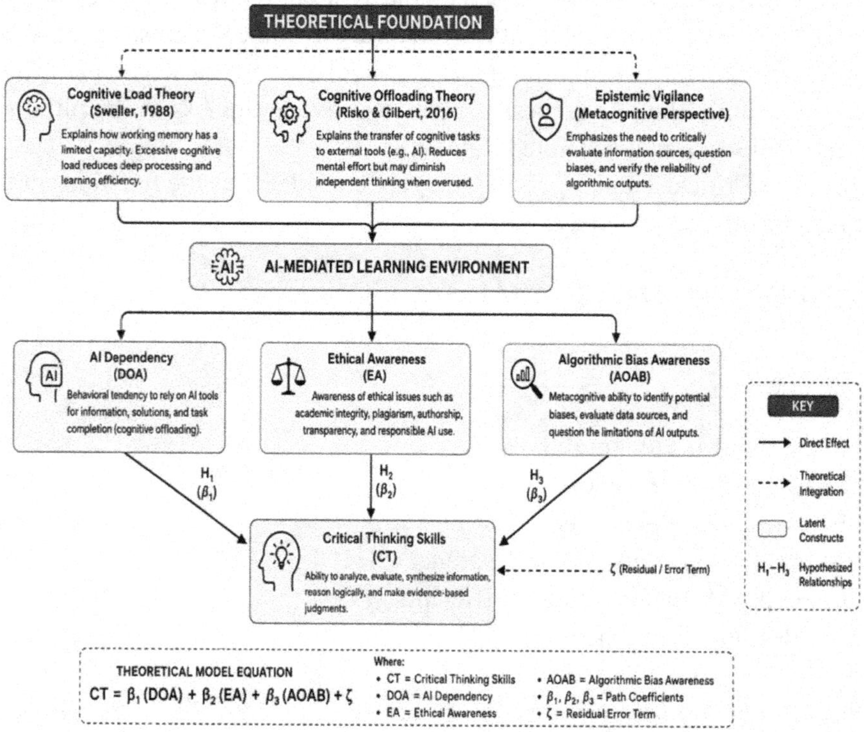

The theoretical relationships discussed in the preceding sections are synthesized into a unified conceptual framework. Drawing upon Cognitive Load Theory, Cognitive Offloading Theory, and Epistemic Vigilance Theory, the framework explains how behavioral reliance on AI systems, ethical considerations, and awareness of algorithmic limitations collectively influence students' critical thinking abilities. The proposed model serves as the theoretical foundation for the subsequent empirical investigation using Partial Least Squares Structural Equation Modeling (PLS-SEM).

METHODOLOGY

The research design was quantitative cross sectional which was used in this study to examine the relationship among the constructs of AI and its relationship with the critical thinking outcome of the university students. The methodological approach adopted was based on the systematic approach of instrument development, data collection and the use of Partial Least Squares Structural Equation Modeling (PLS-SEM). A general workflow of the methodology used is shown in Figure 2.

Figure 2. Sequential research and data processing architecture

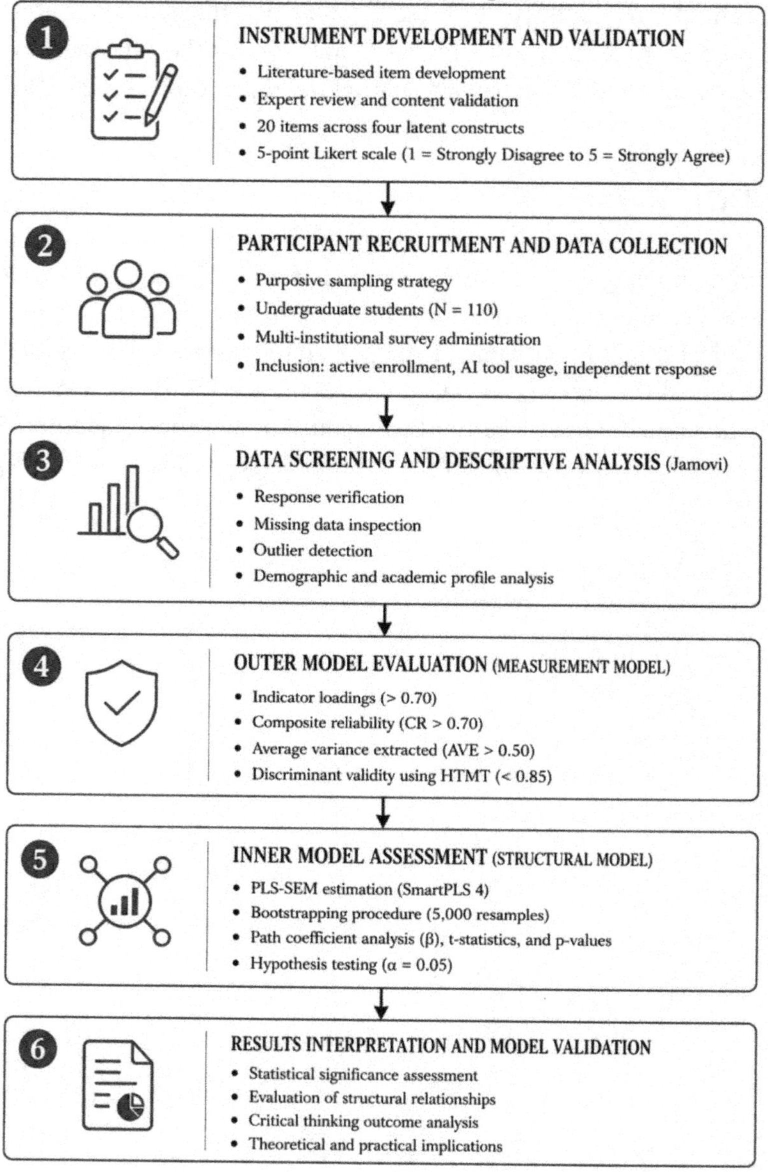

Figure 2. Sequential research workflow illustrating instrument preparation, participant recruitment, measurement model validation, and structural model assessment.

The methodology was designed to ensure both measurement reliability and structural validity while accommodating the relatively small sample size and exploratory nature of the proposed framework.

Methodological Framework and Research Design

The research design used in this study was the quantitative cross-sectional research design approach, which aimed at finding out the effect of AI related behavioral and cognitive factors on students' critical thinking skills in AI mediated learning environments. The quantitative approach was deemed to be appropriate as it was mainly to examine theoretically derived relationships between latent constructs and to test a predictive structural model with data from a specified population.

The cross-sectional design was used as the data were collected from the participants at one point in time, allowing the existing perceptions, attitudes and behavioral tendencies regarding the use of generative AI to be assessed. This design is commonly used in educational technology and behavioral studies where the goal is to determine if there is a statistically significant relationship between variables, but experimental conditions are not controlled.

The methodological framework combines the theory-driven construct specification with the data-driven model validation with the Partial Least Squares Structural Equation Modeling (PLS-SEM). The proposed framework assesses the level of contribution of three elements (AI Dependency (DOA), Ethical Awareness (EA), Algorithmic Bias Awareness (AOAB)) to the development of Critical Thinking Skills (CT).

Figure 3. Mixed-paradigm cognitive-behavioral triangulation matrix

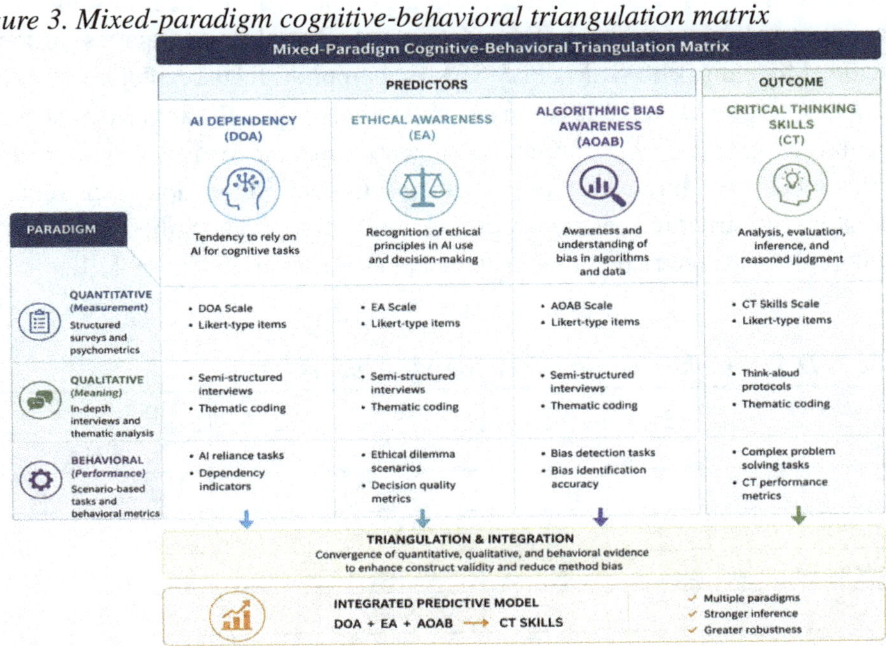

The conceptual architecture of the analytical framework is shown in Figure 3. The analytical procedure was divided into three steps. The first step was to specify and test the measurement model for the constructs to test the constructs' reliability and validity. Second, convergent and discriminant validity tests were used to check the validity of the measures. Third, the structural model was estimated to explore the proposed relationships between latent variables and to ascertain whether any of the latent variables could predict critical thinking outcomes.

The study focused on the higher education students of institutions that are more and more incorporating generative AI tools into their academic activities. The target group were students who use information retrieval, content generation, learning support, and assignment preparation applications assisted by AI regularly.

A purposive sampling approach was used to ensure that the participants have enough experience in using generative AI technologies. This sampling method is well suited when the goal of the research is to find respondents who have particular knowledge, behaviors or experiences related to the constructs being studied.

The participants had to meet three criteria to participate in the study: (i) have to be active student at a university; (ii) be using generative AI tools regularly for academic work; and (iii) not be able to use an external source to complete the questionnaire. To ensure meaningful assessment of AI-related behaviors and perceptions while providing greater response validity these criteria were developed.

Of the 110 responses, 110 were considered complete and consistent in answering the questions and used in the data collection. Although the number of samples was relatively small, it was thought that adequate for Partial Least Squares Structural Equation Modeling (PLS-SEM). PLS-SEM is appropriate for the exploratory research and is able to provide reliable estimates with relatively small samples, as stated by Hair and Alamer (2022). The number of subjects is more than the minimum required for this model structure with three exogenous and one endogenous constructs, for estimating the structural relationships and conducting the hypothesis testing. The demographic characteristic of the respondents is summarized in Table 1.

Table 1. Demographic characteristics of participants

Characteristic	Category	Distribution (%)
Gender	Male	34.5
	Female	65.5
Age Group	18–20 Years	92.1
Academic Background	STEM	71.8
	Non-STEM	28.2
AI Usage Frequency	Continuous Academic Usage	84.5

The demographic characteristics reported in Table 1 indicate a predominantly young and digitally active student population, thereby providing an appropriate context for examining AI-mediated learning behaviors and critical thinking development.

Ethical Considerations

Ethical principles were observed throughout the research process. Participation in the study was voluntary, and respondents were informed about the purpose of the research prior to completing the questionnaire. Informed consent was obtained from all participants before data collection commenced. To protect participant privacy, no personally identifiable information was collected, and all responses were recorded anonymously. The collected data were used exclusively for academic research purposes and were analyzed in aggregate form to ensure confidentiality and data protection.

Instrument Development and Measurement Structure

The measurement instrument was developed through an extensive review of prior literature on artificial intelligence adoption, ethical technology usage, algorithmic literacy, and critical thinking assessment. The questionnaire was designed to capture four theoretically grounded latent constructs: AI Dependency (DOA), Ethical Awareness (EA), Algorithmic Bias Awareness (AOAB), and Critical Thinking Skills (CT).

A total of twenty measurement items were included in the final instrument, with five indicators assigned to each construct. All items were measured using a five-point Likert scale ranging from 1 (Strongly Disagree) to 5 (Strongly Agree). The Likert scaling approach was selected because it enables efficient measurement of perceptions, attitudes, and behavioral tendencies while maintaining statistical suitability for multivariate analysis.

Figure 4. Instrument architecture and constructs distribution

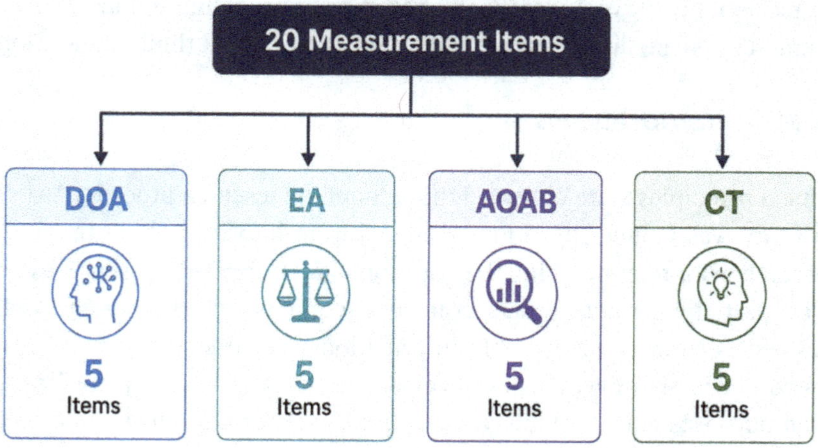

The instrument architecture is illustrated in Figure 4. The balanced distribution of indicators across constructs enhances measurement consistency and facilitates reliable estimation of latent variable relationships. Furthermore, all constructs were modeled reflectively, assuming that observed indicators represent manifestations of the underlying latent variables.

Table 2. Latent construct measurement framework

Construct	Sample Item
DOA	I frequently rely on AI tools to complete academic tasks
EA	I consider ethical implications when using AI
AOAB	AI outputs may contain hidden biases
CT	I critically evaluate information before accepting it

Prior to the main analysis, the instrument was reviewed to ensure conceptual clarity, content relevance, and alignment with the theoretical definitions of each construct. Table 2 summarizes the operational definitions and measurement focus associated with the four latent variables included in the study.

Data Processing and Statistical Analysis

Data analysis was conducted using a two-stage analytical procedure. Initially, descriptive statistics and preliminary data screening were performed using Jamovi to identify missing values, response inconsistencies, and potential outliers. The screening process ensured that only complete and valid responses were retained for subsequent analysis.

Following data preparation, the proposed research model was evaluated using Partial Least Squares Structural Equation Modeling (PLS-SEM) implemented through SmartPLS. PLS-SEM was selected because it is particularly suitable for exploratory research, prediction-oriented studies, and complex models involving multiple latent constructs. In addition, the technique demonstrates robustness when applied to relatively small sample sizes and does not impose strict distributional assumptions on the observed data.

Figure 5. PLS-SEM analytical pipeline

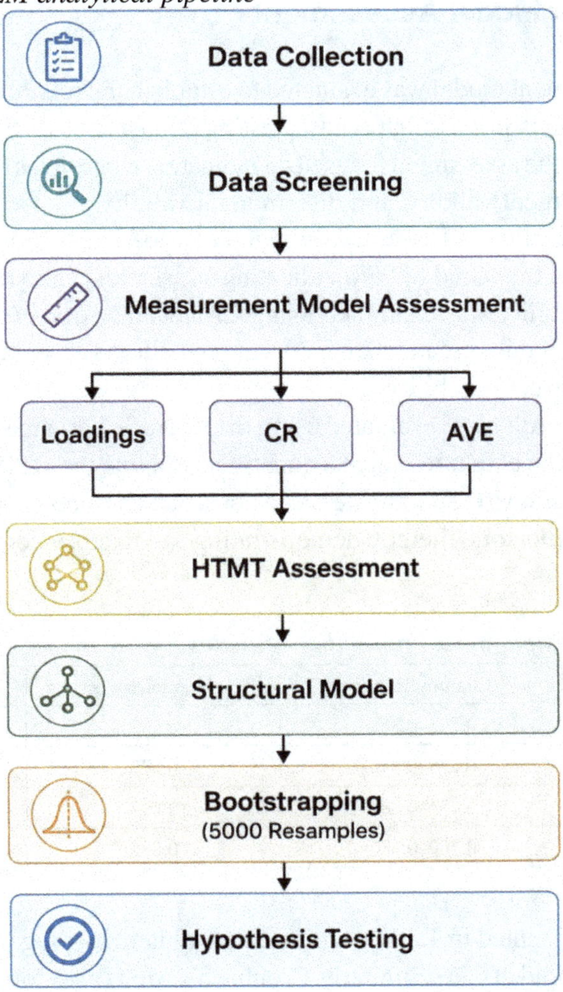

The analytical procedure followed the recommendations of Hair and Alamer (2022) and consisted of two major stages: (i) assessment of the measurement model and (ii) assessment of the structural model. The sequential analytical workflow employed in the study is illustrated in Figure 5.

The analysis commenced with the evaluation of indicator reliability, internal consistency reliability, convergent validity, and discriminant validity. Subsequently, the structural model was estimated to examine the hypothesized relationships among the latent variables. Statistical significance was determined through a bootstrapping procedure involving 5,000 resamples, enabling the estimation of standard errors, confidence intervals, and significance levels for all structural paths.

Measurement Model Assessment

The measurement model was evaluated to establish the reliability and validity of the latent constructs prior to hypothesis testing. Consistent with established PLS-SEM guidelines, the assessment focused on indicator reliability, internal consistency reliability, convergent validity, and discriminant validity.

Indicator reliability was assessed through outer loadings, with values exceeding the recommended threshold of 0.70 indicating satisfactory item reliability. Internal consistency reliability was examined using Cronbach's Alpha (α) and Composite Reliability (CR). Values greater than 0.70 were considered acceptable and indicative of adequate construct reliability.

Convergent validity was evaluated using the Average Variance Extracted (AVE), which measures the extent to which a construct explains the variance of its indicators. AVE values above 0.50 indicate that a construct captures more than half of the variance of its indicators, thereby demonstrating satisfactory convergent validity.

Table 3. Measurement model reliability statistics

Construct	Loading Range	Cronbach's α	CR	AVE
DOA	0.793–0.880	0.901	0.926	0.716
EA	0.775–0.840	0.878	0.910	0.670
AOAB	0.784–0.887	0.897	0.924	0.708
CT	0.769–0.886	0.888	0.918	0.691

The results presented in Table 3 indicate that all item loadings exceeded the recommended threshold of 0.70. Similarly, Cronbach's Alpha and Composite Reliability values for all constructs were substantially above the minimum acceptable level of 0.70, confirming strong internal consistency reliability. Furthermore, all AVE values exceeded the threshold of 0.50, providing evidence of satisfactory convergent validity.

To assess discriminant validity, the Heterotrait–Monotrait Ratio (HTMT) criterion was employed. HTMT values below 0.85 indicate that conceptually distinct constructs are empirically distinguishable from one another. The analysis revealed that all HTMT values remained below the recommended threshold, confirming adequate discriminant validity and supporting the distinctiveness of the four latent constructs included in the model.

Collectively, these findings demonstrate that the measurement instrument possesses satisfactory psychometric properties and is suitable for subsequent structural model evaluation.

Structural Model Assessment

Following confirmation of measurement reliability and validity, the structural model was assessed to examine the hypothesized relationships among AI Dependency (DOA), Ethical Awareness (EA), Algorithmic Bias Awareness (AOAB), and Critical Thinking Skills (CT).

The structural model was estimated using a non-parametric bootstrapping procedure with 5,000 resamples. Bootstrapping is recommended in PLS-SEM because it does not require normal data distribution assumptions and provides robust estimates of standard errors, t-statistics, confidence intervals, and significance levels for structural path coefficients.

The structural model is represented as:

$$CT = \beta_1(DOA) + \beta_2(EA) + \beta_3(AOAB) + \zeta$$

where CT denotes Critical Thinking Skills, DOA represents AI Dependency, EA represents Ethical Awareness, AOAB represents Algorithmic Bias Awareness, β_1–β_3 represent standardized structural path coefficients, and ζ denotes the residual error term.

The significance of each hypothesized relationship was evaluated using standardized path coefficients (β), t-values, and p-values at the 95% confidence level ($\alpha = 0.05$). In addition to path significance testing, the explanatory power of the model was assessed through the coefficient of determination (R^2), which indicates the proportion of variance in Critical Thinking Skills explained by the predictor constructs. Where appropriate, predictive relevance (Q^2) and effect size measures (f^2) may also be examined to provide additional evidence regarding model performance and predictive capability.

Figure 6. PLS-SEM structural path model

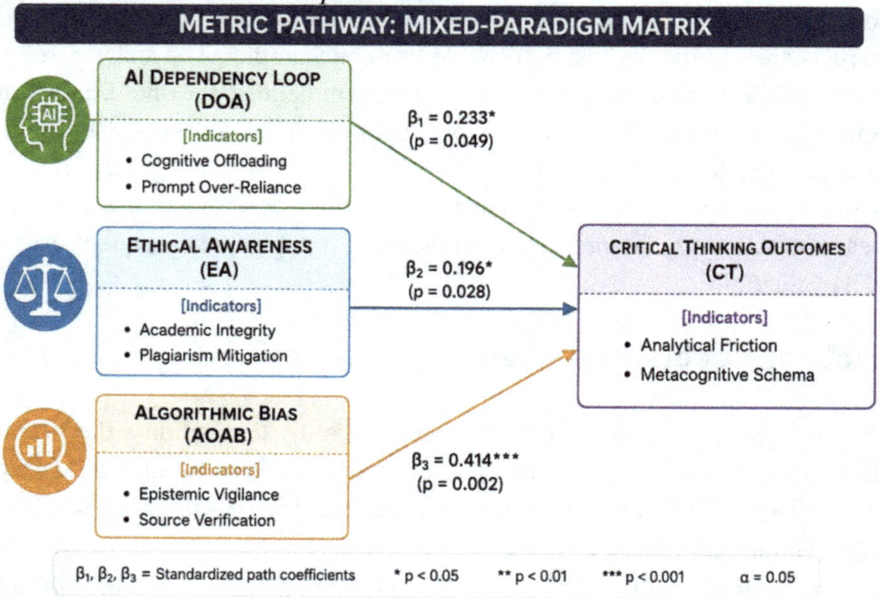

The estimated structural relationships are presented in Figure 6, while the corresponding hypothesis-testing results are summarized in Table 4. The findings indicate that AI Dependency, Ethical Awareness, and Algorithmic Bias Awareness each exert a statistically significant positive influence on Critical Thinking Skills. Among the three predictors, Algorithmic Bias Awareness demonstrates the strongest effect, suggesting that students who possess a greater understanding of algorithmic limitations and potential biases are more likely to exhibit enhanced critical thinking abilities in AI-supported learning environments.

Table 4. Structural path assessment results

Hypothesis	Relationship	β	p-value	Decision
H1	DOA → CT	0.233	0.049	Supported
H2	EA → CT	0.196	0.028	Supported
H3	AOAB → CT	0.414	0.002	Supported

The structural model therefore provides empirical support for all proposed hypotheses and confirms the relevance of AI-related cognitive and behavioral factors in shaping critical thinking outcomes among university students.

RESULTS

The psychometric properties of the measurement model obtained were satisfactory, so that the research instrument used was reliable and valid. The item loadings were greater than the recommended 0.70, with all items having adequate item reliability. In the same way, the internal consistency (Composite Reliability) ranged from 0.910 to 0.926, and the convergent validity (AVE) ranged from 0.670 to 0.716, indicating the good internal consistency and convergent validity of the instrument. In addition, the discriminant validity was confirmed, since all the values of HTMT were under the recommended value of 0.85, meaning that the constructs are empirically different.

Results from the structural model assessment indicated that all three proposed predictors were significant predictors of Critical Thinking Skills. AI Dependency had a positive relationship with Critical Thinking Skills ($\beta = 0.233$, $p = 0.049$), indicating that the use of AI in learning can have a positive impact on cognitive skills when done properly. Ethical Awareness also had a significant positive correlation with Critical Thinking Skills ($\beta = 0.196$, $p = 0.028$), further emphasizing the significance of responsible and reflective use of AI. In addition, Algorithmic Bias Awareness was the most significant predictor ($\beta = 0.414$, $p = 0.002$) that students who are aware of the limitations and potential bias of AI systems are more likely to engage in critical evaluation and analytical reasoning. Together, these results highlight the need for AI literacy, ethical consciousness, and critical thinking in cultivating higher-order thinking skills in AI-based learning environments.

DISCUSSION

This study's results indicate that the constructs of AI Dependency, Ethical Awareness, and Algorithmic Bias Awareness have a significant impact on Critical Thinking Skills of university students. The findings offer meaningful insights into the changing dynamics of AI and cognitive abilities in education. With the rise of generative AI in learning contexts, it is crucial to understand how students engage with this technology in order to measure its educational benefits and potential pitfalls.

The findings indicate that critical thinking in AI-supported learning contexts is not merely a function of the use of AI technologies, but also depends on the students' capacity to reflect on and act with AI systems in an informed, ethical and critical way. The results lend credence to the claim that it is not just the technology that matters in the educational implications of AI, but how learners think about and behave with the technology's output. These observations feed into the current debate about the role of technology in supporting students' independent thinking and learning in higher education.

AI Dependency and Critical Thinking

The results indicate a significant positive relationship between AI Dependency and Critical Thinking Skills. This finding is particularly noteworthy because concerns surrounding AI adoption often emphasize the possibility that excessive reliance on intelligent technologies may reduce independent reasoning and encourage cognitive offloading. While previous research has suggested that students may become increasingly dependent on AI-generated explanations, summaries, and recommendations, the present findings indicate that AI dependency does not necessarily undermine critical thinking when AI tools are used appropriately.

One possible explanation is that students increasingly employ AI systems as cognitive support mechanisms rather than as substitutes for learning. Generative AI technologies provide rapid access to information, alternative viewpoints, and problem-solving strategies that may stimulate intellectual curiosity and analytical evaluation. Rather than eliminating cognitive effort, AI can create opportunities for learners to compare perspectives, identify inconsistencies, and explore complex issues from multiple angles. Such interactions may contribute to the development of analytical reasoning and evaluative thinking.

The findings also align with contemporary perspectives on cognitive augmentation, which suggest that digital technologies can extend human cognitive capabilities by reducing routine information-processing demands and allowing greater focus on higher-order cognitive activities. From this perspective, AI dependency should not be viewed exclusively as a negative phenomenon. Instead, its influence may depend on the manner in which students engage with AI outputs. Learners who critically evaluate AI-generated information are more likely to benefit from AI assistance than those who accept algorithmic responses without reflection.

At the same time, the findings should not be interpreted as evidence that unrestricted AI reliance is universally beneficial. Excessive dependence on AI without active engagement may still limit opportunities for independent reasoning and problem-solving. Consequently, educators should encourage students to use AI as a complementary learning resource while maintaining responsibility for evaluating, verifying, and synthesizing information independently.

Ethical Awareness and Critical Thinking

Ethical Awareness was found to exert a significant positive influence on Critical Thinking Skills. This result highlights the importance of responsible technology use and suggests that ethical reasoning forms an integral component of critical engagement with AI systems. Students who demonstrate greater awareness of issues such as academic integrity, transparency, accountability, and responsible AI utilization appear more likely to evaluate information carefully before accepting or applying it.

The relationship between ethical awareness and critical thinking may be explained by the reflective nature of ethical decision-making itself. Ethical reasoning requires individuals to assess consequences, consider alternative perspectives, evaluate competing arguments, and justify decisions based on established principles. These processes closely resemble the cognitive activities associated with critical thinking. As a result, students who actively consider the ethical implications of AI use may naturally develop stronger analytical and evaluative capabilities.

The findings also reinforce recent discussions regarding AI literacy in higher education. While technical proficiency remains important, effective AI literacy extends beyond operational skills and includes ethical understanding, responsible decision-making, and awareness of potential risks associated with AI-generated content. Students who recognize issues such as plagiarism, authorship, misinformation, and transparency are more likely to engage critically with AI systems rather than using them unreflectively.

From an educational perspective, these findings emphasize the need for institutions to incorporate AI ethics into curricula and digital literacy programs. As AI technologies become increasingly embedded within academic activities, students must be equipped not only with technical competencies but also with the ethical judgment necessary to use these tools responsibly. Encouraging ethical reflection can therefore contribute to both responsible AI adoption and the development of critical thinking skills.

Algorithmic Bias Awareness and Critical Thinking

Among the three predictors examined in this study, Algorithmic Bias Awareness emerged as the strongest determinant of Critical Thinking Skills. This finding suggests that students who recognize the limitations, biases, and potential inaccuracies of AI systems are more likely to engage in analytical reasoning and independent evaluation of information.

Artificial intelligence systems are often perceived as objective and impartial because they rely on computational processes and large-scale datasets. However, researchers have consistently demonstrated that algorithmic systems can inherit and reproduce biases present in training data, design decisions, and implementation contexts. Students who are aware of these limitations are less likely to accept AI-generated outputs unquestioningly and more likely to engage in verification, source evaluation, and critical reflection.

The strong relationship observed in this study indicates that algorithmic bias awareness functions as a form of epistemic vigilance. Individuals who understand that AI-generated information may be incomplete, inaccurate, or biased are motivated to examine evidence more carefully and consider alternative interpretations. Such behaviors are fundamental characteristics of critical thinking and support informed decision-making in digital environments.

Furthermore, awareness of algorithmic bias may help students resist automation bias, a tendency to over-rely on recommendations produced by intelligent systems. By recognizing that AI outputs are subject to limitations, students are encouraged to maintain intellectual autonomy and exercise independent judgment. Consequently, the findings highlight the importance of integrating discussions of algorithmic fairness, transparency, and accountability into educational programs focused on AI literacy.

Educational and Theoretical Implications

The findings of this study have important implications for both educational practice and future research. From an educational perspective, the results suggest that institutions should move beyond simply encouraging AI adoption and instead focus on cultivating students' ability to engage critically with AI technologies. Educational initiatives should emphasize ethical reasoning, algorithmic awareness, source verification, and reflective evaluation of AI-generated content.

Curriculum designers and educators should develop learning activities that require students to compare AI-generated responses with scholarly sources, identify potential biases, and justify their conclusions through evidence-based reasoning. Such approaches can help ensure that AI functions as a tool for intellectual enhancement rather than a replacement for independent thought.

From a theoretical perspective, this study contributes to the growing body of literature on AI-assisted learning by integrating behavioral, ethical, and cognitive dimensions within a single explanatory framework. While previous studies have frequently examined AI adoption, ethical concerns, or critical thinking independently, the present research demonstrates that these factors are interconnected and collectively influence cognitive outcomes. The proposed framework therefore provides a foundation for future investigations examining the long-term effects of AI integration on learning, reasoning, and intellectual development in higher education.

Practical Implications for Higher Education

The findings of this study offer several important implications for higher education institutions seeking to integrate artificial intelligence into teaching and learning processes. As generative AI technologies become increasingly accessible, universities must move beyond a technology-adoption perspective and focus on developing students' capacity to engage critically and responsibly with AI-generated information.

First, educators should incorporate AI literacy as a core component of contemporary education. AI literacy should extend beyond technical proficiency and include the ability to evaluate the accuracy, reliability, and credibility of AI-generated content. Students should be encouraged to compare AI outputs with scholarly sources, identify inconsistencies, and critically assess the quality of generated information before using it in academic work. For example, instructors may design classroom activities in which students compare AI-generated explanations with peer-reviewed journal articles and identify factual inaccuracies, missing information, or unsupported claims. Such exercises can strengthen analytical reasoning while familiarizing students with the strengths and limitations of AI systems.

Second, the significant influence of Ethical Awareness on Critical Thinking Skills highlights the need for institutions to integrate AI ethics into curricula. Educational programs should address issues such as academic integrity, transparency, authorship, privacy, accountability, and responsible AI use. By fostering ethical reasoning, universities can help students become more reflective and responsible users of AI technologies. For instance, educators can introduce case studies involving the misuse of AI-generated assignments, plagiarism concerns, or data privacy violations and encourage students to discuss appropriate ethical responses. These discussions can help learners understand the broader implications of AI use beyond immediate academic benefits.

Third, the strong effect of Algorithmic Bias Awareness suggests that students should be educated about the limitations and potential biases embedded within AI systems. Universities can support this objective by incorporating discussions of algorithmic fairness, transparency, and bias detection into digital literacy and research methodology courses. For example, students may be asked to generate responses from an AI tool using prompts related to social, cultural, or historical topics and then analyze whether the outputs exhibit stereotypes, omissions, or biased representations. Such activities can encourage learners to question algorithmic outputs and develop habits of verification and critical evaluation.

Fourth, institutions should provide professional development opportunities for faculty members to ensure effective and responsible integration of AI technologies into teaching practices. Many educators are still adapting to the rapid emergence of generative AI tools and may require guidance regarding their pedagogical use. Workshops, training programs, and institutional guidelines can help instructors design AI-enhanced learning experiences while maintaining academic rigor. Faculty development initiatives may also support the creation of assessment strategies that encourage critical thinking rather than simple AI-assisted content generation.

Finally, assessment practices may require reconsideration in response to widespread AI adoption. Traditional assignments that focus primarily on information recall or content reproduction may become increasingly vulnerable to AI-assisted completion. Consequently, educators should design assessments that emphasize critical analysis, problem-solving, reflection, argument development, and evidence-based reasoning. For example, students may be required to critique an AI-generated essay, identify weaknesses in its argumentation, verify cited evidence, or explain how they improved the output using independent research. Such assessment approaches encourage students to engage actively with AI tools while maintaining intellectual responsibility and critical judgment.

Collectively, these practical recommendations suggest that the future of AI in higher education should not be centered solely on technological adoption but on fostering responsible, ethical, and critically informed engagement with intelligent systems. By developing AI literacy, ethical awareness, and algorithmic bias awareness, universities can help students leverage the benefits of artificial intelligence while preserving the higher-order cognitive skills essential for academic success and lifelong learning.

Beyond immediate classroom applications, the findings suggest that higher education institutions should adopt a strategic approach to AI integration that balances technological innovation with cognitive development. As AI tools become increasingly embedded within educational ecosystems, universities must ensure that students develop the critical thinking, ethical reasoning, and evaluative skills necessary to navigate complex digital environments. Such an approach can help institutions maximize the benefits of AI while minimizing risks associated with overreliance, misinformation, and algorithmic bias.

Beyond immediate classroom applications, the findings suggest that higher education institutions should adopt a strategic approach to AI integration that balances technological innovation with cognitive development. As AI tools become increasingly embedded within educational ecosystems, universities must ensure that students develop the critical thinking, ethical reasoning, and evaluative skills necessary to navigate complex digital environments. Such an approach can help institutions maximize the benefits of AI while minimizing risks associated with overreliance, misinformation, and algorithmic bias.

LIMITATION AND FUTURE RESEARCH

While this study contributes to the growing body of knowledge on artificial intelligence and critical thinking in higher education, several limitations should be acknowledged. Recognizing these limitations is important for appropriately interpreting the findings and identifying opportunities for future research.

First, the study employed a cross-sectional research design, which captures participants' perceptions and behaviors at a single point in time. Although this approach is effective for examining relationships among constructs, it does not permit definitive conclusions regarding causality. The observed associations between AI Dependency, Ethical Awareness, Algorithmic Bias Awareness, and Critical Thinking Skills should therefore be interpreted as correlational rather than causal. As the adoption of generative AI technologies continues to evolve rapidly, students' attitudes, behaviors, and usage patterns may also change over time. Future research could employ longitudinal research designs to investigate how sustained exposure to AI technologies influences critical thinking development, ethical awareness, and cognitive engagement across different stages of academic progression.

Second, the sample consisted of 110 university students, which, although adequate for PLS-SEM analysis, may limit the generalizability of the findings to broader populations. The participants were selected based on their experience with generative AI technologies and represented a specific educational context. Consequently, the findings may not fully reflect the experiences of students from different educational systems, age groups, academic disciplines, or cultural backgrounds. Future studies may benefit from larger and more diverse samples drawn from multiple institutions and geographical regions. Such investigations would enhance the external validity of the findings and provide a more comprehensive understanding of how AI-related behaviors influence critical thinking across diverse educational settings.

Third, the study relied on self-reported questionnaire responses, which are inherently subject to certain limitations. Participants may unintentionally overestimate or underestimate their behaviors, perceptions, or levels of critical thinking due to social desirability bias, recall bias, or subjective interpretation of survey items. Although measures were taken to ensure anonymity and encourage honest responses, self-reported data cannot entirely eliminate these concerns. Future investigations could incorporate alternative data collection approaches, such as behavioral observations, learning analytics, academic performance indicators, or experimental tasks designed to directly assess critical thinking abilities. Combining self-reported measures with objective assessments would provide a more robust evaluation of the relationships examined in the present study.

Another limitation relates to the scope of the conceptual framework. While the study focused on AI Dependency, Ethical Awareness, and Algorithmic Bias Awareness as predictors of Critical Thinking Skills, numerous additional factors may influence students' cognitive engagement in AI-mediated learning environments. Variables such as digital literacy, self-regulated learning, technology acceptance, trust in AI, cognitive engagement, learning motivation, and academic self-efficacy may also play important roles in shaping how students interact with AI technologies. Future research could extend the proposed framework by incorporating these variables and examining potential mediating or moderating effects. Such investigations would contribute to a more comprehensive understanding of the complex mechanisms underlying AI-supported learning behaviors.

Furthermore, the rapid pace of technological advancement presents an additional challenge for educational research. Generative AI systems continue to evolve in terms of functionality, accessibility, and sophistication. As newer AI models become increasingly capable of producing human-like responses, the nature of students' interactions with these systems may also change. Consequently, findings obtained within the current technological context may require periodic re-evaluation as AI technologies continue to develop. Future studies should therefore examine emerging AI tools and investigate whether advancements in AI capabilities influence patterns of dependency, ethical awareness, algorithmic bias awareness, and critical thinking outcomes.

Future research may also benefit from adopting mixed-method and interdisciplinary approaches. Qualitative methods such as interviews, focus groups, and case studies could provide deeper insights into students' experiences, perceptions, and decision-making processes when using AI technologies. Such approaches would complement quantitative findings by revealing the contextual factors that shape AI-related behaviors. In addition, interdisciplinary collaborations involving education, psychology, computer science, ethics, and data science could generate more holistic perspectives on the implications of AI integration within educational environments.

Finally, comparative studies across different educational systems and cultural contexts represent a promising direction for future research. Educational policies, technological infrastructure, institutional support mechanisms, and cultural attitudes toward technology may influence how students engage with AI systems and develop critical thinking skills. Comparative investigations involving universities from different countries could help identify contextual factors that either facilitate or hinder responsible AI use. Such knowledge would contribute to the development of evidence-based educational strategies and policy recommendations for the effective and ethical integration of artificial intelligence in higher education.

Overall, despite these limitations, the present study provides valuable insights into the relationships among AI Dependency, Ethical Awareness, Algorithmic Bias Awareness, and Critical Thinking Skills. By identifying both the strengths and constraints of the current research, this chapter establishes a foundation for future investigations aimed at understanding the long-term cognitive, behavioral, and educational implications of artificial intelligence in higher education.

CONCLUSION

The increasing adoption of generative artificial intelligence in higher education has created new opportunities and challenges for student learning and cognitive development. This chapter investigated the influence of AI Dependency (DOA), Ethical Awareness (EA), and Algorithmic Bias Awareness (AOAB) on Critical Thinking Skills (CT) among university students. By integrating these dimensions within a unified analytical framework, the study contributes to a deeper understanding of how AI-related behaviors and perceptions shape critical thinking in technology-enhanced learning environments.

The findings suggest that critical thinking is not determined solely by the extent of AI usage but is also influenced by students' awareness of ethical responsibilities and their ability to recognize the limitations and potential biases of AI systems. In particular, algorithmic bias awareness emerged as a significant factor, highlighting the importance of fostering critical evaluation of AI-generated information rather than encouraging passive acceptance of automated outputs. Ethical awareness further reinforces responsible AI engagement, while AI dependency demonstrates a more nuanced relationship with critical thinking when supported by reflective and informed use practices.

The chapter offers both theoretical and practical contributions. From a theoretical perspective, it extends existing research on AI-assisted learning by integrating behavioral, ethical, and cognitive dimensions within a single framework. From a practical perspective, the findings emphasize the need for higher education institutions to prioritize AI literacy, ethical reasoning, and critical evaluation skills alongside technological adoption. Educators should encourage students to question, verify, and critically assess AI-generated content to ensure that AI functions as a tool for intellectual enhancement rather than a substitute for independent reasoning.

Despite its contributions, the study is subject to certain limitations, including the use of a cross-sectional design and a sample drawn from a specific student population. Future research may expand this work through longitudinal investigations, larger and more diverse samples, and the inclusion of additional factors such as digital literacy, trust in AI, self-regulated learning, and academic performance. Such efforts will further advance understanding of the complex relationship between artificial intelligence and critical thinking in contemporary educational settings.

In conclusion, the effective integration of artificial intelligence in education requires a balanced approach that combines technological innovation with ethical awareness and critical reflection. Developing these competencies will be essential for preparing learners to navigate increasingly AI-driven academic and professional environments.

REFERENCES

Akhtar, P., Papadopoulos, T., Khan, H., Ghouri, A. M., Shamim, S., & Ashraf, A. (2026). Risk, generative AI, disinformation control, global supply chains, and social impacts. *Technological Forecasting and Social Change*, *226*, 124609. DOI: 10.1016/j.techfore.2026.124609

Facione, P. (1990). Critical thinking: A statement of expert consensus for purposes of educational assessment and instruction (The Delphi Report).

Floridi, L., & Cowls, J. (2022). A unified framework of five principles for AI in society. *Machine learning and the city: Applications in architecture and urban design*, 535-545.

Hair, J., & Alamer, A. (2022). Partial Least Squares Structural Equation Modeling (PLS-SEM) in second language and education research: Guidelines using an applied example. *Research methods in applied linguistics, 1*(3), 100027.

Mehrabi, N., Morstatter, F., Saxena, N., Lerman, K., & Galstyan, A. (2021). A survey on bias and fairness in machine learning. *ACM Computing Surveys*, *54*(6), 1–35. DOI: 10.1145/3457607

O'Neil, C. (2017). *Weapons of math destruction: How big data increases inequality and threatens democracy*. Crown.

Paul, R., & Elder, L. (2019). *The miniature guide to critical thinking concepts and tools*. Bloomsbury Publishing USA.

Risko, E. F., & Gilbert, S. J. (2016). Cognitive offloading. *Trends in Cognitive Sciences*, *20*(9), 676–688. DOI: 10.1016/j.tics.2016.07.002 PMID: 27542527

Skulmowski, A. (2023). The cognitive architecture of digital externalization. *Educational Psychology Review*, *35*(4), 101. DOI: 10.1007/s10648-023-09818-1

Sweller, J. (1988). Cognitive load during problem solving: Effects on learning. *Cognitive Science*, *12*(2), 257–285. DOI: 10.1207/s15516709cog1202_4

Zhang, Y., Zhang, J., Yue, S., Lu, W., Ren, J., & Shen, X. (2024). Mobile generative AI: Opportunities and challenges. *IEEE Wireless Communications*, *31*(4), 58–64. DOI: 10.1109/MWC.006.2300576

Chapter 14
Over-Automation in Higher Education:
Ethical Risks and Human-Centered AI

Narendra Rathnaraj
http://orcid.org/0000-0002-8389-0816
PSG College of Technology, India

Firdaus Bashir
PSG College of Technology, India

ABSTRACT

Over-automation in education arises when AI systems move from supportive tools to default authorities in teaching learning system. This is done without proportional safeguards. While AI can enhance personalisation and efficiency, chronic reliance can reshape cognition and behavior by encouraging cognitive offloading, weakening critical thinking, and normalising "output-following" overdependent reasoning. This chapter argues that the most consequential harms emerge from the institutionalisation of AI reliance that diffuses responsibility, reduces learner agency, and embeds procedural injustice. The chapter develops a Human-Cantered Ethical Risk Taxonomy of Over-Automation in Education across classroom and institutions. It maps six recurring risk clusters, including accountability, responsibility, pedagogical complacency, procedural injustice, metacognition, and erosion of learner agency. The chapter concludes with actionable design and policy recommendations for responsible AI use in education that protects learner agency, trust, and critical thinking while retaining efficiency gains.

DOI: 10.4018/979-8-3373-9484-8.ch014

1. INTRODUCTION: OVER-AUTOMATION AS AN EDUCATIONAL ETHICS RISK

There is a quiet but consequential shift underway in higher education. Across universities and colleges worldwide, artificial intelligence systems now sit at consequential junctures in students' academic lives: grading essays, screening applications, flagging potential misconduct, recommending courses, predicting dropout risk, and even mediating disciplinary proceedings. The pace of this adoption has outrun the institutional frameworks needed to govern it responsibly. What began as a pragmatic response to scale — too many students, too few faculty, too much data — has gradually evolved into a structural dependency that carries serious ethical implications for learner agency, pedagogical integrity, and institutional accountability.

The term 'over-automation' does not refer to automation per se. AI tools in education can serve genuinely useful functions: reducing administrative burden, enabling timely feedback at scale, and identifying students who may need early support. The ethical problem arises when these tools migrate from the periphery to the center of educational decision-making — when they cease to augment human judgment and begin to substitute for it. This substitution is rarely announced; it accumulates gradually, driven by institutional efficiency pressures, vendor incentives, and the cognitive comfort of delegating difficult decisions to seemingly objective systems.

Over-automation, as used in this chapter, describes the condition in which AI-mediated processes occupy consequential roles in teaching, assessment, advising, or integrity monitoring without adequate mechanisms for human review, contestability, transparency, or accountability. This is a systems-level condition rather than a product-level failure: a given AI tool may function precisely as designed while still producing harmful outcomes when embedded in institutional arrangements that strip away the human judgment the tool was meant to support, not replace.

The harms that follow from over-automation are not evenly distributed. Students from historically marginalized groups — those whose writing styles, accents, faces, or academic trajectories diverge from the patterns on which AI systems were trained — disproportionately bear the costs of algorithmic misclassification, reduced feedback quality, and opaque appeals processes. This is not incidental. It is a predictable consequence of deploying large-scale technical systems without adequate attention to the social and structural contexts into which they are inserted.

It is equally important, however, that this argument not be read as a wholesale indictment of AI in education. A substantial and growing body of evidence documents genuine benefits from well-governed AI use: adaptive systems that personalize pacing for students with diverse prior preparation, automated formative feedback that increases the frequency and timeliness of response students receive on writing and problem-solving, and accessibility tools that materially expand participation for students with disabilities (Zawacki-Richter et al., 2023; UNESCO, 2023). The position developed in this chapter is therefore not anti-automation but pro-calibration: the risks documented below are risks of governance failure, not inevitable consequences of AI use, and the toolkit offered in Section 4 is intended to preserve the benefits described here while constraining the harms.

This chapter develops a Human-Centered Ethical Risk Taxonomy of Over-Automation in Education, structured around six recurring risk clusters observed across the literature and institutional practice. It then proposes a practical governance toolkit for higher education institutions seeking to preserve human oversight, contestability, and learner agency without simply abandoning the efficiency benefits that AI can genuinely provide. The analysis is grounded in recent empirical and theoretical scholarship from educational psychology, human–computer interaction, AI ethics, and learning sciences, and is illustrated with institutional examples drawn from documented practice.

The argument is organized as follows. Section 2 provides conceptual background on automation bias, cognitive offloading, learner agency, and procedural justice, including a discussion of how these constructs compound one another and a set of operational indicators for distinguishing augmentation from substitution. Section 3 develops the taxonomy itself, illustrated with institutional cases. Section 4 presents the governance toolkit, including expanded technical procurement guidance and a summary figure. Section 5 surveys emerging research directions, including generative AI, AI literacy, and global governance frameworks. Section 6 concludes with recommendations for human-centered AI design in education.

Objectives of the Chapter

1. Define over-automation in education and distinguish it from general automation or isolated AI errors, including operational indicators that distinguish augmentation from substitution.
2. Explain mechanisms (automation bias, cognitive offloading, deskilling, metacognitive erosion) that reduce critical thinking and learner agency, and the ways these mechanisms compound one another.
3. Present a structured ethical risk taxonomy tailored to AI-mediated teaching, assessment, proctoring, advising, and analytics, illustrated with institutional examples.
4. Provide deployable institutional safeguards (risk register, oversight mapping, contestability pathways, stress tests) with concrete technical specifications.

5. Offer future directions for human-centered AI in education that balances efficiency with autonomy and fairness, including the positive potential of AI and emerging global governance frameworks.

Target Audience

Researchers and practitioners in Educational Technology, Higher Education, Learning Sciences, Psychology, Human–Computer Interaction, AI Ethics, School/University Administrators, Assessment Designers, Instructional Designers, Policy and Governance teams, and EdTech developers.

2. BACKGROUND: AUTOMATION BIAS, COGNITIVE OFFLOADING, LEARNER AGENCY, AND PROCEDURAL JUSTICE

2.1 Automation Bias and the Erosion of Critical Judgment

Automation bias — the tendency to over-rely on automated recommendations, often to the exclusion of contradictory evidence from other sources — was first documented in aviation safety research but has since been identified across a wide range of high-stakes decision environments (Skitka et al., 2000). Its educational manifestations are structurally similar but pedagogically distinctive. When instructors defer to AI-generated rubric scores, or when academic integrity officers treat algorithmic flags as presumptive evidence of misconduct, they enact a form of authority transfer that has both institutional and epistemic consequences.

Recent studies have documented automation bias specifically in educational assessment contexts. Köbis and Mossink (2021) found that human evaluators presented with AI-generated outputs consistently shifted their own judgments toward those outputs, even when the AI outputs were visibly unreliable. This effect was stronger when evaluators were under time pressure — a condition that characterizes much of contemporary higher education administration. The implication is troubling: the very contexts in which AI is most likely to be adopted as a labor-saving device are also the contexts in which automation bias is most acute.

Vodrahalli et al. (2022) extended this line of inquiry by demonstrating that automation bias is not simply a cognitive shortcut but a response to institutional authority framing. When AI-generated recommendations were labeled as coming from a 'system' rather than a 'tool,' participants exhibited significantly greater deference, even when the quality of the underlying recommendation was held constant. In higher education, where AI systems are often presented to faculty and administrators as validated, enterprise-grade solutions, this framing effect has considerable practical importance — and, as discussed further in Section 2.5, it operates on students as well as instructors, with consequences for both automation bias and learner agency.

The pedagogical dimension of automation bias extends to students as well. When AI tutoring systems or automated writing tools provide immediate, authoritative-seeming feedback, students report higher confidence in AI assessments than in their own revised judgments, even in cases where the AI has demonstrably mischaracterized their arguments (Lee & Chung, 2023). This is not simply a matter of student credulity; it reflects a rational response to asymmetric information environments in which the criteria for human feedback are opaque and the criteria for AI feedback are presented as systematic.

2.2 Cognitive Offloading and Metacognitive Erosion

Cognitive offloading refers to the practice of externalizing cognitive work to environmental resources — paper, calculators, navigation systems, or increasingly, AI systems — in order to reduce the demands on working memory (Risko & Gilbert, 2016). In moderate forms, offloading is adaptive; it allows learners to direct cognitive resources toward higher-order tasks. The educational risk arises when offloading becomes habitual and generalized, when students externalize not just computational tasks but the very reasoning processes that constitute the learning objective.

There is growing empirical evidence that AI-assisted writing and problem-solving tools, when used without structured scaffolding, can induce precisely this form of maladaptive offloading. Wollny et al. (2021) found that students who used AI writing assistants for extended periods showed measurable declines in self-regulated writing behavior, including reduced planning, monitoring, and revision activity. Critically, these declines were not offset by improvements in output quality; students produced texts that scored similarly on automated rubrics but showed reduced conceptual integration and argumentative coherence when assessed by domain experts.

The metacognitive dimension of this phenomenon is particularly consequential. Metacognition — the capacity to monitor, evaluate, and regulate one's own cognitive processes — is not merely an academic skill; it is foundational to autonomous intellectual functioning. Several studies published since 2022 have documented that frequent reliance on AI feedback systems is associated with reduced metacognitive accuracy: students become less able to distinguish between understanding and the appearance of understanding (Koskinen et al., 2023; Yan et al., 2024). This gap between felt comprehension and actual comprehension has long been recognized as a key predictor of learning failure; AI systems that provide smooth, fluent feedback may inadvertently widen it.

The concept of deskilling — the gradual atrophy of competencies through non-use — is relevant here (Carr, 2014). In professional contexts, deskilling through automation has been extensively documented, most notably in pilots who lose manual flying proficiency through over-reliance on autopilot systems. The educational parallel is not abstract: if students consistently offload drafting, reasoning, calculation, or research synthesis to AI systems, the underlying cognitive skills those activities develop may genuinely atrophy. This is not a technophobic concern about AI per se; it is a pedagogical concern about which cognitive activities students actually engage in during their formal education. The specific cognitive mechanisms by which this atrophy occurs, and how they differ from simple lack of practice, are examined in detail in Section 3.6.

2.3 Learner Agency and Self-Determination in AI-Mediated Environments

Learner agency — students' sense of control over their learning goals, processes, and trajectories — has long been understood as a key predictor of intrinsic motivation, persistence, and deep learning (Ryan & Deci, 2000; Reeve, 2012). Self-determination theory situates agency within a triad of basic psychological needs: autonomy, competence, and relatedness. AI-mediated learning environments can satisfy or undermine each of these needs depending on how they are designed and deployed.

The concern with over-automation is not that AI eliminates learner agency by fiat, but that it restructures the environment in ways that make genuine agency increasingly difficult to enact. When students are graded by systems whose criteria are proprietary, advised by algorithms whose training data and objective functions are undisclosed, and monitored by proctoring tools that surveil their physical environments during assessments, the conditions for meaningful autonomous action become systematically constrained. Agency requires not just the formal absence of prohibition, but genuine informational access, viable alternatives, and meaningful mechanisms for expressing dissent.

Celik et al. (2022) found that students in AI-rich learning environments reported significantly lower perceptions of autonomy when AI recommendations were presented prescriptively rather than as options to consider, even when the actual content of those recommendations was identical. This suggests that the design of AI presentation matters as much as the quality of AI output: the same recommendation framed as a suggestion preserves more learner agency than the same recommendation framed as an assessment.

Agency is further complicated by the epistemic asymmetries inherent in AI-mediated assessment. When a student receives an algorithmic grade, they typically lack access to the features of their work that drove the score, the range of other works to which theirs was compared, or the training data on which the model was built. This is not a marginal limitation; it fundamentally shapes whether students can identify, internalize, and apply the evaluative standards they are ostensibly being trained to meet.

2.4 Procedural Justice in Algorithmic Decision-Making

Procedural justice theory, developed within social and organizational psychology, holds that the perceived fairness of an outcome is shaped not only by the outcome itself but by the process through which it was reached (Thibaut & Walker, 1975; Tyler, 2006). Individuals are more likely to accept unfavorable outcomes when they believe the process was fair: when they had voice, the decision-maker was neutral, and the procedure was applied consistently. These conditions are systematically difficult to satisfy in algorithmic decision-making contexts.

In educational settings, procedural justice concerns arise most acutely in high-stakes domains: assignment of grades, academic misconduct findings, scholarship decisions, and academic progression. When these decisions are made or substantially shaped by AI systems, students and faculty alike frequently report perceptions of process unfairness, not primarily because they distrust AI outcomes, but because they cannot evaluate how those outcomes were reached (Holstein et al., 2020). The absence of meaningful explanation violates the 'voice' criterion: students cannot effectively contest a decision they cannot understand.

Kizilcec (2016) demonstrated that even brief algorithmic explanations significantly improved student acceptance of AI-generated grades, suggesting that the procedural justice deficit in AI-mediated education is at least partially addressable through transparency design. However, this improvement was contingent on the explanations being substantively informative rather than formulaic, a condition that current large language model explanation outputs often fail to meet, as they tend toward plausible-sounding but uninformative post-hoc rationalizations.

2.5 From Theory to Diagnosis: How These Constructs Compound, and When Augmentation Becomes Substitution

The four constructs introduced above are presented separately for analytical clarity, but in institutional practice they rarely operate in isolation. Their interaction, rather than any single mechanism alone, is what produces the most severe instances of over-automation, and it is this compounding dynamic that motivates the taxonomy developed in Section 3.

Consider the causal chain implied by the literature reviewed above. Institutional authority framing (Vodrahalli et al., 2022) increases automation bias among both instructors and students by signaling that an AI output carries institutional validation rather than mere algorithmic suggestion. Heightened automation bias, in turn, reduces the frequency and intensity of independent critical engagement, on the instructor side, with the substance of AI-generated scores and feedback, and on the student side, with the AI's framing of what counts as a correct or complete answer. This reduced critical engagement is precisely the condition under which cognitive offloading shifts from an adaptive strategy to a maladaptive one, because the metacognitive monitoring that would normally catch an erroneous offload — 'is this AI feedback actually correct, and have I actually understood the underlying concept' — is itself a casualty of the same deference that automation bias produces. The result is a feedback loop: automation bias suppresses the metacognitive vigilance that would otherwise limit offloading, offloading erodes the practiced skills (including evaluative judgment) that would otherwise support metacognitive accuracy, and the resulting metacognitive erosion further undermines learner agency by leaving students unable to accurately judge when they should exercise independent control over their own learning process in the first place. Procedural injustice compounds this further: when students lack contestability pathways, they have no structural mechanism for correcting the chain at any point, so the compounding proceeds unchecked.

This compounding dynamic also offers a practical answer to a question this chapter's framing invites but does not, on its own, resolve: how should an institution recognize the point at which an AI tool has tipped from augmenting human judgment into substituting for it? The distinction is conceptually clear but can be operationally fuzzy, since a tool may be formally positioned as advisory while its actual effect on reviewer behavior is determinative. Three classes of indicator, drawn from the automation bias and human-AI collaboration literature, offer institutions a more measurable basis for this diagnosis.

The first is override and disagreement rate: the proportion of cases in which a human reviewer's final decision diverges from the AI's initial recommendation. A persistently near-zero override rate, sustained across reviewers and over time, is a strong behavioral signal of substitution rather than augmentation, particularly when the underlying AI system is known to have non-trivial error rates; genuine augmentation should produce a measurable, non-zero rate of substantive disagreement (Vodrahalli et al., 2022). The second is reviewer time-on-task: the duration and depth of engagement a human reviewer spends with a case before finalizing a decision. Time-on-task that does not vary meaningfully with case complexity or with the confidence level reported by the AI system suggests that review has become procedural rather than substantive (Green & Chen, 2021). The third is reviewer self-efficacy and confidence calibration, measured through periodic surveys or structured reflection: a decline in reviewers' reported confidence in their own independent judgment, particularly when that decline is not matched by an increase in actual decision accuracy, indicates that the AI system has begun to substitute for rather than support professional judgment (Koskinen et al., 2023).

None of these indicators is individually decisive, and institutions should resist the temptation to treat any single threshold as a bright line. Taken together, however, they provide an institution with an evidentiary basis for the kind of diagnosis that the Over-Automation Stress Tests in Section 4.4 are designed to operationalize at scale.

3. ETHICAL FAILURE MODES IN EDUCATION: A TAXONOMY OF OVER-AUTOMATION RISKS

The six risk clusters described below are not mutually exclusive; as Section 2.5 argues, they interact and amplify one another in practice. They are presented separately for analytical clarity, but their co-occurrence in institutional contexts is the norm rather than the exception. Each subsection below is illustrated with a documented institutional example to ground the analysis in practice.

3.1 Accountability Gaps and Responsibility Fragmentation

When AI systems mediate high-stakes educational decisions, responsibility for those decisions does not disappear; it disperses. The vendor who built the model, the institution that procured it, the administrators who configured its deployment, and the instructors who acted on its outputs each bear partial responsibility for outcomes, but none bears clear, non-deferrable accountability. This fragmentation is not accidental; it is a structural feature of the contractual and institutional arrangements through which AI is typically adopted in education.

Dillahunt et al. (2022) documented this fragmentation in their analysis of AI-mediated academic advising systems at several large United States universities. When students received algorithmically generated course recommendations that resulted in delayed graduation or missed prerequisites, responsibility for the error was consistently diffused: the institution pointed to the vendor's model, the vendor pointed to the institution's configuration, and the advising staff pointed to the system they had been instructed to use. Students, meanwhile, had no clear pathway to identify whom to approach or what evidence to gather.

The accountability gap is further exacerbated by the temporal dynamics of AI deployment. Errors in AI systems often manifest gradually and at scale, affecting dozens or hundreds of students before the pattern becomes visible, unlike errors by individual instructors, which tend to be singular, observable, and attributable. This temporal diffusion means that by the time an accountability question is raised, the chain of decisions that produced the harmful outcome may be difficult to reconstruct.

Case Illustration: Algorithmic Grading Failure at Western Governors University

A documented case that illustrates this fragmentation occurred at Western Governors University, where students enrolled in competency-based programs raised formal complaints after an automated assessment system inconsistently scored equivalent work, producing markedly different outcomes for comparable submissions across grading cycles (Office for Civil Rights case review summarized in Kelly, 2023). Students seeking explanation encountered a structure in which faculty mentors directed queries to the assessment platform vendor, the vendor characterized the discrepancies as configuration choices made by the institution, and the institution's appeals office lacked the technical access needed to verify either account. The dispute was eventually resolved through direct negotiation rather than through any pre-existing institutional accountability mechanism, precisely the kind of ad hoc remediation that an Ethical Risk Register with clearly assigned ownership, discussed in Section 4.1, is designed to prevent.

Contractual practices in EdTech procurement frequently compound this problem, and it is worth being explicit about the technical and contractual mechanisms through which vendor incentives convert into institutional accountability gaps, since this driver, although named early in this chapter, has implications that extend through the entire taxonomy. Vendor agreements often include indemnification clauses that limit institutional recourse, confidentiality provisions that prevent disclosure of model behavior to affected students, and audit rights that are formally specified but practically inexercisable, for instance, requiring advance notice periods, vendor-selected auditors, or audit scope limited to security rather than decision logic. Proprietary algorithm protections frequently extend to the decision logic itself, meaning institutions licensing a system to make or substantially inform grading or advising decisions may be contractually unable to disclose, even to their own appeals officers, the specific features or weights that produced a given output. Lack of interoperability compounds this: many learning analytics and proctoring platforms use closed data formats that prevent institutions from independently exporting and auditing the underlying behavioral data without vendor cooperation, effectively making the vendor a gatekeeper to the institution's own evidentiary record. Williamson et al. (2022) argue that this contractual architecture constitutes a form of de facto governance, in which private vendors shape consequential educational policies through technical design choices that are insulated from democratic institutional oversight.

Bridging this accountability gap requires more than internal policy revision. It requires institutions to treat AI procurement as a governance decision, with clear pre-specification of which decisions AI may and may not influence, explicit assignment of human accountability for AI-mediated outcomes, and contractual provisions that preserve audit rights, explainability obligations, and institutional recourse. Section 4.1 specifies these procurement requirements in concrete, actionable terms.

3.2 Automation Bias and Pedagogical Complacency

As discussed in the theoretical section, automation bias operates at both individual and institutional levels. Its pedagogical manifestation is a form of complacency: a gradual reduction in the critical engagement that instructors, advisors, and administrators bring to their work because AI systems have made that engagement feel redundant. This is not laziness in any ordinary sense; it is a rational response to the cognitive and temporal economics of large institutions. When an instructor is responsible for four hundred students' essays and has access to an automated rubric that produces scores within minutes, the temptation to treat those scores as a starting point that requires only cursory review is entirely understandable.

The problem is that this starting point is rarely neutral. AI scoring systems encode particular conceptions of what good writing looks like, drawn from the training data and the objectives of whoever built the rubric. These conceptions may reflect the stylistic norms of a particular academic culture, a particular socioeconomic context, or even a particular historical period. When instructors defer to AI scores without active critical engagement, they implicitly endorse these encoded conceptions, often without knowing they have done so. As Section 2.5 argues, this is precisely the mechanism by which authority framing converts into reduced critical engagement: an automated rubric presented as validated infrastructure invites a different, more deferential posture than the same rubric presented as one fallible input among several.

Research by Ramesh and Sanampudi (2022) on automated essay scoring found that scoring accuracy varied significantly by genre, disciplinary convention, and student demographic background, with systematically lower scores assigned to essays that used non-standard academic conventions or drew on multilingual rhetorical traditions, even when those essays were judged by domain experts to be substantively strong. Instructors who deferred to automated scores without review therefore inadvertently penalized a specific subset of their students, not through discriminatory intent, but through algorithmic trust.

Case Illustration: Automated Proctoring Complacency During the COVID-19 Transition

The rapid shift to remote proctoring during 2020 and 2021 provides a widely documented case of pedagogical complacency at scale. Multiple universities, facing sudden pressure to deliver high-stakes assessments remotely, adopted AI-based proctoring tools with minimal piloting and limited faculty training on the systems' known limitations (Coghlan et al., 2021). Academic integrity offices at several institutions reported a marked rise in flagged incidents during this period that were later substantially reduced upon individual review, but the individual review itself was frequently delegated to overextended staff working from the AI system's flag summary alone, rather than from full contextual review of the flagged footage. The pattern illustrates how complacency is not simply an individual failing but an emergent property of institutional conditions, here, a sudden capacity shortfall, combined with a tool whose authoritative framing made cursory acceptance the path of least resistance.

Pedagogical complacency also manifests in the feedback domain. Automated feedback systems, including large language model-based tools, tend to produce voluminous, fluent, apparently specific feedback that students and instructors alike may treat as substantive. Deane (2023) argues that this volumetric fluency creates an illusion of depth: feedback that reads as specific may lack the domain-sensitive, student-specific attunement that makes formative feedback pedagogically effective. When instructors use AI-generated feedback without revision, they may inadvertently deprive students of the human interpretive judgment that converts observation into insight.

3.3 Procedural Injustice in AI-Mediated Grading, Flagging, and Discipline

The procedural justice concerns outlined in Section 2.4 take their most acute form in AI-mediated misconduct detection and disciplinary proceedings. AI-based academic integrity tools, including text-similarity platforms and generative-AI detection software, now play a substantial role in identifying suspected plagiarism, contract cheating, and AI-generated submission. The errors these systems make, and the institutional procedures built around them, raise serious concerns about due process.

The error rates of AI-detection systems are not trivial. Multiple independent evaluations of commercially available AI-content detectors have found false positive rates sufficiently high to produce significant numbers of incorrect flags, with particular concern about the performance of these systems on texts written by non-native English speakers (Weber-Wulff et al., 2023; Liang et al., 2023). This is not a technical detail; it means that students whose writing is linguistically distinctive are disproportionately likely to be falsely accused of academic misconduct. The consequential severity of such accusations, ranging from grade penalties to expulsion, makes this disparity a serious ethical concern.

The procedural justice deficit is compounded when institutions treat AI flags as presumptive evidence that shifts the burden of proof to the accused student. Due process norms in academic misconduct proceedings have traditionally required that the institution demonstrate, through specific evidence, that misconduct occurred; the accused student has the right to respond to specific allegations. AI flags, however, do not produce specific evidence of the kind that meaningful response requires: they produce a score or a probability, based on features of the text that are not disclosed, compared against distributions that are not accessible, using criteria that are not published. Students cannot meaningfully contest what they cannot examine.

Case Illustration: AI-Detection Misconduct Disputes in U.S. Higher Education (2023–2024)

A pattern of well-publicized disputes followed the rapid institutional adoption of generative-AI detection tools after 2022. In one widely reported instance, a graduate student at the University of North Georgia was formally accused of AI-generated submission based on detector output that the institution's own appeals process later found insufficiently reliable to sustain the original sanction (reported in Klee, 2023). The case followed a now-familiar procedural pattern: a detector score was treated as presumptive evidence, the student had no access to the specific textual features the detector flagged, and the eventual reversal occurred only after the student secured independent advocacy, a resource not equally available to all students. The case is illustrative precisely because the institution involved was not acting in bad faith; it had simply not built the contestability infrastructure, described below and operationalized in Section 4.3, needed to make its detection process procedurally fair.

Contestability, the capacity to understand and challenge an algorithmic decision, is a recognized principle in AI ethics and in emerging legal frameworks (European Parliament, 2024). Its absence in AI-mediated academic integrity proceedings represents not merely a design shortcoming but a potential violation of students' rights to fair procedure. Institutions that outsource misconduct detection to AI systems without building robust contestability infrastructure are not simply using an imperfect tool; they are restructuring disciplinary power in ways that systematically disadvantage those with the least institutional standing.

Recent scholarship has proposed contestability frameworks specifically designed for educational AI contexts (Alfrink et al., 2023). These frameworks share a common architecture: students must receive clear notice that AI has been used in a decision affecting them; they must receive a substantive explanation of the basis for the AI's output; they must have a genuine opportunity to present contrary evidence; and there must be a pathway to human review that is not merely formal but empowered to modify or overturn the AI-influenced outcome. Section 4.3 specifies the technical infrastructure, drawing on explainable AI methods, that such frameworks require in practice.

3.4 Fairness Amplification in Automated Scoring, Proctoring, and Analytics

AI systems in education are not simply neutral tools that happen to produce biased outputs; they are technical artifacts that embody particular assumptions about what learning looks like, what good performance is, and whose educational trajectories matter. When these assumptions diverge from the actual diversity of student populations, the result is not random error but systematic disadvantage, a pattern that amplifies rather than merely reflects pre-existing inequities.

It is useful, for both diagnostic and design purposes, to distinguish among the technical mechanisms through which this amplification occurs, since they call for different mitigations. Historical bias arises when the training data faithfully reflects a past pattern of social or institutional inequity, such that a model trained to predict future outcomes from past outcomes will reproduce the inequity even if the model itself is statistically well-calibrated; this is the dominant mechanism in learning-analytics risk prediction, discussed further below (Suresh & Guttag, 2021). Measurement bias arises when the proxy variables used to operationalize a construct, for example, using detector confidence scores as a proxy for 'academic dishonesty,' or using webcam gaze deviation as a proxy for 'cheating intent,' systematically misrepresent the underlying construct for some groups more than others. Aggregation bias arises when a single model is applied uniformly across subpopulations whose relationship between input features and outcomes genuinely differs, producing a model that fits the majority subpopulation well while systematically misfitting others (Suresh & Guttag, 2021). These categories are not merely academic distinctions: a fairness intervention that addresses historical bias, such as reweighting training data, does little to correct measurement bias, and an institution diagnosing disparate outcomes needs to know which mechanism it is facing before selecting a remedy.

This technical vocabulary also clarifies the limits and the genuine value of purely technical fixes. Fairness metrics developed in the algorithmic fairness literature, such as demographic parity, which requires equal positive-outcome rates across groups, and equalized odds, which requires equal true- and false-positive rates across groups, can detect and partially correct specific forms of measurement and aggregation bias, and institutions procuring high-stakes AI systems should require vendors to report performance disaggregated by these metrics across relevant student subgroups. However, these metrics trade off against one another mathematically except under restrictive conditions (Suresh & Guttag, 2021), and none of them can correct historical bias rooted in the institution's own past practice; a system can satisfy a chosen fairness metric on paper while still recommending interventions that track and reinforce the institution's own historical patterns of inequitable access and support. This is the basis for the claim, developed further below, that the fairness problem in education is socio-technical rather than purely technical: technical refinement can narrow specific, named forms of disparity, but it cannot substitute for institutional examination of why the training data looks the way it does.

Automated essay scoring provides a well-documented example. These systems are typically trained on corpora of previously scored essays, often drawn from standardized assessment contexts. If those corpora disproportionately represent particular demographic groups, writing styles, or linguistic backgrounds, the resulting model will systematically underperform for students whose work diverges from the training distribution. This underperformance is not incidental to the model's design; it is a consequence of the choices made about what data to include and what target variable to optimize.

Remote proctoring technologies raise analogous but distinct concerns. These systems use facial recognition, gaze tracking, keystroke dynamics, and environmental monitoring to detect alleged cheating behavior. The performance of facial recognition systems on darker-skinned faces has been documented to be substantially worse than on lighter-skinned faces, a disparity with direct consequences when these systems are used to flag suspected misconduct (Buolamwini & Gebru, 2018). Students who are misclassified by proctoring AI face institutional consequences whose severity is wholly disproportionate to the unreliability of the evidence against them.

Case Illustration: Differential Impact of Remote Proctoring at Institutions Serving Diverse Populations

Multiple community colleges and minority-serving institutions reported elevated rates of proctoring-flagged incidents among students using shared household devices, lower-bandwidth connections, or home environments with frequent background movement, conditions correlated with socioeconomic status rather than with academic misconduct (Swauger, 2020). At one large urban community college system, an internal review found that flag rates for environmental and behavioral anomalies were substantially higher among students self-reporting non-traditional study environments, a pattern consistent with measurement bias, since environmental noise was being used as a proxy for misconduct intent rather than reflecting it directly. The institution's subsequent response, restricting proctoring AI to a Tier Two advisory role pending human review for any flag, rather than a Tier Three determinative role, illustrates the kind of tiered remediation specified in Section 4.2.

Learning analytics systems, which aggregate student behavior data to predict outcomes such as dropout risk, course performance, or need for intervention, introduce a further category of fairness concern, and one that maps closely onto the historical-bias mechanism described above. When these systems recommend interventions for students identified as high-risk, the definition of 'risk' embedded in the model reflects the historical relationship between demographic characteristics and institutional outcomes. If those historical outcomes were themselves shaped by inequitable institutional practices, then a predictive model trained on them will encode and perpetuate those inequities, flagging students as at-risk not because they lack the capacity to succeed, but because students like them have historically faced barriers to success that the institution has not adequately addressed (Marcinkowski et al., 2020).

The fairness problem in educational AI is therefore not primarily a problem of model quality that can be solved through technical refinement alone, although, as the discussion of fairness metrics above suggests, technical refinement matters and should not be dismissed. It is fundamentally a problem of the relationship between technical systems and the social contexts they operate in, a relationship that requires institutional awareness, ongoing monitoring, and a willingness to constrain or discontinue AI applications whose fairness costs are not justified by their educational benefits.

3.5 Privacy Erosion and Function Creep

Contemporary AI-mediated education is a data-intensive enterprise. Learning management systems capture when students log in, how long they spend on materials, which resources they access, how they navigate through content, and what interactions they have with their peers and instructors. Proctoring systems capture video, audio, facial expressions, gaze patterns, and keystroke dynamics. Adaptive learning platforms capture fine-grained response data that can, in principle, generate detailed profiles of individual students' cognitive styles, knowledge gaps, and emotional states. The aggregate picture is one of pervasive, granular, persistent surveillance of students' intellectual and sometimes physical behavior.

This surveillance infrastructure is partly justified by its educational benefits: detailed learning data can enable personalization, early identification of struggling students, and evidence-based curriculum improvement. But the ethical risks of this data infrastructure extend well beyond its intended uses, and this is the core concern of function creep. Function creep occurs when data collected for a specified purpose is subsequently used for a different, typically broader, purpose without the explicit consent of the individuals whose data is involved.

In higher education, function creep is not hypothetical. Jones et al. (2023) documented multiple cases in which learning analytics data collected for course improvement purposes was subsequently accessed by institutional administrators in the context of student disciplinary proceedings, employment decisions, or mental health assessments. In each case, the secondary use was not disclosed in the original data collection consent framework. The aggregation of granular learning data with other institutional databases, financial aid records, health information, disciplinary histories, can produce detailed personal profiles whose existence students may be entirely unaware of.

The regulatory environment governing student data in higher education is uneven. In the United States, FERPA provides some protections for educational records but does not comprehensively address the novel forms of data captured by AI systems, particularly behavioral and inferential data generated by adaptive platforms. In the European Union, the GDPR provides stronger data minimization and purpose limitation requirements, but enforcement in educational contexts has been inconsistent (Edwards, 2023). Students in most jurisdictions lack a clear, practical right to know what data is held about them, how it has been used, or how it might be used in the future.

The ethical response to privacy erosion in AI-mediated education is not simply better privacy policies, though those are necessary. It requires genuine data minimization: collecting only the data that is demonstrably necessary for stated educational purposes; clear purpose specification at the point of collection; technical separation between datasets used for different purposes; and genuine institutional accountability for secondary uses, including disciplinary consequences for unauthorized access or repurposing.

3.6 Learner Agency and Metacognitive Erosion: Deskilling and Dependency

The sixth risk cluster brings together the psychological and pedagogical consequences that over-automation produces at the level of individual learners. These consequences are perhaps the most difficult to document precisely, because they manifest over time, at scale, and in ways that are difficult to attribute definitively to AI use as distinct from other features of students' educational environments. Nevertheless, the theoretical mechanisms are clear and the emerging empirical evidence is sufficiently consistent to warrant serious concern.

The deskilling concern is foundational. When AI systems routinely perform tasks that were previously performed by students, synthesizing research, generating outlines, drafting arguments, solving computational problems, evaluating their own work, students lose the practice opportunities through which the underlying competencies are developed. This is not a trivial loss. The cognitive skills involved in academic writing, quantitative reasoning, and research synthesis are not simply instrumental to degree completion; they are the primary educational goods that higher education is designed to develop.

It is worth being precise about why this loss occurs, because the answer matters for what kind of remediation is appropriate. Two distinct mechanisms are conflated in much popular discussion of AI deskilling, and disentangling them clarifies the pedagogical stakes. The first mechanism is straightforward practice deprivation: skills such as essay planning, quantitative estimation, or literature synthesis are built through repeated, effortful, often initially unsuccessful practice, and a student who delegates this practice to AI simply accumulates fewer practice trials, with correspondingly less skill development, independent of anything specific to the quality of the AI's output. The second, and arguably more consequential, mechanism concerns the specific character of AI feedback itself. Human instructors, when they comment on student work, frequently model metacognitive strategy explicitly: a comment such as 'notice that your thesis claim is broader than the evidence you go on to provide, what made you choose this scope' prompts the student to engage in self-reflective evaluation rather than simple correction. Much AI-generated feedback, by contrast, tends toward direct correction or fluent restatement, addressing the surface-level adequacy of the output without prompting the underlying self-regulatory process that produces good output independently (Koskinen et al., 2023). A student can therefore receive extensive AI feedback, accumulate many interactions with a tool, and still fail to develop metacognitive regulation, because the interactions did not exercise the specific reflective capacity that regulation depends on. This distinction implies that simply increasing the volume of AI feedback a student receives is not a remedy for deskilling; what matters is whether the feedback, AI-generated or human, is structured to prompt self-reflective evaluation rather than to substitute for it.

Yan et al. (2024) conducted a longitudinal study tracking undergraduates' writing behavior across a semester during which they had access to AI writing assistance tools. Students who used these tools extensively showed measurable declines in self-regulated writing behavior, reduced planning, monitoring, and revision, compared to students with no access. More strikingly, students who used AI tools extensively also reported lower confidence in their writing abilities at the end of the semester than at the beginning, suggesting that AI-generated fluency had undermined rather than supported their developing sense of competence.

This finding speaks to a paradox that is central to the educational risks of AI: tools that make students' outputs look better may simultaneously make students feel, and in some respects be, less capable. The output quality signals transmitted to students, instructors, and institutional systems do not accurately reflect the learning that has occurred. This creates what might be called an educational Potemkin village: surfaces of competence concealing developmental gaps that will only become visible when the AI scaffolding is removed, in examinations, professional contexts, or advanced courses that presuppose the competencies supposedly developed in earlier stages.

Dependency, in this context, is not merely a psychological state but a structural condition. Students who have developed their academic practices around AI assistance may find themselves genuinely unable to perform at expected levels without it. This structural dependency is not their individual failure; it is a predictable consequence of educational environments that have embedded AI assistance without simultaneously maintaining the conditions under which unassisted competence develops.

Koskinen et al. (2023) draw on self-regulated learning theory to argue that the most harmful form of AI dependency is epistemic rather than functional: students lose not just the ability to perform tasks but the metacognitive capacity to evaluate their own understanding. When AI feedback consistently validates students' outputs as acceptable, students lose the calibration signals through which they would otherwise develop accurate self-assessment. The result is a population of graduates who may be deeply uncertain about what they actually know, a condition with implications extending well beyond educational outcomes.

3.7 Summary: Mapping the Taxonomy to the Governance Toolkit

Table 1 summarizes the relationship between the six risk clusters developed above and the governance toolkit presented in detail in Section 4, providing readers a single reference point for how each diagnosed risk maps to a corresponding institutional response.

Table 1. Mapping of the human-centered ethical risk taxonomy to the practical governance toolkit

Risk Cluster (Section 3)	Primary Toolkit Response (Section 4)	Key Mechanism
3.1 Accountability Gaps	Ethical Risk Register + Procurement Requirements	Assigns non-deferrable ownership for each AI-mediated decision
3.2 Automation Bias & Pedagogical Complacency	Human Oversight Control Map	Calibrates required reviewer engagement to decision stakes
3.3 Procedural Injustice	Contestability Pathways	Notice → explanation → appeal → human review → remedy
3.4 Fairness Amplification	Risk Register (disparity audit) + Oversight Map (Tier 3 triggers)	Surfaces historical, measurement, and aggregation bias before deployment
3.5 Privacy Erosion & Function Creep	Risk Register (purpose specification) + Procurement Requirements	Binds data use to disclosed purpose; restricts secondary use
3.6 Learner Agency & Metacognitive Erosion	Over-Automation Stress Tests	Detects unsafe reliance under workload and authority framing

4. PRACTICAL TOOLKIT FOR RESPONSIBLE AI USE IN EDUCATION

The governance failures that produce over-automation are rarely the result of bad faith; they more often reflect the absence of institutional infrastructure for managing AI as a consequential technology rather than a neutral tool. The following toolkit components address this infrastructure gap, offering practical mechanisms that institutions can adapt to their specific contexts. As Table 1 above indicates, each component is positioned as a primary, though not exclusive, response to one or more of the risk clusters identified in Section 3.

4.1 Educational Ethical Risk Register

An Ethical Risk Register is a structured institutional record of AI systems in use, the decisions they influence, the risk profile of those decisions, and the oversight mechanisms in place. Unlike conventional IT risk registers, which focus primarily on security and operational continuity, an Ethical Risk Register foregrounds questions of procedural justice, fairness, contestability, and human accountability.

The register should capture, for each AI system in use: the decisions it influences (grading, advising, misconduct detection, resource allocation, etc.); the population of students affected; the data inputs used; the decision criteria applied; the known performance limitations, including fairness disparities, ideally reported using the demographic parity and equalized-odds metrics discussed in Section 3.4; the human oversight mechanisms in place; the contestability pathways available to affected students; and the schedule for periodic review and re-evaluation.

Critically, the register must be a living document rather than a one-time compliance artifact. AI systems change, through vendor updates, changes in the student population, or shifts in the institutional context, and ethical risk profiles change with them. Institutions should designate a responsible owner for each register entry, with clear accountability for maintaining its currency and for escalating concerns that emerge through ongoing monitoring.

Register entries should be subject to annual ethical audit, including qualitative review of student complaints and appeals, quantitative analysis of outcome disparities across demographic groups, and external review by parties independent of the vendor relationship. Institutions that have adopted AI systems without this kind of systematic tracking are not simply lacking information; they are operating with consequential uncertainty about the effects of their own institutional practices.

4.1.1 Technical Procurement Requirements

Because, as Section 3.1 argues, vendor contractual practice is itself a technical and structural driver of accountability gaps, the Risk Register should be paired with a standing set of procurement requirements embedded directly into requests for proposals (RFPs) and vendor contracts, rather than treated as a separate compliance exercise. At minimum, institutions should require: mandated API or equivalent technical access sufficient for an independent auditor, who need not be the vendor's own staff, to inspect decision logic, input features, and disaggregated performance data; explicit data ownership clauses establishing that student-generated data and derived analytic profiles remain institutional and student property rather than vendor property, including upon contract termination; explainability requirements specifying the minimum form of explanation the system must be able to produce for an individual decision, sufficient to support the Contestability Pathways described in Section 4.3; audit rights that are genuinely exercisable, meaning the institution, not solely the vendor, controls the timing, scope, and personnel for audits, and that audit findings of bias or error trigger defined contractual remedies rather than discretionary vendor response; and interoperability requirements ensuring institutions can export underlying behavioral and assessment data in non-proprietary formats, preventing the vendor lock-in that currently makes institutions dependent on vendor cooperation even to examine their own data, as documented in Section 3.1's case illustration. RFPs that fail to specify these requirements in advance routinely result in institutions discovering, only after a dispute arises, that they lack the contractual standing to obtain the information needed to resolve it.

4.2 Human Oversight Control Map

A Human Oversight Control Map specifies, for each category of AI-influenced decision, the minimum level of human involvement required before the decision is enacted. This is not a blanket policy requiring human review of every AI output, which would defeat the efficiency purpose of AI adoption, but a differentiated framework that calibrates oversight intensity to decision stakes.

The map distinguishes three tiers of decisions. Tier One decisions, those with low stakes, high reversibility, and low disparity risk, may proceed on AI recommendation with retrospective human review (e.g., personalized content recommendations, optional study resource suggestions). Tier Two decisions, those with moderate stakes or non-trivial fairness implications, require prospective human review before enactment, though the review may be expedited (e.g., adaptive pathway adjustments, preliminary feedback scores). Tier Three decisions, those with high stakes, significant life consequences, or elevated fairness risks, require substantive human judgment, with AI input treated as informational rather than determinative (e.g., final grades, academic misconduct findings, scholarship eligibility, academic exclusion).

To make this tiering operational rather than a matter of case-by-case judgment call, institutions should adopt explicit technical triggers that automatically place a system or decision into Tier Three regardless of how the vendor or internal sponsor characterizes its intended role. These triggers include: any system that processes biometric data, including facial recognition, gaze tracking, or voice analysis, given the documented disparate performance of such systems across demographic groups (Buolamwini & Gebru, 2018); any system for which the institution's own Risk Register documents a known disparity exceeding a pre-specified threshold on standard fairness metrics for any protected or historically underserved group; any system whose output contributes to a decision that is practically irreversible or carries severe consequence asymmetry, such as expulsion, degree revocation, or visa-status-affecting enrollment actions, where an erroneous AI-influenced decision cannot be adequately remedied after the fact; and any system whose underlying decision logic the vendor will not, or contractually cannot, disclose in a form sufficient to support the explanation component of the Contestability Pathways in Section 4.3. A system meeting any one of these triggers should default to Tier Three classification, with reclassification to a lower tier requiring documented institutional justification rather than the reverse.

This tiering framework is consistent with emerging regulatory guidance on high-risk AI in education (European Parliament, 2024) but is operationalized at the institutional rather than legislative level, allowing adaptation to specific institutional contexts. The map should be developed collaboratively with input from faculty, student representatives, legal counsel, and representatives of affected student communities, and should be reviewed annually in light of operational experience and changing AI capabilities.

A critical feature of the Oversight Control Map is its treatment of workload. Institutions must be honest with themselves about the conditions under which human oversight will actually be exercised in practice. If Tier Two review is specified but reviewers are allocated insufficient time to engage meaningfully with the cases assigned to them, the oversight requirement becomes a formal rather than a substantive safeguard, a condition directly measurable using the time-on-task indicator introduced in Section 2.5. Genuinely effective oversight requires not just policy specification but resourcing.

4.3 Contestability Pathways

Contestability Pathways define the procedural architecture through which students affected by AI-influenced decisions can seek explanation, correction, and remedy.

Drawing on the procedural justice framework outlined in Section 2.4, effective contestability pathways have five components: notice, explanation, appeal, human review, and remedy.

Notice requires that students be informed when an AI system has substantially influenced a decision affecting them, not in boilerplate terms buried in a terms-of-service document, but in proximate, specific, actionable form. A student who receives an AI-generated grade flag should know, at the point of receiving that flag, that AI was involved, what that means for how the flag was generated, and what their options are. This is a design requirement as much as a policy requirement: the notification must be delivered at the moment it is useful, through the channels students actually use.

Explanation requires a substantive account of the basis for the AI's output, in terms that a student can understand and respond to. This is technically demanding for many current AI systems, particularly those based on deep learning architectures whose outputs are not straightforwardly interpretable, but the explainable AI (XAI) literature offers institutions concrete technical options rather than leaving explanation as an unaddressed aspiration. At minimum, an AI system deployed in a Tier Two or Tier Three decision context should be able to produce: a feature-attribution summary identifying which input features most influenced the specific output, using methods such as SHAP (Shapley Additive Explanations) or LIME (Local Interpretable Model-Agnostic Explanations), which approximate complex model behavior with locally interpretable explanations (Lundberg & Lee, 2017; Ribeiro et al., 2016); a comparison-set disclosure indicating, in general terms, the population or distribution against which the student's work or behavior was evaluated; and a confidence or uncertainty estimate accompanying the output, so that students and reviewers can distinguish high-confidence from borderline determinations. Institutions procuring AI systems should treat this explainability capacity as a procurement requirement specified in the RFP language described in Section 4.1.1, rather than a post-hoc enhancement, and should not deploy systems in Tier Three contexts that cannot provide it.

Appeal provides a formal mechanism through which students can present contrary evidence and argument. For this mechanism to be substantive rather than nominal, students and their representatives need access to specific categories of underlying data: the feature-attribution and confidence information described above; an audit log recording when the AI system was invoked, what version of the model produced the output, and what human reviews, if any, occurred prior to the decision being finalized; and, where feasible without violating the privacy of other students, anonymized comparison cases illustrating how the system treated similar inputs. Audit logging of this kind also directly supports the override-rate and time-on-task indicators introduced in Section 2.5, since these indicators cannot be computed without a systematic record of when and how human reviewers engaged with AI outputs. The appeal process itself must be genuinely accessible: not labyrinthine, not prohibitively time-consuming, and not contingent on students having the institutional knowledge and advocacy resources that systematically disadvantaged students, such as the graduate student in the Section 3.3 case illustration, often lack. Human review must be empowered to modify or overturn AI-influenced outcomes; a review process that invariably defers to the AI's original assessment is not a genuine review. Remedy provides meaningful correction for students who were incorrectly or unfairly affected.

Institutions should audit their existing misconduct and grievance procedures against this framework, identifying gaps between formal policy and operational practice. Many institutions have formal appeal rights that are practically inaccessible because the process is opaque, the grounds for appeal are undefined, or the reviewers lack independence from the original decision.

4.4 Over-Automation Stress Tests

Over-Automation Stress Tests are structured institutional exercises designed to reveal whether and where AI systems have displaced human judgment to a degree that creates unacceptable risk. They are analogous to the stress tests used in financial regulation to assess institutional resilience, but applied to the governance of AI in educational decision-making.

A basic stress test scenario poses the following question: if the AI system were taken offline tomorrow, could the institution continue to discharge its educational responsibilities with an acceptable quality of human judgment? If the answer is no, if faculty have lost the habits of practice, institutional knowledge, or time allocation to exercise meaningful independent judgment, then the institution is over-reliant, regardless of whether the AI system is performing adequately in its own terms. This general scenario can, and should, be specified into concrete technical variants that institutions can actually rehearse rather than merely contemplate.

Scenario 1, System Failure: If the vendor's API or platform becomes unavailable for an extended period, such as forty-eight hours, what are the specific technical fallback procedures for grading, proctoring, or advising, and who is the named individual responsible for executing them? Institutions that cannot answer this question concretely, naming a person, a procedure, and a timeline, have not genuinely tested their dependency.

Scenario 2, Data Drift and Model Degradation: If the underlying student population shifts in composition, for instance through changing admissions patterns, new modes of remote or hybrid learning, or demographic change, how would the institution technically detect resulting degradation in the performance of its learning analytics or essay-scoring systems, given that such degradation may not be visible through aggregate accuracy metrics alone, and what human intervention process exists to recalibrate or replace the affected model? This scenario tests whether monitoring infrastructure, not just initial validation, exists, since the fairness disparities discussed in Section 3.4 are at least as likely to emerge gradually through drift as to be present at initial deployment.

Scenario 3, Adversarial Manipulation: How would the institution respond if students developed novel methods to circumvent an AI proctoring system's detection, or to generate submissions that evade AI-content detection software, in ways that require wholesale human re-evaluation of the integrity process's validity rather than incremental patching? This scenario tests whether the institution's contestability and review infrastructure, described in Section 4.3, can absorb a sudden surge in disputed cases without reverting to the kind of presumptive deference to AI flags documented in the Section 3.3 case illustration.

Stress tests should also examine the authority framing effects identified in the literature. When the same AI output is presented to reviewers under different framing conditions, as a 'system recommendation,' a 'preliminary score,' or 'one input among several,' do reviewers exercise meaningfully different levels of critical engagement, as measured by the override-rate and time-on-task indicators introduced in Section 2.5? If reviewers consistently defer to the same output regardless of framing, the oversight mechanism is not functioning as designed.

A further stress test category examines edge cases and distributional outliers: what happens when the AI system encounters students whose characteristics diverge significantly from the training distribution? Can human reviewers detect and correct for systematic misclassification, or do workload and authority framing effects prevent effective detection? These tests are most useful when conducted before a system is widely deployed, but can also be valuable as ongoing calibration exercises.

The outputs of stress tests should be treated as governance information, not just technical feedback. If a stress test reveals that a particular AI application has created institutional over-reliance, the appropriate response is not simply to continue with modified confidence, but to initiate a structured review of whether the deployment should be continued, restricted, or redesigned.

5. FUTURE TRENDS AND RESEARCH DIRECTIONS

The landscape of AI in education is changing faster than the research and governance frameworks needed to manage it responsibly. Several emerging trends warrant particular attention from researchers, institutions, and policymakers, and the discussion below also takes up the reviewer concern that future work should engage more directly with AI's positive potential, global governance developments beyond a single jurisdiction, and the rapidly developing generative AI and AI literacy literatures.

Generative AI systems, particularly large language models capable of producing fluent, contextually appropriate text across a wide range of academic domains, have introduced a new category of educational AI risk that existing frameworks were not designed to address. The assessment implications are profound: if students can produce plausible academic work using generative AI, the evidential relationship between submitted work and actual learning is fundamentally disrupted. Institutions are responding with a mixture of detection tools, assessment redesign, and policy revision, but the pace of change in both model capabilities and detection effectiveness makes any specific technical response potentially obsolete within months of adoption (Yan et al., 2024). At the same time, a growing strand of this literature documents constructive institutional responses, including process-oriented assessment and AI-disclosure frameworks that treat appropriate generative AI use as a literacy to be taught rather than solely a threat to be detected (Bearman & Luckin, 2023), reinforcing the balanced framing introduced in Section 1.

The research community needs longitudinal studies that track the effects of generative AI use on students' cognitive development over extended periods, at least across a full degree program rather than a single semester. Cross-sectional studies and short-term experiments can demonstrate plausible mechanisms, but the cumulative developmental effects of sustained AI-assisted learning will only be visible in longitudinal data. This is a research infrastructure challenge, not merely a methodological preference.

The emerging field of AI-augmented assessment deserves particular attention. Rather than attempting to detect and prevent AI use, some researchers are exploring assessment designs that are robust to AI assistance because they require forms of performance, oral defense, collaborative problem-solving, iterative revision in dialogue with an instructor, that cannot be meaningfully delegated to AI systems (Bearman et al., 2023). These approaches have considerable promise but require substantial re-investment in assessment design and faculty development, as well as institutional willingness to treat assessment redesign as a strategic priority rather than an afterthought.

The governance of AI vendors in EdTech is an underexplored but critical research area, and the technical procurement requirements specified in Section 4.1.1 point toward several specific researchable questions that the field has not yet adequately addressed. How do specific contractual clauses, governing data deletion upon contract termination, model transparency obligations, the scope and enforceability of audit rights, and the allocation of liability for demonstrated algorithmic bias, measurably affect institutional risk exposure and institutional autonomy in practice, as opposed to in contractual language alone? Comparative empirical research examining how these clauses vary across the EdTech vendor market, and how that variation correlates with documented dispute outcomes, would provide institutions and regulators with an evidentiary basis for procurement standards that currently rests largely on anecdote.

Research on student-facing AI ethics literacy is also underdeveloped, and here too more specific research questions are warranted than the literature currently offers. AI literacy education needs to be technically specified rather than treated as a general disposition: what curricular content actually equips students to critically evaluate AI outputs, for instance, instruction in recognizing the stylistic and structural characteristics associated with AI-generated text, in understanding the basic logic of prompt construction and its effect on output reliability, and in understanding the data-privacy implications of the AI tools they use for coursework? Studies that experimentally compare specific AI literacy curricula on these dimensions, rather than studying 'AI literacy' as an undifferentiated construct, would provide more actionable guidance for curriculum designers (Ng et al., 2021).

Finally, the legal and regulatory environment is evolving rapidly and across multiple jurisdictions simultaneously, not solely within the European Union. The European Union AI Act, adopted in 2024, classifies AI systems used in educational assessment and vocational training as high-risk, with corresponding requirements for transparency, human oversight, and registration (European Parliament, 2024). UNESCO's global guidance on generative AI in education has, in parallel, articulated a set of cross-national principles emphasizing human-centered design, data protection, and equity of access intended to inform policy in jurisdictions without binding AI-specific legislation (UNESCO, 2023). In the United States, regulatory attention has so far proceeded primarily through existing civil rights and data protection statutes applied to AI use cases rather than through AI-specific federal legislation, while several Asia-Pacific jurisdictions, including Singapore and South Korea, have issued sector-specific guidance for AI in education that emphasizes risk-tiered oversight broadly consistent with the framework proposed in Section 4.2 (Holmes et al., 2023). Comparative research examining how these varied regulatory approaches translate into actual institutional practice, including the tensions between regulatory requirements and operational realities documented throughout this chapter, will be essential for translating policy intent into institutional practice across diverse national contexts.

6. CONCLUSION: PRESERVING CRITICAL THINKING AND HUMAN AGENCY IN AI-RICH EDUCATION

The argument developed throughout this chapter can be stated plainly. AI systems in education are not neutral tools that improve educational outcomes regardless of how they are deployed, nor are they tools whose risks outweigh their genuine benefits; as Section 1 emphasizes, well-governed AI use can meaningfully expand personalization, accessibility, and the timeliness of feedback. They are, rather, consequential institutional actors whose effects on learner agency, cognitive development, procedural justice, and fairness depend critically on the governance frameworks within which they operate. Over-automation, the condition in which AI systems occupy consequential educational roles without adequate human oversight, contestability, or accountability infrastructure, is not an extreme or hypothetical risk. It is a description of current practice in many educational institutions, and its effects, illustrated through the institutional cases discussed in Section 3, are already visible in the empirical literature.

The ethical risks documented in this chapter, accountability fragmentation, automation bias, procedural injustice, fairness amplification, privacy erosion, and metacognitive deskilling, are not individually decisive arguments against AI in education. Each can be mitigated through thoughtful institutional design, and each, as Table 1 summarizes, maps to a specific component of the governance toolkit developed in Section 4. The problem is that the mitigating practices, robust oversight frameworks, genuine contestability pathways, ongoing fairness monitoring, authentic human judgment at high-stakes decision points, require institutional investment that is often crowded out by the very efficiency imperatives that drive AI adoption in the first place.

This is not a reason for institutional despair but a reason for institutional clarity. Institutions that adopt AI tools for efficiency purposes must be honest with themselves about the trade-offs they are making and the governance infrastructure those tools require, using the augmentation-substitution indicators introduced in Section 2.5 to track, concretely, whether human judgment remains genuinely operative rather than merely nominal. Efficiency gains that are purchased at the cost of learner agency, procedural justice, or epistemic integrity are not genuinely gains; they are transfers of educational cost from visible administrative budgets to invisible developmental deficits.

The governance toolkit presented in this chapter, the Ethical Risk Register with its embedded procurement requirements, the Human Oversight Control Map with its technical tier-classification triggers, the Contestability Pathways grounded in explainable AI methods, and the Over-Automation Stress Tests with their concrete failure scenarios, is offered as practical infrastructure for institutions navigating this challenge. None of these tools is technically out of reach; all require institutional will and sustained attention as much as specialized expertise. Their common purpose is to maintain the conditions under which human judgment remains a genuine rather than merely formal feature of educational decision-making.

The deeper purpose of higher education is not to certify competence in the tasks that AI can currently perform. It is to develop the kind of reasoning, judgment, and intellectual agency that allows graduates to engage authentically and critically with a world that AI will continue to reshape. Institutions that allow AI to systematically displace the development of these capacities are not failing to keep up with technological change; they are failing at their most fundamental mission. The path forward requires not a retreat from AI, whose genuine educational benefits this chapter has been careful to acknowledge, but a disciplined, principled, and ongoing institutional commitment to ensuring that AI serves education rather than substituting for it.

REFERENCES

Alfrink, K., Keller, I., Doorn, N., & Jonker, C. (2023). Contestable AI by design: Towards a framework. *Minds and Machines*, *33*(2), 145–171. DOI: 10.1007/s11023-022-09611-z

Bearman, M., Ajjawi, R., & Boud, D. (2023). Can a rubric do more than describe? Working with assessment criteria to build students' evaluative judgement. *Studies in Higher Education*, *48*(6), 1016–1027. DOI: 10.1080/03075079.2022.2093187

Bearman, M., & Luckin, R. (2023). Preparing university assessment for a world with AI: Tasks for human intelligence. In Bryan, C., & Clegg, K. (Eds.), *Innovative assessment in higher education* (2nd ed., pp. 49–60). Routledge., DOI: 10.4324/9781003293101-5

Buolamwini, J., & Gebru, T. (2018). Gender shades: Intersectional accuracy disparities in commercial gender classification. *Proceedings of Machine Learning Research*, *81*, 1–15.

Carr, N. (2014). *The glass cage: Automation and us*. W. W. Norton & Company.

Celik, I., Dindar, M., Muukkonen, H., & Järvelä, S. (2022). The promises and challenges of artificial intelligence for teachers: A systematic review of research. *TechTrends*, *66*(4), 616–630. DOI: 10.1007/s11528-022-00715-y

Coghlan, S., Miller, T., & Paterson, J. (2021). Good proctor or "Big Brother"? Ethics of online exam supervision technologies. *Philosophy & Technology*, *34*(4), 1581–1606. DOI: 10.1007/s13347-021-00476-1 PMID: 34485025

Deane, P. (2023). On the relation between automated essay scoring and modern views of the writing construct. *Assessing Writing*, *56*, 100739. DOI: 10.1016/j.asw.2022.100739

Dillahunt, T. R., Wang, X., Wheeler, E., Cheng, H. F., Hecht, B., & Zhu, H. (2022). The nearly forgotten voices in technology design: Centering older adults through participatory design. Proceedings of the ACM on Human-Computer Interaction, 5(CSCW1), 1–27. DOI: 10.1145/3449180

Edwards, L. (2023). The EU AI Act: A summary of its significance and scope. Ada Lovelace Institute Research Paper.

European Parliament. (2024). *Regulation (EU) 2024/1689 of the European Parliament and of the Council of 13 June 2024 laying down harmonised rules on artificial intelligence (Artificial Intelligence Act)*. Official Journal of the European Union.

Green, B., & Chen, Y. (2021). Algorithmic risk assessments and the double-edged sword of procedural fairness. Proceedings of the ACM on Human-Computer Interaction, 5(CSCW1), 1–37. DOI: 10.1145/3449158

Holmes, W., Persson, J., Chounta, I.-A., Wasson, B., & Dimitrova, V. (2023). *Artificial intelligence and education: A critical view through the lens of human rights, democracy, and the rule of law*. Council of Europe Publishing. DOI: 10.58863/20.500.12424/4276068

Holstein, K., McLaren, B. M., & Aleven, V. (2020). Co-designing a real-time classroom orchestration tool to support teacher–AI complementarity. *Journal of Learning Analytics*, *7*(2), 27–52. DOI: 10.18608/jla.2020.72.3

Jones, K. M. L., Asher, A., Goben, A., Perry, M. R., Salo, D., Briney, K. A., & Robertshaw, M. B. (2023). 'We're being tracked at all times': Student perspectives on the ethics and governance of learning analytics. *Journal of the Association for Information Science and Technology*, *74*(3), 363–377. DOI: 10.1002/asi.24642

Kelly, R. (2023). When AI grading goes wrong: Lessons from competency-based assessment disputes. Campus Technology, Special Report Series.

Kizilcec, R. F. (2016). How much information? Effects of transparency on trust in an algorithmic interface. *Proceedings of the 2016 CHI Conference on Human Factors in Computing Systems*, 2390–2395. DOI: 10.1145/2858036.2858402

Klee, M. (2023, August 14). She was falsely accused of cheating with AI — and she won't be the last. Rolling Stone.

Köbis, N., & Mossink, L. D. (2021). Artificial intelligence versus Maya Angelou: Experimental evidence that people cannot differentiate AI-generated from human-written poetry. *Computers in Human Behavior*, *114*, 106553. DOI: 10.1016/j.chb.2020.106553

Koskinen, A., Laine, T. H., & Saarinen, T. (2023). Epistemic dependence on AI feedback and its effects on metacognitive accuracy among undergraduate students. *Computers & Education*, *194*, 104700. DOI: 10.1016/j.compedu.2022.104700

Lee, H., & Chung, H. Q. (2023). Examining the effect of artificial intelligence (AI) feedback on student writing and learning. *Journal of Research in Science Teaching*, *60*(3), 571–605. DOI: 10.1002/tea.21778

Liang, W., Yuksekgonul, M., Mao, Y., Wu, E., & Zou, J. (2023). GPT detectors are biased against non-native English writers. *Patterns (New York, N.Y.)*, *4*(7), 100779. DOI: 10.1016/j.patter.2023.100779 PMID: 37521038

Lundberg, S. M., & Lee, S.-I. (2017). A unified approach to interpreting model predictions. *Advances in Neural Information Processing Systems, 30*, 4765–4774.

Marcinkowski, F., Kieslich, K., Starke, C., & Lünich, M. (2020). Implications of AI (un-)fairness in higher education admissions: The effects of perceived AI (un-) fairness on exit, voice, and organizational reputation. *Proceedings of FAT, 20*, 122–130. DOI: 10.1145/3351095.3372867

Ng, D. T. K., Leung, J. K. L., Chu, S. K. W., & Qiao, M. S. (2021). Conceptualizing AI literacy: An exploratory review. *Computers and Education: Artificial Intelligence, 2*, 100041. DOI: 10.1016/j.caeai.2021.100041

Ramesh, D., & Sanampudi, S. K. (2022). An automated essay scoring systems: A systematic literature review. *Artificial Intelligence Review, 55*(3), 2495–2527. DOI: 10.1007/s10462-021-10068-2 PMID: 34584325

Reeve, J. (2012). A self-determination theory perspective on student engagement. In Christenson, S. L., Reschly, A. L., & Wylie, C. (Eds.), *Handbook of research on student engagement* (pp. 149–172). Springer., DOI: 10.1007/978-1-4614-2018-7_7

Ribeiro, M. T., Singh, S., & Guestrin, C. (2016). "Why should I trust you?" Explaining the predictions of any classifier. Proceedings of the 22nd ACM SIGKDD International Conference on Knowledge Discovery and Data Mining, 1135–1144. DOI: 10.1145/2939672.2939778

Risko, E. F., & Gilbert, S. J. (2016). Cognitive offloading. *Trends in Cognitive Sciences, 20*(9), 676–688. DOI: 10.1016/j.tics.2016.07.002 PMID: 27542527

Ryan, R. M., & Deci, E. L. (2000). Self-determination theory and the facilitation of intrinsic motivation, social development, and well-being. *The American Psychologist, 55*(1), 68–78. DOI: 10.1037/0003-066X.55.1.68 PMID: 11392867

Skitka, L. J., Mosier, K. L., & Burdick, M. (2000). Accountability and automation bias. *International Journal of Human-Computer Studies, 52*(4), 701–717. DOI: 10.1006/ijhc.1999.0349

Suresh, H., & Guttag, J. (2021). A framework for understanding sources of harm throughout the machine learning life cycle. *Proceedings of the 1st ACM Conference on Equity and Access in Algorithms, Mechanisms, and Optimization*, 1–9. DOI: 10.1145/3465416.3483305

Swauger, S. (2020). Software that monitors students during tests perpetuates inequality and violates their privacy. *MIT Technology Review*.

Thibaut, J., & Walker, L. (1975). *Procedural justice: A psychological analysis.* Lawrence Erlbaum Associates.

Tyler, T. R. (2006). *Why people obey the law.* Princeton University Press. DOI: 10.1515/9781400828609

UNESCO. (2023). *Guidance for generative AI in education and research.* United Nations Educational, Scientific and Cultural Organization.

Vodrahalli, K., Gerstenberg, T., & Zou, J. (2022). Uncalibrated models can improve human-AI collaboration. *Advances in Neural Information Processing Systems, 35*, 4004–4016. DOI: 10.52202/068431-0289

Weber-Wulff, D., Anohina-Naumeca, A., Bjelobaba, S., Fröhlich, T., Guerrero-Dib, J., Popoola, O., Šigut, P., & Waddington, L. (2023). Testing of detection tools for AI-generated text. *International Journal for Educational Integrity, 19*(1), 26. DOI: 10.1007/s40979-023-00146-z

Williamson, B., Bayne, S., & Shay, S. (2022). The datafication of teaching in Higher Education: Critical issues and perspectives. *Teaching in Higher Education, 27*(3), 287–300. DOI: 10.1080/13562517.2020.1748811

Wollny, S., Schneider, J., Di Mitri, D., Weidlich, J., Rittberger, M., & Drachsler, H. (2021). Are we there yet? A systematic literature review on chatbots in education. *Frontiers in Artificial Intelligence, 4*, 654924. DOI: 10.3389/frai.2021.654924 PMID: 34337392

Yan, L., Sha, L., Zhao, L., Li, Y., Martinez-Maldonado, R., Chen, G., Van Der Graaf, J., Láng, J., Moreno-Marcos, P. M., & Gašević, D. (2024). Practical and ethical challenges of large language models in education: A systematic literature review. *British Journal of Educational Technology, 55*(1), 90–112. DOI: 10.1111/bjet.13370

Zawacki-Richter, O., Marín, V. I., Bond, M., & Gouverneur, F. (2023). Systematic review of research on artificial intelligence applications in higher education — Where are the educators? *International Journal of Educational Technology in Higher Education, 20*, 39. DOI: 10.1186/s41239-023-00400-z

KEY TERMS AND DEFINITIONS

Augmentation-Substitution Indicators: Measurable behavioral signals, including override and disagreement rates, reviewer time-on-task, and reviewer self-efficacy, used to determine empirically whether an AI system is supporting human judgment or has displaced it in practice.

Automation Bias: The systematic tendency to over-trust or defer to automated recommendations, even in the presence of contradictory information, leading to reduced exercise of independent human judgment in consequential decisions.

Cognitive Offloading: The practice of externalizing cognitive tasks to environmental tools or systems in order to reduce the demands on working memory; educationally problematic when it becomes habitual and extends to tasks whose cognitive engagement constitutes the primary learning objective.

Contestability: The institutional capacity of individuals affected by algorithmic decisions to understand the basis of those decisions, present contrary evidence, and access meaningful human review and remedy.

Deskilling: The gradual atrophy of cognitive competencies resulting from non-use, typically because those competencies have been delegated to automated systems; in educational contexts, refers to the erosion of academic skills through sustained AI assistance.

Explainable AI (XAI): A set of technical methods, including feature-attribution techniques such as SHAP and LIME, designed to render the outputs of complex AI systems interpretable to human users, supporting contestability and informed human oversight.

Function Creep: The use of data or systems for purposes beyond those originally specified and consented to; in educational AI contexts, often involves the secondary use of learning analytics data in disciplinary or employment decisions.

Learner Agency: The degree of control, autonomy, and self-determination that students exercise over their learning goals, processes, and trajectories; a key predictor of intrinsic motivation and deep learning.

Metacognition: The capacity to monitor, evaluate, and regulate one's own cognitive processes, including accurate self-assessment of comprehension, strategy selection, and learning progress.

Over-Automation: The institutional condition in which AI systems occupy consequential roles in educational decision-making, including teaching, assessment, advising, or integrity monitoring, without adequate mechanisms for human oversight, contestability, transparency, or accountability.

Procedural Justice: The perceived fairness of a decision process, encompassing voice (the opportunity to present one's case), neutrality (impartiality of the decision-maker), and consistency (equal treatment across cases); relevant to the legitimacy of AI-mediated educational decisions.

Responsibility Fragmentation: The diffusion of accountability for AI-mediated harms across multiple actors, including vendors, institutions, administrators, and instructors, such that no individual or entity bears clear, non-deferrable responsibility for an outcome.

Chapter 15
Students in the AI Age: Learning, Dependency, and Cognitive Growth Among Economics Students in Higher Education

Francis Arthur
http://orcid.org/0000-0001-7792-6563
University of Cape Coast, Ghana

Abena Yeboah Abraham
http://orcid.org/0000-0002-4454-155X
Koforidua Technical University, Ghana

Mark Inkoom
http://orcid.org/0009-0008-2797-6712
University of Cape Coast, Ghana

ABSTRACT

The rapid integration of artificial intelligence (AI) into higher education is transforming how students access information, solve problems, and engage with learning. While AI offers significant benefits, concerns have emerged regarding cognitive dependency, reduced critical thinking, and diminished intellectual autonomy. This chapter examines the implications of AI-mediated learning for economics students, whose academic development depends on analytical reasoning, model-based thinking, and critical evaluation. Drawing on Cognitive Offloading Theory, Dual-Process Theory, Self-Regulated Learning Theory, Automation Bias, and Neuroplasticity, the chapter proposes the AI-Cognitive Dependency and Growth Framework (AI-

DOI: 10.4018/979-8-3373-9484-8.ch015

CDGF). The framework explains how AI engagement can lead to either cognitive dependency or cognitive growth, providing guidance for responsible AI-supported learning in higher education.

1. INTRODUCTION

1.1 The Rise of Artificial Intelligence in Higher Education

Artificial intelligence has become one of the defining forces reshaping higher education in the twenty-first century (Arthur, 2026). Across universities, AI is no longer limited to institutional administration or experimental educational technologies; it is increasingly embedded in teaching support, academic writing, feedback systems, learning analytics, student advising, research assistance, and assessment-related practices (Bond et al., 2024; Crompton & Burke, 2023). Earlier applications of AI in higher education were often associated with intelligent tutoring systems, adaptive learning platforms, automated assessment, and learning analytics (Ouyang & Jiao, 2021; Zawacki-Richter et al., 2019). However, the emergence of generative AI has widened the scale and visibility of AI use because students can now interact with systems that generate explanations, examples, summaries, arguments, codes, calculations, and academic drafts from ordinary language prompts (Kasneci et al., 2023; Yan et al., 2024).

This development has changed the meaning of academic support. Generative AI systems can provide conversational explanations, simplify difficult concepts, generate outlines, translate academic language, suggest research directions, and assist with problem solving in ways that appear immediate and personalized (Chan & Hu, 2023; Ogunleye et al., 2024). For many students, this means that learning support is no longer restricted to lecture rooms, textbooks, office hours, or peer discussions. Instead, support is available continuously through tools that respond instantly and adapt their outputs to the learner's prompt (Batista et al., 2024; Belkina et al., 2025). This expansion has transformed how students access knowledge, organize ideas, and approach academic tasks, making AI a major influence on contemporary learning behavior (Markauskaite et al., 2022).

1.2 AI and the Changing Nature of Student Learning

AI-supported learning represents a shift from information scarcity to information abundance. In traditional academic settings, students often had to search for relevant sources, read across different materials, compare ideas, interpret evidence, and construct responses through sustained intellectual effort. In AI-mediated settings, students can ask an AI system to summarize a paper, explain a theory, generate examples, solve a quantitative problem, or propose a structure for an essay within seconds (Kasneci et al., 2023; Lo, 2023). This shift can improve access to learning resources, especially when AI is used to clarify difficult content, provide timely feedback, and support students who require additional scaffolding (Cavalcanti et al., 2021; Seo et al., 2021).

The same shift also changes the learner's role. When AI provides explanations, suggestions, and solutions, students may become active evaluators of AI outputs, but they may also become passive consumers of automated responses. Ouyang and Jiao (2021) distinguish between AI-directed, AI-supported, and AI-empowered learning, showing that the educational role of AI depends on whether learners remain recipients, collaborators, or leaders in the learning process. This distinction is important because AI can either support student agency or quietly reduce the learner's responsibility for thinking. When students use AI to plan, monitor, evaluate, and revise their learning, it can support self-regulated learning (Arthur et al., 2026; Jin et al., 2023; Lan & Zhou, 2025). However, when they use it mainly to obtain answers or complete tasks quickly, the learning process may become efficient without becoming intellectually deep.

The quality of student learning therefore depends not only on access to AI, but also on students' capacity to use AI critically. AI literacy is important because students need to understand how AI systems work, why their outputs may be limited, and how automated responses should be questioned before being accepted (Arkorful et al., 2025; Laupichler et al., 2022; Ng et al., 2021). Without such literacy, students may confuse the fluency of an AI-generated explanation with accuracy, validity, or understanding. This is particularly important because large language models often present responses in confident and coherent language, even when the reasoning may be incomplete, the evidence may be weak, or the interpretation may be misleading (Tlili et al., 2023; Yan et al., 2024).

1.3 The Cognitive Question in AI-Mediated Learning

The most important issue raised by AI in higher education is not only whether students can use it, but what repeated use does to the way they think. Higher education is expected to develop independent reasoning, critical judgment, intellectual discipline, and the ability to work through complexity (Bearman et al., 2023; Markauskaite et al., 2022). If students increasingly rely on AI systems to explain concepts, frame arguments, interpret evidence, solve problems, and evaluate alternatives, then AI use becomes a cognitive issue, not merely a technological one. The concern is that AI may support learning in the short term while weakening the habits of effort, uncertainty tolerance, and analytical struggle that make deep learning possible (Gerlich, 2025; Zhai et al., 2024).

This concern is closely connected to cognitive offloading and dependency. Cognitive offloading involves using external tools to reduce mental effort, and it is not inherently harmful because students have always used books, calculators, notes, diagrams, and software to extend their cognitive capacities (Gerlich, 2025; Peng & Yeh, 2025; Wang et al., 2026). The educational risk emerges when students offload the central reasoning activities that learning is supposed to cultivate, such as questioning assumptions, comparing explanations, justifying arguments, interpreting evidence, and evaluating conclusions (Zhai et al., 2024). Recent studies suggest that generative AI dependency may influence students' academic achievement, self-efficacy, and technological dependence, especially when learners begin to treat AI as the primary source of academic direction rather than as a support for their own reasoning (Jia et al., 2025; Peng et al., 2026; Shahzad et al., 2025; Zhang & Xu, 2024).

The cognitive concern also intersects with academic integrity. Early debates about ChatGPT in higher education focused strongly on plagiarism, authorship, cheating, and assessment security because generative AI can produce text that appears original and academically acceptable (Cotton et al., 2023; Perkins, 2023). These concerns remain important, but they are not sufficient. A student may use AI without directly violating academic rules and still avoid the reasoning process that an assignment was designed to develop. The deeper question is therefore not only whether AI-generated work is submitted dishonestly, but whether students are still practicing the cognitive operations that higher education is meant to strengthen.

1.4 Why Economics Education Requires Special Attention

Economics education requires special attention because the discipline depends on abstract reasoning, model-based analysis, logical argumentation, data interpretation, and policy judgment (Arthur et al., 2025). To learn Economics is not merely to remember definitions, reproduce diagrams, or calculate answers; it is to understand how assumptions shape models, how incentives influence behaviour, how scarcity creates trade-offs, and how policy choices produce intended and unintended consequences. Critical thinking in Economics involves both the technical tools of analysis and the broader capacity to apply those tools to complex social and economic problems (Siegfried & Colander, 2022). Recent work on university Economics students also emphasizes the need to assess critical thinking as a domain-specific skill rather than as a general academic ability detached from disciplinary reasoning (Tarasova et al., 2025).

This makes AI use among Economics students particularly important. Empirical evidence from Ghanaian higher education shows that Economics students' intention and actual use of ChatGPT are shaped by perceived usefulness, trust, and expectations about learning support (Salifu et al., 2024). Similarly, research on Economics students' use of generative AI indicates that students may be motivated by the desire to automate routine tasks, save time, and compensate for limited experience (Balytska et al., 2024). These findings suggest that AI is already becoming part of how Economics students organize academic work and respond to learning demands.

The promise is clear, AI can help Economics students obtain explanations of difficult concepts, practice problem solving, receive examples, and test alternative interpretations. Bröse et al. (2026) show that ChatGPT can serve as an automated Economics tutor for basic knowledge-oriented tasks, although the same study also notes limitations related to narrow explanations, errors, and overconfident responses. The risk is equally clear. If students use AI to obtain conclusions without examining assumptions, tracing causal logic, interpreting data, or evaluating policy consequences, they may complete Economics tasks without developing economic thinking. Since Economics education depends on reasoning through uncertainty and weighing alternatives, excessive AI reliance may weaken the analytical habits that the discipline seeks to build (Siegfried & Colander, 2022; Balytska et al., 2024).

1.5 Purpose and Structure of the Chapter

Against this background, this chapter examines learning, dependency, and cognitive growth among Economics students in the age of AI. The chapter does not reject AI, because AI can expand access to learning support, personalize feedback, and assist students in navigating difficult academic content (Chan & Hu, 2023; Lim et al., 2023). At the same time, the chapter does not treat AI as a neutral solution to educational challenges, because its effects depend on how students use it, how lecturers guide it, and how institutions design learning tasks around it (Kumar et al., 2024; Mah & Groß, 2024). The central argument is that AI should support students' cognitive development rather than replace the intellectual effort through which understanding is formed.

The chapter is guided by three objectives. First, it examines how AI is changing student learning in higher education through generative AI systems, AI tutoring tools, and AI-assisted academic support. Second, it explains why Economics education deserves special attention because of its reliance on abstract reasoning, model-based thinking, data interpretation, and policy evaluation. Third, it develops a conceptual explanation of AI dependency by drawing on cognitive offloading theory, dual-process cognition, self-regulated learning theory, automation bias, and neuroplasticity.

The chapter proceeds in five main sections. Following this introduction, Section Two discusses artificial intelligence and learning in higher education, focusing on the types of AI tools used by university students, the benefits of AI-supported learning, emerging concerns about dependency, and current research gaps. Section Three examines the cognitive demands of Economics education, with attention to abstract reasoning, problem framing, data interpretation, and policy evaluation. Section Four presents the theoretical foundations of the chapter by explaining how cognitive offloading, dual-process cognition, self-regulated learning, automation bias, and neuroplasticity illuminate the possible cognitive effects of AI-mediated learning. Section Five conceptualizes AI dependency in higher education by identifying its forms, characteristics, and psychological drivers.

The chapter contributes to current debates by reframing AI in higher education as a question of cognitive growth rather than technological efficiency alone. For Economics education, this reframing is necessary because the purpose of learning is not simply to help students produce faster answers, but to develop learners who can question assumptions, evaluate evidence, reason through uncertainty, and make informed judgments. The chapter therefore argues that AI should be positioned as a partner in economic thinking, not as a replacement for the intellectual labour through which economic understanding is developed.

2. ARTIFICIAL INTELLIGENCE AND LEARNING IN HIGHER EDUCATION

2.1 Types of AI Tools Used by University Students

Artificial intelligence in higher education is not a single technology, but a broad family of tools that support different aspects of student learning. Recent reviews show that AI is used in universities for tutoring, assessment, feedback, writing support, learning analytics, prediction, recommendation, and adaptive learning (Bond et al., 2024; Crompton & Burke, 2023). Earlier discussions of AI in higher education focused largely on intelligent tutoring systems, automated assessment, adaptive platforms, and learning analytics, where AI was mainly embedded within institutional systems or course platforms (Ouyang & Jiao, 2021; Zawacki-Richter et al., 2019). The current AI landscape is broader because students now use both institutionally provided systems and publicly available tools that operate outside formal university control.

The most visible category of AI tools used by university students is generative AI. These systems include large language models and related applications that can generate text, explanations, summaries, outlines, examples, translations, codes, and problem-solving steps in response to user prompts (Kasneci et al., 2023; Lo, 2023). Students use such tools to clarify difficult concepts, prepare assignments, generate ideas, improve academic writing, summarize readings, and rehearse possible responses to questions (Chan & Hu, 2023; Ogunleye et al., 2024). In this sense, generative AI has become attractive because it combines the functions of a search engine, writing assistant, tutor, editor, and conversational partner within one accessible interface.

A second category is AI tutoring systems. These tools are designed to guide learners through content, provide hints, adapt to student performance, and support practice-based learning. Intelligent tutoring systems have a longer history in educational technology, but recent AI developments have made tutoring more conversational, flexible, and responsive to student prompts (Ouyang & Jiao, 2021; Seo et al., 2021). In higher education, AI tutoring can support students by providing explanations, diagnosing misconceptions, and offering step-by-step guidance on academic tasks (Cavalcanti et al., 2021). In Economics education specifically, Bröse et al. (2026) show that ChatGPT can perform some tutoring functions by explaining economic concepts and supporting basic problem-solving, although its limitations require students and educators to remain cautious.

A third category involves AI-assisted analytics and modelling tools. These include learning analytics dashboards, predictive systems, automated feedback tools, statistical assistants, coding assistants, and modelling platforms that help students and institutions interpret data, monitor progress, and make decisions about learning (Cavalcanti et al., 2021; Mah & Groß, 2024). For students, such tools may support quantitative analysis, visualization, simulation, forecasting, and interpretation of complex datasets. For universities, they may help identify students who need support, track learning engagement, and personalize academic interventions (Kumar et al., 2024; Zawacki-Richter et al., 2019). However, because these tools can influence how learners interpret evidence and make academic decisions, they also raise questions about transparency, data ethics, and overdependence on automated judgments.

2.2 Benefits of AI-Supported Learning

The first major benefit of AI-supported learning is personalization. AI tools can adjust explanations, examples, feedback, and recommendations to students' needs, allowing learners to request clarification at different levels of difficulty (Jin et al., 2023; Lan & Zhou, 2025). This is particularly useful in higher education, where students enter classrooms with different levels of prior knowledge, confidence, language proficiency, and access to academic support. Generative AI can help students revisit difficult ideas, ask follow-up questions, and receive alternative explanations when they do not understand a concept in its original form (Chan & Hu, 2023). When used appropriately, this kind of support can reduce barriers to participation and help students become more active in managing their own learning.

A second benefit is immediate feedback and scaffolding. Feedback is central to learning because it helps students identify errors, revise their work, and improve their understanding. AI-supported feedback systems can provide quick responses on writing, problem-solving, quiz performance, coding, and conceptual understanding (Cavalcanti et al., 2021). In online learning environments, AI can also affect learner-instructor interaction by providing forms of support that complement, rather than completely replace, human teaching presence (Seo et al., 2021). When students use AI feedback to compare answers, revise explanations, and monitor progress, it can support self-regulated learning processes such as planning, monitoring, evaluation, and reflection (Jin et al., 2023; Lan & Zhou, 2025).

A third benefit is efficiency and accessibility. AI tools can reduce the time students spend searching for basic information, formatting ideas, organizing drafts, translating content, or locating examples (Batista et al., 2024; Belkina et al., 2025). This efficiency can be valuable when students use the time saved to deepen analysis, consult additional sources, or improve the quality of their work. AI may also improve accessibility by supporting students who face language barriers, limited academic support, disability-related challenges, or difficulties with confidence and participation (Lim et al., 2023). In this respect, AI has the potential to widen learning opportunities, particularly when it is embedded within inclusive pedagogical practices rather than used only as a shortcut for task completion.

2.3 Emerging Concerns about AI Dependency

Despite these benefits, AI-supported learning has raised growing concerns about dependency. AI dependency occurs when students rely on AI not merely as a support tool, but as the main source of explanation, direction, judgment, and academic production. Zhai et al. (2024) show that overreliance on AI dialogue systems may affect students' cognitive abilities, including critical thinking, analytical reasoning, and decision-making. Gerlich (2025) similarly links frequent AI tool use with cognitive offloading and possible weakening of critical thinking when users transfer too much mental work to automated systems. This suggests that the central risk is not AI use itself, but the gradual replacement of student reasoning with automated reasoning.

One concern is overreliance on automated solutions. When students repeatedly ask AI to solve problems, generate assignments, or produce interpretations, they may become less willing to engage with difficult tasks independently. Jia et al. (2025) associate generative AI dependency with academic achievement through psychological mechanisms such as self-efficacy, while Zhang and Xu (2024) discuss the paradox between students' confidence and technological dependence in task completion. These findings suggest that AI may improve task performance while also changing students' beliefs about their own ability to complete academic work without assistance. In the long term, this may weaken learner autonomy if students begin to treat AI as the first and final authority in learning.

Another concern is reduced engagement with complex tasks. Higher education requires students to struggle with difficult ideas, compare evidence, tolerate uncertainty, and revise their thinking. However, AI tools can make complex tasks appear easier by producing polished explanations and structured responses without requiring the student to go through the reasoning process. Bearman et al. (2023) argue that AI in higher education must be examined critically because it changes educational relationships, practices, and assumptions about learning. Markauskaite et al. (2022) also emphasize that learners need new capabilities in a world where AI is increasingly entangled with human learning. These concerns are important because ease of access does not automatically produce depth of understanding.

Academic integrity is another major concern. Generative AI can produce essays, summaries, reflections, and responses that may be submitted as student work, raising questions about authorship, originality, and assessment validity (Cotton et al., 2023; Perkins, 2023). However, academic integrity should not be reduced only to cheating. The deeper issue is whether assessments still measure students' own understanding, reasoning, and judgment when AI can perform many parts of the task. Tlili et al. (2023) show that ChatGPT presents both opportunities and ethical challenges in education, including issues of trust, responsibility, and appropriate use. Therefore, institutions must address not only misconduct, but also the redesign of assessment for an AI-mediated learning environment.

2.4 Current Research Gaps

Although research on AI in higher education is expanding rapidly, important gaps remain. One major gap is the limited disciplinary focus of much existing research. Many studies discuss AI in higher education generally, but fewer examine how AI affects learning in specific disciplines with distinctive cognitive demands (Bond et al., 2024; Crompton & Burke, 2023). This is important because the meaning of AI-supported learning may differ across fields. For example, AI use in writing-intensive courses may raise different issues from AI use in statistics, programming, Economics, laboratory science, or policy analysis. In Economics education, where students must reason with models, data, assumptions, incentives, and policy trade-offs, AI dependency may have consequences that general higher education studies do not fully capture.

A second gap is the limited use of cognitive and psychological explanations. Much of the AI education literature focuses on adoption, perception, ethics, academic integrity, and institutional policy. These themes are necessary, but they do not fully explain how AI use may shape students' thinking habits, motivation, confidence, effort regulation, and tolerance for difficult reasoning. Studies on overreliance and cognitive offloading have begun to address this problem, but more work is needed to explain how AI affects the internal processes of learning across time (Gerlich, 2025; Zhai et al., 2024). Without this cognitive focus, AI research may overemphasize visible outcomes such as speed, convenience, and performance while underexamining deeper changes in reasoning and judgment.

A third gap is the need for conceptual frameworks. Current AI debates often move between optimism and fear, presenting AI either as a solution to educational challenges or as a threat to academic standards. Such oppositions are not sufficient for guiding higher education practice. What is needed are frameworks that explain the conditions under which AI supports learning, the conditions under which it creates dependency, and the pedagogical strategies that can preserve student agency. Markauskaite et al. (2022) argue that the relationship between AI and human learning must be rethought in terms of the capabilities learners need in an AI-rich world. For Economics education, this means developing a framework that positions AI as a support for economic thinking rather than a substitute for the cognitive effort through which economic understanding is developed.

3. COGNITIVE DEMANDS OF ECONOMICS EDUCATION

3.1 Nature of Economic Thinking

Economics education is cognitively demanding because it requires students to move beyond memorizing concepts toward disciplined forms of abstract reasoning, model-based analysis, and logical argumentation. Economic thinking involves explaining how individuals, firms, governments, and institutions make choices under conditions of scarcity, incentives, constraints, uncertainty, and trade-offs. This means that students must learn to reason from observable economic events to the underlying relationships that connect decisions, markets, policies, and outcomes. Siegfried and Colander (2022) explain that critical thinking in Economics requires students to understand both the technical tools of economic reasoning and the broader judgments needed to apply those tools meaningfully. Similarly, Tarasova et al. (2025) emphasize that critical thinking among Economics students should be assessed as a domain-specific competence because economic reasoning depends on disciplinary concepts, models, and forms of evidence.

A major feature of economic thinking is abstraction. Economic models simplify complex realities by focusing on selected variables and relationships, such as demand and supply, incentives and behavior, inflation and unemployment, or cost and benefit. This abstraction helps students identify patterns that may not be immediately visible in everyday experience. However, economic abstraction also requires students to understand the assumptions on which models are built, the conditions under which those models apply, and the limitations of using simplified representations to explain complex social realities. Jhun (2023) argues that economists often reason with multiple models because no single model fully captures the complexity of an economic system. This makes model-based thinking central to Economics education because students must learn not only to apply models, but also to evaluate their relevance, scope, and limitations.

Economic thinking also requires logical argumentation. Students must be able to make claims, support those claims with economic theory or empirical evidence, and defend the reasoning that connects evidence to conclusions. A student may draw a demand and supply diagram correctly but still fail to think economically if they cannot explain why the curve shifts, what assumption is being made, or how the model applies to a particular context. Siegfried and Colander (2022) make this distinction important by showing that Economics education requires both "little-think" reasoning within models and "big-think" judgment about how economic reasoning applies to broader social issues. Therefore, the nature of economic thinking is not mechanical calculation alone; it is the disciplined use of concepts, assumptions, models, and evidence to explain economic behavior and evaluate economic problems.

3.2 Skills Required for Economic Analysis

The first major skill required for economic analysis is critical thinking. Economics students must learn to question assumptions, evaluate explanations, identify causal relationships, and judge the strength of evidence. This is important because economic issues rarely have simple or single explanations. For instance, inflation may be explained through demand-side pressures, cost-push factors, exchange rate depreciation, monetary expansion, supply shocks, or expectations. Students therefore need the ability to compare explanations rather than accept the first available answer. Tarasova et al. (2025) argue that critical thinking among Economics students should be understood through domain-specific tasks, which means that students demonstrate critical thinking when they use economic concepts and evidence to analyze economic problems. In the same way, Siegfried and Colander (2022) argue that teaching Economics should involve helping students think critically about both economic tools and their application to real-world issues.

Problem framing is another essential skill in economic analysis. Before students solve an economic problem, they must first decide what kind of problem it is, what assumptions matter, and which model or concept is most appropriate. For example, unemployment can be framed as a labor market problem, a macroeconomic demand problem, a skills mismatch problem, a structural inequality problem, or a policy coordination problem. Each framing leads to a different explanation and a different possible intervention. Jhun's (2023) discussion of multi-model reasoning is useful here because economic problems often require students to consider more than one model before arriving at a defensible interpretation. This means that problem framing is not a preliminary activity outside economic reasoning; it is part of the reasoning itself.

Data interpretation is also central to economic analysis because modern Economics depends heavily on quantitative evidence, statistical reasoning, and empirical judgment. However, economic data do not interpret themselves. Students must learn to identify patterns, distinguish correlation from causation, recognize uncertainty, interpret statistical outputs, and connect empirical results to economic theory. This requires more than technical calculation because a regression coefficient, graph, index, or forecast becomes meaningful only when students can explain what it shows, what it does not show, and what assumptions shape its interpretation. Tarasova et al. (2025) support this point by treating critical thinking in Economics as a domain-specific skill that involves the interpretation and evaluation of economic evidence.

Policy evaluation represents one of the highest levels of economic analysis. Students must learn to assess policy alternatives by considering efficiency, equity, incentives, distributional consequences, unintended effects, and long-term outcomes. A subsidy, tax policy, interest rate decision, or exchange rate intervention cannot be judged only by whether it produces an immediate technical result. It must also be evaluated in relation to who benefits, who loses, what trade-offs emerge, and what alternative policies may be more appropriate. Jhun (2023) explains that economic reasoning often involves model uncertainty, which is especially relevant to policy evaluation because different models may lead to different conclusions. Therefore, policy evaluation requires students to reason under uncertainty rather than simply apply fixed formulas.

3.3 Risks of AI-Driven Cognitive Substitution in Economics

The cognitive demands of Economics education make AI-driven cognitive substitution a serious concern. AI-driven cognitive substitution occurs when AI does not merely support students' learning, but performs the reasoning processes that students are expected to develop. Generative AI can explain concepts, summarize theories, solve numerical problems, generate policy arguments, interpret graphs, and produce model-based explanations. These functions can be useful when students use them to compare ideas, test their understanding, or identify gaps in their reasoning. However, they become risky when students use AI outputs as replacements for their own abstraction, model selection, evidence evaluation, and logical argumentation. Gerlich (2025) links frequent AI use to cognitive offloading when users transfer mental effort to external systems, while Zhai et al. (2024) show that overreliance on AI dialogue systems may weaken students' cognitive abilities, including critical thinking and analytical reasoning.

This risk is particularly relevant because Economics students are already using generative AI for academic purposes. Salifu et al. (2024) found that Economics students' behavioral intention and use of ChatGPT in Ghanaian higher education were shaped by perceived usefulness, trust, and learning expectations. Balytska et al. (2024) also found that Economics students may use generative AI to automate routine tasks, save time, and compensate for limited academic or practical experience. These findings show that AI is becoming part of how Economics students manage learning tasks. The problem is not that students use AI, but that repeated use for speed and convenience may gradually reduce their engagement with the difficult reasoning processes through which economic understanding is formed.

One major risk is reduced analytical struggle. Learning Economics requires students to work through uncertainty, revisit assumptions, compare explanations, correct errors, and justify conclusions. This intellectual struggle is not a weakness in the learning process; it is part of how conceptual mastery develops. Bröse et al. (2026) show that ChatGPT can perform some Economics tutoring functions, but they also identify limitations related to errors, narrow explanations, and overconfident responses. This suggests that students who depend on AI explanations without critical evaluation may miss both the inaccuracies in the output and the deeper learning that comes from constructing explanations independently.

A second risk is loss of conceptual mastery. Students may learn how to prompt AI effectively without understanding the economic reasoning behind the response. They may produce an acceptable explanation of elasticity, inflation, market failure, fiscal policy, or opportunity cost without being able to reproduce the logic independently. This creates a gap between academic performance and actual understanding. Gerlich (2025) warns that cognitive offloading may reduce the need for users to exercise their own critical thinking, while Zhai et al. (2024) associate AI overreliance with possible reductions in students' cognitive engagement. In Economics education, this means that students may appear competent because they can produce correct-looking answers, even though they may not have developed the reasoning habits required for independent economic analysis.

The challenge, therefore, is not to remove AI from Economics education, but to prevent AI from replacing the cognitive work that gives Economics its educational value. Students should be guided to use AI to ask better questions, compare competing explanations, identify assumptions, test model logic, and critique automated outputs. They should not use it only to obtain conclusions. Economics education in the AI age must therefore protect abstract reasoning, model-based analysis, logical argumentation, data interpretation, and policy judgment. If these cognitive demands are preserved, AI can become a support for economic thinking. If they are bypassed,

AI may produce faster answers while weakening the intellectual foundations of Economics learning.

4. THEORETICAL FOUNDATIONS

4.1 Cognitive Offloading Theory

Cognitive Offloading Theory provides a useful lens for explaining how learners use external tools to support, extend, or reduce internal mental effort. Cognitive offloading refers to the use of external actions, objects, or technologies to reduce the cognitive demands that would otherwise be handled through internal memory, attention, or reasoning (Risko & Gilbert, 2016). This idea is consistent with broader theories of distributed and extended cognition, which argue that human thinking is often supported by tools, symbols, environments, and technologies beyond the mind itself (Clark & Chalmers, 1998). In educational contexts, cognitive offloading is therefore not unusual. Students use notebooks to store information, calculators to perform computations, textbooks to organize knowledge, diagrams to visualize relationships, and digital tools to retrieve information.

The value of cognitive offloading depends on what is being offloaded and why it is being offloaded (Burnett & Richmond, 2026). When students use external tools to reduce unnecessary cognitive burden, they may be able to focus attention on higher-order reasoning and conceptual understanding. For example, using a calculator may free the learner from repetitive arithmetic so that attention can be directed toward interpreting economic meaning. Similarly, using a graphing tool may help students visualize relationships among variables without spending all their effort on manual construction. In this form, cognitive offloading can support learning because it reorganizes effort rather than eliminates it (Risko & Gilbert, 2016).

However, the same logic becomes problematic when offloading turns into cognitive outsourcing. In this chapter, cognitive outsourcing refers to the transfer of core reasoning processes to AI systems in ways that reduce the learner's own participation in thinking. This distinction is important because AI can now do more than store information or perform routine calculations. Generative AI can explain theories, write arguments, interpret data, summarize evidence, generate examples, and recommend conclusions. When students use AI to support these tasks, the tool may extend their thinking. When they use AI to replace their own questioning, interpreting, evaluating, and justifying, the tool may weaken the cognitive effort needed for learning.

This theory is especially relevant to Economics education. Economics students are expected to reason through models, assumptions, trade-offs, evidence, and policy implications. These tasks require cognitive effort because students must decide which concepts apply, what evidence matters, and how conclusions should be justified. AI may help reduce unnecessary confusion by explaining unfamiliar concepts or providing alternative examples. However, if AI carries out the central reasoning process, students may arrive at economic answers without developing economic understanding. Cognitive Offloading Theory therefore supports the chapter's argument that AI should be used to assist economic reasoning without removing the intellectual effort through which reasoning capacity is formed.

4.2 Dual-Process Theory of Cognition

Dual-Process Theory explains human cognition through the interaction between two broad forms of thinking: fast, automatic, intuitive processing and slower, deliberate, reflective processing. Kahneman (2003) presents this distinction in relation to bounded rationality and behavioral economics, showing that human judgment is often shaped by heuristics, shortcuts, and limits in deliberate reasoning. Evans (2008) similarly explains that dual-process accounts distinguish between automatic forms of thinking and controlled forms of reasoning. Evans and Stanovich (2013) further clarify this distinction by describing Type 1 processing as fast, autonomous, and low in cognitive effort, while Type 2 processing is slower, reflective, and demanding of attention and working memory.

This theoretical distinction is important for AI-mediated learning because generative AI can encourage students to move quickly from question to answer. AI-generated responses often appear fluent, organized, and confident. This fluency may invite quick acceptance, especially when students are under pressure to complete assignments, solve problems, or understand difficult material. From a dual-process perspective, the concern is that students may rely on fast acceptance rather than slow evaluation. In other words, AI may make learning appear easier while reducing the learner's engagement in reflective judgment.

The risk is not merely that AI may provide inaccurate responses. The deeper concern is that AI may strengthen habits of heuristic processing. A student may accept an AI explanation because it sounds clear, not because it has been examined against theory, evidence, context, or logic. This matters because higher education depends on the development of reflective thinking. Students are expected to evaluate claims, identify assumptions, recognize limitations, compare alternatives, and revise conclusions. These are Type 2 processes because they require sustained attention, deliberate analysis, and willingness to work through uncertainty (Evans & Stanovich, 2013).

Dual-Process Theory is particularly relevant to Economics education because economic reasoning is not usually a matter of immediate intuition. Students must slow down to examine whether an explanation of inflation, unemployment, market failure, fiscal policy, or exchange rate movement is theoretically coherent and empirically defensible. They must also learn that the first plausible explanation may not be the strongest explanation. In Economics, therefore, AI should not be designed merely to provide immediate answers. It should be used to activate reflective reasoning by asking students to compare assumptions, identify missing evidence, test causal logic, and consider alternative models. Dual-Process Theory therefore supports the chapter's position that AI must guide students from quick acceptance toward deliberate economic judgment.

4.3 Self-Regulated Learning Theory

Self-Regulated Learning Theory explains learning as an active process in which students plan, monitor, control, and evaluate their own learning. Zimmerman (2002) describes self-regulated learners as students who set goals, observe their progress, adjust their strategies, and evaluate learning outcomes. Pintrich (2004) also explains self-regulated learning as a process involving cognition, motivation, behavior, and context. This means that learning is not only about receiving information; it is also about how students manage attention, effort, strategy use, feedback, and reflection. Panadero (2017) further emphasizes that self-regulated learning involves metacognitive and motivational processes that help learners take responsibility for their own academic development.

This theory is highly relevant to AI-supported education because the educational value of AI depends on how students regulate their interaction with the tool. AI can support self-regulated learning when it helps students clarify goals, identify gaps in understanding, seek feedback, revise weak answers, and reflect on learning progress. In this sense, AI can operate as a scaffold for metacognition rather than as a substitute for learning. Jin et al. (2023) connect AI-supported learning with metacognitive, cognitive, behavioral, and motivational regulation, while Lan and Zhou (2025) position AI-empowered self-regulated learning around planning, monitoring, reflection, and adaptive learning. These contributions suggest that AI becomes educationally valuable when students remain active regulators of their own learning.

However, AI can also weaken self-regulation when students use it to avoid monitoring their own understanding. A student who immediately asks AI for a final answer may no longer pause to identify what they do not understand, why they are confused, or which strategy would help them learn. This creates a problem because metacognition depends on the learner's awareness of knowledge gaps and learning strategies. When AI removes the need for students to plan, monitor, and evaluate, it may reduce the very self-regulatory processes that support deep learning. The danger is therefore not AI feedback itself, but feedback that is consumed passively rather than used reflectively.

In Economics education, self-regulated learning is essential because economic understanding develops through repeated cycles of interpretation, testing, revision, and justification. Students must monitor whether they understand the assumptions of a model, whether they can interpret a graph, whether their data interpretation supports their conclusion, and whether a policy recommendation follows logically from the evidence. AI can support this process when it prompts students to explain their reasoning, compare alternative policies, identify weak assumptions, and revise conclusions. However, if AI simply produces final answers, it may reduce students' opportunity to regulate their own thinking. Self-Regulated Learning Theory therefore supports the argument that AI should be used to promote metacognitive engagement, reflective learning, and intellectual responsibility.

4.4 Automation Bias

Automation Bias explains the tendency of individuals to give excessive trust to automated systems, especially when those systems appear accurate, authoritative, or efficient. Parasuraman and Riley (1997) explain that human interaction with automation can involve misuse when users overrely on automated systems and fail to monitor them appropriately. Goddard et al. (2012) define automation bias as the tendency to accept automated recommendations even when those recommendations are incomplete or incorrect. This theory is relevant to AI-mediated learning because students may accept AI outputs not because they have evaluated them, but because the outputs are produced by a system perceived as intelligent.

In higher education, automation bias may occur when students treat AI-generated explanations, summaries, calculations, or policy arguments as reliable without subjecting them to academic scrutiny. The confidence and fluency of AI outputs can make them appear more authoritative than they actually are. This is important because generative AI does not understand in the human sense; it produces responses based on patterns in data and language. Therefore, an AI-generated answer may be coherent but conceptually weak, relevant but incomplete, or confident but inaccurate. Automation Bias Theory helps explain why students may overlook these weaknesses when they trust the system more than their own critical judgment.

The concept of appropriate reliance is useful here. Appropriate reliance means that users should neither reject automated advice automatically nor accept it uncritically; they should judge when the system is useful and when human evaluation is necessary (Schemmer et al., 2023). In education, this means that students must learn how to verify AI-generated claims, compare them with course materials, check evidence, and identify assumptions. For Economics students, appropriate reliance is especially important because economic problems often involve uncertainty, competing models, and context-specific judgments. AI may offer a policy recommendation, but students must still ask whether the recommendation accounts for trade-offs, distributional effects, institutional constraints, and unintended consequences.

Automation Bias therefore strengthens the theoretical argument of this chapter. It shows that AI dependency is not only a matter of convenience; it is also a matter of trust. When students trust AI outputs without scrutiny, they may stop practicing the evaluative judgment that Economics education requires. AI-supported Economics learning must therefore train students to question automated outputs, not merely use them. The goal is not suspicion of AI, but disciplined trust. Students should learn to ask when AI is useful, when it is limited, and when economic reasoning must override automated fluency.

4.5 Neuroplasticity and Cognitive Development

Neuroplasticity provides a developmental perspective on why repeated cognitive behaviors matter for learning. Neuroplasticity refers to the brain's capacity to change in response to experience, practice, training, and environmental demands. Kleim and Jones (2008) explain that experience-dependent plasticity is shaped by principles such as repeated use, specificity, intensity, and salience. May (2011) also explains that adult brain structure can change in response to learning and experience. These ideas are important for education because they suggest that cognitive capacities are strengthened through repeated use and practice.

This theory must be applied carefully to AI in education. It would be inaccurate to claim that AI automatically damages students' brains or directly destroys their ability to think. Neuroplasticity does not support such a simplistic argument. Rather, it suggests a more careful point: the habits students repeatedly practice are likely to shape the capacities they continue to develop. If students repeatedly practice questioning assumptions, interpreting data, comparing explanations, and defending conclusions, these forms of reasoning are more likely to become stronger. If they repeatedly outsource those processes to AI, they may receive less practice in the cognitive activities that higher education is expected to cultivate.

Neuroplasticity therefore connects closely with the concern about cognitive outsourcing. Learning is not only about producing correct answers; it is also about repeatedly engaging in the mental activities that make correct reasoning possible. For Economics students, this repeated engagement is central. Students must practice abstract reasoning, model-based analysis, data interpretation, causal explanation, and policy evaluation. These capacities are not developed through passive exposure to answers. They are developed through use, feedback, correction, reflection, and revision. This is why AI must be positioned carefully within Economics education.

The long-term implication is that AI should be used to exercise students' reasoning, not bypass it. AI can provide prompts, examples, counterarguments, and feedback that help students practice economic thinking. It can ask students to justify why a model applies, identify what evidence is missing, explain the assumptions behind a policy recommendation, or revise a weak argument. In this form, AI becomes a practice environment for cognitive development. However, when AI supplies final explanations without requiring student reasoning, it may reduce the repeated intellectual activity through which economic judgment grows. Neuroplasticity therefore supports the chapter's broader theoretical claim that AI in Economics education should be designed for cognitive growth, not cognitive replacement.

These theoretical perspectives provide a coherent foundation for the chapter. Cognitive Offloading Theory explains how AI can either support or replace internal reasoning. Dual-Process Theory explains why AI convenience may encourage fast acceptance unless students are guided toward reflective evaluation. Self-Regulated Learning Theory explains why students must remain active planners, monitors, and evaluators of their own learning. Automation Bias explains why students may trust AI outputs without adequate scrutiny. Neuroplasticity explains why repeated cognitive habits matter for long-term intellectual development. Together, these theories justify the central argument of the chapter: AI should be used in Economics education as a scaffold for disciplined thinking, not as a substitute for the cognitive effort through which economic understanding is formed.

5. AI DEPENDENCY IN HIGHER EDUCATION

5.1 Conceptualising AI Dependency

The increasing presence of artificial intelligence in higher education has created new opportunities for academic support, but it has also introduced a deeper concern about student dependency. AI dependency may be understood as a pattern of repeated reliance on AI systems for academic explanation, task completion, problem-solving, interpretation, decision-making, and confidence-building in ways that reduce the learner's independent cognitive engagement. This definition does not suggest that every use of AI is dependent or harmful. Students may use AI productively to clarify difficult concepts, receive feedback, organize ideas, and improve learning strategies (Chan & Hu, 2023; Jin et al., 2023). Dependency begins to emerge when AI becomes the first and most trusted source of academic direction, rather than one support among several learning resources.

The defining feature of AI dependency is not simply frequency of use, but the learner's relationship with the tool. A student may use AI often and still remain cognitively active if they question outputs, compare them with course materials, revise weak responses, and use the tool to deepen understanding. In contrast, another student may use AI less frequently but still show dependency if they cannot begin, continue, or complete academic work without automated assistance. Recent studies on generative AI dependency suggest that problematic reliance may be associated with academic performance, self-efficacy, stress, anxiety, and students' confidence in their own ability to complete academic tasks (Jia et al., 2025; Liu et al., 2026). Therefore, AI dependency should be conceptualized as both behavioral and cognitive, involving what students do with AI and how they come to perceive their own academic capacity in relation to it.

AI dependency also has an epistemic dimension because it affects how students judge knowledge. When students repeatedly accept AI-generated explanations as sufficient, they may begin to treat automated fluency as a substitute for evidence, theory, and disciplinary reasoning. Farhi et al. (2023) show that students recognize both the usefulness and ethical concerns of ChatGPT, indicating that AI use is already tied to questions of trust, reliability, and academic responsibility. Similarly, Uppal and Hajian (2025) discuss students' perceptions of ChatGPT in relation to academic enhancement, procrastination, and ethical concerns. These concerns suggest that dependency is not only about convenience; it is also about whether students maintain responsibility for verifying, questioning, and justifying what they learn.

In higher education, AI dependency should therefore be distinguished from AI support. AI support occurs when students use AI to extend learning while retaining responsibility for reasoning, judgment, and reflection. AI dependency occurs when students transfer these responsibilities to the system. This distinction is important because higher education is not only concerned with whether students can produce correct answers, but whether they can explain, defend, and evaluate those answers. In Economics education, this distinction becomes especially important because students must understand the assumptions, evidence, models, and trade-offs behind economic claims. If AI use leads students to prioritize quick completion over disciplined reasoning, then dependency becomes a threat to cognitive growth.

5.2 Forms of AI Dependency

AI dependency in higher education can appear in at least three related forms: informational dependency, cognitive dependency, and decision dependency. Informational dependency occurs when students rely on AI as their primary source of academic information. In this form, students may ask AI to define concepts, summarize readings, explain theories, generate examples, and identify relevant sources before consulting textbooks, peer-reviewed articles, lectures, or instructors. This is understandable because generative AI makes information access fast, conversational, and convenient. Studies on students' acceptance of ChatGPT show that perceived usefulness, ease of use, performance expectations, and technological literacy influence students' intention to use AI tools in higher education (Al-Mamary et al., 2024; Strzelecki, 2024). However, informational dependency becomes problematic when students mistake AI-generated summaries for sufficient academic engagement.

Informational dependency is particularly risky because AI outputs may appear organized and authoritative while lacking disciplinary depth, contextual accuracy, or source transparency. Students may receive a neat explanation of inflation, market failure, elasticity, or fiscal policy, but may not know whether the explanation reflects the relevant course content, empirical context, or theoretical assumptions. Grassini (2024) emphasizes that students' acceptance of ChatGPT in higher education is shaped by factors that can make the tool attractive for academic use, while Tiwari et al. (2024) show that students' adoption of ChatGPT is influenced by the perceived benefits of using the technology. These patterns show why informational dependency can grow quietly: the tool appears useful because it reduces search effort, but it may also reduce sustained reading, comparison of sources, and independent synthesis.

Cognitive dependency is deeper than informational dependency because it involves reliance on AI for reasoning itself. In this form, students do not only ask AI what something means; they ask AI to construct the logic, interpret evidence, solve problems, generate arguments, and explain conclusions. Cognitive dependency is closely connected to cognitive offloading because students transfer mental effort from themselves to external systems (Risko & Gilbert, 2016). While offloading can support learning when it reduces unnecessary burden, it becomes risky when students outsource the core cognitive activities that academic learning is meant to develop. Gerlich (2025) links AI use to concerns about cognitive offloading and critical thinking, while Zhai et al. (2024) connect overreliance on AI dialogue systems with possible risks to students' cognitive abilities.

Decision dependency represents a third form of reliance. It occurs when students depend on AI to choose what to write, which answer to trust, which interpretation to accept, which method to apply, or which policy position to defend. In higher education, this may appear when students ask AI to select a thesis statement, determine the best answer to an assignment, recommend a conclusion, or evaluate the quality of their work without further human or disciplinary scrutiny. Niu et al. (2024) discuss AI autonomy in higher education from a uses and gratifications perspective, showing that students' interaction with AI may be shaped by what they expect the system to provide. In academic settings, this matters because decision-making is part of learning. Students develop judgment by choosing among alternatives, experiencing uncertainty, defending positions, and revising weak choices.

Decision dependency is especially concerning in Economics education because economic analysis often involves competing explanations and uncertain policy choices. AI may recommend a policy intervention, but students must still decide whether the recommendation is theoretically sound, empirically justified, socially equitable, and contextually appropriate. Smerdon (2024) shows that AI adoption in essay-based assessment raises questions about student usage and performance, which is relevant because assessment tasks often require students to make and defend academic decisions. If AI makes these decisions for students, assessment may capture the quality of AI-supported production rather than the student's own economic judgment.

5.3 Psychological Drivers of Dependency

AI dependency is partly sustained by psychological drivers that make automated assistance attractive to students. One major driver is cognitive ease. Cognitive ease refers to the comfort associated with tasks that feel simple, fluent, and low in effort. Generative AI increases cognitive ease because it provides immediate responses, organized explanations, and polished language without requiring students to move slowly through uncertainty. This can be helpful when students are genuinely stuck, but it can also encourage students to prefer AI-generated clarity over the more demanding work of reading, comparing, questioning, and revising. Revesai (2025) frames generative AI dependency as an emerging academic concern because students may increasingly rely on AI for academic performance. In this sense, dependency grows when ease becomes more attractive than understanding.

A second driver is effort avoidance. Higher education often requires students to engage in difficult tasks that demand patience, concentration, and repeated revision. However, AI can reduce the perceived cost of academic work by generating answers, explanations, and drafts almost instantly. Uppal and Hajian (2025) link students' perceptions of ChatGPT with academic enhancement, procrastination, and ethical concerns, suggesting that AI may be attractive not only because it supports learning, but also because it helps students manage delay, pressure, and task avoidance. Liu et al. (2026) further connect academic stress with students' dependency on generative AI, suggesting that students under pressure may turn to AI as a way of reducing anxiety and performance burden. These dynamics show that dependency may be driven not only by curiosity or innovation, but also by emotional relief.

A third driver is reduced intellectual perseverance. Intellectual perseverance refers to the willingness to remain engaged with difficult ideas, unresolved questions, and demanding reasoning processes. This quality is central to university learning because deep understanding often develops through confusion, correction, and sustained effort. When AI provides immediate answers, students may spend less time struggling productively with complex tasks. Zhang and Xu (2024) describe a paradox in which generative AI may support task completion while also increasing technological dependence. This paradox is important because a student may feel more capable when using AI, while becoming less willing to work independently without it.

For Economics students, these psychological drivers are especially important because the discipline demands sustained analytical effort. Students must compare models, interpret data, test assumptions, evaluate trade-offs, and defend policy conclusions. These tasks are intellectually demanding because they rarely produce simple or final answers. If students rely on AI mainly for cognitive ease, effort reduction, and quick reassurance, they may avoid the productive struggle through which economic reasoning develops. AI dependency in Economics education therefore threatens not only academic integrity, but also the formation of analytical habits, conceptual confidence, and independent judgment.

This section therefore conceptualizes AI dependency as a multi-dimensional problem involving information, cognition, decision-making, and psychology. Informational dependency affects how students access and trust knowledge. Cognitive dependency affects how they reason, interpret, and construct meaning. Decision dependency affects how they choose, judge, and defend academic positions. Psychological drivers such as cognitive ease, effort avoidance, and reduced intellectual perseverance explain why dependency can become attractive even when students understand the risks. The challenge for higher education is therefore not to prohibit AI use, but to design learning environments in which AI supports rather than replaces student agency. For Economics education, this means ensuring that AI use strengthens students' ability to question assumptions, evaluate evidence, reason through uncertainty, and make independent judgments.

6. THE AI-COGNITIVE DEPENDENCY AND GROWTH FRAMEWORK

6.1 Overview of the Framework

The AI-Cognitive Dependency and Growth Framework is proposed to explain how economics students' engagement with generative artificial intelligence can produce two contrasting learning outcomes: cognitive growth or cognitive dependency. In higher education, AI tools such as ChatGPT, Gemini, Claude and other large language models are increasingly used for explanation, summarisation, writing support, problem-solving, data interpretation and idea generation. UNESCO recognises that generative AI is reshaping how knowledge is produced and validated, and therefore calls for education systems to develop human capacity, regulation and policy so that AI supports rather than weakens learning (Holmes & Miao, 2023). Similarly, the

OECD has warned that AI in education requires careful governance to ensure that it enhances learning rather than replacing human judgement and effort (OECD, 2023).

For economics students, the issue is especially important because economics education depends heavily on analytical reasoning, model-building, interpretation of evidence, mathematical logic, diagrammatic explanation and policy judgement. Students may use AI productively to clarify concepts such as elasticity, inflation, fiscal policy, market failure, opportunity cost, econometric interpretation and development theory. However, the same tools may also encourage shortcut learning if students rely on AI-generated answers without verifying assumptions, interpreting models or independently constructing arguments. Recent evidence suggests that generative AI can improve performance and reduce mental effort, but this reduction in effort may become problematic when it replaces deeper learning processes (Deng et al., 2025).

The framework therefore rests on a central proposition: AI use becomes educationally beneficial when it augments students' thinking, but it becomes harmful when it substitutes for students' reasoning, judgement and intellectual effort. This proposition is consistent with research on cognitive offloading, which shows that learners may delegate mental tasks to external tools. Cognitive offloading is not inherently negative; calculators, notebooks and search engines all support learning. The problem arises when offloading becomes excessive and weakens independent reasoning, self-regulation and critical evaluation (Gerlich, 2025; Lodge & Loble, 2026).

The framework consists of four interrelated domains: AI Learning Engagement, Psychological Mediators, Cognitive Dependency Trajectories, and Cognitive Growth Outcomes (see Figure 1). In all, these domains explain how students move from AI use to either cognitive development or cognitive dependency.

Figure 1. AI-cognitive dependency and growth framework

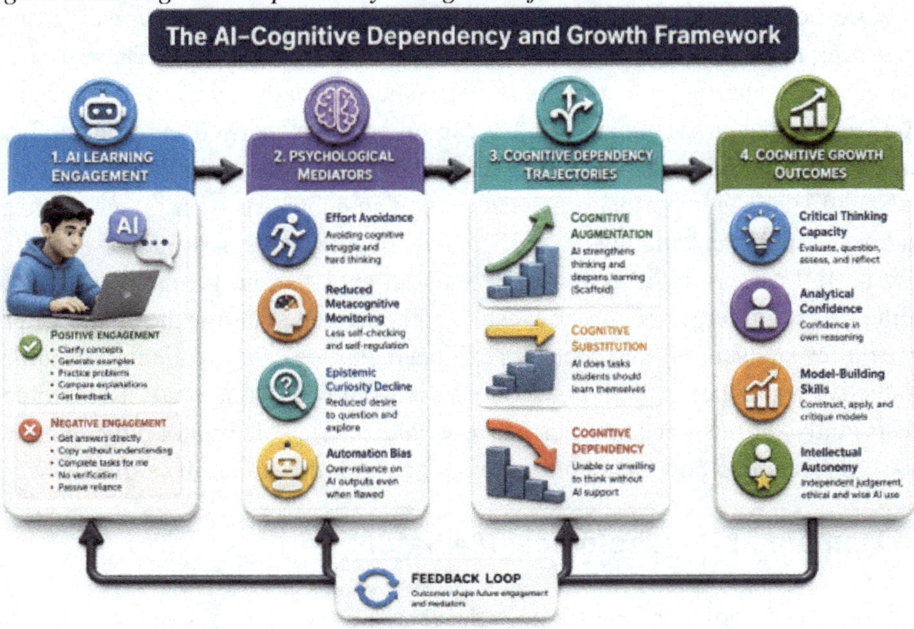

6.2 Domain 1: AI Learning Engagement

AI learning engagement refers to the ways economics students interact with AI tools during academic work. These interactions may be constructive, passive or dependent. Constructive engagement occurs when students use AI as a learning partner to clarify difficult concepts, test their understanding, generate examples, compare explanations, practise calculations or receive feedback on drafts. For example, an economics student may ask AI to explain the difference between demand-pull inflation and cost-push inflation, then compare the response with lecture notes and textbook explanations. In this case, AI supports learning without replacing the student's responsibility to evaluate and internalise the concept.

Evidence from economics education indicates that students are beginning to use AI for research support, explanation, summarisation and academic writing. A recent study on artificial intelligence in economic education found that economics students use AI tools to support learning and academic tasks, although their perceptions vary depending on usefulness, reliability and concerns about responsible use (Czapski & Pyra, 2026). Similarly, work on economics students' use of generative AI suggests that perceived usefulness, ease of use and academic relevance influence students' willingness to adopt such tools (Balytska et al., 2024).

Positive engagement patterns include using AI to clarify economic terminology, simulate policy debates, interpret graphs, generate practice questions, compare competing theories and improve the structure of academic writing. These uses can support active learning when students remain intellectually involved. Kasneci et al. (2023) argue that large language models can support personalised learning, feedback and content generation, but they also require users to understand their limitations.

Negative engagement patterns occur when students use AI as a substitute for reading, thinking, calculating, modelling or evaluating. This may include asking AI to write full essays, solve assignments without explanation, generate answers for online quizzes, interpret regression results without understanding the model, or produce policy analysis without checking evidence. In such cases, students may appear productive while their underlying economic reasoning remains weak. This problem is especially serious in economics because students must learn not only "what the answer is" but also how assumptions, evidence and models produce that answer.

6.3 Domain 2: Psychological Mediators

The second domain of the framework identifies the psychological mechanisms that shape whether AI engagement leads to growth or dependency. Four mediators are particularly important: effort avoidance, reduced metacognitive monitoring, epistemic curiosity decline and automation bias (see Figure 2).

Effort avoidance occurs when students use AI to escape cognitively demanding tasks. Economics learning often requires sustained effort: reading theoretical arguments, solving numerical problems, drawing graphs, interpreting data and evaluating policy trade-offs. If AI provides immediate answers, students may be tempted to avoid the productive struggle that supports learning. Deng et al. (2025) found that ChatGPT interventions can reduce mental effort while improving some learning outcomes, but reduced effort becomes risky when it prevents knowledge retention and transfer.

Reduced metacognitive monitoring refers to weakened self-checking and self-regulation. Metacognition involves students' ability to ask: Do I understand this concept? Can I explain it without help? Is this answer correct? What evidence supports this claim? Fan et al. (2025) warn that generative AI may encourage "metacognitive laziness", where learners become less active in monitoring their own understanding. In economics, this may appear when a student accepts an AI explanation of exchange rate depreciation without checking whether the assumptions fit a floating or fixed exchange rate regime.

Epistemic curiosity decline refers to a reduction in students' desire to investigate, question and explore knowledge. Economics education should cultivate curiosity about how markets work, why inequality persists, how policy affects welfare and why economic models simplify reality. If students repeatedly receive ready-made AI explanations, curiosity may shift from "How can I understand this?" to "What can AI produce for me?" This can weaken the habit of inquiry that is central to economic reasoning.

Automation bias refers to the tendency to over-rely on automated systems, even when their outputs may be wrong or incomplete. Georgetown's Center for Security and Emerging Technology defines automation bias as over-reliance on automated systems, which can lead people to favour system recommendations even when contradictory information is available (Kahn et al., 2024). In economics learning, automation bias may occur when students accept an AI-generated policy recommendation without questioning data quality, ideological assumptions, model limitations or contextual relevance.

Figure 2. Overview of psychological mediators

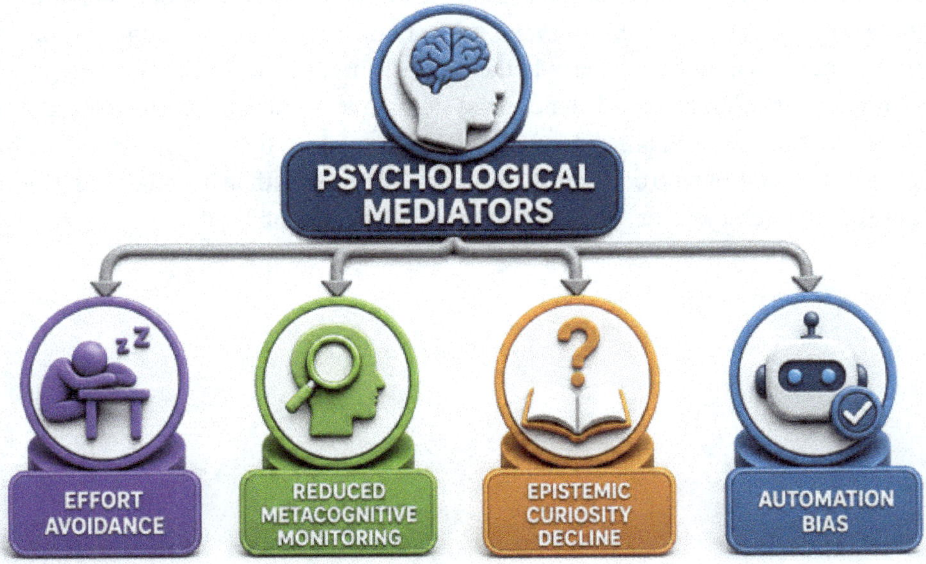

6.4 Domain 3: Cognitive Dependency Trajectories

The third domain explains the possible pathways students may follow as they use AI in learning. The framework identifies three trajectories: cognitive augmentation, cognitive substitution and cognitive dependency (see Figure 3).

Cognitive augmentation is the most desirable trajectory. Here, AI strengthens rather than replaces student thinking. Students use AI to extend their learning, test arguments, receive feedback and deepen understanding. For example, a student studying market structures may ask AI to compare perfect competition, monopoly and oligopoly, but then independently draws diagrams, explains welfare losses and relates the concepts to real-world industries. In this trajectory, AI functions as a scaffold.

Cognitive substitution occurs when AI begins to perform tasks that students should be learning to do themselves. For instance, an economics student may ask AI to interpret a regression table, write the entire interpretation and produce policy implications without understanding coefficients, significance levels or model assumptions. The student completes the task but does not develop analytical competence. This reflects what scholars describe as the risk of performance gains without genuine learning (Yan et al., 2025).

Cognitive dependency is the most problematic trajectory. It occurs when students become unable or unwilling to undertake academic reasoning without AI support. Dependency may be visible when students cannot begin assignments without AI, cannot explain AI-generated answers, cannot solve basic economic problems independently or cannot evaluate whether an AI output is valid. Zhai et al. (2024) warn that over-reliance on AI dialogue systems may reduce students' capacity for independent decision-making. Gerlich (2025) also found that cognitive offloading mediated the relationship between AI tool use and lower critical thinking, suggesting that excessive reliance can weaken cognitive development.

Figure 3. Snapshot of cognitive dependency trajectories

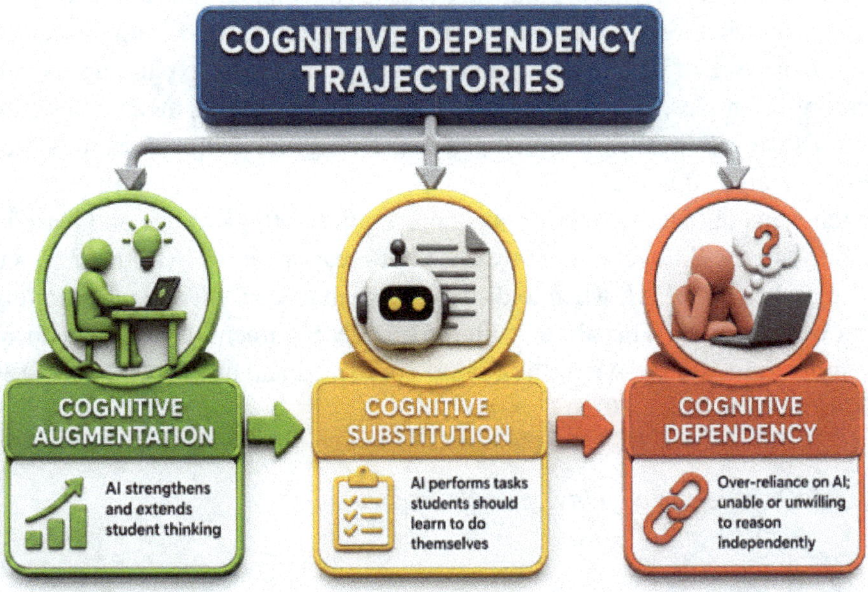

6.5 Domain 4: Cognitive Growth Outcomes

The fourth domain focuses on the outcomes that should result from responsible AI use. The framework identifies four key outcomes for economics students: critical thinking capacity, analytical confidence, model-building skills and intellectual autonomy (see Figure 4).

Critical thinking capacity refers to students' ability to evaluate assumptions, identify weaknesses in arguments, assess evidence and recognise limitations. Economics requires critical engagement because models simplify reality and policy recommendations often involve trade-offs. AI can support critical thinking if students are trained to interrogate outputs rather than accept them passively. Holmes and Miao (2023) emphasises the need for learners to develop human-centred capacities in the age of generative AI.

Analytical confidence refers to students' belief that they can reason through economic problems independently. This differs from confidence in using AI. A student may be confident in prompting AI but still weak in economic analysis. The goal is for AI-supported learning to increase students' confidence in their own reasoning, not merely their confidence in using tools.

Model-building skills are central to economics education. Students must learn how to construct, apply and critique models such as demand and supply, Keynesian income determination, production possibility frontiers, IS-LM frameworks, game theory matrices and econometric models. AI may assist by explaining models or generating examples, but students must still practise building models themselves. Over-reliance can weaken this competence if AI-generated explanations replace hands-on analytical work.

Intellectual autonomy refers to students' ability to think, judge and learn independently. In the AI age, autonomy does not mean avoiding AI; rather, it means knowing when to use AI, when to distrust it, when to verify it and when to rely on one's own reasoning. This aligns with the broader argument that higher education must move from simple AI prohibition to guided, ethical and critical use (OECD, 2023; Holmes & Miao, 2023).

Figure 4. Overview of cognitive growth outcomes

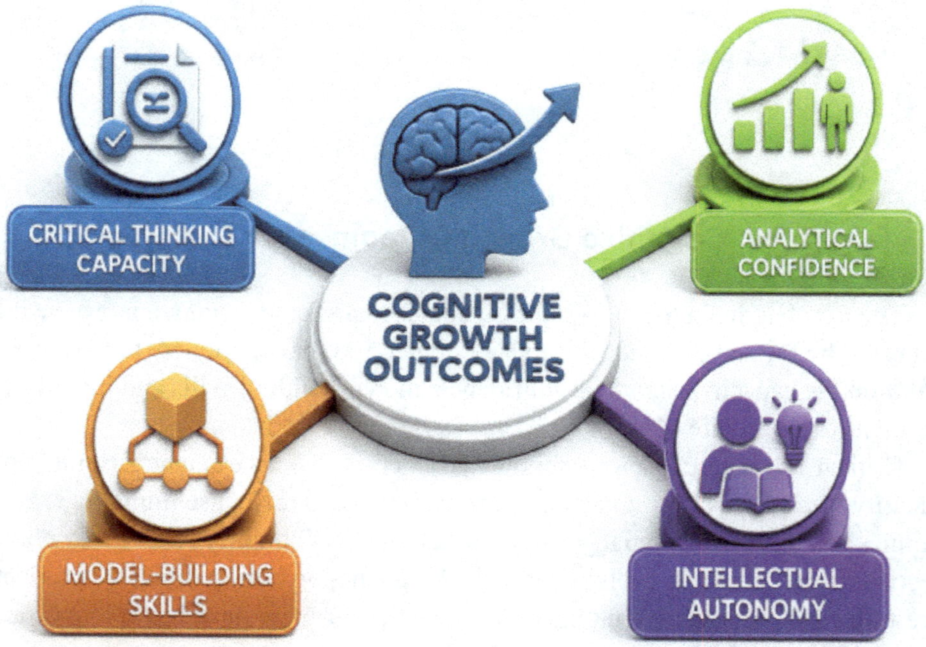

6.6 Framework Dynamics

The AI-Cognitive Dependency and Growth Framework is dynamic rather than linear. AI engagement does not automatically produce dependency, nor does it automatically produce growth. The outcome depends on how students use AI, how lecturers design learning tasks, how institutions regulate AI use and how students monitor their own thinking.

A positive developmental pathway begins with purposeful AI learning engagement. Students use AI to clarify concepts, test examples and receive formative feedback. Strong metacognitive monitoring then helps them verify outputs, identify errors and connect AI explanations to economic theory. This leads to cognitive augmentation, where AI strengthens learning. Over time, students develop critical thinking, analytical confidence, model-building skills and intellectual autonomy.

A negative developmental pathway begins with convenience-driven AI engagement. Students use AI mainly to avoid effort, complete assignments quickly or produce polished answers. Reduced metacognition, declining curiosity and automation bias then increase the likelihood of cognitive substitution. If this pattern continues, students may develop cognitive dependency, where AI becomes a replacement for independent economic reasoning.

The framework therefore suggests that the educational value of AI depends less on access to the tool and more on the quality of learning design around the tool. For economics students, AI should be embedded within tasks that require explanation, verification, comparison, reflection and independent modelling. For example, instead of asking students to submit an essay generated with AI assistance, lecturers may require students to compare an AI-generated explanation of inflation with textbook evidence, identify errors, revise the explanation and defend their judgement orally. Such tasks encourage AI-supported cognitive growth rather than AI-driven dependency.

In practical terms, the framework recommends that economics lecturers design AI-resilient assessments that require students to show their reasoning process. These may include handwritten model construction, oral defence of policy arguments, AI-output critique assignments, data interpretation tasks, reflective AI-use logs and in-class problem-solving. Institutions should also provide clear AI literacy policies so that students understand acceptable use, disclosure expectations and the limits of AI-generated knowledge.

In all, the framework contributes to higher education by offering a balanced model. It avoids both technological optimism and technological panic. AI is neither a guaranteed learning solution nor an inevitable threat to cognition. Its effect depends on whether students are guided to use it as a tool for thinking or allowed to use it as a substitute for thinking. For economics students, the central challenge is therefore not simply learning with AI, but learning how to remain intellectually active, critical and autonomous in an AI-mediated academic environment.

7. IMPLICATIONS FOR ECONOMICS EDUCATION

The AI-Cognitive Dependency and Growth Framework provides important implications for economics education in an era where generative artificial intelligence is becoming an increasingly common learning companion. The framework suggests that the educational value of AI depends not simply on its availability but on how it is integrated into teaching, curriculum design, technological systems, and institutional policies. If appropriately managed, AI can support cognitive augmentation and intellectual growth. However, when used uncritically, it may encourage cognitive substitution and dependency. Consequently, economics educators, curriculum developers, technology designers, and institutional leaders must adopt approaches that prioritise human reasoning, critical judgement, and intellectual autonomy.

7.1 Implications for Teaching and Pedagogy

The framework highlights the need for pedagogical approaches that preserve and strengthen students' cognitive engagement while benefiting from the affordances of AI technologies.

7.1.1 Designing Cognitively Demanding Tasks

Economics instruction should increasingly focus on designing learning activities that require higher-order thinking rather than simple information retrieval. Since AI systems can rapidly generate definitions, explanations, and summaries, assignments that merely require reproduction of information may no longer effectively assess learning. Instead, lecturers should develop tasks that require students to compare competing economic theories, evaluate policy alternatives, interpret economic data, critique assumptions, and justify decisions using evidence.

For example, rather than asking students to define inflation, instructors may require them to compare AI-generated explanations of inflation with textbook interpretations, identify inaccuracies, and evaluate the implications of different policy responses. Such activities encourage analytical reasoning and prevent students from becoming passive recipients of AI-generated content.

7.1.2. Encouraging Analytical Struggle

Productive learning often involves cognitive effort and intellectual struggle. Educational psychology research has consistently shown that deeper learning occurs when learners actively engage with challenging tasks rather than receiving immediate answers. Economics education particularly depends on students grappling with abstract concepts, mathematical reasoning, policy trade-offs, and model construction.

The framework therefore suggests that lecturers should create opportunities for students to work through economic problems before consulting AI tools. Activities such as case analyses, problem-based learning, classroom debates, and economic simulations can encourage students to develop reasoning skills before receiving technological assistance. AI should serve as a supplementary learning resource rather than a replacement for analytical effort.

7.1.3. Limiting Passive AI Use

The framework further recommends reducing opportunities for passive AI consumption. Students should not be encouraged to accept AI outputs without scrutiny. Instead, lecturers should promote verification, critique, and reflection. Assignments can require students to explain how they used AI, identify limitations in AI-generated responses, and demonstrate independent reasoning alongside AI-supported work.

Such practices reinforce the principle that AI should augment learning rather than substitute for cognitive engagement. This approach aligns with contemporary calls for responsible and transparent AI use in higher education (Holmes & Miao, 2023).

7.2 Implications for Curriculum Design

The framework also has important implications for curriculum development within economics programmes.

7.2.1. AI Literacy in Economics Programmes

As AI technologies become integrated into economic analysis, research, forecasting, and policy evaluation, economics graduates will require AI literacy as a core professional competence. However, AI literacy should extend beyond technical proficiency. Students must understand how AI systems generate outputs, their limitations, potential biases, ethical implications, and appropriate applications within economic contexts.

Economics curricula should therefore include dedicated learning outcomes related to AI literacy. Topics may include algorithmic decision-making, data ethics, responsible AI use, AI-supported economic modelling, and critical evaluation of AI-generated information. Such competencies will prepare graduates to work effectively in increasingly AI-mediated professional environments.

7.2.2. Integrating Metacognitive Training

The framework identifies reduced metacognitive monitoring as a key mechanism contributing to cognitive dependency. Consequently, economics curricula should explicitly incorporate metacognitive training. Students need opportunities to reflect on how they learn, how they use AI, and how they evaluate the quality of information generated by technological systems.

Reflective journals, learning portfolios, self-assessment activities, and AI-use reflections can help students develop greater awareness of their cognitive processes. Such interventions encourage learners to monitor their understanding, recognise knowledge gaps, and maintain responsibility for their own learning. Metacognitive competence is particularly important in economics because effective economic reasoning requires continual evaluation of assumptions, evidence, and analytical approaches.

7.3 Implications for AI System Design

The framework suggests that responsibility for preventing cognitive dependency does not rest solely with educators and students. AI developers also play an important role in shaping learning behaviours.

7.3.1. Human-Centred AI Learning Systems

Educational AI systems should be designed according to human-centred principles that prioritise learning rather than convenience alone. Human-centred AI places the learner's cognitive development at the centre of technological design. Instead of simply delivering answers, AI systems should encourage questioning, reflection, explanation, and evidence evaluation.

For economics education, AI systems could be designed to prompt students to explain their reasoning before receiving complete solutions. They could ask learners to identify assumptions underlying economic models or evaluate alternative policy options before providing recommendations. Such features would encourage active engagement rather than passive dependence.

7.3.2. Tools that Promote Thinking Rather than Substitution

The framework proposes that educational AI should function as a cognitive scaffold rather than a cognitive replacement. AI systems can support thinking by providing hints, guiding questions, conceptual prompts, and feedback rather than fully completed answers.

For example, when students ask how fiscal policy influences unemployment, an AI learning system could guide them through relevant economic principles, encourage them to consider competing theoretical perspectives, and prompt them to apply concepts to specific economic contexts. Such an approach strengthens reasoning and model-building skills while reducing the likelihood of cognitive substitution.

7.4 Implications for Policy and Institutional Governance

Institutions of higher education have a critical role in ensuring that AI integration supports learning rather than undermines it. The framework suggests that universities should move beyond simplistic approaches that either prohibit AI use entirely or permit unrestricted adoption.

Instead, institutions should develop comprehensive AI governance frameworks that promote responsible and educationally beneficial use. These frameworks should establish clear guidelines regarding acceptable AI use, disclosure requirements, academic integrity expectations, and ethical considerations.

Universities should also provide AI literacy training for both students and academic staff. Faculty development programmes can help lecturers redesign assessments, integrate AI responsibly into teaching, and identify strategies for maintaining cognitive engagement. Similarly, student training initiatives can promote critical evaluation of AI outputs and responsible technology use.

Assessment policies should also be reconsidered. Traditional take-home assignments may become increasingly vulnerable to inappropriate AI use. Institutions may therefore need to adopt more authentic assessment approaches, including oral examinations, reflective portfolios, case analyses, problem-solving exercises, and project-based assessments that emphasise reasoning processes rather than final products.

Ultimately, institutional governance should seek to create environments in which AI supports intellectual development while preserving the central role of human judgement, creativity, and critical thinking.

8. Future Research Directions

Although research on AI in higher education is expanding rapidly, significant knowledge gaps remain regarding its long-term cognitive consequences. The AI-Cognitive Dependency and Growth Framework highlights several priorities for future investigation.

Need for Case and Longitudinal Studies

Most existing studies examine AI use over relatively short periods. Consequently, little is known about the long-term effects of sustained AI engagement on cognitive development. Longitudinal studies are needed to examine whether repeated reliance on AI influences students' critical thinking, problem-solving abilities, academic performance, and intellectual independence over time. Such research would help determine whether cognitive dependency develops gradually and whether specific educational interventions can mitigate its effects.

Future studies should also incorporate case studies, institutional examples, and evidence from diverse educational contexts to better understand how variations in pedagogical practices, technological infrastructure, and policy environments shape AI use and its cognitive consequences in higher education.

Neuroscientific Research on AI Use

The cognitive implications of AI-assisted learning remain insufficiently understood at the neurological level. Future studies could employ neuroscientific methods such as neuroimaging, eye-tracking, and cognitive load measurement to investigate how AI influences attention, memory, reasoning, and information processing.

Understanding these mechanisms would provide valuable insights into how AI affects learning and how educational systems can optimise its use.

Discipline-Specific AI Learning Research

Current research often treats AI use as a general educational phenomenon. However, the cognitive demands of disciplines differ considerably. Economics requires analytical reasoning, mathematical modelling, evidence interpretation, and policy evaluation. Consequently, the effects of AI use among economics students may differ from those observed in disciplines such as literature, engineering, medicine, or computer science.

Future research should therefore examine discipline-specific patterns of AI engagement and their implications for learning outcomes.

Measurement of AI Dependency

A major limitation in the current literature is the absence of robust instruments for measuring AI dependency. Future studies should develop and validate scales capable of assessing different dimensions of dependency, including behavioural reliance, cognitive substitution, reduced metacognitive monitoring, and diminished intellectual autonomy.

Reliable measurement tools would facilitate empirical testing of the proposed framework and support evidence-based interventions.

9. CONCLUSION

The rapid emergence of generative artificial intelligence has created unprecedented opportunities and challenges for economics education. While AI technologies can enhance learning, improve access to information, and support academic productivity, they also raise important concerns regarding cognitive dependency, effort avoidance, reduced metacognitive engagement, and automation bias.

The AI-Cognitive Dependency and Growth Framework provides a conceptual explanation of how these contrasting outcomes emerge. The framework demonstrates that AI engagement influences learning through psychological mediators that shape whether students follow trajectories of cognitive augmentation, cognitive substitution, or cognitive dependency. Ultimately, these trajectories affect critical thinking capacity, analytical confidence, model-building skills, and intellectual autonomy.

The central argument of the framework is that the educational value of AI depends on how it is used. AI should function as a tool that strengthens human thinking rather than replaces it. Economics education must therefore prioritise pedagogical practices, curricula, technologies, and policies that promote active reasoning, reflective judgement, and independent analysis.

As higher education continues to adapt to the AI era, maintaining a balance between technological innovation and human cognitive development will be essential. The future of economics education should not be characterised by competition between humans and artificial intelligence, but by the cultivation of graduates who can use AI critically, ethically, and intelligently while retaining the intellectual capacities that define meaningful learning and sound economic reasoning.

REFERENCES

Al-Mamary, Y. H. S., Shamsuddin, A., Abdul Hamid, N. A., & Alshallaqi, M. (2024). Exploring factors influencing university students' intentions to use ChatGPT: The role of technological literacy and perceived support. *Future Business Journal, 10*, 119. Advance online publication. DOI: 10.1186/s43093-024-00406-5

Arkorful, V., Arthur, F., Boateng, E., Ofosu-Koranteng, M., Salifu, I., Attom, E. R., Tetteh, S. A., Quayson, E., Asare-Bediako, S., & Nortey, S. A. (2025). Exploring artificial intelligence literacy among basic school teachers in Ghana. *Discover Education*, *4*(1), 250. DOI: 10.1007/s44217-025-00630-3

Arthur, F. (2026). Modelling the nexus between artificial intelligence usage and graduate capital dimensions: A PLS-SEM approach. *European Journal of Education*, *61*(1), e70484. DOI: 10.1111/ejed.70484

Arthur, F., Opoku, E., Inkoom, C., Suradji, S. D., & Inkoom, M. (2026). Where there is will, there is AI: Linking expectancy-value beliefs, generative AI use and self-regulated learning among economics students. *European Journal of Education*, *61*(3), e70743. DOI: 10.1111/ejed.70743

Arthur, F., Yidana, M. B., & Acquah, B. Y. S. (2025). Self-regulated learning among higher education economics students: Does gender and academic level matter? *Cogent Education*, *12*(1), 1–22. DOI: 10.1080/2331186X.2025.2579351

Balytska, M., Rašticová, M., Versal, N., Honchar, I., Prykaziuk, N., & Tkalenko, N. (2024). What drives economics students to use generative artificial intelligence? *Knowledge and Performance Management*, *8*(2), 51–64. DOI: 10.21511/kpm.08(2).2024.05

Batista, J., Mesquita, A., & Carnaz, G. (2024). Generative AI and higher education: Trends, challenges and future directions from a systematic literature review. *Information (Basel)*, *15*(11), 676. Advance online publication. DOI: 10.3390/info15110676

Bearman, M., Ryan, J., & Ajjawi, R. (2023). Discourses of artificial intelligence in higher education: A critical literature review. *Higher Education*, *86*(2), 369–385. DOI: 10.1007/s10734-022-00937-2

Belkina, M., Daniel, S., Nikolic, S., Haque, R., Lyden, S., Neal, P., Grundy, S., & Hassan, G. M. (2025). Implementing generative AI in higher education: A systematic review of case studies. *Computers and Education: Artificial Intelligence*, *8*, 100407. Advance online publication. DOI: 10.1016/j.caeai.2025.100407

Bond, M., Khosravi, H., De Laat, M., Bergdahl, N., Negrea, V., Oxley, E., Pham, P., Chong, S. W., & Siemens, G. (2024). A meta systematic review of artificial intelligence in higher education: A call for increased ethics, collaboration, and rigour. *International Journal of Educational Technology in Higher Education, 21*(1), 4. Advance online publication. DOI: 10.1186/s41239-023-00436-z

Bröse, N., Spielmann, C., & Tode, C. (2026). ChatGPT as economics tutor: Capabilities and limitations. *International Review of Economics Education, 51*, 100337. Advance online publication. DOI: 10.1016/j.iree.2025.100337

Burnett, L. K., & Richmond, L. L. (2026). Meta-analytic investigations of the effect of cognitive offloading on memory-based task performance and interindividual variability. *Memory & Cognition, 54*(1), 144–168. DOI: 10.3758/s13421-025-01743-8 PMID: 40500483

Cavalcanti, A. P., Barbosa, A., Carvalho, R., Freitas, F., Tsai, Y. S., Gašević, D., & Mello, R. F. (2021). Automatic feedback in online learning environments: A systematic literature review. *Computers and Education: Artificial Intelligence, 2*, 100027. Advance online publication. DOI: 10.1016/j.caeai.2021.100027

Chan, C. K. Y., & Hu, W. (2023). Students' voices on generative AI: Perceptions, benefits, and challenges in higher education. *International Journal of Educational Technology in Higher Education, 20*(1), 43. Advance online publication. DOI: 10.1186/s41239-023-00411-8

Clark, A., & Chalmers, D. (1998). The extended mind. *Analysis, 58*(1), 7–19. DOI: 10.1093/analys/58.1.7

Cotton, D. R. E., Cotton, P. A., & Shipway, J. R. (2023). Chatting and cheating: Ensuring academic integrity in the era of ChatGPT. *Innovations in Education and Teaching International, 61*(2), 228–239. DOI: 10.1080/14703297.2023.2190148

Crompton, H., & Burke, D. (2023). Artificial intelligence in higher education: The state of the field. *International Journal of Educational Technology in Higher Education, 20*(1), 22. Advance online publication. DOI: 10.1186/s41239-023-00392-8

Czapski, G., & Pyra, M. (2026). Artificial Intelligence in Economic Education: Adoption, Uses and Student Perceptions in Higher Education. *European Research Studies, 29*(1), 551–568. DOI: 10.35808/ersj/4330

Deng, R., Jiang, M., Yu, X., Lu, Y., & Liu, S. (2025). Does ChatGPT enhance student learning? A systematic review and meta-analysis of experimental studies. *Computers & Education, 227*, 105224. DOI: 10.1016/j.compedu.2024.105224

Evans, J. St. B. T. (2008). Dual-processing accounts of reasoning, judgment, and social cognition. *Annual Review of Psychology, 59*(1), 255–278. DOI: 10.1146/annurev.psych.59.103006.093629 PMID: 18154502

Evans, J. St. B. T., & Stanovich, K. E. (2013). Dual-process theories of higher cognition: Advancing the debate. *Perspectives on Psychological Science, 8*(3), 223–241. DOI: 10.1177/1745691612460685 PMID: 26172965

Fan, Y., Tang, L., Le, H., Shen, K., Tan, S., Zhao, Y., Shen, Y., Li, X., & Gašević, D. (2025). Beware of metacognitive laziness: Effects of generative artificial intelligence on learning motivation, processes, and performance. *British Journal of Educational Technology, 56*(2), 489–530. DOI: 10.1111/bjet.13544

Farhi, F., Jeljeli, R., Aburezeq, I., Dweikat, F. F. I., Al-Shami, S. A., & Slamene, R. (2023). Analyzing the students' views, concerns, and perceived ethics about ChatGPT usage. *Computers and Education: Artificial Intelligence, 5*, 100180. Advance online publication. DOI: 10.1016/j.caeai.2023.100180

Gerlich, M. (2025). AI tools in society: Impacts on cognitive offloading and the future of critical thinking. *Societies (Basel, Switzerland), 15*(1), 6. Advance online publication. DOI: 10.3390/soc15010006

Goddard, K., Roudsari, A., & Wyatt, J. C. (2012). Automation bias: A systematic review of frequency, effect mediators, and mitigators. *Journal of the American Medical Informatics Association : JAMIA, 19*(1), 121–127. DOI: 10.1136/amiajnl-2011-000089 PMID: 21685142

Grassini, S., Aasen, M. L., & Møgelvang, A. (2024). Understanding university students' acceptance of ChatGPT. *Applied Artificial Intelligence, 38*(1), 2371168. Advance online publication. DOI: 10.1080/08839514.2024.2371168

Holmes, W., & Miao, F. (2023). *Guidance for generative AI in education and research.* Unesco Publishing.

Jhun, J. (2023). Multi-model reasoning in economics: The case of COMPASS. *Philosophy of Science, 90*(4), 836–854. DOI: 10.1017/psa.2023.69

Jia, W., Pan, L., & Neary, S. (2025). Effect of generative AI dependency on university students' academic achievement: The mediating role of self-efficacy and moderating role of perceived teacher caring. *Behavioral Sciences (Basel, Switzerland), 15*(10), 1348. Advance online publication. DOI: 10.3390/bs15101348 PMID: 41153138

Jin, S. H., Im, K., Yoo, M., Roll, I., & Seo, K. (2023). Supporting students' self-regulated learning in online learning using artificial intelligence applications. *International Journal of Educational Technology in Higher Education*, *20*(1), 37. Advance online publication. DOI: 10.1186/s41239-023-00406-5

Kahn, L., Probasco, E. S., & Kinoshita, R. (2024). *AI Safety and Automation Bias*. Center for Security and Emerging Technology. DOI: 10.51593/20230057

Kahneman, D. (2003). Maps of bounded rationality: Psychology for behavioral economics. *The American Economic Review*, *93*(5), 1449–1475. DOI: 10.1257/000282803322655392

Kasneci, E., Sessler, K., Küchemann, S., Bannert, M., Dementieva, D., Fischer, F., Gasser, U., Groh, G., Günnemann, S., Hüllermeier, E., Krusche, S., Kutyniok, G., Michaeli, T., Nerdel, C., Pfeffer, J., Poquet, O., Sailer, M., Schmidt, A., Seidel, T., & Kasneci, G. (2023). ChatGPT for good? On opportunities and challenges of large language models for education. *Learning and Individual Differences*, *103*, 102274. Advance online publication. DOI: 10.1016/j.lindif.2023.102274

Kleim, J. A., & Jones, T. A. (2008). Principles of experience-dependent neural plasticity: Implications for rehabilitation after brain damage. *Journal of Speech, Language, and Hearing Research: JSLHR*, *51*(1), S225–S239. DOI: 10.1044/1092-4388(2008/018) PMID: 18230848

Kumar, V., Ashraf, A. R., & Nadeem, W. (2024). Will artificial intelligence drive advancements in higher education? A tri-phased exploration. *Technological Forecasting and Social Change*, *201*, 123258. Advance online publication. DOI: 10.1016/j.techfore.2024.123258

Lan, M., & Zhou, X. (2025). A qualitative systematic review on AI empowered self-regulated learning in higher education. *npj Science of Learning*, *10*, Article 21. https://doi.org/DOI: 10.1038/s41539-025-00319-0

Laupichler, M. C., Aster, A., Schirch, J., & Raupach, T. (2022). Artificial intelligence literacy in higher and adult education: A scoping literature review. *Computers and Education: Artificial Intelligence*, *3*, 100101. Advance online publication. DOI: 10.1016/j.caeai.2022.100101

Lim, W. M., Gunasekara, A., Pallant, J. L., Pallant, J. I., & Pechenkina, E. (2023). Generative AI and the future of education: Ragnarok or reformation? A paradoxical perspective from management education. *International Journal of Management Education*, *21*(2), 100790. Advance online publication. DOI: 10.1016/j.ijme.2023.100790

Liu, X., Zhang, Y., Chen, W., & Li, H. (2026). Academic stress and university students' dependency on generative artificial intelligence: A multiple mediation model using PLS-SEM. *BMC Psychology*, *14*(1), 216. Advance online publication. DOI: 10.1186/s40359-026-03986-9 PMID: 41547828

Lo, C. K. (2023). What is the impact of ChatGPT on education? A rapid review of the literature. *Education Sciences*, *13*(4), 410. Advance online publication. DOI: 10.3390/educsci13040410

Lodge, J. M., & Loble, L. (2026). *Artificial intelligence, cognitive offloading and implications for education*. University of Technology Sydney.

Mah, D. K., & Groß, N. (2024). Artificial intelligence in higher education: Exploring faculty use, self-efficacy, distinct profiles, and professional development needs. *International Journal of Educational Technology in Higher Education*, *21*(1), 58. Advance online publication. DOI: 10.1186/s41239-024-00490-1

Markauskaite, L., Marrone, R., Poquet, O., Knight, S., Martinez-Maldonado, R., Howard, S., Tondeur, J., De Laat, M., Buckingham Shum, S., Gašević, D., & Siemens, G. (2022). Rethinking the entwinement between artificial intelligence and human learning: What capabilities do learners need for a world with AI? *Computers and Education: Artificial Intelligence*, *3*, 100056. Advance online publication. DOI: 10.1016/j.caeai.2022.100056

May, A. (2011). Experience-dependent structural plasticity in the adult human brain. *Trends in Cognitive Sciences*, *15*(10), 475–482. DOI: 10.1016/j.tics.2011.08.002 PMID: 21906988

Ng, D. T. K., Leung, J. K. L., Chu, S. K. W., & Qiao, M. S. (2021). Conceptualizing AI literacy: An exploratory review. *Computers and Education: Artificial Intelligence*, *2*, 100041. Advance online publication. DOI: 10.1016/j.caeai.2021.100041

Niu, J., Geng, Z., & Chen, X. (2024). The role of artificial intelligence autonomy in higher education: A uses and gratifications perspective. *Sustainability (Basel)*, *16*(3), 1276. Advance online publication. DOI: 10.3390/su16031276

OECD. (2023). *Artificial Intelligence in science: Challenges, opportunities and the future of research*. OECD Publishing., DOI: 10.1787/a8d820bd-

Ogunleye, B., Zakariyyah, K. I., Ajao, O., Olayinka, O., & Sharma, H. (2024). A systematic review of generative AI for teaching and learning practice. *Education Sciences*, *14*(6), 636. Advance online publication. DOI: 10.3390/educsci14060636

Ouyang, F., & Jiao, P. (2021). Artificial intelligence in education: The three paradigms. *Computers and Education: Artificial Intelligence*, *2*, 100020. Advance online publication. DOI: 10.1016/j.caeai.2021.100020

Panadero, E. (2017). A review of self-regulated learning: Six models and four directions for research. *Frontiers in Psychology*, *8*, 422. Advance online publication. DOI: 10.3389/fpsyg.2017.00422 PMID: 28503157

Parasuraman, R., & Riley, V. (1997). Humans and automation: Use, misuse, disuse, abuse. *Human Factors*, *39*(2), 230–253. DOI: 10.1518/001872097778543886

Peng, J. L., & Yeh, S. L. (2025). Cognitive offloading in short-term memory tasks: Trust toward tools as a moderator. *International Journal of Human-Computer Interaction*, *41*(21), 13382–13393. DOI: 10.1080/10447318.2025.2474449

Peng, X., Sun, K., Shan, X., & Zhang, J. (2026). Empowerment or dependency? A systematic review of the impacts of intelligent assessment and generative AI on learners' self-beliefs and cognitive agency in music education. *Frontiers in Psychology*, *17*, 1776445. DOI: 10.3389/fpsyg.2026.1776445 PMID: 41783302

Perkins, M. (2023). Academic integrity considerations of AI large language models in the post-pandemic era: ChatGPT and beyond. *Journal of University Teaching & Learning Practice*, *20*(2). Advance online publication. DOI: 10.53761/1.20.02.07

Pintrich, P. R. (2004). A conceptual framework for assessing motivation and self-regulated learning in college students. *Educational Psychology Review*, *16*(4), 385–407. DOI: 10.1007/s10648-004-0006-x

Revesai, Z. (2025). Generative AI dependency: The emerging academic crisis and its impact on student performance: A case study of a university in Zimbabwe. *Cogent Education*, *12*(1), 2549787. Advance online publication. DOI: 10.1080/2331186X.2025.2549787

Risko, E. F., & Gilbert, S. J. (2016). Cognitive offloading. *Trends in Cognitive Sciences*, *20*(9), 676–688. DOI: 10.1016/j.tics.2016.07.002 PMID: 27542527

Salifu, I., Arthur, F., Arkorful, V., Nortey, S. A., & Osei-Yaw, R. S. (2024). Economics students' behavioural intention and usage of ChatGPT in higher education: A hybrid structural equation modelling-artificial neural network approach. *Cogent Social Sciences*, *10*(1), 2300177. Advance online publication. DOI: 10.1080/23311886.2023.2300177

Schemmer, M., Kühl, N., Benz, C., Bartos, A., & Satzger, G. (2023). Appropriate reliance on AI advice: Conceptualization and the effect of explanations. *Proceedings of the 2023 CHI Conference on Human Factors in Computing Systems*, 1–18. https://doi.org/DOI: 10.1145/3581641.3584066

Seo, K., Tang, J., Roll, I., Fels, S., & Yoon, D. (2021). The impact of artificial intelligence on learner-instructor interaction in online learning. *International Journal of Educational Technology in Higher Education*, *18*(1), 54. Advance online publication. DOI: 10.1186/s41239-021-00292-9 PMID: 34778540

Shahzad, M. F., Xu, S., & Zahid, H. (2025). Exploring the impact of generative AI-based technologies on learning performance through self-efficacy, fairness & ethics, creativity, and trust in higher education. *Education and Information Technologies*, *30*(3), 3691–3716. DOI: 10.1007/s10639-024-12949-9

Siegfried, J. J., & Colander, D. (2022). What does critical thinking mean in teaching economics? The big and the little of it. *The Journal of Economic Education*, *53*(1), 71–84. DOI: 10.1080/00220485.2021.2004278

Smerdon, D. (2024). AI in essay-based assessment: Student adoption, usage, and performance. *Computers and Education: Artificial Intelligence*, *7*, 100288. Advance online publication. DOI: 10.1016/j.caeai.2024.100288

Strzelecki, A. (2024). Students' acceptance of ChatGPT in higher education: An extended Unified Theory of Acceptance and Use of Technology. *Innovative Higher Education*, *49*(2), 223–245. DOI: 10.1007/s10755-023-09686-1

Tarasova, K., Gracheva, D., Talov, D., Orel, E., & Dementiev, A. (2025). Measuring changes in critical thinking skills among university economics students: Insights from domain-specific assessment. *Studies in Higher Education*. Advance online publication. DOI: 10.1080/03075079.2025.2484423

Tiwari, C. K., Bhat, M. A., Khan, S. T., Subramaniam, R., & Khan, M. A. I. (2024). What drives students toward ChatGPT? An investigation of the factors influencing adoption and usage of ChatGPT. *Interactive Technology and Smart Education*, *21*(3), 333–355. DOI: 10.1108/ITSE-04-2023-0061

Tlili, A., Shehata, B., Adarkwah, M. A., Bozkurt, A., Hickey, D. T., Huang, R., & Agyemang, B. (2023). What if the devil is my guardian angel? ChatGPT as a case study of using chatbots in education. *Smart Learning Environments*, *10*(1), 15. Advance online publication. DOI: 10.1186/s40561-023-00237-x

Uppal, K., & Hajian, S. (2025). Students' perceptions of ChatGPT in higher education: A study of academic enhancement, procrastination, and ethical concerns. *European Journal of Educational Research, 14*(1), 199–211. DOI: 10.12973/eu-jer.14.1.199

Wang, J. (2026). Cognitive offloading through digital tools and its relationship with critical thinking, task persistence, and learning depth. *Frontiers in Psychology, 17*, 1781101. DOI: 10.3389/fpsyg.2026.1781101 PMID: 41909580

Yan, L., Greiff, S., Lodge, J. M., & Gašević, D. (2025). Distinguishing performance gains from learning when using generative AI. *Nature Reviews Psychology, 4*(7), 435–436. DOI: 10.1038/s44159-025-00467-5

Yan, L., Greiff, S., Teuber, Z., & Gašević, D. (2024). Promises and challenges of generative artificial intelligence for human learning. *Nature Human Behaviour, 8*(10), 1839–1850. DOI: 10.1038/s41562-024-02004-5 PMID: 39438686

Zawacki-Richter, O., Marín, V. I., Bond, M., & Gouverneur, F. (2019). Systematic review of research on artificial intelligence applications in higher education: Where are the educators? *International Journal of Educational Technology in Higher Education, 16*(1), 39. Advance online publication. DOI: 10.1186/s41239-019-0171-0

Zhai, C., Wibowo, S., & Li, L. D. (2024). The effects of over-reliance on AI dialogue systems on students' cognitive abilities: A systematic review. *Smart Learning Environments, 11*(1), 28. Advance online publication. DOI: 10.1186/s40561-024-00316-7

Zhang, Y., & Xu, W. (2024). The paradox of self-efficacy and technological dependence: Unraveling generative AI's impact on university students' task completion. *The Internet and Higher Education, 65*, 100978. Advance online publication. DOI: 10.1016/j.iheduc.2024.100978

Zimmerman, B. J. (2002). Becoming a self-regulated learner: An overview. *Theory into Practice, 41*(2), 64–70. DOI: 10.1207/s15430421tip4102_2

Chapter 16
Toward Human-Centered AI in Economics Education:
Designing Artificial Intelligence for Thinking, Not Cognitive Replacement

Abena Yeboah Abraham
http://orcid.org/0000-0002-4454-155X
Koforidua Technical University, Ghana

Francis Arthur
http://orcid.org/0000-0001-7792-6563
University of Cape Coast, Ghana

Mark Inkoom
http://orcid.org/0009-0008-2797-6712
University of Cape Coast, Ghana

ABSTRACT

Artificial intelligence (AI) is increasingly shaping learning processes in higher education, raising concerns about cognitive dependency and the erosion of critical thinking. These concerns are particularly significant in economics education, where analytical reasoning, judgement, and problem-solving are essential. This chapter conceptually examines how human-centred AI design can support cognitive development rather than replace it. Drawing on Human-Centred AI, Cognitive Load Theory, Self-Regulated Learning Theory, Dual-Process Theory, and insights from neuroscience, the chapter proposes the Human-Centered AI for Economic Thinking

DOI: 10.4018/979-8-3373-9484-8.ch016

(HCAI-ET) Framework. The framework offers design and pedagogical principles that promote cognitive engagement, metacognition, intellectual autonomy, and responsible AI integration in economics education.

1. INTRODUCTION AND CONTEXT

The rapid integration of artificial intelligence (AI) into higher education represents one of the most significant pedagogical transformations of the twenty-first century. Once regarded as a supplementary educational technology, AI has increasingly become embedded in the ways students search for information, generate ideas, solve problems, analyse data, and construct academic arguments (Kasneci et al., 2023; Labadze et al., 2023; Tlili et al., 2023). The emergence of generative AI and large language models has accelerated this transformation by making intelligent support systems more accessible, conversational, and responsive across disciplinary contexts (Bhullar et al., 2024; Chiu, 2024). Consequently, AI has moved from the periphery of educational practice to the centre of contemporary debates about learning, thinking, authorship, and academic responsibility.

Across higher education, AI tools are increasingly supporting tasks that traditionally depended on students' independent cognitive effort, including explanation seeking, problem-solving, writing support, feedback generation, literature synthesis, data interpretation, and assessment preparation (Chiu et al., 2023; Farrokhnia et al., 2024; Xia et al., 2024). While these developments have expanded opportunities for personalised learning and academic support, they have also raised important questions about the changing nature of student engagement. The central issue is no longer whether students will use AI, but whether such use strengthens or weakens the cognitive capacities that higher education seeks to cultivate (Markauskaite et al., 2022; Yang et al., 2021).

These concerns are particularly significant in Economics education, where learning extends beyond memorising concepts to developing analytical reasoning, abstraction, model-based thinking, and evaluative judgement (Arthur et al., 2025). Economics students are expected to interpret complex market and social phenomena, assess trade-offs, work with assumptions, and apply theoretical models to real-world problems (Bröse et al., 2026; Salifu et al., 2024). Such intellectual practices require sustained engagement with evidence, uncertainty, and competing explanations. As AI tools increasingly provide instant explanations, worked solutions, forecasts, and model interpretations, a critical question emerges: can AI support and deepen economic thinking rather than replace it?

Recent evidence suggests that AI adoption among Economics and business students is growing rapidly, with learners perceiving AI tools as valuable for academic support, performance improvement, and knowledge access (Acquah et al., 2025; Duong et al., 2023; Gao et al., 2024). Salifu et al. (2024), for example, found that Economics students' use of ChatGPT is shaped by trust, perceived usefulness, and learning expectations, while Bröse et al. (2026) demonstrated that ChatGPT can function as an effective tutor for understanding economic concepts and problem-solving processes. Although these findings highlight the instructional potential of AI, they also raise important questions about the quality and depth of learning when students rely on systems that can explain, summarise, calculate, and evaluate on their behalf.

The challenge is therefore not limited to concerns about inaccurate information or algorithmic bias. More fundamentally, AI may alter how students think, the effort they invest in learning, and the ways they evaluate knowledge claims (Essel et al., 2024; Gerlich, 2025; Stadler et al., 2024). Repeated reliance on AI to bypass difficult reasoning tasks may reduce students' willingness to grapple with conceptual uncertainty, scrutinise assumptions, and trust their own interpretive judgement. This risk has been discussed through concepts such as cognitive offloading, automation bias, reduced critical thinking, and overdependence on intelligent systems (Gerlich, 2025; Lee et al., 2025; Stadler et al., 2024). Although cognitive offloading has long been part of human learning through tools, texts, and technologies, excessive and unreflective reliance may undermine the productive mental effort necessary for deep understanding. As Stadler et al. (2024) argue, large language models can reduce mental effort while potentially compromising reflective inquiry, suggesting that convenience and performance gains may come at the expense of intellectual development.

Human-centered AI provides an important framework for addressing these concerns by emphasising what AI should enable learners to become rather than merely what AI can accomplish. Instead of replacing human reasoning, human-centered approaches prioritise augmentation, agency, transparency, trust, ethical responsibility, and human flourishing (Fu & Weng, 2024; Khosravi et al., 2022; Yang et al., 2021). In educational settings, this requires AI systems and pedagogical practices that encourage students to question, compare, justify, reflect, and revise their thinking. Educational success should therefore be assessed not only in terms of efficiency or task completion, but also in relation to deeper understanding, intellectual autonomy, and responsible judgement (Markauskaite et al., 2022; Tuomi, 2024).

Within this perspective, AI literacy becomes essential for responsible learning. Students must understand not only how to use AI tools, but also how such systems generate responses, where their limitations lie, and how their outputs should be critically evaluated (Long & Magerko, 2020; Ng et al., 2021; Southworth et al., 2023). For Economics students, this involves interrogating AI-generated explanations, identifying underlying assumptions, assessing causal claims, and comparing automated outputs with economic theory and contextual evidence. Without such competencies, learners may confuse fluency with accuracy and automated explanations with genuine understanding.

The pedagogical role of lecturers and curriculum designers is therefore crucial in determining whether AI promotes cognitive development or cognitive replacement. AI can support self-regulated learning when used to facilitate planning, monitoring, feedback seeking, and reflection (Jin et al., 2023; Xu et al., 2025). However, without appropriate guidance, students may employ AI primarily for answer generation and shortcut learning. Economics educators must consequently design learning activities that require students to explain their reasoning, defend assumptions, critique AI outputs, and connect automated responses to economic concepts, empirical realities, and ethical considerations.

The African and Ghanaian higher education context offers a particularly important lens for examining these issues. AI adoption in these settings occurs alongside broader concerns regarding digital inequality, graduate employability, curriculum relevance, and knowledge production in the Global South. Evidence from Ghanaian Economics students indicates increasing engagement with ChatGPT and related tools, influenced by perceived usefulness, trust, curiosity, and performance expectations (Acquah et al., 2025; Salifu et al., 2024). At the same time, questions remain regarding access, institutional policy, academic preparedness, and students' capacity to use AI critically rather than dependently. These realities underscore the need to understand AI not merely as a technological innovation, but as a pedagogical and cognitive intervention.

Against this background, this chapter examines the implications of generative AI for Economics education through a human-centered lens that prioritises cognitive augmentation over cognitive replacement. Drawing on insights from human-centered AI, cognitive psychology, self-regulated learning, dual-process theory, cognitive load theory, and neuroplasticity, the chapter explores how AI influences students' thinking effort, judgement, autonomy, and learning habits (Khosravi et al., 2022; Markauskaite et al., 2022; Xu et al., 2025). Rather than rejecting AI or embracing it uncritically, the chapter argues that AI should function as a cognitive partner that supports students in questioning assumptions, evaluating alternatives, reflecting on evidence, and developing the analytical discipline required for economic reasoning.

The central argument is that the educational value of AI depends not merely on its capacity to improve efficiency or provide instant support, but on its ability to strengthen learners' cognitive agency. While AI can expand access to knowledge, enhance feedback processes, and assist students in navigating complex economic concepts, its long-term contribution to higher education rests on whether it promotes critical thinking, metacognitive engagement, and intellectual autonomy. By advancing a Human-Centered AI for Economic Thinking perspective, this chapter contributes to ongoing debates on responsible AI in higher education and provides a conceptual foundation for designing AI-supported learning environments that preserve independent thought and meaningful learning among Economics students.

2. PURPOSE AND SCOPE OF THE CHAPTER

The purpose of this chapter is to develop a conceptual argument for human-centered AI in Economics education, with particular attention to how AI can be designed and used to support students' thinking rather than replace it. Building on current debates on responsible AI, learner agency, AI literacy, and assessment transformation, the chapter positions Economics education as a disciplinary context in which the cognitive consequences of AI use require careful scholarly attention (Chan, 2023; Laupichler et al., 2022; Yang et al., 2024). The central concern of the chapter is not whether AI should be used in higher education, but how its use can be aligned with the intellectual purposes of Economics learning.

The scope of the chapter is deliberately conceptual. It does not present primary empirical data, statistical results, classroom experiments, or technical AI system development. Instead, it synthesises literature from human-centered AI, cognitive psychology, neuroscience, self-regulated learning, and Economics education to clarify how AI may influence students' reasoning, judgment, autonomy, and metacognitive engagement. This approach is consistent with conceptual scholarship, which seeks to organise existing knowledge, clarify relationships among concepts, and develop frameworks that offer new ways of understanding an emerging problem (Jaakkola, 2020; Jabareen, 2009).

The chapter is also bounded by its focus on Economics students in higher education. Although the discussion has relevance for other fields, Economics is treated as a distinctive learning context because it requires students to work with models, assumptions, data, uncertainty, trade-offs, and policy consequences. The chapter therefore focuses on AI use in relation to economic thinking, rather than on AI adoption in education generally. It also does not examine AI as a purely technical innovation, institutional productivity tool, or replacement for lecturers. Rather, it examines AI as a pedagogical and cognitive support system whose educational value depends on whether it strengthens students' capacity to reason independently.

Within this scope, the chapter pursues five related objectives. First, it examines the psychological and cognitive risks associated with AI-supported learning in Economics education. Second, it synthesises insights from cognitive psychology, neuroscience, and educational theory to explain how AI may shape thinking effort, judgment, and learner autonomy. Third, it proposes a Human-Centered AI for Economic Thinking Framework that positions AI as a cognitive partner rather than a cognitive replacement. Fourth, it identifies design and pedagogical principles that encourage critical questioning, metacognitive reflection, effortful reasoning, and intellectual independence. Finally, it contributes to broader debates on responsible AI adoption in higher education by showing how AI can be integrated without weakening the cognitive purposes of disciplinary learning.

The expected contribution of the chapter is therefore both conceptual and pedagogical. Conceptually, it reframes AI in Economics education as a question of cognitive agency rather than technological efficiency alone. Pedagogically, it offers a basis for designing AI-supported learning environments that require students to question, justify, revise, and evaluate AI-generated outputs. This contribution extends current discussions on academic integrity, assessment redesign, and human-AI collaboration by foregrounding what students should still be able to understand and decide for themselves in an AI-mediated learning environment (Bittle & El-Gayar, 2025; Hwang & Lee, 2025; Weng et al., 2024).

3. CONCEPTUAL AND THEORETICAL FOUNDATIONS

This chapter is grounded in an interdisciplinary theoretical position that treats AI in Economics education as more than a technological issue. It is also a cognitive, pedagogical, ethical, and developmental issue. Since the chapter argues for AI that supports thinking rather than replaces it, no single theory is sufficient to explain the relationship between AI use, student reasoning, and the development of economic judgment. The chapter therefore draws on Human-Centered AI, Cognitive Load Theory, Self-Regulated Learning Theory, Dual-Process Theory, and Neuroplasticity to explain how AI may either strengthen or weaken students' cognitive agency. These perspectives provide the foundation for understanding AI as a system that must be deliberately designed to support effortful reasoning, metacognitive engagement, critical judgment, and intellectual autonomy.

3.1 Human-Centered AI (HCAI)

Human-Centered AI (HCAI) provides the principal design perspective underpinning this chapter. It emphasises that intelligent systems should augment human capabilities, preserve human control, foster trust, and promote ethical responsibility rather than displace human judgement (Yang et al., 2021; Shneiderman, 2020). Within education, this approach shifts attention from technological performance alone to the broader effects of AI on learners, educators, and learning environments.

Yang et al. (2021) argue that human-centered AI in education should make learning processes more visible and support learners' understanding and agency.

Similarly, Fu and Weng (2024) highlight transparency, fairness, privacy, autonomy, and accountability as essential considerations in responsible educational AI practices. These principles provide an important framework for understanding how AI systems can be integrated into learning environments while maintaining learner participation and critical engagement.

In Economics education, the HCAI perspective is particularly relevant because disciplinary learning involves reasoning about assumptions, evidence, trade-offs, and uncertainty. Markauskaite et al. (2022) and Hwang and Lee (2025) suggest that educational technologies are most effective when they complement rather than replace higher-order thinking processes. HCAI therefore offers a useful lens for examining the relationship between AI tools and the development of economic reasoning and judgement.

3.2 Cognitive Load Theory

Cognitive Load Theory explains learning in terms of the limitations of working memory and the cognitive demands imposed by instructional activities. Sweller (1988) argues that learning is hindered when tasks overload working memory, while later developments distinguish between intrinsic, extraneous, and germane forms of cognitive load (Paas et al., 2003; Sweller et al., 2019). This distinction provides an important basis for analysing the educational effects of AI-supported learning.

AI technologies can reduce extraneous cognitive load by clarifying instructions, organising information, and providing timely feedback (Jin et al., 2023; Sweller et al., 2019). However, learning also depends on productive cognitive effort that contributes to knowledge construction and schema development. Stadler et al. (2024) observe that large language models may reduce mental effort during academic tasks while influencing the depth of student inquiry. Cognitive Load Theory therefore offers a framework for understanding how AI-mediated support may interact with both learning efficiency and meaningful cognitive engagement.

Within Economics education, this perspective is relevant because students regularly work with abstract models, quantitative relationships, graphical representations, and policy analyses that require sustained cognitive processing. The theory thus provides a basis for examining how AI support can influence the balance between reducing unnecessary complexity and maintaining productive intellectual effort.

3.3 Self-Regulated Learning Theory

Self-Regulated Learning Theory provides a framework for understanding how learners actively manage their own learning through planning, monitoring, strategy use, reflection, and self-evaluation. Zimmerman (2002) describes self-regulated learners as those who are able to set goals, observe their progress, adjust their strategies, and evaluate their learning outcomes. This theory is highly relevant to AI-supported education because the value of AI depends not only on what the tool can generate, but also on how learners use, question, and regulate their engagement with AI outputs.

In generative AI environments, self-regulation becomes even more important because students can easily move from learning support to answer dependency (Xu et al., 2025; Risko & Gilbert, 2016). AI can assist learners by providing feedback, prompts, examples, explanations, and opportunities for revision. Jin et al. (2023) show that AI applications can support self-regulated learning when they are used to guide students' planning, monitoring, and reflection. Similarly, Xu et al. (2025) emphasise the importance of metacognitive support in generative AI learning environments, arguing that students need support to evaluate their understanding and regulate their learning processes. These insights suggest that AI should be designed to strengthen students' self-regulatory capacities rather than reduce their responsibility for learning.

For Economics students, self-regulated learning is essential because economic understanding develops through iterative reasoning (Arthur et al., 2025). Students must identify what they do not understand, revisit assumptions, compare theoretical explanations, interpret data carefully, and revise their conclusions. AI can support this process when it asks students to explain why a demand curve shifts, justify the assumptions behind a model, compare alternative policy interventions, or reflect on the limitations of a forecast. However, when AI is used only to produce final answers, students may lose opportunities to monitor and regulate their own thinking. Self-Regulated Learning Theory therefore supports the chapter's argument that AI should be designed to promote metacognition, reflection, and intellectual responsibility.

3.4 Dual-Process Theory

Dual-Process Theory explains human reasoning through the interaction between fast, automatic, intuitive forms of thinking and slower, more deliberate, analytical forms of thinking. Kahneman (2003) links this distinction to bounded rationality and behavioural economics, showing that human judgment is often shaped by heuristics, biases, and limits in reflective reasoning. Evans (2008) and Evans and Stanovich (2013) further explain that Type 1 thinking is fast and automatic, while Type 2 thinking is slower, more effortful, and more reflective. This distinction is central to the chapter because AI convenience may encourage students to rely on fast acceptance rather than slow evaluation.

Generative AI tools often produce fluent, confident, and well-structured responses. This fluency can make AI-generated content appear reliable even when it contains weak reasoning, hidden assumptions, incomplete evidence, or inaccurate claims. When students encounter such outputs, they may be tempted to accept them quickly because doing so reduces effort. Lee et al. (2025) suggest that generative AI use may reduce cognitive effort and affect critical thinking confidence, raising concerns about how users evaluate automated outputs. From a dual-process perspective, this means that AI may strengthen surface-level processing when learners rely on convenience, fluency, and speed instead of reflective analysis.

This issue is especially important for Economics education because economic reasoning requires slow and deliberate thinking. Students must not only know what an AI system says about inflation, unemployment, market failure, or fiscal policy; they must examine whether the explanation is theoretically coherent, empirically justified, and contextually appropriate. A human-centered approach to AI should therefore be designed to activate reflective thinking. Instead of giving students only final answers, AI systems should ask them to compare assumptions, identify possible biases, test the logic of claims, and consider alternative interpretations. Dual-Process Theory therefore helps explain why AI in Economics education must be designed to move students from quick acceptance to critical evaluation.

3.5 Neuroplasticity and Use-Dependent Brain Development

Neuroplasticity and use-dependent brain development provide a developmental perspective on why repeated learning habits matter. Neuroplasticity refers to the brain's capacity to change in response to experience, practice, and learning. Evidence from neuroscience shows that repeated training and experience can shape brain structure and function over time (Draganski et al., 2004; May, 2011). Kleim and Jones (2008) also explain that experience-dependent plasticity is shaped by principles such as "use it or lose it" and "use it and improve it," suggesting that capacities that are repeatedly exercised may be strengthened, while those that are underused may receive less reinforcement.

This perspective must be applied carefully to AI in education. It would be inaccurate to claim that AI use automatically weakens the brain or damages students' reasoning. However, the literature on cognitive offloading shows that humans often use external tools to reduce internal cognitive effort (Risko & Gilbert, 2016). Such offloading is not inherently negative. Students have always used calculators, textbooks, notes, search engines, and peer discussion to support thinking. The concern emerges when cognitive outsourcing becomes habitual and replaces the repeated practice of reasoning, judging, and reflecting. Gerlich (2025) argues that AI tools may intensify cognitive offloading in ways that raise concerns for critical thinking, especially when users depend on automated systems for tasks that require independent judgment.

For Economics education, the implication is that students need repeated practice in the cognitive activities that define the discipline. They must learn to frame economic problems, reason through causal relationships, interpret evidence, analyse trade-offs, and defend conclusions. If these processes are repeatedly outsourced to AI, students may complete academic tasks while receiving less practice in the mental activities that build economic expertise. Neuroplasticity and use-dependent learning therefore support the chapter's argument that AI should be used to exercise students' reasoning rather than bypass it. AI should prompt practice, feedback, revision, and reflection so that students continue to strengthen the cognitive habits required for independent economic judgment.

3.6 Integrated Theoretical Position of the Chapter

Generally, these theories provide a coherent foundation for the chapter's central argument. Human-Centered AI establishes the design principle that AI should augment rather than replace human capability (Yang et al., 2021). Cognitive Load Theory explains why AI should reduce unnecessary cognitive burden while preserving the productive mental effort needed for learning (Sweller et al., 2019). Self-Regulated Learning Theory shows that students must remain active agents who plan, monitor, evaluate, and reflect on their learning (Zimmerman, 2002). Dual-Process Theory explains why AI-generated convenience may encourage fast, uncritical acceptance unless students are guided toward slower and more analytical reasoning (Evans & Stanovich, 2013; Kahneman, 2003). Neuroplasticity and use-dependent brain development further remind us that repeated cognitive habits matter for the long-term development of reasoning capacity (May, 2011).

This integrated theoretical position is relevant to Economics education because the discipline depends on reasoning under uncertainty, evaluating assumptions, interpreting evidence, and making judgments about competing alternatives. The chapter therefore treats AI not as a neutral technological addition to the Economics classroom, but as a cognitive influence that can shape how students learn to think. If designed poorly, AI may encourage dependency, reduce productive struggle, and weaken reflective judgment. If designed from a human-centered perspective, however, AI can become a scaffold for deeper learning by prompting students to question, justify, revise, compare, and evaluate. This theoretical foundation therefore justifies the chapter's broader claim that AI in Economics education must be designed for thinking, not merely for task completion.

4. ECONOMICS EDUCATION AND THE RISK OF COGNITIVE REPLACEMENT

A primary risk in AI-mediated Economics education is the gradual substitution of economic reasoning with automated answer production. Economics is not merely a technical discipline concerned with calculations, diagrams, and definitions; it is a cognitive discipline that requires students to frame problems, interpret models, evaluate assumptions, compare alternatives, and make judgments under conditions of uncertainty (Cohen, 2024; Thompson, 2025). The development of economic understanding depends on students' ability to move between abstract theory and real-world complexity, especially when analysing trade-offs, incentives, scarcity, market behaviour, policy effects, and welfare consequences. As Sollosy and McInerney (2022) argue in relation to business education, the rise of AI requires educators to rethink what students should know and how they should learn in an AI-rich environment. In Economics education, this means that AI should not simply improve the speed of academic task completion; it should protect the reasoning practices through which students become economically literate thinkers.

The concern becomes more pronounced when generative AI systems are used to produce explanations, solve numerical problems, interpret graphs, summarise readings, or propose policy recommendations without requiring students to engage in the underlying logic of the task. Shen and Zhu (2025) note that ChatGPT has practical applications in Economics teaching, but they also highlight deficiencies that require strategic pedagogical attention. Similarly, Bröse et al. (2026) show that ChatGPT can perform several functions associated with an automated Economics tutor, while also presenting limitations that students and educators must recognise. These studies suggest that generative AI may support Economics learning, but only when students remain cognitively involved in evaluating the accuracy, assumptions, and relevance of AI-generated outputs. Without this involvement, students may appear to complete economic tasks successfully while bypassing the reasoning processes that give such tasks educational value.

This bypassing of reasoning is closely linked to automation bias and over-reliance. Automation bias occurs when individuals give excessive weight to automated recommendations, even when such recommendations are incomplete, misleading, or require further human scrutiny (Parasuraman & Riley, 1997). In educational contexts, this may happen when students treat AI-generated answers as authoritative because they are fluent, structured, and confidently presented. Zhai et al. (2024) warn that over-reliance on AI dialogue systems can affect students' critical cognitive capabilities, including decision-making, analytical reasoning, and critical thinking. This is especially relevant to Economics education, where a polished explanation of inflation, taxation, unemployment, or exchange rates may still contain weak assumptions, omitted variables, or inappropriate generalisations. When students accept such outputs uncritically, they risk confusing rhetorical fluency with economic validity.

The risk of cognitive replacement is also connected to the "out-of-the-loop" problem in automation. Endsley and Kiris (1995) explain that when automated systems take over key functions, human users may lose situation awareness, become less vigilant, and experience reduced ability to intervene effectively when the system fails. In Economics education, a similar problem may occur when AI systems perform the interpretive work that students are supposed to practise. If students repeatedly rely on AI to explain models, interpret data, or justify policy choices, they may become less attentive to the steps through which economic conclusions are reached. This does not mean that AI should be excluded from Economics classrooms. Rather, it means that AI use must be structured so that students remain "in the loop" as active interpreters, evaluators, and decision-makers.

The same concern appears in recent debates on critical thinking and academic integrity. Essien et al. (2024), in their study of AI text generators in UK business schools, show that generative AI raises important questions about the development of higher-order thinking in higher education. Dalalah and Dalalah (2023) further caution that AI detection tools can produce false positives and false negatives, suggesting that academic integrity cannot be protected only through technological policing. Bittle and El-Gayar (2025) similarly argue that generative AI has intensified concerns about academic integrity and requires a broader research and policy agenda. These debates matter for Economics education because the problem is not only whether students submit AI-generated work. The deeper problem is whether students still understand, question, and defend the economic reasoning behind the work they submit.

For example, a student may ask an AI tool to explain the likely effect of fuel subsidy removal on inflation, exchange rates, household welfare, and government expenditure. The AI system may generate a coherent response that mentions rising transport costs, fiscal consolidation, and possible inflationary pressure. However, a closer economic analysis would require the student to ask further questions: What is the structure of the economy? How dependent are households on transport-intensive goods? What exchange rate regime is in place? How credible is fiscal policy? What compensatory measures are available for vulnerable groups? If the student merely submits the AI-generated response, the task becomes an exercise in answer reproduction. If the student interrogates the response, tests its assumptions, and situates it within economic theory and empirical context, the same AI output becomes a stimulus for deeper thinking.

These risks indicate that the central challenge is not AI usage itself, but the design and positioning of AI within Economics learning environments. AI can support students by offering explanations, examples, simulations, feedback, and alternative perspectives. However, it can also promote dependency when it is used mainly to produce answers, reduce effort, or bypass analytical struggle. The future of AI in Economics education should therefore be guided by pedagogical safeguards that preserve disciplinary reasoning, metacognitive engagement, and student agency. Such safeguards include asking students to critique AI outputs, identify assumptions, compare competing explanations, justify policy recommendations, and reflect on the limits of automated reasoning. In this way, AI can be positioned not as a substitute for economic thought, but as a carefully governed tool for strengthening the habits of inquiry, judgment, and intellectual independence that define Economics education.

5. THE HUMAN-CENTERED AI FOR ECONOMIC THINKING (HCAI-ET) FRAMEWORK

The rapid integration of generative artificial intelligence into higher education has created new possibilities and risks for economics education (Acquah et al., 2025; Arthur, 2026a). AI systems can support students by explaining difficult concepts, generating examples, assisting with data interpretation, and providing feedback on written work (Arthur, 2026a; Arthur, 2026b). However, these same systems can also encourage passive learning, shortcut thinking, and cognitive dependency when students use them to obtain complete answers without engaging in the reasoning process. This concern is particularly significant in economics education because learning economics requires more than memorising definitions. Students must develop the capacity to interpret evidence, construct and critique models, evaluate assumptions, compare policy options, and reason through trade-offs.

The Human-Centered AI for Economic Thinking (HCAI-ET) Framework is proposed as a conceptual model for guiding the responsible design and use of AI systems in economics education. The framework is grounded in the principle that AI should enhance human reasoning rather than replace it. UNESCO's guidance on generative AI in education stresses the need for human capacity development and a human-centred vision of AI use in education and research (Cukurova & Miao, 2024). Similarly, the OECD AI Principles emphasise trustworthy AI that respects human rights, democratic values, transparency, and human-centred governance (OECD, 2023).

The HCAI-ET Framework responds to a growing concern in AI-supported learning: students may become efficient at producing outputs while becoming less capable of independent thought. Recent research on AI and cognitive offloading suggests that frequent reliance on AI tools may reduce critical thinking when learners delegate substantial cognitive work to external systems. Gerlich (2025) found that increased AI usage was significantly associated with lower critical thinking skills, with cognitive offloading acting as a key mediating mechanism. The study suggests that excessive dependence on AI may reduce opportunities for deep cognitive engagement, analytical reasoning, and independent problem-solving (Gerlich, 2025). In higher education, Zhai et al. (2024) study on over-reliance on AI dialogue systems also warns that excessive dependence on AI may weaken independent decision-making and cognitive engagement. These concerns are especially relevant to economics, where students must learn how to think like economists rather than merely reproduce economic explanations.

The HCAI-ET Framework therefore proposes that AI in economics education should be designed around four interdependent dimensions: AI Design Orientation, Cognitive Engagement Mechanisms, Psychological Safeguards Against Dependency, and Cognitive and Developmental Outcomes. Together, these dimensions explain how AI systems can be structured to promote economic reasoning, analytical confidence, and intellectual autonomy.

Figure 1. Human-Centered AI for Economic Thinking (HCAI-ET) framework

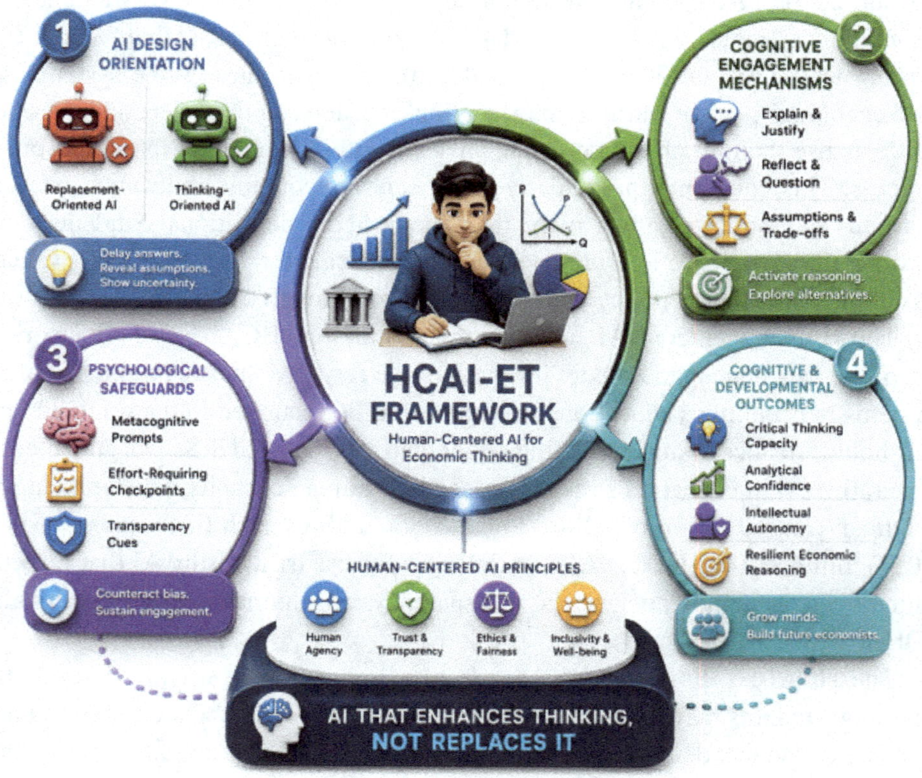

5.1 AI Design Orientation

The first dimension of the HCAI-ET Framework concerns the orientation of AI design. It distinguishes between replacement-oriented AI and thinking-oriented AI. Replacement-oriented AI refers to systems that provide complete answers, full interpretations, ready-made essays, solved calculations, or finished policy arguments with minimal requirement for student reasoning. In economics education, this may occur when a student asks an AI tool to "explain the causes of inflation," "solve this elasticity problem," "interpret this regression output," or "write a policy recommendation," and the system immediately supplies a polished response. While such outputs may appear helpful, they can bypass the intellectual processes through which students learn to analyse economic problems.

Replacement-oriented AI is attractive because it is efficient. However, its educational risk is that efficiency may be mistaken for learning. A student may submit a coherent AI-generated explanation of fiscal policy without understanding the multiplier process, crowding-out effects, or the assumptions behind Keynesian and classical interpretations. In such cases, AI produces performance without necessarily producing competence.

Thinking-oriented AI, by contrast, is designed to keep students cognitively active. Rather than immediately providing final answers, it prompts students to reason, justify, compare, question, and revise. In economics education, a thinking-oriented AI tool might ask students to identify the assumptions behind a demand and supply model before giving feedback. It might require students to explain why a tariff creates deadweight loss before showing the welfare diagram. It might ask students to compare short-run and long-run effects before presenting a macroeconomic policy analysis.

This design orientation aligns with UNESCO's AI Competency Framework for Students, which identifies four core dimensions of AI competence: a human-centred mindset, ethics of AI, AI techniques and applications, and AI system design. The framework emphasises the development of responsible, ethical, and critically engaged AI users and co-creators rather than passive consumers of AI technologies (UNESCO, 2024). It also reflects UNESCO's view that AI should protect human agency and support the development of human capabilities.

The HCAI-ET Framework advocates for AI systems that delay complete answers, provide partial scaffolding, reveal uncertainty, and make assumptions visible. This does not mean AI should be made unnecessarily difficult to use. Rather, it means AI should be designed to preserve the learner's responsibility for thinking.

5.2 Cognitive Engagement Mechanisms

The second dimension of the framework focuses on the mechanisms through which AI can stimulate economic thinking. If AI systems are to support learning rather than replace cognition, they must be designed to activate reasoning processes. Three mechanisms are particularly important: prompted explanation and justification, reflection triggers and counterfactual questioning, and explicit representation of assumptions and trade-offs.

Prompted explanation and justification requires students to explain their reasoning before receiving AI feedback. In economics, this may involve asking students to first state why a demand curve slopes downward, why inflation may reduce purchasing power, or why a government subsidy may create both benefits and inefficiencies. The AI system can then respond by identifying gaps, correcting misunderstandings, and asking further questions. This approach prevents students from becoming passive recipients of finished explanations.

Reflection triggers and counterfactual questioning encourage students to consider alternative possibilities. Economics is a discipline of trade-offs, assumptions, and conditional reasoning. A good AI learning system should therefore ask questions such as: What happens if consumer income changes? What if the economy is operating below full employment? How would the analysis differ under perfect competition and monopoly? What assumptions are required for this model to hold? Such questions support deeper economic reasoning because they require students to move beyond surface-level answers.

Explicit representation of assumptions and trade-offs is especially important in economics education. Economic models simplify reality, but students often struggle to recognise the assumptions behind those simplifications. The threshold concepts literature in economics shows that students often experience difficulty with foundational economic ideas that transform how they understand the discipline (Carrasco-Aguilar et al., 2026). For this reason, AI tools should not simply generate model-based answers. They should expose the assumptions underlying those answers.

For example, if a student asks AI whether minimum wage laws increase unemployment, a thinking-oriented system should not simply provide a one-sided answer. It should indicate that the response depends on assumptions about labour market structure, elasticity of demand for labour, monopsony power, enforcement, and the size of the wage increase. This type of interaction helps students understand that economic reasoning involves conditional judgement rather than mechanical answer production.

5.3 Psychological Safeguards Against Dependency

The third dimension of the HCAI-ET Framework addresses psychological risks associated with AI use. Even well-designed AI tools may promote dependency if students are not guided to monitor their own thinking. The framework therefore proposes three safeguards: metacognitive prompts, effort-requiring checkpoints, and transparency cues.

Metacognitive prompts encourage students to examine their own understanding. Before presenting a solution, an AI tool may ask: What do you already know about this concept? Which part of the problem is unclear? Can you explain the answer in your own words? What evidence supports your interpretation? Such prompts encourage students to monitor their learning rather than outsource judgement to AI.

This is important because over-reliance on AI may reduce students' active monitoring of their own knowledge. Research on AI and cognitive offloading suggests that when learners delegate too much cognitive work to external tools, their critical thinking may weaken (Gerlich, 2025). In economics education, this may occur when students allow AI to interpret data, construct arguments, and evaluate policy options without checking whether they personally understand the reasoning.

Effort-requiring checkpoints are design features that require students to attempt part of a task before receiving help. For example, an AI economics tutor may ask students to draw a demand and supply diagram, identify equilibrium, or predict the effect of a tax before showing the correct analysis. These checkpoints preserve productive struggle, which is necessary for conceptual growth. They also reduce the tendency to use AI as a shortcut.

Transparency cues remind students that AI outputs may be incomplete, biased, context-insensitive, or incorrect. This safeguard directly addresses automation bias. Georgetown University's Center for Security and Emerging Technology (CSET) defines automation bias as the tendency of individuals to over-rely on automated systems, often favouring system recommendations even when contradictory information is available (Kahn et al., 2024). In economics, automation bias may cause students to accept AI-generated conclusions without questioning the data, assumptions, ideological framing, or model limitations behind them.

Transparency cues may include statements such as: This answer depends on assumptions. Check the data source. Consider alternative models. This interpretation may not apply to all economies. Verify with course materials. Such cues help students treat AI as a fallible tool rather than an authority.

5.4 Cognitive and Developmental Outcomes

The final dimension of the HCAI-ET Framework focuses on the long-term outcomes that human-centred AI should support. These outcomes include sustained critical thinking capacity, stronger analytical confidence, preservation of intellectual autonomy, and resilient economic reasoning skills.

Sustained critical thinking capacity is essential because economics students must evaluate evidence, identify assumptions, interpret competing theories, and make reasoned policy judgements. AI should therefore support students in questioning and testing ideas (Vendrell & Johnston, 2026). It should not merely provide polished answers that reduce the need for evaluation. Kasneci et al. (2023) argue that large language models offer opportunities for personalised learning and feedback, but their educational use must be accompanied by awareness of limitations and risks.

Analytical confidence refers to students' belief that they can reason through economic problems independently (Walsh et al., 2021). This is different from confidence in using AI. A student may know how to prompt AI effectively but still lack confidence in drawing diagrams, interpreting coefficients, or explaining policy trade-offs. The goal of HCAI-ET is to ensure that AI strengthens students' confidence in their own economic reasoning.

Preservation of intellectual autonomy is central to the framework. Human-centred AI should help students become better thinkers, not more dependent users. Intellectual autonomy means that students can decide when AI is useful, when it should be questioned, and when independent reasoning is required. This aligns with the OECD's emphasis on trustworthy AI systems that remain understandable and accountable to humans (OECD, 2023).

Resilient economic reasoning skills refer to students' ability to apply economic concepts across unfamiliar contexts (Tarasova et al., 2026). For example, a resilient economics student should be able to use demand and supply reasoning to analyse housing markets, food prices, labour markets, or exchange rates without requiring AI to generate the entire analysis. AI can support this skill by providing feedback and alternative examples, but students must still practise transferring concepts independently.

The HCAI-ET Framework therefore does not reject efficiency. Rather, it argues that efficiency should not come at the expense of cognitive development. In economics education, the most valuable AI systems will be those that help students slow down where thinking matters, question where assumptions are hidden, and reason where answers appear easy.

5.5 Synthesis of the HCAI-ET Framework

The HCAI-ET Framework contributes to AI in education by shifting attention from whether students should use AI to how AI should be designed to support disciplinary thinking. In economics, the central question is not simply whether AI improves productivity, but whether it strengthens students' capacity to think economically.

The framework suggests that replacement-oriented AI increases the risk of cognitive dependency because it encourages passive reception, effort avoidance, and automation bias. Thinking-oriented AI, by contrast, supports cognitive growth by requiring explanation, justification, reflection, and assumption-checking. The framework therefore proposes a movement from AI as answer-provider to AI as reasoning partner.

In practical terms, economics educators and AI developers should design AI-supported learning systems that ask before answering, scaffold before solving, reveal uncertainty before concluding, and require judgement before recommendation. Such systems would be especially useful in topics such as demand and supply analysis, inflation, unemployment, economic growth, public finance, international trade, development economics, and econometrics.

The framework also has implications for institutional AI policies. Universities should not merely focus on detecting AI misuse. They should promote AI learning designs that protect intellectual effort and preserve human agency. UNESCO's guidance on generative AI in education highlights the need for regulation, policy, and human capacity development to ensure that AI benefits learners and educators (Adarkwah et al., 2026; Holmes & Miao, 2023; Prastyo & Bagaskoro, 2025). The HCAI-ET Framework offers one way of operationalising that human-centred vision within economics education.

Generally, the framework advances the argument that AI should be designed for thinking, not cognitive replacement. In the context of economics education, this means helping students reason through complexity, evaluate assumptions, interpret evidence, and develop the intellectual autonomy required for responsible economic judgement.

5.6 Classroom Applications of the HCAI-ET Framework

The HCAI-ET Framework can be operationalised through classroom activities that require students to engage actively with AI rather than passively consuming generated responses. The following examples illustrate how human-centred AI principles can be embedded within economics teaching and learning.

Example 1: Demand and Supply Analysis (Microeconomics)

Students are required to construct a demand and supply diagram independently and predict the effects of a specific tax on equilibrium price, quantity, consumer surplus, producer surplus, and deadweight loss before consulting an AI system. The AI tool subsequently provides feedback, identifies overlooked assumptions, and asks students to justify their reasoning. In this way, AI functions as a scaffold for conceptual understanding rather than a substitute for economic analysis.

Example 2: Inflation Analysis and Policy Evaluation (Macroeconomics)

Students use AI to generate explanations of inflationary pressures and policy responses, but they must compare the outputs with textbook models and empirical evidence from their own economy. Learners are required to identify oversimplifications, challenge assumptions, and revise the AI-generated explanations using established economic theories. This activity promotes critical evaluation and contextual reasoning.

Example 3: Regression Interpretation and Model Critique (Econometrics)

Students first interpret regression coefficients, significance levels, and model assumptions independently before consulting AI-generated interpretations. Classroom discussions then focus on differences between students' analyses and AI outputs, particularly regarding causality, omitted variables, and contextual relevance. Such exercises strengthen analytical reasoning while exposing students to the limitations of automated interpretations.

Example 4: Policy Alternatives in Development Economics

Students employ AI tools to generate alternative policy recommendations for addressing poverty, unemployment, or inequality. They subsequently evaluate these recommendations using development theories, empirical evidence, and local socioeconomic contexts. Oral presentations and reflective essays require students to defend their conclusions and explain why certain AI-generated proposals were accepted, modified, or rejected. This approach reinforces intellectual autonomy and evidence-based judgement.

These examples demonstrate that the HCAI-ET Framework does not seek to limit AI use but rather to structure its application in ways that preserve explanation, justification, reflection, and independent economic reasoning.

Table 1 shows an illustrative classroom application of the HCAI-ET.

Table 1. Illustrative classroom applications of the HCAI-ET

Framework	AI Role	Student Cognitive Task	Expected Outcome
Demand and Supply Analysis	Feedback and scaffolding	Draw diagrams and justify tax effects	Stronger conceptual understanding
Inflation and Policy Evaluation	Generate alternative explanations	Critique assumptions and compare evidence	Critical economic reasoning
Regression Interpretation	Provide comparative interpretations	Evaluate coefficients and model assumptions	Improved analytical competence
Development Policy Analysis	Generate policy options	Defend recommendations using evidence	Greater intellectual autonomy

5.7 Evaluating the Effectiveness of the HCAI-ET Framework

The effectiveness of the HCAI-ET Framework should be assessed not only through academic performance but also through indicators of cognitive engagement, critical thinking, and intellectual autonomy. Multiple evaluation approaches may therefore be employed to determine whether AI-supported learning contributes to deeper economic understanding.

Evaluation Indicator 1: Critical Thinking Capacity

One important measure involves students' ability to evaluate competing economic explanations, identify assumptions, critique AI-generated arguments, and justify policy recommendations. Assessment tasks that require independent analysis, argumentation, and evidence-based reasoning provide important indicators of whether AI functions as a tool for cognitive augmentation rather than cognitive replacement.

Evaluation Indicator 2: Reflective AI-Use Journals and Learning Logs

Reflective journals and AI-use logs enable students to document how they engaged with AI during coursework, explain which outputs they accepted or rejected, and describe how AI influenced their understanding of economic concepts. Such reflections provide evidence of metacognitive engagement, self-regulated learning, and responsible AI use.

Evaluation Indicator 3: Oral Assessments and Classroom Presentations

Oral examinations, classroom presentations, and viva-style assessments offer valuable measures of independent understanding. Students who have developed genuine economic competence should be able to defend their reasoning, explain assumptions, and respond to questions without relying exclusively on AI-generated materials. These approaches help distinguish deep learning from superficial task completion.

Evaluation Indicator 4: Pre- and Post-Intervention Measures

Pre- and post-intervention assessments may be used to examine changes in analytical confidence, critical thinking dispositions, and perceptions of intellectual autonomy. Surveys, structured interviews, and classroom observations can provide complementary evidence regarding students' experiences within AI-supported learning environments and the extent to which the framework promotes meaningful cognitive development.

Evaluation Indicator 5: Institutional and Policy-Level Assessment

From an institutional perspective, evaluation may include monitoring patterns of AI use, the quality of students' reasoning in assessments, and compliance with AI literacy and disclosure requirements. Universities implementing the framework may also examine whether AI-supported pedagogies improve student engagement while preserving independent problem-solving abilities and disciplinary thinking.

Table 2 presents illustrative indicators for evaluating the effectiveness of the HCAI-ET Framework.

Table 2. Illustrative indicators for evaluating the effectiveness of the HCAI-ET framework

Evaluation Dimension	Example Methods	Evidence of Framework Effectiveness
Critical Thinking Capacity	Essay critiques, policy analysis tasks, AI-output evaluations	Ability to identify assumptions, justify arguments, and evaluate evidence
Metacognitive Engagement	Reflective journals, AI-use logs, learning portfolios	Greater self-monitoring and responsible AI use
Independent Economic Reasoning	Oral examinations, presentations, viva assessments	Ability to explain concepts and defend arguments without AI dependence
Analytical Confidence and Autonomy	Pre- and post-intervention surveys, interviews, classroom observations	Increased confidence in solving economic problems independently
Institutional Implementation	AI disclosure records, assessment quality reviews, AI literacy monitoring	Improved engagement alongside sustained intellectual independence

Generally, these evaluation strategies recognise that the success of the HCAI-ET Framework should not be judged solely by efficiency or academic performance. Rather, its effectiveness depends on whether students become more reflective, analytically confident, and intellectually autonomous thinkers who can apply economic reasoning independently while using AI responsibly as a cognitive support tool.

5.7. Empirical Support for the HCAI-ET Framework

Recent empirical evidence provides strong support for the principles underlying the Human-Centered AI for Economic Thinking (HCAI-ET) framework. A meta-analysis by Ilgun Dibek et al. (2025) found that AI-supported educational interventions produced moderate improvements in students' higher-order thinking skills, although the effects varied according to the type of AI tool and instructional context. Similarly, Saritepeci and Yildiz Durak (2024) demonstrated that integrating AI into design-based learning enhanced students' creative self-efficacy and reflective thinking, suggesting that AI can contribute positively to cognitive development when embedded within learner-centred and participatory pedagogies. These findings align with the HCAI-ET proposition that AI should function as a thinking-oriented partner that encourages explanation, reflection, and active engagement rather than merely delivering finished answers. The evidence therefore reinforces the framework's emphasis on preserving students' cognitive involvement through prompts, scaffolding, and opportunities for independent reasoning.

Similarly, emerging research highlights the risks of excessive reliance on AI, thereby strengthening the need for the psychological safeguards proposed within the HCAI-ET framework. Zhai et al. (2024) reported that over-reliance on AI dialogue systems may weaken critical thinking, analytical reasoning, and independent decision-making as learners increasingly favour efficient cognitive shortcuts over deliberate cognitive effort. Likewise, Revesai (2025) found that dependency on generative AI among university students was associated with diminished critical thinking, weaker writing skills, and lower academic performance. Complementing these findings, Li et al. (2026) showed that higher task complexity increased AI dependency through elevated cognitive load and future anxiety, whereas stronger task motivation reduced excessive reliance on AI. Collectively, these studies support the HCAI-ET framework's emphasis on metacognitive prompts, transparency cues, effort-requiring checkpoints, and human-centred design principles that enable AI to augment, rather than replace, students' economic reasoning, intellectual autonomy, and long-term cognitive development.

6. IMPLICATIONS FOR HIGHER EDUCATION AND POLICY

The Human-Centered AI for Economic Thinking (HCAI-ET) Framework offers important implications for higher education institutions seeking to integrate artificial intelligence into teaching and learning without compromising students' cognitive development. As AI technologies become increasingly embedded within educational environments, universities must ensure that technological innovation enhances rather than diminishes critical thinking, intellectual autonomy, and disciplinary competence. The framework therefore provides guidance for educators, curriculum developers, AI designers, and policymakers who are responsible for shaping the future of AI-supported learning in economics education.

6.1. Implications for Economics Educators

The framework suggests that economics educators should move beyond viewing AI merely as a productivity tool and instead approach it as a cognitive partner that can either support or undermine learning depending on how it is used. Teaching practices should therefore prioritise thinking-oriented AI integration that encourages students to analyse, evaluate, justify, and reflect rather than simply obtain answers.

Economics lecturers should design learning activities that require students to explain assumptions, critique AI-generated analyses, compare alternative economic interpretations, and defend policy recommendations using evidence. Such approaches help ensure that students remain actively involved in the reasoning process. For example, rather than allowing students to submit AI-generated policy briefs, lecturers may require students to identify limitations within AI-generated recommendations and explain how economic theory supports or challenges those recommendations.

The framework also highlights the importance of creating opportunities for productive cognitive struggle. Students should be encouraged to grapple with economic concepts, interpret data independently, and construct models before consulting AI tools. In this way, AI becomes a scaffold for learning rather than a substitute for intellectual effort.

6.2. Implications for Curriculum Designers

The framework further suggests that curriculum designers should incorporate explicit cognitive safeguards within AI-supported learning environments. Economics curricula can no longer focus solely on disciplinary content; they must also prepare students to engage critically and responsibly with AI technologies.

One important implication is the integration of AI literacy within economics programmes. Students should develop an understanding of how AI systems generate outputs, the limitations of predictive models, the potential for algorithmic bias, and the ethical implications of AI-assisted decision-making. Such knowledge is particularly important in economics, where data interpretation and policy analysis increasingly rely on computational tools.

Curriculum designers should also embed metacognitive development throughout economics programmes. Reflective activities, AI-use journals, self-assessment exercises, and critical evaluation tasks can help students monitor their own learning processes and reduce the likelihood of cognitive dependency. By strengthening students' awareness of how they think, learn, and evaluate information, institutions can promote more responsible AI engagement.

In addition, assessment practices should be redesigned to prioritise reasoning processes rather than merely evaluating final outputs. Oral defences, case analyses, simulation exercises, policy critiques, and reflective portfolios may provide more effective measures of student learning in AI-enhanced educational environments.

6.3. Implications for AI Developers

The HCAI-ET Framework also has significant implications for developers of educational AI systems. Current AI applications often prioritise efficiency, speed, and convenience. While these features offer clear benefits, they may unintentionally encourage passive learning and cognitive substitution if students receive complete solutions without engaging in the underlying reasoning process.

The framework therefore advocates for the development of AI systems that promote reasoning transparency. Such systems should make assumptions explicit, reveal uncertainty, encourage questioning, and provide opportunities for reflection before delivering conclusions. Rather than functioning as answer-generating machines, educational AI systems should serve as cognitive facilitators that support inquiry and analysis.

For economics education specifically, AI systems could incorporate prompts that require students to justify assumptions, identify economic trade-offs, interpret graphical relationships, and evaluate alternative policy scenarios. AI tools could also provide multiple perspectives on economic issues, helping students recognise that many economic questions involve competing theories and context-dependent interpretations rather than universally correct answers.

Transparency features should also be incorporated into AI systems. Students should be informed when outputs are based on incomplete information, uncertain evidence, or simplified assumptions. Such transparency can reduce automation bias and encourage more critical engagement with AI-generated content.

6.4. Implications for Policymakers and Institutional Governance

At the policy level, the framework emphasises the need to balance technological innovation with cognitive sustainability. While governments and higher education institutions are increasingly investing in AI technologies, equal attention must be given to safeguarding the intellectual capacities that higher education seeks to develop.

Institutional AI policies should therefore extend beyond academic integrity concerns to address broader educational objectives. Universities should establish guidelines that promote responsible AI use while preserving critical thinking, independent judgement, and disciplinary competence. These guidelines should clearly define acceptable AI use, disclosure requirements, and expectations regarding student engagement with AI-generated content.

Policymakers should also support investments in AI literacy initiatives for both students and educators. Faculty development programmes are particularly important because lecturers play a central role in shaping how AI is integrated into learning environments. Without adequate preparation, educators may struggle to design learning experiences that leverage AI effectively while preventing dependency.

At the national level, higher education regulatory bodies may consider incorporating AI literacy and responsible AI use into programme accreditation standards. Such measures would encourage institutions to adopt a more systematic and human-centred approach to AI integration.

Ultimately, the framework suggests that successful AI governance should not focus solely on controlling technology. Rather, it should seek to cultivate educational environments where AI supports human development, intellectual growth, and informed decision-making.

7. CONCLUSION

The rapid expansion of artificial intelligence within higher education has fundamentally altered the educational landscape. AI technologies are increasingly capable of generating explanations, solving problems, analysing data, and producing sophisticated written content. As a result, the central question facing higher education is no longer whether students will use AI, but how AI can be integrated in ways that strengthen rather than weaken human cognition.

This challenge is particularly important within economics education. Economics graduates frequently assume roles that require complex reasoning, evidence-based decision-making, policy analysis, forecasting, and strategic judgement. Their effectiveness depends not only on access to information but also on their ability to think critically, evaluate assumptions, interpret uncertainty, and make informed decisions in complex environments.

The Human-Centered AI for Economic Thinking (HCAI-ET) Framework offers a conceptual response to these challenges. The framework argues that AI should be designed and implemented in ways that preserve human agency, encourage cognitive engagement, and support intellectual development. Through its interconnected dimensions of AI Design Orientation, Cognitive Engagement Mechanisms, Psychological Safeguards Against Dependency, and Cognitive and Developmental Outcomes, the framework provides a structured approach for understanding how AI can contribute to meaningful learning while reducing the risk of cognitive dependency.

A central contribution of the framework is its distinction between replacement-oriented AI and thinking-oriented AI. Whereas replacement-oriented systems risk encouraging passive learning and cognitive substitution, thinking-oriented systems promote reasoning, reflection, and active engagement. The framework therefore shifts attention from technological efficiency alone to the broader educational purpose of developing capable and independent thinkers.

The chapter ultimately argues that the future of AI in economics education should not be defined by the replacement of human intelligence but by its enhancement. Human-centred AI offers a pathway for combining technological innovation with the preservation of critical thinking, analytical confidence, intellectual autonomy, and resilient economic reasoning. By placing cognitive growth at the centre of AI design and educational practice, higher education institutions can harness the benefits of artificial intelligence while safeguarding the human capacities that remain essential for learning, leadership, and responsible economic decision-making.

8. LIMITATIONS AND SUGGESTIONS FOR FUTURE RESEARCH

This chapter is conceptual in nature and is therefore limited by the absence of empirical evidence to validate the proposed HCAI-ET Framework within actual economics classrooms. The framework synthesises insights from multiple theoretical perspectives and existing literature, but its effectiveness in promoting critical thinking, intellectual autonomy, and responsible AI use remains to be tested. Future studies should employ experimental, longitudinal, and mixed-method designs to examine how human-centred AI interventions influence students' economic reasoning, metacognitive skills, cognitive engagement, and dependency on AI tools across different educational contexts. Such empirical investigations would help refine the framework and establish its practical applicability in economics education.

REFERENCES

Acquah, B. Y. S., Arthur, F., Salifu, I., Mensah, E., Opoku, E., Abam Nortey, S., & Tetteh, S. A. (2025). Modelling economics students' use of ChatGPT and academic performance: Insights from self-determination theory and epistemic curiosity. *Discover Artificial Intelligence*, *5*(1), 134. Advance online publication. DOI: 10.1007/s44163-025-00373-y

Adarkwah, M. A., Ercan, A. M., Schneider, K., & Bayar, E. (2026). Generative artificial intelligence policy: A qualitative UNESCO framework analysis. *Journal of University Teaching & Learning Practice*, *23*(2), 1–38. DOI: 10.53761/801ryw41

Arthur, F. (2026a). Agentic AI in Economics Education: Fostering Autonomous and Empowered Learning. *Inspirations in AI Innovation*, 21.

Arthur, F. (2026b). Modelling the nexus between artificial intelligence usage and graduate capital dimensions: A PLS-SEM Approach. *European Journal of Education*, *61*(1), e70484. DOI: 10.1111/ejed.70484

Arthur, F., Yidana, M. B., & Acquah, B. Y. S. (2025). Self-regulated learning among higher education economics students: Does gender and academic level matter? *Cogent Education*, *12*(1), 1–22. DOI: 10.1080/2331186X.2025.2579351

Bhullar, P. S., Joshi, M., & Chugh, R. (2024). ChatGPT in higher education: A synthesis of the literature and a future research agenda. *Education and Information Technologies*, *29*(16), 21501–21522. DOI: 10.1007/s10639-024-12723-x

Bittle, K., & El-Gayar, O. (2025). Generative AI and academic integrity in higher education: A systematic review and research agenda. *Information (Basel)*, *16*(4), 296. Advance online publication. DOI: 10.3390/info16040296

Bröse, N., Spielmann, C., & Tode, C. (2026). ChatGPT as economics tutor: Capabilities and limitations. *International Review of Economics Education*, *51*, 100337. Advance online publication. DOI: 10.1016/j.iree.2025.100337

Carrasco-Aguilar, Á., Shu, Z., Camacho-Ruiz, M., & Arias-Oliva, M. (2026). Integrating AI and Visual Tools in Economics Education: Enhancing Pedagogy Through Mermaid and Large Language Models. In *Teaching Innovations in Economics: Integrating Artificial Intelligence and Emerging Technologies* (pp. 235–254). Springer Nature Switzerland. DOI: 10.1007/978-3-032-08213-8_11

Chan, C. K. Y. (2023). A comprehensive AI policy education framework for university teaching and learning. *International Journal of Educational Technology in Higher Education*, *20*(1), 38. Advance online publication. DOI: 10.1186/s41239-023-00408-3

Chiu, T. K. F. (2024). Future research recommendations for transforming higher education with generative AI. *Computers and Education: Artificial Intelligence*, *6*, 100197. Advance online publication. DOI: 10.1016/j.caeai.2023.100197

Chiu, T. K. F., Xia, Q., Zhou, X., Chai, C. S., & Cheng, M. (2023). Systematic literature review on opportunities, challenges, and future research recommendations of artificial intelligence in education. *Computers and Education: Artificial Intelligence*, *4*, 100118. Advance online publication. DOI: 10.1016/j.caeai.2022.100118

Cohen, A. J. (2024). What do we want students to (know and) be able to do: Learning outcomes, competencies, and content in literacy-targeted principles courses. *The Journal of Economic Education*, *55*(2), 128–145. DOI: 10.1080/00220485.2023.2282016

Cukurova, M., & Miao, F. (2024). *AI competency framework for teachers*. UNESCO Publishing.

Dalalah, D., & Dalalah, O. M. A. (2023). The false positives and false negatives of generative AI detection tools in education and academic research: The case of ChatGPT. *International Journal of Management Education*, *21*(2), 100822. Advance online publication. DOI: 10.1016/j.ijme.2023.100822

Draganski, B., Gaser, C., Busch, V., Schuierer, G., Bogdahn, U., & May, A. (2004). Neuroplasticity: Changes in grey matter induced by training. *Nature*, *427*(6972), 311–312. DOI: 10.1038/427311a PMID: 14737157

Duong, C. D., Vu, T. N., & Ngo, T. V. N. (2023). Applying a modified technology acceptance model to explain higher education students' usage of ChatGPT: A serial multiple mediation model with knowledge sharing as a moderator. *International Journal of Management Education*, *21*(3), 100883. Advance online publication. DOI: 10.1016/j.ijme.2023.100883

Endsley, M. R., & Kiris, E. O. (1995). The out-of-the-loop performance problem and level of control in automation. *Human Factors*, *37*(2), 381–394. DOI: 10.1518/001872095779064555

Essel, H. B., Vlachopoulos, D., Essuman, A. B., & Amankwa, J. O. (2024). ChatGPT effects on cognitive skills of undergraduate students: Receiving instant responses from AI-based conversational large language models. *Computers and Education: Artificial Intelligence, 6*, 100198. Advance online publication. DOI: 10.1016/j.caeai.2023.100198

Essien, A., Bukoye, O. T., O'Dea, X., & Kremantzis, M. (2024). The influence of AI text generators on critical thinking skills in UK business schools. *Studies in Higher Education, 49*(5), 865–882. Advance online publication. DOI: 10.1080/03075079.2024.2316881

Evans, J. S. B. T. (2008). Dual-processing accounts of reasoning, judgment, and social cognition. *Annual Review of Psychology, 59*(1), 255–278. DOI: 10.1146/annurev.psych.59.103006.093629 PMID: 18154502

Evans, J. S. B. T., & Stanovich, K. E. (2013). Dual-process theories of higher cognition: Advancing the debate. *Perspectives on Psychological Science, 8*(3), 223–241. DOI: 10.1177/1745691612460685 PMID: 26172965

Farrokhnia, M., Banihashem, S. K., Noroozi, O., & Wals, A. (2024). A SWOT analysis of ChatGPT: Implications for educational practice and research. *Innovations in Education and Teaching International, 61*(3), 460–474. DOI: 10.1080/14703297.2023.2195846

Fu, Y., & Weng, Z. (2024). Navigating the ethical terrain of AI in education: A systematic review on framing responsible human-centered AI practices. *Computers and Education: Artificial Intelligence, 7*, 100306. Advance online publication. DOI: 10.1016/j.caeai.2024.100306

Gao, Z., Cheah, J.-H., Lim, X.-J., & Luo, X. (2024). Enhancing academic performance of business students using generative AI: An interactive-constructive-active-passive (ICAP) self-determination perspective. *International Journal of Management Education, 22*(2), 100958. Advance online publication. DOI: 10.1016/j.ijme.2024.100958

Gerlich, M. (2025). AI tools in society: Impacts on cognitive offloading and the future of critical thinking. *Societies (Basel, Switzerland), 15*(1), 6. Advance online publication. DOI: 10.3390/soc15010006

Holmes, W., & Miao, F. (2023). *Guidance for generative AI in education and research.* Unesco Publishing.

Hwang, Y., & Lee, J. H. (2025). Exploring students' experiences and perceptions of human-AI collaboration in digital content making. *International Journal of Educational Technology in Higher Education*, *22*(1), 44. Advance online publication. DOI: 10.1186/s41239-025-00542-0

Ilgun Dibek, M., Sahin Kursad, M., & Erdogan, T. (2025). Influence of artificial intelligence tools on higher order thinking skills: A meta-analysis. *Interactive Learning Environments*, *33*(3), 2216–2238. DOI: 10.1080/10494820.2024.2402028

Jaakkola, E. (2020). Designing conceptual articles: Four approaches. *AMS Review*, *10*(1–2), 18–26. DOI: 10.1007/s13162-020-00161-0

Jabareen, Y. (2009). Building a conceptual framework: Philosophy, definitions, and procedure. *International Journal of Qualitative Methods*, *8*(4), 49–62. DOI: 10.1177/160940690900800406

Jin, S.-H., Im, K., Yoo, M., Roll, I., & Seo, K. (2023). Supporting students' self-regulated learning in online learning using artificial intelligence applications. *International Journal of Educational Technology in Higher Education*, *20*(1), 37. Advance online publication. DOI: 10.1186/s41239-023-00406-5

Kahn, L., Probasco, E. S., & Kinoshita, R. (2024). *AI Safety and Automation Bias*. Center for Security and Emerging Technology., DOI: 10.51593/20230057

Kahneman, D. (2003). Maps of bounded rationality: Psychology for behavioral economics. *The American Economic Review*, *93*(5), 1449–1475. DOI: 10.1257/000282803322655392

Kasneci, E., Seßler, K., Küchemann, S., Bannert, M., Dementieva, D., Fischer, F., Gasser, U., Groh, G., Günnemann, S., Hüllermeier, E., Krusche, S., Kutyniok, G., Michaeli, T., Nerdel, C., Pfeffer, J., Poquet, O., Sailer, M., Schmidt, A., Seidel, T., & Kasneci, G. (2023). ChatGPT for good? On opportunities and challenges of large language models for education. *Learning and Individual Differences*, *103*, 102274. Advance online publication. DOI: 10.1016/j.lindif.2023.102274

Khosravi, H., Shum, S. B., Chen, G., Conati, C., Tsai, Y.-S., Kay, J., Knight, S., Martinez-Maldonado, R., Sadiq, S., & Gašević, D. (2022). Explainable artificial intelligence in education. *Computers and Education: Artificial Intelligence*, *3*, 100074. Advance online publication. DOI: 10.1016/j.caeai.2022.100074

Kleim, J. A., & Jones, T. A. (2008). Principles of experience-dependent neural plasticity: Implications for rehabilitation after brain damage. *Journal of Speech, Language, and Hearing Research: JSLHR*, *51*(1), S225–S239. DOI: 10.1044/1092-4388(2008/018) PMID: 18230848

Labadze, L., Grigolia, M., & Machaidze, L. (2023). Role of AI chatbots in education: Systematic literature review. *International Journal of Educational Technology in Higher Education, 20*(1), 56. Advance online publication. DOI: 10.1186/s41239-023-00426-1

Laupichler, M. C., Aster, A., Schirch, J., & Raupach, T. (2022). Artificial intelligence literacy in higher and adult education: A scoping literature review. *Computers and Education: Artificial Intelligence, 3*, 100101. Advance online publication. DOI: 10.1016/j.caeai.2022.100101

Lee, H.-P., Sarkar, A., Tankelevitch, L., Drosos, I., Rintel, S., Banks, R., & Wilson, N. (2025). The impact of generative AI on critical thinking: Self-reported reductions in cognitive effort and confidence effects from a survey of knowledge workers. In *Proceedings of the 2025 CHI Conference on Human Factors in Computing Systems* (pp. 1–22). Association for Computing Machinery. https://doi.org/DOI: 10.1145/3706598.3713778

Li, H., Yang, F., & Liu, J. (2026). Task complexity and AI dependency among college students: The mediating roles of cognitive load, future anxiety, and task motivation. *BMC Psychology, 14*(1), 552. DOI: 10.1186/s40359-026-04204-2 PMID: 41787504

Long, D., & Magerko, B. (2020). What is AI literacy? Competencies and design considerations. In *Proceedings of the 2020 CHI Conference on Human Factors in Computing Systems* (pp. 1–16). Association for Computing Machinery. https://doi.org/DOI: 10.1145/3313831.3376727

Markauskaite, L., Marrone, R., Poquet, O., Knight, S., Martinez-Maldonado, R., Howard, S., Tondeur, J., De Laat, M., Shum, S. B., Gašević, D., & Siemens, G. (2022). Rethinking the entwinement between artificial intelligence and human learning: What capabilities do learners need for a world with AI? *Computers and Education: Artificial Intelligence, 3*, 100056. Advance online publication. DOI: 10.1016/j.caeai.2022.100056

May, A. (2011). Experience-dependent structural plasticity in the adult human brain. *Trends in Cognitive Sciences, 15*(10), 475–482. DOI: 10.1016/j.tics.2011.08.002 PMID: 21906988

Ng, D. T. K., Leung, J. K. L., Chu, S. K. W., & Qiao, M. S. (2021). Conceptualizing AI literacy: An exploratory review. *Computers and Education: Artificial Intelligence, 2*, 100041. Advance online publication. DOI: 10.1016/j.caeai.2021.100041

Organisation for Economic Co-operation and Development. (2023). *OECD Employment Outlook 2023: Artificial Intelligence and the Labour Market*. OECD Publishing.

Paas, F., Renkl, A., & Sweller, J. (2003). Cognitive load theory and instructional design: Recent developments. *Educational Psychologist, 38*(1), 1–4. DOI: 10.1207/S15326985EP3801_1

Parasuraman, R., & Riley, V. (1997). Humans and automation: Use, misuse, disuse, abuse. *Human Factors, 39*(2), 230–253. DOI: 10.1518/001872097778543886

Prastyo, P. A., & Bagaskoro, G. (2025). AI governance and strategic priorities: Mapping national AI policies in the OECD. *Artificial Intelligence in Learning, 1*(4), 301–314. DOI: 10.63913/ail.v1i4.33

Revesai, Z. (2025). Generative AI dependency: The emerging academic crisis and its impact on student performance—A case study of a university in Zimbabwe. *Cogent Education, 12*(1), 2549787. DOI: 10.1080/2331186X.2025.2549787

Risko, E. F., & Gilbert, S. J. (2016). Cognitive offloading. *Trends in Cognitive Sciences, 20*(9), 676–688. DOI: 10.1016/j.tics.2016.07.002 PMID: 27542527

Salifu, I., Arthur, F., Arkorful, V., Abam Nortey, S., & Osei-Yaw, R. S. (2024). Economics students' behavioural intention and usage of ChatGPT in higher education: A hybrid structural equation modelling-artificial neural network approach. *Cogent Social Sciences, 10*(1), 2300177. Advance online publication. DOI: 10.1080/23311886.2023.2300177

Saritepeci, M., & Yildiz Durak, H. (2024). Effectiveness of artificial intelligence integration in design-based learning on design thinking mindset, creative and reflective thinking skills: An experimental study. *Education and Information Technologies, 29*(18), 25175–25209. DOI: 10.1007/s10639-024-12829-2

Shen, Z., & Zhu, W. (2025). The application of ChatGPT in economics teaching: Scenarios, deficiencies and strategies. In *Proceedings of the 2025 International Conference on Implementing Generative AI into Telecommunication and Digital Innovation*. Association for Computing Machinery. https://doi.org/DOI: 10.1145/3771792.3774392

Shneiderman, B. (2020). Human-centered artificial intelligence: Reliable, safe & trustworthy. *International Journal of Human-Computer Interaction, 36*(6), 495–504. DOI: 10.1080/10447318.2020.1741118

Sollosy, M., & McInerney, M. (2022). Artificial intelligence and business education: What should be taught. *International Journal of Management Education, 20*(3), 100720. Advance online publication. DOI: 10.1016/j.ijme.2022.100720

Southworth, J., Migliaccio, K., Glover, J., Glover, J., Reed, D., McCarty, C., Brendemuhl, J., & Thomas, A. (2023). Developing a model for AI across the curriculum: Transforming the higher education landscape via innovation in AI literacy. *Computers and Education: Artificial Intelligence*, *4*, 100127. Advance online publication. DOI: 10.1016/j.caeai.2023.100127

Stadler, M., Bannert, M., & Sailer, M. (2024). Cognitive ease at a cost: LLMs reduce mental effort but compromise depth in student scientific inquiry. *Computers in Human Behavior*, *160*, 108386. Advance online publication. DOI: 10.1016/j.chb.2024.108386

Sweller, J. (1988). Cognitive load during problem solving: Effects on learning. *Cognitive Science*, *12*(2), 257–285. DOI: 10.1207/s15516709cog1202_4

Sweller, J., van Merriënboer, J. J. G., & Paas, F. (2019). Cognitive architecture and instructional design: 20 years later. *Educational Psychology Review*, *31*(2), 261–292. DOI: 10.1007/s10648-019-09465-5

Tarasova, K., Gracheva, D., Talov, D., Orel, E., & Dementiev, A. (2026). Measuring changes in critical thinking skills among university economics students: Insights from domain-specific assessment. *Studies in Higher Education*, *51*(3), 649–664. DOI: 10.1080/03075079.2025.2484423

Thompson, A. (2025). Bridging mathematical proficiency and economic reasoning: A commentary on calculus in undergraduate economics education. *International Journal of Research in Undergraduate Mathematics Education*, *11*(4), 773–780. DOI: 10.1007/s40753-026-00295-9

Tlili, A., Shehata, B., Adarkwah, M. A., Bozkurt, A., Hickey, D. T., Huang, R., & Agyemang, B. (2023). What if the devil is my guardian angel: ChatGPT as a case study of using chatbots in education. *Smart Learning Environments*, *10*(1), 15. Advance online publication. DOI: 10.1186/s40561-023-00237-x

Tuomi, I. (2024). Beyond mastery: Toward a broader understanding of AI in education. *International Journal of Artificial Intelligence in Education*, *34*(1), 20–30. DOI: 10.1007/s40593-023-00343-4

UNESCO. (2024). *AI competency framework for students*. United Nations Educational, Scientific and Cultural Organization. https://unesdoc.unesco.org/ark:/48223/pf0000391105

Vendrell, M., & Johnston, S. K. (2026). Scaffolding critical thinking with generative AI: Design principles for integrating large language models in higher education. *Computers and Education: Artificial Intelligence*, 100572.

Walsh, P., Owen, P., & Mustafa, N. (2021). The creation of a confidence scale: The confidence in managing challenging situations scale. *Journal of Research in Nursing : JRN*, *26*(6), 483–496. DOI: 10.1177/1744987120979272 PMID: 35265154

Weng, X., Xia, Q., Gu, M., Rajaram, K., & Chiu, T. K. F. (2024). Assessment and learning outcomes for generative AI in higher education: A scoping review on current research status and trends. *Australasian Journal of Educational Technology*, *40*(6), 37–55. DOI: 10.14742/ajet.9540

Xia, Q., Weng, X., Ouyang, F., Lin, T.-J., & Chiu, T. K. F. (2024). A scoping review on how generative artificial intelligence transforms assessment in higher education. *International Journal of Educational Technology in Higher Education*, *21*(1), 40. Advance online publication. DOI: 10.1186/s41239-024-00468-z

Xu, X., Qiao, L., Cheng, N., Liu, H., & Zhao, W. (2025). Enhancing self-regulated learning and learning experience in generative AI environments: The critical role of metacognitive support. *British Journal of Educational Technology*, *56*(5), 1842–1863. Advance online publication. DOI: 10.1111/bjet.13599

Yang, S. J. H., Ogata, H., Matsui, T., & Chen, N.-S. (2021). Human-centered artificial intelligence in education: Seeing the invisible through the visible. *Computers and Education: Artificial Intelligence*, *2*, 100008. Advance online publication. DOI: 10.1016/j.caeai.2021.100008

Yang, Y., Luo, J., Yang, M., Yang, R., & Chen, J. (2024). From surface to deep learning approaches with generative AI in higher education: An analytical framework of student agency. *Studies in Higher Education*, *49*(5), 817–830. DOI: 10.1080/03075079.2024.2327003

Zhai, C., Wibowo, S., & Li, L. D. (2024). The effects of over-reliance on AI dialogue systems on students' cognitive abilities: A systematic review. *Smart Learning Environments*, *11*(1), 28. DOI: 10.1186/s40561-024-00316-7

Zimmerman, B. J. (2002). Becoming a self-regulated learner: An overview. *Theory into Practice*, *41*(2), 64–70. DOI: 10.1207/s15430421tip4102_2

About the Contributors

Pandimurugan Vellaisamy is an Associate Professor in the Department of Computer Science and Engineering at Acharya University, Karakul, Bukhara Region, Uzbekistan. He has over 17 years of academic experience, including more than seven years of post-Ph.D. teaching and research experience. His research interests include Artificial Intelligence, Machine Learning, Computer Networks, Cybersecurity, Health Informatics, and the Internet of Things (IoT). Dr. Pandimurugan has authored 50 Scopus-indexed publications, including 16 SCI-indexed journal articles, along with several book chapters and patents. His research focuses on AI- and IoT-enabled healthcare, particularly AI in health informatics, medical image analysis, disease prediction, medical data security and wearable security.

***

A. Chinnasamy is currently an Assistant Professor in the Department of Data Science And Business Systems, with nearly 15 years of academic experience. He holds a B.E., M.E., and Ph.D., and has demonstrated expertise in areas such as vehicular ad hoc networks (VANETs), Internet of Things (IoT), machine learning, and wireless communication. Dr. Chinnasamy has made significant research contributions, with 13 publications indexed in Scopus, 4 in Web of Science, and a total of 22 in Google Scholar. His work has garnered over 100 citations, reflecting his impact in the field. He has authored book chapters, published in reputed journals, and presented at both national and international conferences. His research includes the development of secure routing protocols for VANETs, anomaly detection in sensor-based cyber-physical systems, and IoT-based health assistance systems. He also holds a granted patent on cooperative sensing and control in IoT networks using machine learning algorithms, and has filed another on emotion recognition for fitness applications. In addition to his research, Dr. Chinnasamy is actively involved in academic leadership and service. He is an Anna University recognized Ph.D. supervisor, guiding nine research scholars, and serves as a reviewer for several SCI journals. He has contributed to curriculum development, coordinated departmental activities, and organized workshops and seminars. His professional memberships include the Computer Society of India (CSI), International Association of Engineers (IAENG), Indian Society for Technical Education (ISTE), and IEEE. Dr. Chinnasamy's dedication to teaching, research, and academic service has established him as a respected educator and researcher in computer science and engineering, with a strong commitment to advancing knowledge in wireless networks, IoT, and intelligent systems.

Abena Yeboah Abraham is currently a Senior Lecturer in the Department of General Studies, Faculty of Business and Management Studies at Koforidua Technical University, Ghana. She holds a Ph.D. in Economics Education from University of Cape Coast, two master's degrees—Master of Philosophy in Economics and Master of Business Administration in Human Resource Management from University of Cape Coast, UCC and Ghana Institute of Management and Public Administration, GIMPA respectively. A Bachelor of Education Degree in Social Science (Economics and Management), from University of Cape Coast. She has extensive experience in university level teaching, executive and adult training. Since 2013, Dr. Abraham has taught courses such as Management, Economics, Managerial Economics, Operations Management, Labour Economics, Research Methods and Human Resource Management at academic and professional training levels. She has published a few research articles in reputed journals and presented in international conferences. Her research interests are interdisciplinary and focus on Economics Education, artificial intelligence in education, Labour Economics, Management, Education and Managerial Economics. As a broad minded individual she is open to partner in collaborative studies and projects that may be interdisciplinary in nature but has a touch of impacting scholarly attention.

Ashraf Alam is currently serving as an Assistant Professor in the Department of Education at NIT Calicut, Kerala, India. He has been recognised among the World's Top 2% Scientists by Stanford University and Elsevier. His academic contributions include more than 80 Scopus-indexed publications and over 100 conference presentations delivered at national and international academic forums. His work has appeared in reputed research publication platforms including Elsevier, Springer, Taylor & Francis, CRC Press, Routledge, Atlantis Press, Springer Nature, Palgrave Macmillan, and IEEE. He earned his Ph.D. from IIT Kharagpur, where his research engaged with foundational concerns in educational policy, curriculum design, educational technology, philosophy of education, innovation in education, educational administration, governance, and pedagogical transformation. His work is grounded in a transdisciplinary orientation that draws from educational sciences, digital pedagogy, curriculum theory, learning analytics, sustainability education, instructional design, artificial intelligence, ethics of technology, and socio-technical studies. Dr. Ashraf's scholarship strives to interrogate and expand the boundaries of educational thought by examining the epistemological, ethical, and social dimensions of digital and post-digital pedagogies. His work critically engages with the changing nature of knowledge production, learner agency, pedagogical mediation, and institutional transformation in technologically saturated educational environments. He is particularly invested in advancing inclusive digital learning, gamified instructional strategies, AI-mediated educational ecosystems, and ethically governed technology integration in education. His research agenda is animated by the pursuit of design-oriented, ethically attuned, and contextually responsive frameworks that can support meaningful educational reform. Through his work, he seeks to contribute to the development of pedagogical models that are not only technologically innovative but also socially just, epistemically inclusive, developmentally sensitive, and aligned with the broader goals of sustainable and human-centred education.

Gültekin Altuntaş is an Associate Professor in the Department of Logistics at Istanbul University's Faculty of Transportation and Logistics. His expertise spans entrepreneurship, management, strategic management, organizational behavior, and human resources. He holds a Ph.D. in Strategic Entrepreneurship (2010), two master's degrees—one in Entrepreneurship from Ball State University, USA (2004) and another in Business Management and Organization from Istanbul University (2021)—and two bachelor's degrees: one in Business Administration from Istanbul University (2002) and another in Management Information Systems from Anadolu University (2019). Since 2011, Dr. Altuntaş has taught courses such as Management, Strategic Management, Entrepreneurship, and Innovation Management at academic and professional training levels. Beyond academia, he actively advises public- and private-sector projects, serves as a peer reviewer for academic journals, and contributes to evaluation boards for technoparks and development agencies.

Francis Arthur, Ph.D, is a researcher and educator in Economics Education with expertise in advanced quantitative research methods, educational technology, and data analytics. He earned his doctorate in Economics Education from the University of Cape Coast and has developed strong methodological competence in Network Analysis, Covariance-Based Structural Equation Modelling (CB-SEM), Partial Least Squares Structural Equation Modelling (PLS-SEM), fuzzy-set Qualitative Comparative Analysis (fsQCA), Latent Profile Analysis, Artificial Neural Networks (ANN), hierarchical and multilevel modelling, and other sophisticated analytical techniques for examining complex relationships in education and economics. His research focuses on artificial intelligence in education, self-regulated learning, academic engagement, teacher self-efficacy, motivational processes, and technology-enhanced pedagogy. He has published extensively in leading international journals and conference proceedings, with studies addressing generative artificial intelligence, digital citizenship, educational metaverse, and innovative teaching and learning in higher education. Dr. Arthur is the recipient of several distinguished honours, including the International Society for Educational Planning Glen Earthman Outstanding Dissertation Award (2025), the Overall Best Presenter in STEM Award at the 5th International Conference of Postgraduate Studies at the University of Cape Coast (2025), and the Outstanding Academic Achievement Award as the Overall Best PhD Student in Economics Education with a CGPA of 4.0 (2024). Also, Dr. Arthur serves on the editorial boards of international journals and is an active peer reviewer for numerous high-impact, Scopus-indexed, and Web of Science journals, including Frontiers in Education, Frontiers in Artificial Intelligence, Journal of Cleaner Production, Interactive Learning Environments, European Journal of Education, Scientific Reports, and PLOS One. Through his scholarship and professional service, Dr. Arthur contributes to the advancement of rigorous, innovative, and policy-relevant research in economics education and the broader field of educational technology.

B.Sridevi completed her Ph.D from Anna University and working as Professor in Velammal Institute of Technology, CHennai. She has more than 20 years of experience in teaching and research. She is currently pursuing 3 funded projects under ICPS,DST and MSME. She has published more than 30 papers in the reputed journals and international conferences. She is owning 3 patents and her research areas are Networks and Image processing

Firdaus Bashir is a dynamic academician and certified trainer, bringing together a powerful blend of expertise in Management and Law. She holds a Ph.D. in Management from Anna University, Chennai, where her research explored the impact of Green Human Resource Management (GHRM) practices on organizational performance in MSMEs, with a focus on the mediating role of green organizational culture. Her academic journey reflects her interdisciplinary strength, holding an MBA with dual specialization in Human Resource Management and Marketing, alongside a BA LL.B. (Hons.) from the School of Indian Legal Thoughts, Mahatma Gandhi University, Kottayam. A Certified Psychometric Test Professional (CTPT) accredited by SHRM and HRCI, and a Junior Chamber International Certified Trainer, she exemplifies a strong commitment to advancing professional development and nurturing talent. She began her career as a Corporate Trainer at Sutherland Global Services, where she led recruitment, assessment, and preplacement training initiatives and later served as Trainer and Training Coordinator at Karpagam University. An active researcher, Dr. Firdaus has presented her work at numerous prestigious academic conferences, both nationally and internationally. Her publications appear in Scopus, Web of Science, and SSCI-indexed journals, reflecting her contribution to key areas such as HRM, AI readiness, and technology acceptance. Beyond the classroom, she has played a vital role in conducting impactful Management Development Programs (MDPs) and training workshops, translating knowledge into practice and empowering professionals across sectors.

D.Sivakami has completed her M.Sc (Nursing) in the Medical Surgical department and she is working as Associate Professor at Velammal College of Nursing. She is having 10 years of teaching experience.

Bilal El-Mansoury, PhD, served as a Postdoc Researcher in Neuroscience at the Royal College of Surgeons in Ireland, University of Medicine and Health Sciences. His work centers on understanding how glial cell dysfunction contributes to the pathophysiology of hepatic encephalopathy and various neurodegenerative disorders. Dr. El-Mansoury also investigated the role of miRNAs in CDKL5 deficiency disorder, with the aim of identifying novel therapeutic targets for this rare epileptic encephalopathy.

Nil Selenay Erden has been serving as an Associate Professor in the field of Organizational Behavior since 2020. She completed her Ph.D. in 2015 with a dissertation titled "Extra-Role Behaviors and Job Creep: Relationships Between Affect, Withdrawal Behaviors, and Organizational Identification." She has been actively engaged in teaching since 2017, offering courses such as Behavioral Sciences, Organizational Behavior, Communication and Reporting, Scientific Research and Publication Ethics, and Statistics in Social Sciences. Her research interests focus on employee attitudes, training effectiveness, and human–artificial intelligence interaction.

G.Pradeep Kumar pursuing his Ph.D from Anna University and working as Assistant Professor in Velammal College of Engineering and Technology, Madurai. He has 16 years of experience in teaching and research. He is currently pursuing 3 funded projects under ICPS,DST and MSME. He has published more than 20 papers in the reputed journals and international conferences. He is owning 3 patents and his research areas are Unmanned systems, Networking and Image processing

Mark Inkoom is a Master's student in Petroleum and Energy Studies at the Institute for Oil and Gas Studies, University of Cape Coast, Ghana. He holds a Bachelor of Education degree in Social Sciences (Economics) and a certificate in AI

Career Essentials from ALX Africa. His research interests are interdisciplinary and include energy policy and planning, climate change and sustainable development, energy economics, resource governance, machine learning applications in petroleum and energy studies, and artificial intelligence in education, with particular interest in AI for social good and technology-enhanced teaching and learning. He is a research collaborator with Heston's Research Group at Walsh University, USA, and teaches various courses at the College of Distance Education Switch Programme, University of Cape Coast. He has co-authored several research papers and is currently involved in ongoing research projects that connect energy, technology, education, and sustainable development.

Hiroshini K is an undergraduate student in the Department of Computer Science and Engineering at Amrita Vishwa Vidyapeetham, Chennai. Her academic interests include artificial intelligence, machine learning, and their applications in real-world domains. She is particularly interested in understanding the impact of emerging technologies such as large language models on human cognition and decision-making. She is passionate about research, problem-solving, and exploring innovative solutions to complex challenges in the field of computing.

K.Vijayalakshmi is working as Assistant Professor in the Department of Computational Intelligence at S.R.M. Institute of Science and Technology, Kattankulathur, Chennai–603 203, Tamilnadu, INDIA. She acquired B.E. Degree in Electronics and Communication Engineering from Valliammai Engineering College, Kattankulathur in 2005. She received M.Tech Degree in Information Technology, 2007 at Sathyabama University, Chennai and completed Ph. D degree in 2019 under the Faculty of Information and communication engineering at Sathyabama University, Chennai. She has over 18 years of experience in teaching and guiding projects for undergraduate and post graduate students. Her research in the field of Wireless Sensor Network. She published various SCI journals, Scopus Indexed journals, various international journals and conferences. Her areas of interest include Artificial Intelligence, Machine Learning and Internet of Things.

K.Kavitha completed her Ph.D from Anna University and working as Associate Professor in Velammal College of Engineering and Technology, Madurai. She has more than 15 years of experience in teaching and research. She is currently having a funded projects under DST and she has published more than 30 papers in the reputed journals and international conferences. She is owning 3 patents and her research areas are Signal Processing and Image processing

Jesi kerenal has completed her B.Sc (Nursing) and she is working as Nursing Tutor at Velammal College of Nursing. She is having 2 years of teaching experience.

P.Suveetha Dhanaselvam completed her Ph.D from Anna University and working as Professor in Velammal College of Engineering and Technology, Madurai. She has 20 years of experience in teaching and research. She is currently pursuing 3 funded projects under ICPS,DST and SERB. She has published more than 30 papers in the reputed journals and international conferences. She is owning 3 patents and her research areas are Signal Processing and Image processing

S. Narendra Rathnaraj is presently working as Assistant Professor at PSG IM in the domain of Marketing specializing in Social Media Marketing. He holds doctoral degree in Management with Leadership as his specialization. He holds a bachelor's degree in Mechanical Engineering, master's degrees in Human Resource Management and Technology Management also Post Graduate Diploma in Labour and Administrative Laws. He has cleared both NET and SET in Management. He previously worked as Guest Faculty in Bharathiar School of Management and Entrepreneur Development, Bharathiar University, Coimbatore. His research experience includes working as Research Fellow under RUSA project and professional experience includes working as Assistant Manager in R&D with Mahindra and Mahindra. He has published several research articles that are listed under UGC, Scopus and Elsevier. Also, he has attended several national and international conferences and has won several best paper awards.

S.Baghavathi Priya is an Associate Professor of Computer Science and Engineering at Amrita Vishwa Vidyapeetham, Chennai. She received gold medal in M.Tech degree. She received Ph.D. from Jawaharlal Nehru Technological University Hyderabad. She has 27 years of experience in teaching and 15 years of experience in research. She has successfully supervised 09 research scholars. She has published around 80 research papers in various conferences and journals. She is the author of the book titled as Operating Systems. She has published 10 book chapters in IGI Global, CRC Press and Wiley Publications. She received best paper award in ICTIS 2015 at Ahmedabad and in CAASR International conference 2017 at Dubai. She received the award of Top 20 influential women educators in Tamil Nadu from the Academic Council of uLektz. She received Active participation woman award from CSI. She is a Life time member in CSI, IAENG and member of ACM.

Krithikha Sanju S is an Assistant Professor in the Department of Information Technology at Sri Sivasubramaniya Nadar College of Engineering, Chennai, India. She received her B.E. degree in Electronics and Communication Engineering from Sethu Institute of Technology in 2015. Following graduation, she worked at IBM as a Technical Associate from July 2015 to June 2016. She pursued her M.E. in Computer Science and Engineering with a specialization in Big Data Analytics at

CEG, Anna University, graduating in 2018. In February 2025, she obtained her Ph.D. in Information and Communication Engineering from CEG, Anna University. Her primary research interests include Natural Language Processing, Image Processing, and Social Network Analysis, with a focus on advanced computational techniques for real-world applications.

S. P. Santhoshkumar received the Bachelor's Degree in Electronics and Communication Engineering from Anna University, Chennai in 2006, the Master's Degree in Software Engineering from Anna University of Technology, Coimbatore in 2011, and the Philosophy of Doctorate degree in Information and Communication Engineering from Anna University, Chennai in 2024, respectively. He is currently working as an Assistant Professor (SG) at the Department of Computer Science and Engineering, School of Computing, Vel Tech Rangarajan Dr. Sagunthala R&D Institute of Science and Technology, Avadi, Chennai. His research areas include Machine Learning, Cloud Computing, Deep Learning, Software Engineering and Web Development. He has quality of publications to his credit, including Journal Articles, Conference Publications, Patents, Books and Book Chapters. Also, he received best faculty awards in national level.

Doni Sugianto Sihotang is a doctoral student in Marketing at Jakarta State University, Indonesia. His academic background includes a Bachelor's degree in Social Anthropology from Universitas Sumatera Utara and a Master's degree in Marketing Management from Jakarta State University. His interdisciplinary training allows him to merge cultural perspectives with marketing and behavioral research methods. His research interests include consumer behavior, digital marketing, tourism marketing, artificial intelligence in marketing, and behavioral analytics. He has contributed to several peer-reviewed publications on topics such as consumer decision-making, destination branding, technology adoption, and sustainable tourism development. He has received multiple academic awards, including the BIMA DRTPM Research Grant from the Indonesian Ministry of Education and the PMDSU Fast-Track Scholarship for outstanding young researchers. His work aims to advance interdisciplinary research that combines anthropology, marketing, and emerging technologies to better understand consumer behavior and digital innovation in developing economies.

V. Sridhar is a distinguished academic leader, researcher, and administrator with over 40 years of experience in engineering education, research, and academic governance. He currently serves as the Rector of Acharya University, Uzbekistan. He holds a B.E. in Electronics and Communication Engineering, an M.E. in Electronics and Telecommunication Engineering, a Ph.D. from IIT Delhi, and completed post-doctoral research at UNITEN, Malaysia. Throughout his career, he has held several key leadership positions, including Acting Vice-Chancellor and Registrar (Evaluation) of VTU, Belagavi, and Principal of PES College of Engineering, Mandya. His expertise spans VLSI design, digital signal processing, biomedical engineering, telemedicine, cryptography, biometrics, and wireless communications. He has guided numerous research scholars, published extensively, secured research grants, and holds a patent in elliptic curve cryptography. A Fellow of IETE and member of IEEE, ISTE, and IMAPS, Dr. Sridhar continues to contribute significantly to higher education, research, and institutional development.

Fernando Vieira holds a degree in Social and Work Psychology, a Master's degree in Clinical and Health Psychology (Childhood and Adolescence), a specialization in Cognitive-Behavioral Therapy, and a PhD in Clinical Psychology from the Institute of Psychology of the University of São Paulo (USP). He has served as a teaching assistant at the Institute of Psychology of USP and has taught at the Faculty of Medicine of USP. He has also been a guest lecturer in the Blended Intensive Programme of Emotional Education at the Polytechnic Institute of Bragança, Portugal.

Index

A

B

C

D

E

G

H

I

L

M

N

O

P

S

T

W

www.ingramcontent.com/pod-product-compliance
Lightning Source LLC
LaVergne TN
LVHW061531290926
849162LV00004B/755